AF692458

Illegal Waste Management Activity in the Process of Bunker Fuel Production

# Illegal Waste Management Activity in the Process of Bunker Fuel Production

## *A Criminological Case Study of Corporate Environmental Crime and Its Enforcement*

Giulia Giardi

eleven

*Published, sold and distributed by Eleven*
P.O. Box 85576
2508 CG The Hague
The Netherlands
Tel.: +31 70 33 070 33
Fax: +31 70 33 070 30
e-mail: sales@elevenpub.nl
www.elevenpub.com

*Sold and distributed in USA and Canada*
Independent Publishers Group
814 N. Franklin Street
Chicago, IL 60610, USA
Order Placement: +1 800 888 4741
Fax: +1 312 337 5985
orders@ipgbook.com
www.ipgbook.com

Eleven is an imprint of Boom uitgevers Den Haag.

ISBN 978-94-6236-738-8
ISBN 978-94-0011-290-2 (e-book)
NUR 741

© 2023 Giulia Giardi | Eleven International Publishing

This publication is protected by international copyright law.
All rights reserved. No part of this publication may be reproduced, stored in a retrieval system, or transmitted in any form or by any means, electronic, mechanical, photocopying, recording or otherwise, without the prior permission of the publisher.

# List of Abbreviations

| | |
|---|---|
| AG | Advocate General |
| BAT | Best Available Techniques |
| Bia | Ministerial Decision on collection of wastes (*Besluit inzamelen afvalstoffen*) |
| Bor | Ministerial Decision on environmental law (*Besluit omgevingsrecht*) |
| BREF | Best Available Techniques Reference Documents |
| CIMAC | International Council on Combustion Engines |
| CJEU | Court of Justice of the European Union |
| CPT | Crime pattern theory |
| EU | European Union |
| EVOA | Dutch abbreviation for EU Regulation 1013/2006 (*Europese Verordening Overbrenging Afvalstoffen*) |
| FP | National Public Prosecutor's Office for Financial, Economic and Environmental Crimes (*Functioneel Parket*) |
| HOI | Port reception facility (*Havenontavantgsinstallatie*) |
| HOV | Port reception facility (*Havenontvangstvoorziening*) |
| IenW | Minister for Infrastructure and Water Management (*Ministerie Infrastructuur en Waterstaat*) |
| ILT | Human Environment and Transport Inspectorate (*Inspectie Leefomgeving en Transport*) |
| IMO | International Maritime Organisation |
| IOD | Investigative and intelligence unit (*Inlichtingen- en Opsporing Dienst*) |
| IPPC | Integrated Pollution Prevention and Control Bureau |
| ISO | International Standards Organisation |
| LAP | Dutch national waste management plan (*Landelijke Afvalbeheerplan*) |
| LMA | Dutch national registry of wastes (*Landelijke meldpunt afvalstoffen*) |
| LMK | National Environmental Chamber (*Landelijke Milieukamer*) |
| LoW | List of Wastes |
| MARPOL | International Convention for the Prevention of Pollution from Ships |

| | |
|---|---|
| MS | Member State |
| NVWA | Netherlands Food and Consumer Product Safety Authority (*Nederlandse Voedsel- en Warenautoriteit* -NVWA) |
| OM | Dutch Public Prosecution Service (*Openbaar Ministerie*) |
| PCBs | Polychlorobiphenyl |
| POPs | Persistent organic pollutants |
| RAT | Routine activities theory |
| REACH | Registration, Evaluation, Authorisation and Restriction of Chemicals |
| RIVM | Dutch National Institute for Public Health and the Environment (*Rijksinstituut voor Volksgesondheid en Milieu*) |
| SCP | Situational crime prevention |
| SMK | Strategic Environmental Chamber (*Strategische Milieukamer*) |
| SP | Sectorplan (Section in the LAP) |
| SZW | Labour Authority (*Nederlandse Arbeidsinspectie/ Inspectie van Sociale Zaken en Werkgelegenheid*) |
| Wabo | General provisions of environmental law (*Wet algemeen bepalingen omgevingsrecht*) |
| WCA | Law on chemical waste (*Wet chemische afvalstoffen*) |
| WED | Law on Economic Crimes (*Wet op economische delicten*) |
| WFD | Waste Framework Directive |
| Wm | Law on environment (*Wet milieubeheer*) |
| WvS | Dutch Code of Criminal Law (*Wetboek van Strafrecht*) |
| WvSv | Dutch Code of Criminal Procedure (*Wetboek van Strafvordering*) |
| Wvvs | Law for the prevention of pollution from ships (*Wet te voorkoming van verontreiniging door schepen*) |

# Cases and Legislation

## International

Basel Convention on the Control of Transboundary Movements of Hazardous Wastes and their Disposal (adopted 22 March 1989, entered into force 5 May 1992) (1989), 28 ILM 657

International Convention for the Prevention of Pollution from Ships (MARPOL), November 2, 1973, entry into force 17.02.1978, 17 I.L.M. 546

International Convention on Civil Liability for Bunker Oil Pollution Damage 2001, entry into force 21 November 2008

Kyoto Protocol to the United Nations Framework Convention on Climate Change, Kyoto, 11 December 1997. 16 February 2005, No. 30822

## EU

Regulation (EC) No 850/2004 of the European Parliament and of the Council of 29 April 2004 on persistent organic pollutants and amending Directive 79/117/EEC, OJ L 158, 30.4.2004, p. 7-49, which has been repealed and replaced by Regulation (EU) 2019/1021 of the European Parliament and of the Council of 20 June 2019 on persistent organic pollutants, OJ L 169, 25.6.2019, p. 45-77

Regulation (EC) 1013/2006 of the European Parliament and of the Council of 14 June 2006 on shipments of waste, OJ L 190, p. 1, 12.07.2006

Regulation (EC) No 1907/2006 of the European Parliament and of the Council of 18 December 2006 concerning the Registration, Evaluation, Authorisation and Restriction of Chemicals (REACH), establishing a European Chemicals Agency, amending Directive 1999/45/EC and repealing Council Regulation (EEC) No 793/93 and Commission Regulation (EC) No 1488/94 as well as Council Directive 76/769/EEC and Commission Directives 91/155/EEC, 93/67/EEC, 93/105/EC and 2000/21/EC (OJ L 396, 30.12.2006, corrected version in OJ L136, 29.5.2007, p. 3

Regulation (EC) No 1272/2008 of the European Parliament and of the Council of 16 December 2008 on classification, labelling and packaging of substances and mixtures amending and repealing Directives 67/548/EEC and 1999/45/EC, and amending Regulation (EC) No 1907/2006 (OJ L 353, 31.12.2008, p. 1)

Directive 2005/35/EC of the European Parliament and of the Council of 7 September 2005 on ship-source pollution and the introduction of penalties for infringement OJ L255, 30.09.2005, p. 11

Directive 2006/12/EC of the European Parliament and of the Council of 5 April 2006 on waste (OJ L 114, 27.4.2006, p. 9-21

Directive 2008/98/EC of the European Parliament and of the Council of 19 November 2008 on waste and repealing certain Directives, OJ L 312, 22.11.2008, p. 3-30

Directive 2009/123/EC of the European Parliament and of the Council of 21 October 2009 amending Directive 2005/35/EC on ship-source pollution and on the introduction of penalties for infringements, OJ L280, 27.10.2009, p. 52

Directive 2010/75/EU of the European Parliament and of the Council of 24 November 2010 on industrial emissions (integrated pollution prevention and control) OJ L 334, 17.12.2010, p. 17–119

Directive 2016/802/EU of the European Parliament and of the Council of 2016 of 11 May 2016 relating to a reduction in the sulphur content of certain liquid fuels (codification), OJ L 132, 21.05.2016, p. 58

Directive 2018/851/EU of the European Parliament and of the Council of 30 May 2018 amending Directive 2008/98/EC on waste, OJ L 150, 14.6.2018, p. 109–140

Directive 2019/883/EU of the European Parliament and of the Council of 17 April 2019 on port reception facilities for the delivery of waste from ships, amending Directive 2010/65/EU and repealing Directive 2000/59/EC, OJ L 151, 7.6.2019, p. 116–142

Commission Decision of 18 December 2014 amending Decision 2000/532/EC on the list of waste pursuant to Directive 2008/98/EC of the European Parliament and of the Council, OJ L 370, 30.12.2014, p. 44–86

Commission Decision of 3 May 2000 replacing Decision 94/3/EC establishing a list of wastes pursuant to Article 1(a) of Council Directive 75/442/EEC on waste and Council Decision 94/904/EC establishing a list of hazardous waste pursuant to Article 1(4) of Council Directive 91/689/EEC on hazardous waste (notified under document number C(2000) 1147) (2000/532/EC)

Commission Regulation (EU) No 1357/2014 of 18 December 2014 replacing Annex III to Directive 2008/98/EC of the European Parliament and of the Council on waste and repealing certain Directives Text with EEA relevance OJ L 365, 19.12.2014, p. 89–96

National – The Netherlands

Wet van 3 maart 1881 – Wetboek van Strafrecht (WvS)

Wet van 22 juni 1950, houdende vaststelling van regelen voor de opsporing, de vervolging en de berechting van economische delicten (WED)

Wet van 26 november 1970, houdende regelen in het belang van het voorkomen of beperken van luchtverontreiniging (Wet inzake luchtverontreiniging – Wil)

Wet van 13 juni 1979, houdende regelen met betrekking tot een aantal algemene onderwerpen op het gebied van de milieuhygiëne (Wet milieubeheer – Wm)

Wet chemische afvalstoffen (Stb. 1981, 696)

Wet van 14 december 1983, houdende regelen ter voorkoming van verontreiniging door schepen (Wet ter voorkoming van verontreiniging door schepen – Wvvs)

Wet van 31 oktober 1991, houdende regelen betreffende de openbaarheid van bestuur

Wet van 6 november 2008, houdende regels inzake een vergunningstelsel met betrekking tot activiteiten die van invloed zijn op de fysieke leefomgeving en inzake handhaving van regelingen op het gebied van de fysieke leefomgeving (Wet algemene bepalingen omgevingsrecht – Wabo)

Besluit van 11 december 2006, houdende regels ter voorkoming van verontreiniging door schepen (Besluit voorkoming verontreiniging door schepen)

Besluit van 19 maart, houdende regels met betrekking tot het inzamelen van bedrijfsafvalstoffen of gevaarlijke afvalstoffen

Besluit van 25 maart 2010, houdende regels ter uitvoering van de Wet algemene bepalingen omgevingsrecht (Besluit omgevingsrecht – Bor)

Regeling van de Staatssecretaris van Infrastructuur en Milieu, van 18 maart 2015, nr. IENM/BSK-2015/52417, houdende vaststelling van criteria ter nadere invulling van de voorwaarden als bedoeld in artikel 5 van de kaderrichtlijn afvalstoffen (Regeling criteria bijproducten kaderrichtlijn afvalstoffen), Staatscourant 2015, 7458

## National – UK

The Environmental Permitting Regulations (England and Wales) 2016, No. 1154

## Case-law

### *EU*

Case C-9/00 Palin Granit Oy and Vehmassalon kansanterveystyön kuntayhtymän hallitus. [2002] ECR 2002 I-03533

Case C-114/01 AvestaPolarit Chrome Oy [2003] ECR 2003 I-08725

Case C-235/02 Criminal proceedings against Marco Antonio Saetti and Andrea Frediani [2004] ECR 2004 I-01005

Case C-457/02 Criminal proceedings against Antonio Nișelli [2004] ECR 2004 I-10853

Case C-121/03 Commission v Spain [2005] ECR I-7569

Case C-194/05 Commission of the European Communities v Italian Republic [2007] ECR 2007 I-11661

Case C-188/07 Commune de Mesquer [2008] ECR I-4501, para. 53, Case C-263/05 Commission vs. Italy [2007] ECR I-11745, para. 32

Joined Cases C- 241/12 and C-242/2012 Shell Nederland Verkoopmaatschappij BV and Shell Belgium [2013].

C-418/97 ARCO Chemie Nederland Ltd [2000] ECR I – 4475

Joined Cases C- 241/12 and C-242/2012 Shell Nederland Verkoopmaatschappij BV and Shell Belgium [2013], Opinion of AG Jääskinen

*National – The Netherlands*

ECLI:NL:RBAMS:2010:BN2149

ECLI:NL:RBAMS:2010:BN2068

ECLI:NL:GHAMS:2011:BR0014

ECLI:NL:GHAMS:2011:BU9237

ECLI:NL:GHAMS:2020:1157

Ontwerpbeschikking ambtshalve gedeeltelijk intrekken vergunning van Wubben Handelsmaatschappij BV, Gedeputeerde Staten van Noord-Brabant, 8 December 2016 [Administrative decision]

*National – UK*

'Agouman v. Leigh' (2009), High Court of Justice, [2016] EWHC 1324 (QB)

# List of Tables and Figures

**Tables**

Table 2.1: Overview of the book summarising methodological aspects relevant for each chapter 79
Table 5.1: The structurally established goals in the waste oil management and bunker fuel production industries 212
Table 7.1: Summary of the answers to the research questions and overview of related book Chapter 318

**Figures**

Figure 1.1: Adapted responsive regulation pyramid 41
Figure 2.1: Comparison of universal scripts used for crime-script analysis of a subway mugging – original from Cornish 1994 and contemporary version from Tompson and Chainey 2011 65
Figure 2.2: Sample table for data collection from dossiers applying the crime scripting method 66
Figure 2.3: Extract from Tompson and Chainey (2011) – Useful questions for the identification of offending conditions and enforcement conditions (p. 11) 68
Figure 3.1: Fractional distillation of crude oil 85
Figure 3.2: The system of petroleum extraction, refinement, and use – emissions and wastes from a finite stock of crude to a finite stock of biosphere 87
Figure 3.3: The stages of bunker fuel production and consumption 91
Figure 3.4: The actors involved at different stages of bunker fuel production 92
Figure 3.5: Physical flows of WOs (row above) and accompanying documents (row below) from use of substance to re-use after treatment 96
Figure 3.6: Overlap between the three stages of the bunker fuel production process and the waste oil management process from generation to re-use 98
Figure 3.7: Permissible operations for (waste) oils under Directive 2008/98 101
Figure 3.8: Market dynamics in the bunker fuel production industry 117
Figure 3.9: Embedded intervention/problem-triangle adapted for organisational crimes 133

Figure 4.1: The formal system of guardianship in the waste oil management industry 147
Figure 4.2: Overview of component Acts in Case 1 153
Figure 4.3: Act 1 – Collecting WOs, activities and actors organised in scenes from Pre-activity to Post-activity 155
Figure 4.4: Act 2 – Documenting the Collection of WOs, activities and actors organised in scenes from Pre-activity to Post-activity 159
Figure 4.5: The influence of fraud and lack of knowledge on the formal system of guardianship in Case 1 160
Figure 4.6: Act 3 – Mixing waste oils, activities and actors organised in scenes from Pre-activity to Post-activity31 162
Figure 4.7: Logic of LAP Sector-plans 164
Figure 4.8: Comparison between processing according to law, Crafty's permit and in reality 167
Figure 4.9: Act 4 – Processing WOs, activities and actors organised in scenes from Pre-activity to Post-activity 168
Figure 4.10: Act 5 – Illegal Movement and receipt of WOs Labelled as Products, activities and actors organised in scenes from Pre-activity to Post-activity 171
Figure 4.11: Overview of component Acts in Case 2 180
Figure 4.12: Act 1 – Producing (Fertilisers and Pesticides), activities and actors organised in scenes from Pre-activity to Post- activity 182
Figure 4.13: Act 2 – Labelling WOs as By-products, activities and actors organised in scenes from Pre-activity to Post- activity 186
Figure 4.14: Act 3 – Limited testing of WOs labelled as by-products, activities and actors organised in scenes from Pre-activity to Post- activity 189
Figure 4.15: Act 4 – Illegal Movement and Receipt of WOs labelled as by-products, activities and actors organised in scenes from Pre-activity to Post-activity 192
Figure 5.1: Legitimate and illegitimate opportunities for goal attainment at the crossroads between waste oil management and bunker fuel production. 217
Figure 5.2: Symbioses and synergies that generate a crime-facilitative system at the overlap between WOM and BFP. 259
Figure 6.1: The agencies involved in the system of guardianship for waste management in the Netherlands 264
Figure 6.2: Extract from "Blauwdruk Team Andante 2017 Engels", p. 3. 271
Figure 6.3: Adapted responsive regulation pyramid 294
Figure 7.1: Intervention script for illegal waste oil management activities in the process of bunker fuel production 323

# Acknowledgements

In German, which happens to have become my family language in recent years, the supervisors of a doctoral candidate are referred to as *Doctorvater* or *Doktormutter*. In the context of completing a PhD, one has a bit more choice about the parents one takes on than with biological parents, but there is never a real guarantee about how well they will raise the *"Doktorkind"* nor how well that *Doktorkind* will do of its own accord. I believe I am one of the luckiest *Doctorkinder* in the world because my *Doktorvätern* have done exactly what every good parent needs to do: they never gave up on me, they never let me give up on myself and they masterfully combined kindness, encouragement, compassion, and firmness in their varied efforts to help me get to doctoral adulthood. Prof. Hans Nelen and dr. Roland Moerland have all the expertise to write their own doctoral parenting book. There were less than a handful of meetings where both were not present; and I can think of none where they had not made the joint effort to formulate a message that would aid me along my path.

Dear Roland, I admire and appreciate how you choose each word that you carefully utter to be precise and to convey the strength of your message. You would never give empty praise, nor gratuitous criticism. You have taught me that self-respect is the basis upon which one traverses (academic) life and that the thoughts and opinions of others are there for us to reflect and build new ideas and perspectives and not construct or destruct ourselves. (That said, your being 'impressed' is the greatest award for my work I could have hoped for.) You bring so much enthusiasm to all your endeavours and you marry it to incredible clear-headedness and piercing analysis – your example will be a guide for many years to come.

Dear Hans, you are the epitome of starting with kindness. Despite there being many reasons for you to consider yourself as above us all, there is not the slightest whiff of arrogance in the way you conduct yourself. Indeed, you show clearly how one's own achievements can never take up so much space as to squeeze out the aspirations of others. You actively make that space and generously pick out each strength you can find so that those around you can thrive. You have continuously helped me see the bigger picture, whether in making a theoretical point or deciding which step to take next in my academic career.

There is no doubt that this book could not exist except for the work of Luuk Boogert, Jos van der Kamp and the other members of the Andante team. You display tirelessness and excitement in the face of what can often seem like insurmountable challenges. As a citizen of this world, I am grateful that you wake up every day and make an effort to achieve justice for us all. As a researcher, I am thankful that you trusted me enough to make me a part of your incredible work. As a young woman at the start of my career, I am deeply appreciative of the honesty, kindness, respect and encouragement you showed me.

It took a number of years for this book to materialise and I have learned to consider 'doing my PhD' as a phase in my life rather than a specific project. I have spent this stage in my life in the company of many people, all of whom it is challenging to list here. Still, I am grateful for all those encounters, however brief. Some friendships, however, are also truly a hallmark of this time in my life and deserve to be acknowledged more explicitly.

Dear Kim, there is so much warmth in your heart, that I can often imagine myself knocking at its door on a cold and windy day and being assured of finding refuge and the possibility to recover within it. Your strong sense of doing right and doing well help me calibrate my own efforts and I can rely on you to figure out all kinds of challenges – ethical or practical, criminological or motherly.

Dear Constantijn, we go on the greatest intellectual adventures together and laugh so much along the way. All the frustrations and twists and turns of life can be endured with so much more ease if one can savour them in good company like yours. You always take me just seriously enough so that I know what I say and feel matters, but you never let me go so far as to fall into any kind of despair.

Dear Marcus, you are the most deeply loyal and just person I know. If gravity were to stop existing all of a sudden, you could be trusted to take on its task. You and Annika are truly like family to me (us) and I look forward to all the years to come where we watch this family grow and evolve.

Dear Andrea, you artfully combine being grounded and ambitious in a way that is so inspiring. Your hard work is pure because not only is it principled, but it is also visibly a source of joy for you. You expect no praise but insist on fairness for all. You always make time and embody the idea that love is truly limitless – how lucky I feel to often be the recipient of these generous gifts!

Dear Ida, you helped me see that the writing process is one that can be delighted in, if only I would stop focusing on getting everything perfect and right instantly. You have taught me resilience and hopefulness as well as loyalty and compassion. Thank you.

Behind the four walls within which the pages of this book were written, life has continued to unfold. Since my childhood, my parents – Maria and Marino – have made all the efforts they could to help me strengthen my character, sharpen my mind, and ignite my curiosity. To this day, they provide the material means that are essential to survive because good books and ideas are often not enough.

Without saying it, I know they have no doubt in my ability to ultimately succeed. Thank you. My acquired parents – Mahnaz Syrus and Mamad Shamskho – assure me a home away from home and give our family enterprise much needed stability and support. They also always insisted that they would do anything to help me finish this project and have been true to their word. Leah Herrmann entered our home to help take care of our young children while the final stages of this life-phase were unfolding. She allowed me to be a mother and a PhD candidate at the same time. She loved and cared for my children in a way that put my heart and conscience at ease so I could focus on producing my so-called third child. Marie Köllhofer – at turns my acquired sister and guardian angel – has been there to celebrate every tiny victory in my life and has helped me pick up the pieces at each moment of crisis without displaying anything other than love and patience throughout.

Siavash Shamskho walks alongside me tirelessly as we figure out this strange, beautiful, and sometimes frustrating thing called life. The strong blasts of the winds of my mood and my alternating extremes of excited ambition and petrified anxiety have never shaken you and I am sure we will go on to achieve many more wonderful things together, laughing and talking each step of the way. Lara and Luca, my beautiful children, have showed me what truly matters in the world. Without that shift in perspective, I would have never finished this.

Aachen, 12th March 2023

# Table of Contents


| | | |
|---|---|---|
| 1 | **Introduction** | 19 |
| 1.1 | Research Questions & Research Aims | 25 |
| 1.2 | Theoretical Approaches & Conceptual Tools | 29 |
| 1.3 | Academic & Societal Relevance | 46 |
| 1.4 | Outline | 49 |
| 2 | **Methods & Methodology** | 51 |
| 2.1 | Research Strategy | 51 |
| 2.2 | Methods of Data Selection, Collection, Reduction, and Analysis | 58 |
| 2.3 | Limitations | 73 |
| 3 | **The Waste-Product Nexus Exploring the Physical, Economic and Regulatory Features of Two Overlapping Industries** | 81 |
| 3.1 | Physical Flows: Oils, Goods, Fuel & Wastes | 83 |
| 3.2 | The Waste Oil Management Services Industry | 100 |
| 3.3 | Markets, Standards and Legislation in the Bunker Fuel Production Industry | 115 |
| 4 | **Deconstructing Two Criminal Events Using Crime Script Analysis** | 139 |
| 4.1 | Formal Guardianship Structures in the Netherlands | 141 |
| 4.2 | Case 1: Waste Collection & Processing | 151 |
| 4.3 | Case 2: Producing Petrochemicals and Waste Oils | 178 |
| 5 | **A Crime-Facilitative System at the Intersection of Two Symbiotic Industries** | 203 |
| 5.1 | Crime-Facilitative Systems, Symbiotic Industries and Organisational Crime | 205 |
| 5.2 | Encouraging Crime: Goals, Provocations, Incentives & Rewards | 211 |
| 5.3 | Facilitating & Encouraging Crime: Opportunities, Efforts & Excuses | 223 |

5.4 Facilitating Crime: Low Risks, Concealment and Capable Guardianship 242

**6 Andante: Exploring an Example of Capable Guardianship** 261
6.1 Andante: An Overview 263
6.2 Andante through the Lenses of Problem-Oriented Policing and Responsive Regulation 286
6.3 Andante through the Lens of Situational Crime Prevention 299

**7 Conclusions** 315
7.1 Summary and Overview of the Book 316
7.2 Developing Crime-Resistance: Intervening at Multi-Level Pinch-Points to Inhibit Crime-Commission 321
7.3 Halting the Treadmill of Law: Learning Experiences from Criminal Law Enforcement and Beyond 335

**Annex I – Additional Materials** 351

**Annex II – Field Work** 353

**Annex III – Details on Waste Oils and Bunker Fuel** 359

**Bibliography** 361

# 1 Introduction

Two clamorous events of global importance and impact have taken place within the 18 months that precede the writing of this introduction: the *Wakashio* spill in July 2020 and the blockage of the Suez Canal trading route in March 2021. At the risk of ageing this manuscript prematurely, I considered it important to begin with these two events, not just because of the magnitude and absurdity of their repercussions. But also, and especially, because they are so representative of the interconnectedness that underlies both causes and effects in the cases of corporate environmental crime that are explored in this book.

Let us begin with the more recent event – the Suez Canal blockage. One of the largest container ships known to man – the Ever Given – tipped over in the Canal on Tuesday 23rd March 2021 where it remained until it was dislodged eight days later. The costs to global trade were initially estimated at roughly $6.7 million per *minute*,[1] in reference merely to the quantity of cargo held up and delayed because hundreds of ships could not traverse the waters at this location. Yet the logistical disruption to the routines of global and globalised trade are challenging to assess with any certainty. We should not, of course, turn a blind eye to the potentially harmful side effects that such hinderances to trade bring. Loss of profits affects the entire supply and distribution chain, not just large companies but also the individual workers who are involved at each stage. Still, this incident is particularly remarkable because it shows how much our current society relies on global(-ised) trade and shipping to sustain the prosperity of mankind. It is astounding to realise that the well-being and happiness of billions of people can potentially be (negatively) affected by the single crossing of a single, albeit very large, ship.

Roughly six thousand kilometres southeast of Suez, and approximately 8 months earlier, another cargo ship – the *Wakashio* – was on its way from Singapore to Tubarão, Brazil. When it reached the height of Mauritius, it ran aground on a coral reef. Within two weeks, oil began leaking from the ship leading to immense damage to flora and fauna at this environmentally precious location. The health

1. Mary-Ann Russon, "The Cost of the Suez Canal Blockage," *BBC News* 29 March 2021; Justin Harper, "Suez Blockage Is Holding up $9.6bn of Goods a Day," *BBC News* 26 March 2021.

of locals was also later reported to have been affected by the spill. At the time of writing, investigations into the causal chain of events have still not been completed, but most sources agree: the lack of compatibility between the engine of the ship and the fuel used to power it is the likely culprit.[2] The fuel that ships consume is called bunker fuel (BF) and it is one of the protagonists of the story that unfolds in the next few hundred pages.

In a nutshell, the most recently devised international rules concerning bunker fuel put a lot of pressure on the actors involved in producing this substance to generate a fuel with the lowest concentration of sulphur possible. As if ripped from the pages of a comic book, the bunker fuel used by the *Wakashio* – and roughly 70% of container ships circulating on global waters in the first half of 2020 – was called Very Low Sulphur Oil (VLSO).[3] VLSO is a magic potion: it contains very little sulphur and very much of almost anything else. A substantial part of it is kerosene, a petroleum derivative normally used to fuel airplanes. And here we see yet another dimension of interconnectedness linked to one more recent event of global importance. The spreading and attempts at containment of the COVID-19 virus in 2020 meant that many airline companies had little to no use for fuel – i.e., kerosene. According to some estimates, air travel dropped by roughly 60% in 2020.[4] So, kerosene went from being a highly valued and valuable product to an inconvenient burden to get rid of with as little costs as possible or, hopefully, with some profit to cover for the lack of consumption by airlines. Luckily, that burden could be lifted by using kerosene to make bunker fuel, which incidentally meant that the relative sulphur content of *that* fuel would also be so low that it would meet the newest and most stringent standards. When life gives you lemons, make bunker fuel!

Not so luckily, this magical potion labelled as VLSO is far from suitable for the running of ship engines. Already in advance of its injection into the engines of the *Wakashio*, economic and state actors alike were aware of the potential problems linked to its consumption.[5] However, this awareness did not amount to concern

2. Nisha Degnarain, "Satellites Make New Discovery About Mauritius Oil Spill Ship Wakashio," *Forbes* 22 January 2021; "New Images Released of Engine Damage Caused by Experimental Low Sulfur Ship Fuel VLSFO," ibid. 24 January 2021; "BP Confirms It Supplied Fuel to Mauritius Oil Spill Ship but Denies Fuel Was Cause," *Forbes* 23 January 2021.
3. Warren Patterson, "Marine Fuels & IMO 2020: So Much for All the Hype," in *THINK Economic and Financial Analysis*, ed. ING (21 July 2020). https://think.ing.com/articles/marine-fuels-imo-2020-so-much-for-all-the-hype
4. Statistic based on oil sales from Singapore – considered as a benchmark for global market. International Air Transport Association, 'Airline Industry Statistics Confirm 2020 Was Worst Year on Record' Press Release, 3 August 2021; "Air Travel Down 60 Per Cent, as Airline Industry Losses Top $370 Billion: Icao," *UN News* 15 January 2021; Wikipedia, "Impact of the Covid-19 Pandemic on Aviation."
5. Degnarain, "New Images Released of Engine Damage Caused by Experimental Low Sulfur Ship Fuel VLSFO"; Marasi News, "Clean Arctic Alliance: How Did Super Pollutant 'Frankenstein' Fuels Come to Market?," (29 January 2020). More recently Chevron has conducted a series of studies to look at compatibility further, see: "Scuffing & Red Deposits after Fuel Transition:

or caution in placing the product on the market. The destruction that resulted in the case of the *Wakashio* is merely a most clamorous and visible example of what such lack of concern has led to. In fact, the costs of pollution from the burning of VLSO by more than 68,000 ships across the world are 'invisible' and 'incalculable',[6] like many other types of environmental harm. And VLSO is just the latest in an interminable string of concoctions that result from the bunker fuel production (BFP) process. The awareness of those taking risks with the well-being of our planet and our health is partial. It is not that they do not know how their actions and omissions may lead to harm: they know that they are likely to lead to some harm, they just do not know the scale and nature of that harm. They also know that they can make millions in profit from manufacturing and selling substances like VLSO.

One of the other protagonists of our story has not yet visibly featured in the events recounted above, although the role of kerosene in VLSO partially hinted at it. That protagonist is waste; and lack of its explicit mention so far has a lot to do with the peculiarities of the two events, but it is also a consequence of both the elusiveness and ubiquitousness of waste. Waste is both noun and verb: for example, kerosene may be *a* waste, or it may be wast*ed*. And, if we think of wasting as a verb and contextualise it into our global system of production and consumption, we may get a glimpse of how diabolical this protagonist is. If the kerosene that was used to make VLSO had merely been abandoned, many would say it was wasted or that it was a waste of a precious resource. Such a perspective rests on a utilitarian worldview, where the value of an object or an action depends on its instrumentality towards a goal; that goal being the efficient consumption of resources to sustain physical and economic life toward eternal growth. Lack of instrumentality means lack of use; in other words: uselessness. Therefore, use*ful*ness is the opposite of wastefulness according to this worldview. Abolishing wasting as an action requires that what is wasted be used as a product instead.

However, waste is not just what is without use. Waste, in fact, is often defined in relation to its harmful effects on the environment and human health. For several decades, environmentalists and policy makers have been engaged in applying the waste label to an increasing number of substances based on the detrimental impact of their management, if the latter is carried out without considering the goal of environmental conservation. The birth of the legal waste label has brought with it procedures, actors and standards that are functional to such conservation. The result is the existence of entire waste management systems and networks,

Causes and Solutions," in *Marine lubricants information bulletin* (Chevron Marine Products LLC, 2021).

6. United Nations, "Review of Maritime Transport 2020 " in *Review of Maritime Transport*, ed. United Nations Conference on Trade and Development (New York2020), p. 37 – the total number of ships of more than 100 gross tonnage circulating in 2020 was more than 98.000.

which are continuously growing in sophistication. However, such systems are not fool proof – waste management firms do not always carry out their activities in accordance with the letter and spirit of the laws that govern their operations. The reasons for such improper management are many, but there are some basic structural arrangements within the waste management services (WMS) industry that make illicit practices possible and appealing.

Wastes come in all shapes and sizes. The ones we are specifically curious about in this book are waste *oils* (WOs).[7] These wastes can physically be blended into the bunker fuel mixtures mentioned before. In fact, numerous substances that are classifiable as (hazardous) waste oils according to the law have repeatedly ended up in bunker fuel over the span of decades.[8] Wastes and waste oils are mishandled in many ways; and there are clamorous examples of this kind of activity too. One of these is the case of yet another ship – the *Probo Koala*.[9]

In 2006, the multinational Trafigura was in search for a waste management firm to handle a large quantity of waste oils it held aboard the *Probo Koala*. Some time prior to this, large quantities of petroleum refinery residues as well as wastes had been loaded and treated on the ship itself to generate a product – naphtha. For that transformation to occur, Trafigura had applied a process called caustic washing, which entails the use of caustic soda to strip substances of impurities.

7. The term 'waste oil' is used throughout this book to indicate several different types of oil (petroleum) based substances that are classifiable as wastes under Dutch and EU law. It should be noted that 'waste oil' can also be considered a *specific* type of waste under these rules, different from others such as 'used lubricants' or 'fuel residues'. I made the choice to use waste oils to simplify the narration. The more specific labels as well as the accompanying references to national or EU rules will be made accordingly to substantiate these more specific labels where this is necessary. Chapter 3 will also go into the details of how waste oils are precisely categorised under the applicable legislation.

8. ACM Spapens, "Vuile Olie: Een Onzichtbaar Probleem Met Grote Gevolgen," *Het tijdschrift voor de politie* 75, no. 8 (2013); A de Buck et al., "Blends in beeld. Een analyse van de bunkerolieketen" (Delft: CE Delft, 2011).

9. Greenpeace & Amnesty International, "The Toxic Truth. About a Company Called Trafigura, a Ship Called Probo Koala and the Dumping of Toxic Waste in Cote D'ivoire," (London: Amnesty International International Secretariat, 2012). UNEP, "UN Environment Releases Independent Audit of Sites Affected by Toxic Waste Dump in Côte D'ivoire," news release, 30 January 2018, 2018, https://www.unenvironment.org/news-and-stories/press-release/un-environment-releases-independent-audit-sites-affected-toxic-waste. "Environmental Audit of the Sites Affected by the Dumping of Toxic Wastes from the "Probo Koala"," (2018). Trafigura, "Trafigura & the Probo Koala," (2016). VROM Tweede Kamer, "Probo Koala in Amsterdam, Feitenrelaas En Relevante Wetgeving," (2006). Hulshof Commissie, "Rapport Van Bevindingen Naar Aanleiding Van Het Onderzoek Van De Gang Van Zaken Rond Aankomst, Verblijf En Vertrek Van De Probo Koala in Juli 2006 Te Amsterdam", ed. Requested by Gemeente Amsterdam (2006); United Nations, "Report of the Special Rapporteur on the Adverse Effects of the Movement and Dumping of Toxic and Dangerous Products and Wastes on the Enjoyment of Human Rights, Okechukwu Ibeanu," (2009). Inspectie Leefomegeving en Transport (ILT), "Heavy Fuel Oil for Sea-Going Vessels on-Road Fuels for West Africa Blended in the Netherlands," (2018). An English translation of the judgment in the Probo Koala case is available at: www.rechtspraak.nl/Organisatie-en-contact/Organisatie/Rechtbanken/Rechtbank-Rotterdam/Nieuws/Documents/English%20translation%20Seatrade.pdf.

The naphtha Trafigura generated yielded it a whopping $19 million in profit. However, there was a large amount of highly toxic waste left over as well – the impurities from the residues mixed with the caustic soda. At first, Trafigura went to a specialised waste oil management firm in Amsterdam to have its waste taken care of. The price attached to this service was very high given the toxicity of the substances, which was discovered only after the wastes were partly offloaded. A decision was made to spare such exorbitant costs and to ultimately take the wastes southwards to the Ivory Coast instead, where the 500 tons of slops were offloaded at the Port of Abidjan. They were then dumped at several locations across the city. The damage that resulted was immense, albeit not immediately visible. Several deaths and severe illnesses were reported and connected to the dumping. Trafigura had received a quote of € 500.000 for the handling of its waste in the Netherlands, in accordance with Dutch and European Union (EU) legislation. The waste management services it received in Abidjan cost a mere € 18.500. The extent of compliance with any rules on environmental and human health protection was null. Thanks to the application of EU, international and national rules, criminal proceedings were initiated against Trafigura and others in the Netherlands. Among those indicted we find Amsterdam Port Services – the company which had initially taken part of the wastes and then returned them to the *Probo Koala*.[10]

Just like the *Ever Given* in Suez and the *Wakashio* in Mauritius, the *Probo Koala* case shows us merely the tip of the illicit waste oil management (WOM) iceberg. However, there is a stark difference between the case of the *Probo Koala* and that of the *Wakashio*: the way they can and have been defined *legally*. While the VLSO used to fuel the *Wakashio* seemingly complied with all the international standards applicable to bunker fuel, the activities performed on the waste oils transported by the *Probo Koala* were in clear contravention of Dutch, European and international laws. In part, these laws govern the management of waste as a specific economic and environmentally relevant activity; however, more general administrative and criminal law provisions were also the basis of the case brought against Trafigura. This disparity in the regulation of the waste oil management and bunker fuel production sectors is an important criminogenic element as will become clear in this book.

The *Probo Koala* proceedings have functioned as a springboard for more intense public scrutiny of firms involved in the waste oil and bunker fuel sectors in the Netherlands. Several (state) actors have been probing into the world of oil with reinforced focus and increased resources. They have attempted to uncover the

10. Commissie, "Rapport Van Bevindingen Naar Aanleiding Van Het Onderzoek Van De Gang Van Zaken Rond Aankomst, Verblijf En Vertrek Van De Probo Koala in Juli 2006 Te Amsterdam"; International, "The Toxic Truth"; Trafigura, "Trafigura & the Probo Koala"; Tweede Kamer, "Probo Koala in Amsterdam, Feitenrelaas En Relevante Wetgeving"; UNEP, "Environmental Audit of the Sites Affected by the Dumping of Toxic Wastes from the 'Probo Koala'."

workings of the industries immersed in this murky and awful substance. Among those actors, there is a group of Dutch police officers who have been working with a specialised public prosecutor for several years. They have been focusing on these very peculiar and endemic crimes. We can refer to them collectively as the Andante team.

Through their efforts, the Andante team and others have found repeated patterns of offending: waste oils are systematically mishandled at different stages of the waste management process. Then, they are systematically introduced into the process of bunker fuel production. These patterns have been observed within the Netherlands, but also across borders. And, partly based on information from other authorities across the globe, the patterns are confirmed to be taking place in several parts of the world. This shows that there is a serious societal and legal problem, which we can condense as 'illegal waste oil management activities in the process of bunker fuel production'. With these terms we indicate different manifestations of the same underlying pattern: substances that are classifiable as waste oils under Dutch and European law are systematically dealt with in ways that are contrary to those rules by corporate actors. Among the forms of mismanagement, we are particularly interested in those instances where waste oils enter the bunker fuel production process. The illegality of such entry is, for the most part, dependent on the boundaries set by waste management legislation, as well as administrative and criminal law.[11] These activities result in environmental degradation and pose risks to human health. We can, therefore, categorise these patterns as a form of corporate environmental crime.

Whether relying on legal definitions of crime or zemiological approaches, this legal and societal problem can also be looked at as a criminological one. It is open to investigation to understand how and why it occurs by using tools developed to study criminogenesis. Criminological analyses also yield important findings on *limiting* criminogenesis through different kinds of responses. Hence, the aim of this

11. There are arguments to be made about using the label 'illicit' or 'questionable' instead of 'illegal' to define the activities that are being studied in this book. By using these broader terms, one could also indicate activities that are not strictly forbidden by the applicable rules. To some extent, I also talk about these kinds of activities and use terms like 'questionable' where appropriate. Furthermore, because part of the data that I use relates to real events, using the term illegal or even criminal opens up the possibility that the individuals or firms that recognise themselves in the descriptions I made would contest the accuracy of such labels. I chose the term 'illegal' because, according to my juridical assessment (and that of state authorities as regards the cases that are analyzed in Chapter 4), there is evidence of rule violation when looking at the facts. The ambiguity of what counts as waste and what counts as product and, in turn, what counts as legal or illegal is itself a fundamental component of the case study and the way harmful activities are justified, concealed, and denied. By taking a firm stance to speak about '*illegal* waste oil management activities', I also want to show that one can take a clear position, in light of the applicable law, but then still explore nuance, which I do throughout the text, yet still not be overtaken by the same ambiguity that excuses acts of environmental degradation.

book is to address the societal, legal, and criminological problem outlined above. How this will be done is discussed in the following Sections.

## 1.1 Research Questions & Research Aims

The goal of this research is to identify the crime facilitative factors of illegal waste oil management activities in the process of bunker fuel production as well as the intervention mechanisms upon these factors to limit its occurrence. The two main research questions are:

1. How and why do illegal waste oil management activities in the process of producing bunker fuel take place?
2. How can illegal waste oil management activities in the process of producing bunker fuel be limited?

The aims underlying these two research questions are exploratory, descriptive, and explanatory. Regarding the former two aims, an important aspect to consider in formulating the research questions was that of data. We have seen that there is a recognisable societal problem, which is criminologically and legally interesting and which needs to be addressed. When I began this research, however, there was little empirical data on what illegal waste oil management in the process of bunker fuel production looked like concretely. Publicly available information was scarce,[12] and hardly any criminological or legal analyses had been published on this specific theme, with some exceptions in the Dutch language.[13] At the time the research project started, several publications in the field of criminology – as well as some other, relevant disciplines – were available and were related to the central themes of the book. These publications provided insight into similar or connected (criminal) activities. The overview presented below – including the specific sources which are cited – is not meant to be complete, rather it is illustrative of the stand of the academic debate at the time.

In the fields of both criminology and law, there were numerous publications on the topics of environmental and corporate crime (studied separately or in combination).[14] Illegal waste activities are repeatedly focused on in publications

12. Hans Marijnissen, "Zaak-Shell: Testcase Voor Aanpak Vervuilde Stookolie," *Trouw* 2013; Ariën Rasmijn, "Zware Stookolie Gelekt in Binnenwater Aruba," *Caribisch Netwerk* 2015; John Vidal, "The World's Largest Cruise Ship and Its Supersized Pollution Problem," *The Guardian* 2016; Fred Pearce, "How 16 Ships Create as Much Pollution as All the Cars in the World," *The Daily Mail* 2013; Jeremy Plester, "Dirty Diesel: Why Ships Are the Worst Offenders," *The Guardian* 2017.
13. Spapens, "Vuile Olie: Een Onzichtbaar Probleem Met Grote Gevolgen"; de Buck et al., "Blends in beeld. Een analyse van de bunkerolieketen"
14. Some examples from green criminology are: Piers Beirne and Nigel South, *Issues in Green Criminology* (Routledge, 2013); Rob White, *Global Environmental Harm: Criminological Perspectives* (Routledge, 2013); Tanya Wyatt, "Issues in Green Criminology: Confronting Harms against Environments, Humanity and Other Animals," *British Journal of Criminology* 48, no. 5 (2008). In

of this kind as a specific form of environmental and/or corporate crime.[15] Furthermore, illegal waste activities have also been studied specifically in relation to (mafia-type) organised crime.[16] Organisational and green criminology scholars have also focused more on explorations of crimes or harm-producing practices linked to the oil sector.[17]

Beyond criminology and law, literature from natural and medical sciences that looks at the way pollution is generated and how it affects the environment and human health has also dealt with issues of illegal waste management and

---

the field of organisational criminology, see, for example: Ronald C Kramer, "Corporate Crime: An Organizational Perspective," *White-collar and economic crime* (1982); Vincenzo Ruggiero, *Organized and Corporate Crime in Europe: Offers That Can't Be Refused* (Dartmouth, 1996); Sally S Simpson and David Weisburd, *The Criminology of White-Collar Crime* (Springer, 2009); Gary Slapper and Steve Tombs, *Corporate Crime* (Harlow: Longman, 1999).

15. Lieselot Bisschop, "Is It All Going to Waste? Illegal Transports of E-Waste in a European Trade Hub," *Crime Law and Social Change* 58, no. 3 (2012); Don Liddick, "The Traffic in Garbage and Hazardous Wastes: An Overview," *Trends in Organized Crime* 13, no. 2-3 (2010); M. H. Wong, "Export of Toxic Chemicals – a Review of the Case of Uncontrolled Electronic-Waste Recycling," *Environmental pollution* 149, no. 2 (2007); Lisa Tompson and Spencer Chainey, "Profiling Illegal Waste Activity: Using Crime Scripts as a Data Collection and Analytical Strategy," *European Journal on Criminal Policy and Research* 17, no. 3 (2011); Rob White and Diane Heckenberg, "Key Vulnerabilities and Limitations in the Management of Hazardous Waste and Its Disposal: A Checklist Assessment Tool," *Journal of Environmental Protection* 2, no. 09 (2011); Karin van Wingerde, *De Afschrikking Voorbij: Een Empirische Studie Naar Afschrikking, Generale Preventie En Regelnaleving in De Nederlandse Afvalbranche* (2012); Wim Huisman, "Tussen Winst En Moraal: Achtergronden Van Regelnaleving En Regelovertreding Door Ondernemingen" (Boom Juridische uitgevers, 2001); Wim Huisman and Judith van Erp, "Opportunities for Environmental Crime: A Test of Situational Crime Prevention Theory," *British Journal of Criminology* 53, no. 6 (2013).
16. A. D'Amato, "Illegal Waste Disposal in the Time of the Mafia: A Tale of Enforcement and Social Well Being," *Journal of Environmental Planning and Management* 55, no. 5 (2012); Monica Massari, "Ecomafias and Waste Entrepreneurs in the Italian Market" (paper presented at the 6th cross-border crime colloquium held in berlin, germany, 2004); Monica Massari and Paola Monzini, "Dirty Businesses in Italy: A Case-Study of Illegal Trafficking in Hazardous Waste," *Global crime* 6, no. 3-4 (2004); Andrew Szasz, "Corporations, Organized Crime, and the Disposal of Hazardous Waste: An Examination of the Making of a Criminogenic Regulatory Structure," *Criminology* 24, no. 1 (1986); Vincenzo Ruggiero and Nigel South, "Green Criminology and Dirty Collar Crime," *Critical Criminology* 18, no. 4 (2010).
17. Hope M Babcock, "A Risky Business: Generation of Nuclear Power and Deepwater Drilling for Offshore Oil and Gas," *Colum. J. Envtl. L.* 37 (2012); Alan A. Block and Thomas J. Bernard, "Crime in the Waste Oil Industry," *Deviant Behavior* 9, no. 2 (1988); Elizabeth A Bradshaw, ""Obviously, We're All Oil Industry": The Criminogenic Structure of the Offshore Oil Industry," *Theoretical Criminology* 19, no. 3 (2015); Matthew B Greife and Paul B Stretesky, "Treadmill of Production and State Variations in Civil and Criminal Liability for Oil Discharges in Navigable Waters," *Routledge International Handbook of Green Criminology. London: Routledge* (2013); Dara O'Rourke and Sarah Connolly, "Just Oil? The Distribution of Environmental and Social Impacts of Oil Production and Consumption," *Annual Review of Environment and Resources* 28, no. 1 (2003); Vincenzo Ruggiero and Nigel South, "Green Criminology and Crimes of the Economy: Theory, Research and Praxis," *Critical Criminology* 21, no. 3 (2013); "Toxic State-Corporate Crimes, Neo-Liberalism and Green Criminology: The Hazards and Legacies of the Oil, Chemical and Mineral Industries," *International Journal for Crime, Justice and Social Democracy* 2, no. 2 (2013).

pollution.[18] Economic analyses also often focus on how to reduce environmental pollution through market and regulatory strategies. In these analyses, pollution is generally defined as an externality in the operation of markets.[19] Along the same philosophical lines, law and economic models or recommendations have also been developed to reduce environmental crimes and harms.[20]

Other relevant bodies of work include corporate regulation and governance, including work on corporate social responsibility and risk-regulation.[21] Lastly, there have been numerous legal analyses of legislation designed to protect the environment, whether regulatory or criminal in nature.[22]

18. I. C. Eze et al., "Long-Term Air Pollution Exposure and Diabetes in a Population-Based Swiss Cohort," *Environ Int* 70 (2014); R. Kelishadi and P. Poursafa, "Air Pollution and Non-Respiratory Health Hazards for Children," *Arch Med Sci* 6, no. 4 (2010); M. Dherani et al., "Indoor Air Pollution from Unprocessed Solid Fuel Use and Pneumonia Risk in Children Aged under Five Years: A Systematic Review and Meta-Analysis," *Bull World Health Organ* 86, no. 5 (2008); Donella Hager Randers Joerrgen Meadows Dennis L. Meadows, *Limits to Growth the 30-Year Update* (London: Earthscan, 2012).
19. SE Shmelev and John R Powell, "Ecological–Economic Modelling for Strategic Regional Waste Management Systems," *Ecological Economics* 59, no. 1 (2006); Christian Almer and Timo Goeschl, "The Sopranos Redux: The Empirical Economics of Waste Crime," *Regional Studies* 49, no. 11 (2015).
20. Susan F. Mandiberg and Michael G. Faure, "A Graduated Punishment Approach to Environmental Crimes: Beyond Vindication of Administrative Authority in the United States and Europe," *Columbia Journal of Environmental Law.* 34, no. 2 (2009); Michael Faure, "The Development of Environmental Criminal Law in the Eu and Its Member States," *Review of European, Comparative & International Environmental Law* 26, no. 2 (2017); Michael Faure, Morag Goodwin, and Franziska Weber, "The Regulator's Dilemma: Caught between the Need for Flexibility & the Demands for Forseeability-Reassessing the Lex Certa Principle," *Alb. LJ Sci. & Tech.* 24 (2013).
21. Christine Parker, "Meta-Regulation: Legal Accountability for Corporate Social Responsibility," (2007); "Twenty Years of Responsive Regulation: An Appreciation and Appraisal," *Regulation & Governance* 7, no. 1 (2013); Christine Parker and Vibeke Lehmann Nielsen, *Explaining Compliance: Business Responses to Regulation* (Edward Elgar Publishing, 2011); Peter N Grabosky, "Green Markets: Environmental Regulation by the Private Sector*," *Law & Policy* 16, no. 4 (1994); Neil Gunningham, Peter N Grabosky, and Darren Sinclair, *Smart Regulation: Designing Environmental Policy*, vol. 514 (Clarendon Press Oxford, 1998); Peter Mascini and Eelco Van Wijk, "Responsive Regulation at the Dutch Food and Consumer Product Safety Authority: An Empirical Assessment of Assumptions Underlying the Theory," *Regulation & Governance* 3, no. 1 (2009); Judith Van Erp and Wim Huisman, "Smart Regulation and Enforcement of Illegal Disposal of Electronic Waste," *Criminology & Public Policy* 9, no. 3 (2010); Ian Ayres and John Braithwaite, *Responsive Regulation: Transcending the Deregulation Debate* (Oxford University Press, 1992); John Braithwaite, "Enforced Self-Regulation: A New Strategy for Corporate Crime Control," *Michigan Law Review* 80, no. 7 (1982); *Regulatory Capitalism: How It Works, Ideas for Making It Work Better* (Edward Elgar Publishing, 2008); John Braithwaite and Peter Drahos, *Global Business Regulation* (Cambridge University Press, 2000).
22. Joonas Alaranta and Topi Turunen, "Drawing a Line between European Waste and Chemicals Regulation," *Review of European, Comparative & International Environmental Law* 26, no. 2 (2017); Ilona Cheyne, "The Definition of Waste in EC Law," *Journal of Environmental Law* 14, no. 1 (2002); Hazel Ann Nash, "The Revised Directive on Waste: Resolving Legislative Tensions in Waste Management?," ibid.21 (2009); P. Rice, "Harmonization of Criminal Environmental Liability Throughout the EU," *Environmental Claims Journal* 15, no. 2 (2003); Eloise Scotford, "Trash or Treasure: Policy Tensions in EC Waste Regulation," *Journal of Environmental Law*

However, the empirical information from these various sources did *not* contain detailed accounts of crime commission processes that could be categorised under the label of illegal waste oil management activities in the process of bunker fuel production. These very peculiar processes were brought to my attention when I encountered the Andante team.[23] Therefore, it was clear that one of the primary aims of the research should be exploratory and descriptive. Without a clear picture of what this phenomenon looked and looks like, it is highly unlikely that we can formulate any explanation of it, let alone make any appropriate recommendations to limit its occurrence. Therefore, the following sub-questions were formulated to achieve two research aims – exploration and description.

a. What do illegal waste oil management (WOM) activities in the process of bunker fuel production (BFP) look like?
b. During which steps of the broader BFP and WOM processes do these illegal activities occur?
c. Which logistical steps and which actions are undertaken by the actors involved?
d. What types of actors are involved?
e. What types of activities do they engage in?
f. What tools do they use to complete these activities?
g. What factors, at different levels of analysis, influence – facilitate or constrain – the actors involved in undertaking the abovementioned logistical steps towards crime-commission?

While description of crime commission processes was considered important, the theoretical criminological literature makes evident that, when appropriately expanded, description can gradually lead to explanation.[24] Therefore, by adding context (see sub-questions a and b) as well as the relationships *between* elements,

---

19, no. 3 (2007); Kimberly K Gregory, "The Basel Convention and the International Trade of Hazardous Waste: The Road to the Destruction of Public Health and the Environment Is Paved with Good Intentions," *Currents: Int'l Trade LJ* 10 (2001); Sabaa Ahmad Khan, "E-Products, E-Waste and the Basel Convention: Regulatory Challenges and Impossibilities of International Environmental Law," *Review of European, Comparative & International Environmental Law* (2016); Jonathan Krueger, "The Basel Convention and the International Trade in Hazardous Wastes," *Yearbook of international co-operation on environment and development* 2002 (2001); Katharina Kummer, "The International Regulation of Transboundary Traffic in Hazardous Wastes: The 1989 Basel Convention," *International and Comparative Law Quarterly* 41, no. 03 (1992).

23. The details of how I met and worked with the Andante team are provided in Chapter 2 and then Chapter 6 delves into the substance of the team's work. At present, it is relevant to know that I got in touch with the Andante team through one of my supervisors' contacts in the Dutch public prosecution service (*Openbaar Ministerie* – OM). We were looking for prosecutors who were dealing with or had dealt with waste crime in an initial, exploratory stage of the research.

24. See Chapter 2 for a discussion of the methodological aspects of how description and explanation are carried out in this research.

we can begin advancing some explanations for this phenomenon. Question (g) makes this explanatory aim concrete.

Furthermore, because of the juridical relevance of the problem as well as the importance of the concept of 'control' in criminological analysis, it was also clear from the outset that no study of criminogenesis would be complete without a specific focus on this aspect. Plus, the aim of developing recommendations for future efforts at limiting this type of crime expressed in the second main research question could not be fulfilled without looking at existing response measures. Therefore, three more sub-research questions needed to be formulated in this respect:

h. What internal as well as external regulations and mechanisms for supervision and control exist that apply to the WOM and BFP sectors?
i. How are these regulations and mechanisms interpreted, applied, and enforced?
j. How can these regulations and mechanisms influence – facilitate or constrain – the occurrence of the criminal activities that take place in the WOM and BFP sectors?

To answer the research questions we have just articulated, we need to use theoretical approaches and conceptual tools to guide us – these are discussed in the next Section. It is important to note here that illegal waste oil management in the process of bunker fuel production is taken as a *case* that needs to be *studied*. I will refer to the entirety of the research as a case study. In Chapter 2, I clarify what the notion of case study means for us from a methodological perspective.

## 1.2 Theoretical Approaches & Conceptual Tools

The exploration and analysis of criminogenesis carried out in this study have been performed by relying on a set of concepts and related theoretical propositions. Situational Crime Prevention (SCP) and crime script analysis (CSA) are used, on the one hand, as specific approaches. Organisational criminology and green criminology, on the other hand, are broader fields of study to which this research belongs and from which we borrow important conceptual tools for analysis. The reasons for choosing each of these theoretical perspectives is explained in the ensuing subsections, where each perspective is also briefly reviewed. The reviews are meant to inform the reader of the most important theoretical and empirical aspects of the bodies of knowledge captured within each perspective, and to highlight the tools that are useful for the present work. Epistemological and ontological considerations linked to the use of theories will be addressed in Chapter 2.

### *Deconstructing Crime Events Using Situational Crime Prevention and Crime-Script Analysis*

One of the perspectives adopted in this work is rooted in the SCP model. This model belongs to a wider family of preventive approaches from the field of environmental criminology. SCP shares a common starting point with other environmental criminological theories: the interest in and study of criminal *events* and the (immediate) *circumstances* in which these events occur.[25] The analysis and understanding of these factors is then used to develop solutions to the problem under study. The following subsection examines the origins and content of SCP to contextualise the conceptual tools, which are used in this study.

#### *Theoretical Foundations of SCP and the Environmental Approach to Explaining and Analysing Crime*

Theories in the field of environmental criminology pay special attention to *crime as an event* as opposed to *criminality* as a *characteristic of an offender* or group of offenders.[26] Traditionally, criminological analysis has placed more emphasis on the latter, leading to the formulation of preventative strategies that centred on changing individuals. In this regard, there is a wealth of scientific literature examining the drivers of criminality – whether biological, psychological or sociological – and the development of individual dispositions to commit crime.[27] The view expounded in these works is based on the premise that the ultimate determining factor of whether a crime will be committed is the existence of a criminal disposition, which leads those possessing it to seek out opportunities to engage in criminal acts.

By contrast, environmental criminologists view the offender as *one component* within a dynamic context. Thus, location, time, motive and methods of offending also become relevant as the aim shifts from transforming the offender to preventing criminal acts.[28] Therefore, the investigator is tasked with understanding crime *events*: such understanding emerges by observing, cataloguing and reflecting on the reality in which these events occur. Contemporary approaches in environmental criminology and crime analysis are grounded in three basic

25. Richard Wortley and Lorraine Mazerolle, *Environmental Criminology and Crime Analysis* (Willan, 2013), p. 1.
26. Richard Wortley and Michael Townsley, ed. *Environmental Criminology and Crime Analysis*, Second ed., Crime Science Series (Oxon: Routledge, 2017).
27. See texts such as: Lanier, M. Essential Criminology. New York: Routledge, 2015 and Newburn, T. Criminology [3rd ed.] London: Routledge, 2017.
28. Townsley, *Environmental Criminology and Crime Analysis*; Rachel Boba, "Crime Analysis and Crime Mapping," (Sage Publications, 2005); Derek B. Cornish and Ronald V. Clarke, "The Rational Choice Perspective," in *Environmental Criminology and Crime Analysis*, ed. Richard Wortley and Michael Townsley (Oxon: Routledge, 2017); Paul Ekblom, "The Conjunction of Criminal Opportunity: A Framework for Crime Reduction Toolkits," *Policing and Reducing Crime Unit Research, Development and Statistics Directorate Home Office: London, UK* (2001).

propositions. Firstly, the nature of the environment in which criminal behaviour occurs has a significant impact on criminal behaviour: (elements of) the scene of a crime may be criminogenic. Secondly, distribution of crime across space and time is non-random: crime is clustered in relation to opportunities present in criminogenic environments. Thirdly, awareness and study of criminogenic environments are useful tools for studying and controlling crime.[29]

Situational crime prevention couches itself in this very perspective and highlights the role opportunities play in *causing* crime.[30] This understanding rests upon certain theoretical assumptions about offenders' decision-making and how criminal opportunities are supplied. As regards the former, proponents of SCP view individuals as beings that engage in purposive behaviour based on *rational choices*.[31] Although rationality is bounded, individuals act based on (complex) cost-benefit evaluations of the situation they are in, factoring in their perception of the positive and negative results of a given decision.[32] Consequently, it is possible to influence individual behaviour *away* from criminal activities by *altering situational circumstances*; i.e. by redesigning criminogenic environments to reduce the perceived supply of opportunities and/or shift the balance between the costs (risks) and rewards of criminal acts and decisions. In the original formulation of the SCP model, offenders' perception of risks, efforts, and rewards are targeted to reconfigure environments in a way that prevents crime.

In terms of distribution of criminal opportunities, SCP draws on routine activities theory (RAT) and crime pattern theory (CPT).[33] RAT sees crime as the product of the coming together of three essential elements: a likely offender, a suitable target and the absence of capable guardians. It is the examination of the characteristics of these three elements that enable us to grasp how a situation leads to crime by generating motivation and opportunity. This explanation is

29. Townsley, Environmental Criminology and Crime Analysis.
30. Karen Bullock, Ronald V. Clarke, and Nick Tilley, *Situational Prevention of Organised Crimes* (Taylor & Francis, 2010); ibid.
31. Townsley, *Environmental Criminology and Crime Analysis*; Ronald V. Clarke, "Situational Crime Prevention," *Crime and justice* 19, no. Building a Safer Society: Strategic Approaches to Crime Prevention (1995); Ronald V Clarke, "Situational Crime Prevention: Theoretical Background and Current Practice," in *Handbook on Crime and Deviance* (Springer, 2009); Ronald V. Clarke, "Situational Crime Prevention," in *Environmental Criminology and Crime Analysis*, ed. Richard and Townsley Wortley, Michael (Oxon: Routledge, 2017); Ronald Clarke and Marcus Felson, *Routine Activity and Rational Choice*, vol. 5 (Transaction Publishers, 1993).
32. Clarke, "The Rational Choice Perspective"; R.V. Clarke, & Felson, M., ed. *Routine Activity and Rational Choice: Advances in Criminological Theory* (Routledge., 1993); Clarke and Felson, *Routine Activity and Rational Choice*, 5; Raymond Paternoster and Sally Simpson, "A Rational Choice Theory of Corporate Crime," in *Routine Activity and Rational Choice: Advances in Criminological Theory* (Routledge, 2017); Alexis Russell Tibbetts Stephen G. Piquero, *Rational Choice and Criminal Behavior: Recent Research and Future Challenges* (New York: Routledge, 2012). There is continued debate about the accuracy, appropriateness as well as the scientific and policy value of rational choice theories. These points are discussed in more detail in Chapter 2.
33. Bullock, Clarke, and Tilley, Situational Prevention of Organised Crimes.

complemented by an account of wider societal forces as factors, which make the convergence of the above elements more likely. Such forces determine the natural rhythms of everyday life – the routines that make up these rhythms then produce circumstances where the three necessary elements of crime come together.[34]

Complementarily, CPT assumes that crime does not occur either randomly nor uniformly across space, time, or society. It recognises that objects, rules and processes are inter-connected. It follows that clustering of crime can be observed and this clustering is a function of the location in which these events take place. Location here is taken in its broadest conception, going beyond a certain geographical space and including a social network or a space of activity.[35] SCP is linked to and builds on these theories. Within the SCP model, crime is the (predictable) outcome of the interaction between motivation and situation: the junction of an opportunity and a willingness to act criminally.

*Principles and Techniques of SCP*

Four important principles must be respected in applying the SCP model: (1) using the approach to understand a single, specific crime at a time; (2) the need to adopt a procedural perspective; (3) the application of SCP to an existing crime problem; and (4) the recognition of the possibility that there may be a series of (complementary) solutions to the problem studied. Each of these principles is briefly discussed in the following paragraphs.

Firstly, the analysis undertaken using SCP must be crime specific. This follows from the fact that situational factors vary for different categories of crime.[36] The present research fulfils this requirement by examining the activity of illegally managing waste oils in the process of making bunker fuel.

Secondly, a procedural approach is necessary: thus, the focus is on the *modus operandi* as seen from the offender's perspective. This leads also to the distinction between motive and motivation. Whereas the former is closely linked to an individual's dispositions; motivation relates more directly to the immediate decision to commit a criminal act, and subsequently also determines the way in which the act will be carried out.[37] Taking this further, a method has been developed for analysing crime problems that allows for the detailed study of the sequence of events that take place leading up to, during and after the commission

34. Clarke, *Routine Activity and Rational Choice: Advances in Criminological Theory;* Marcus Felson, "Routine Activities and Crime Prevention:: Armchair Concepts and Practical Action," in *Crime Opportunity Theories* (Routledge, 2017); "The Routine Activity Approach," in *Enviornmental Criminology and Crime Analysis*, ed. Richard & Townsley Wortley, Michael (Oxon: Routledge, 2017).
35. P. J. Brantingham, Brantingham, P. L., and Andresen, M. A., "The Geometry of Crime and Crime Pattern Theory," in *Environmental Criminology and Crime Analysis*, ed. Richard and Townsley Wortley, Michael (Oxon: Routledge, 2017).
36. Clarke, "Situational Crime Prevention."
37. Bullock, Clarke, and Tilley, Situational Prevention of Organised Crimes.

of a crime. This analysis is done by using a 'crime-script' as a conceptual tool. By employing this method, it is possible to extrapolate "pinch-points" for intervention by identifying the opportunities that make the crime appealing to and possible for the offender, and that can be "blocked" in order to limit its occurrence.[38] CSA will feature prominently in this work as it will be used as one of the main tools of analysis.

Thirdly, SCP is driven by the aim of solving an existing crime problem. Unlike other strategies within environmental criminology, such as 'crime prevention through environmental design' and 'design against crime',[39] SCP is not anticipatory in its preventive stance. Rather, it begins by observing and exploring a problem that is already present.[40] Once more is known about the problem, it is analysed to understand its main determinants. On the basis of hypotheses made regarding these determinants, solutions are also identified, implemented and studied. The measures put into place based on these considerations are then evaluated.[41] By focusing on an existing crime problem, SCP can readily be applied in the field, where insights are generated and then tested immediately. The crime events we discuss in this book are representative of a type of ongoing criminal activity. While certain aspects of the *modi operandi* that are discussed here may have evolved or may simply be different, the basic characteristics of both crimes and their facilitating conditions remain consistent and, therefore, currently relevant.

Finally, given that through the use of SCP many points for intervention and opportunity reduction are likely to be found, it is important to recognise that a multiplicity of solutions can exist and may be necessary to ensure effective disruption of criminal activities. Consequently, an assortment of techniques has

38. Ibid.
39. Crime prevention through environmental design (CPTED) was first proposed by C. Ray Jeffrey and later expanded on by Oscar Newman, Tim Crowe and Paul Ekblom. CPTED puts theoretical ideas and empirical evidence about how the built environment influences the distribution of crime-opportunities into practice. CPTED includes ways of managing, building and designing physical settings. C. Ray Jeffery, *Crime Prevention through Environmental Design* (Beverly Hills [Calif.]: Sage Publications, 1971); Oscar Newman, *Defensible Space: Crime Prevention through Urban Design* (New York: Collier Books, 1973); Timothy D. Crowe and Institute National Crime Prevention, *Crime Prevention through Environmental Design: Applications of Architectural Design and Space Management Concepts*, 2nd ed. ed. (Boston, Mass: Butterworth-Heinemann, 2000); Paul Ekblom, "Deconstructing Cpted... and Reconstructing It for Practice, Knowledge Management and Research," *European Journal on Criminal Policy and Research* 17, no. 1 (2011). The same logic has been applied by proponents of 'design against crime', from which Paul Ekblom stands out as a founding father. His work with Clarke on SCP more generally has focused on this aspect of managing situations. Design against Crime: Crime Proofing Everyday Products, (Boulder, Colo.: Lynne Rienner Publishers, 2012).
40. Clarke, "Situational Crime Prevention."
41. Ibid. Given the combination of these steps and approaches, SCP comes within the domain of 'action research', defined as a process involving a spiral of steps, "each of which is composed of a circle of planning, action and fact-finding about the result of the action." (Kurt Lewin, "Action Research and Minority Problems," *Journal of Social Issues* 2, no. 4 (1946).

been proposed.[42] In line with the theoretical roots of the SCP model, these techniques have been subdivided into five main categories: reduction of rewards; increase in risks; increase in effort; reduction of provocations; and removal of excuses. The first three categories were already introduced in the original presentation of the model and are linked to the rational choice (RC) perspective.[43] The latter two derive from subsequent re-elaborations and relate more closely to the offender's perceptions and psychology. Environmental conditions may, in fact, supply the means through which personal inhibitions and the self-perceived criminality of the offender are reduced – excuses. Environmental conditions may also influence and lead to the formation of a criminal motivation – provocations.[44]

More recently, a sixth category has been advanced: 'providing opportunities'. This entails ensuring a supply of alternative, legal opportunities in contrast to criminal opportunities.[45] When these are low or absent, the possibilities of the offence occurring increase.[46] This category will not be used in the analysis of criminal events in Chapter 4, but it will be discussed in relation to interventions and guardianship in Chapter 6. In fact, in both Chapters 6 and 7 the range of techniques that belong to all six categories will also inform both the reflection on existing responses and the formulation of recommendations for developing new interventions.

The question now arises: How can we capture the environmental conditions that the different concepts discussed in the preceding paragraph refer to? We need a tool to help us systematically explore criminal events. This tool should help us proceed through each event sequentially, making the chronology of actions move to the background so that we can identify the means, rewards, risks, provocations, and excuses that are present at each stage. That tool is the crime-script.

*The Procedural Analysis of Crime: The Development of CSA as an Investigative Tool*

SCP offers researchers a set of concepts with which to deconstruct crime events. By uncovering the *process* behind criminal acts, it becomes easier to select and

42. The 25 Techniques Table is reproduced in Annex I.
43. Clarke, "Situational Crime Prevention."
44. Martha J. Smith and Ronald V. Clarke, "Situational Crime Prevention: Classifying Techniques Using "Good Enough" Theory," in *The Oxford Handbook of Crime Prevention*, ed. Brandon C. Welsh Martha J. Smith Ronald V. Clarke David P. Farrington (Oxford University Press, 2012); Derek Blaikie Cornish and Ronald V Clarke, "Opportunities, Precipitators and Criminal Decisions: A Reply to Wortley's Critique of Situational Crime Prevention," *Crime prevention studies* 16 (2003); Richard Wortley, "Situational Precipitators of Crime," in *Environmental Criminology and Crime Analysis*, ed. Richard Wortley and Michael Townsley (Oxon: Routledge, 2017).
45. Joshua D. Freilich and Graeme R. Newman, "Providing Opportunities: A Sixth Column for the Techniques of Situational Crime Prevention," in *Organized Crime, Corruption and Crime Prevention: Essays in Honor of Ernesto U. Savona*, ed. Stefano Caneppele and Francesco Calderoni (Cham: Springer International Publishing, 2014).
46. This category is not explored in our analysis of criminogenesis *per se*, but we discuss it further in Chapter 6 when reflecting on the question of interventions to reduce crime.

analyse single decisions and actions that take place over time and space. In this sense, both the RC perspective and CSA can be seen as heuristic devices. They do not necessarily explain *why* a crime occurs or provide definitive answers to the question of how to eliminate crime entirely, but they can be used to unveil the "choice structuring properties" of criminal events.[47] The original formulation of the crime-script concept derives from cognitive psychology where schemas are developed to conceptualise the cognitive structures within which perceptions and representations of past experiences and behaviours can be organised.[48] These cognitive processes are recognised as having two functions: (1) assisting with the categorisation of reality and; (2) acting upon and within that reality in a routinized manner.[49] Schemas can be of different kinds, whether relating to the self, to other persons, to one's and others' roles and, finally, to events. Event schemas relate to the knowledge structure regarding actions and sequences of actions within a specific context.

The crime-script tool was devised by combining the schema concept with ideas from the crime-event model – as conceptualised in environmental criminology – and RC. The event schema described above is extracted and used by an external observer to investigate and single out the different component stages of a specific crime-commission process. The investigator puts himself in the shoes of the perpetrator and views the reality – the setting – in which a specific crime is committed. Therefore, the decisions, actions and resources that are necessary to successfully complete the crime at each stage can be observed, categorised and understood.[50] The second objective in developing the concept of a crime-script was that of enhancing the possibility of finding useful points of intervention

47. Marco Zanella, "Script Analysis of Corruption in Public Procurement," *Cognition and Crime: Offender Decision Making and Script Analyses* (2013).
48. Benoit LeClerc and Richard Wortley, *Cognition and Crime: Offender Decision Making and Script Analyses / Edited by Benoit Leclerc and Richard Wortley*, ed. Benoit LeClerc and Richard Wortley, Crime Science Series (Routledge (Firm)) (Abingdon, Oxon; New York: Routledge, 2014).
49. Derek B Cornish, "The Procedural Analysis of Offending and Its Relevance for Situational Prevention," *Crime prevention studies* 3 (1994).4.
50. Ibid.;LeClerc and Wortley, *Cognition and Crime: Offender Decision Making and Script Analyses / Edited by Benoit Leclerc and Richard Wortley*; Hervé Borrion, "Quality Assurance in Crime Scripting," *Crime Science* 2, no. 1 (2013); Nicholas Gilmour, "Understanding Money Laundering–a Crime Script Approach," *Eur. Rev. Organ. Crime* 1, no. 2 (2014); Graham Hancock and Gloria Laycock, "Organised Crime and Crime Scripts: Prospects for Disruption," in *Situational Prevention of Organised Crimes*, ed. Karen Bullock, Ronald Victor Gemuseus Clarke, and Nick Tilley (Collumpton: Willan Publishing, 2010); Alice Hutchings and Thomas J Holt, "A Crime Script Analysis of the Online Stolen Data Market," *British Journal of Criminology* 55, no. 3 (2015); Julie Lacoste and Pierre Tremblay, "Crime and Innovation: A Script Analysis of Patterns in Check Forgery," *Crime Prevention Studies* 16 (2003); William D Moreto and Ronald V Clarke, "11 Script Analysis of the Transnational Illegal Market in Endangered Species," *Cognition and Crime: Offender Decision Making and Script Analyses* (2013); Tompson and Chainey, "Profiling Illegal Waste Activity: Using Crime Scripts as a Data Collection and Analytical Strategy."

when analysing crime events,[51] thus creating a clear link between the use of the crime-script tool and the aims of SCP. Accordingly, crime-scripts have been used as a template to comprehensively capture crime-commission processes in a standardised and systematic manner.

CSA is used in *this* study to deconstruct criminal events, or rather to *re-construct* the crime commission processes that took place during each event by cataloguing and examining the logistical steps that made up those processes.[52] Each logistical step in a crime-commission process includes actors, decisions, and actions. The details of how such reconstruction has been performed in this study are provided in Chapter 2.

*Unravelling the Context behind the Situation: Using Organisational and Green Criminology to Investigate Criminogenesis and Develop Interventions*

Using CSA and SCP can help us to break down a criminal event to identify the situational characteristics in which it occurs. However, this cataloguing of situational characteristics is limited – it does not tell us how those characteristics themselves were generated and by which processes and dynamics a specific situation materialised the way it did. The theoretical pillars supporting SCP – namely RAT and CPT – point towards 'social structure' for answers about how situations are created. RAT specifically points to the socially structured premises behind the coming together of motivated offenders, suitable targets, and incapable guardians.

We have classified the social phenomena, which we want to describe and explain, as corporate environmental crimes. Therefore, organisational and green criminology are pertinent sources for the conceptual tools that we can use for our analysis. Each is now briefly described in turn. The main concepts from these sub-disciplines that will be used in this book are also mentioned and they will be elaborated on in more detail in the Chapters where they are used.

*Organisational Criminology*

Organisational criminology is not a tightly defined field of inquiry. Its outer boundaries are often determined more by what it is *not* than what it is.[53] Organisational criminals are not blue collar, but possibly white collar. They do not carry out more traditional forms of crime, usually thought of as including varieties of interpersonal violence or engaging in explicitly criminalised trades.

51. Derek B Cornish, "Crimes as Scripts" (paper presented at the Proceedings of the international seminar on environmental criminology and crime analysis, 1994).
52. Nicholas Lord et al., "A Script Analysis of the Distribution of Counterfeit Alcohol across Two European Jurisdictions.", p. 257; Cornish, "The Procedural Analysis of Offending and Its Relevance for Situational Prevention.", p. 162 citing Ekblom and Johnson.
53. The notion of organisational crime has been chosen as an umbrella term to cover the criminological study of white-collar and corporate crime.

Organisational crimes are not simple but often result from complex processes involving several individuals and organisations. Maybe most importantly, organisational crimes are not responded to and labelled in the same way as more traditional forms of crime. Often, organisational crimes are either not crimes under the law or they are not detected, investigated, and prosecuted to the same extent. Offenders are also not afforded the same level of public reprobation as perpetrators of traditional crimes. Yet, this does not mean that organisational crimes are any less harmful or destructive. On the contrary, a paradox that the field of organisational criminology tries to highlight is that some of the gravest injustices we witness today effectively go unnoticed, unpunished, and unchanged.[54]

Let us narrow down the concepts and theories from organisational criminology that are relevant for this study. The crimes we are looking at are carried out in the context of legitimate business transactions – in the waste oil management and bunker fuel production sectors. They do not involve any direct interpersonal violence. They are carried out by individuals, who are working for corporations. The illegitimate actions of these individuals further the interests – increase in profits or reduction of costs – of the corporations.[55] The actions lead to harm to human health and the environment. Many of these activities are also partly forbidden by law or even criminalised.[56] Furthermore, the activities happen repeatedly or even, one might argue, structurally. The cases we look at are not exceptional, rather they are quite normal.

Based on these premises, three main explanatory models and frameworks, which fall under the category of organisational criminology, have been selected

54. J. Albanese, "Corporate Criminology: Explaining Deviance of Business and Political Organizations," *Journal of criminal justice* 12, no. 1 (1984); Benson and Simpson, *Understanding White-Collar Crime: An Opportunity Perspective*; William Chambliss, "State Organized Crime," *Making law: The State. Law, and Structural Contradictions* (1993); James William Coleman, "Toward an Integrated Theory of White-Collar Crime," *American Journal of Sociology* 93, no. 2 (1987); David Kauzlarich and Dawn L. Rothe, "Crimes of the Powerful," in *Encyclopedia of Criminology and Criminal Justice*, ed. Gerben Bruinsma and David Weisburd (New York, NY: Springer New York, 2014); Kramer, "Corporate Crime: An Organizational Perspective"; Ronald C Kramer, Raymond J Michalowski, and David Kauzlarich, "The Origins and Development of the Concept and Theory of State-Corporate Crime," *Crime & Delinquency* 48, no. 2 (2002); M Lanier, *Essential Criminology* (New York: Routledge, 2015); Passas, "Anomie and Corporate Deviance"; Ruggiero, *Organized and Corporate Crime in Europe: Offers That Can't Be Refused*; Simpson and Weisburd, *The Criminology of White-Collar Crime*; Slapper and Tombs, *Corporate Crime*; Edwin Hardin Sutherland, Gilbert Geis, and Colin Goff, *White Collar Crime: The Uncut Version*, vol. 58 (New Haven, CT: Yale University Press 1983).
55. Marshall Barron Yeager Peter C. Clinard, *Corporate Crime* (New Brunswick, NJ: Transaction Publ, 2006).
56. Shrager and Short define organisational crime as: "Illegal acts of omission or commission of an individual or a group of individuals in a formal organization in accordance with the operative goals of the organization, which have serious physical or economic impact on employees, consumers, or the general public." Laura Shill Schrager and James F. Short, "Toward a Sociology of Organizational Crime," *Social Problems* 25, no. 4 (1978).p. 408. See also Friedrichs.O. Friedrichs David, "Crimes of the Powerful and the Definition of Crime," in *The Routledge International Handbook of the Crimes of the Powerful* (Routledge, 2015).

for the analysis in this book. They emphasise the 'macro level', i.e., the structural forces that characterise a setting and make corporate crime possible and appealing. The concepts are: crime-facilitative system, criminogenic industry, and state-facilitated state corporate crime. A crime-facilitative system is multi-organisational in nature, i.e., it involves several individuals or separate corporate entities that act within a common structure. That common structure is legal, normative, economic and organisational. The structural dynamics encourage and facilitate crime because they lower risks of detection while increasing incentives and opportunities for illegal activities.[57] A criminogenic industry is a sector of the economy distinguished by a set of specialised activities or specific products.[58] In our case study, there are two industries that are relevant: that of waste oil management services and that of bunker fuel production. There are several models that look at criminogenic features of industries, however, the main concept that is used in this book sees industry as its own level of analysis, where there are peculiar interactions between business and government, which give rise to structural dynamics that enable and facilitate crime.[59] This notion of industry is partly derived from the framework on state-corporate crime, which is also drawn on throughout this book. State-corporate crime has been defined as: "illegal or socially injurious actions that result from a mutually reinforcing interaction between (1) policies and/or practices in pursuit of the goals of one or more institutions of political governance and (2) policies and/or practices in pursuit of the goals of one or more institutions of economic production and distribution."[60] This concept is important because it continuously brings our attention back to the relationship between government and business, as well as their common goals. Each of the concepts just listed will be described in more detail in the Chapters where they are applied.

*Responsive Regulation and Organisational Crime*

Another important concept connected to organisational criminology is that of 'responsive regulation'. This concept is particularly relevant for answering the second main research question and the connected sub-questions. The literature on and related to responsive regulation tries to explore the question of how mechanisms of intervention – enacted by both the public and private sectors – can be set up to reduce corporate offending. The notion of 'responsiveness'

57. Needleman and Needleman, "Organizational Crime: Two Models of Criminogenesis."
58. Norman K Denzin, "Notes on the Criminogenic Hypothesis: A Case Study of the American Liquor Industry," *American Sociological Review* (1977); Harvey A Farberman, "A Criminogenic Market Structure: The Automobile Industry," *The Sociological Quarterly* 16, no. 4 (1975); Gilbert Geis, "The Heavy Electrical Equipment Anti-Trust Cases of 1961," in *Criminal Behavior Systems*, ed. M and Quinney Clinard, R (New York: Holt, Rinehart and Winston, 1967); Coleman, "Toward an Integrated Theory of White-Collar Crime."
59. Bradshaw, ""Obviously, We're All Oil Industry": The Criminogenic Structure of the Offshore Oil Industry."
60. Kramer, Michalowski, and Kauzlarich, "The Origins and Development of the Concept and Theory of State-Corporate Crime." p. 271.

in this context has evolved in parallel to other conceptual developments in criminology. Situational crime prevention, which has customarily been applied to more traditional forms of crime, was criticised for its rational choice foundations. Such criticism has led to the creation of an expanded set of techniques of intervention. At the same time, similar doubts have been raised in the realm of organisational criminology and corporate regulation. These doubts have laid the groundwork for responsive regulation. In the next paragraphs, we look at how the concept has evolved and why it is relevant for our investigation of interventions in this book.

Theoretically and empirically, many have argued and shown that simply manipulating the costs and benefits of situations does not eliminate criminal or undesired behaviour. Indeed, this kind of criticism is frequently levelled against any regulatory or enforcement strategies that are grounded in deterrence and rational choice theories more generally. It has been repeatedly shown that state interventions are so poorly generating deterrent effects that deterrence-based measures explain neither violations nor compliance. Based on this evidence, alternative models have been developed to understand the dynamics behind both why corporations do not abide by the law and how they can be supported in complying. Within the SCP framework the categories of reducing provocations, removing excuses and providing opportunities play a similar role.

In the corporate regulation literature, a distinction that has been popular among scholars is that between amoral rational calculators, political citizens, and organizationally incompetent entities.[61] Each of the three typologies leads to certain implications regarding the characteristics and qualities of regulatory strategies and regulatory agents. Incompetent organisations require something akin to instruction manuals or warning signals to become aware of the mistakes they make or the skills they lack. Therefore, teaching or training as well as some form of accounting can help such organisations to build competence and make fewer mistakes. Of course, accountants and teachers would then have to be highly skilled themselves to support competence-building accurately and adequately. Amoral rational calculators would need to be threatened or rewarded into compliance. Regulation for these entities means letting them know that someone is watching and will take action when they do something wrong. This approach is often referred to as 'regulator as policeman'. While expertise may

61. John T. Scholz, "Cooperation, Deterrence, and the Ecology of Regulatory Enforcement," *Law & Society Review* 18, no. 2 (1984); Robert A. Kagan and John T. Scholz, "The "Criminology of the Corporation" and Regulatory Enforcement Strategies," in *Enforcing Regulation* (Springer Netherlands: Dordrecht, 1984); Gary Slapper and Steve Tombs, *Corporate Crime*, Longman Criminology Series (Harlow: Pearson Longman, 1999). Another, complementary perspective that needs to be mentioned here is that developed by Henk van de Bunt, whereby a company's ability to comply is connected to its 'social responsiveness'. See: van de Bunt, Henk G., and Wim Huisman. "Organizational Crime in the Netherlands." *Crime and Justice* 35 (2007): 217-60, p. 234 and van de Bunt, Henk G. *Organisatiecriminaliteit*. (Arnhem: Gouda Quint, 1992).

not be as important here *if* the wrongful behaviour is easily identifiable, a lot of resources would need to be, in any case, expended to maintain a credibly high rate of detection and swiftness in response. Of course, such an approach is premised on the existence of clear standards that can be enforced. For the third typology, the political citizen, dialogue – in the sense of a direct and enduring exchange between regulator and regulated entity – becomes explicitly relevant. Political citizens must be convinced and persuaded that what the regulator says is right and fruitful. Such persuasion must appeal to the self-interest of the citizen. Regulating means giving advice or even negotiating.

The topic of regulatory responsiveness has also been taken up in organisational *criminology*. The notion of responsive regulation builds on the integrated theory of organisational crime (ITOC, also known as the theory of tipping points), which looks at the relationship between corporate employees and their social environment. One of the theoretical pillars of the ITOC are the notions of strain and social control. According to the ITOC, individuals and organizations strive towards certain goals and, in that process, may be faced with obstacles or frustration. These obstacles can be overcome by embarking upon illegitimate courses of action. However, the decision to take such paths must first be definitionally viable.[62]

According to the ITOC, the purpose of regulatory strategies should be to tip definitions in favour of *compliance with* as opposed to *resistance against* regulation. The theory also incorporates insights from the labelling perspective,[63] therefore, a distinction is further made between stigmatisation and (reintegrative) shaming. Supplying definitions favourable to compliance should not include hostile and confrontational methods that attack the identity of the regulatory targets. Rather they should firmly highlight the shamefulness of the acts while at the same time respectfully rely on and encourage the targets' capacity to improve and comply. Consequently, regulating towards compliance should have two dimensions. The first is substantive, whereby the actual definition of what is good behaviour – respecting the law, protecting the environment – is provided and prioritised. The second dimension is procedural – dialogue must be fair, cooperative and display respect, trust and belief in the targets' capacity to comply.[64]

62. John Braithwaite, "Criminological Theory and Organizational Crime " *Justice Quarterly* 6, no. 3 (1989).

63. The labelling perspective emphasizes the relationship between behaviours and their definition within a specific social group. When the group considers a certain behaviour or activity as non-conformist or deviant, it attaches a negatively charged label to it – crime, which leads to further negative consequences for the individual or group labelled thus. Without the existence of such labels, there would be no crime. Becker, *Outsiders: Studies in the Sociology of Deviance*; Erving Goffman, *Stigma: Notes on the Management of Spoiled Identity* (London: Penguin, 1963).

64. Ayres and Braithwaite, Responsive Regulation: Transcending the Deregulation Debate.

Responsive regulation, which has built on this initial line of reasoning, is often associated with (and some say even *reduced* to) the 'responsive regulation pyramid'.[65] We can use a modified version of the pyramid to grasp this concept better and to visualise it alongside the other concepts mentioned so far. We can think of responsiveness as having three dimensions: responsiveness of the measures in relation to the needs of the target; responsiveness in attitude and function based on the behaviour of the target; and responsiveness in terms of the nature of the intervention (extern/internal), depending on the capacity to (self-)regulate of the target.

The central portion of the pyramid in Figure 1.1 shows us measures look, if they are responsive to the characteristics of the target. This aspect of responsive regulation means that regulators should advance pragmatically along the pyramid based on the initial and subsequent behaviours manifested by the regulated entities. The fundamental premise is that, in any encounter, one always begins at the bottom of the pyramid, giving the target of regulation maximum freedom in choosing how and whether to comply. It opens up the space for dialogue, persuasion, education and clarification, all of which are important for regulatory targets corresponding to the different models we discussed at the beginning of this subsection.

**Figure 1.1 Adapted responsive regulation pyramid**

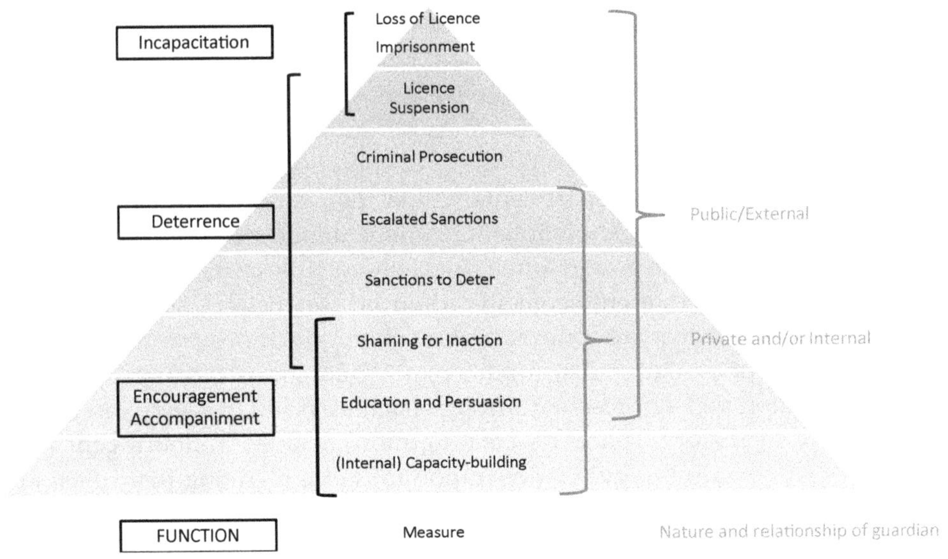


65. Peter Mascini, "Why Was the Enforcement Pyramid So Influential? And What Price Was Paid?," *Regulation & Governance* 7, no. 1 (2013).

Only when these attempts fail, does the regulator begin adopting rationales and using measures higher up the pyramid. Warnings and shaming are issued before any sanctions are applied. The warnings are important because they signal to the targeted entity that something needs to change, thereby raising awareness and giving the opportunity to ask for assistance and then make wilful decisions for which consequences can be expected. Those consequences can be found either further up the sanctions pyramid, when the choice made is to continue violating the law; or they can be further down the pyramid when even small steps towards compliance are taken.[66]

Each of these gradual steps is also connected to the attitude of the guardians involved, which is depicted on the left-hand side of the pyramid using the term 'function'. The gradual movement from encouragement to incapacitation means that the regulated entity will not be stigmatised and, therefore, alienated; rather a firm but fair increase in the severity of the attitude and measures can foster commitment to compliance. This aspect of responsiveness draws from the ITOC discussed previously and meets the *needs* underlying the target's behaviours.

One last concept linked to the ITOC and responsive regulation needs to be discussed: enforced self-regulation. The premises are much the same as for the other two ideas; however, this notion adds an important mechanism when thinking of regulating not just a single corporation but an *entire industry* as well as who should take on this task – outsiders or insiders. According to the ideas of enforced self-regulation,[67] states should create broad guidelines, principles and targets that provide the outermost boundaries for corporate activities in a given sector. In response to these outer boundaries, businesses must develop their own guidelines and rules, based on their expertise about the substantive aspects of the trade they are involved in. These must then be submitted to state agencies for approval. Once approved, they are binding. Corporations that are large enough should also have specialised departments within their internal structure that can effectively assess and facilitate compliance. These departments can have direct contact to state agencies to report offending, where it is particularly serious or where it is felt that external enforcement would be beneficial. Continued lack of compliance or lack of adequate communication about violations can be monitored by state agencies, but as a secondary mechanism. Where industries appear to avoid and resist regulation and enforcement through such a system, the state can take up more and more regulatory 'space' by creating more detailed and stringent rules. The notion of enforced self-regulation is important in highlighting that rule*making* is just as important as rule enforcement both for maximising innovation and production as well as for protecting welfare interests. This move from private or

66. Graham Dukes, John Braithwaite, and James P Moloney, *Pharmaceuticals, Corporate Crime and Public Health* (Edward Elgar Publishing, 2014).
67. Braithwaite, "Enforced Self-Regulation: A New Strategy for Corporate Crime Control." See also literature on meta-regulation, which adopts a similar rational, in note 21above.

internal responsibility to public or external responsibility for fostering compliance is shown on the right side in Figure 1.1 From this perspective, responsiveness in connected to the ability of the targets to self-regulate effectively.

The responsiveness of both economic organisations and regulatory agents that we have explored in the preceding paragraphs makes something very clear. Regulatory plurality is essential: plurality in assumptions about the generative forces of both violation and compliance. Plurality in attitudes and approaches, firm but fair instead of only accommodating or coercive. Plurality in relationships and in the regulatory network.

In this book, insights from the literature on corporate regulation reviewed in the preceding paragraphs are used to complement the analysis of a specific set of crime events and responses: those investigated by the Andante *police* team. Both the events and the team were embedded in a wider regulatory context, where activities of waste oil management and bunker fuel production are influenced by rules and actors at several levels. Some of these actors are state authorities, others are not. Some have explicit monitoring and enforcement powers, which include the use of administrative and criminal law measures, others are market participants or just members of society more generally. We will not systematically apply the ideas of responsive regulation and the related ITOC or enforced self-regulation to all such actors, but we should keep them in mind as we explore different facets of regulation and guardianship in Chapters 3 to 6.

*Green Criminology*

Green criminology[68] broadly consists in the study of environmental harm that results in negative consequences to ecosystems, humans, and animals. Specifically, it explores *how* and *under what circumstances* these harms occur. The way in which these issues are studied and the methods employed are those furnished by criminological theories, models and frameworks; nevertheless, much of the literature in the field of green criminology also adopts perspectives and tools from other disciplines, making this area of research inherently open and multi-disciplinary. Green criminology has, in fact, been described as a "rendezvous discipline" in that it brings together and orients different efforts to provide insight and solutions to environmental issues.[69] Ultimately, green criminology urges

68. The term 'green criminology' is used specifically to avoid ambiguities and to grasp the two main elements: use of criminology and focus on 'green' issues. There is some debate among scholars debate on problems of using the term 'green' because of association with political parties that focus on environmental issued. Some scholars have proposed the 're-' claiming of 'environmental criminology' instead. However, for this book that would create unnecessary confusion because environmental criminology is understood in this work as the impact of environmental (situational) conditions on the incidence and occurrence of crime.
69. Although no single theory underpins this branch of criminological inquiry, a number of streams can be identified within this approach, each characterised by certain premises and notions.

researchers to undertake investigations into issues of environmental harm, using tools from different disciplines, and to acknowledge the "inter-connectedness of social and ecological phenomena".[70]

It is important to recognise that there is a marked difference between the study of 'green crimes' and the adoption of a "green criminological *perspective*". The latter refers to the idea that engaging in green criminological analysis requires a shift in focus and a different conceptualisation of environmental problems, of their causes and of their effects. This redirection of the criminological effort leads to a *critical* analysis of reality and, even more so, of the way we study and explain it. The criticism, thus, also extends to the little attention paid by criminologists to environmental harms and green crimes more generally. In this sense, the preponderance of criminological analyses of street crimes or more 'traditional' forms of crime is seen as a consequence of the dependence on socially (and legally) constructed definitions of wrongful or harmful behaviour. Even more important, however, is that the focus on traditional crimes is a source of legitimisation of a system, which accepts environmental harm as a necessary side-effect of its functioning and, therefore, does not question its occurrence. It follows that green criminology scholars express the need to re-focus and reconceptualise the interest of criminological inquiry: the selection and examination of an object of study should depend upon considerations of harm, justice, and equality rather than pre-existing notions of acceptability codified in law and negotiated by 'powerful' members of society.

---

Beirne and South, *Issues in Green Criminology*; Avi Brisman and Nigel South, "A Green-Cultural Criminology: An Exploratory Outline," *Crime Media Culture* 9, no. 2 (2013); Carole Gibbs et al., "Introducing Conservation Criminology Towards Interdisciplinary Scholarship on Environmental Crimes and Risks," *British Journal of Criminology* 50, no. 1 (2010); Michael J. Lynch, "The Meaning of Green: Contrasting Criminological Perspectives," *Theoretical criminology* 7, no. 2 (2003); Michael J. Lynch and Paul B. Stretesky, "Similarities between Green Criminology and Green Science: Toward a Typology of Green Criminology," *International Journal of Comparative and Applied Criminal Justice* 35, no. 4 (2011); Gorazd Mesko, Nigel South, and Rob White, "Special Issue: Green Criminology Editors' Introduction," *Crime Law and Social Change* 59, no. 3 (2013); Angus Nurse, "Exploring Green Criminology: Towards a Green Criminological Revolution," *Journal of Environmental Law* 27, no. 2 (2015); Frank Pearce, "Issues in Green Criminology: Confronting Harms against Environments, Humanity and Other Animals," *Theoretical Criminology* 13, no. 2 (2009); Ruggiero and South, "Green Criminology and Dirty Collar Crime"; "Critical Criminology and Crimes against the Environment," *Critical Criminology* 18, no. 4 (2010); Holger Schmidt, "A Green Branch of Criminology? Thoughts on Green Criminology," *Kriminologisches Journal* 45, no. 4 (2013); Nigel South, "A Green Field for Criminology? A Proposal for a Perspective," *Theoretical Criminology* 2, no. 2 (1998); Rob White, ed. *Transnational Environmental Crime: Toward an Eco-Global Criminology* (Routledge, 2011); *Global Environmental Harm: Criminological Perspectives;* Rob White and Diane Heckenberg, *Green Criminology: An Introduction to the Study of Environmental Harm* (New York; London: Routledge, Taylor & Francis Group, 2014); Wyatt, "Issues in Green Criminology: Confronting Harms against Environments, Humanity and Other Animals."

70. Rob White, *Global Environmental Harm: Criminological Perspective.* See also: Beck, Ulrich, and Mark Ritter. *Risk Society: Towards a New Modernity. Theory, Culture & Society.* (London: Sage, 1992).

Green criminology and organisational criminology share an acute awareness of problems of definition and power. Behind the lack of a properly applied label that signals responsibility for harm and wrongdoing, there may lie structural arrangements that help actors avoid that label. Or, even when such a label is applied, the consequences of it may differ substantially compared to those linked to the criminal label that is applied for more traditional forms of crime. Environmental harm is often dealt with through administrative and regulatory law, relegated to the realm of technical malfeasance. It is not stigmatised as real crime, but merely as a morally innocent incompatibility between normal (economic) activities and overly prudent, complicated rules. An important and revelatory characteristic of the rules that are designed to protect the environment is that they establish permissible amounts of harm to occur. Of course, criminal law does the same in the case of the most egregious acts, like murder, by still furnishing exceptions such as self-defence.

However, when it comes to environmental damage, this boundary of permissible harm is both more malleable and less conservative. We, as a society, seem to be more tolerant when it comes to environmental degradation. It is in this regard that a green criminological perspective is important for this study. Green criminology is as much about the way we generate rules and regulations for environmental protection and how we enforce them as it is about the way that harm is physically generated in the first place. Indeed, it sees these two aspects as sides of the same coin. It forces us to always go back and check what even the best implementation and application of a rule means in terms of environmental conservation or degradation concretely. And, in turn, what that tells us about our society and the legal and industrial structures within it.

Therefore, in this study, green criminology is our smoke detector. As long as the fire of environmental destruction is still burning, even if the flames are barely visible and we are only unknowingly breathing in the smoke, green criminology will signal it. Even when we discuss innovative policies in the field of environmental protection that are designed to reduce waste, for example, we will take a second look and think about its broader implications, within a global neoliberal system that still defines environmental harm as a mere externality. The most important concept that will be used for this purpose is that of the 'Treadmill of Law', which focuses on how state-corporate symbioses lead to the generation of rules, definitions and enforcement practices that are not as protective of the environment as they could and should be.[71]

71. Paul B. Stretesky, Michael A. Long, and Michael J. Lynch, "Does Environmental Enforcement Slow the Treadmill of Production? The Relationship between Large Monetary Penalties, Ecological Disorganization and Toxic Releases within Offending Corporations," *Journal of Crime and Justice* 36, no. 2 (2013); Paul B Stretesky, Michael A Long, and Michael J Lynch, *The Treadmill of Crime: Political Economy and Green Criminology* (Routledge, 2013); Michael J. Lynch, Paul B. Stretesky, and Michael A. Long, "The Treadmill of Production and the Treadmill of

## 1.3 Academic & Societal Relevance

Bunker fuel is a carbon-based fuel the burning of which leads to the emission of carbon dioxide ($CO_2$) as well as other pollutants. Among those pollutants, we find particulate matter, also known as aerosols, "which include particles that can cool or heat the Earth's climate by reflecting or absorbing the radiation of the sun." One type of particulate matter that is highly prevalent in emissions coming from the burning of bunker fuel is black carbon. But there are several types of pollutants that are emitted by ships burning bunker fuel.

> *"Ambient air pollution accounts for an estimated 4.2 million deaths per year due to stroke, heart disease, lung cancer and chronic respiratory diseases. Around 91% of the world's population lives in places where air quality levels exceed [the limits set by the World Health Organisation]."*[72]
>
> *"Black carbon is estimated to be responsible for approximately 15 per cent of the current excessive warming of global temperatures. In addition, short-term reductions in black carbon can potentially delay the impact of global warming by approximately 10 years."*[73]

These two quotes plainly reveal the importance of any investigation into practices that contribute to carbon emissions and pollution, which then increase the risks of harm to human health and the environment. The kinds of activities that can fall under this category are several and very diverse in character and scale. Just to remain in the realm of waste management and emissions from the consumption of fuel, we could also conduct research into the dependence on petroleum for the running of cars and lorries or look at the use of coal to power entire countries. We could also zoom down into the detail of why the members of a single household or even several small villages do not separate their wastes so that items may be adequately recycled instead of being lumped all together and dumped. These are all worthwhile topics for research given the urgency of dealing with the problems of pollution and environmental degradation that loom over us right now; and the dire consequences of which only the coming generations will be able to truly experience in all their horror.

But, without wanting to take any merit away from the pursuit of these other possible avenues for research, it is important to consider that not all polluting activities are born equal. Some have much more impact on the overall health of human beings and the planet. And some are particularly challenging to overcome because they are entrenched with- and operate in support of legal and legitimate

Law: Propositions for Analyzing Law, Ecological Disorganization and Crime," *Capitalism Nature Socialism* 31, no. 1 (2020).

72. World Health Organisation, "Ambient (Outdoor) Air Pollution," https://www.who.int/news-room/fact-sheets/detail/ambient-(outdoor)-air-quality-and-health.

73. European Commission – DG Environment, "Air Pollution and Climate Change," https://ec.europa.eu/environment/integration/research/newsalert/pdf/24si_en.pdf, p. 4.

structures of production and consumption. Indeed, their intimate connection with the structures that underly the operation of economic and legal systems sometimes makes them invisible or untouchable, meaning that it becomes even more important to shine some light on them. Otherwise, we may be unable to take any action to limit their occurrence. The corporate environmental crimes that are discussed in this book belong to this category of human health- and environment-endangering practices. Pollution from ships that consume bunker fuel is estimated to contribute to roughly 3% of worldwide $CO_2$ emissions. And what is worse, some projections hold that emissions from international shipping will increase by 50% in the next 30 years.[74]

The academic relevance of this research hinges partly on its societal one. The efforts and resources that a research project demands should, in my opinion, be used to do more than merely solve intellectual puzzles. Scholars have a responsibility to investigate social reality in a way that contributes to either increasing prosperity or reducing adversity. However, the academic relevance of this book also has other dimensions. Social research can have different purposes depending on the type of knowledge that one aims to generate. These purposes are reflected in the research questions that guide a given project. In turn, different types of research questions and purposes can characterise a project as being an example of either basic or applied research. Basic research includes studies that try to explore, describe, explain, understand, or make predictions about social phenomena. In contrast, applied research includes studies that aim to change social situations directly; evaluate social intervention programmes; and assess the social impacts of projects, or of either technological or policy changes. The academic relevance of a study can be linked back to any one of these eight purposes.

The data that have been gathered and analysed for this book had not been previously used for social research purposes. In the case of the data on the work of the Andante team, we can even say that access of this kind is virtually unprecedented. The data on the crime events is slightly different. Although other scholars have discussed similar cases of illegal waste oil management activities in the process of bunker fuel production, this research looks at cases that are 'new' from an academic standpoint. Additionally, the level of detail that data from criminal investigation files provides increases the degree of relevance for exploratory research. Overall, the data on both crimes and responses that has been made available prompts an exploratory purpose and then triggers a descriptive one. Thanks not just to the availability but also the *character* of the data, we can develop *detailed* descriptions of crimes and responses as well as the context in which these unfold. And, thanks to the employment of the theoretical concepts

74. International Maritime Organisation, "Fourth Greenhouse Gas Study 2020," https://www.imo.org/en/OurWork/Environment/Pages/Fourth-IMO-Greenhouse-Gas-Study-2020.aspx.

and frameworks discussed in Section 2, we can also venture some explanations for the social phenomena, which are explored and described. Furthermore, the data available on the work of the Andante team specifically gives some space for understanding the experience of a specific set of people in responding to the crimes that are studied in this book. However, this last purpose is pursued to a limited extent.

The findings and reflections that I present in this book may form the basis for prediction, yet this is not an aim of the research I have undertaken. The matter of generalisability is discussed in more detail in Chapter 2. I also cannot characterise the work done over the last years as a form of applied research; although a strong desire to bring about change and improvement has fuelled my endeavours throughout. I have, at no stage, designed interventions or attempted to carry out an evaluation of existing interventions. This point needs to be stressed particularly in relation to my analysis of responses, and specifically of the work of the Andante team.

Nevertheless, I sincerely hope that I can, even if to a very small extent, contribute to some future amelioration of the reality that is depicted in this book. In fact, this book may be relevant not just for scholars but also for practitioners. It pragmatically and practically addresses a very precise societal problem and catalogues some of the existing solutions to that problem. Policy makers, enforcement agents and businesses in the waste oil management and bunker fuel production sectors may draw some useful insights from this book to inform their activities. Hopefully, they would do so in a way that further promotes environmental conservation and the protection of human health.

Lastly, I would like to address the position of this book within the wider literature in the fields of organisational and environmental criminology. The main framework that configures the overall analysis presented in the coming pages is that of SCP. The work presented here sticks to the five categories of techniques of SCP – increasing efforts and risks as well as reducing rewards, provocations, and excuses – but it also adds a new level of depth in applying these now well-known concepts. While the theoretical work on SCP as well as CPT and RAT is clearly premised on awareness of structural determinants of situational features, most of the studies in which SCP is applied do not address the aspect of social structure in detail. The uniqueness of this book lies in the clear link that is made between the situation and the context. This link is made thanks to the integration of organisational criminology into the explanatory framework. Contributions in the field of organisational criminology are not generally as interested in the minutiae and intricacies of crime events that can be teased out by using tools such as crime-script analysis. Therefore, the novelty of the approach taken here is two-fold as it enriches both theoretical perspectives it draws from by integrating them. This is true for the analysis of both criminogenesis as well as of responses.

## 1.4 Outline

The case study unfolds over six substantive chapters, preceded by Chapter 2, which concerns methodological procedures and considerations. In Chapter 3, we sail along the flows of oil, goods, fuel, and wastes to see how the two industries are physically structured and connected. Then, we adopt different analytical lenses – legal and economic – to look at the bunker fuel and waste oil industries separately. Chapter 4 begins with a review of criminal and administrative law enforcement measures, which complement the specific rules that govern the two industries and demonstrate how the legal structure enters situations in the arrangement of a formal system of guardianship. Chapter 4 then explores the criminogenic situations by unravelling two representative criminal events using CSA to uncover the choice-structuring properties of those events. Chapter 5 takes us to the overlap between waste oil management and bunker fuel production. There we discuss the dynamics within that industrial and relational space to see how they generate a crime-facilitative system. Chapter 6 focuses on the aspect of responses, particularly the history, experience, and legacy of the Andante team. Chapter 7 concludes the book by threading together the findings from the preceding chapters from which I develop a series of reflections and recommendations.

# 2 Methods & Methodology

In this Chapter, we first examine the research strategy I adopted to answer the research questions. Then we look at how I completed the various stages of the research: from how I identified and accessed the sources of the data that I collected through to how I analysed those data. Finally, we consider to what extent the findings presented in this book can be generalised as well as other limitations.

## 2.1 Research Strategy

The following paragraphs outline the choices that I made regarding my research strategy and my assumptions in making those choices. The last portion of this subsection is dedicated to the role of law and legal research within my research strategy.

*Induction, Retroduction & the Role of (Criminological) Theories and Concepts*

In Chapter 1, I formulated a series of research questions:
1. How and why do illegal waste oil management activities in the process of producing bunker fuel take place?
2. How can illegal waste oil management activities in the process of producing bunker fuel be limited?
   a. What do illegal waste oil management (WOM) activities in the process of bunker fuel production (BFP) look like?
   b. During which steps of the broader BFP and WOM processes do these illegal activities occur?
   c. Which logistical steps and which actions are undertaken by the actors involved?
   d. What types of actors are involved?
   e. What types of activities do they engage in?
   f. What tools do they use to complete these activities?
   g. What factors, at different levels of analysis, influence – facilitate or constrain – the actors involved in undertaking the abovementioned logistical steps towards crime-commission?

h. What internal as well as external regulations and mechanisms for supervision and control exist that apply to the WOM and BFP sectors?
i. How are these regulations and mechanisms interpreted, applied, and enforced?
j. How can these regulations and mechanisms influence – facilitate or constrain – the occurrence of the criminal activities that take place in the WOM and BFP sectors?

These research questions show us that there are three purposes underlying the research in this book, which are: to explore, describe, and explain a social phenomenon. Exploration and description can be performed by using the *inductive strategy*. Induction presupposes an external observer who catalogues reality. Through this exercise, patterns, and associations between elements of that reality may become apparent. These associations may hint at relationships between the relevant elements but cannot furnish causal explanations. The recurrence of elements or patterns can lead to empirical generalisations or even theoretical propositions.[1] I used the inductive strategy to answer the 'what' and 'how' questions by also applying the existing theoretical concepts, which we reviewed in Chapter 1. *Through* these concepts, I got an initial impression of how the situations and contexts in which the crimes I was interested in look like and operate. The concepts helped me to make sense of the reality I was observing.

For the portion of the research that focuses on explanation, I drew on the theoretical pillars underlying situational crime prevention (SCP), which have been discussed in Section 2 of Chapter 1 (routine activities theory and crime pattern theory). Although SCP is usually applied on the micro – or individual – level, its theoretical premises connect the micro setting of crimes and the offenders' decisions in those settings to broader, structural arrangements. Therefore, it is possible to link descriptions and analyses of situations with descriptions and analyses of contexts when using SCP. To help me in generating such a multi-level analysis, which is explicitly referred to in sub-question (g), I drew on the ideas of critical realism and the retroductive research strategy.

Critical realism and the retroductive strategy can be understood through the notion of "mechanism-context-outcome configurations."[2] Agency and social structure are the components of a mechanism: when an individual decides and acts, he does so based on the resources and possibilities available to him. Although action is only attributable to human agents, the *way* they act is constrained and

1. Norman W. H. Blaikie, *Designing Social Research: The Logic of Anticipation*, 2nd ed. ed. (Cambridge, UK;: Polity Press, 2010); Howard Saul Becker, *Tricks of the Trade: How to Think About Your Research While You're Doing It* (Chicago: Univ. of Chicago Press, 2011).
2. R. A. Y. Pawson, "Middle-Range Realism," *European Journal of Sociology* 41, no. 2 (2000).

facilitated by *socialstructures*.[3] Therefore, both human agency and social structures need to be investigated to understand the functioning of mechanisms.[4]

SCP relies on three theoretical pillars. One of these concerns the 'agent' portion of the retroductive mechanism, i.e., the fact that human beings make (bounded) rational choices. The other two pillars are connected to the social structure component of the mechanism as well as the contextual element. Crime pattern theory states that crime is clustered based on the distribution of opportunities. Certain parts of social structure are consistently shaped in ways that create incentives or reduce the constraints for certain forms of crime.[5] Routine activities theory identifies crime as resulting when three features are present: a motivated offender, a suitable target, and the lack of a capable guardian. The simultaneous presence of these features can be traced back to 'social structure' i.e., the patterns of daily life that characterise a specific population or geographic setting. The foregoing brings us to the conclusion that, to conceptualise mechanisms as accurately as possible, we need to investigate which actors are involved in bringing about the outcomes we want to explain; what positions they occupy within the social structure; and what rights, obligations, interests, and avenues of action they have given their position within the social structure. Chapter 3 of this book addresses this need.

The logic just outlined, which is inspired by the retroductive strategy, means that I will draw more and more from the existing literature in both organisational and green criminology to make sense of the structure and context in which the crimes occur. In the retroductive strategy, this use of concepts could lead to the development of a model, including the formulation of a series of hypotheses that would then be deductively tested. I have not gone as far as testing hypotheses

3. According to critical realists, social structure has certain characteristics that make it possible to identify entire sets of available resources or possible choices. One such characteristic is that there are different 'categories' of individuals who have certain sets of rights, obligations, and interests. In our study, for example, we can say that all waste management firms in a certain jurisdiction, which have a permit for handling certain WOs, are subject to a similar set of rights and obligations and may even face similar market conditions. However, this account of how social structure and human agency interact should not lead us to view individual actions as pre-determined. On the contrary, critical realism supports the idea that individuals can respond to their circumstances in creative ways. In fact, "social events of interest must be understood as the result of the interplay over time between (antecedent) social structure and (subsequent) human agency."( Paul Lewis, "Realism, Causality and the Problem of Social Structure," *Journal for the theory of Social Behaviour* 30, no. 3 (2000). 260.)
4. There is a body of literature dedicated to bringing together critical realism, the retroductive research strategy and SCP. See, for example: Ray Pawson, "The ABC of Evaluation," *American Journal of Evaluation* 26, no. 4 (2005); Pawson, "Middle-Range Realism"; Ray Tilley Nick Pawson, *Realistic Evaluation* (London: Sage, 2007).
5. Felson 1994 Marcus Cohen Lawrence E. Felson, "Human Ecology and Crime: A Routine Activity Approach," *Human Ecology* 8, no. 4 (1980); Marcus Felson, "Linking Criminal Choices, Routine Activities, Informal Control, and Criminal Outcomes," in *The Reasoning Criminal* (Springer, 1986).

in this research, although Chapters 3, 4 and 5 show some deductive logic being applied to study the case at the 'macro' level.

Given the above, the relationship between theory and my analysis and findings can be summarised in the following terms. In this study, theories and concepts have had three functions: sensitising, systematising, and aiding explanation. I needed a coherent set of notions that could help me make sense of the complexity of the events I was studying. As I learned more about the crimes and their contexts, labels like 'opportunity' or 'risk' took on more precise meaning – I could link them to specific situational conditions or even individual experiences. Therefore, the concepts helped me, first, to *make* some meaningful *observations*,[6] and then to consistently reflect on the data that emerged from the observations. Through that reflection the definitions of the concepts evolved. As these definitions matured and solidified, so did the lines that formed the analytical structure that I applied to the reality I was trying to understand. I began to categorise and systematise what I observed more and more in relation to these theoretical concepts – and their gradually more concrete definitions – as I applied them to my case.

My primary concern in this research has not been that of testing theories, hypotheses, or refining the detailed, precise definitions of theoretical notions. Nor did my engagement with empirical data aspire to the generation of entirely new theories. I selected the concepts and theories discussed in Chapter 1 without applying rigid definitional boundaries or attempting to operationalise them in minute detail.

### *The Role of Law and (Empirical) Legal Research*

The research presented in this book is primarily criminological in nature, and the results of my analysis are supposed to further criminological understanding of the crimes that will be explored as well as the responses to those crimes. At the same time, legal rules have played an important role in the research. My academic training as well as the theoretical tools I selected for my analysis mean that I have placed an emphasis on this aspect of the case study. However, this emphasis is not sufficient to characterise this book as a traditional doctoral thesis in law, which means my analysis of legislation and judgments will not be as detailed as one would expect in such a piece. The use of legal research is elaborated on further in the paragraphs below.

---

6. Unlike the positivist tradition, I explicitly acknowledge that observation is theory-laden. For a discussion on this see: Blaikie, *Designing Social Research: The Logic of Anticipation*; Thomas S. Kuhn, *The Structure of Scientific Revolutions* (University of Chicago Press, 1970); Paul Feyerabend, *Against Method* (London: Verso, 2010); A. F. Chalmers, *What Is This Thing Called Science?* (Indianapolis: Hackett Publishing Company, Inc., 2015).

The research has two aims: (1) to understand how and why illegal waste activity in the bunker fuel sector occurs; and (2) to examine which measures currently exist to tackle this issue. In this context, legal analysis is relevant and necessary for three reasons, two of which are more related to the first aim of the research and one of which is linked to the second aim.

1. How and why the crimes occur:
   a. Defining the object of study.
   b. Explaining the social phenomenon.
2. Existing response measures:
   c. Assessing intervention mechanisms and their practical implementation.

**Defining the object of study**: waste management is a regulated activity, and illegal waste activity can be defined, broadly speaking, as the handling of waste in contravention of existing rules on waste management. In this sense, knowledge of the applicable law is necessary to determine which types of behaviour are permissible in this domain.[7] More specifically, analysis of the legal framework provides (partial) answers to the questions:

- What are waste oils?
- How can different types of waste oils be categorised?
- Who may handle waste oils?
- How may and should waste oils be handled?

To answer these questions, the approach that I take is one that is *internally focused*; in other words, one that looks *in* the law and not beyond it.[8] Naturally, the findings from this analysis filter into the criminological understanding of the characteristics of the actors involved in illegal waste activities. The requirements stemming from the legal framework influence the types of actors who can be present in the waste industry and the activities that they are allowed to carry out. Nevertheless, this portion of the research focuses on what the law says about waste management; therefore, the method of *doctrinal legal research* is the one that needs to be employed. This method, used by scholars and practitioners alike,

7. This means that in this study the activities and behaviours that are being studied are defined in relation to the legally-established boundary of permissible conduct, which is not an unproblematic choice. In fact, in criminology several scholars argue that the way criminal behaviour is legally circumscribed and how the 'criminal' label is attached are more a reflection of the way (the powerful members of) society choose to include and exclude certain groups and individuals than what is truly wrong or right. For a discussion on this, see: W. Morrison, "What Is Crime? Contrasting Definitions and Perspectives," in *Criminology*, ed. Chris Hale, K. Hayward, A. Wahidin, and E. Wincup (Oxford: Oxford University Press, 2013); Howard Saul Becker, *Outsiders* (N.Y.: Fress Press, 1966); Jeff Hayward Keith J. Morrison Wayne Presdee Mike Ferrell, *Cultural Criminology Unleashed* (2016).
8. What this means is that this internal approach does not concern itself with issues of justice or fairness. Nor does it venture to look at underlying assumptions (or intervention theories) that inspire and shape laws.

requires the selection of an issue (see the questions formulated in the bullet points above); the search for and **I**dentification of the applicable legal **R**ules and related authoritative guidance on the interpretation of those rules; the **A**pplication of the rules to the problems being investigated and the drawing of **C**onclusions (IRAC).[9] By adopting this method, we can develop a clearer understanding of how illegal waste oil management activities occur on a micro level – which rules are violated and how. The same exercise should be performed in the domain of bunker fuel production. However, as we will see in more detail in Chapter 3, the bunker industry is much more sparsely regulated. Therefore, the sources that need to be accessed to answer the questions in relation to bunker fuel are slightly different. The questions that need to be formulated for this industry are:

- What is bunker fuel?
- Who may produce bunker fuel?
- How may bunker fuel be produced and consumed?

Regarding the scope of application of the doctrinal method, we should keep in mind that the core empirical material that has been used for this book concerns crimes that took place within the jurisdiction of Dutch police and public prosecution authorities. The reasons for choosing the Netherlands as the setting in which both crimes and responses should be studied is explained in the first part of Section 2 below when describing the Andante *programma* as a source of data.

Because of the nature of the (criminal) activities we want to unravel and explain, we need to examine mainly EU law. Rules regarding bunker fuel production and waste oil management mostly fall under the domain of environmental law, where the EU takes a leading role in promulgating legislation.[10] We also need to take into account the related national implementing measures. Indeed, the Dutch national legal framework is relevant for us also beyond the implemented EU or international legislation pertaining to waste and bunker fuel. Administrative and criminal law designate even broader boundaries of what acceptable (business) conduct is – they are analysed at the beginning of Chapter 4. These areas of law are also the basis of most enforcement powers and activities. Administrative and criminal law are also nationally-circumscribed, as are the agencies that derive their mandates from said rules. We consider this latter observation in more detail below.

Legal analysis is necessary and relevant when seeking **macro level explanations** for illegal waste activities. With reference to the concept of industry as a

9. Mark van Hoecke, *Methodologies of Legal Research: What Kind of Method for What Kind of Discipline?* (Oxford: Hart, 2013); Mike Chui Wing Hong McConville, *Research Methods for Law* (Edinburgh: Edinburgh University Press, 2017); Michael Mason Julie Salter, *Writing Law Dissertations: An Introduction and Guide to the Conduct of Legal Research* (Harlow: Longman, 2011).
10. This is discussed in more detail in Chapter 3.

criminogenic context,[11] we should identify and scrutinise the legal framework governing and shaping actions within the sectors of waste oil management and bunker fuel production. Here the approach is an *integrated* one, where legal analysis is combined with methods from other disciplines, namely criminology and sociology.[12] Once the applicable legal rules are identified, they are analysed beyond their purely legal significance to determine how they function in specific circumstances. 'Function' has a precise connotation in this type of analysis: we are interested in *how rules may facilitate or constrain criminal and harmful activities.* Legal rules do this by opening avenues of action – i.e., by circumscribing permissibility. They attach consequences to violations, thereby generating costs and risks. They also contribute to populating the definitional universe of actors in the waste oil management and bunker fuel production sectors. The boundaries of permissibility and *acceptability* are influenced by legal rules and their interpretation by policymakers, judicial authorities, enforcement agents, and economic actors. Such interpretations may, in turn, be connected to the power and interests of specific categories of actors. The relevant legislation will again be international, European, and national (Dutch) in both the domains of waste oil management and bunker fuel production. We apply this method partly in Chapter 3 and then in Chapter 5.

Three steps – one doctrinal and two empirical – are needed to understand how current **mechanisms that exist to prevent and contrast** illegal waste activities function. First, we need to see which powers are given by the legal framework to different agents for monitoring and enforcing the application of waste management and bunker fuel production rules. This requires a *doctrinal* method (discussed above and applied in Chapter 3 as well as Chapter 4). Subsequently, we need to investigate how these rules are used by the relevant actors in practice through an *empirical* analysis, which is carried out in two ways. First, the criminal cases we analyse in this study give some indications regarding potentially problematic and challenging areas of enforcement. Using crime-script analysis in Chapter 4, we – somewhat implicitly – look at deficiencies in monitoring and enforcement by examining cases where guardianship did not inhibit the occurrence of criminal activities. Second, we look at the work of a police team that has unfolded over several years in Chapter 6, where the largest amount of empirical evidence regarding responses is presented is reviewed. Chapter 6 is an exploration of the law in action.

Ultimately, all the findings from the exploration of the three legal aspects outlined above can feed into a set of recommendations for improvement of the

11. The theoretical notion of a criminogenic industry is discussed in more detail in Chapters 3 and 5.
12. Hoecke, *Methodologies of Legal Research: What Kind of Method for What Kind of Discipline*; McConville, *Research Methods for Law*; Salter, *Writing Law Dissertations: An Introduction and Guide to the Conduct of Legal Research.*

frameworks that regulate waste oil management and bunker fuel production. Therefore, legal notions and measures will also be part of the recommendations that I will formulate in the final Chapter of this book.

## 2.2 Methods of Data Selection, Collection, Reduction, and Analysis

In the following paragraphs, we look at the methods I applied in implementing the research strategy outlined in the previous Section. We begin by looking at the primary, secondary and tertiary sources, which furnished the data used for the analysis and my relationship to both the sources and the data themselves. Then, we explore the notion of a case study and what it means for how the data is selected, organised, and analysed. Lastly, we look at the way I collected, reduced, and analysed the data.

### *Sources of Data and the Researcher's Stance*

In social research there is hierarchy of sources of data that specifies which types of information are optimal to answer a given research question. Depending on the level of analysis one chooses, the direct experience of an individual, group, organisation, or institution may be most relevant. 'Directness' is the key word. Starting from the premise that I am an *external* observer of the phenomena that I have researched, it has been my task to get as close as possible to the crime events that are problematised and investigated in this book.

In an ideal social research world, I would have been present during the commission of criminal acts and talked about them openly with the perpetrators of those acts – casually sipping coffee as waste oils and bunker fuel were being blended together – to try and understand what they were doing, how they saw it, and why they were carrying out those activities.[13] Alas, this is not an ideal social research world, so I have had to make do with the next, next best thing. The next best thing would have been a (retrospective) conversation with a perpetrator. And maybe also with someone in a similar position as the perpetrator, but who chose to comply with the law instead of violating it.[14] I only got as far as the meticulous documentation of a criminal event that police and public prosecution authorities have carried out.[15] From a social research perspective my source of data on crime events comes with plenty of baggage.

13. Blaikie, *Designing Social Research: The Logic of Anticipation*.
14. Studies like that of Huisman are illuminating in this respect. (Wim Huisman, "Tussen Winst En Moraal: Achtergronden Van Regelnaleving En Regelovertreding Door Ondernemingen" (Boom Juridische uitgevers, 2001).
15. That is still better than I had hoped for before starting the research. I had banked on judgments and abstract descriptions of decade-old cases. So, the next, next best thing has been a treasure trove I will always be grateful for.

Police and public prosecutors are allowed to collect selected information based on a circumscribed mandate.[16] They begin digging and documenting only when there is at least a whiff of suspicious behaviour (which they are able to detect); and continue gathering information when that suspicion is confirmed.[17] They rarely probe into the intimate lifeworld of suspects, especially when they are suspected of corporate environmental crime instead of the murder of a friend.[18] They actively look for crime motivators and opportunities surrounding the crime event. They look for the truth, but a truth that fits into their task to indict, prosecute, and convict suspects. All the data on crime events that I had access to is skewed by the position, tendencies, assumptions, and mandate of these agencies. This made my life easier when it came to collecting and reducing the data for my criminological analysis, but it also narrowed my outlook down substantially.

Of course, not all the information I have used for this research has been generated through police investigations. A large part of my reflections centres on the structures that contextualise the criminal events. In this respect, I have had substantial freedom to learn about: how petroleum is refined into products; which rules apply to processes involving petroleum use and the management of waste; what the markets for bunker fuel and waste oil management look like; and which policies have been enacted over the years in respect of these substances. Handbooks, scholarly articles, technical treatises, policy documents, judgments, and the texts of applicable legislation have been directly accessible to me. Relying on these other sources can be seen, to some extent, as a form of triangulation.[19]

Another aspect of the research has been that of looking at existing responses to the crimes. In that respect, I was extremely fortunate that the police and prosecution agents who had opened up their investigation dossiers also made me privy to their own functioning (my access is discussed in the paragraphs immediately below). This was an occasion that I had not anticipated or hoped for at the outset. I had made no plan to systematically collect data regarding the direct experience and practice of enforcement. My initial strategy was to see enforcement externally, in the same way I wanted to look at the context of crimes. Instead, I got to see police in action. The social, legal, and economic context in which the Andante team worked is virtually the same as that in which the crimes materialised. In that sense, my sources of data for describing and analysing the context of guardians are those cited above. However, in the case of Andante, I was able to get a better *understanding* of how they, as enforcement agents, experienced that context – how it constrained and facilitated their work.

---

16. The impact that relying on this source of data has on the validity of my findings is discussed in the last Section of this Chapter.
17. Suspicion has objective characteristics provided by the legal framework and subjective ones that emerge from the application of legal procedures by individuals onto reality. I may have selected far more or far fewer cases to look at if I had been shown the preliminary evidence the police had.
18. Especially when asking 'why' questions, this information is very important.
19. See also the discussion on limitations in Section 3 below.

*The Andante Programma and Access to Primary Data*

About two months into the start of this doctoral research (Autumn 2015), my supervisor contacted a Dutch public prosecutor with whom he had previously been in touch for other projects. He enquired whether she knew anyone within the *Openbaar Ministerie* (OM – Public prosecution service of the Netherlands) who was either currently working on or had previously dealt with cases of waste crime or waste trafficking. We were then put in touch with a prosecutor working at the *Functioneel Parket*, which is a specialised department of the public prosecution service that focuses on economic and environmental crimes.

We set up a meeting with this prosecutor: all three of us – my supervisor, co-supervisor, and me – went to the offices of the prosecutor twice and we also invited him once to Maastricht. It was during these meetings that we outlined my original research aims and questions, and we also got a better understanding of the cases that he had been working on until that point. All meetings and conversations as well as other field visits are listed in Annex II and are referenced accordingly throughout the book.

The prosecutor we spoke to clarified that the cases he was dealing with were forms of *corporate* crime: all the actors involved were legal entities, their representatives, or employees. During our conversations, it became very clear that we were all interested in uncovering the causes environmentally harmful practices connected to the management of waste. The prosecutor shared that he thought it would be important for the crimes he had been investigating and prosecuting to also be explored from an academic perspective. In view of that aim, he would be willing to allow me to read through the dossiers that the police team he was working with had developed and were still developing. He invited me to explore how I could make sense of the crime events from a criminological perspective.

The dossiers he was referring to had been put together by a special group of police officers. In 2012, the Andante *programma* was set up to systematically investigate crimes in the Dutch waste oil branch. The initial goal of the *programma* was to look at the process of de-bunkering, which is when ships release (remnants of) their fuel to entities located at sea-ports. This is done because the fuel is unsuitable, undesirable or has already been used and needs to be discharged before new fuel can be loaded onto the ship. This focus was premised on the then recent *Probo Koala* case, where Dutch waste oil management companies were found to have acted in contravention of Dutch and EU rules on waste management.[20] These companies were located at ports and should have handled the hazardous waste oils of the *Probo Koala* in an environmentally sound manner; instead, they only partly treated the wastes and then returned them to the ship because Trafigura (the company using the ship) had been unwilling to pay for proper treatment. The *Probo Koala* case was one example of more systematic wrongdoing

20. See Chapter 1 for a summary of the case and the relevant references.

in the sector. Dutch authorities, however, consistently found themselves at a disadvantage when trying to reconstruct the chain of actors and events underlying these recurring harms. The *programma* was supposed to serve as a knowledge-generating pool whereby the process of waste oil management and bunker fuel production could be better understood. This understanding would also make it easier to pinpoint and document wrongdoing.[21] At the same time, the investigators would move from indications of criminal activities (*aanwijzingen*) – that were discovered through checks, reports made to the authorities, or intelligence-based signals – to investigations of the facts. A number of these investigations matured into fully-fledged indictments, and, ultimately, were brough before criminal courts.

Based on these initial conversations, my supervisors, the prosecutor, and I agreed to formalise our exchanges. Through my supervisor, I applied to the *Parket Generaal*, which is the managing department of the OM, for access to the dossiers in function of my research. I was granted access to the physical files connected to the Andante *programma*. I would be able to read through those files and take anonymised notes and would have to receive approval from the prosecutor in charge of the dossiers before making my analysis public. Part of that approval would hinge on adequate anonymisation and not jeopardising the ongoing investigations.

I was welcomed into the offices of the Andante team in Amsterdam, where the files were physically held. One of the officers of the team was assigned to accompany me to sift through the information available. He gave me an overview of all the cases that they were working on and explained the way the *programma* functioned. The team had developed a structure to group the cases based on similarities in *modi operandi*. I had several conversations with this officer, and it was through these conversations that I determined which cases to focus on in more detail for the crime-script analysis (I explain this process further below when discussing data selection and collection). The dossiers contained one or more *'proces verbaal'*, which are official police records in written form in which they document facts that they have observed and statements they have obtained from a suspect or witness. These reports were connected to annexes (*bijlagen*), which were usually documents from the companies being investigated, such as e-mail exchanges, certificates of products, records of the movement of substances from different machines or tanks, results from sample-testing of substance, and so on. The dossiers provided chronological and detailed accounts of crime events unfolding over finite periods of time. During these crime events, multiple criminal acts took place, but all were attributable to a company and/or its representatives. Sometimes the same criminal act would be repeated several times and, in other parts of the dossiers, distinct but linked criminal acts were recorded.

21. See Section 1 of Chapter 6 for more details on the *programma*.

I was allowed to request access to all dossiers, even if they were not of the cases I was focusing on. Sometimes, based on observations or questions I had, the officer accompanying me would point me in the direction of other information in the dossiers or even to judgments that had already been issued or specialised literature. I was also allowed to speak to all members of the team about the dossiers or about the investigations more generally. I collected data for this research between July 2016 and February 2020, but I accessed the investigation dossiers specifically in two stages between October and December 2016 and then between September and November 2017. I collected other types of data on the Andante team as a group of enforcement agents as well, and this data collection took place also at other locations – I explain and describe this further below. The conditions under which I was allowed to use the information in the dossiers were: that my reproduction of the facts of the cases should not jeopardise ongoing investigations; and that anonymity should be preserved. (See also ethical considerations discussed below.)

The opportunity to draw from the rich well of information that Andante put at my disposal meant I had to make some choices about the scope of my research. In my initial research proposal, I had indicated that I wanted to look at and compare two jurisdictions: Italy and the Netherlands. However, the data I would have had access to in Italy was not truly comparable to that being furnished by Andante. Furthermore, the time and resources that my field work in the Netherlands required precluded me from expending a commensurate amount of time looking at Italian cases. Therefore, based on the empirical material that became available about not just crimes but also responses, my supervisors and I concluded that it was wisest to restrict the scope of the research to the Netherlands, and particularly the legal portion of the research to rules applicable in that territory.

### *Choosing a Case – Conducting a Study*

In this book, the notion of 'case study' indicates three things. First, it is a method of data *selection*. Second, it indicates a unit of analysis. Third, it suggests an approach to investigation.[22] We look at each in turn in the following paragraphs. A case study may also serve different functions.[23] These functions depend partly on the research questions and can result in several (sub-)cases being studied, depending on whether the aims of the research are more descriptive or explanatory

22. Blaikie, *Designing Social Research: The Logic of Anticipation*.
23. Case studies can serve as illustrations of social reality at different levels of complexity They may play different functions in the development of theory. If separated into single or multiple, case studies, they may have comparative uses, whereby a more experimental approach can be adopted to come to more general findings. Robert K Yin, *Applications of Case Study Research* (Sage, 2011); *Case Study Research: Design and Methods* (Sage publications, 2013).

and whether the goal is to generate or apply theory.[24] Conducting a case study – especially when of a single case – raises interesting issues regarding both generalisability and theory-generation. We also discuss these issues in Section 3.

First, let us consider that the case that we study in this book has been selected as a means to understand a broader societal issue.[25] We live in a time where illegal waste activity is part of our reality. It is a social phenomenon, which we problematised in Chapter 1 and which can manifest itself in different ways. One such way, and one such *case,* is that where illegal waste activity is part of the process of making bunker fuel. The methodological issue that arises in using a case in this way is that of the generalisability of the findings from this research to the broader issue of illegal waste activity, itself a form of corporate environmental crime. This way of seeing a case study also hints at the function of this research. Therefore, the case is used as an *instrument*.

At the same time, the goals of the research were not to generate more general theoretical conclusions and propositions. Most of the analysis is geared towards understanding the dynamics within the case itself. The data that I used have also *not been previously analysed*. Consequently, the case study is partly *intrinsic* because there is value in studying the case for its own sake and not just because it is illustrative of a broader social issue.

In a case study, research questions can be explored by looking at a single unit – an event, program, activity, process or even an individual's life – that is bounded in time, space, and activity. This is the second way of defining a case study. In this book, our unit of analysis – our case – is a *process,* itself made up of events. The latter have occurred at least in part in the Netherlands between 2012 and 2016. The regulatory and economic context of those events still exists, albeit some changes have taken place since their occurrence.[26] But the broader processes of waste oil management and bunker fuel production are ongoing. What is different here compared to the notion of a case study as a form of data selection is that a 'unit' presupposes a "mode of organising data".[27] From the perspective of the researcher, all the information gathered and analysed for the purpose of the study is connected and bound together in some way. All the

---

24. *Applications of Case Study Research; Case Study Research: Design and Methods.* Blaikie, *Designing Social Research: The Logic of Anticipation;* Robert E. Stake, "Qualitative Case Studies," in *The Sage Handbook of Qualitative Research,* ed. Norman K. Lincoln Yvonna S. Denzin (Thousand Oaks: Sage Publications, 2005).
25. This is different than saying that a case study is a method in itself for answering a research question. For example, a survey or an ethnographic study are used to answer a research question and case studies are seen as another method to do the same.
26. Where relevant, I mention which legislation and relevant judicial interpretation was applicable at the time of the criminal events and what the current applicable rules are, including any important differences in substance.
27. Blaikie, *Designing Social Research: The Logic of Anticipation.* 188. William J. Hatt P. K. Goode, *Methods in Social Research* (New York1952). 339.J. Cresswell, *Research Design* (Sage Publications, 2014); J. Clyde Mitchell, "Case and Situation Analysis," *The Sociological Review* 31, no. 2 (1983).

data has been collected in function of analysing a central problem, namely illegal waste oil management activities in the process of bunker fuel production. The two representative criminal cases that will be analysed in Chapter 4 ground the rest of the analysis – making sense of the situations and contexts that characterise those events is the work carried out in the other chapters.

The third way of understanding a case study is in reference to the approach and methods that are used. In fact, case studies are often characterised as designs where several different methods are combined. Regarding the combination of methods for this research, several procedures have been used to collect data: content analysis of documents and records, legal research and analysis, open interviews, expert interviews, and unstructured observations. We zoom into methods of data collection, reduction, and analysis in the coming paragraphs.

*Data on Crime Events at the Micro Level – Crime-Script Analysis*

*Data Collection and Reduction*

Crime-script analysis furnished both the concepts and method for data collection and reduction on crime-events, the results of which are provided in Chapter 4. The data collected using this method was described above in the paragraphs on the Andante *programma.* Other criminologists that have used crime-script analysis cite police investigation files as a suitable source of data for conducting crime-script analyses, albeit as an incomplete one as it will not contain *all* the information about the crime-commission process.[28]

In the original proposal for CSA, a distinction exists between universal scripts, *meta*scripts, *proto*scripts, scripts and tracks. These script forms encompass different levels of abstraction. Universal scripts are described as "scenes arranged into a sequential order which further the overall action [and] offer standardized guidelines for constructing scripts at the track-level, whatever the state of knowledge about the offense in question."[29]

Universal scripts are the most abstract: they provide the least concrete information about individual crime-commission processes but are useful for understanding almost any crime event. According to the original presentation of CSA, a universal script is composed of the following scenes: Preparation, Entry, Pre-Condition, Instrumental Precondition, Instrumental Initiation, Instrumental Actualisation, Doing, Post-Condition and Exit.[30] However, simplified versions of the universal script, which are more often employed, include only four scenes:

28. Benoit Leclerc, "Crime Scripts," in *Environmental Criminology and Crime Analysis*, ed. Richard Wortley and Michael Townsley (Abingdon: Routledge, 2017); Karen Clarke R. V. G. Tilley Nick Bullock, "Situational Prevention of Organised Crimes," (2013).
29. Derek B Cornish, "The Procedural Analysis of Offending and Its Relevance for Situational Prevention," *Crime prevention studies* 3 (1994)., p. 161-162.
30. Ibid.

Preparation, Pre-Activity, Activity, and Post Activity.[31] The two versions are compared in Figure 2.1. Here we can also see what each of these elements of the universal script refers to when concretely applied to a criminal event.

**Figure 2.1 Comparison of universal scripts used for crime-script analysis of a subway mugging – original from Cornish 1994 and contemporary version from Tompson and Chainey 2011.**

| Adapted Universal Script (Tompson & Chainey 2011) | Original Universal Script (Cornish 1994) | Facts of Crime Event |
|---|---|---|
| Preparation | Preparation | Meet and greet on hunting ground |
| Pre-activity | Entry | Entry into underground system |
| | Pre-condition | Travel to hunting ground |
| | Instrumental pre-condition | Waiting/circulating at hunting ground |
| | Instrumental initiation | Selecting victim and circumstance |
| Activity | Instrumental actualisation | Close-in/preparation |
| | Instrumental actualisation | Striking at victim |
| | Doing | Take money, jewellery, etc. |
| | Post-condition | Escape from scene |
| Post-activity | Exit | Exit from system |

This basic template, however, is not satisfactorily applicable to the cases we are interested in analysing. Indeed, other scholars have attempted to use CSA to examine organised, organisational, or generally more complex forms of crime, and have had to adapt the crime-script tool to the needs of these types of analyses.[32] One interesting suggestion, which has been formulated in the specific case of analysing illegal waste activity, is that of using 'Acts' to break-down the criminal

31. See e.g. Lisa Tompson and Spencer Chainey, "Profiling Illegal Waste Activity: Using Crime Scripts as a Data Collection and Analytical Strategy," *European Journal on Criminal Policy and Research* 17, no. 3 (2011), p. 9. For reviews of the application of crime-script analysis, see: Leclerc, "Crime Scripts." Hashem Dehghanniri and Hervé Borrion, "Crime Scripting: A Systematic Review," *European Journal of Criminology* 18, no. 4 (2021).
32. Helen Cockbain Eleanor Laycock Gloria K. Brayley, "The Value of Crime Scripting: Deconstructing Internal Child Sex Trafficking," *Policing*, no. 5 (2011); Bullock, "Situational Prevention of Organised Crimes"; Marco Zanella, "Script Analysis of Corruption in Public Procurement," in *Cognition and Crime: Offender Decision Making and Script Analyses*, ed. Benoit Wortley Richard Leclerc (Abingdon Routledge, 2014); Nicholas Lord et al., "A Script Analysis of the Distribution of Counterfeit Alcohol across Two European Jurisdictions," *Trends in Organized Crime* 20, no. 3 (2017); Spencer P. Chainey and Arantza Alonso Berbotto, "A Structured Methodical Process for Populating a Crime Script of Organized Crime Activity Using Osint," ibid. (2021).

process into smaller chunks.[33] This suggestion is coherent with the theatrical metaphor that underlies the CSA approach: a series of scenes are grouped together to form an Act. In that proposal, the Acts are, in turn, defined by referring to the stages that compose the legal/legitimate management of waste: creation, storage, collection, transport, treatment and disposal – of wastes.[34] The Acts become synonymous with the different stages.[35]

Now we can consider how the universal script that I used for data collection looked like, based on the foregoing reflections. We have established that the universal script should contain Acts that correspond to distinct logistical steps for each crime event. These Acts were not labelled *a priori*, rather they reflect the specific steps that I identified in analysing the criminal events. I then thought about which scenes make up each Act. The comparison made in Figure 2.1 is useful for this purpose. The scenes distinguished by Cornish in the first column were developed with the aim of eliciting offender accounts,[36] thus having in mind the possibility to inquire about very specific details of the crime commission process. They were also designed for types of crime involving very direct, interpersonal, and concrete *humanly performed* activities. Many of the activities I explored in this study involve mechanical and chemical processes: human actors are somewhat removed from the action. Even where this is not the case (for example, when documents are forged) it is not that specific techniques of forgery are used that require examination of scenes like 'instrumental actualisation'. Rather, there may be some psychological processes, such as considering forgery of the document as a necessary part of the mechanical procedure of collecting waste, that are relevant to the scripting process. Such psychological processes could be unravelled by splitting the Act up into very detailed scenes.

**Figure 2.2 Sample table for data collection from dossiers applying the crime scripting method**

| Act / Scene | Act 1 (e.g. collection) | | Act 2 (e.g. forgery) | | Act 3 (e.g. mixing) | |
|---|---|---|---|---|---|---|
| | Offending Conditions | Enforcement Conditions | Offending Conditions | Enforcement Conditions | Offending Conditions | Enforcement Conditions |
| Pre-activity | | | | | | |
| Activity | | | | | | |
| Post- activity | | | | | | |

33. Tompson and Chainey, "Profiling Illegal Waste Activity: Using Crime Scripts as a Data Collection and Analytical Strategy." p. 8.
34. Ibid. p. 8-9.
35. Ibid.
36. Cornish, "The Procedural Analysis of Offending and Its Relevance for Situational Prevention."

However, by doing this I would have run into the obstacle of not having the data to support any such analysis – I would have had to speak to the employees forging the documents. Therefore, given both the nature of the crimes being studied and the nature of the data available, I made the choice to use a simplified universal script, which consists of three scenes: Pre-activity, Activity and Post-activity.[37] By choosing to use CSA in this way for data collection and reduction, I ended up having an action within a criminal event as the smallest unit of analysis. That action classifies as part of either Pre-Activity, Activity or Post-Activity Scenes within an Act. Several Acts form a complex criminal event. The universal script template that I used for the analysis in Chapter 4 is displayed in Figure 2.2.

*Data Analysis*

Breaking complex criminal events down into Acts, Scenes, and actions is the method of *scripting*. However, scripting also requires us to insert information that distinguishes a given action. The script must, therefore, be completed with details about the actors perpetrating the crimes, the steps they take, and the tools they use to do this. Furthermore, the aim of scripting crime events is to uncover the "choice-structuring properties" of the situations in which they occurred. SCP provides us with five categories – risks, efforts, rewards, provocations, and excuses – to guide the collection and reduction of data.

Furthermore, four categories of factors have been proposed to break down each Scene: 'prerequisites', 'facilitators', 'responsibility' and 'legislation and regulation'. Prerequisites and facilitators are grouped together as 'offending conditions'; and responsibility and legislation and regulation as 'enforcement conditions' (see Figure 2.3).

Prerequisites are described as "likely preconditions that need to be satisfied before illegal activity is initiated". Identifying them means "identify[ing] the props (or tools) that the offender will have used to commit the illegal waste activity; [and that] these may be cognitive or physical tools."[38] The information gathered from the police files told me a lot about physical tools that are used in the three criminal events we are interested in. However, cognitive processes and perceptions were beyond the scope of this study for the reasons outlined above. Nevertheless, we can say something about the choices actors make by looking at their ultimate behaviour. The information from each case concerning prerequisites is summarised in the relevant sub-sections of Chapter 4. This information was first reduced into tables like the one portrayed in Figure 2.2.

37. Tompson and Chainey, "Profiling Illegal Waste Activity: Using Crime Scripts as a Data Collection and Analytical Strategy.", p. 9.
38. Ibid. p. 10.

**Figure 2.3 Extract from Tompson and Chainey (2011) - Useful questions for the identification of offending conditions and enforcement conditions (p. 11)**

| Condition | | Relevant questions to consider |
|---|---|---|
| *Offending conditions* | *Prerequisites* | What physical equipment is required? |
| | | What human resources are required? |
| | | What knowledge is required? |
| | | Is there an awareness of the rewards of legitimate choices? |
| | *Facilitators* | Is this a reciprocal interaction between cast members? |
| | | What rewards are on offer? |
| | | What is the perceived risk of being caught? |
| | | What are the perceived costs of being caught? |
| *Enforcement conditions* | *Responsibility* | What agency has responsibility for the enforcement of this activity? |
| | | What powers are available to enforce this activity? |
| | *Legislation and regulations* | What legislation governs this activity? |
| | | What permit conditions are related to this activity? |

Table 3. Relevant questions (to attempt to answer) to help populate the script with an understanding of offending and enforcement conditions.

The questions on 'enforcement conditions' help to identify which agency is best placed, in legal terms, to intervene and stop the (criminal) activities that are occurring and how it can do this.[39] Such information is vital for reconstructing the process of guardianship. The data on the legal framework underlying the activities of guardians has been collected using the legal research methods discussed above and is presented in Chapter 3 as well as in the first Section of Chapter 4. Based on this initial legal analysis, I could pinpoint at which stage a guardian would have had the power to intervene. In reference to the facts of the specific cases, I also determined where guardians had or had not intervened, thus contributing to lowering the risks and costs of engaging in criminal activities. The data on these aspects of the criminal events are analysed in Chapter 4.

*Ethical Considerations*

It is important to explicitly mention that the information regarding crime events that I used for my analysis was obtained without the suspects, defendants, or witnesses being aware of it. In that sense, none of these individuals could consent to my use of their (personal) data. The reason for this is obvious, but nonetheless needs to be mentioned. At the time I was collecting the data on the criminal events, the cases were still being either investigated by the police or had been investigated but not yet brought before a criminal court for adjudication. Contacting the individuals involved to ask for consent would have run the risk of interfering with

39. Ibid. p. 11.

the investigations and prosecutions. This impossibility also has implications for the validity and generalisability of my findings, which I discuss at the end of Section 3 below.

Although we could not seek explicit consent from suspects, defendants, and witnesses, my supervisors and I made the decision to forge ahead. Because the events that were investigated are forms of corporate crime, the type of personal information in the dossiers was different than that in other types of investigations. Under Dutch law, companies can be held criminally responsible for violating the law. Therefore, suspects, defendants, and associated entities were mostly legal entities or individuals in their roles as employees or representatives of these entities. There were of course biographic details of the latter or of witnesses included in the dossiers, such as the full name and home address. However, these details were not interesting to me. For the most part, I tried to focus on the activities instead of the actors themselves. I was careful to anonymise all my notes: no real company names are included in them; and, where individuals were somehow relevant to the narrative of an event, I always replaced names with functions, such as 'director', 'employee' or 'permit issuer'.

I also did my best to reduce the detail in recounting each crime event to the greatest extent possible in order to avoid that the company and connected individuals could later be identified. In fact, one of the cases that I had initially chosen to script was later removed from the study as some of the most important facts to describe the *modus operandi* were too distinct to adequately anonymise the case.

I collected most of the data in the dossiers by making anonymised written notes while reading the investigation files. I then filled in the tables described above on my computer with fewer recognisable details. My notebook and laptop were stored safely throughout the research. The process of recording and safeguarding the data was discussed with and approved by the prosecutor in charge of team.[40] This book has been reviewed by the prosecutor to check for accuracy and to be assessed for possible breaches of privacy or endangering ongoing investigations. The data have been stored in accordance with the rules set by Maastricht University.

*Data on Guardianship and Interventions: Studying the Case of Andante*

*Data Collection and Reduction*

I sat in the offices of the Andante team for a total of 30 days over a timespan of three years – on those occasions I was primarily there to work with the dossiers on criminal cases. However, I also spent considerable time with the team members besides doing my individual work. Furthermore, I spent five days with them while

40. A data management protocol was drawn up and agreed upon between myself and the prosecutor.

they conducted checks on ships and lorries transporting wastes and bunker fuel blend components, in collaboration with other state authorities. Additionally, on nine occasions, I had conversations and conducted interviews with members of the team and the prosecutor.

Most of the data that I collected regarding the Andante team and other enforcement agencies is in the form of unstructured observations. Those observations took place in a 'natural' setting.[41] I sat in briefings in the same way that other officers or agents would. On some occasions, however, members of the team would deliver brief presentations specifically for my benefit. The latter I have classified as expert interviews instead of unstructured observations as the aim of these was mostly to provide further details about the cases I was analysing. The team also shared several documents that they produced with me: some were more related to the cases I was analysing; many were about the functioning of the team itself and their methods. I have labelled these documents accordingly in Annex II. I also carried out a series of interviews with members of the police team that were focused on their professional history and how they came to be part of the Andante team. The aim of those interviews was to delve deeper into both the history and characteristics of the team.

The collection of data on Andante started rather unintentionally. It was incidental to the data collection I was performing regarding the criminal events themselves. The plan had been to sit in the offices of the team for a few days a week over several months and quietly read through the dossiers, take notes, and ask questions when needed. My presence in their offices was about the safety of the information in the files. That information could not physically leave the offices, except in the anonymised form of my notes and reflections.

However, besides the questions that I had on the cases I was analysing, I was often informally conversing with the various team members. We talked about their work on the cases, but also their experience in the team more generally. I was always invited to join during coffee, lunch, and cigarette breaks, and was privy to the conversations that took place among team members during those moments. These conversations meant that I quite organically got to know the team and not just the crimes they were investigating.

*Data Analysis*

As I discovered more about the team itself and noted down this information, I found myself requiring some sort of systematising framework to make sense of this social microcosm. Because SCP was the main structuring approach for this research project, the initial concepts I used were borrowed from there. Increasing risks was the category into which I could pigeonhole the work of the team and the stories of other agents and agencies they told me about. The techniques belonging to that

41. Blaikie, *Designing Social Research: The Logic of Anticipation.*

category – e.g., extending guardianship and strengthening formal surveillance – were initially helpful to capture some of the nuance I was observing and hearing. The more foundational concept of capable guardianship often provided a broader net into which the varied information I received could fall.

However, the most fitting notion I could retrieve in the literature connected to SCP was that of problem-oriented policing (POP).[42] Although never formally established as a POP team, many of the features of Andante's operation resembled what I read about this prevention and enforcement strategy. POP is itself connected to SCP, especially in terms of the outlook that agents can take in trying to resolve crime-problems. As we will see in Chapter 6, I also needed to refer to the notion of responsive regulation to reflect on the work of the team because the body of literature connected to responsive regulation is best suited to understanding the nature and quality of responses to corporate offending (see Chapter 1). It provided a yardstick against which to reflect on the experiences of Andante and their collaborators.

Based on the increasing data that I was exposed to and my continuous reflections using the abovementioned theoretical concepts, I began of my notes to then carry out a thematic analysis.[43] I also set up extra in-depth interviews with team members. Unfortunately, of the mountain of data that I collected during my time with the team, only a fraction has been used in this book. It became clear after some time that I would not have had the time to continue collecting and working on these data within the framework of my PhD project. Most of them remain buried in my notebooks and I hope I may be able to revive this avenue of research in the future. Suffice to say, that I abandoned the more elaborate plan of coding a larger dataset using Atlas.ti and I returned to a simpler, manual approach for reviewing my notes, the interview transcripts, and the documents of the team using theoretical concepts to structure my collection and analysis. More details are found in Chapter 6.

*Ethical Considerations*

The members of the Andante team as well as the other enforcement agents I encountered during my field visits were informed of my presence and the fact

42. "Herman Goldstein's problem-oriented policing concept is a comprehensive prescription for improving the way in which the police do business. It calls for the police to understand their work in a new light, to recognize that what they are called upon to do is to address a wide range of problems that threaten the safety and security of communities, including, but not limited to what is commonly viewed as serious crime. The concept calls for the police to improve their understanding of the underlying conditions that give rise to community problems and to respond to these problems through a much wider range of methods than they have conventionally used." (Michael S. Scott, *Problem-Oriented Policing: Reflections on the First 20 Years* (US Department of Justice, Office of Community Oriented Policing Services, 2000), p. 2). I talk about problem-oriented policing in more detail in Chapter 6.
43. Clarke, Victoria, Virginia Braun, and Nikki Hayfield. "Thematic analysis." *Qualitative psychology: A practical guide to research methods* (2015): 248.

that I was present in function of conducting my doctoral research. I made the disclaimer that I would take notes of my observations and conversations with them and asked for explicit consent when I recorded an interview. In Chapter 6, some quotes from the interviews have been used directly: The individuals whose voices those quotes capture have been informed of their use and have read the manuscript. Therefore, they had the possibility of checking whether the portions of the interviews that I used misrepresented what they conveyed to me at the time they were recorded.

I collected most of the data on responses by making anonymised written notes during or immediately after my field visits and conversations. I recorded interviews, which I then anonymised during the transcription phase. Several of the interviews were conducted in Dutch, and I translated them personally to protect the data. I also took notes during each interview. My notebook and recording device were stored safely throughout the research. The process of recording and safeguarding the data was discussed with and approved by the prosecutor in charge of team.[44]

*Data on the Macro Level: 'Detailed Description' and the Importance of Context in Explaining the Case*

In Chapter 1, the case of illegal waste management activity in the process of bunker fuel production was classified as a form of corporate environmental crime. We saw in Section 1 above, that context and social structure are important explanatory elements according to SCP because they supply the conditions that motivate offenders, remove or inhibit guardianship, and generate suitable targets. Structural and contextual factors that are associated with and used to explain corporate and environmental crime are often, but not always, different than those that are included in explanations of more traditional forms of crime.[45] Therefore, explaining the crimes that are analysed in this book meant that I had to pay special attention to the bodies of literature, which in Chapter 1 were categorised under the terms organisational and green criminology.

The structural and contextual factors that are highlighted in both green and organisational criminology revolve around regulatory and enforcement arrangements; economic conditions, including the distribution of economic power;

44. A data management protocol was drawn up and agreed upon between myself and the prosecutor.
45. Some authors have attempted to find a general explanation to crime, without making distinctions between traditional and organisational offending, e.g.: Michael R. Hirschi Travis Gottfredson, *A General Theory of Crime* (Stanford, Calif.: Stanford Univ. Press, 1998). Other authors have used theories developed for traditional forms of crime and applied them to organisational crimes, e.g.: John Braithwaite, "Criminological Theory and Organizational Crime " *Justice Quarterly* 6, no. 3 (1989); Robert Agnew, "Building on the Foundation of General Strain Theory: Specifying the Types of Strain Most Likely to Lead to Crime and Delinquency," *Journal of Research in Crime and Delinquency* 38, no. 4 (2001).

and the normative or definitional features of a setting. I carried out literature reviews in these two sub-disciplines in order to identify the key concepts that would guide my research on structure and context.

The kinds of information I gathered against this theoretical backdrop mostly falls into three categories:

a) Legal and policy documents that outline the range of permissible and acceptable actions in the two industries, including which type of actors may operate within them and under what conditions. The conditions include what kinds of consequences can be expected upon violation of the rules. Legal documents include legislation, judicial decisions, and soft law instruments such as industry standards. (See also the second part of Section 1 above on legal research.)
b) Sector specific technical documents or manuals, including guidance published by state entities regarding the nature and use of substances that are defined as waste oils or bunker fuel.
c) Academic literature that describes and analyses the two industrial sectors, which also includes empirical data and is not merely a theoretical exploration.

These types of data collected and the analysis performed do not show if and how the actual offenders perceived the situational conditions that are generated by structural and contextual characteristics and what role they played in the ultimate decision to commit crime. However, they supply a great deal of the detailed and thick description that is needed for the case study.[46]

## 2.3 Limitations

### *Generalisability vs Transferability*

> *The goal [of the research] is not to produce a standardised set of results that any other careful researcher in the same situation or studying the same issues would have produced. Rather it is to produce a coherent and illuminating description of and perspective on a situation that is based on and consistent with detailed study of that situation.*[47]

46. Michael Bassey, "Pedagogic Research: On the Relative Merits of Search for Generalisation and Study of Single Events," *Oxford review of education* 7, no. 1 (1981).
47. J. W. Schofield, "Increasing the Generalizability of Qualitative Research" in *Social Research: Philosophy, Politics and Practice*, ed. M. Hammersley (London: Sage 1993). 202P.

> *An important criterion in judging the merits of a case study is the extent to which the details are sufficient and appropriate for* [*an individual*] *in a similar situation to relate his decision-making to that described in the case study.*[48]

These two quotes are taken from literature that discusses how general statements about social reality may be derived from case studies. As mentioned in the preceding section, the notion of case study also refers to a form of data selection. In social research that is characterised as 'quantitative' in nature, researchers use procedures like probability sampling. These procedures may qualify a certain sample of data as *representative* (of a population). The same cannot be done when choosing a case study. Indeed, generalisability of findings based on such representativeness may not be sought after by the researcher who studies a case at all. In that sense, the first quote captures the intent and function behind much of case study – and one may say of qualitative – research more generally: providing accurate, profound, and detailed descriptions and analyses of certain social situations. This is a fitting definition for the work that is presented in this book.

Another approach to generalisability that we can reflect on is that evinced in the second quote above. This kind of generalisability hinges on the 'transferability' or 'relatability' of the case *vis-à-vis* other similar cases. At first, it may be possible to perform 'natural generalisation': we can recognise similarities and repetitive patterns when comparing the characteristics of the case being studied with similar social situations. Taken from this perspective, applying theoretical concepts like opportunity, risk, reward and so on can make these patterns visible in this case and then comparable to other cases. When context is also described and analysed in sufficient depth, it may also then be possible to detect whether there is congruence between the context of the case and other social situations.[49] Therefore, the data and conclusions in this research are transferable or relatable in the sense of the second quote at the beginning of this section. Especially since the cases analysed in this study can be considered 'typical' because certain characteristics – e.g., the *modi operandi*, the (types of) actors involved, the guardianship structures – are common to several cases.

Definitively proving that a specific case is 'typical' is a virtually impossible feat,[50] yet it is still arguable. My claim rests on two sources. First, conversations with experts – the members of the Andante team, including the specialised prosecutor – who have been conducting investigations in the waste and oil sectors

48. Bassey, "Pedagogic Research: On the Relative Merits of Search for Generalisation and Study of Single Events." 85.
49. Blaikie, *Designing Social Research: The Logic of Anticipation.*
50. Margaret Diane Preissle Judith Tesch Renata Goetz Judith Preissle LeCompte, *Ethnography and Qualitative Design in Educational Research* (Bingley, U.K.: Emerald Group Pub., 2008); William Foote Whyte King Kathleen Whyte, *Learning from the Field: A Guide from Experience* (Beverly Hills, Calif.: Sage, 1984).

for decades. Based on their experience, they have been able to develop templates of how these crimes tend to occur. Indeed, as we shall see in Chapter 6, the Andante project is itself an attempt at identifying broader trends and characteristics in this type of offending with the aim of improving responses. The careful and reflexive work of the team has yielded an answer to the question of what typical cases look like. I have built on that.

Second, we need to consider existing (academic) literature on illegal waste activities, including broader investigations into corporate and environmental crimes as well as narrower investigations into (crime in) the waste oil management and bunker fuel production sectors. These more scholarly investigations show which types of trends continuously pop up in relation to these types of criminal activities. As I delved into the detailed data on criminal events, I was able to recognise many features that I had seen in the literature. There were no fundamental inconsistencies with what was reported in these secondary sources. Nor did activities in the criminal events strike me as unexpected or inexplicable based on the information I gathered about similar crimes as well as the context in which those events materialised. It made sense why the activities were happening so systematically.

*Responses: Generalising the Andante Experience*

The data on Andante provide various illustrations of guardianship *vis-à-vis* a specific form of crime. For example, we can see how Andante monitored, investigated, and intervened against a waste oil collection firm or how they cooperated with other agents in this process. Based on these findings, we can develop more general insights on interventions in cases of illegal waste activities and corporate environmental crimes. When we discover what has made Andante capable guardians, we may transfer some of those insights to other guardians.

For example, one element that will repeatedly return in our findings is that of (technical) knowledge. The Andante team members have been able to, first, identify and then, competently investigate crimes because they know enough about the waste oil management and bunker fuel production processes to detect wrongdoing. These activities are highly complex and lack of sufficient knowledge blinds all potential guardians. So, individual citizens, who have no special guardianship function for enforcing legal rules on waste oil management are also inhibited in their own possibilities for guardianship by lack of sufficient knowledge. Each of us could campaign for more stringent rules on fuel quality if we were aware of how such fuel is made. This type of analytic generalisability[51] is applied 'horizontally' – i.e., other guardians for the *same kind of crime* may develop the requisite skills to intervene more successfully. However, we could generalise 'vertically' as well for corporate environmental crimes: Theoretical and empirical

51. Yin, *Applications of Case Study Research.*

literature contains plenty of evidence that knowledge plays a huge role in aiding the concealment of corporate environmental crimes. Knowledge possessed by guardians increases their ability to detect corporate environmental crimes. This example of knowledge serves to show how transferability functions with regard to the analysis of data that was gathered on responses for this study.

### *Validity*

There are nine limitations to this research that need to be addressed in more detail and which impact the validity of the findings presented in this book.

First, the data used for the crime-script analysis are secondary: they were collected (*ex-post facto*) by criminal enforcement agents, whose aim was different than mine. Therefore, by using these data, I automatically integrated the perspective and methods of those agents into the material I used. While crime-opportunities are relevant for an investigation, what is ultimately documented in a police report are provable facts that are relevant for attributing criminal responsibility, based on the standards that apply within the rules of criminal procedure.

Second, the use of police-generated data suffers from several limitations. As already stated, these limitations are connected to the mandate of police and other criminal justice authorities, but they extend further. Police do not and cannot detect all crime and they may have (structurally perpetuated) biases that impact their detection practices. Connected to detection is the issue of reporting. Not all crime is immediately consciously experienced by victims, especially in cases of corporate and environmental crime, or victims may not turn to authorities at all. Police control is also not uniform in either breadth or effectiveness, which then impacts both detection and reporting as well.[52] Using data from police or other (criminal) law enforcement agencies, therefore, means that not just the biases but also the practices and procedures of individual agents and organisations are 'baked into' the data as well. The only way to disentangle the primary data from those other ingredients is to increase the number of sources one uses through triangulation.[53]

Third, the data that I used do not capture the *experience* of the individuals involved in the events. Situational crime prevention and crime-script analysis

52. The following contributions discuss the peculiarities of using police-generated data in more detail: Maguire, Mike, and Susan McVie. "The Oxford Handbook of Criminology." Essay. In Crime Data and Criminal Statistics: A Critical Reflection. Oxford University Press, 2017; Maguire, Mike. "The Oxford Handbook of Criminology." Essay. In Criminal Statistics and the Construction of Crime. Oxford University Press, 2012; Coleman, Clive, and Jenny Moynihan. Understanding Crime Data: Haunted by the Dark Figure. Crime and Justice. Buckingham: Open University Press, 1996.

53. For a discussion on triangulation, see: Wincup, Emma, Kathy Salter Hampson, Ella Holdsworth, and Joanna Large. Criminological Research: Understanding Qualitative Methods (version 2nd edition.). London: SAGE Publications, 2017, p. 10-12.

presume the bounded rationality of the offender, and they also require that the offender's perspective and perception be included in understanding the choice to commit crime. All my conclusions about risks, rewards, efforts, provocations, and excuses are externally assessed based on the connections that I drew from reading the facts of the cases and by researching the contexts in which they occurred. However, the voices of the perpetrators were not included to confirm or deny my assessment.

Fourth, my assessment about situational factors is skewed because I have used it to explain offending. Just like the voices of perpetrators are missing from my account, so are those of employees and representatives of firms that operate in the same contexts and under very similar situational conditions, who have *not* violated the law.

Fifth, my research has been circumscribed in terms of levels and units of analysis. It has not looked at the *intra*-organisational dimension, i.e., the social dynamics and procedural features that operate within a specific firm (whether that is a waste management company, a petrochemical producer, or a surveyor, to name a few possible candidates). Some of the theories discussed in this book actually require this aspect to be integrated into the analysis for explaining criminogenesis. In line with the points just outlined, even on the intra-organisational (or meso) level, it would be important to explore examples of firms that comply as well as firms which do not in order to get a fuller picture.

Sixth, because regulations as well as market dynamics have been shown to play an important role in this case study, looking at how crimes unfold in different jurisdictions, which adopt diverse regulatory regimes or strategies would have been recommendable. It would also be especially interesting to see the magnitude of difference between jurisdictions within the EU/EEA and then between EU/EEA countries and others in different parts of the globe, especially where important ports are located.

The seventh aspect to consider when thinking about the validity of my findings is connected to the portion of the research that focuses on responses. Even though the data on Andante as a team is, to a great extent, primary in nature, it still suffers from two limitations. The first is that much of the information I gathered is self-reported. For example, when the officers were interviewed about how and why they were appointed to the team or talked about the team's history and impact, the information they shared was based on their subjective experience. The second is that there are other authorities that have dealt with these types of industrial activities and which I have not spent time with or interviewed extensively. Among those authorities the ILT is the most important. This is the Dutch Human Environment and Transport Inspectorate (*Inspectie Leefomgeving en Transport*), which has a mandate to monitor compliance with and enforce waste management rules.[54] The experience of these other agents would have given me a more complete picture of state enforcement.

The eighth issue that needs to be addressed is my own relationship to the Andante team. Throughout the research, it often felt like the Andante team and I were on a common mission against environmental crime. This attitude was a catalyst for open conversation; however, it also meant that I was prone to understanding the motivations and perspective of the team and bringing them unconsciously into my own work. If I had overcome the second and third limitations listed just above by introducing the perspective of offenders and non-offenders into my work, I could have made up for the bias somewhat, but this was not possible for both ethical reasons (outlined above) and because such a research design would not have been possible for me to carry out in practice.

At the same time, I deliberately and systematically reflected on my interactions with the Andante team in my field notes and reported back both what I observed and my own thoughts about the observations as well as about the team more generally to my supervisors at regular intervals. I recall several meetings where fascination and excitement were accompanied by an equal measure of critical reflection.

Lastly, the theoretical concepts and frameworks that I used for my analysis are based on imperfect assumptions about the way human beings and society function. The most obvious problem is my use of rational choice theory, which has been amply criticised by many scholars.[55] I think the SCP framework's evolution, which has led to the inclusion of categories like 'provocations' and 'excuses', and the fact that it has always acknowledged that motivation and opportunity ultimately emerge from the way social reality is structured already go a long way to addressing some of the criticism. I also agree with Clarke's statement that SCP is a pragmatic tool that is "good enough" and has proven its validity through the results of its implementation.[56] If the recommendations that are based on

54. I did, however, get the possibility to speak with some ILT agents during my work with Andante. See Annex II for details.

55. Graham Farrell, "Situational Crime Prevention and Its Discontents: Rational Choice and Harm Reduction Versus 'Cultural Criminology'," in *Crime Opportunity Theories* (Routledge, 2017); David Garland, "Governmentality and the Problem of Crime: Foucault, Criminology, Sociology," *Criminological Perspectives. Essential Readings* (2003); David Garland and Richard Sparks, "Criminology, Social Theory and the Challenge of Our Times," *Brit. J. Criminology* 40 (2000); Jock Young, "Searching for a New Criminology of Everyday Life: A Review Of 'the Culture of Control'," review of Searching for a New Criminology of Everyday Life: A Review of 'The Culture of Control', David Garland, *The British Journal of Criminology* 43, no. 1 (2003); Alexis Russell Tibbetts Stephen G. Piquero, *Rational Choice and Criminal Behavior: Recent Research and Future Challenges* (New York: Routledge, 2012); Willem De Haan and Jaco Vos, "A Crying Shame: The over-Rationalized Conception of Man in the Rational Choice Perspective," *Theoretical Criminology* 7, no. 1 (2003).

56. Martha J. Smith and Ronald V. Clarke, "Situational Crime Prevention: Classifying Techniques Using "Good Enough" Theory," in *The Oxford Handbook of Crime Prevention*, ed. Brandon C. Welsh Martha J. Smith Ronald V. Clarke David P. Farrington (Oxford University Press, 2012).

my findings would be implemented in practice, then maybe we could imagine evaluating their external validity. Indeed, it is a personal wish to, one day, design and setup an action research project that draws from these findings to test them out in the hope of developing more insights and tools that lead to reducing and preventing the kinds of harm that are discussed in this book.

Table 2.1 below provides an overview of the book and summarises the main points discussed in this Chapter. It includes the themes addressed as well as the strategy, methods, sources of data, and theoretical concepts that are relevant for each chapter.

Table 2.1 Overview of the book summarising methodological aspects relevant for each chapter.

| Chapter | Theme | Strategy/Methods/Concepts | Research Questions |
|---|---|---|---|
| 1 | Introduction | Literature review:<br>– Existing literature on the topic<br>– Theoretical concepts applies in the book | N/A |
| 3 | Exploring the context in which the crimes occur: the waste oil management and bunker fuel production industries | – Inductive<br>– Literature review<br>– Content analysis<br>– Doctrinal legal research<br>– Criminogenic industry<br>– Routine activities theory (macro level) | What do illegal waste oil management (WOM) activities in the process of bunker fuel production (BFP) look like?<br>During which steps of the broader BFP and WOM do these illegal activities occur?<br>What internal as well as external regulations and mechanisms for supervision and control exist that apply to the WOM and BFP sectors? |
| 4 | Reconstructing events to identify the situational conditions that lead to criminal behaviour | – Inductive<br>– Crime-script analysis<br>– Doctrinal legal research<br>– Empirical legal research<br>– Situational crime prevention<br>– Elements of the retroductive research strategy | All research sub-questions |
| 5 | Macro-level criminological analysis of the context and structures to see how | – Inductive<br>– Literature review<br>– Content analysis<br>– Integrated legal research | What factors influence – facilitate or constrain – the actors involved in undertaking the abovementioned logistical steps towards crime-commission? |

| Chapter | Theme | Strategy/Methods/Concepts | Research Questions |
|---|---|---|---|
| | they generate the situational conditions discussed in Chapter 4 | – Crime-facilitative system<br>– Criminogenic industry<br>– State-corporate symbiosis<br>– Organisational criminology<br>– Elements of the retroductive research strategy | How are these regulations and mechanisms interpreted, applied, and enforced?<br>How can these regulations and mechanisms influence – facilitate or constrain – the occurrence of criminal activities that take place in the WOM and BFP sectors?<br>(Further research questions are formulated in Chapter 5, inspired by the theoretical concepts that are applied there.) |
| 6 | Responses to the crimes under study with a focus on the experience of a specific group of police enforcement agents | – Inductive<br>– In-depth interviews<br>– Participant observation<br>– Content analysis<br>– Empirical legal research<br>– Situational crime prevention<br>– Problem-oriented policing<br>– Corporate (responsive) regulation<br>– Organisational criminology | What internal as well as external regulations and mechanisms for supervision and control exist that apply to the WOM and BFP sectors?<br>How are these regulations and mechanisms interpreted, applied, and enforced?<br>How can these regulations and mechanisms influence – facilitate or constrain – the occurrence of criminal activities that take place in the WOM and BFP sectors? |

# 3 The Waste-Product Nexus

## Exploring the Physical, Economic and Regulatory Features of Two Overlapping Industries

Our case unfolds at the intersection of two industrial areas of activity: we have the world of bunker fuel (BF) on the one hand, and that of hazardous waste oil (WO) management on the other. Both these areas of activity are fraught with complex processes and numerous actors. The dynamics generated by the interplay of such processes and actors – within each and at the overlap between the two industries – lead to the emergence of conditions that facilitate crime. Understanding the resulting crimes, therefore, requires us to understand these two industries first. The attractiveness of choosing to handle hazardous waste oils in a way that is both contrary to law *and* harmful to the environment partly depends on the circumstances – the needs and pressures – that exist in the waste oil management services (WOMS) industry. Similarly, using waste to produce bunker fuel is appealing and possible because the bunker fuel industry encourages and facilitates it being so. Hence, in this Chapter, we journey through these two industries trying to imagine ourselves operating within them in order to feel the temptations, the pressures and the normalness, which facilitate the criminal activities that we later deconstruct in Chapter 4.

To explore these two industries, we need to identify relevant elements that systematise the bulk of information that exists in relation to them. Literature from organisational criminology can help us in this respect. Several relevant elements or categories of elements can be found within this subdiscipline.[1] No analysis

1. One contribution lists relationships, physical, historical, political and economic aspects as relevant.(Norman K Denzin, "Notes on the Criminogenic Hypothesis: A Case Study of the American Liquor Industry," *American Sociological Review* (1977). Another states that industries can be understood in reference to policy, legislation, lobbying, research and technology, the availability of natural resources, the relevant clients and customers, public opinion and the harm the industry produces. (Elizabeth A Bradshaw, ""Obviously, We're All Oil Industry": The Criminogenic Structure of the Offshore Oil Industry," *Theoretical Criminology* 19, no. 3 (2015). Larger categories that have been mentioned when looking at criminogenic systems are the "normative, legal, economic and organisational features" of an industry. Martin L Needleman and Carolyn Needleman, "Organizational Crime: Two Models of Criminogenesis," *The Sociological Quarterly* 20, no. 4 (1979). Even broader are the concepts of business, administrative and social environments, which, in turn, subsume various collections of elements listed in the literature. Wim Huisman, "Tussen Winst En Moraal: Achtergronden Van Regelnaleving En Regelovertreding Door Ondernemingen" (Boom Juridische uitgevers, 2001). Much narrower

can capture everything that the numerous elements and groupings covered by different scholars try to include. There is no consistent and proven list of relevant elements that need to be explored to study criminogenesis. However, market conditions as well as the regulatory and normative functions of legislation and standards are continuously reiterated in the literature. The analysis of the data on criminal events carried out in this study confirms the relevance of these two aspects. Yet, we cannot make sense of either of those wider categories of elements without looking at the physical processes that they accompany.

Therefore, in this analysis, we choose to focus on *three* specific *sets* of elements: First, the physical substances that are central in the industries that contextualise our case; second, the economic characteristics of each industry; and third, the standards, rules and legislation that have a regulatory function in each of the industries. We can imagine that all three sets of elements in relation to the two industries generate a system, which, in turn, forms the context of our case study. In this Chapter, we try to depict the breadth and range of the system by cataloguing its various elements and noting the spaces in which there is an overlap between the industries. Later, in Chapter 5, we will zoom into this overlapping space specifically and analyse it in more depth using the notions of 'crime-facilitative system' and 'symbiosis'.

In Section 1, we look at all the relevant physical *flows* in the system.[2] This way of looking at the physical dimension of the industries allows us to see how the system lives. The overarching physical flow is that of oil substances that become wastes and then become products (again). Sections 2 and 3 are focused on the waste oil management services industry and the bunker fuel production (BFP) industry, respectively. Within each Section, we look at the applicable rules and economic features in turn. For the waste sector, we begin with the relevant legislation because this industry is dependent on legislation and policy for its existence. The waste management services (WMS) market is a consequence of the framework created by the state through legislation and definitions. The basic concept of waste is a social and legislative construction – to understand this construction, we need to take a step back and see how substances that end up being labelled as wastes come into existence first physically, then legally, and only after that economically.

---

analyses look only at economic features of industries such as entry barriers, product concentration and product differentiation, price elasticity and the growth of demand. (Harvey A Farberman, "A Criminogenic Market Structure: The Automobile Industry," *The Sociological Quarterly* 16, no. 4 (1975); William N Leonard and Marvin Glenn Weber, "Automakers and Dealers: A Study of Criminogenic Market Forces," *Law and Society Review* (1970). Literature that is focused on the dynamics between state and economy returns to more the abstract and familiar theoretical concepts of goals, social controls, constraints, oversight and guardianship. (Ronald C Kramer, Raymond J Michalowski, and David Kauzlarich, "The Origins and Development of the Concept and Theory of State-Corporate Crime," *Crime & Delinquency* 48, no. 2 (2002).

2. The notion of 'flows' taken from complex systems theory, see notes 13 and 14 below for an explanation of flows in relation to other system elements.

The opposite is true of the bunker fuel sector. To this day, hard law as well as state-generated measures and mechanisms are scarce in this industry. The market is much freer and can operate with little 'external' regulation. Therefore, looking at how the physical reality of the bunker fuel sector has been managed economically is our starting point. Regulatory efforts to curb the effects of this market's operation on human well-being are secondary and reactive to such effects. For both industries, we also need to consider formal guardianship structures because they affect the constellation of incentives and pressures too. The issue of enforcement is discussed in the conclusions of the Chapter along with some broader observations.

## 3.1 Physical Flows: Oils, Goods, Fuel & Wastes

We consider four physical flows in this section. The first is that of petroleum from extraction and into all the various applications this remarkable substance has.[3] The second and third flows are intimately linked: goods and their components flow across the earth on ships. In turn, bunker fuel flows through a manufacturing process and into the engines of such ships. The fourth flow is that of wastes generally and waste oils specifically, which is accompanied by a corresponding flow of documents.[4] All these flows interact and overlap, creating the physical structures that contextualise our case. We explore each flow in terms of processes and procedures applied to the substances, as well as the actors that perform them. Following these flows helps us to learn about the features of the substances and actors as elements in the relevant industrial systems.

### *The Flow of Oil: Extraction, Expansion, Emission*

> *Oil's ubiquity has produced various "regimes of living – configurations of normative, technical, and political elements that are brought into alignment in problematic and uncertain situations" – around its heterogeneous uses and deployments.*[5]

To overcome the separation between industries and really look at the flows that traverse the breadth of processes in our case study, we need to find a common denominator. Peeling back the labels we attach to substances that say – this is a waste, this is a product, this is bunker fuel, a lubricant, a pesticide, or a hazardous danger, we find that the common denominator is oil. Once extracted, whether

---

3. 'Petroleum' and 'oil' are used interchangeably throughout this Chapter.
4. As will be seen in this and later Sections, several substances that are traded in the context of the industries we are exploring require some form of accompanying documentation or labels to inform those purchasing and consuming them of their content and quality. However, in the case of waste and its movement, such documents take on particularly high significance and can influence situations in ways that substantially either constrain or facilitate crime.
5. Hannah Appel, Arthur Mason, and Michael Watts, *Subterranean Estates: Life Worlds of Oil and Gas* (Cornell University Press, 2015). 27.

on land or offshore, petroleum travels into a series of mechanical and chemical processes and enters into our lives in multiple forms, many of which we do not even realise. Our study is not a technical treatise on crude oil refinement processes nor a deep exploration of the world of oil, (however much such areas of knowledge are interesting and pertinent for a thorough understanding of our case).[6] Our interest here is circumscribed to the following four points:

1. The finite nature of petroleum and of a petroleum-based economy.
2. The versatility of petroleum and its consequent pervasiveness.
3. The specific uses of petroleum that are relevant for our case.
4. The relationship between the consumption of petroleum and the finite nature of a clean and healthy environment.

If we take points one and four in the above list, we see clear arguments in favour of reducing our societal dependence on oil. Our petroleum-based economy is unsustainable, from cradle to grave. There is not enough oil to continue supporting the lifestyles that have been created based on its use. Lifestyles not just of individuals but of entire countries and global networks.[7] And there are not enough resources in our environment to sustain these lifestyles either. So, why have we not kicked our addiction to oil? Points two and four give us a clue. There is a good chance that as you read these words you are in the proximity of something that is made of a petroleum derivative or brought to you thanks to fuels and lubricants that power all sorts of movement: machinery, cars, trucks, planes, trains, and ships. Interestingly, all these applications of oil can be relevant for us, with some having a more evident or direct link to our case than others. Let us look at the process of oil distillation to understand this better.

---

6. See, for example: Pete Newell, *Globalization and the Environment: Capitalism, Ecology and Power* (John Wiley & Sons, 2013); Steve Coll, *Private Empire: Exxonmobil and American Power* (Penguin, 2012); Hope M Babcock, "A Risky Business: Generation of Nuclear Power and Deepwater Drilling for Offshore Oil and Gas," *Colum. J. Envtl. L.* 37 (2012); Roy Whitehead Jr and Walter Block, "Environmental Justice Risks in the Petroleum Industry," *Wm. & Mary Envtl. L. & Pol'y Rev.* 24 (2000); Melissa Luisa Jarrell, *Environmental Crime and the Media: News Coverage of Petroleum Refining Industry Violations* (LFB Scholarly Pub., 2007); Dale C Spencer and Amy Fitzgerald, "Three Ecologies, Transversality and Victimization: The Case of the British Petroleum Oil Spill," *Crime, Law and Social Change* 59, no. 2 (2013); Michael J Lynch, Paul B Stretesky, and Ronald G Burns, "Slippery Business: Race, Class, and Legal Determinants of Penalties against Petroleum Refineries," *Journal of Black Studies* 34, no. 3 (2004); Judith E Koons, "Earth Jurisprudence and the Story of Oil: Intergenerational Justice for the Post-Petroleum Period," *USFL Rev.* 46 (2011); Dara O'Rourke and Sarah Connolly, "Just Oil? The Distribution of Environmental and Social Impacts of Oil Production and Consumption," *Annual Review of Environment and Resources* 28, no. 1 (2003); Walter E Block and Roy Whitehead, "Environmental Justice Risks in the Petroleum Industry," in *Philosophy of Law* (Springer, 2019).
7. Appel, Mason, and Watts, Subterranean Estates: Life Worlds of Oil and Gas.

**Figure 3.1 Fractional distillation of crude oil**

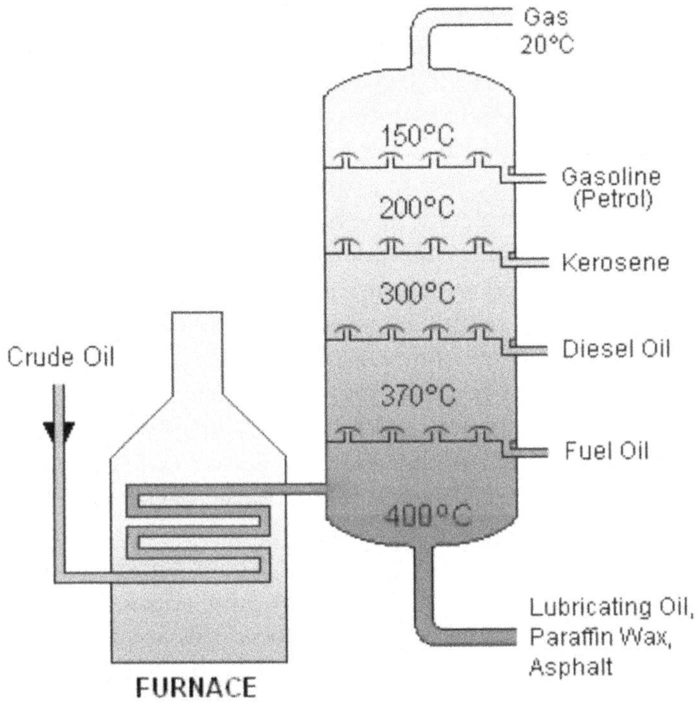


In Figure 3.1, we see that, once extracted, crude oil is heated up in a furnace from which it streams into a distillation tower, where different trays collect the components of the oil.[8] Each tray collects different hydrocarbon molecules. The separation occurs due to the pressure and heat applied to the crude oil: at different boiling points, different types of hydrocarbon molecules are left on the trays.[9] Every barrel of crude oil we see entering this process is transformed into different products, which are then sold on. Examples of these different products are listed in Figure 3.1. A variety of *further* methods of refinement follow this initial distillation, contingent on what is most profitable to sell. Depending on the final product that should be generated, oil can go through several further instances of fractional distillation, and it can also be mixed with other substances that either enhance or purify the hydrocarbon base.

8. Wikimedia Commons contributors, "File:Crude Oil Distillation-en.svg," *Wikimedia Commons*, https://commons.wikimedia.org/w/index.php?title=File:Crude_Oil_Distillation-en.svg&oldid=491221543 (accessed April 9, 2023).
9. For a simplified explanation of fractional distillation, see: BBC, "Fractional Distillation," https://www.bbc.co.uk/bitesize/guides/zyvc6fr/revision/1. Christopher Lux Jonathan Fisher, *Bunkers: An Analysis of the Practical, Technical and Legal Issues* (Banbury: Petrospot Ltd, 2004).

There are distinctive demands for diverse types of hydrocarbon molecules, differing per geographical location and related regulatory and economic contexts.[10] Ultimately, we see that the process of refinement is influenced by three factors. Two of these – regulations as well as demand for specific petroleum products – vary per market and jurisdiction. The third derives from the quality of crude oil at the source. All these factors lead to uncertainties. Margins are often tight in this business and profit needs to be *squeezed* out of every drop of oil.

At every stage of both the initial distillation process and the further refinement procedures that each stream of petroleum traverses, we also have some form of emission into the atmosphere and generation of wastes. Refining can be understood as removing the unwanted and/or mixing in additional ingredients in the hydrocarbon blend. For example, naphtha is used for petro*chemical* production; therefore, after it is refined and purified from several elements during distillation, it is combined with other substances to make things like solvents, pesticides, or creams, to name a few. That combination yields the desired products but also other substances, i.e., possible wastes. Another example is residues, at the bottom of Figure 3.1 (labelled as paraffin, asphalt, etc.), which have several destinations. They are the basis of bunker fuel, which is a key element in our case study. Residues are also precursors to lubricants, which can be used in various industries to support the functioning of machinery. Once used, all these substances become wastes. Again, each of these different processes and procedures are accompanied by emissions into the biosphere. Of course, the most visible emission is if wastes from these processes are simply released. Disposing of oil wastes at sea was a common (and accepted) practice just a few decades ago.[11] But emissions and wastes come in several forms and the re-use of wastes itself produces more emissions and wastes. Therefore, the flow of oil is also a flow of wastes and emissions, as can be seen in Figure 3.2.

---

10. In Europe, for example, diesel and distillates are more popular, whereas in the US there is a higher demand for gasoline because of the respective prevalence of diesel- and gasoline-fuelled cars in these two regions. We also see that regulations that require, for example, lowering of sulphur content in fuel products influence the refining process – purification of products from such substances requires the application of more complex technologies. Bottom line: The more refinement the crude oil needs, the more money needs to be spent. The cost of refinement impacts the price of the products that are sold on. Refineries are also faced with the challenge that each batch of crude oil has its own characteristics: the quality of the crude oil can vary from location to location and from extraction to extraction.
11. ACM Spapens, "Vuile Olie: Een Onzichtbaar Probleem Met Grote Gevolgen," *Het tijdschrift voor de politie* 75, no. 8 (2013). Environmental Protection Agency, "Learn About Ocean Dumping," https://www.epa.gov/ocean-dumping/learn-about-ocean-dumping#:~:text=The%20 Ocean%20Dumping%20Ban%20Act, at%20sea%20using%20shipboard%20incinerators; James A Rogers, "Ocean Dumping," *Envtl. L.* 7 (1976); Willard Bascom, "The Disposal of Waste in the Ocean," *Scientific American* 231, no. 2 (1974); Donat-P Häder, "Dumping of Toxic Waste into the Oceans," in *Anthropogenic Pollution of Aquatic Ecosystems* (Springer, 2021).

**Figure 3.2 The system of petroleum extraction, refinement, and use - emissions and wastes from a finite stock of crude to a finite stock of biosphere**

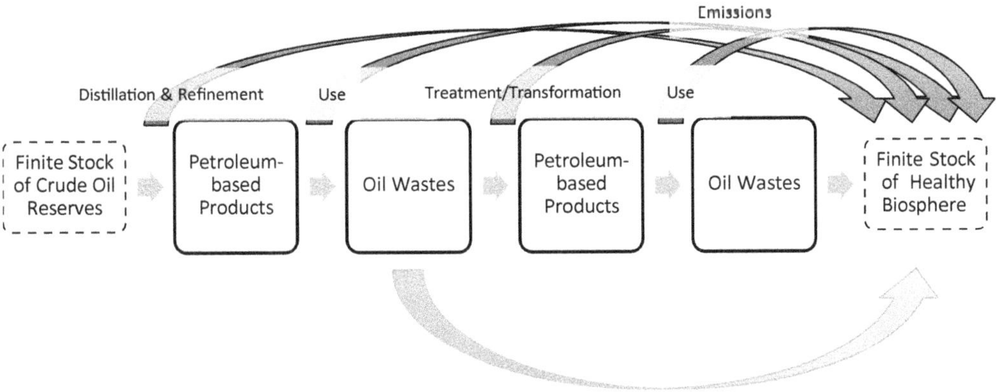


What we also see in Figure 3.2 is the finite nature of both the stock of crude oil that is being extracted and of the biosphere's capacity for absorbing toxins that are released as petroleum is extracted, processed, and consumed. The notion of a 'stock' comes from the literature on complex systems and industrial ecology.[12] It indicates a defined and measurable entity that can amass or be drained. In this context, we use it to refer to the finite energy sources, which are also known as non-renewable precisely because there is a limited amount. The stock cannot amass new units at a speed that is commensurate to our draining of it. Because of the disparity in accumulation and depletion rate, we are essentially emptying out the stock of petroleum before it can be refilled. In similar fashion, there is a finite amount of 'healthy biosphere':[13] the introduction of pollutants into the biosphere

12. "Stocks are entities that can accumulate or be depleted, such as a bathtub, which fills with water from a faucet. [...] A technique commonly used to distinguish a stock from a flow is to consider what would happen in the system if time were to stop. Stocks, which are accumulations, would continue to exist. Stocks change over time because of the actions of flows into and out of them. Flows disappear because they are actions." (Donella H. Wright Diana Meadows, *Thinking in Systems: A Primer* (2015).
13. "The biosphere is sometimes thought of as one large ecosystem—a complex community of living and nonliving things functioning as a single unit. More often, however, the biosphere is described as having many ecosystems. Biosphere Reserves [are influenced by various activities]. People play an important part in maintaining the flow of energy in the biosphere. Sometimes, however, people disrupt the flow. For example, in the atmosphere, oxygen levels decrease and carbon dioxide levels increase when people clear forests or burn fossil fuels such as coal and oil. Oil spills and industrial wastes threaten life in the hydrosphere. The future of the biosphere will depend on how people interact with other living things within the zone of life." (National Geographic, "Biosphere.") See, also: Donella Meadows, Jorgen Randers and Dennis Meadows, *Limits to Growth the 30-Year Update* (London: Earthscan, 2012).

depletes it. We are also draining the stock of our healthy biosphere too quickly,[14] making it essentially finite.

The tensions that derive from the continuous draining of these two finite stocks are important for us. We lack the primary resources to sustain the current regimes of living referred to in the quote at the beginning of the Section, therefore we need to find replacements. Some replacements – such as full reliance on renewable energy sources – may shift regimes of living so drastically that they upset the balances of power and habit that have been built around a petroleum-fuelled society. Other replacements may maintain the status quo a little longer because they essentially make the use of petroleum *more efficient*, thereby extending it in time. The former option has the potential to also reduce the negative impact on our biosphere's regenerative stock, while the latter continues to pollute and reduce our planet's natural resources in terms of clean air.

Transforming waste oils into products perpetuates and prolongs our reliance on oil for the functioning of our economy. It may be better than dumping waste oils. It may be better than extracting more crude oil. But it is still a method of burning fossil fuels to sustain production and transport. It still requires the use of the same physical flows and the involvement of the same groups of actors who manage (and profit from) those flows. Let us take a closer look at one of these oil flows – that of bunker fuel into ship engines.

### *The Flow of Goods and the Flow of Fuel: What Is Bunker Fuel and Why Do We Need It?*

In the eighteenth century, steam engines were integrated into ships, triggering the development of marine engineering. Since that time, innovation in this sector has been shaped, in great part, by new discoveries in terms of fuel sources and types, with consequent designing of more and more powerful and sophisticated engines.

When crude oil was discovered in the mid-nineteenth century, it had an impact on shipping as well. Over time, as using oil became commercially feasible, steam engines were redesigned into diesel engines.[15] Since this advancement, bunker fuel of differing qualities has been the principal substance powering the movement of vessels worldwide. In turn, the cost of fuel and the way it is stored and runs through the motors of ships has greatly contributed to shaping the shipping sector. The way shipping is currently carried out is a *direct consequence* of the opportunities bunker fuel has created. Partly thanks to the nature of bunker fuel, shipping has become the backbone of the *cheap* flow of goods and their component parts across the globe.[16] Cargo ships transport almost everything that we own. According to

14. The rate at which we introduce these pollutants – which is itself directly a product of our consumption of fossil fuels – and the rate at which the generation of the elements of a healthy biosphere are not commensurate.
15. Fisher, Bunkers: An Analysis of the Practical, Technical and Legal Issues.
16. Ibid.

some estimates, 90% of all our objects and material possessions have travelled to us in a cargo on a cargo ship.[17]

Behind this flow of goods runs the flow of bunker fuel through the engines of (commercial) shipping. Bunker fuel can be described by looking at its physical characteristics: it is brown to black liquid with a characteristic odour. It is often portrayed as thick and treacly and is known to be highly viscose, especially in comparison to other petroleum products. Alternatively, we can look at it in terms of its composition. Bunker fuel is the result of blending together different substances, the most important of which are residues from the crude oil refinement process of distillation (see bottom of Figure 3.1 above).[18] It is essentially made up of different *streams* of residues, most of which are 'heavy' in nature – like those from the initial process of petroleum distillation – with the addition of 'lighter' residues known as blend components (BCs), (or also known as cutter stocks).[19]

The flow of residual materials into bunker blends is the result of the historical development of marine engineering we began exploring in the preceding paragraphs. In the 1950s, it was established that marine engines could operate on *heavy* fuels, which are usually at the bottom in the distillation process portrayed in Figure 3.1 above. In subsequent years, an ever-growing number of seafarers and shipowners embraced this possibility, also due to the relatively low prices of oil bunkers. However, the general increase in crude oil prices that occurred in the 70s had a significant impact on the quantity and manner of fuel consumption in the shipping sector as well. At the same time, demand began increasing for products like gasoline, lubricants, and aviation fuels, which meant crude oil refining processes evolved to accommodate these new sources of profit, thus detracting supply from the heavy fuels segment of the market. We can imagine this in reference to Figure 3.1 by visualising more oil being pushed to the higher

17. OECD, "Ocean Shipping and Shipbuilding," https://www.oecd.org/ocean/topics/ocean-shipping/. It is important to note that estimates differ and it is unclear exactly how these percentages are calculated by the different sources. A joint report from the OECD and the International Transport Forum speaks of 80% of the global trade volume, for example. ( OECD and International Transport Forum, "Navigating Towards Cleaner Maritime Shipping: Lessons from the Nordic Region," (2020). The United Nations Conference on Trade and Development (UNCTAD) publishes a yearly *Review of Maritime Transport*, where a distinction is made between tanker trade, main bulk, cargo and other dry cargo. Technically, all of this could classify as cargo shipping, therefore, all the fuel consumed by the ships supporting the movement of these different categories of cargo would be included in the estimate of percentage of global trade. UNCTAD looks at the amount of tons loaded to calculate trade volume. In 2021, the UNCTAD maintained that "over 80% of the volume of international trade in goods is carried by sea, and the percentage is even higher for most developing countries." (OECD, "Review of Maritime Transport," (2021).
18. A de Buck et al., "Blends in beeld. Een analyse van de bunkerolieketen," (Delft: CE Delft, 2011). 29.
19. Ibid. p. 21 The other components can be: gasoil, light cycle gasoil and heavy cycle gasoil and, occasionally, kerosene, carbon black, used lubricants or shale oil. Fisher, *Bunkers: An Analysis of the Practical, Technical and Legal Issues.*

trays in distillation towers leaving less at the bottom. So, increase in oil prices and decreased availability of heavy fuels meant that diesel engine builders decided to focus on ensuring a higher degree of efficiency, which included modifying engines to enable them to burn *lower quality* (read: cheaper) fuels. The ultimate result was a growing and worrisome decrease in the quality of marine fuel to the point that problems in handling and engine damage became very prevalent.

We should keep in mind that engines on ships are able to burn the worst quality substances at temperatures of roughly 400°C. For these engines to be negatively affected in functioning, the worst of the worst kind of materials would have to have been injected into them. Imagine then, how bad the quality of fuels would have to be to make engine damage a significant problem. Indeed, it was in response to these challenges – thought to be in the past – that numerous stakeholders, including the International Standards Organisation (ISO), began working on the first marine fuel standards in the 1980s.

Nevertheless, problems linked to consumption of low-grade bunker fuel continue to be felt by the shipping sector today – with the Wakashio case being a prominent and terrifying contemporary example – on two fronts. A first set of difficulties is linked to the quality of fuel in relation to the functioning of engines. Regardless of standards, this is still a problem, which is caused in great part by the habitual use of bunker fuel as a dumping ground for wastes. A second set of challenges stems from the pressures to change due to growing environmental awareness. In fact, the regulations that are in place are not just limited in scope, they can even have troublesome side effects. Such regulations have focused on very specific individual elements in bunker fuel, such as sulphur concentration.

Because bunker fuel is a blend, focusing on one characteristic of the product can lead to the use of increasing quantities of potentially harmful substances to decrease the concentration of a single element. If all we check for when blending these substances is sulphur content – and sulphur content tends to be high in residues – then we need to add more and more and more of the other, also highly harmful, substances to the mix. Bunker fuel flows through engines and engines do not discriminate against sulphur, or toxins, and they only rarely discriminate against wastes. Indeed, only on *some* occasions has the quality of fuel negatively impacted the mechanical functioning of ships in a visible manner. However disastrous such events turn out to be, they are relatively few in relation the volume of shipping traffic world-wide. For the most part, the full impact of the flow of bunker fuel is neither consciously considered by consumers of the goods that travel thanks to this flow, nor by standard-setters, whether state or industry-based. Therefore, the flow continues and carries with it all the toxins from ship engines into our seas and air.[20] Next, we zoom in on how bunker fuel is made to understand this point better.

*The Flow of Residues: Who Makes Bunker Fuel and How?*

The exact recipe for blending the various elements of which bunker fuel is made up of is currently based on detailed marine fuel quality specifications. The elements are added together at differing ratios to match 'specs'. However, the *primary* targets to consider in blending have long been and continue to be viscosity and density. Others include flash point, ash and, in more recent years, sulphur content. The full list of specifications, however, is long and complex; but it suffices to say that most, if not all, entries on that list relate to physical-chemical properties. Ultimately, in making the calculations about how much of each component element to include in a blend, "the objective of the blender is to purchase low-value residual base material and increase its value by adding small amounts of blend components [and to ensure that] [t]he end product [will] have a value higher than that of the basic components used."[21]

**Figure 3.3 The stages of bunker fuel production and consumption.**

Bunker fuel production has three distinct phases, which are represented in Figure 3.3. First, the generation of residues from distillation of crude oil; second, the generation and purchase of blend components; and third, the blending of the former and the latter to produce a final product. We can also add a fourth and final stage, where bunker fuel is ultimately *consumed*, as this clarifies the interactions at play in the stages of production.

The principal categories of firms present in the bunker fuel industry are refineries, traders, suppliers, terminals, and ship owners. We will discuss each in turn, but we should be aware that there may be instances where the lines between these categories are not so clear-cut. The largest firms operating in this

20. Bunkers: An Analysis of the Practical, Technical and Legal Issues. Neil Cockett, Neil Cockett on Bunkers (London; Hong Kong: LLP, 1997); W. D. Ewart, Bunkers: A Guide for the Ship Operator (London: Fairplay Publications, 1982); William L. Leffler, Petroleum Refining for the Non-Technical Person (Tulsa, Okla., USA: PennWell Books, 1985); Vaclav Smil, Oil: A Beginner's Guide (Oneworld Publications, 2018); Energy and Civilization: A History (Cambridge, Mass; London: The MIT [Massachusetts Institute of Technology] Press, 2018).
21. de Buck et al., "Blends in beeld. Een analyse van de bunkerolieketen." 30.

industry – which are also some of the largest market players in the broader, global *oil industry* – can cover most, if not all, the activities carried out by the single firms. They may do so sequentially, in the sense of from start to finish by covering all the steps involved in making bunker fuel and then selling it. Or they may be present intermittently at several stages in the process, with their activities in one stage not necessarily linking to the next.[22] In Figure 3.4 we use the model presented above concerning the stages of production and consumption of bunker fuel to help us to systematise the various actors in relation to each other and in relation to the bunker fuel production process itself.[23]

**Figure 3.4 The actors involved at different stages of bunker fuel production**

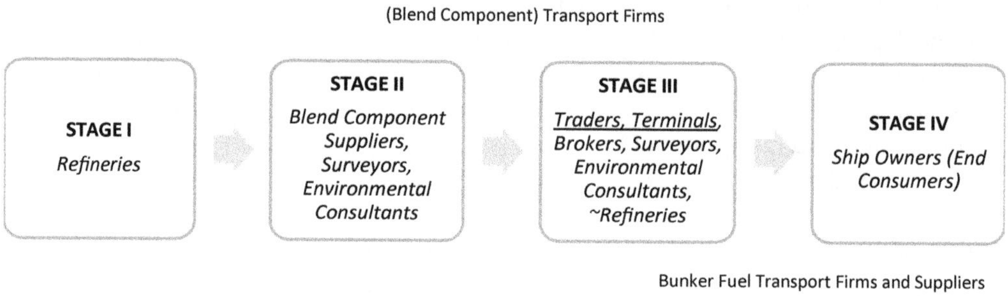


A central node in the network of this industry is the *Terminal* where the various ingredients – residues and blend components – come together and are blended to make bunker fuel (Stage III in Figure 3.4). This node, however, can be characterised as logistical rather than social or economic. A *Terminal* is merely a location, which may even be rented out for single uses, where the technology necessary for blending is present and operational. Terminals are also locations where bunker fuel is stored. Within the economic and social network of bunker fuel production, a parallel to this logistically central node are actors known as *Traders*. Traders may actually never be in physical possession of bunker fuel or its component elements, but they retain legal ownership and control of them at this fundamental stage of the process where the different components are purchased and come together to make a final product. The product is then sold on to *End Consumers,* which we looked at in the preceding subsection on the shipping sector generally. Ownership means that Traders direct the blending process: they determine which components come together and in what way. Traders can be of two kinds: independent or part of larger oil companies. Among the independent Traders, there are a number who have very strong market positions and have large quantities of liquid capital, some having a turnover of around € 190 billion a year,

22. Ibid. 48.
23. Ibid. 48.

which makes them powerful and influential global market players. The economic strength of these firms is paralleled by their relative obscurity – not much is known about them generally.[24]

In this process of making bunker fuel, Stage II is particularly interesting for our case study. While the entirety of the process involves residues, Stage II is where residues have an even wider definition. It is where residues may correspond with wastes or former wastes. If we return to our common denominator – oil – we can say that Stage I is linked to the first distillation procedure crude oil goes through. Then, Stage II makes it possible for all the other, subsequent procedures that are applied along the flow of oil to enter bunker fuel production as well. That is where flows of waste become relevant.

*The Flow of Wastes and the Flow of Documents: Physical and Social Processes*

Actors in the Bunker Fuel Production Process

- *Refineries*, which are the source of the base residues and which may also carry out some of the activities normally reserved for Terminals, namely the storage of BF (Stage I and sometimes Stage III).
- *Blend component suppliers,* who physically handle and supply specific components other than residues (Stage III).
- *Bunker fuel suppliers*, who directly and physically supply the finished product to ships. Like in the case of Traders, BF suppliers can be either independent or part of larger oil companies. The most active firms in this category usually supply the residues from their own refineries and then purchase BCs from others to bring the final product up to specifications. A study conducted in 2011 states that the market share of independent suppliers is equal to 60% (Stage III).
- *(Bunker fuel) transportation firms,* which are specialised in delivering BF using vessels for inland waters (between Stage III and Stage IV). There are also firms that transport BCs, however, in most cases either the seller or buyer (between Stages II and III) will provide the means to transport these substances.
- *Brokers,* that support the making of sales agreements between sellers and buyers of BF and receive a fee for carrying out this activity. The number of sales conducted through Brokers has been characterised as 'substantial' (Stage III).
- *Ship owners,* who own the vessels that consume BF. They may directly select and purchase the final BF product (Stage IV) or this may be done by Charterers instead.
- *Charterers,* are the actors who actually use vessels for business purposes. They enter into a contractual agreement with ship owner for the use of the vessel.

24. Ibid.

The agreement also specifies whether they or the ship owners are responsible for selecting and purchasing BF for a given span of time or journey.

- *Surveyors*, whose task it is to test samples of BCs or BF in an independent manner in support of the trade in these substances (Stage II and Stage III).
- *Environmental bureaus* or *environmental departments of larger firms*, which support firms in complying with the applicable legislation by providing information or assisting with administrative procedures (e.g. compilation of certificates attesting composition and quality of the product) (Stage II and Stage III).

Waste is in the eye of the beholder, or rather the discarder. According to the EU law definition, the term waste means "any substance or object which the holder discards or intends or is required to discard."[25] In the context of our case, we need to reflect on the intentions and obligations to 'discard' along the oil refinement and consumption routes. As petroleum flows from wells into distillation towers, through various procedures and into the machinery of end users, wastes are continually generated.[26] Several moments along the oil consumption route include the creation of waste (see Figure 3.2 above). Legally, there are numerous definitions for what we conventionally term 'waste oils' in this book. Directive 2008/98, for example, provides the following definition for waste oils: "any mineral or synthetic lubrication or industrial oils which have become unfit for the use for which they were originally intended, such as used combustion engine oils and gearbox oils, lubricating oils, oils for turbines and hydraulic oils."[27] However, there are both broader and narrower categories of wastes connected to oil use and refinement under both international and Dutch law. we find more specific definitions for different types of 'waste-containing oils' (*oliehoudende afval*).[28]

Definitions tell us about where these waste flows originate and the properties that the wastes have due to these origins, including how toxic and hazardous they are. Waste legislation definitions also correspond to permissible actions. Therefore,

25. Art. 3(1) Directive 2008/98/EC of the European Parliament and of the Council of 19 November 2008 on waste and repealing certain Directives, OJ L 312, 22.11.2008, p. 3-30 (Waste Framework Directive). See also the definition in Art. 2.1 of the Basel Convention.
26. Some of them, as we will see in Chapter 4, are never even labelled as wastes, but merely as by-products.
27. Art. 3(3).
28. See Section 2 below for the details on national law. Some examples in international law include: 'waste mineral oils unfit for their originally intended use (Basel Convention, Annex VIII, A3020); waste tarry residues arising from refining, distillation and any pyrolytic treatment of organic materials (Basel Convention, Annex VIII, A3190); waste oils/water hydrocarbons/water mixtures, emulsions (Basel Convention, Annex VIII, A4060). Part 2 of Annex V of Regulation (EC) 1013/2006 also lists several different types of wastes. For example, Chapter 05 "Wastes from petroleum refining, natural gas purification and pyrolytic treatment of coal"; or Chapter 13 "Oil wastes and wastes of liquid fuels (except edible oils, and those in chapters 05, 12"; or within Chapter 16, number 16 07 "wastes from transport tank, storage tank and barrel cleaning (except 05 and 13)" and 16 07 08* "wastes containing oil".

origins of wastes are also an important determinant in their legally defined flow *towards* an ultimate destination. This flow goes through several types of waste management service (WMS) procedures. These procedures show us what the flow of waste can look like.

A specific source of waste oils has been, and continues to be, the shipping sector. The functioning of vessels requires the use of different oils, such as lubricants and fuels. Towards the middle of the twentieth century, the general, global practice was for ships to dispose of their wastes at sea. But this became more and more problematic over time as it led to increasing pollution of the coasts with disastrous effects.[29] The international community, and specifically the International Maritime Organisation (IMO), took on this challenge by adopting an agreement in 1973 – the International Convention for the Prevention of Pollution from Ships (MARPOL).[30] This instrument only entered into force in 1983 when the required number of signatories was obtained, which is also when the relevant measures were transposed into national law by the Netherlands through the *Wet ter voorkoming van verontreiniging door schepen* (*Wvvs*).[31] Through this piece of legislation a specific waste collection process was created, leading to a new activity and actor in waste and waste oil management: the port reception facility (*havenontvanginstallaties* – HOI – or *havenontvangstvoorziening* – HOV). Any waste coming from ships is collected at these facilities since that time. Therefore, waste oils that come from the shipping sector usually flow through these facilities.

Another important legal instrument to consider that created a need for specific waste oil management services and that has shaped the physical flow of waste oils is EU Regulation 1013/2006,[32] which mirrors international rules applicable to the Netherland and other EU Member States (MSs) by virtue of the Basel Convention on Transboundary Movements of Wastes.[33] The Basel Convention includes waste oils in its Annex VIII classification, which means they are considered hazardous wastes and must be treated as such. This categorisation creates legal restrictions on where and by which entities these wastes may be handled. It is illegal to deliver

29. See note 12 above.
30. International Convention for the Prevention of Pollution from Ships (MARPOL), November 2, 1973, entry into force 17.02.1978, 17 I.L.M. 546. In the EU, MARPOL is transposed through a series of Directives and Commission Implementing Decisions. Directive (EU) 2019/883 of the European Parliament and of the Council of 17 April 2019 on port reception facilities for the delivery of waste from ships, amending Directive 2010/65/EU and repealing Directive 2000/59/EC, OJ L 151, 7.6.2019, p. 116-142 is the most recent version of the Directive. At the time of the unfolding of the events in the cases analysed in Chapter 4 Directive 2000/59 was still applicable.
31. Wet van 14 december 1983, houdende regelen ter voorkoming van verontreiniging door schepen (Wet ter voorkoming van verontreiniging door schepen – Wvvs).
32. Regulation (EC) 1013/2006 of the European Parliament and of the Council of 14 June 2006 on shipments of waste, OJ L 190, p. 1, 12.07.2006. The Regulation is referred to colloquially through the Dutch acronym EVOA (*Europese Verordening voor de Overbrening van Afvalstoffen*) in the Netherlands.
33. Basel Convention on the Control of Transboundary Movements of Hazardous Wastes and their Disposal (adopted 22 March 1989, entered into force 5 May 1992) (1989), 28 ILM 657.

waste oils to countries and firms that do not possess the requisite technologies and permits to handle these particularly dangerous wastes.

Just like in the case of other types of waste, waste oil management services include several procedures (collection, transportation, treatment, etc.).[34] Policy and legislation stress the importance of separate collection and handling of waste oils – *vis-à-vis* other types of waste and between different waste oil streams. Not just in case of the various waste oils from ships, but generally.[35] Through treatment procedures waste oils can be 'regenerated' and subsequently re-enter the market as products: the oils in this case should be used again in the same way as they were initially.[36]

**Figure 3.5 Physical flows of WOs (row above) and accompanying documents (row below) from use of substance to re-use after treatment**

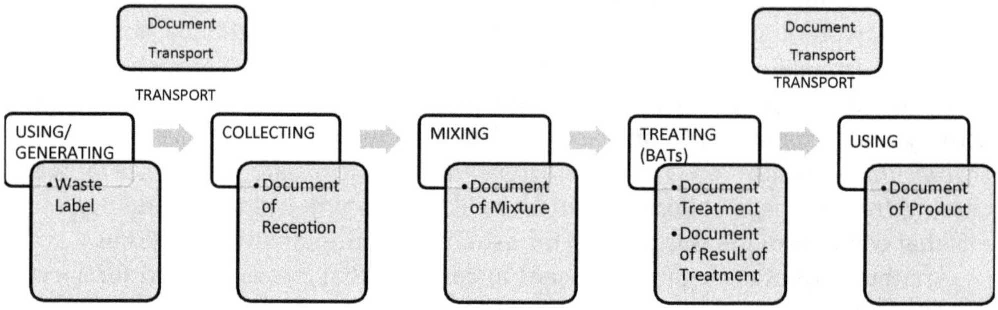


Abstractly, treatment of waste oils is like treatment of other wastes: it requires the use of technologies and techniques that can achieve certain results in an acceptable manner. The concept of 'best available techniques' (BATs) is important here. The use of the BATs is prescribed in waste management legislation.[37] It indicates that flows of waste need to traverse the technology that most efficiently treats wastes

34. Waste management is usually divided up into different processes and corresponding actors. Art. 3 Directive 2008/98 distinguishes between waste holder, waste producer, collection, prevention, treatment, recovery recycling and disposal.
35. "The separate collection of waste oils remains crucial to their proper management and the prevention of damage to the environment from their improper disposal." Rec. 44 Directive 2008/98/EC.
36. For more details on this, see Section 2 below.
37. Art. 3(20) of the Waste Framework Directive refers to the definition of BATs contained in the Industrial Emissions Directive (formerly, the integrated pollution prevention and control (IPPC) Directive). "'[B]est available techniques' means the most effective and advanced stage in the development of activities and their methods of operation which indicates the practical suitability of particular techniques for providing the basis for emission limit values and other permit conditions designed to prevent and, where that is not practicable, to reduce emissions and the impact on the environment as a whole." (Art. 3(10) Directive 2010/75/EU of the European Parliament and of the Council of 24 November 2010 on industrial emissions (integrated pollution prevention and control) OJ L 334, 17.12.2010, p. 17-119.)

and that also has the lowest negative environmental impact as possible.[38] The techniques vary depending on the nature of the wastes being treated, but they also evolve over time. The notion of BATs is incorporated into the system of waste management so that firms operating in this sector have the room for manoeuvre required to foster innovation, which, in turn, ultimately contributes to better results for the environment.[39] Yet, it also means that physical waste flows are often redirected in concert with such innovation. In practice, this means that the flow of waste oils will change with changes in technology. National legislation and policy provide detailed prescriptions on which techniques and technology are compatible with each waste oil type.[40] The first table in Annex III (labelled Table 24 from the text of origin) gives a detailed overview of waste oil streams relevant for our case and the related permissible treatment procedures and/or BATs. These streams are outlined in the legislation and policies that were in vigour when the facts of the two criminal cases that are analysed in Chapter 4 unfolded. The applicable rules in the Netherlands have changed since that time: this is discussed in the next section of this Chapter as well as in Chapter 4. From the information on the oil streams, we can also visualise what the physical flow of waste oils looks like in the example provided in Figure 3.6.

38. Best available techniques are connected to the permit conferral system within the waste management framework. National (and local) authorities have to remain up to date with the developments of best available techniques and monitor existing permits or confer new permits in accordance with the parameters that are set out in the Best Available Techniques Reference Documents (BREFs). These documents are drawn up under the aegis of the European Commission. The European Integrated Pollution Prevention and Control (IPPC) Bureau, which is a unit of one of the scientific institutes of the European Commission's Joint Research Centre – the Institute for Prospective Technological Studies – is tasked with managing and documenting information exchanges between the relevant authorities in the Members States as well as industrial actors. Based on these exchanges, the IPCC Bureau develops BREFs for specific industries or industrial installations. For a discussion on this topic, see: Harald Schoenberger, "Integrated Pollution Prevention and Control in Large Industrial Installations on the Basis of Best Available Techniques – the Sevilla Process," *Journal of Cleaner Production* 17, no. 16 (2009); Jutta Geldermann et al., "Proposal for an Integrated Approach for the Assessment of Cross-Media Aspects Relevant for the Determination of "Best Available Techniques" Bat in the European Union," *The International Journal of Life Cycle Assessment* 4, no. 2 (1999); Irina Tikhonova et al., "Best Available Techniques and Best Environmental Management Practices: Collaboration between Industries and Regions," *Procedia Environmental Science, Engineering and Management* 8, no. 2 (2021).

39. In the next Section we explore this in more detail by looking at the framework and content of the Dutch national waste management plan and how it defines and dictates the different techniques that apply to different waste streams.

40. This is discussed in more detail in Section 2.

**Figure 3.6 Overlap between the three stages of the bunker fuel production process and the waste oil management process from generation to re-use.**

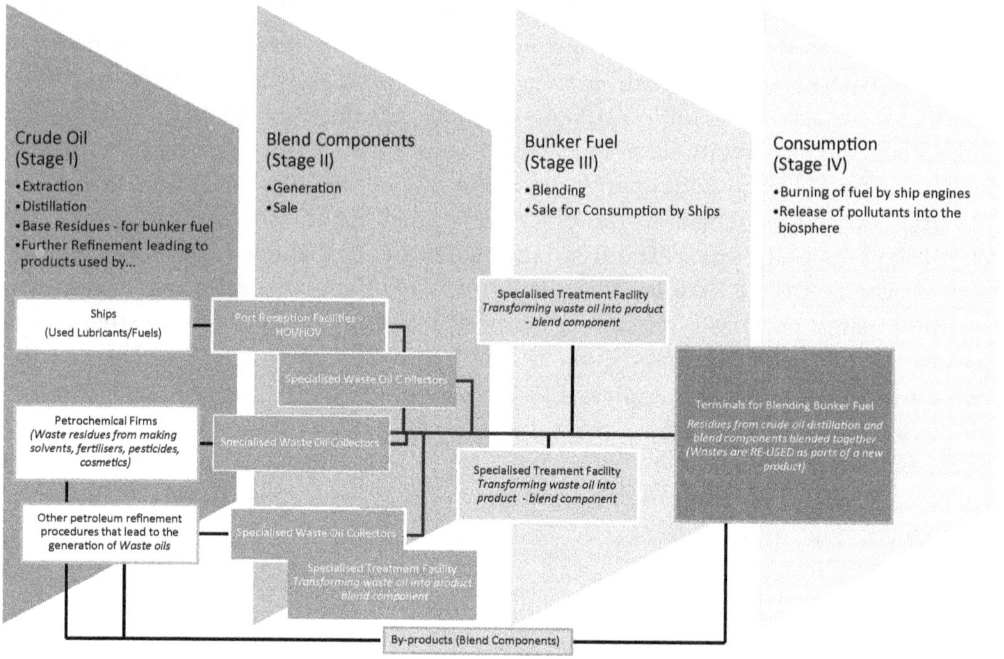


Furthermore, a parallel flow of documents that accompanies that of waste oils is also portrayed in Figure 3.6. This is a 'parallel' flow because it is physically separate from that of the wastes. Human beings and organisations are responsible for the intellectual process of labelling substances as wastes as well as the physical attribution and connection of those labels to substances. The label is not inherent to the substance – wastes have no ontological reality but are socially constructed. Waste management policies and legislation are the most important sources for the parameters that are used for such social construction. For example, a waste is labelled as hazardous when it possesses certain qualities such as a threshold concentration of a certain toxin.[41]

Nevertheless, parameters are not always as easy to apply and require a degree of interpretation. Therefore, policy and legislation are filtered through human agents who handle 'wastes'. The distance between the parallel flows of waste and their accompanying documents comes in the form of the human practise of labelling. The two flows never meet but are always separated by the exercise of agency by certain individuals and organisations. Assuming the label is applied in accordance with the letter and spirit of the law, the gap between the two

41. See the full list here: https://echa.europa.eu/de/hazardous-waste-properties-ann-3-dir-2008-98 (last accessed 30 July 2022).

flows remains constant as both documents and substances follow the same route. Therefore, Figure 3.6 should be read as representing a *legally correct* movement of both documents and waste oils. In Chapter 4, we will see how these flows look when legal rules are *not* adhered to.

Now that we have seen what the different physical flows that are relevant in our case study look like separately, it is important for us to see how they function together. Flows of oil, fuel, goods, and wastes are all intertwined in different ways. One such way is when the waste oil management services and bunker fuel production industries overlap. This overlap is a physical one having two dimensions. On the one hand, there is an overlap in the physical properties and flows of substances. On the other hand, there are actors who operate – whether legitimately or not – at the crossroads of the two industries, who may handle both categories of substances. Indeed, there may be situations where it *is* legally acceptable for waste oils to be used in the process of generating bunker fuel. At the same time, waste oils have been repeatedly introduced into the bunker fuel production process in illegal and questionable ways. Figure 3.6 captures both scenarios and helps us to contextualise our case within the two broader industrial processes. Here we see the physical movement of waste oil substances – regardless of how they are or should be labelled by disposers and waste management operators – represented by the smaller rectangles, which are connected to each other. The bunker fuel production process is represented by the three large trapeziums in Figure 3.6.

First, these substances are generated through oil refinement procedures and oil consumption practices. Second, they are collected and handled by different actors in various ways, without the actors necessarily complying with the applicable legislation. The documents accompanying these substances attest to their transformation from wastes to tradable products (again, without this necessarily having taken place physically or legitimately) and assist their introduction into the blending stage of bunker fuel production. Lastly, wastes, blended with residues and other blend components are sold on as bunker fuel to End Users at Stage III of the bunker fuel production process. These blends are ultimately consumed by ships carrying goods across the globe, and then toxins are released into the biosphere (recall also Figure 3.2, above).

Under a set of strictly circumscribed conditions, which include the use of special technologies,[42] such a physical flow may be legally acceptable in the case of a small selection of waste oils. In most cases, which are typified by the crime events we will see in Chapter 4, this physical flow is *not* legitimate. And from the perspective of environmental conservation, any and all such flows are at least questionable;

42. See the two tables reproduced in Annex III, which show the types of wastes that, if properly treated, may be used in the production of bunker fuel (labelled table 24 from original text) and residues that are usable as blend components (labelled table 1 from original text), respectively.

and lead to some degree of degradation and harm. Adding another layer of reflection, we could say that from the perspective of situational crime prevention, the characteristics of the substances involved in these physical flows as well as the routine nature of the flows, result in a condition of 'low efforts'. Actors wishing to introduce waste oils into the bunker fuel production process need not exert themselves too much. 'Rewards' are also easily accessible: this route to profit is open to those who wish to take it. The coming Sections are dedicated to exploring the legal and economic characteristics that may affect the physical flows discussed until now.

## 3.2 The Waste Oil Management Services Industry

The process of managing waste has mostly developed in response to legislative impulses. Over the years, a corpus of rules and guidelines has been established to respond to the production of waste and to control its handling. The activities that have emerged in implementing and applying these rules have led to the creation of a waste (management services) market. Hence, any analysis of the waste industry needs to start by examining the detailed structure that the legal framework has created for its operation. In this Section, we first look at the applicable rules, which tell us which activities are incentivised or discouraged in the industry. After that, we reflect on the economic forces that are at work within the waste oil management services industry.

### *The Legal Rules Applicable to Waste Oil Management Services*

The following paragraphs address which behaviours are permissible and desirable according to the legal framework. The main instrument that we examine is Directive 2008/98/EC, known as the Waste Framework Directive (WFD), which is the cornerstone of waste legislation in the EU as well as its Member States. At the national level, the Dutch Environmental Protection Law (*Wet milieubeheer* – Wm) is the most important piece of legislation for our case.[43] Waste management legislation applies to substances or objects that are classified as wastes. This may seem like an obvious point, but that does not make it trivial. In fact, the question of the definition of waste is at the core of the criminal activities we are exploring. Therefore, in this subsection, we begin by looking at the boundary between waste and non-waste and what that means for our case. Then we look at how different waste labels (i.e., different waste types) must be handled and the implications this has for our analysis.

43. *Wet van 13 juni 1979, houdende regelen met betrekking tot een aantal algemene onderwerpen op het gebied van de milieuhygiëne.* Chapter 10 regulates waste management activities generally.

*Treating Waste Oils or Making Products?*

The WFD indicates different avenues of action based on the waste/non-waste distinction – they are portrayed in Figure 3.7.

**Figure 3.7 Permissible operations for (waste) oils under Directive 2008/98.**

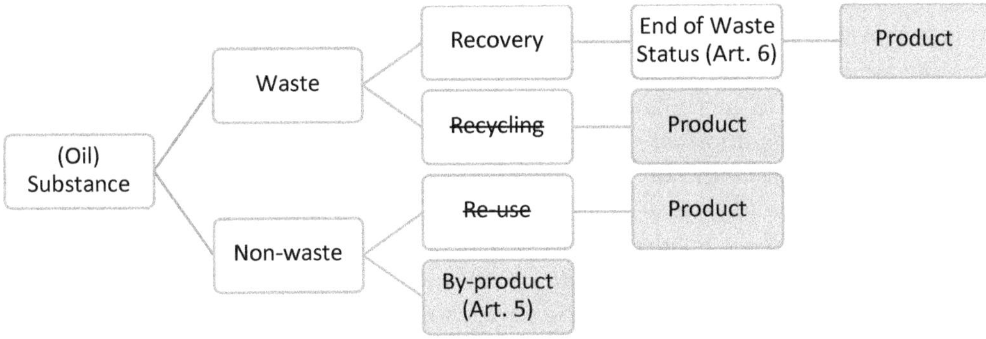


These avenues offer the possibility for firms to fulfil two aims: managing waste and generating usable products. We can distinguish between these various options based on the nature of the 'transformative process' an object or waste needs to go through. Where recovery and recycling operations have taken place,[44] substances and objects "*cease to be waste*" and may receive 'end-of-waste status' in accordance with Article 6 WFD. (In our case, we are talking about hazardous waste oils. The Directive's definition of recycling excludes energy recovery or "reprocessing into materials that will be used as fuels" for waste oils.[45] Therefore, we can *only* speak of recovery once substances are identified as wastes.) Alternatively, there may be instances where something *never becomes a waste*: this is the case of re-use and 'by-products' defined and regulated in Article 5. The grey boxes in Figure 3.7 show when a substance can (re-)enter the market as a product based on these distinctions.

44. Arts. 10 and 11.

45. The distinction between recovery and recycling is that recycling involves *further reprocessing beyond recovery* Art. 3(13). 3 (17): "'recycling' means any recovery operation by which waste materials are reprocessed into products, materials or substances whether for the original or other purposes." Recovery is defined as "any operation the principal result of which is waste serving a useful purpose by replacing other materials, which would otherwise have been used to fulfil a particular function, or waste being prepared to fulfil that function, in the plant or in the wider economy." (Art. 3(15) The reality of the waste management process, however, means that these distinctions are not always clear cut. 'Recovery' includes those operations between the moment of disposal and recycling that are necessary for recycling to take place, for example. Therefore, the distinction that are outlined above need to be understood as general rules that must be applied to each individual case depending on the origins and characteristics of the waste. In Chapter 4 this application will be carried out in relation to the specific facts and circumstances of the two criminal cases that will be analysed there.

At the bottom of Figure 3.7, we find what may happen to oil substances that are not labelled as wastes. These situations may seem to be beyond the scope of our analysis – we are interested in cases where *wastes* have entered the bunker fuel production process. Nevertheless, we look at where this has happened illegally, or at least questionably. Substances that are correctly labelled as wastes generally under the law may also correctly become products – violations in such situations revolve around mishandling *after* the waste label has been applied.

Illegalities and questionable practices also occur *at the moment of theapplication of the waste label*. In fact, we could argue that a lot of waste crime occurs in that process of labelling and that we are blind to it because of the concealment function such labelling has. Some of these illegalities are linked to the application of the wrong type of *specific* waste label: for example, an oil waste may be categorised as 'liquid fuel and oil residues' (*vloeibare brandstof- en olierestanten*) but it may in reality be 'waste oil' (*afgewerkte olie*).[46] In such a case, the rules that are being violated are the ones discussed in the paragraphs below on 'end-of-waste'.

However, there may be substances that formally never enter the realm of waste management because the entities handling them do not identify them as wastes to begin with. This is the case of re-usable substances and by-products. The definition of these substances circumscribes the outer limits of the waste management framework. Beyond those limits, the protections that the framework provides – in terms of permissible activities as well as guardianship structures – are no longer applicable. None of the criminal cases fall under the category of waste/re-usable product (hence, the strikethrough in Figure 3.7.[47] Therefore, we must move on to the notion of by-product.

46. Waste oil within the meaning of Art. 3(3) WFD. The former is covered by Sectorplan 59 and the latter by Sectorplan 56. Sectorplans are discussed below. This assertion will become clearer in Chapter 4 in the analysis of the two criminal cases where we will also see how the mis-application of the waste label works in practice and how it happens in contravention of both the letter and spirit of the rules discussed in this Section.

47. The European Commission (EC) specifies that "re-use is a means of waste *prevention*; it is not a waste-management operation [emphasis added]." The notion of re-use exists to avoid the unnecessary and inefficient possibility that the waste label is applied to an object or substance that is in conditions that make it usable. Because the definition of waste depends on the user's intention to discard, some objects or substances may become legally entangled in the waste management framework, but this may be undesirable. For example, a shipping firm may purchase a certain amount of fuel and already fill up the ship's tanks with it, but then realise that it needs less. Assuming the tanks are clean, and that fuel has not been contaminated or altered, the firm may choose to remove the excess amount and sell it on. (European Commission, "Guidance on the Interpretation of Key Provisions of Directive 2008/98/EC on Waste," (2012). As mentioned in note 43 above, the nuances in applying the waste label to a substance or object are challenging to capture without referring to specific facts of a case, including the consideration of the characteristics of both the (potential) discarder and the waste or substance in question. In Chapter 4 these details will be included in the analysis to examine the process whereby the waste label was mis-applied in the specific circumstances of the two criminal cases. An example to show this nuance was provided by one of the members of the Andante team: "If I get rid of petrol because water got into it, it is waste. If you get that water out, the petrol can be used for its

*By-products*

The rules governing by-products were developed through the case-law of the CJEU[48] which clarified the legal boundary between waste and by-product that applies to production residues. Production residues are substances that emerge from procedures used to make *other*, primary products first. Article 5(1) WFD codifies the case-law that was developed prior to the enactment of the 2008 Directive. In the Netherlands, Article 5(1) is reproduced *verbatim* in Article 1.1(6) Wm.[49]

Four cumulative criteria must be met for a production residue to be considered a by-product: (a) further use of the substance or object is certain; (b) the substance or object can be used directly without any further processing other than normal industrial practice; (c) the substance or object is produced as an integral part of a production process; and (d) further use is lawful. The European Commission provides non-binding guidance on each of these criteria.[50] It is beyond the scope of our discussion to go into the details of how each of the conditions in Article 5(1) should be interpreted – the Commission also repeatedly states that an assessment must be carried out on a case-by-case basis by the relevant manufacturer and national authorities.[51] However, there are some points that are important to highlight for our case study.

original purpose: combustion. So after successful dewatering, there is end-of-waste. Is that reuse? I don't think so, because fuel can only be used once. Dewatering is a recovery operation, that is, a recycling operation that treats the waste for its original purpose (R3: recovery of organic matter). If I don't want to dispose of the petrol, but dewater myself, the petrol does not get waste status. Dewatering is then not a recovery operation. See ch. B6 of LAP 3." [translated from Dutch by author] (Personal communication 11.08.2022).

48. A diverse set of manufacturers had often found themselves in possession of 'production residues' – materials and substances that were not deliberately made products but could still be used. Waste management legislation appeared to have such a broad scope that would also include production residues.

49. Art. 5(2) allows for standardized rules, guidelines, and procedures to be developed at either EU or national level for certain by-products. What this means is that there is agreement and automatic acceptance of certain substances coming from specified processes as by-products. When these exist at EU level, they supersede any national provisions in the same sector. Until now, no such agreement exists for blend components (blend components) at EU level. There are also no rules in the Netherlands on blend components. The national legal basis for such rules would be art. 1.1 (7) *Wm.*

50. Commission, "Guidance on the Interpretation of Key Provisions of Directive 2008/98/Ec on Waste." More recently, the Commission has issued a new document to incorporate changes made to the Waste Framework Directive in 2018. These changes – and the related guidance – are not applicable to the criminal cases we will look at in Chapter 4. The Directive has been amended by Directive (EU) 2018/851 of the European Parliament and of the Council of 30 May 2018 amending Directive 2008/98/EC on waste, OJ L 150, 14.6.2018, p. 109-140. The related Commission guidance is: "Commission Notice on Technical Guidance on the Classification of Waste (2018/C 124/01)," (2018).

51. "A decision on whether or not a particular substance or object is a by-product must in the first instance be made by the producer of the substance or object, together with the competent national authorities, based on the applicable national legislation transposing the WFD." "Guidance on the Interpretation of Key Provisions of Directive 2008/98/EC on Waste." p. 15.

The first criterion is the residue's certainty of use. Certainty is determined by the market in which the residue may be placed after it is generated. Specifically, manufacturers must consider how 'solid' or 'sound' supply and demand for the objects or substances are, as well as the potential gains that may come from selling them.[52] The relevant markets in our case are those for blend components and bunker fuel. We go into more detail regarding legal and market conditions in the bunker fuel production process in the next Section;[53] however, now we can anticipate some aspects. There is a high demand for blend components, yet this is combined with very low product differentiation. Therefore, the threshold for a marketable blend component is not very high. Consequently, we could say that there is a solid market and great potential for financial gain under Article 5(1)(a) WFD.

The second criterion is whether the residue may be used directly after it is generated, which means it does not need to be processed any further. Further processing is defined as anything more than 'normal industrial practice'.[54] As we saw in Section 1, the 'blending' stage is central to bunker fuel production – all the various substances that make up bunker fuel come together here. It is 'normal' that several substances are put together at differing ratios to attain something that measures up to industry standards. When one or more of the blend components is not optimal, the ratios can be adapted. For example, in one of its investigations, the Andante team discovered that some blend components of very poor quality were being blended at a ratio of 1 to 9. For every 1 portion of extremely problematic blend components (read: very hazardous waste oils in need of sophisticated treatment), they added 9 parts of blend components possessing more desirable properties. The companies providing the poor-quality blend components were still making very large profits because they were, in fact, using unprocessed wastes, which they had been originally contracted and paid to treat using expensive technologies.[55] This instance of blending was no different than the blending that was performed for non-wastes. If the criterion is what is normal in the industry, it does not exclude these substances because, from a purely physical or economic perspective, they are not problematic.

52. Ibid. 16 citing case-law from CJEU: Case C-9/00 *Palin Granit Oy and Vehmassalon kansanterveystyön kuntayhtymän hallitus.* [2002] ECR 2002 I-03533, para 39.; Case C-114/01 *AvestaPolarit Chrome Oy* [2003] ECR 2003 I-08725.; Case C-235/02 *Criminal proceedings against Marco Antonio Saetti and Andrea Frediani* [2004] ECR 2004 I-01005; Case C-121/03 *Commission v Spain* [2005] ECR I-7569.

53. All the information on the bunker fuel industry discussed here is also discussed in Sections 1 and 3 of this Chapter. Please refer to those parts for more detailed explanations, including the relevant references.

54. Commission, "Guidance on the Interpretation of Key Provisions of Directive 2008/98/Ec on Waste." 17-18 citing case-law from CJEU: Case C-194/05 *Commission of the European Communities v Italian Republic* [2007] ECR 2007 I-11661; Case C-457/02 *Criminal proceedings against Antonio Niselli* [2004] ECR 2004 I-10853.

55. Criminal investigation file "Case 3" from the Andante project. Field Notes 04.12.2018.

The third criterion requires residues to be directly generated as part of the industrial process that is geared towards making the primary product. Because 'normal industrial practice' is also relevant in this assessment,[56] we can apply the arguments just discussed above for the third criterion. Ultimately, it makes no difference at the stage of the process where something resembling a blend component is first generated, if what comes out can be blended in Stage III of bunker fuel production. Blending as a procedure eliminates the need to carry out many other forms of preparation and processing leading up to it.

The fourth and final criterion is the most decisive as it counterbalances economic aspects with legal safeguards. Article 5(1)(d) specifies that 'lawful' means "the substance or object fulfils all relevant product, environmental and health protection requirements for the specific use and will not lead to overall adverse environmental or human health impacts." In our case, the relevant requirements are the rules applicable to blend components and bunker fuel, as well as chemicals' legislation. Blend components and bunker fuel are scarcely regulated through hard law measures. The only exception being Sulphur content of bunker fuel, i.e., not directly of blend components.

The EU Commission states that fulfilling the applicable industry standards is a sign of lawfulness.[57] There *are* industry standards; however, they are applicable only to the final bunker fuel product, not to its individual components. The *indirect* standard for blend components on that basis is that they be suitable for blending to make fuel that complies with the industry specifications. But specifications, whether directly or indirectly applied, contain little to no limitations that are relevant for protecting human health and the environment. Plus, let us not forget that the process of blending facilitates compliance with specifications, even if the individual components are of very poor quality.[58]

Regulation 18 of MARPOL Annex VI, which is the international law basis that sets limits on the concentration of $SO_x$ and $NO_x$ in bunker fuel, prohibits the inclusion of "any added substance or chemical waste that: jeopardises the safety of ships or adversely affects the performance of machinery; or is harmful

56. Commission, "Guidance on the Interpretation of Key Provisions of Directive 2008/98/Ec on Waste." 18-19. The Commission refers to the documents that have been developed by its scientific research departments on best available techniques. These are known as BREF documents. (See note 37 above for more details on best available techniques and BREFs more generally). At the time of the unfolding of the facts of the two cases analysed in Chapter 4, there was no Commission BREF document for waste oils. Since that time, a document has been developed, and it can be found at: Benoit Zerger Antoine Pinasseau, Joze Roth, Michele Canova, Serge Roudier, "Best Available Techniques (Bat) Reference Document for Waste Treatment ", ed. European IPPC Bureau (Seville, Spain: European Union, 2018).

57. Commission, "Guidance on the Interpretation of Key Provisions of Directive 2008/98/EC on Waste." 19-20.

58. de Buck et al., "Blends in beeld. Een analyse van de bunkerolieketen."

to personnel; or contributes overall to additional air pollution."[59] The thresholds of acceptability for these three negative side effects are not provided. Nor are there standardised testing mechanisms to assess whether chemical wastes are even present in the final blend, let alone in any single blend component. Besides being tautological in respect of waste legislation, this provision is unhelpful in making a true determination of whether a production residue is a waste or a by-product.

Nevertheless, there are other, more clearly defined and more easily testable prohibitions. For example, when PCBs are present at a certain concentration in oil (50 ppm) or there are persistent organic pollutants, Article 7 Regulation (EC) 850/2004 applies.[60] Such substances are, *by definition*, wastes and need to be handled and treated following specific procedures before they can be used as products. It is legally forbidden to label these substances by-products.

*REACH*[61]

Next, we need to consider rules stemming from the regulation of chemicals. In the EU, we look to the REACH – Registration, Evaluation, Authorisation and Restriction of Chemicals – framework for this purpose.[62] When a firm produces a new *hazardous* chemical, it must make use of a registration process, which is administered by national entities responsible for implementing and enforcing REACH. Registration includes the name of the product; a serial number; the characteristics of the product – including information on health and environmental risks stemming from the manufacturing and use of the product; and the production techniques used to manufacture that product. The relevant national

59. Regulation 18 – Fuel oil quality, (a) (iii), Chapter 3 – Requirements for control of emissions from ships, Annex VI- Regulations for the Prevention of Air Pollution from Ships, International Convention for the Prevention of Pollution from Ships (MARPOL), November 2, 1973, entry into force 17.02.1978, 17 I.L.M. 546.
60. Regulation (EC) No 850/2004 of the European Parliament and of the Council of 29 April 2004 on persistent organic pollutants and amending Directive 79/117/EEC, OJ L 158, 30.4.2004, p. 7-49, which has been repealed and replaced by Regulation (EU) 2019/1021 of the European Parliament and of the Council of 20 June 2019 on persistent organic pollutants, OJ L 169, 25.6.2019, p. 45-77. Art. 7 still governs the relationship to the waste definition and related management procedures.
61. It is important to note that REACH is discussed here as an aspect to consider in the case where a substance could be classifies as a by-product, i.e., there substances is not a waste. The applicability of REACH would be an indication connected to the last criterion in Art. 5(1) that the substance's use is lawful. In fact, Art. 2(2) REACH Regulation states: "Waste as defined in Directive 2006/12/EC of the European Parliament and of the Council is not a substance, preparation or article within the meaning of Art. 3 of this Regulation." (Directive 2006/12/EC has been replaced by Directive 2008/98/EC.)
62. Regulation (EC) No 1907/2006 of the European Parliament and of the Council of 18 December 2006 concerning the Registration, Evaluation, Authorisation and Restriction of Chemicals (REACH), establishing a European Chemicals Agency, amending Directive 1999/45/EC and repealing Council Regulation (EEC) No 793/93 and Commission Regulation (EC) No 1488/94 as well as Council Directive 76/769/EEC and Commission Directives 91/155/EEC, 93/67/EEC, 93/105/EC and 2000/21/EC (OJ L 396, 30.12.2006, corrected version in OJ L136, 29.5.2007, p. 3).

authority must approve the substance and the production technique. Once a certain production technique and substance are approved, they can be used and sold freely within the EU, as long as they comply with the details included in the registration.[63]

Some blend components and their relevant production procedures are registered under REACH.[64] Therefore, the lawfulness criterion enshrined in Article 5(1)(d) may be fulfilled if the production residue is a substance that is registered in this way. However, a very important aspect of this is that the *procedure* for generating the particular substance *also* coincides with the relevant registration. In practice, a manufacturer would have to be generating a primary product through a process that also normally integrates a REACH-registered manufacturing procedure, which, in turn, yields a REACH-compliant chemical. This is not impossible, but it is a high threshold to achieve.

Article 5(1)(d) also provides a broader safety net by referring to overall environmental and human health impacts. In lieu of a standardised definition of measurable thresholds, the Commission provides a comparative test. Would treatment leading to 'end-of-waste' status mean that the product is safer to use than simply using it as a by-product directly? If the answer is yes, then the residue is a waste.[65] Such situations are then covered by Article 6 WFD, which we explore below.

63. Title II, Chapter 1, REACH Regulation. For an overview of the authorities involved in applying and enforcing REACH, see Section 1 of Chapter 4. For a discussion on REACH and its implementation more generally, see: E Spencer Williams, Julie Panko, and Dennis J Paustenbach, "The European Union's Reach Regulation: A Review of Its History and Requirements," *Critical reviews in toxicology* 39, no. 7 (2009); Kathrin Schwirn et al., "Environmental Risk Assessment of Nanomaterials in the Light of New Obligations under the Reach Regulation: Which Challenges Remain and How to Approach Them?," *Integrated Environmental Assessment and Management* 16, no. 5 (2020); Nabila Arfaoui, Eric Brouillat, and Maïder Saint Jean, "Policy Design and Technological Substitution: Investigating the Reach Regulation in an Agent-Based Model," *Ecological Economics* 107 (2014). There are also scholars who look at the boundary between chemicals' and waste legislation more specifically, for example: Joonas Alaranta and Topi Turunen, "How to Reach a Safe Circular Economy?—Perspectives on Reconciling the Waste, Product and Chemicals Regulation," *Journal of Environmental Law* 33, no. 1 (2021); R Stewart, "Eu Legislation Relating to Electronic Waste: The Weee and Rohs Directives and the Reach Regulations," in *Waste Electrical and Electronic Equipment (Weee) Handbook* (Elsevier, 2012); MPM Janssen and FA van Broekhuizen, "Waste Handling and Reach: Recycling of Materials Containing Svhcs: Daily Practice Challenges," (2017).

64. For a discussion of the relationship between REACH and blend components for bunker fuel production, see: M.H. Broekman & J. Bakker, "Milieurisico's Van Specifieke Stoffen in Bunkerolie in Zeeschepen: Onderzoek Van De Literatuur En De Reach-Dossiers," (Bilthoven: Rijksinstituut voor Volksgezondheid en Milieu (RIVM), 2016).

65. Commission, "Guidance on the Interpretation of Key Provisions of Directive 2008/98/EC on Waste." 20.

*A Waste (Label) Is Born*

If a substance is not a by-product according to the criteria outlined above, then it is a waste (assuming the holder discards, intends to or is obliged to discard it). Once this is determined, several obligations arise for those handling said substance. Foremost among these is the accurate labelling of the waste. Article 7(1) WFD introduces the "List of Waste" (LoW), which is a binding inventory of wastes.[66] The LoW specifies the labels and codes applicable to different waste streams. When a waste is assigned a specific code, this influences the way it may be transported and treated.[67] Codes referring to hazardous wastes include an "*".[68] In the Netherlands, the codes from the LoW are referred to as EURAL codes.[69] The movements of wastes are notified through a centralised system – the *Landelijk Meldpunt Afvalstoffen* (LMA)[70] by entering the relevant codes electronically.[71]

66. Commission Decision of 3 May 2000 replacing Decision 94/3/EC establishing a list of wastes pursuant to Art. 1(a) of Council Directive 75/442/EEC on waste and Council Decision 94/904/EC establishing a list of hazardous waste pursuant to Art. 1(4) of Council Directive 91/689/EEC on hazardous waste (2000/532/EC). Commission Decision 2014/955/EU of 18 December 2014 amending Decision 2000/532/EC on the list of waste pursuant to Directive 2008/98/EC of the European Parliament and of the Council, OJ L 370, 30.12.2014, p. 44-86. See also the European Commission's guidance document: European Commission, "Commission Notice on Technical Guidance on the Classification of Waste " (2018).
67. Categorisation in the LoW also influences recyclability of wastes.
68. Para. 4, Annex, Commission Decision 2000/532/EC. Substances which are not categorised as hazardous in this list may, nevertheless, be considered hazardous waste under the conditions set out in Art. 3(2) jo. Commission Regulation 1357/2014 (Art. 7(2)).
69. EURAL codes are composed of 12 ciphers: the first five are a working number assigned by the *Landelijk Meldpunt Afvalstoffen (LMA)* – the national database for recording of waste movements. The last seven ciphers are a unique tracking number. Furthermore, wastes are also labelled with a *goederencode* (Harmonized System Code), composed of ten ciphers, the first six of which are internationally harmonised.
70. Several state authorities have access to the data of the LMA and can use the data to track waste trends and movements as well as identify possible mistakes or wrongdoing. This is discussed in further detail in Section1 of Chapter 4.
71. Art. 10.37 (2) Wm allows hazardous and industrial wastes to be given only to entities that are registered in the official list of waste collectors in the Netherlands (available through the NIWO website, under VIHB list, https://ondernemersloket.niwo.nl/home/publicatie/zoek-vihb-registraties) (Art. 10.45(1)(a) Wm) or those having a permit in accordance with Art. 10.48 Wm. Where wastes are given to such an entity certain information (*inter alia*, date of release, quantity, common name, manner of management, address of destination) must be registered by the entity releasing the wastes, and this information needs to be stored for a period of five years (Art. 10.38 Wm). Art. 10.39 Wm requires that the same information indicated above must be sent to the entity receiving the wastes along with a description of the nature, characteristics, and composition of the wastes. All of this information must also be included in labels that physically accompany the wastes (10.39 (1) (b) Wm). The entity receiving the waste has to register the information mentioned in Art. 10.38(1) Wm upon receiving the wastes (Art. 10.40 Wm). Art. 10.44 Wm further specifies that any transport of hazardous or industrial wastes must always be accompanied by documents as described in Art. 10.39 Wm. The aforementioned provisions implement Arts. 17, 19, 35 and 36 of Directive 2008/98/EC, which cover the issues of traceability of wastes, labelling of hazardous wastes, keeping a detailed record by entities who manage waste, and the prohibition of uncontrolled waste management, respectively.

Another important instrument for determining the label assigned to wastes is Regulation 1013/2006, known as EVOA in the Netherlands. It sets up a series of mechanisms that should prevent harm to human health and the environment that derives from the movement of hazardous wastes. Part of the logic of the Regulation is that entities that do not have the appropriate means should not be able to handle hazardous wastes. Wastes may be delivered only to territories and firms that have been approved by the relevant national authorities.[72] Regulation 1013/2006 focuses on constraining the *movement* of wastes – it relies on accurately applying waste labels so that handling and treatment are commensurate to hazardousness and risk.

Waste labels do not just indicate what a substance is and where it may go, but also what may be done with it. This includes whether it may be mixed with other wastes and whether it may be recycled, recovered, or landfilled. The WFD imposes four obligations in the handling of substances labelled as waste oils.[73] Different types of waste oils should be collected separately if technically possible, and not mixed together where this is economically and technically feasible.[74] They should be handled in accordance with the waste hierarchy contained in Article 4 and in accordance with the standards on environmental protection evinced in Article 13. Furthermore, if the waste oils are hazardous,[75] they must be collected separately and cannot be mixed with other wastes.[76] Mixing within this definition also includes "diluting of hazardous substances." Firms may be exempted from the latter obligation under certain conditions.[77]

72. Art. 3 lays out the general procedural framework, which categorises different types of waste and the relative obligations to notify the relevant national authority of the intention to move the wastes across borders into the territory of competence of said authority. The authority must then consent to the movement of the waste to a suitable facility having the technology necessary for the handling of that type of waste and the related permit. In some instances, the national authorities have pre-consented to transport to specific entities, however, notification is still required. The rules concerning notification are included in Art. 4. Art. 5 further requires that firms releasing the wastes and the firms receiving them must conclude a contract that includes details on the nature of the wastes and the manner in which they should be handled and treated.
73. Art. 21.
74. Art. 18.
75. Annex III to the WFD lists a series of hazardous properties that substances may possess. If a WO contains such substances, it is considered hazardous. Annex III has now been replaced by Commission Regulation 1357/2014 (Commission Regulation (EU) No 1357/2014 of 18 December 2014 replacing Annex III to Directive 2008/98/EC of the European Parliament and of the Council on waste and repealing certain Directives Text with EEA relevance OJ L 365, 19.12.2014, p. 89-96)
76. Art. 18 Directive 2008/98/EC.
77. First, they must possess a permit in accordance with art. 23 WFD (Art. 18 (2) (a)). Second, the mixing operations must be carried out in conformity with the "best available techniques"(Art. 18 (2) (b)). Lastly, the mixing must comply with art. 13 and must not increase adverse impacts on human health and the environment (Art. 18 (2) (c)).

*'End of Waste'*
Let us now focus on the branch that grows from the definition of an oil substance as a waste, linked to Article 6 WFD, which is portrayed at the top of Figure 3.7. Two sets of obligations are relevant: the first concerns permit obligations and the second includes the characteristics of treatment operations, which the firms that have permits can carry out.[78] The procedures for requesting, granting, and monitoring compliance with permits are found in national law, like the specific techniques that can be applied to waste oil substances for them to receive end-of-waste status.

Article 10.48 Wm specifies that the handling of certain categories of hazardous and industrial wastes may be limited to entities that have obtained a permit from the competent authority where this is determined through generally applicable administrative rules developed by the Minister for Infrastructure and Water Management (*Infrastructuur and Waterstaat – IenW*).[79][80] Article 9 of the Ministerial Decision on collection of wastes (*Besluit inzamelen afvalstoffen – Bia*)[81] states that a permit should be obtained where a firm wishes to collect oil wastes and ship-generated wastes. Furthermore, Article 2.1 (2) of the Ministerial Decision on environmental law (*Besluit omgevingsrecht – Bor*)[82] obliges entities, which wish to process oil wastes, industrial wastes, and hazardous wastes to obtain a permit for doing so. Annex I, Part C *Bor* includes several categories of activities for which this obligation exists.[83] In our case, a permit must be obtained from the Provincial authority. This means that it is the Provincial authority who will also be carrying

78. Art. 23 WFD requires that treatment of waste be carried out by firms that have obtained a permit from the competent authority. The permit then provides the blueprint for each individual firm's operations as it includes the "types and quantities of wastes that may be treated" as well as the technical requirements and methods to be adopted for each operation (Art. 23 (1) (a), (b) and (d)).
79. The Wm refers to "*Onze Minister*", which in Art. 1.1 is defined as "*Minister van Infrastructuur en Milieu*" (translated: Infrastructure and Environment). This ministry was replaced by that of *Infrastructuur and Waterstaat* (*IenW*) in 2017. Since 2017, environmental matters may fall under the purview of other ministries, such as that for Economic Affairs and Climate Policy (*Economiche Zaken en Klimaat*) or Agriculture, Nature and Food Quality (*Landbouw, Natuur en Voedselkwaliteit*) as well. However, the Ministry for Infrastructure and Water Management is the relevant one for our case because waste management falls under the tasks of the *IenW*.
80. Art. 2.1(i) of the Dutch General Environmental Law Provisions (*Wet algemene bepalingen omgevingsrecht – Wabo*) prohibits the carrying out of regulated activities that lead to damage to the physical environment without a valid permit. Art. 2.3(b) Wabo prohibits the carrying out of such activities in violation of permit conditions. (*Wet van 6 november 2008, houdende regels inzake een vergunningstelsel met betrekking tot activiteiten die van invloed zijn op de fysieke leefomgeving en inzake handhaving van regelingen op het gebied van de fysieke leefomgeving.*)
81. Besluit van 19 maart, houdende regels met betrekking tot het inzamelen van bedrijfsafvalstoffen of gevaarlijke afvalstoffen.
82. Besluit van Besluit van 25 maart 2010, houdende regels ter uitvoering van de Wet algemene bepalingen omgevingsrecht.
83. Category 4.4 refers to storing oil wastes, Category 5.4 includes storage of both oil wastes and fuel oils, and Category 28.4 refers to the processing of hazardous and industrial wastes.

out front line monitoring and compliance activities in respect of the companies whose activities we are interested in.

Article 10.3 Wm states that the Minister for Infrastructure and Water Management will determine a national waste management plan every six years.[84] The most recent version of the National Waste Management Plan of the Netherlands (*Landelijke afvalbeheerplan* – LAP) is LAP 3 and it entered into force on 28 December 2017.[85] The criminal events that we will analyse in Chapter 4 took place prior to this date and the applicable rules can be found in the preceding plan, LAP 2.[86] The LAP deals with the means of managing specific waste types (also referred to as streams) according to their particular characteristics.[87] The LAP divides the rules applicable to different waste streams into Sector-plans (*sectorplannen* -SP). Each SP delineates the waste stream it applies to and specifies the minimum standards of how that waste stream should be processed.[88]

The LAP provides a link between the moment something is recognised and labelled as a waste until it reaches its ultimate end, which may turn out to be a new beginning. Indeed, one of the outcomes of processing of some waste streams using certain techniques can be that the wastes are recovered.[89] Wastes that have undergone recovery operations could become products.[90] These recovery operations must be in accordance with the provisions of the SP that applies to the specific waste. There are a series of SPs, which cover "oil containing wastes": these are numbers 55, 56, 58, 59, 60, 61, 62 and 63.[91]

84. This implements Art. 28 of Directive 2008/98/EC, which requires all Member to develop a waste management plan to generate environmentally sound waste management practices.
85. The LAP is reviewed periodically by policy makers. Reviews incorporate any relevant legislative changes that have occurred at international, EU and national level, including the implementation of new (minimum) treatment standards. The LAP is also geared towards reaching any waste management goals – which often come in the form of waste reduction targets – by manipulating waste streams. For example, the goal may be set (at EU or national level) for plastic wastes to be reduced to a certain amount. The LAP can provide techniques for recycling of plastics, which reduces the amount of plastic that is simply disposed of, or tariffs applied to plastic generation. The LAP can also respond to changes in the market. For example, if a new use for a treated waste is found, the treatment operations can be codified into the LAP; this would also ensure that smaller quantities of the relevant wastes are ultimately disposed. Furthermore, there may be a link between the LAP entries and technological advancements. If new, more environmentally friendly ways of treating wastes are developed, including new ways to transform wastes into products, then this can be included in the LAP as well.
86. For major modifications between the *LAP* 2 and *LAP* 3, see: https://lap3.nl/documenten/overzicht/.
87. Art. 10.7(3) Wm.
88. See: https://lap3.nl/sectorplannen/oliehoudend/). The numbering of these Sector-plans has remained consistent through LAP 2 and LAP 3..
89. Conceptualised as "*nuttige toepassing*" in the Dutch version of the WFD and in the national implementing measures. This means that the wastes can be literally 'usefully applied' again.
90. Art. 1.1(6) *Wm*.
91. For the full list of waste substances that might be found in bunker fuel, refer the first table in Annex III (labelled Table 24 from the text of origin) where these are linked to their classification and to a description of the minimum standards for treatment.

The minimum standards for each waste stream indicated in the enumerated Sector-plans have a common logic: if the desired outcome is a *usable fuel oil for ships*, the technology used to process the wastes must go beyond dividing oils from water and sediment fractions. This would require several different stages of distillation and cleaning.[92] Where this (technological) standard of purification of the waste substances cannot be achieved, the only option for dealing with most waste oils is to burn them in cement ovens. This point will become clearer in Case 1 in Chapter 4. In that case, the company involved did not adhere to the minimum standards of the Sector-plans that applied to the wastes it was collecting.

***

From a criminological perspective, we can say that the availability of *legal* means to profit is somewhat restricted in the waste oil management industry. The rules for appropriately and safely transforming waste oils into products – specifically blend components – are strict and necessitate the use of very expensive technologies. Compliance with these rules has high monetary costs, which brings us to the broader question of how the economic features of the waste industry may generate a series of criminogenic incentives and pressures.

### *Economic Pressures and Incentives in the Waste (Oil) Management Services Market*

Scholars from different schools of thought in criminology have focused on the economic dynamics that characterise an industry in various ways. Among those studying organisational offending, some have often underlined how lack of competition or other deviations from 'ideal' free market conditions create criminogenic pressures. Others have focused more on how the normalised traditions of commerce, coupled with little oversight incentivise crime.[93] There are also criminologists that look at legitimate business sectors to determine their vulnerability to organised crime infiltration.[94] The latter perspective is particularly relevant for analysing the waste sector. Indeed, the waste industry is a notorious fertile breeding ground of all kinds of upper- and underworld criminal activities. The following analysis draws mainly on this body of literature.

92. See the first table in Annex III – labelled table 24 from the original text – for an overview of the procedures that should be applied to different waste streams in order for them to be transformed into blend components in accordance with LAP 2, which was the applicable waste management plan at the time when the facts of the two cases analysed in Chapter 4 took place.

93. See note 1 above for a more detailed overview of the literature.

94. Tom Vander Beken and Stijn Van Daele, "Legitimate Businesses and Crime Vulnerabilities," *International journal of social economics* 35, no. 9/10 (2008). Jim Baird, Robin Curry, and Paulo Cruz, "An Overview of Waste Crime, Its Characteristics, and the Vulnerability of the Eu Waste Sector," *Waste Management & Research* 32, no. 2 (2014); Nicholas Dorn, Stijn Van Daele, and Tom Vander Beken, "Reducing Vulnerabilities to Crime of the European Waste Management Industry: The Research Base and the Prospects for Policy," *Eur. J. Crime Crim. L. & Crim. Just.* 15 (2007).

A pivotal aspect of the WMS market is that it works in reverse because waste has a negative value. Although waste is, in some sense, supplied, waste generators are actually on the demand side of the economic exchange because the legal framework obliges them to seek out waste management services. At the same time, the services offered to manage waste can have very high value. The more stringently a waste and its treatment are regulated, the higher the profit margins may be for a firm that is willing to cut corners in its management, because it can legitimately charge high service costs without necessarily undertaking the necessary operations. From an economic perspective, such a firm would need to be discouraged either through the supply and demand relationship with the waste generator or through the application of external constraints.

The former option is problematic for two reasons. First, there is an *inelastic demand*, meaning that waste is produced regardless of the price of the management services. The generation of waste depends on the processes and conditions that *precede* its creation; and these are not directly influenced by the existence or costs of waste management procedures, once those generative processes or conditions have been completed. Demand is not affected by the 'quality' of service, including its legality beyond the initial instance of collection.

Second, disposers pay when they relinquish waste, not when the waste management operation is performed. Payment does not hinge on the operation taking place in accordance with any agreements; nor is there the possibility to withhold payment when such agreements or even generally applicable rules are violated. Further, in most cases,[95] the disposer discharges legal responsibility for any adverse effects the waste may have along with the waste itself, which disincentivises any inquiry by the disposer on the fate of the wastes. Consequently, in economic and in legal terms, there is *no incentive stemming from the services-contract relationship for the entities managing wastes to comply with any applicable rules.* In fact, some speak of the "seductive opportunity" that a waste treatment firm is faced with once in possession of the waste;[96] namely to minimize costs of treatment as much as possible in order to keep more of the profit from having taken the waste from the disposer for a fee.

The external constraints to wrongdoing often come in the form of permit requirements, which impose a degree of pressure on waste management firms.

95. Note, however, that a shift has been taking place in more recent years towards the application 'extended producer responsibility' (EPR), which may alter this characteristic of the waste sector. Most notably, Directive (EU) 2018/851 has been adopted in the EU. It amends the Waste Framework Directive to include enhanced protection through EPR. For a discussion on this, see: Katrien Steenmans, "Extended Producer Responsibility: An Assessment of Recent Amendments to the European Union Waste Frameworks Directive," *Law Env't & Dev. J.* 15 (2019); Chris Backes, "The Waste Framework Directive and the Circular Economy," in *Research Handbook on Eu Environmental Law* (Edward Elgar Publishing, 2020).
96. Huisman, "Tussen Winst En Moraal: Achtergronden Van Regelnaleving En Regelovertreding Door Ondernemingen."

Permit requirements create costs because they are linked to the possession and operation of specific technologies. Companies make large investments to participate in this market; therefore, high returns are necessary for them to survive. The costs in terms of capital, time and effort required to keep up with the standards that filter through the permit requirement can sometimes be at odds with the trends in demand for specialised WMS. The conditions for legally providing supply are not organically linked to demand, and this may generate criminogenic pressures.

Seeking other lucrative means of waste management, such as 'transformation' into products is one way these pressures may be alleviated. The lack of flexibility at the input side of the economic exchange (wastes 'supplied' *vis-à-vis* technology possessed) can be countered if the market for the products that come out of the transformation is open, accessible, and competitive enough to enter. Moreover, law and policy allow and encourage a transformation of wastes into products; therefore, the incentives to achieve and sustain this transformation are high. With certain wastes, this policy-led incentive is matched by particular characteristics of the substances being handled that make them especially prone to these transformative practices. Waste oils are an example of such substances: they are transformable but also can merely give the impression of having been transformed, even when they have not received adequate treatment.

The transformability of wastes is also linked to a final important criminogenic economic feature of the industry. Waste is considered to have 'low integrity', which means high opportunities for counterfeiting. The low integrity of wastes derives from the fact that they can easily be misrepresented as something else. Waste oils are particularly prone to such misrepresentations as they resemble many other oils. Extensive – as well as expensive – testing is required to determine their precise composition. Furthermore, wastes are easily mixed with each other or with non-waste or non-hazardous substances, thus making it possible to dilute the 'undesirable content', even when faced with testing or inspection. This is especially true in the case of liquid wastes and waste oils. Those purchasing products that were formerly wastes must, therefore, rely on the willingness of the supplier to reveal the proper nature and history of the goods,[97] which is often accomplished by providing documentation. However, documentation itself can be manipulated to the benefit of the supplier, so that it conceals the negative characteristics – or the lack of necessary qualities – of the product that was formerly a waste. Why such manipulation may take place is evident from the above discussion of costs and pressures.

***

97. Tom Vander Beken, The European Waste Industry and Crime Vulnerabilities (Maklu, 2007).

Waste management finds itself at a crucial point in the global commodity chain. It is both at the 'end', where goods – and other substances needed to make goods – end up, and at the 'beginning', where the chain re-starts because of recycling, re-use, and recovery.[98] Waste management functions as an engine that transforms a finite, linear process of global commodity production and consumption into one that is perpetual and circular.[99] This legally sanctioned transformative potential of waste has a counterpart in the system of documenting waste management activities. The system can be hijacked through fraud. The transformative potential of wastes corresponds to that of their accompanying documents. Documents that may conceal the wasteful nature of substances and reframe or rebrand them as (by-) products destined for bunker fuel production. And, engines of ships can run on such waste-containing blends, irrespective of how they are labelled. The next Section looks at the bunker fuel production industry, where said wastes often end up.

## 3.3 Markets, Standards and Legislation in the Bunker Fuel Production Industry

It is remarkable to see how two industries can be diametrically opposed in their regulatory features even though their central products are so complementary. In the same way that the waste oil sector is stringently legally regulated, the bunker fuel production industry is virtually free of direct and specialised legislative constraints. The economic dynamics of supply and demand – and the related characteristics of the actors involved in production and consumption – are what fundamentally structures the patterns of day-to-day operations in this sector. That is not to say that there is no legislation whatsoever that applies to bunker fuel specifically. But, for the most part, the bunker fuel production industry regulates itself. Therefore, understanding the structural features of the bunker fuel production industry means we need to understand its economic dynamics first. Only after that, can we look at the different degrees of regulation – from standards

98. Ibid. Please note that, from a strictly legal perspective, the terms re-use, recycling and recovery always have to be contextually applied based on the specific facts and circumstances of the case. Here they are used to characterise the possible functions and outcomes of waste management as an economic activity more generally.

99. At the time of the facts of the two criminal cases, which we will analyse in Chapter 4, the notion of a circular economy already existed but it was not explicitly part of the EU and Dutch policy framework for waste reduction and management. Since that time, industrial ecology – the discipline from which the concept of circular economy is derived – has informed more and more of the policy initiatives taken at European and national levels. We discuss this briefly in Section 3 of Chapter 5 and then return to reflect on this development in more detail in the concluding Chapter of the book. The true circularity of waste management processes is questionable even though the legislative and policy language used in relation to this industry suggests it to be desirable and feasible. In fact, waste management is most often merely a prolongation of use instead of a properly set up element in a within a broader organisation of 'circularity'.

to hard law, from self-imposed constraints to the direct limitations provided by the state.

*Market Dynamics in the Bunker Fuel Production Process*

The market dynamics that characterise the different stages of bunker fuel production and consumption are portrayed in Figure 3.8. In the first and third stages, we witness greater market concentration, with fewer players as well as fewer sources and locations: the market at these points in the bunker fuel production process is virtually oligopolistic.[100] In Figure 3.8, these stages are represented in larger boxes with a thicker outline to show the relatively greater power and market concentrations *vis-à-vis* the other stages. Oligopolies are a consequence of the nature of the substances and technologies featuring in Stages I and III. In Stage I, obtaining residual materials requires direct connection to the process of distilling crude oil. A primary requirement for this is access to oil wells and exploration capital, which mostly means very high investments. In Stage III, blending bunker fuel requires cost-effective access to large terminals where blending can take place. Furthermore, selling and trading bunker fuel also necessitates a prominent position on the market. There are high entry barriers for traders – the main actors involved in Stage III and those who legally control bunker blends.

Requirements of this kind are absent in Stage II, which means that the market here is more open and competitive as opposed to oligopolistic. The dotted line in Figure 3.8 represents the porousness of the blend component market. At this point in the production process, competition is high among (potential) producers of blend components for two reasons. The first is connected to the historical development of this part of the process. Over time, traditional blend components like diesel have shifted to other markets where their sale yields greater profits. For example, in Europe diesel powered automobiles have become more and more popular. Selling diesel to millions of car owners and users is much more profitable than using it as a blend component. Therefore, the new-found uses for traditional blend components have made them increasingly expensive, which has led to mounting pressure to find novel and cheaper substitutes.[101] We see this in Figure 3.8, where the arrow on the bottom left pointing upwards signals this mounting pressure towards Stage II.

100. de Buck et al., "Blends in beeld. Een analyse van de bunkerolieketen."

101. de Buck et al., "Blends in beeld. Een analyse van de bunkerolieketen"; Fisher, *Bunkers: An Analysis of the Practical, Technical and Legal Issues.*

**Figure 3.8 Market dynamics in the bunker fuel production industry**

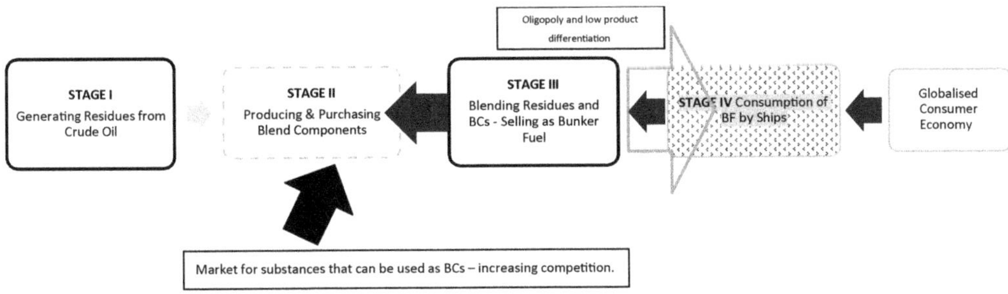


Second, there are few mechanisms for controlling the quality of blend components. This is attributable, for the most part, to the characteristics of bunker fuel generally and blend components specifically. The parameters to determine what a good blend component is are few and leave ample room for manoeuvre.[102] In fact, a good blend component is essentially any substance that yields a decent fuel according to the ISO Standard, when mixed with base residues. There is no official or standardised concept of a blend component producer or production process either. Licencing requirements are indirect and tangential, based on the nature of the substances being handled by the producers in question. For example, if the substances classify as chemicals that are subject to regulatory restrictions, there may be the need for firms to obtain a permit in accordance with the national measures that implement REACH. But REACH does not apply to all substances that can be used as blend components. In economic terms, this means there is little to no product differentiation for blend components as well as few entry barriers for producers, both of which also then contribute to the openness of the market at Stage II.

Once bunker fuel is generated through blending in Stage III, it is sold on to end consumers in Stage IV. The characteristics of the consumption of bunker fuel generate specific pressures towards Stage III, which then trickles down into the rest of the bunker fuel production process. We saw, in Section 1, that demand for bunker fuel comes, for the most part, from the world of cargo shipping. In that world, maintaining low transportation costs is of fundamental importance. It sustains the current globalised system of production and ensures that consumeristic and trade-centred globalisation continues to thrive.

The economic concept of 'monopsony' is useful in understanding the implications of the foregoing for the bunker fuel production process. With this concept, economists indicate a market where there is a single buyer of a certain

102. This was briefly discussed in Section 1 where bunker fuel and its production process were first introduced and is explained in more detail in the sub-sections immediately below.

product.[103] However, it is also used to define other, more common, situations. For example, there may be more than one large supermarket in a given region, however, the group of large supermarkets represents virtually the only avenue for farmers and other producers to sell their products. Essentially, this set of supermarkets wields tremendous power over the producers and can dictate the conditions for purchasing goods, from quality to price. This has numerous effects for the market, which can be both positive and negative. For example, end consumers who shop at the large supermarkets will benefit from low prices, but the producers will also have to endure low profits.

The cargo shipping sector functions in a similar way in respect of the bunker fuel production process. It is the largest and predominant avenue for consumption of bunker fuel. However, before going further in the application of the concept of monopsony to Stage III, we must underline a fundamental difference to the example of the large supermarkets just given. In the supermarket example, goods go through supermarkets to the final consumers. In that process, they traverse a monopsony. But bunker fuel is consumed in function of globalised trade. Ships carry goods that are sold on further. Therefore, the ultimate consumer at the other end of the bunker fuel production process does not buy bunker fuel itself, rather he purchases goods which are available to him at a certain location and for a certain price through, amongst other things, the consumption of bunker fuel by ships. The ultimate consumer pays not only for the product itself but also for the process whereby that product reaches him. Consequently, *to keep prices low for consumers all over the world, the price of bunker fuel must also be kept low*. Therefore, it is unsurprising that the characteristics of the substances and processes involved in the production of the fuel, which allows the global economy to run, are themselves greatly influenced by this ultimate pressure to maintain low costs for consumers.[104] This pressure is shown using the black arrows moving from right to left in Figure 3.8.

Yet, we must not forget the market characteristics of the process at Stage III itself because it offers a strong counterbalance to the condition of monopsony we have just analysed. A relatively small number of firms sells bunker fuel.[105] We have already described Stage III as being a virtual oligopoly. Therefore, although the pressure for low prices of bunker fuel exerted by the shipping sector in Stage

103. To understand the concept of monopsony better and to see how it is usually applied to labour markets, see: Roger D Blair and Jeffrey L Harrison, *Monopsony in Law and Economics* (Cambridge University Press, 2010); Samuel Muehlemann, Paul Ryan, and Stefan C. Wolter, "Monopsony Power, Pay Structure, and Training," *ILR Review* 66, no. 5 (2013).

104. Examples of contributions where the connection between neoliberalism and consumerism is addressed are: Collins, Victoria E, and Dawn Lynnette Rothe. *The Violence of Neoliberalism: Crime, Harm and Inequality*. New York: Routledge, 2020; Harvey, David. A Brief History of Neoliberalism. Oxford: Oxford University Press, 2005; Cohen, Lizabeth. A Consumer's Republic: The Politics of Mass Consumption in Postwar America. New York: Knopf, 2003.

105. de Buck et al., "Blends in beeld. Een analyse van de bunkerolieketen"; Fisher, *Bunkers: An Analysis of the Practical, Technical and Legal Issues*.

IV can be felt by those selling it, the latter are powerful enough to impact the market in two ways. First, they filter that pressure further down to Stage II (shown using the larger arrow from Stage III to Stage II in Figure 3.8). Second, they make it challenging for the shipping sector to effectively respond to product-quality related issues.

Regarding the latter point, it may be argued that the shipping sector could respond to the detrimental effects of poor-quality bunker fuel by seeking out suppliers that produce higher quality bunker fuel. This can be considered a market-based response and a solution to the problem we are exploring. By shifting demand, they could provoke supply to change. Nonetheless, this is not happening and may have little to no effect. The reasons for this are two-fold. First, the practices we are analysing that occur in Stages II and III are highly prevalent, which leaves the shipping sector with few possibilities to escape this problem by finding qualitatively better alternatives. We could capture this in a statement like, "bunker fuel is just generally bad."[106] Moreover, the lack of transparency, of product differentiation, and of competition at Stage III make it particularly challenging for members of the shipping sector to make informed, alternative decisions in response to this problem. We could typify this in a statement such as "all bunker fuel looks the same and, if we don't buy it from these people, it is unlikely that we will find another source for it." (See the large grey arrow moving from left to right between Stage III and Stage IV.)

Second, the cargo shipping sector itself is formed by several actors with differing interests and goals (shown with the pattern inside the Stage IV box). And these interests and goals are often unrelated to concerns for environmental preservation. A distinction must be made between ship owners, charterers, crews and employees, and insurance companies. Ship owners are insured for damages to their vessels, just like charterers are insured for issues arising when goods they wish to transport do not arrive at their destination or are delivered late.[107] Although the quality of bunker fuel is very low from an environmental perspective in general and because of criminal practices like the ones we are analysing, it is still 'good enough' for ships to run on, most of the time. In fact, the scenarios where shipments do not arrive, arrive late or where crew members or port staff are immediately physically harmed because of the poor quality of bunker fuel are relatively rare. Therefore, the losses incurred in these cases are often compensated and resolved through insurance schemes.[108] The wider, more devastating, and longer-term effects of these practices are mostly unnoticed, undetected or impossible to causally link to specific culprits once their effects have materialised. And the actors in Stage IV have priorities that distance them from taking a proactive stance to protect the environment at their own financial

106. Ibid.

107. See the discussion on the Bunkers Convention below.

108. See the discussion on the Bunkers Convention below.

expense.[109] The bunker fuel industry and the shipping sector, therefore, are structured in such a way that no internal, market-based solution currently appears possible. There is no internal pressure to change because of the deadlock of forces that results from the flow of economic incentives and pressures we have just explored.

Nevertheless, just like we saw in the case of waste management, there is always the possibility that states may choose to intervene through legislative measures to alter market forces. It may even be the case that industry actors themselves generate guidelines, standards or even lobby for some form of (external) regulation, when it would benefit the market. Indeed, the bunker fuel sector is not entirely unregulated as we see in the following subsections.

### *Standards and Legislation in the Bunker Fuel Industry*

In this subsection we explore constraints and controls that apply to actors in the bunker fuel production industry. We survey the constellation of measures, ranging from industry standards to hard law instruments, by referring to the different stages of bunker fuel production.

#### *Stages II to III: Blending Components*

In 1987 the ISO published ISO 8217 (Petroleum Products – Fuels (class F) – Specifications of marine fuels) in response to industry-wide demand for more uniformity in bunker fuel quality and labelling. Until the 1970s, substances that were being used to fuel stationary, on-land, machinery engines were defined as one and the same as fuels for ships or other large locomotive objects. Differentiation among fuels was largely informal, with confusing labels being applied without specific criteria. With time, the wish to have greater clarity and uniformity was expressed in the fuel oil industry at large, especially by actors using fuels for ships. It was in this climate that the British Standards Agency and then the ISO developed the basic blueprint for ISO 8217. Apart from the ISO, another agency that was interested in harmonising marine fuel quality standards at the time was the International Council on Combustion Engines (CIMAC). CIMAC's concerns centred more on the suitability of fuels for older and newer engines to reflect the interests of engine manufacturers and users, whom they represent(ed). Such focus led them to develop a separate set of recommendations,

109. de Buck et al., "Blends in beeld. Een analyse van de bunkerolieketen"; Fisher, *Bunkers: An Analysis of the Practical, Technical and Legal Issues*; Neil Cockett, *Neil Cockett on Bunkers* (London; Hong Kong: LLP, 1997); W. D. Ewart, *Bunkers: A Guide for the Ship Operator* (London: Fairplay Publications, 1982); William L. Leffler, *Petroleum Refining for the Non-Technical Person* (Tulsa, Okla., USA: PennWell Books, 1985); Vaclav Smil, *Oil: A Beginner's Guide* (Oneworld Publications, 2018); *Energy and Civilization: A History* (Cambridge, Mass; London: The MIT [Massachusetts Institute of Technology] Press, 2018).

the first of which was published in 1986.[110] For the criminal events that we will analyse in Chapter 4, the 2012 edition of ISO 8217 is applicable. Currently, the 2017 version applies, but it is being reviewed,[111] and we can expect a new standard in 2022.[112][113]

The quality of bunker fuel as a final product can be assessed through ISO 8217. This assessment takes several forms. One is that of testing procedures. There are two main types of bunker fuels within the Standard – distillates and residual fuels – and within these types there are different categories of fuel– DMX, DMA, DMB and DMZ are distillates, whereas RMA, RMB, RMD, RME, RMG and RMK are residual fuels. For each category the Standard provides maximum and/or minimum values or percentages of different parameters as well as the related testing procedures. For example, the density of a fuel at 15°C should be maximum 890,0kg/m$^3$ for the DMA category – this can be ascertained using testing procedures standardised under ISO 3675 or ISO 12185. Another form of assessment provided in the Standard is that of visual inspection: for example, under the entry of "Appearance", the Standard states "Clear and bright".

Besides parameters for assessment, the Standard also provides a definition of bunker fuel: "the fuels shall be homogenous blends of hydrocarbons derived from petroleum refining." It adds that the fuel should not contain inorganic acids or used lubricating oils. The presence of used lubricating oil cannot be tested directly. Instead, the Standard provides parameters of maximum concentration of zinc, phosphorous and calcium that, if exceeded, indicate that used lubricating oils *may* be present. In fact, the Standard does not cover many aspects of fuel quality as is demonstrated by the following quote taken from a manual that is widely used within the industry:

> *Q: If I order fuel to comply with the current International Standard will they cover all the possible quality characteristics?*

110. Fisher, *Bunkers: An Analysis of the Practical, Technical and Legal Issues*. 54-58. By 1990, only the CIMAC recommendations and ISO 8217:1987 were used as reference points for fuel specifications (The BSI had developed and updated Standard in 1989, which was identical to the ISO 8217:1987). A later version of ISO 8217, which was published in 1996 came much closer to the CIMAC recommendations (p. 58). New versions of ISO 8217 were published in 2005, 2010, 2012 and 2017 (ISO Website).
111. https://www.iso.org/committee/47414.html; https://www.iso.org/standard/80579.html (accessed 30 July 2022) under the name ISO/AWI 8217 by the ISO/TC 28/SC4 Committee A supplementary set of specifications were published in 2019 – ISO/PAS 23263:2019 – and they are also currently applicable. These specifications make it possible to adapt fuels that are covered by ISO 8217 to also comply with the 0,5% sulphur cap that entered into force in January 2020.
112. https://www.iso.org/obp/ui/#iso:std:iso:pas:23263:ed-1:v1:en (accessed 30 July 2022).
113. https://www.cimac.com/cms/upload/Publication_Press/WG_Publications/CIMAC_WG07_2011_Guideline_Fuel_Quality_Ignition_Combustion.pdf (accessed 30 July 2022). For its part, CIMAC also continued to issue new recommendations and their 2011 version is the most recent. As in the past, the main difference between the CIMAC recommendations and ISO 8217 lies in CIMAC's focus on engine performance.

> *A: No. Although the International Standard includes the main quality parameters it will never cover all the strange contaminants that may find their way into marine fuels. At the end of the day, the Standard provides a good benchmark but a fuel can be unfit for use and still meet the basic quality limits within the tables of the Standard.*[114]

The Standard gives partial guidance and information, at best. While generally useful for operational purposes, the Standard – and the related testing procedures – are virtually mute on issues of toxicity, hazardousness, and environmental impact. The parameters that are necessary for trading among industry actors are not the same as those that may interest the broader public. The quote also clearly states that a fuel may not even be fit for use, although it complies with the Standard. Nevertheless, there is a provision in the Standard and the CIMAC Recommendations according to which "the fuels should not include any added substance or chemical waste which either: i) jeopardises the safety of ships or adversely affects the performance of machinery; or ii) is harmful to personnel; or iii) contributes to overall additional air pollution.

That said, while all other parameters in the Standard have a corresponding set of testing procedures, this additional note regarding the safety of fuels does not include a standardised and effective means to check whether the batch being sold or purchased pollutes more or less than usual; or whether it contains chemicals and wastes that it should not. Some literature exists detailing the kinds of testing and results that may reveal signs of wastes or added hazardousness. However, the additional testing or additional attention required to make such assessments goes beyond the normal evaluation of a fuel against the specifications included in the Standard. Standardised testing based on ISO 8217 can be performed in two weeks, but expedited testing can be done in 24 hours, albeit at a very high cost.[115] Applying those procedures would slow down shipping substantially; and lead to undesirable competitive disadvantages for the traders involved.[116] The Standard does not itself furnish parameters and procedures to prevent the blending of wastes or other dubious and dangerous substances into bunker fuel in general.[117]

---

114. de Buck et al., "Blends in beeld. Een analyse van de bunkerolieketen"; Fisher, *Bunkers: An Analysis of the Practical, Technical and Legal Issues*. 53.
115. Rebecca Prentiss Pskowski, "Bad Bunker: Fuel Contamination Claims, Imo 2020, and the Houston Problem," *Tul. Mar. LJ* 44 (2019).
116. Richard Staring, Bisschop, Lieselot; Roks, Robby; Brein, Elisabeth; van de Bunt, Henk, "Drug Crime in the Port of Rotterdam," (Rotterdam: City of Rotterdam Department of Public Safety; Public Prosecutor's Office; Police; Customs; Erasmus University Rotterdam, 2019); Anna Sergi and Alexandria Reid, *Ports, Crime and Security: Governing and Policing Seaports in a Changing World* (Policy Press, 2021); Leonid Lantsman, *Seaport Vulnerability to Criminal Networks: A Mixed Method Approach to Measuring Criminological Vulnerability in the Top 30 Us Container Ports* (City University of New York, 2017).
117. Although Clause 5 Annex B "Deleterious Materials" of the ISO 8217 Standard does provide something of a procedure that looks at the whole production chain. It reads as follows: Identifying and determining the concentration of a material that causes the fuel to be

The prohibitive reference to chemical wastes is the only part of the Standard that looks at the components that go *into* bunker fuel. In deciding what to blend together, companies producing bunker fuel are very flexible and have no specific set of rules to follow. But there are other sources of constraint that apply tangentially to bunker fuel. Chemicals' regulation is one such source.

Many substances that are used in the making of bunker fuel are classified as petrochemicals subject to certain EU rules, including REACH, which we already mentioned in Section 2 when discussing the distinction between by-products and wastes. However, the regulation of individual substances that are used as blend components is no guarantee of safety or environmental protection once these substances are blended into the bunker fuel mixture. The reasons for this are two-fold.

First, because there is no prescribed set of rules about the exact components of bunker fuel, there is also no way of testing and then predicting the consequences of consuming certain blends. *Each batch of bunker fuel is unique.* And this uniqueness leads to uncertainty and unpredictability. In 2016, the Dutch National Institute for Public Health and the Environment (RIVM)[118] published a report on the environmental risks of using specific substances in bunker fuel for shipping. In their summary,[119] they state the following when talking about how bunker fuel is the result of the blending of several substances to match certain parameters:

> *To what extent the emission of these blend materials is an additional risk to the environment [beyond the already acknowledged emissions of sulphur dioxide, nitrogen oxides, particulate matter, and heavy metals] is unknown.*[120] *Because the composition of the marine fuel by ship is different, it is not possible to ascertain the nature and extent of the emissions from the flue gases.*[121]

unacceptable for use can be difficult given that: a) each fuel is a unique, complex blend of hydrocarbon species; b) a wide range of materials from different sources can enter the marine supply chain from the production, handling and transport systems; c) various analytical techniques are used to detect specific chemical species with no standardized approach; and d) in most cases, sufficient data are not available with respect to the effects of any one specific material, or combinations thereof, on the variety of marine machinery systems in service, on personnel or on the environment. It is therefore not practical to require detailed chemical analysis for each delivery of fuels beyond the requirements listed in Table 1 or Table 2. Instead, a refinery, fuel terminal or any other supply facility, including supply barges and truck deliveries, should have in place adequate quality assurance and management of change procedures to ensure that the resultant fuel is compliant with the requirements of Clause 5.

118. Rijksinstituut voor Volksgesondheid en Milieu.
119. M.H. Broekman & J. Bakker, "Milieurisico's Van Specifieke Stoffen in Bunkerolie in Zeeschepen: Onderzoek Van De Literatuur En De Reach-Dossiers," (Bilthoven: Rijksinstituut voor Volksgezondheid en Milieu (RIVM), 2016). 5.
120. The portion of the summary immediately before this part reads: "It is known that ocean shipping contributes substantially to air pollution due to emissions of sulfur dioxide, nitrogen oxides, particulate matter and heavy metals such as nickel. Less well known is that sea vessels also emit pollutants such as ultrafine particles and black carbon."
121. Flue gas (sometimes called exhaust gas or stack gas) is the gas that emanates from combustion plants and which contains the reaction products of fuel and combustion air and residual

Second, we are not just ignorant about what goes into any single batch of bunker fuel and, consequently, the quantitative measure of pollution each batch produces. We also do not know the full nature of this pollution in qualitative terms. When reviewing the scientific literature on the burning of several substances known to be commonly found in bunker fuel, the RIVM concludes:

> *The scientific literature lacks studies about the environmental impact of these blend materials in marine fuel. The varying composition of the fuel that is created makes it difficult to measure the environmental impact of blended substances into the marine fuel by ship. In addition, a standardized method fails to measure the chemical composition of environmentally harmful substances in the fuel and the emission of pollutants in the flue gases.*[122]

And this last statement regarding the measurement of the chemical composition of environmentally harmful substances extends even to those blend components that are covered by the REACH framework. The RIVM states that, even where some of the substances entering the blends are covered by REACH certifications,[123] "there is no (mandatory) risk assessment of effects on the environment" applicable to these blend components.[124] Therefore, even where a substance is recognised as a chemical whose use should be restricted, that does not automatically lead to any evaluation of its toxicity, and certainly not of what the consequences would be of mixing it with other (toxic) substances and burning it as fuel.

The degree of uncertainty evinced in these quotes is even more problematic if we consider the scale of international shipping as well as the invisibility and latency of the consequences of pollution. While some fuel batches are of such poor quality that they lead to horrific and immediately tangible scenarios like that of the recent *Wakashio* spill, most do not. From Stages II to III, the bunker fuel production process dangerously lacks guidance for both those working within it and those who end up dealing with the consequences of what is manufactured in the relevant procedures. We cannot protect ourselves and our environment from unknown types and quantities of pollution. Some small steps have been taken to remedy this situation and they have resulted in hard law measures being developed at international and European level. We explore these next.

---

substances such as particulate matter (dust), sulfur oxides, nitrogen oxides, and carbon monoxide. (James G. Speight, "3 – Unconventional Gas," in *Natural Gas (Second Edition)*, ed. James G. Speight (Boston: Gulf Professional Publishing, 2019).

122. Bakker, "Milieurisico's Van Specifieke Stoffen in Bunkerolie in Zeeschepen: Onderzoek Van De Literatuur En De Reach-Dossiers." 5.

123. See above discussion on relationship between chemicals legislation and waste management as well as the coming subsection about REACH certifications and blend components.

124. Bakker, "Milieurisico's Van Specifieke Stoffen in Bunkerolie in Zeeschepen: Onderzoek Van De Literatuur En De Reach-Dossiers." 5.

*Stages III to IV: The Sale and Purchase of Bunker Fuel*

At the time of the adoption of the Kyoto Protocol in 1997,[125] the governmental representatives of 84 countries from all over the world made a commitment to reduce greenhouse gas emissions to slow down global warming. Those representatives also made an explicit decision to *exclude* bunker fuel-related emissions from their commitments.[126] The agreement to avoid commitment has characterised discussions on this topic in subsequent intergovernmental conferences in 2007, 2009, 2010, 2011 and 2012. One of the most contentious matters underlying this lack of commitment has been the difficulty of determining which countries should be responsible for setting limits on emissions from bunker fuel consumption, as well as enforcing such limits.[127]

The political question of responsibility has been compounded by the technical question of how reduction in emissions can be achieved practically. Devising and applying significant changes to several hundreds of thousands of vessels or altering the production and distribution mechanisms of large, complex, and extremely costly industrial installations would require not just intelligent solutions but herculean efforts. An important actor in that regard is the International Maritime Organisation (IMO). International conferences have repeatedly delegated the question of emission reduction to the IMO as it has the technical competence to explore questions of regulation connected to shipping at an international level. The existence of such a specialised body has, in some sense, enabled politicians to avoid the very difficult question of dealing with bunker fuel emissions.[128]

---

125. Kyoto Protocol to the United Nations Framework Convention on Climate Change, Kyoto, 11 December 1997. 16 February 2005, No. 30822. Signatories are now 102 (See, https://treaties.un.org/Pages/ViewDetails.aspx?src=TREATY&mtdsg_no=XXVII-7-a&chapter=27&clang=_en).
126. Sebastian Oberthür, "Institutional Interaction to Address Greenhouse Gas Emissions from International Transport: Icao, Imo and the Kyoto Protocol," *Climate Policy* 3, no. 3 (2003).
127. This is linked to the more general regime of attributing responsibility under Kyoto and subsequent agreements whereby developing countries are treated exceptionally while at the same time there is use of an equality principle. Political compromise vs needs of environmental protection. For a discussion, see: Christoph Böhringer, The Kyoto Protocol: A Review and Perspectives, Oxford Review of Economic Policy, Volume 19, Issue 3, September 2003, p. 451-466; Grunewald, N., & Martinez-Zarzoso, I. (2016). Did the Kyoto Protocol fail? An evaluation of the effect of the Kyoto Protocol on CO2 emissions. Environment and Development Economics, 21(1), 1-22.
128. Henrik Selin et al., "Mitigation of Co2 Emissions from International Shipping through National Allocation," *Environmental Research Letters* 16, no. 4 (2021); Harilaos N. Psaraftis and Christos A. Kontovas, "Decarbonization of Maritime Transport: Is There Light at the End of the Tunnel?," *Sustainability* 13, no. 1 (2021); Dirk Heine and Susanne Gäde, "Unilaterally Removing Implicit Subsidies for Maritime Fuels," *International Economics and Economic Policy* 15, no. 2 (2018); Yubing Shi, "Are Greenhouse Gas Emissions from International Shipping a Type of Marine Pollution?," *Marine Pollution Bulletin* 113, no. 1 (2016); "Reducing Greenhouse Gas Emissions from International Shipping: Is It Time to Consider Market-Based Measures?," *Marine Policy* 64 (2016); Thomas Gehring and Benjamin Faude, "A Theory of Emerging Order within Institutional Complexes: How Competition among Regulatory International Institutions Leads

The IMO's technical specialisation has not been matched by its political strength in bringing about consensus amongst state parties. Although it has been tasked with devising technical, operational, and market-based-measures to encourage the reduction of emissions from bunker fuel consumption, the reach of its interventions has been limited. In fact, the most tangible outcome of the IMO's efforts in regulating the hazards of bunker fuel consumption is the creation of Annex VI to MARPOL,[129] which marginally regulates the content and characteristics of bunker fuel. Through Annex VI, the IMO has developed a series of obligatory limits to the concentration of sulphur and nitric oxides that may be present in bunker fuel.

While Annex VI applies to the final bunker fuel product, it remains mute on the individual blend components that are used to make bunker fuel. Therefore, much like the ISO standard discussed previously, the rules are applied to a finished product and compliance therewith can be ascertained by testing only a few characteristics of that *finished* product. Annex VI does not regulate the bunker fuel production *process*.[130] Furthermore, the regulation of $SO_x$ or $NO_x$ content is problematic in itself because of the nature of the blending process, as discussed in Sections 1 and 2 of this Chapter. It does not guarantee environmental safety and human health protection. In fact, it may have quite dangerous unintended side effects, especially once the fuel is burned by engines.

The currently applicable limits were not yet in force at the time in which the facts of the two cases that we will analyse in Chapter 4 took place. Nevertheless, the process of *attempting* to regulate the bunker fuel industry and its central product is relevant for us to understand the dynamics and relationships that characterise this sector. These dynamics and relationships generate patterns in the distribution of pressures and incentives that contextualise the criminal events we will explore.

---

to Institutional Adaptation and Division of Labor," *The Review of International Organizations* 9, no. 4 (2014); Judith van Leeuwen and Kristine Kern, "The External Dimension of European Union Marine Governance: Institutional Interplay between the Eu and the International Maritime Organization," *Global Environmental Politics* 13, no. 1 (2013).

129. MARPOL has been implemented into EU law through Directive 2005/35/EC and later Directive (EU) 2016/802. In the Netherlands, the provisions of MARPOL and the two Directives are implemented into national law through the *Wvvs* and the Law on Air Pollution (*Wet inzake luchtverontreiniging – Wil*). (Directive 2005/35/EC of the European Parliament and of the Council of 7 September 2005 on ship-source pollution and the introduction of penalties for infringement, OJ L255, 30.09.2005, p. 11. Directive (EU) 2016/802 of the European Parliament and of the Council of 2016 of 11 May 2016 relating to a reduction in the sulphur content of certain liquid fuels (codification), OJ L 132, 21.05.2016, p. 58. *Wet van 26 november 1970, houdende regelen in het belang van het voorkomen of beperken van luchtverontreiniging.*

130. This is in sharp contrast to the regulation of waste management where several parameters are developed and re-developed in order to make the process of waste management more environmentally sound.

*The Role of Surveyors and Environmental Bureaus*

In the world of shipping, fostering trust among trading partners has always been an important activity. Long distances between ports of origin and destination meant that losses – due to accident or malevolence – were many. Avoiding and redressing losses is a core component of how this world functions, which means insurance as well as third-party inspectors have a special function in allowing this sector to run smoothly. Inspectors are supposed to check goods, whether they are being transported or consumed by the ships. Through their independent work, problems and damage can be limited or adequately redressed. While inspectors initially focused on the goods that were being transported, the increasingly poor quality of fuel in the second half of the 20th Century created the opportunity for these third-party figures to introduce themselves in the bunker fuel inspection business: this activity is known as *surveying*.

Surveyors test samples against ISO 8217 and other parameters; then they interpret results so that both producers and users of fuel can understand the quality, nature, and consequences of using the products they handle. Surveyors are private, for-profit entities, without any state-mandated powers. Nevertheless, part of the services they offer is to check compliance with applicable rules. Indeed, as environmental laws have increased in quantity and degree of protection, surveyors have increasingly taken on an image of 'environmental consultants', whose task it is to contribute to environmental conservation through their activities. However, the fact remains that bunker fuel traders and buyers pay for their services to receive information about the products they are handling.[131]

Another actor that has emerged more recently is the environmental bureau. These entities serve either within larger bunker fuel trading companies or as external consultants. Their function is more administrative in nature, as they do not carry out testing of samples, but focus more on the documents that are necessary for holding, transporting, and using oil substances. They should

131. de Buck et al., "Blends in beeld. Een analyse van de bunkerolieketen.", Laura Poggi et al., "Recent Developments in Remote Inspections of Ship Structures," *International Journal of Naval Architecture and Ocean Engineering* 12 (2020); Brian J Beck, "Liability of Marine Surveyors for Loss of Surveyed Vessels: When Someone Other Than the Captain Goes Down with the Ship," *Notre Dame L. Rev.* 64 (1989). Becoming a marine surveyor, a sub-specialty of which is to be a bunker surveyor, requires undergoing training through institutions such as the Lloyd's Maritime Institute (see: https://www.lloydmaritime.com/en/index). There is a Singaporean Standard according to which the different institutions can award the bunker surveyor certification, that is the SS 600 (See: https://www.mpa.gov.sg/web/portal/home/port-of-singapore/services/bunkering/bunkering-standards/singapore-standard-code-of-practice-for-bunkering-ss600, (accessed 30 July 2022). Examples of companies that offer this service are: SGS (https://www.sgs.com/en/services/bunker-survey-testing-and-inspection, (accessed 30 July 2022); and Intertek (https://www.intertek.com/lintec/bunker-survey/, (accessed 30 July 2022), amongst others.

function as a compliance department or consultant, with a focus on environmental regulations.[132]

Surveyors and environmental bureaus are mentioned here because their role is relevant to Stage III in bunker fuel production, namely when bunker fuel is sold and delivered. It is at this time that surveyors can test the samples that are taken upon delivery of the fuel. This is also the moment where documents are exchanged. Those documents are prepared with the help of environmental bureaus and attest to the characteristics of the fuel. Documents reflect the results of sample testing, but they are always humanly generated. A systematic review of bunker delivery notes (BDNs) – the special forms that accompany bunker fuel when it is ultimately delivered to the final consumer – showed that these were often incomplete, inaccurate, and frequently fabricated without any verifiable connection to the physical product they referred to.[133]

The samples of fuel are the means through which the surveyors, ship owners or charterers, as well as traders can establish whether the fuel matches ISO specifications and complies with the limits set out in Annex VI to MARPOL. Testing may be broader than that, depending on the needs of the parties involved. These same samples have to be stored on board for 12 months following the delivery of the bunker in case any damage occurs due to its use or transport. In such cases, civil liability may be established, as we see next.

*Stage IV: Bunker Fuel Consumption*

Our exploration of the flows of petroleum in Section 1 demonstrated that emissions and wastes emerge from several procedures occurring *prior* to the blending of residues and blend components to make bunker fuel. In that sense, pollution accompanies the procedures that serve as precursors to the blending process. Yet the most obvious connection between bunker fuel and its pollutant effects is at the stage of its consumption by ships. While the foregoing paragraphs looked at how such pollution can be limited by setting parameters that apply to bunker fuel as a product *before* it is consumed, now we consider those rules that create responsibilities and obligations after the fuel starts flowing through the engines of ships.

The most important instrument in that regard is the International Convention on Civil Liability for Bunker Oil Pollution Damage (Bunkers Convention).[134] As

132. de Buck et al., "Blends in beeld. Een analyse van de bunkerolieketen."

133. Helen Sampson et al., "Greener Shipping? A Consideration of the Issues Associated with the Introduction of Emission Control Areas," *Maritime Policy & Management* 43, no. 3 (2016); Ivar Tønnensen, 01 February 2002, 2002, https://www.gard.no/web/updates/content/53293/controlling-bunker-costs; International Bunker Industry Association (IBIA) & Baltic and International Maritime Council (BIMCO), "Bimco & Ibia Bunekring Guide," (2018).

134. International Convention on Civil Liability for Bunker Oil Pollution Damage 2001, entry into force 21 November 2008. The choice to regulate the adverse impacts of shipping by using liability and compensation mechanisms is grounded in a provision of the UN Convention on the Law

the name suggests, this is a regulatory instrument. It provides the legal basis for claims against polluters to be brought to civil courts;[135] and it obliges potential polluters (defined here as registered shipowners) to be insured against incidents of environmental damage attributable to them.[136] The insurance – whether as a policy or other form of financial security – covers the costs linked to the reinstatement following environmental impairment as well as costs to prevent further impairment.[137] The obligation to be insured applies only to vessels having a gross tonnage greater than 1000.[138]

It is beyond the scope of this Section to explore the Convention in detail. What is relevant for us is to see how its provisions influence the constellation of definitions, incentives and pressures that characterise the bunker fuel *production* industry. In relation to the substance of "bunker oil", the Convention states that it is "any hydrocarbon mineral oil, including lubricating oil, used or intended to be used for the operation or propulsion of the ship, and any residues of such oil."[139] This definition does little to reduce the ambiguities we discussed above. There is no element of it that would encourage those who benefit from the use of bunker fuel to demand a more environmentally friendly substance than that currently being supplied to them. The strength of the Convention's constraining potential rests on the notion of 'pollution damage'. It entails the "loss or damage caused outside the ship by contamination resulting from the escape or discharge of bunker oil from the ship, wherever such escape or discharge may occur."[140] In that respect, the extremely broad definition of bunker fuel serves as a safety net for claimants.[141] The purpose of the Convention is not to *prescribe* how fuel should be manufactured, but to *compensate* for whatever may happen when even the most questionably generated fuel is released into the environment. The next matter is to see how compensation can be obtained and what this means for the incentives and pressures in the bunker fuel industry.

Once (a threat of) pollution damage is ascertained, the ship owner is strictly liable to provide compensation for it.[142] The question of accountability reveals

---

of the Sea 1982, specifically Art. 235(3), which obliges states to cooperate in implementing and developing international law on liability and compensation, and mentions the need to develop criteria and procedures for payment of adequate compensation including 'compulsory insurance or compensation funds'.

135. International Convention on Civil Liability for Bunker Oil Pollution Damage 2001, entry into force 21 November 2008.
136. Art. 7(1).
137. Art. 1(9) (a) and (b).
138. Art. 7(1).
139. Art. 1(5).
140. Art. 1(9) (a-b).
141. Nicholas Gaskell and Craig Forrest, "Marine Pollution Damage in Australia: Implementing the Bunker Oil Convention 2001 and the Supplementary Fund Protocol 2003," *University of Queensland Law Journal, The* 27, no. 2 (2008).131.
142. Art. 3. Paras. (3) and (4) provide defences against liability.

some of the more injurious aspects of the consumption of bunker fuel.[143] We hinted at them previously when talking about the economic characteristics of the bunker fuel market: the complexity, variety and fragmented nature of the global shipping sector pose great challenges to environmental protection. The Bunkers Convention holds ship owners responsible for pollution damage,[144] which also means ship owners must bear the cost of the mandatory insurance that should be obtained to cover risks for such damage. Therefore, we could deduce that ship owners, as customers in the bunker fuel market, may demand more environmentally friendly fuels in order to minimise the risks and costs associated with bunker fuel consumption. This would keep their premiums low.

However, ship owners are not necessarily those who purchase bunker fuel. Each ship and, potentially, each journey a ship makes comes with its own 'charter party'. A charter party is the contractual agreement between the owner of a ship and the user of the ship – the charterer. It is rare that these two actors coincide. Provisions for the distribution of responsibilities and costs are made through the charter party. There are standardised forms for charter parties; however, each agreement is different.[145] It may be the case, for example, that a ship owner selects and purchases the bunker fuel used for a given journey. But it may also be the case that the charterer does so instead, without necessarily being contractually conferred the onus of repairing environmental damage linked to bunker fuel consumption in accordance with the Bunkers Convention.[146] Therefore, it is rather difficult to make any general statement about how the potential burden of bearing costs for environmental damage that the Convention creates may ultimately constrain ship owners or charterers. And this means it is also challenging to say how such potential costs influence the decision to purchase a specific batch of bunker fuel, having a given price and risk attached to it. Add to that the complication that such risk is virtually impossible to estimate as shown above in the quotes from the RIVM study.

Beyond the question of the Convention's scope *ratione personae,* we need to also consider who *applies* the Convention in practice. The obligation to obtain insurance, whereby a ship may not operate without being covered, is connected to the state

143. For an overview of the history of international regulation of shipping, see: Gaskell and Forrest, "Marine Pollution Damage in Australia: Implementing the Bunker Oil Convention 2001 and the Supplementary Fund Protocol 2003."
144. Art. 1(3) defines ship owner as: "The owner, including the registered owner, bareboat charterer, manager and operator of the ship."
145. Pskowski, "Bad Bunker: Fuel Contamination Claims, Imo 2020, and the Houston Problem"; The Editors of Encyclopaedia Britannica, "Charter Party (Contract)," in *Encyclopedia Britannica* (2018); Ling Zhu, "Compensation Issues under the Bunkers Convention," *WMU Journal of Maritime Affairs* 7, no. 1 (2008); Charles L Trowbridge, "History, Development, and Characteristics of the Charter Concept," *Tul. L. Rev.* 49 (1974).
146. Art. 1(3) has a widened definition of shipowner: "including the registered owner, bareboat charterer, manager and operator of the ship."

where a ship is registered; or the flag state of that ship, in absence of registration.[147] A system of certification has been set in place, whereby ships cannot traverse the waters of State Parties without having such certificates. The certificates attest to the fact that the ship owner is insured.[148]

The possibility to bring a claim against a ship owner for environmental impairments is connected to the location where the damage occurred. The territory, territorial seas, exclusive economic zone (EEZ) or, in absence of an EEZ, the space spanning a maximum of 200 nautical miles from the baseline of the territorial sea of a State Party determine the jurisdictional boundaries for claims made under the Convention.[149] Furthermore, the Convention requires that a final judgment made by a court having jurisdiction should be recognised by and enforceable in each State Party.[150]

No data has been systematically collected regarding the number of claims made on the basis of the Convention. Therefore, it is challenging to provide an accurate picture of which Courts have been petitioned, how the proceedings and judgments turned out or how they are enforced.[151] The most important point, however, is still that the Convention is not prescriptive as regards the bunker fuel product or the production process. It is *compensatory*: its function is to ensure that, once damage has already materialised, there are sufficient resources to try and remedy it. Like compulsory insurance for automobiles, it functions as a fall back. *Un*like in the case of automobiles, there are no mechanisms *before* the occurrence of damage that are actively geared to increasing safety. Driving a car requires one to be trained to preserve the safety of all on the road. Cars need to go through several stages of safety tests before they can be marketed. Insurance is just another element in a complex, albeit imperfect and not fool-proof system. The Bunkers Convention is merely a drop in a virtually empty bucket of precautionary measures. The lack of adequate regulation of the bunker fuel sector also inhibits the empowerment of guardians to intervene and prevent or stop wrongdoing. Sadly, *nulla poena sine lege* rings all too true in the bunker fuel sector, but it is hardly the hallmark of a free and just society. The question of enforcement in both the bunker fuel and waste oil management sectors is considered below.

### *Enforcement at the Waste-Product Nexus and Concluding Remarks*

Waste oil management and bunker fuel production are two overlapping industries. Substances and documents travel from one to the other, carrying with them

147. Art. 1(10).
148. Art. 7.
149. Art. 9(1) and Art. 2(a)(i) and (ii).
150. Art. 10.
151. Some recent US cases have been analysed in: Pskowski, "Bad Bunker: Fuel Contamination Claims, Imo 2020, and the Houston Problem."

hazards to the environment and profits to corporate actors. Waste management firms, petrochemical manufacturers, industrial complexes, users of machinery, as well as the global cargo shipping sector are all physically and economically interlinked by virtue of the existence of these two industries. Sometimes,[152] some of these actors behave in ways that are illegal, and we will see two detailed examples of such illegal behaviours in the next Chapter.

But before we can zoom in on those details, we can take a moment to approach these flows of substances and documents through the optic of routine activities theory because this will help us set up our analysis later.[153] In this Chapter, we have reconstructed the "routine legitimate activities [that] provide the wherewithal to commit offenses or to guard against others who do so, [and that] may also provide offenders with suitable targets."[154] The suitable targets in our case study are waste oils, blend components, and bunker fuel, as well as the documents that are supposed to accompany these substances. It is the regular and routinised flow of these substances that shows us who potential offenders are. In the waste oil management and bunker fuel production industries, we have a series of actors that are both pressured and incentivised to commit questionable and criminal acts. These actors can be broadly defined as *holders* of substances that *should* be *legally defined* as wastes. Therefore, waste management firms as well as companies that generate wastes can belong to this category. And, whether they do so knowingly or not, companies involved in the manufacturing of bunker fuel also fall under this definition because often waste oils end up in the blends they make. Therefore, we can confidently say that potential targets and offenders regularly converge in space and time. The question is then, where are those "others" who "guard against [the commission of] offenses"?

In Figure 3.9, we see two triangles. The inner one reflects the crime-generation process and it is complemented by a second, outer triangle that helps formulate interventions. The outer triangle conceptualises those "others" we have just hinted at – the guardians. Guardianship may take many forms, depending on its focus. The triangle portrayed in Figure 3.9 has been slightly modified to avoid confusion. In the original version of the triangle, the intervention role linked to the target/ victim (at the base of the triangle) is labelled 'guardian'.[155]

---

152. It is difficult to establish exactly how often the rules are violated and how much harm is caused by these violations. See Chapter 2 for a more thorough discussion of generalizability of the findings reported in this book.
153. The routine activities approach – as well as its relationship to situational crime prevention – is discussed in Chapter 1.
154. Marcus Felson and Lawrence E. Cohen, "Human Ecology and Crime: A Routine Activity Approach," *Human Ecology* 8, no. 4 (1980). 393.
155. Ronald V. & Eck Clarke, John, "Become a Problem Solving Crime Analyst – in 55 Small Steps," (London: Jill Dando Institute of Crime Science, University College London, 2003).

In *this* study, guardian and guardianship are the broadest concepts, with which we indicate all those actors and activities that may promote compliance and/or inhibit offending generally.[156] Hence, we replaced the name for the narrower role by using custodian instead. We also need to adapt not the name, but the *definitions* of the other guardians included in the embedded triangle so that they match the characteristics of the crimes we are exploring in this study.[157]

**Figure 3.9 Embedded intervention/problem-triangle adapted for organisational crimes**

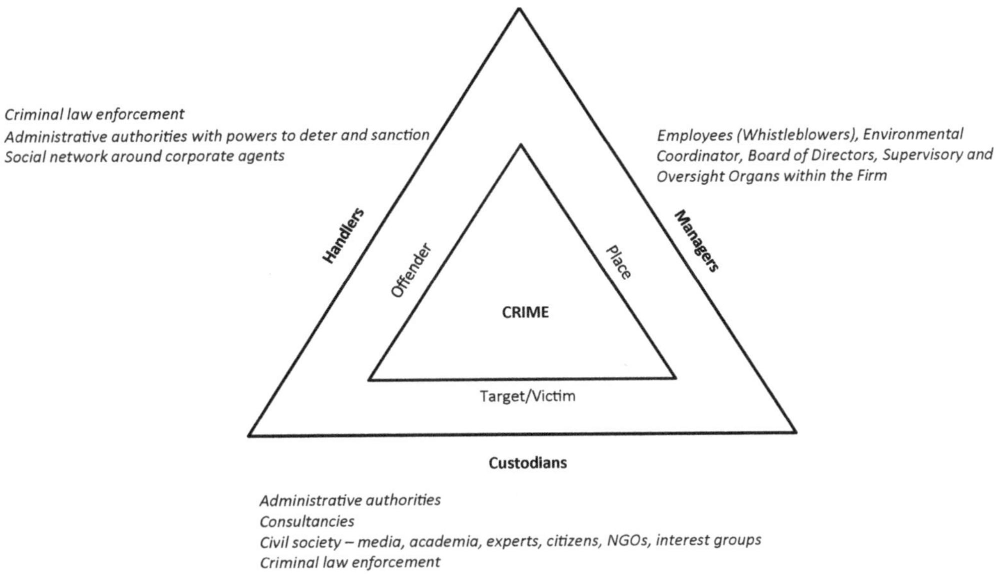


For organisational crimes, the distinctions between handler, manager and custodian are not so easily drawn.[158] Firstly, the place (right side, inner triangle) where crimes occur is often the premises of businesses, indeed the places are usually even business *transactions*. This overlap distorts the triangle and its

156. In fact, in the original formulation of the routine activities approach guardianship was defines as "any spatio-temporally specific supervision of people or property by other people which may prevent criminal violations from occurring."
157. The original definitions are as follows: A handler is someone who knows the offender well – a family member, a friend or a teacher, for example – and can influence or control the offender. A manager is someone who is responsible for controlling behaviour in a given place. A custodian [guardian in the original formulation] is often the same person as the victim themselves when speaking of more traditional forms of crime, such as the person who owns the property that is stolen (Clarke, "Become a Problem Solving Crime Analyst – in 55 Small Steps.")
158. In her work on trust Shapiro explains this collapse of the roles in reference to the asymmetries that fiduciary relationship are born out of and perpetuate (Susan P. Shapiro, "Collaring the Crime, Not the Criminal: Reconsidering the Concept of White-Collar Crime," *American Sociological Review* 55, no. 3 (1990).

dynamics as offenders are often also managers because it is their task to control the business transactions 'where' the crimes occur. Of course, some firms have dedicated compliance and oversight personnel or departments, which may instead be seen as the managers. In any case, we could say that managers in our case are the employees of the firms themselves, possibly also any individuals or entities that are responsible for ensuring compliance or oversight *within* the firms. The internal environmental bureaus mentioned in Section 3 are another example.

Next, we must re-think the notion of custodian along these same lines. If the targets are substances, documents, and industrial processes, then offenders are once again the relevant guardians. It is their task to safeguard these 'objects'. Indeed, it is their specialised privilege and duty to do so.[159] We entrust the management of our wastes to specialised firms, for example. However, the target/ victim distinction may now help us to identify a broader set of *custodians*. Who would be best placed to protect the environment and our health, which are the victims of these types of crime? Many would argue that the state plays an important role in this regard; so, we could say that the custodians of the *victims* are state-authorised, monitoring and enforcement agencies as well as policymakers. Civil society also plays an important role here, which has become more obvious with regard to environmental harm in recent years.

Lastly, we have the handlers, those who exert sufficient influence and control over the potential offenders (left side of the triangle in Figure 3.). Do corporations have parents, teachers, or friends, as indicated in the definition of handlers for more traditional forms of crime? Is there a social network of corporations? Maybe a better way of looking at it is to move past the corporate form. Employees and agents of corporations form a social network that exerts influence and generates (informal) social control. Is this what is actually meant by handler in the context of the problem-triangle? We could argue that, yes, these are the so-called handlers, or that they are one set of handlers, and that other individuals and entities like family members form another set, outside the workplace. Of course, any other state-authorised agents could formally try to influence and control the behaviour of offenders, as we have mentioned in the case of custodians. Probation and police officers are counted as handlers when it comes to traditional offenders, for example. This would also be true for organisational crimes.

Therefore, while law enforcement agents are not the only guardians that may be in a position to disrupt criminal activities, their absence or incapability converging in space and time with targets and offenders is still relevant to understanding criminogenesis. Indeed, in the case of organisational crimes, where many of the other guardians are intra-organisationally tied with offenders, we could argue that

159. In Section 4 of Chapter 5, we will look at the notion of trust again in more detail.

there is almost an organic convergence between all three elements as a motivated offender would be an unlikely capable guardian at the same time.[160]

Having seen how the applicable rules as well as the economic dynamics within the two industries may incentivise or pressure actors into criminal conduct, we now need to discover which instruments and choices are available to law enforcement agents who want to limit illegalities in the waste oil managements services and bunker fuel production sectors. These instruments are also generated by the same legal rules that apply to potential offenders. Which powers of intervention do enforcement agents dispose of? And how do these agents and their powers fit into the broader picture of incentives, pressures, and definitions we have been drawing in this Chapter?

In answering these questions, we need to recall that, although the industries we have been discussing are global in nature, both legislation and enforcement connected to these industries are nationally circumscribed. Even though international and even European rules apply to some of the activities we have reviewed until now, the mechanisms for ensuring compliance or responding to violations are always dependent on the arrangements made within a specific state for that purpose. Indeed, our analysis in this book is grounded in criminal events that have taken place, at least in part, within the territory of the Netherlands, and that have been responded to by Dutch authorities. However, we can make some more general observations regarding enforcement within these industries, without getting into the details of the specific agencies and rules in the Netherlands. The latter will be discussed at the beginning of the next Chapter in function of the crime-script analysis and again later in Chapter 6 where we look at the Andante team in more detail.

For both industries, administrative and criminal law rules are applicable. The administrative rules are those cited in this Chapter. They centre around permissible waste management activities, and the manufacturing, use, sale, and transport of chemicals. Administrative enforcement agents may monitor activities by firms in these sectors; specifically, they can trace the movement of substances from one entity to another by examining accompanying documentation. They may also test substances to see that they correspond to the documents, although (thorough) testing is rare because it is expensive and may not always satisfactorily

160. There are many assumptions in this argument, which make it problematic. First, the corporate form should not blind us to the individuality of the various persons that work within that form. Their individuality also means they may be differently motivated or there may be some persons who are not criminally motivated at all and even wish to halt criminal activities. Indeed, within a corporation the roles of handler, manager and guardian may be taken on responsibly an in favour of compliance with the law. Second, the offender in routine activities theory is an individual who perpetrates predatory offences. Replacing that offender with a corporation is problematic for translating the theory. Still, the point that offender and guardian, in some sense, coincide, is at the core of important work in the field of organizational criminology, specifically that of Shapiro on trust (Shapiro, "Collaring the Crime, Not the Criminal: Reconsidering the Concept of White-Collar Crime."

reveal the true nature of the substances. Administrative and criminal law rules are connected to the permits held by companies operating in the two sectors. Firms that do not comply with permit conditions can be warned and then sanctioned through fines and permit withdrawal. Criminal law agents may also exercise their powers based on more general criminal law provisions, such as fraud or endangering physical health by trading in hazardous substances without notifying buyers of the true nature of the product.[161]

Several *different* agencies may have powers of intervention at different stages of the procedures of waste management and bunker fuel production. Sometimes these powers can be exercised concurrently; other times, a single agency may be competent for one stage of the process and another agency for the next stage of the same process, depending on the classification of the substance or procedure involved at that stage. No single department operates across the two industries and at the overlap between the two, with a birds-eye view of all the physical and economic flows we have discussed until now.[162]

When we reflect on enforcement *at the overlap* of the waste oil management services and bunker fuel production industries, three characteristics come to mind: it is fragmented, asymmetric and it encourages criminogenic symbioses. The former two characteristics are conducive to the third. Let us look at each in turn as we describe enforcement.

Fragmentation makes detecting wrongdoing difficult and means the pattern of enforcement is inconsistent, at best. This fragmentation is due to three reasons. First, criminal activities take place at the overlap of two *legally distinct* industries. Waste oil management is regulated and enforced through sector-specific legislation, which is connected to specialised agents through explicit and circumscribed mandates conferring competence to them. The same is true for those hard law rules that apply to the bunker fuel sector. The distinctness of the legal regimes functions as a veil: enforcement agencies in the waste sector cannot see past the realm of waste management into that of bunker fuel, and vice versa.

Second, the legal regimes of each industry are internally fragmented, which also leads to fragmented enforcement. Waste management legislation is designed to be specific not just to waste *vis-à-vis* other substances and objects, but also to make distinctions among waste streams. When it comes to waste oils, this fragmentation is even more problematic. A major source of waste oils is the shipping sector. We saw in Section 1 that, by virtue of obligations under MARPOL, we have specialised waste collection facilities at ports (HOVs and HOIs). These are regulated and monitored separately from other waste oil collectors. There are also

161. The legal provisions are discussed in Section 1 of Chapter 4.
162. The ILT has powers that allow it to monitor waste management activities as well as the movement of chemicals. However, these two issues are dealt with by two different departments. See Chapter 4 for more details on the division of enforcement tasks in the Netherlands.

several different kinds of waste oil streams, each of which needs to be handled in a unique way, although *all* could be wrongfully introduced into bunker fuel.

Third, we have been looking at two industries that are global in their extension but are not regulated uniformly in all parts of the world. Even within the EU – which is a relatively homogenous regulatory space – there are many differences among the applicable rules and enforcement practices. In great part, this problem stems not from the two industries themselves but from their inherent connection to the world of shipping and how regulation of this sector has developed historically. Actions that are undertaken in the shipping sector – and their effects – can be intervened upon based on two types of competence: that of the flag state or that of the port state.

Flag states are notoriously unwilling and incapable of enforcing rules, which is why so many of them are chosen as flag states in the first place. Port states have a better track record in this regard; however, they are under immense pressure to be lenient in both the formulation of restrictions and in their enforcement. Ports are sources of wealth (redistribution) on a grand scale. A successful port can substantially alter the economic conditions of a region or country. Competition levels among ports are very high: Making substantial alterations to enforcement practices in a port, which may have a constraining effect on trade, can lead to economic devastation for the port and the localities it is connected to. The race to the bottom that is often lamented when talking about globalisation generally is characteristic of the relationships between ports across the globe.[163]

The fragmentation that derives from the flag state/port state distinction is also connected to the second characteristic of enforcement, namely that it is asymmetric. Asymmetry here has four dimensions. First, there is the global-local dimension: economic patterns that are global are not regulated globally and this asymmetry has criminogenic potential.[164] Second, there is an asymmetry between the two industries: waste management is stringently regulated and enforced, but bunker fuel production is scarcely regulated, and it is very difficult for any state enforcement to take place. At the same time, these two industries are physically, legally, and economically connected. Third, there is an asymmetry in knowledge between the private economic actors who operate in the industries and the public state enforcement agents. This latter asymmetry is characteristic of organisational

163. John NK Mansell, *Flag State Responsibility: Historical Development and Contemporary Issues* (Springer Science & Business Media, 2009); Michael Galley, "Ship Registration, Owner Anonymity and Sub-Standard Shipping," in *Shipbreaking: Hazards and Liabilities* (Springer, 2014); Mia Mahmudur Rahim, Md Tarikul Islam, and Sanjaya Kuruppu, "Regulating Global Shipping Corporations' Accountability for Reducing Greenhouse Gas Emissions in the Seas," *Marine Policy* 69 (2016); Carlos Felipe Llinás Negret, "Pretending to Be Liberian and Panamanian; Flags of Convenience and the Weakening of the Nation State on the High Seas," *J. Mar. L. & Com.* 47 (2016); Jeremy Firestone and James Corbett, "Maritime Transportation: A Third Way for Port and Environmental Security" (paper presented at the Widener L. Symp. J., 2002).

164. Nikos Passas, "Globalization, Criminogenic Asymmetries and Economic Crime," *Eur. JL Reform* 1 (1999).

crime more generally. Lastly, there is an asymmetry between the importance of the bunker fuel sector for international trade and the degree of oversight that is actually exercised by states. The immense clout powering the engines of millions of ships is virtually unchecked, which means that enforcement agents are even less knowledgeable *vis-à-vis* this sector than in the waste sector.

Based on our reflections on fragmentation and asymmetries, we can argue that the overlap between waste oil management services and bunker fuel production is characterised by criminogenic symbioses. These symbioses are generated between state and private actors within the two industries and at the overlap between them. The symbioses occur because the legitimate goals that are pursued by those actors are distorted or their implementation is not adequately fostered by the mechanisms of enforcement and control that exist. We will reflect on this symbiosis in Chapter 5, but we first need to see how it plays out in practice by analysing two criminal cases in Chapter 4.

# 4 Deconstructing Two Criminal Events Using Crime Script Analysis

Our journey into the worlds of waste oil management and bunker fuel production now continues as we venture closer to the activities of firms operating in these two industries. Our focus is on *criminal* activities:[1] when waste oils are managed in contravention of Dutch as well as EU rules and are used as blend components in the bunker fuel production process. We look at two cases, which represent patterns in *modi operandi* as well as violations of two branches of waste management legislation. The patterns were identified during the Andante project.[2] The team observed that there were several sources of waste oils that were illegally being introduced into bunker blends, which could be clustered around two processes. Each of these processes also corresponded to certain separate patterns in the way the offences were carried out, although there were commonalities as well. The first case concerns waste oils coming from collection and treatment processes. Treatment supposedly leads to usable products and the case is connected to the notion of 'end-of-waste'. The second case revolves around the operations of a petrochemical production firm, which deals with the waste oils emerging from its manufacturing processes in the way that is most profitable: selling them as blend components. It is connected to the 'by-product' label as well as the REACH framework. The analysis of both cases is functional to answering the following research questions:[3]

a. What does the illegal sale, transport and blending of waste oils in the process of producing bunker fuel look like?
b. During which steps of the bunker fuel production and waste oil management processes do these activities [illegal sale, transport and blending of waste oils] occur?

---

1. The events are characterized as criminal here because the activities that take place are pursuable under Dutch criminal law. In the research questions, the term illegal is used because the questions address these types of activities more generally and not just as they manifest in the Netherlands or how they are defined under Dutch law. In an EU context, however, the label illegal can usually be applied without difficulty.
2. See Chapter 2 for more details on the selection of the two cases and the Andante project.
3. These questions (particularly numbers 2, 4, 8, and 9) have already partly been addressed in Chapter 3, and cross-references are made where appropriate.

c. Which logistical steps and which actions are undertaken by the actors involved?
d. What types of actors are involved?
e. What types of activities do they engage in?
f. What tools do they use to complete these activities?
g. What factors, at different levels of analysis, influence – facilitate or constrain – the actors involved in undertaking the abovementioned logistical steps towards crime-commission?
h. What internal as well as external regulations and mechanisms for supervision and control exist that apply to the WOM and BFP sectors?
i. How are these regulations and mechanisms interpreted, applied and enforced?
j. How can these regulations and mechanisms influence – facilitate or constrain – the occurrence of the criminal activities that take place in the WOM and BFP sectors?

To answer these questions, we use tools and concepts from crime script analysis and situational crime prevention, both of which are connected to routine activities theory.[4] In both of the cases that we analyse, the targets are waste oils, blend components and bunker fuel. The offenders are individuals and corporations that operate in different industries: waste oil management services, petrochemical production, and bunker fuel production. Guardians are, theoretically, all those individuals or entities that may be able to (physically) intervene and stop the completion of a criminal act.

However, the scope of this Chapter is somewhat narrower, partly because of the type of data that were available for reconstructing the criminal events.[5] In this Chapter, we focus on two types of guardians. On one hand, we have administrative and criminal law enforcement agents who act on behalf of the state and who have powers granted to them by law to inspect, monitor, and enforce the rules applicable to waste oil management and bunker fuel production. We refer to these as formal guardians. We speak about a formal system of guardianship when we look not only at the guardians themselves but also at the tools they can use according to the law. The formal system of guardianship also includes any other legally imposed measures that are supposed to support oversight: such as documents and record-keeping. On the other hand, we have potential guardians. They are actors or entities who, because of their access to information regarding the crime, could themselves frustrate or inhibit its completion. Alternatively, they could report the information to a formal guardian. Potential guardians do not have a legally imposed responsibility to exercise oversight.

4. See Chapter 1 and the end of Chapter 3 for a discussion of routine activities theory.
5. See Chapter 2 for details regarding the nature and sources of data used in this analysis.

These three basic factors – targets, offenders, and guardians – are not just statically observed in our analysis. Rather, by examining the dynamic interaction between them, we can reach conclusions about the risks, efforts, rewards, excuses, and provocations that characterise these crime events. Therefore, when thinking about what factors either facilitate or constrain the logistical steps that make up criminal events to answer question (g.), we need to keep in mind the following assertion from situational crime prevention:[6]

***Crime will occur when: efforts & risks are low and rewards, provocations & excuses are high.***

The Chapter is divided into three Sections. First, we briefly look at how the formal system of guardianship is structured in the Netherlands. This helps us to see who has powers of intervention in the respective cases and in which legal provisions these powers are grounded. Knowing who may intervene is then helpful for reconstructing the pattern of enforcement as it unfolded in practice for each case. The second and third Sections are each dedicated to the analysis of one of the crime events: this analysis is both legal and criminological in nature. For each act of each event, we see which legal provisions are violated and then discuss the way the crime unfolds by referring to criminological concepts. The Chapter then rounds off with some reflections where common findings from both cases are brought together, in light of the above theoretical assertion.

## 4.1 Formal Guardianship Structures in the Netherlands

In Chapter 3, we saw that waste oil management and bunker fuel production are two overlapping industries, which are, nevertheless, legally distinct. This legal separateness manifests itself in practice through separate systems of guardianship. In this Section, we look at how waste management legislation and rules applying to bunker fuel production are enforced through administrative and criminal law measures in the Netherlands.

### *Administrative and Criminal Law Enforcement of Waste Management Legislation*

Dutch law ensures that both administrative and criminal law agents may monitor, intervene, and sanction activities of firms in the WOMS sector. These powers have three different bases: First, those that extend from the permit relationship. Second, those connected to the movement and transportation of wastes. Third, there are powers and sanctions grounded in criminal law.

Local authorities – the municipality or province – are first in line to ascertain whether a firm is handling the waste-categories included in its permit and

6. See Chapter 1 for a more detailed elaboration of the theoretical framework.

whether it is doing so appropriately.[7] Within the Dutch legal framework there is a distinction between different waste streams and different activities that can be performed with specific wastes. This distinction influences which authorities are responsible for issuing permits. The general rule set out in the ministerial Decision on environmental law is that municipalities are responsible for the issuing of permits and monitoring compliance therewith.[8] However, there can be exceptions. In fact, where a firm wishes to process industrial and hazardous wastes it must obtain a permit from the provincial authority.[9] This is the case for waste oils.

*Omgevingsdiensten* (environmental services – ODs) are regional agencies that can also act through the permit relationship. There are currently 29 ODs in the Netherlands, and they may use administrative law measures to monitor compliance with permits and even issue sanctions for violations. Some ODs dispose of special officers – *buitengewone opsporingsambtenaren* (BOAs), who have criminal law powers, which they use for their enforcement tasks. ODs as well as local and provincial authorities monitor permits related to waste *treatment and storage*, which are obtained under Wabo rules.

The Human Environment and Transport Inspectorate (*Inspectie Leefomgeving en Transport* – ILT) is another important agency involved in the enforcement of environmental laws, and especially waste management activities. It primarily works at a national level. Violations of permits for *collection* of waste can be followed up by the ILT, which may then choose to use administrative or criminal law measures – including sanctions in the form of fines – to address them. In fact, the ILT, although formally an administrative agency, disposes of a range of

7. Art. 18.18 Wet milieubeheer (Wm) prohibits acting in contravention of permit conditions. *Wet van 13 juni 1979, houdende regelen met betrekking tot een aantal algemene onderwerpen op het gebied van de milieuhygiëne (Wet milieubeheer)*. Meanwhile, the Wabo has replaced the Wm in this respect. Old Wm permits are now considered permits under 2.2 Wabo, with 2.3.a Wabo taking the place of 18.18 Wm.
8. Art. 7.1 Besluit van Besluit van 25 maart 2010, houdende regels ter uitvoering van de Wet algemene bepalingen omgevingsrecht (Besluit omgevingsrecht – Bor).
9. Bijlage I, Onderdeel C Bor.

regulatory powers,[10] including an investigative and intelligence unit – *Inlichtingen- en Opsporing Dienst* (IOD).[11]

The ILT is primarily responsible for monitoring the movement of (hazardous) wastes within the Netherlands and across borders,[12] in accordance with Regulation (EC) 1013/2006.[13] Notifications of such movements as well as the registration of pre-approved firms, which may receive certain categories of hazardous wastes

---

10. There are four types of measures that can be used under administrative law to obtain compliance and punish violations. First, the administrative authority (the municipality, province, or ILT) may issue a warning (*bestuurlijke waarschuwing*) after having ascertained that undesirable or illegal behaviour risks or is taking place. Second, the administrative authority may impose an order under penalty (*last onder dwangsom*). The order may require a firm to stop a certain activity or to do something, which may include repairing damage that has already taken place. It may also require a firm to stop violations that have repeatedly taken place. The penalty is triggered when the order is not complied with. Third, administrative authorities may impose an executive order (*bestuursdwang*). The aims of the order may be to prevent, limit, or resolve damage resulting from a violation or to demand compliance with the applicable rules. The fourth type of administrative measure involves the (temporary) withdrawal of a firm's permit (in the case of the movement of hazardous wastes regulated in Regulation 103/2006, this withdrawal is required in accordance with Art. 9(8) Regulation 1013/2006). The withdrawal may include a contestation (*bezwaar*) of the permit. Criminal law measures may also be used by the ILT. These include a preliminary measure (*voorlopige maatregel*) based on Art. 28 WED; the imposition of an administrative penalty (*bestuurlijke strafbeschikking*) (art. 257ba (2) WvSv); or the initiation of criminal proceedings through the filing of a criminal complaint (*proces-verbaal*).
11. The ILT/IOD focuses on organised crime, crimes having an international dimension and what has been translated as crimes of a subversive (*ondermijnend*) nature.
12. There are also agencies and networks that facilitate exchanges and learning or even indirectly participate in enforcement of waste management rules at the European and international level. For example, both EUROPOL and Eurojust have groups or individuals that focus on corporate and environmental crime as part of their efforts to facilitate cross-border investigations and prosecution of cases having cross-border characteristics. A small group of public prosecutors from EU countries have also set up an informal network – the European Network of Prosecutors for the Environment (ENPE) as well. This non-profit association has grown to include members from outside the EU and beyond the European continent. Among their working groups, there is one specifically devoted to exploring the causes of waste crime in violation of rules on waste shipments covered by Regulation 1013/2006 and the Basel Convention. The European Union Network for the Implementation and Enforcement of Environmental Law (IMPEL) brings together environmental authorities from the EU Member States as well as other countries to share best practices. It sets up workshops, seminar and contributes to research efforts all aimed at implementing environmental law. IMPEL is partly funded by the European Commission. INTERPOL has also set up a Pollution Crime Working Group that looks at the movement of waste across borders. The Basel Secretariat is an important entity as well, as it is responsible for supporting the implementation of the Basel Convention in the Sate Parties. It operates under the administration of the United Nations Environmental Program (UNEP). The International Network for Environmental Compliance and Enforcement (INECE) works on a global level and includes both governmental and non-governmental partners for conferences and other information and knowledge sharing events. One of the focuses of INECE has been that of environmental issues connected to ports.
13. Regulation (EC) 1013/2006 of the European Parliament and of the Council of 14 June 2006 on shipments of waste, OJ L 190, p. 1, 12.07.2006.

(from abroad) are within the purview of the ILT.[14] Dutch law also classifies the movement of hazardous wastes in contravention of the provisions of Regulation 1013/2006 as a violation of the *Wet milieubeheer* (Wm).[15] Police and Customs agencies also have criminal law inspection, investigation, and enforcement powers in respect of the movement of hazardous wastes.[16][17]

Lack of compliance with the administrative law rules that were discussed in Chapter 3 can lead to the imposition of administrative and then criminal law measures.[18] To detect violations, authorities can do one of three things: they can visit the premises of firms, check transports, or remotely review the records of waste management firms that are registered through the *Landelijke Meldpunt*

14. The Wm delegates powers to the Minister for Infrastructure and Water Management (Arts. 18.2b (1) (b) & 18.2b (2) Wm). Art. 5.10 Wabo further provides that the Minister for Infrastructure and Water Management can issue an administrative decision *vis-à-vis* a firm that handles hazardous wastes that fall under Regulation 1013/2006. The Minister has delegated these to the Inspector-General of the ILT, which, in turn, has delegated them to the individual inspectors of the ILT. (*Wet van 6 november 2008, houdende regels inzake een vergunningstelsel met betrekking tot activiteiten die van invloed zijn op de fysieke leefomgeving en inzake handhaving van regelingen op het gebied van de fysieke leefomgeving* (*Wet algemene bepalingen omgevingsrecht – Wabo*). (See: https://www.ilent.nl/onderwerpen/afvaltransport-evoa/toezicht-en-handhaving/bevoegdheden).
15. Regulation 1013/2006 is transposed into arts. 10.56 (1) & (2) and 10.60 Wm. The latter reproduces the activities that are permitted and forbidden in the Regulation. The Wm indicates that the Minister for Infrastructure and Water Management is responsible for the implementation of Regulation 1013/2006 into the Dutch legal system, including its enforcement (art. 10.58). The Minister's responsibility for administrative enforcement of Regulation 1013/2006 is covered by art. 18.2b Wm. Violations of art. 10.60 Wm are also classified as violations of art. 1a WED – this is the basis for criminal law measures that are activated upon violation of Regulation 1013/2006 in the Netherlands. For more details on the content of Regulation 1013/2006 see Section 2 of Chapter 3 and the related references.
16. Art. 141 of the Dutch Code of Criminal Procedure (WvSv) lists the agencies and authorities which are tasked with the investigation of criminal facts. Art. 9 of the VROM Decision refers to art. 141 WvSv in relation to the enforcement of Titale 10.7 Wm, the *Besluit inzameling afvalstoffen*, Regeling inzameling afvalstoffen, and the cross-border movement of (hazardous) wastes. (*Besluit aanwijzing ambtenaren VROM-regelgeving van 16 december 2004*). VROM stands for *Volkshuisvesting, Ruimtelijke Ordening en Milieubeheer* (Housing, Spatial Planning and the Environment) and was the name of a Ministry the tasks of which have been absorbed into other ministries, amongst which we find the Ministry for Infrastructure and Water Management today.
17. Customs agents are part of the Dutch Tax Authority (*Belastingdienst*) – the criminal law (investigative and intelligence branch) of the Tax Authority – *Fiscale inlichtingen- en opsporingsdienst* – FIOD) is, therefore, also the one that uses criminal law measures where customs issues arise in matters of waste transports. The ILT is still primarily responsible and FIOD must work alongside and under the guidance of the ILT when carrying out its tasks in this domain. See: Douane (Ministerie van Financiën), "40.04.00 Overbrenging Afvalstoffen (Evoa)," https://www.belastingdienst.nl/bibliotheek/handboeken/html/boeken/HVGEM/overbrenging_afvalstoffen_evoa_-de_handhaving_van_de_afvalstoffenwetgeving.html.
18. See note 304above.

*Afvalstoffen* (LMA).[19] Checks are often conducted based on knowledge of prior offending as well as other forms of intelligence or risk-based analyses.[20]

Criminal law also provides a basis for investigations and sanctions. This includes both the Law on Economic Crimes (*Wet op de economische delicten* – WED) and the Code of Criminal Law (*Wetboek van Strafrecht* – WvS).[21] Article 1a WED criminalises conduct that infringes provisions of the Wm.[22] Article 6(1) WED specifies that such crimes may be punished by a fine of the fifth category or a term of imprisonment of up to six years.[23] The use of criminal law measures (for investigation) is triggered by an 'indication' (*aanwijzing*) that criminal activities have taken place.[24] There is no defined order in terms of competence among the above cited authorities about which one should be the first to respond.[25]

19. The LMA is described in more detail in Section 2 of Chapter 3. There are other databases that are accessible to authorities. For example, movements of waste across borders are connected to the database of forms holding EVOA-permits. The VIHB is the national list of registered waste-collectors, handlers, brokers and transporters (see also note 71 in Chapter 3).
20. On its website of the ILT states: "The ILT carries out its inspections on the basis of risk profiles. Priority is given to checking waste exports to non-OECD countries and countries that were the last to join the European Union. [Author's translation] Original: *"De ILT voert de controles uit op basis van risicoprofielen. De controle van afvalexport naar niet-OESO-landen en landen die als laatste zijn toegetreden tot de Europese Unie heeft hierbij prioriteit."* Inspectie Leefomgenving en Transport (Ministerie van Infrastructuur en Waterstaat), "Toezicht En Interventies," https://www.ilent.nl/onderwerpen/afvaltransport-evoa/toezicht-en-handhaving/toezicht-en-interventies.
21. Wet van 22 juni 1950, houdende vaststelling van regelen voor de opsporing, de vervolging en de berechting van economische delicten (Wet op de economische delicten – WED). Wet van 3 maart 1881 – Wetboek van Strafrecht (WvS).
22. The relevant provisions of the Wm are those relating to the movement and transportation of wastes covered by Regulation 1013/2006 (see note 309above); and those on waste management more generally (Title 10). When the waste label is not applied to a substance that is a waste, and that substance is handled by various actors, which are not waste management firms, this means that there is no existing permit relationship that grounds compliance and enforcement efforts. In this respect, arts. 10.37 (2) and 10.55 Wm are central because they prohibit the handling of hazardous wastes by entities that do not possess the necessary technology and permits. It is on *this* basis that other criminal and administrative law powers of investigation and sanctioning can be used.
23. A fine of the fifth category is equal to € 90.000. Fine categories are defined in art. 23 WvS.
24. Which does *not* mean there must be a 'suspicion' of criminal wrongdoing as defined in art. 27 WvSv.
25. Depending on the circumstances one or several agencies may have competence and respond first. Besides the already mentioned ILT/IOD, Police, Provinces and ODs, there are also other Dutch supervisory bodies that have powers delegated to them by different ministries, such as *Algemene Inspectiediensten* (AIDs), which fall under the Ministry for agriculture, nature and food quality; or the *Staatstoezicht op de Mijnen* (SodM); or local water authorities (*waterschappen*). Nevertheless, there are some arrangements in place for determining how supervisory and monitoring competences should be exercise. For example, an agreement has been signed by the Ministry of Infrastructure and Water Management and the Ministry of Finance, which respectively lead the ILT and *Belastingdienst* (Tax Authority). This agreement describes the division of responsibilities and tasks for the purposes of enforcement in the realm of waste management, specifically as pertains to the movement and transportation of waste. Ministerie van Infrastructuur en Waterstaat, "Convenant Inzake De Samenwerking Tussen Het Ministerie Van Infrastructuur En Waterstaat Het Ministerie Van Financien Buj De Uitvoering Van Wettelijke

Because the management of waste is inherently tied up with the creation of documents that attest to the nature and record the movement of wastes, most criminal cases also include some form of fraud. Article 225 WvS criminalises the falsification of documents.[26] There are also other criminal law provisions that may be violated in the types of cases we are examining.[27] Articles 174(1) and 175(1) WvS criminalise the selling or marketing of products that are harmful to human health and the environment, without the purchaser being informed of their harmful nature. They apply when documents do not reveal the fact that substances are wastes or where the substances are portrayed as different wastes than they are.[28] In the Netherlands, both natural and legal persons may be held criminally liable.[29]

Figure 4.1 portrays the formal system of guardianship in relation to the process of waste oil management. The portions in black are those directly linked to waste management legislation or criminal law provisions as well as the agencies that can act on these bases – this is the formal system of guardianship in the realm of waste management.

---

Taken Op Het Beliedsterrein Van Het Ministerie Van Infrastructuur En Waterstaat Door De Douane," (2018). "Bijlage 1 – Convenant Inzake De Samenwerking Tussen Het Ministerie Van Infrastructuur En Waterstaat Het Ministerie Van Financien Buj De Uitvoering Van Wettelijke Taken Op Het Beliedsterrein Van Het Ministerie Van Infrastructuur En Waterstaat Door De Douane," (2018).

26. Art. 225 WvS states: 1. He who falsely prepares or falsifies a document intended to serve as proof of an offence, with the intent to use it as genuine and unaltered or to have it used by others, shall be punished as guilty of forgery with imprisonment of not more than six years or a fine of the fifth category.
2. The same punishment is imposed upon anyone who wilfully uses the forged or falsified document as if it were genuine and uncorrected, or wilfully delivers or possesses such a document, knowing or having reason to suspect that it is intended for such use. [Author's translation.]

27. Environmental crime in the Netherlands is handled through a combined system whereby damage to the environment is directly criminalized through provisions in the WvS (Arts. 157, 158, 161quater, 161quinquies, 171, 172, 173, 173a, 173b, 429 (4)) and then through the WED that makes a link to sectoral legislation, which administratively regulates activities that may have detrimental impacts on human health and the environment. The obligation to transpose Directive 2008/99/EC on environmental crimes in the Netherlands did not lead to any changes in Dutch legislation as this combined system was deemed to be adequate for the purposes of transposition.

28. When this is done knowingly, a fine of the fifth category or a term of imprisonment of maximum 15 years may be applied (Art. 174(1) WvS). Where this leads to death, the punishment will be life imprisonment or a maximum penalty of 30 years or a fine of the fifth category. Where this is done recklessly, a fine of the fourth category or imprisonment of up to one year may apply (art. 175 (1) WvS). Where this leads to death, the punishment will be a maximum imprisonment of two years or a fine of the fourth category.

29. Art. 51 WvS states that a company may be held criminally liable – liability may be connected to offences of natural or legal persons. It is also interesting to note that the notion of 'organised crime' as defined in Art. 140 WvS may also be applied. Indeed, one of the avenues explored during the Andante project was the possibility of defining the criminal activities they were investigating as a form of organised crime – this idea was later no longer pursued (Interview no. 7 on 20.02.2020).

Waste management is generally regulated under administrative law, but there may be different specialised domains of administrative law that are relevant to different portions of waste management or of tangential activities. The dashed lines represent the link between port, local authorities (including ODs) or the ILT, and the waste management procedures.[30] These authorities have powers of oversight through administrative rules and can impose measures and sanctions on that basis. The thicker, double-dashed lines between the by-product or product portions of the process and the ILT on the top right-hand side also represent administrative law rules, but these are outside the scope of waste management legislation. The powers of port authorities in relation to activities and substances at ports are also administrative in nature. They are portrayed with dotted lines at the bottom right-hand side as they are also separate from the rules on waste management.

Criminal law rules encompass the entirety of the process as they relate more generally to official documents as well as harms that derive from improper handling of substances, regardless of which industrial process are involved. The continuous black lines represent the connection between state agents and the waste management process that is derived from criminal law provisions or powers. Customs, Police, the ILT and (BOAs) in ODs may act based on the violation criminal law rules, however, the ILT, Customs and ODs can do so because of the link with waste management legislation, whereas the Police has a more general mandate in this respect.

**Figure 4.1 The formal system of guardianship in the waste oil management industry**

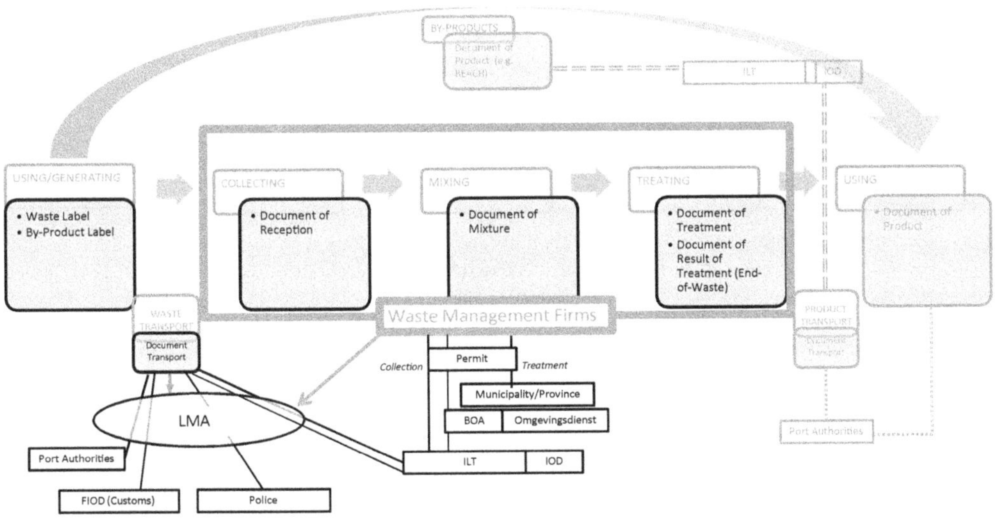


30. The role of port authorities in the process of waste management is discussed in more detail in Section 2 of Chapter 3.

All the above cited authorities may also observe the movement of wastes remotely through the LMA.[31] The LMA is portrayed as an oval with dashed lines as the obligation to record movements of waste and report them to the LMA is covered in the Wm, i.e., in administrative law.

*Administrative and Criminal Law Enforcement Measures in the Bunker Fuel Production Industry*

There are three domains that are relevant for law enforcement purposes in the BFP industry. The first is that of the manufacturing, movement, and use of chemicals covered by REACH.[32] The second domain is that of compulsory labelling of hazardous and chemical substances; and it partly overlaps with REACH obligations. The third domain revolves around bunker-fuel related pollution and damages. The latter is, legally speaking, separate from the first two. Nevertheless, there are areas of overlap between each of these domains as well as with that of enforcement for WOMS.

In the Netherlands, three administrative agencies are responsible for the monitoring of chemicals, as well as the related used of special and specific labels that accompany those chemicals.[33] In the context of our case, the powers of the ILT are relevant because it is responsible for monitoring and enforcing REACH in respect of manufacturers, importers, and dealers of chemicals for *professional* use.[34]

31. However, the LMA does not necessarily contain the records of all movements of waste *across borders* that take place under EVOA. But the Ministry for Infrastructure and Water Management disposes of a list of permit holders and approved entities under EVOA.
32. Regulation (EC) No 1907/2006 of the European Parliament and of the Council of 18 December 2006 concerning the Registration, Evaluation, Authorisation and Restriction of Chemicals (REACH), establishing a European Chemicals Agency, amending Directive 1999/45/EC and repealing Council Regulation (EEC) No 793/93 and Commission Regulation (EC) No 1488/94 as well as Council Directive 76/769/EEC and Commission Directives 91/155/EEC, 93/67/EEC, 93/105/EC and 2000/21/EC (OJ L 396, 30.12.2006, corrected version in OJ L136, 29.5.2007, p. 3). For a more detailed discussion on REACH, see Chapter 3.
33. These are the ILT, the Labour Authority (*Nederlandse Arbeidsinspectie/ Inspectie van Sociale Zaken en Werkgelegenheid* – SZW), and the Netherlands Food and Consumer Product Safety Authority (*Nederlandse Voedsel- en Warenautoriteit* -NVWA). Each of these agencies has a specific focus. The *Inspectie* SZW focuses on professional and industrial users of REACH-covered substances. They specialise on work-safety related issues. The NVWA focuses on producers, transporters and traders of REACH-covered substances destined for consumers. The Mines-authority (*Staatstoezicht op de Mijnen*) of the Netherlands also has some tasks in enforcing REACH where this is connected to mining. The Customs agency may also be involved in the enforcement of REACH. Chapter 9 Wm covers REACH-related rules. Administrative enforcement of REACH is regulated under Chapter 18 Wm (art. 18.2b (1) refers to the Minister for Infrastructure and Water Management and art. 18.2b (2) to the Minister for Economic Affairs as well as the Minister for Social Affairs and Employment, and the Minister for Health, Welfare and Sport. Violations of Title 9 Wm are also classified as violation of the WED (art. 1a (1°) and (2°) WED and art. 9.3 en 9.3a Wm. Art. 1(4) WED also includes the violations rules under the *Warenwetbesluit* (Decision on the Law on Goods) as criminal law violations.)
34. See also Rijksoverheid, "Handhaving Reach En Clp," https://chemischestoffengoedgeregeld.nl/content/handhaving.

As mentioned above, the ILT disposes of a criminal law investigative unit (IOD) as well as a range of both administrative and criminal law powers to enforce rules.[35] Substances that are wastes may *not* be labelled as REACH products,[36] which means the system for enforcement discussed in the preceding subsection will be triggered when this rule is violated.

All substances that end up in bunker fuel as well as bunker fuel itself must be accompanied by a special document that informs those handling them of the characteristics and potential hazards of those substances. This document is called a (material) safety data sheet (SDS).[37] It must accompany substances. This obligation concerning accompanying documents is separate from any labelling obligations that may derive from the concurrent applicability of the REACH framework to the same substance. Transporting hazardous substances without this document is a punishable offence.[38]

When bunker fuel is supplied to an end user, a special document is also included – this is called a bunker delivery note (BDN).[39] It is similar to the

---

35. See note 304above for more details about the range of powers the ILT disposes of. The other agencies have similar powers that they can use *vis-à-vis* firms and individuals that are within their focus.
36. Art. 2(2) Regulation (EC) No 1907/2006 (REACH).
37. Art. 31(3) Regulation (EC) No 1907/2006 (REACH) states that an SDS provides a mechanism for transmitting appropriate safety information on substances and mixtures where: a substance or a mixture meets the criteria for classification as hazardous according to CLP; or a substance is persistent, bioaccumulative and toxic (PBT) or very persistent and very bioaccumulative (vPvB), according to the criteria given in Annex XIII of REACH, or; a substance is included in the candidate list for eventual authorisation according to Art. 59(1) of REACH for any other reasons. Under certain conditions some mixtures which do not meet the criteria for classification as hazardous according to CLP also require an SDS to be prepared or be made available request (See Art. 31(3) of REACH, and notes to tables 3.4.6, 3.6.2, 3.7.2, 3.8.3 and 3.9.4 of Annex I of CLP. CLP is the Regulation that governs the classification and labelling of chemical and hazardous substances: Regulation (EC) No 1272/2008 of the European Parliament and of the Council of 16 December 2008 on classification, labelling and packaging of substances and mixtures amending and repealing Directives 67/548/EEC and 1999/45/EC, and amending Regulation (EC) No 1907/2006 (OJ L 353, 31.12.2008, p. 1). See also: European Chemicals Agency (ECHA), "Guidance on the Compilation of Safety Data Sheets (Version 4.0)," (2020). Globally, there is a system in place for the harmonised categorisation and labelling of hazardous and substances and chemicals, which is called the Globally Harmonized System of Classification and Labelling of Chemicals (GHS). This system is relevant for the formulation of Safety Data Sheets. It was first published in 2002 (United Nations, Globally Harmonized System of Classification and Labelling of Chemicals (GHS, 2003); the currently applicable version is United Nations, Globally Harmonized System of Classification and Labelling of Chemicals (GHS Rev. 9, 2021). Art. 9.3a. Wm transposes the provisions of Regulation 1272/2008.
38. Art. 1a 1° WED cites the Wm and specifically Art. 9.3.3 Wm, which implements REACH into national law. For substances that are not covered by REACH the obligation to have an SDS is covered by Art. 9.3a.3(1) Wm, which is also listed in Art. 1a 1° WED.
39. The Bunker Delivery Note (BDN) is the delivery note for the bunkered fuel. This is required to include data on the fuel delivered. MARPOL Annex VI, Appendix V provides a list of information that should be included in the BDN. See also ILT Website: Inspectie Leefomgenving en Transport (Ministerie van Infrastructuur en Waterstaat), "Marine Fuels Quality," https://english.ilent.nl/themes/l/legislation-merchant-shipping/marine-fuels-quality. Regulation 18 (3-6) Annex VI,

SDS in terms of its function to inform those handling the substances of their characteristics and hazardousness, but specific to bunker fuel. Sometimes, the information included in the SDS (or the BDN) can serve as an indication that waste oils have been illegally introduced into the bunker fuel production process. Formal guardians who review such documents need to have sufficient experience and expertise to be able to notice these indications. However, neither the SDS nor the BDN would ever clearly state that wastes are contained in the substance to which these documents are connected. It is illegal for bunker fuel to contain "chemical wastes";[40] and it is also illegal to transport hazardous waste oils without documentation that explicitly and clearly labels them as wastes.

Enforcement in the realm of bunker fuel trading and consumption is very different from that of chemicals or wastes. The rules that apply relate to product characteristics or any damage that the product may cause. Much of the work of enforcement occurs *ex post facto*: once damage has materialised, authorities must establish who can be held liable to compensate for the damage. To make this possible, MARPOL as well as the related EU and national rules, create a system of sample-taking. Samples are taken when bunker fuel is delivered; and they are linked to the bunker delivery note mentioned before. Samples must be kept on board for 12 months, while the BDN should be available for checks for three years.[41]

If damage occurs, the sample of the fuel being consumed by the ship at the time of the relevant incident can be tested. The testing of samples forms part of investigations into the legal and practical consequences of damage linked to bunker fuel use and handling. As an adjunct to this system, there is a compliance mechanism to ensure that samples are appropriately taken and stored.[42] Sample-taking is also the means to ascertain whether a certain batch of bunker complies with the limits on sulphur oxides ($SO_x$) and nitrogen oxides ($NO_x$) set out in Annex VI of MARPOL.[43] It is also prohibited to introduce wastes into bunker fuel, which connects back to the rules and measures discussed in the preceding subsection.[44] Authorities do not take or check samples each time each ship bunkers at a given port – this would be virtually impossible given the volume of traffic. However, if they choose to conduct checks to ascertain compliance with rules on

International Convention for the Prevention of Pollution from Ships (MARPOL), November 2, 1973, entry into force 17.02.1978, 17 I.L.M. 546. Implemented into the *Wet van 14 december 1983, houdende regelen ter voorkoming van verontreiniging door schepen* (*Wet ter voorkoming van verontreiniging door schepen – Wvvs*) through *Besluit van 11 december 2006, houdende regels ter voorkoming van verontreiniging door schepen* (*Besluit voorkoming verontreiniging door schepen*).

40. Regulation 18(1)(a)(iii) Annex VI, MARPOL.
41. Regulation 18(3-6).
42. See Section 3 Chapter 3 regarding the taking of samples connected to the BDN for more details on how this compliance mechanism functions.
43. Regulation 14 Annex VI covers sulphur oxides and Regulation 13 Annex VI applies to nitrogen oxides (MARPOL).
44. Regulation 18(1)(a)(iii) Annex VI, MARPOL.

bunker fuel content and quality, this will require the use of the samples taken mandatorily under MARPOL. Other samples may be taken in addition to these as well.

Just as is the case for waste oil management, more general criminal law provisions apply in cases of fraud as well as where human health and the environment are endangered or harmed due to concealment of the true properties of substances. ILT and Police are also then empowered to intervene in these situations.[45]

Although not connected to any administrative or criminal law provisions, there are some actors and tools that support oversight within the bunker fuel industry that should be mentioned as they will also feature in the second case we analyse. These include entities that advise manufacturers of chemical substances and bunker fuel traders about product quality and characteristics. They can be external environmental bureaus or surveyors. Alternatively, some companies may have internal environmental departments that serve this function. These entities are connected to the administrative law system insofar as they support the generation of REACH certificates and safety data sheets in accordance with the applicable rules. However, they have no legal obligations under either system. Responsibility for the accuracy of the documents remains with the companies who manufacture, sell, and transport the substances.[46]

## 4.2 Case 1: Waste Collection & Processing

In the first criminal event we are exploring, the focus is on waste collection and processing activities undertaken by Crafty Collectors (referred to in abbreviated form as Crafty). Upon receipt of several *different* wastes – used oils, oil-containing wastes, residues – Crafty mixes them together and then processes them using a 'gravity separation' system. Oil and water have different properties – including different masses – and they are immiscible, which means they can be separated by simply letting gravity do its work. That is the basic mechanism behind gravity separation technology. This technology is perfectly suited for oil-water compounds. However, the wastes that Crafty inputs into the gravity separation system are not *only* simple oil-water compounds, but also other types of waste oils (WOs).[47] In fact, Crafty even mixes simple oil-water compounds together with

45. Arts. 225, 174 and 175 WvS. See also subsection on enforcement in the waste oil management industry for more details on the application of these provisions.

46. Surveyors or environmental bureaus may however be complicit in a situation where fraud or another criminal act takes place, but this has to be assessed based on the facts of the case. Section 3 of Chapter 3 also discusses these actors and their function in the bunker fuel industry.

47. The difference between wastes that are mentioned here is discussed as part of the analysis of the case in the following subsections. 'Waste oil' is a label used to generically refer to wastes that contain oils and/or that result from the use of oils. The hazardousness of these wastes varies.

other WOs and then subjects these *mixtures* to gravity separation, which is contrary to general waste legislation and to Crafty's permit conditions.

When *simple* oil-water compounds undergo gravity separation, the oil that is extracted can be used again.[48] Depending on the nature and characteristics of the oil that was in the input waste, the outcome of the gravity separation process may be a product, which can be used as a blend component. However, Crafty applies gravity separation to wastes that require more complex processing to become suitable blend components. Gravity separation applied to these types of wastes does not treat them sufficiently for them to stop being wastes. Therefore, the outcome of the process is, in fact, a slightly different, re-packaged *waste oil*. In the following sections we explore how this happens. For our analysis, the criminal event is divided into five *Acts* (see Figure 4.2).[49]

During *Act 1 – Collecting Waste Oils*, we look at the part of the process where Crafty Collectors retrieves or receives waste oils. In *Act 2 – Documenting the Collection of Waste Oils*, Crafty modifies the documents that accompany the waste oils upon their arrival, thus committing fraud. *Act 3 – Mixing Waste Oils* and *Act 4 – Processing Waste Oils* concern the procedures to which Crafty subjects the waste oils it has received, including creating mixtures of different waste oils and applying gravity separation. Crafty labels the wastes that emerge from the gravity separation process as products and sells these as blend components. In *Act 5 – Illegally Moving and Receiving Waste Oils Labelled as Products*, Crafty Collectors delivers the wastes without appropriate documentation to third parties, which are not equipped to handle waste oils.

48. For a more detailed discussion of the definition as well as the implications – legal and practical – of waste recovery see Section 2 of Chapter 3 on the waste oil management services industry.
49. The function of 'Acts' in the crime-scripts is discussed in Chapter 2.

**Figure 4.2 Overview of component Acts in Case 1**

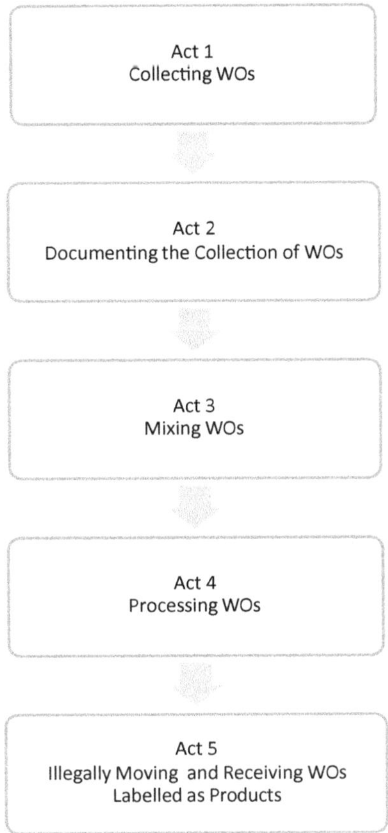


## *Act 1 – Collecting Waste Oils*

### *Reconstructing the Crime Event*

In *Act 1*, Crafty Collectors collects or receives various waste oils and oil-containing wastes,[50] which we can refer to collectively as waste oils,[51] from other waste

50. The legal provisions that apply to 'collection' are not the same as those applying to 'receipt' because the latter are connected to Crafty's permit for processing wastes. See note 56 below for more details.
51. For example, the investigators documented eight deliveries of ship waste from inland and sea-ships, mixes of bilge water and used oils; five deliveries of compounds labelled as oil-water mixture; and six deliveries of ship waste from inland and sea-ships, used oils and bilge water (mixed). (Criminal investigation file "Case 1" from the Andante project. Field Notes 20-21.10.2016; Field Notes 27.10.2016; Field Notes 28.10.2016.)

collectors or directly from entities[52] that need to discard them.[53] Some instances of this collection and receipt are problematic for two reasons: Firstly, Crafty does not have the technology to handle these WOs safely. Secondly, Crafty's permit does not cover these substances. In fact, Crafty Collectors has obtained a permit from the provincial administrative authority of Wasteland to receive simple oil-water compounds. The permit allows Crafty to subject these simple compounds to gravity separation. More complex waste oils that cannot be adequately treated using this method cannot be handled by Crafty.

Crafty's actions constitute a breach of Articles 2.1(i) and 2.3(a) Wabo.[54] Article 2.1(e)(i) or (ii) prohibits the carrying out of regulated activities that lead to damage to the physical environment without a valid permit and Article 2.3(a) prohibits the carrying out of such activities in violation of permit conditions. Waste management generally, and collection specifically, fall under the definition of a regulated activity that can lead to physical environmental damage. By receiving and collecting wastes that are not included in its permit conditions Crafty is acting against the limitations imposed by it, but also performing activities for which it has no permit, hence the violation of both provisions.[55]

*Act 1* can be broken down into scenes using the crime script tool. Each scene includes an activity (in the box) and actors performing the activity (to the right of the box). By receiving and/or collecting wastes it cannot legally and technically handle, Crafty Collectors violates the law. This is the focus of the *Activity* scene (see Figure 4.3). In the *Post-activity* scene this illicit collection is concealed through the manipulation of the accompanying documents, which is discussed in further detail in the analysis of *Act 2*.

*Examining Offending and Enforcement Conditions*

We can further enrich the crime script with information concerning offending conditions, which means we must, firstly, uncover what prerequisites, in terms of physical equipment, human resources and knowledge are necessary to complete the crime commission process. Secondly, we need to consider which agencies and

52. Ship waste can come directly from ships, but most often is first collected by specialised entities located at ports (port reception facilities, see Chapter 3 for more details on these actors). Used oils can also come from ships, e.g., remnants of bunker fuel, but there were also used oils from industrial machinery, including lubricant oils. (Criminal investigation file "Case 1" from the Andante project. Field Notes 20-21.10.2016; Field Notes 27.10.2016; Field Notes 28.10.2016.)
53. Criminal investigation file "Case 1" from the Andante project. Field Notes 20-21.10.2016; Field Notes 27.10.2016; Field Notes 28.10.2016.
54. Art. 18.18 Wm now under Art. 2.3(a) Wabo. See Section 1 above for more details about the rules applicable to the issuing of permits within the waste management industry.
55. Criminal investigation file "Case 1" from the Andante project. Field Notes 20-21.10.2016; Field Notes 27.10.2016; Field Notes 28.10.2016.

agents have the possibility or obligation to monitor and intervene according to the applicable legislation as well as the measures at their disposal.[56]

Regarding prerequisites, we see that between the *Activity* and *Post-activity* scenes the documents certifying the nature and quality of the waste oils are disjoined from the waste oils themselves. In the *Post-activity* scene, it is the manipulation of the documents that provides the means to conceal the illegal activity (i.e., the reception of waste oils contrary to legislation and permit conditions). We will see that the activities central to *Acts 3* to *5* are also partly concealed by this initial manipulation of the documents. The documents are supposed to function as a tool for guardianship; however, here we see them become a facilitating instrument for the perpetration of several offences. Therefore, the manipulation of the documents has two results: first, it reduces the risk of the illegal activities being discovered by functioning as a means of concealment; second, it hampers the system for controlling the crime.

**Figure 4.3 Act 1 - Collecting WOs, activities and actors organised in scenes from Pre-activity to Post-activity**

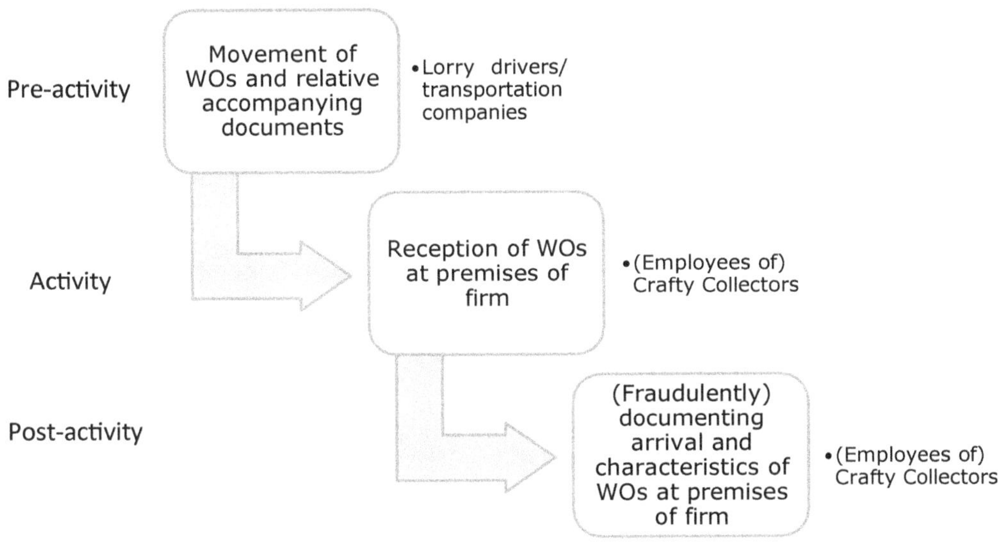


We see another important factor facilitating the crime-commission process if we consider the prerequisite of knowledge. Although the actions that take place during *Act 1* and the tools used to realise them are not particularly complex, understanding the meaning and implications of these actions requires certain

56. For an overview of how the crime-script tool functions and how data has been collected and reduced using this tool, see Chapter 2 and the related Annexes.

knowledge. During the *Pre-activity* scene, where the lorry driver[57] has physical control of the waste oils, his lack of knowledge regarding what types of substances may be received by Crafty Collectors has an enabling function. The lorry driver cannot determine whether he is facilitating an illicit activity, therefore, it is difficult for him to act as a guardian, which again decreases Crafty's risk of getting caught.

Crafty Collectors has had different permits at different moments of its operation.[58] Its most recent permit, however, was issued by the Provincial Authority of the Wasteland Province (hereafter referred to as Wasteland Province) given that Crafty wants to process hazardous and industrial wastes.[59] Therefore, Wasteland Province has the powers and task to ascertain whether Crafty is complying with the limitations of its permit as regards the types of wastes it can receive, collect, and handle.

The remarks made about knowledge as an important factor in empowering potential guardians to frustrate the occurrence of the crime are also relevant when we look at the formal system of guardianship. The lack of expertise of the employees of the Wasteland Province was ascertained by the police in their investigations.[60] When confronting the employee that issued the permit to Crafty, whom we shall call Mr. Smith, the investigators discovered that he did not understand the meaning and implications of the permit conditions himself.[61]

57. In most cases a lorry driver, however, waste oils can be transported using a variety of means: lorries, ships, or trains. Furthermore, the conductors of the transport vehicles can be employees of logistics companies, employees of the entities sending their wastes to Crafty Collectors or employees of Crafty itself that work as part of the transport division. To simplify the narration of events we refer to these actors universally as 'lorry drivers'.
58. It is important to note that the matter of the permit has been somewhat simplified here to facilitate a clearer reconstruction of the events. From a legal perspective, there are clear distinctions between waste collection, waste storage and waste processing/treatment. Firms need permits related to each of these specific activities and different authorities are in charge of monitoring compliance with each permit. So, for example, waste collection falls under the competence of the ILT and the Minister for Infrastructure and Water Management while processing is connected to Wabo and is monitored by Provinces and ODs (see Section 1 above for clarifications on the various authorities). Therefore, a firm may possess both a collector's permit and a Wabo permit and be monitored by both the ILT and the competent OD at the same time. Depending on the subsequent actions of the firm the constellation of competent authorities shifts. If a waste collected transfers wastes to another collector, then the ILT is competent to also look at the transfer, but if the waste is given over to a firm that has a permit for storage or processing, then Provinces and ODs could also be involved in monitoring the movement of the waste. Furthermore, it may even be the case that a firm has a permit for collecting wastes that covers certain waste types and a permit for processing wastes that covers a more restricted set of waste types.
59. Criminal investigation file "Case 1" from the Andante project. Field Notes 20-21.10.2016; Field Notes 27.10.2016; Field Notes 28.10.2016.
60. Criminal investigation file "Case 1" from the Andante project. Field Notes 20-21.10.2016; Field Notes 27.10.2016; Field Notes 28.10.2016.
61. Shared in written communication with one of the investigating officers dated 12.12.2018: There were two departments at the province working on the permit at the time. That is the permit issuing department (Mr. Smith) and the permit enforcing department (the one that physically checks the company for compliance with the permit). These two departments communicate poorly with each other. Therefore, this is now organised differently in *Omgevingsdiensten*

This made it impossible for him to be aware of whether Crafty was compliant with legislation generally and its permit conditions specifically. It may also have influenced other abilities to exercise guardianship, including making decisions about whether to mandate a check of the premises based on looking at the records of waste flows to and from Crafty in the LMA. We see how the ability of the formal guardians is further hindered by the actions of Crafty Collectors in *Act 2*.

*Act 2 – Documenting the Collection of Waste Oils*

*Reconstructing the Crime Event*

Waste legislation requires that all movement and management of hazardous wastes be recorded and accompanied by adequate documentation.[62] The documents accompanying hazardous waste oils contain numerous details regarding their characteristics. This information includes, amongst other things, a series of European and International codes that refer to the quality and nature of the wastes and their hazardousness. In the Netherlands, these are referred to as EURAL codes. All codes play a dual function: first, they facilitate tracking and statistics gathering. Second, they form part of the system of guardianship in the waste sector by limiting the legally viable actions of waste handlers as well as supporting monitoring and inspection.

In *Act 2*, the employees of Crafty Collectors manipulate accompanying documents and the firm's own records to conceal various criminal activities. This is an act of forgery within the meaning of Article 225 WvS, which punishes the falsification of documents that are intended to serve as proof of any fact, with the intent to use them as if they were genuine and unadulterated. The accompanying documents serve this function in that they are designed to certify the characteristics of the wastes which they accompany. The consequent false record keeping also contravenes Article 10.40 Wm, which requires entities receiving wastes to keep a record of, *inter alia*, the nature, characteristics, composition and given name of the wastes.

Crafty Collectors creates entries in its records that do not correspond to reality, beyond those reflecting the manipulated documents discussed above. For example, it registers the receipt of waste oils from firms (in other countries) that did not transfer waste oils to it at all. In these instances, Crafty itself collected the WOs

(Environmental Departments), where all permit issuers and enforcers now sit together and communicate more with each other). [Original: *Er waren toen twee afdelingen bij de provincie bezig met de vergunning. Dat is de vergunningverlening (Mr. Smith) en de vergunning handhavers (degene die het bedrijf fysiek controleren op het naleven van de vergunning). Deze twee afdelingen communiceren slecht met elkaar. Vandaar dat men dit nu anders heeft ingericht naar Omgevingsdiensten, waar alle vergunningverleners en handhavers nu bij elkaar zitten en meer met elkaar communiceren).*]

62. Art. 10.40 Wm creates the obligation to report the movement (receipt) of wastes and Art. 10.41 Wm makes it obligatory to keep accurate records. Additionally Art. 2(3) *Besluit melden bedrijfsafvalstoffen en gevaarlijke afvalstoffen* also applies.

from firms that should not have handled the oils themselves or that should not have passed them on to Crafty because it lacked the technical and legal ability to handle the wastes. Crafty Collectors generates a false paper trail through its records to conceal these illicit activities.

The steps that are taken in respect of accompanying documents are the following: Firstly, original copies, on white paper, are drawn up by the waste collectors and/or the firms who wish to dispose of the waste seen in *Act 1*. Then, two copies of these documents, made on yellow and purple paper,[63] travel with the related waste to the place of destination. The purple document is a carbon copy of the yellow document. When the waste oils that arrive are not covered by Crafty Collectors' permit or are received from entities that should not handle waste oils, Crafty's employees change the EURAL codes by hand to make it appear as if the substances are legally acceptable. The new codes written by the employees often omit the "*" symbol, which indicates the hazardous nature of the substance and, frequently, the numerical sequence is also altered.

It is also often the case that Crafty itself – like many other waste collection firms – explicitly and openly takes on the responsibility of assigning a specific code to the wastes it receives. A collector can do this under the guise of its legal entitlements and its professional expertise. In practice, this means that the initial document is drawn up by Crafty – there is no need to modify the document formulated by the waste generator, Crafty merely draws up a fraudulent document from the start. A waste generator can contact Crafty and notify it that it wishes to dispose of some waste oils and then describe the oils as part of this notification. Crafty then draws up the documents that will later accompany the physical movement of the wastes.[64]

The purple carbon copy, which also bears the modifications made by Crafty's employees, is taken back by the lorry driver who delivered the WOs to keep as part of his records.[65] Crafty keeps the illicit WOs and the yellow copy. It then registers the entry of the wastes in its records using the newly assigned, fraudulent codes.[66] In Figure 4.4, *Act 2* is broken down into scenes.

The records that are referred to in the *Post-activity* scene are forwarded monthly to the *Landelijk Meldpunt Afvalstoffen* (LMA).[67] Inaccuracies in the records that are

63. Further information regarding the characteristics of the waste as well as copies of the transport documents are also sent to Crafty Collectors electronically.

64. This was clarified in a written communication with one of the investigating officers dated 12.12.2018.

65. One of the ways police investigators reconstructed the manipulation of documents, and related illicit waste activities was by looking at documents from the lorry drivers.

66. Criminal investigation file "Case 1" from the Andante project. Field Notes 20-21.10.2016; Field Notes 27.10.2016; Field Notes 28.10.2016.

67. For more information regarding the LMA and its function within the system of waste management, see Section 1 above and Section 2 of Chapter 3.

forwarded to the LMA lead to an inaccurate picture what types of wastes are handled by what firms on the national territory for policy makers, thereby also hindering good policy making.[68]

**Figure 4.4 Act 2 – Documenting the Collection of WOs, activities and actors organised in scenes from Pre-activity to Post-activity**

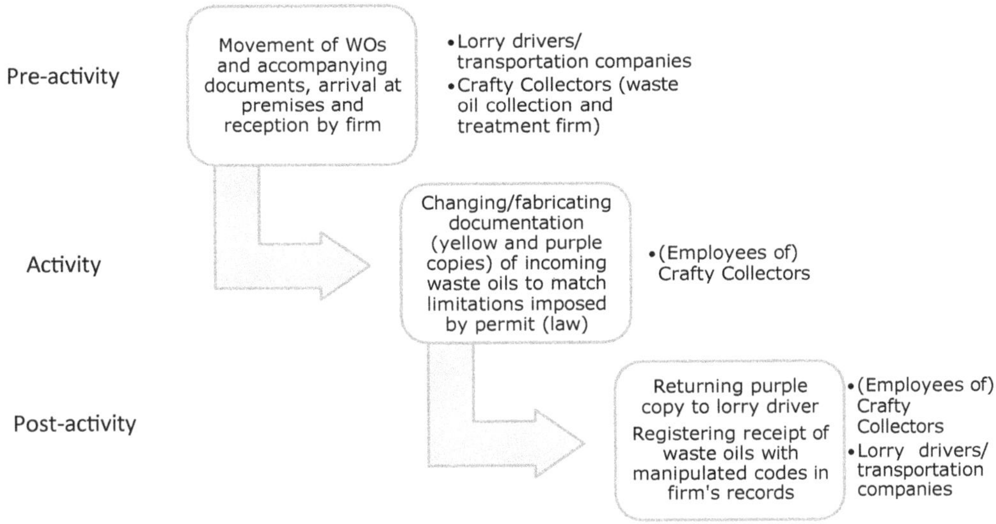


*Examining Offending and Enforcement Conditions*

If we reflect on the prerequisites necessary to complete *Act 2*, two elements stand out. First, the physical requirement of using documents. Second, the requirement of knowledge of types of waste that can be legally handled by the firm. The documents have different roles and functions in each scene. In the *Pre-activity* scene, they facilitate the movement – the illicit collection and receipt – of the WOs. Then, they are the main object of the *Activity* scene as they are fraudulently modified. Finally, they are the basis for false entries in the registration system of the firm in the *Post-activity* scene. It is this last step which supports the concealment of several other illicit activities occurring in the other *Acts*. The knowledge prerequisite guides *how* the documents are manipulated in the *Activity* scene. The documents can be tailored to match the types of waste oils the permit allows Crafty Collectors to handle, mix, and transform into products.

Therefore, as already discussed for *Act 1*, we see that the documents that should function as tools of guardianship are abused and become a means for the perpetration of the crime. This is especially true where guardianship is exercised by merely checking the *records* that are kept by Crafty Collectors remotely as

68. We will return to the point of policymaking and recording of waste movements in Chapter 7.

opposed to verifying the accuracy of the records *vis á vis* the actual practices of the company. When Mr. Smith of the Wasteland Province checks these records, he gets a picture of a compliant waste collection and processing facility. In this way, the manipulation of documents and records examined in the *Activity* and *Post-activity* scenes of *Act 2*, respectively, are of fundamental importance in shielding Crafty Collectors from the risk of discovery by official guardians.

**Figure 4.5 The influence of fraud and lack of knowledge on the formal system of guardianship in Case 1**

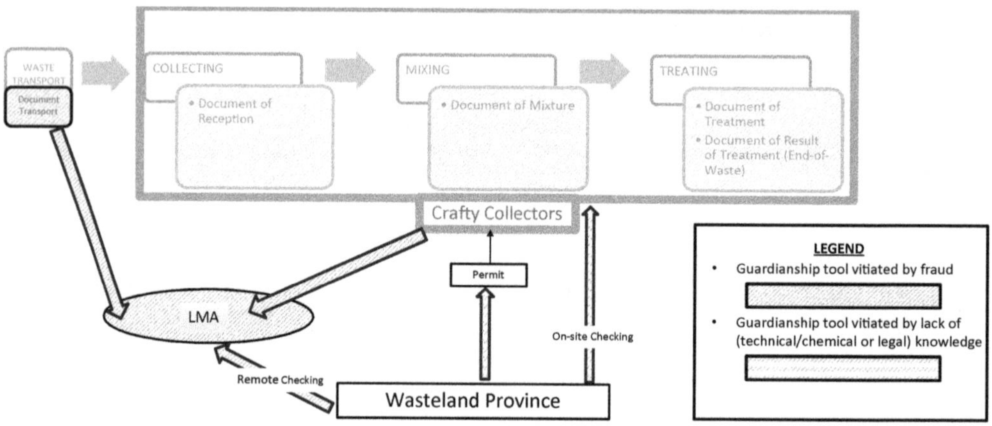


In Figure 4.5, we see how the formal system of guardianship is constructed for activities occurring in Case 1. The focus is on the guardianship functions of the local administrative authority (Wasteland Province), but the observations extend to other agencies that can exercise guardianship by virtue of the powers granted to them by the legal framework (ILT, Police and Customs). The arrows pointing away from Wasteland Province represent powers or measures grounded in the legal framework, which can be used to exercise oversight. The legend indicates two patterns to show how the tools for guardianship may become ineffective. The first pattern indicates those tools for guardianship, which have been vitiated by the fraudulent actions of Crafty Collectors' employees, thus becoming facilitators and means of commission rather than inhibitors to the criminal actions. More specifically, if we examine the fraudulent use of the registration system by Crafty Collectors, which supplies data into the LMA, we see that the records contained in this system are inaccurate. Therefore, the system becomes a shield to the ascertaining the factual reality of the practices being conducted by the firm.

The second pattern indicates those tools for guardianship, which are made less effective by a lack of knowledge on the part of the guardian. This lack of knowledge can be of two kinds: first, lack of information because monitoring and checks are not carried out at all or not carried out in a way that ensure the collection of all necessary information. Second, lack of technical understanding and insight to be able to make an informed and accurate assessment of whether the firm being monitored is complying with the applicable rules and what to look for to make such an assessment.[69] The impact of lack of knowledge on the system of guardianship – specifically, on the issuing of permits and monitoring compliance therewith – is discussed further when looking at the way waste is handled and processed by Crafty Collectors in *Acts 3* and *4*.

*Act 3 – Mixing Waste Oils*

*Reconstructing the Crime Event*

*Act 3* focuses on the initial procedures to which the wastes that reached Crafty Collectors in *Act 1* are subjected. Given the different characteristics of the various waste oils, they should be sorted separately for subsequent individual, specialised treatment.[70] However, Crafty Collectors simply mixes them together, which is less costly.[71] The physical characteristics of the waste oils facilitate the execution of this decision materially and the previous manipulation of documents and records facilitates it juridically. Therefore, manipulation of the transport documents and company records is considered as central to the *Pre-activity* scene.

69. The latter form of lack of knowledge extends to the lorry driver, who we mentioned in Act 1. However, the lorry driver is only a potential guardian given his position within the crime event: he does not have any powers prescribed by law to effect control in the process of waste management.
70. Different wastes are categorised into different Sector-plans depending on their origin and characteristics. The Sector-plans applicable to the wastes that Crafty handles are numbers 53, 56, 58, 59 and 63 In each of these, it is specified that wastes belonging to one stream should not be mixed with wastes belonging to another stream. Mixing of hazardous wastes is also generally prohibited by Art. 10.54a *Wm*, which implements Art. 18 Directive 2008/98/EC. See also *Regeling scheiden en gescheiden houden van gevaarlijke afvalstoffen*, https://wetten.overheid.nl/BWBR0009515/2011-03-05.
71. If Crafty were to follow the instructions relating to each waste stream, it would have to have separate tanks and various types of technology tailored to each waste stream. This is much more expensive than using common tanks and a single technology. See Act 4 for more details on this.

**Figure 4.6** **Act 3 – Mixing waste oils, activities and actors organised in scenes from Pre-activity to Post-activity**

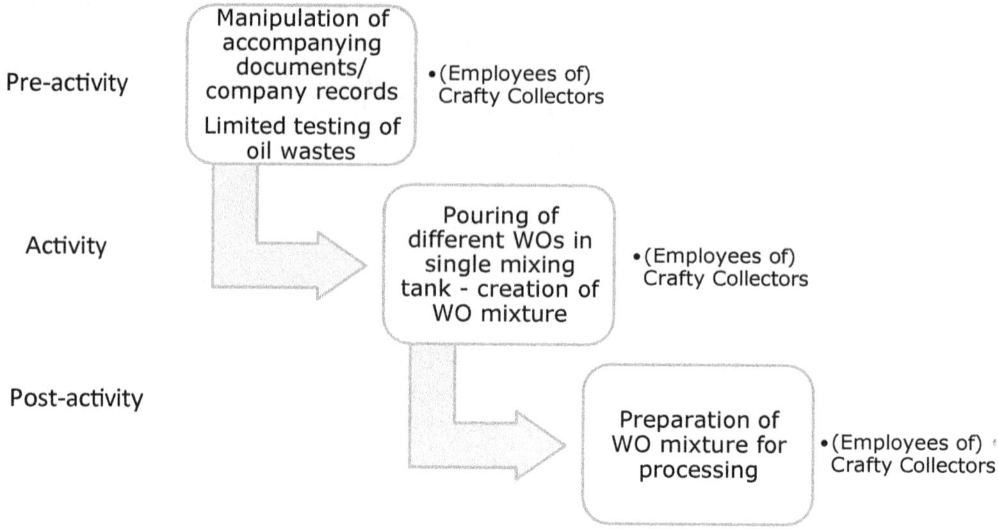


Before mixing the waste oils together, Crafty conducts a series of tests on samples from the different waste oils it has collected and received. These tests are very limited as they only look at five aspects: flashpoint, viscosity, PCB, chlorine, and water content.[72] Through these five parameters it is not possible to determine which pollutants are in the wastes and what the exact composition of these wastes is. This is problematic in two respects: First, there are limitations on which types of wastes can be mixed together. These limitations are based on the presence or absence of certain substances in the wastes.[73] Without testing for these substances, Crafty Collectors cannot determine whether it can legally mix the wastes together. Second, when a firm wishes to regenerate waste oils, and therefore, to transform them into newly usable products, one of the requisites of the treatment process is that it eliminates certain harmful substances.[74] Without testing for these substances, it is not possible to design the treatment process in a way that adequately removes them. Therefore, this lack of testing is also particularly relevant when examining *Act 4*. No further tests are conducted

72. These five aspects are important for the production of bunker fuel. They may also be useful pieces of information to know whether wastes should be mixed together and what treatment possibilities exist. However, for these latter two aims, even more information would actually be required – these parameters are not sufficient. Indeed, these limited parameters cater clearly to the need of generating blend components for bunker fuel. Criminal investigation file "Case 1" from the Andante project. Field Notes 20-21.10.2016; Field Notes 27.10.2016; Field Notes 28.10.2016.
73. Substances cited specifically in the Sector-plans include PCBs, halogens, PAKs, heavy metals, chemicals, preservatives, coolants, etc. see Part I of SP 56, SP 58, SP 59 and SP63.
74. Part I of SP 56, SP 58, SP 59 and SP63.

after the waste oils are mixed together in the *Activity* scene. However, the five parameters are very important if the aim is making a blend component for bunker fuel. Figure 4.6 shows the component scenes of *Act 3.*

*Examining Offending and Enforcement Conditions*

Crafty Collectors must keep records of everything that happens on its premises.[75] Tanks are used to store waste oils, and each tank has a serial number. When anything enters or exits a tank, it is registered as part of the 'tank administration'. The information contained in each tank's administration states where the waste oils that are stored in it (temporarily) came from by using the serial numbers of the tank(s), which previously held the waste oil(s). In our case, the tank administration is not manipulated fraudulently.[76]

Mixing substances together means that their origins are materially hidden: they can no longer be distinguished from each other and any testing of the substances will show the composite result of the mixture, not the individual characteristics of each ingredient that went into the mixture. The tank administration creates the possibility to untangle the components from the mixture on paper. Therefore, it is a tool through which guardianship can be exercised; in other words, it generates an opportunity for social control.

We now break down the offending conditions present in *Act 3.* A distinction should be made between containers and tanks holding waste oils and the waste oils themselves. This distinction is important because the characteristics of the waste oils facilitate the commission of the crime. However, the use of tanks and tank administration facilitates *discovery* and reconstruction of the crime after it has occurred.

Nevertheless, the tank administration can only be a useful means of control if the guardian using it can understand the implications of what he finds in the administration. The guardians should follow the stream of oil through the various storage tanks to the original disposer or collector that we saw in *Act 1.* After that, the guardian must also recognise which entities Crafty Collectors can plausibly receive waste oils from lawfully or which types of waste oils Crafty can legally handle. Such a process requires a lot of time, concentration, as well as technical and legal expertise.

75. This is not a legal requirement, but a practical and technical matter that relates to the management of substances and use of machinery by a firm like Crafty.
76. The investigating officers explained that it is not in the interest of a waste collector to manipulate the tank administration itself because accurately keeping track of the flows of substances through different tanks is important for proper functioning of the internal procedures of the firm. (Interview no. 7 on 20.02.2020 and written communication with one of the investigating officers dated 12.12.2018)

*Act 4 – Processing (Treating) Waste Oils*

*Reconstructing the Crime Event*

In *Act 4* we look at the portion of the criminal events where the WOs are subjected to gravity separation. Before looking at how Crafty Collectors processes the WOs, we need to consider how it *should* do so according to the applicable rules. The Dutch national waste management plan (*Landelijke afvalbeheerplan* – LAP) specifies which actions can be undertaken in respect of different waste streams:[77] it says how wastes can be handled, whether they can be mixed and under what circumstances and what the outcomes may be if certain specific technological procedures are applied to specific streams.[78] The LAP is divided into Sector-plans – each applies to different wastes.

We can understand the logic of the Sector-plans as follows: a certain input (type of waste/waste stream) is matched with a process, more specifically, each Sector-plan lays down some 'minimum requirements' for the processing of that waste. The processing can lead to a certain outcome, which may be the generation of a usable product (see Figure 4.7). In each Sector-plan we find a delineation of the scope, thus the input/waste type it applies to, and then the description of the minimum standards for processes that may be applied to that waste type in order for it to be recovered (i.e., to receive 'end-of-waste' status).[79]

**Figure 4.7 Logic of LAP Sector-plans**

77. For more details about the LAP and its relationship to waste management legislation more generally, see Section 2 of Chapter 3.
78. There are a series of Sector-plans, which cover "oil containing wastes": 55, 56, 58, 59, 60, 61, 62 and 63 (see: Rijkswaterstaat (Ministerie van Infrastructuur en Waterstaat), "Oliehoudend Afval," https://lap3.nl/sectorplannen/oliehoudend/.) The numbering of these Sector-plans has remained consistent through LAP 2 and LAP 3. For major modifications between the *LAP* 2 and *LAP* 3, see: "Lap 2," https://lap3.nl/overig/lap-archief/lap-2-0/.
79. Recovery operations are not one and the same as the process whereby a waste receives end of waste status, because there may be several steps of recovery between the moment a waste begins being treated and when it finally becomes a product. See Chapter 3 for a more detailed discussion of the different waste management procedures more generally.

Sector-plans 53,[80] 56,[81] 58[82] and 59[83] are the ones that are relevant in *Crafty's* case

Following the above logic in view of the facts of the present case, we can formulate the following questions in relation to each of the components shown in Figure 4.7 included in square brackets following each of the questions:

1. What types of waste does Crafty Collectors receive? How can they be classified under the Dutch LAP? Does this classification change once the mixing process takes place in *Act 3?* [**Input: Waste stream/type**]
2. What type of technology is suitable to properly transform the types of WOs handled by Crafty Collectors into usable fuel products for ships? [**Process**]

---

80. Sector-plan 53 is different to other SPs as it only applies to the collection phase in the waste management process. It applies to waste from ships and includes: wastes containing oils and grease from ships; cargo remains; watery wastes and slops; cargo-related wastes; other wastes coming from vessels (p. 1). According to this SP, waste from ships changes categorisation once it is brought on land for treatment. In most cases, the waste will then be treated like other industrial wastes, and other SPs will apply (p. 1, 3) Ministerie van Infrastructuur en Waterstaat, Landelijk Afvalbeheerplan, Sectorplan 56, Afgewerkte olie – Tekst sectorplan (kern van het beleid), 28.11.2017.
81. Sector-plan 56 applies to waste oils, which includes used oil from internal combustion engines and gearboxes, used lubricating oil, used oil for turbines, and used hydraulic oils. These oils can contain harmful substances such as PCBs and halogens. Sector-plan 56 lists the following when demarcating its scope of application: "used oil refers to both mineral and synthetic used lubricating, system or hydraulic oils (such as used oil from combustion engines and gearboxes, as well as lubricating oil, oil for turbines and hydraulic oils), including mixtures of these" (p. 1). Sector-plan 56 further specifies that the covered waste oils can be split up into three sub-categories: a) waste oils containing a PCB concentration above 0,5 mg/kg; b) waste oils that contain a concentration of halogens (chlorine, fluorine, bromine, iodine, and astatine) above 1000 mg/kg; and c) other used oils, which do not contain PCBs and halogens at the concentration specified for sub-categories a and b and that have not been mixed or collected together with other substances. With "other substances" the Sector-plan indicates those which are different in nature and function than the used oils in question (p. 1). Ministerie van Infrastructuur en Waterstaat, Landelijk Afvalbeheerplan, Sectorplan 56, Afgewerkte olie – Tekst sectorplan (kern van het beleid), 28.11.2017.
82. Sector-plan 58 concerns oil/water compounds, oil/water/silt compounds and oil-containing sludges. Sector-plan 58 differentiates between three sub-categories: a) oil/water (o/w) mixes, and oil/water/sediment (o/w/s) mixes; b) o/w and o/w/s mixes coming from ships; and c) other oil-containing sludges. As concerns sub-category b, Sector-plan 58 only applied to the processing stage, while Sector-plan 53 applies to the collection stage of waste management. Ministerie van Infrastructuur en Waterstaat, Landelijk Afvalbeheerplan, Sectorplan 58, *Olie/water mengsels, olie/water/slib mengsels en oliehoudende slibben*- Tekst sectorplan (kern van het beleid), 28.11.2017.
83. Sector-plan 59 governs liquid fuel oils and oil residues. The wastes covered by this Sector-plan can be divided into two sub-categories: a) liquid fuel residues such as, but not limited to, liquid fuel residues that are released when emptying storage tanks or transport equipment (of vehicles or vessels), unless it concerns fuel residues as part of oil-containing washing waters), and batches of fuel that does not meet specifications (off-spec batches); b) unused oils (e.g. lubricating oil), or oil-containing wastes released during the emptying of storage tanks or transport equipment (of vehicles or vessels), unless it concerns waste oil as part of oil-containing washing waters), or batches of oil that does not meet specifications (off-spec batches). Ministerie van Infrastructuur en Waterstaat, Landelijk Afvalbeheerplan, Sectorplan 59, *Vloeibare brandstof- en olierestanten*- Tekst sectorplan (kern van het beleid), 28.11.2017

3. What type of technology does Crafty Collectors have according to its permit? [**Process**]
4. What type of technology does Crafty Collectors *actually* have and use to process the WOs? [**Process**]
5. What is the outcome of Crafty inputting the wastes described in answer to question 1 into the process identified in question 4, a waste or a usable product? [**Outcome**]

**Waste stream/type:** Crafty receives numerous types of waste oils and oil-containing wastes. These vary from lubricating and fuel oils from industrial installations, to wastes originating from ships. Different Sector-plans apply to the different wastes (53, 56, 58 and 59).[84] Nevertheless, these classifications become irrelevant once *Crafty* mixes all the wastes that it collects and receives together in *Act 3*.[85] The mixtures that emerge do not correspond to any of the specific Sector-plans listed above, which makes it very difficult to determine how the wastes should be properly processed, let alone whether a usable product can be generated from their processing.

**Process:** The mixture of wastes created in *Act 3* does not fall under any specific Sector-plan, which means we cannot ascertain the exact standards for processing it by looking at a (53, 56, 58 and 59), we see that in all cases, if the desired outcome is a usable fuel oil for ships, the technology used to process the wastes must go beyond dividing oils from water and sediment fractions, it must include some form of reduction of hazardous substances. Furthermore, given that the oil mixtures are often complex (especially when actions as those discussed in *Act 3* take place) refinement using fractional distillation technology is often necessary as well as a means of removing hazardous substances. Such processes would require several different stages of distillation and cleaning – these have been depicted in Image A of Figure 4.8.

According to its permit, Crafty Collectors owns and uses a unit for liquid fuel oils and oil residues, which removes water and sediment from these substances. Such a unit would be a suitable technology for processing some wastes that fall under Sector-plan 59. However, it does not tackle the presence of contaminants; nor does it support fractional distillation, making it unsuitable for the waste oil mixtures Crafty handles. In *reality*, Crafty has a simple gravity separation unit. This type of

84. More details regarding different waste oils streams, their definition under the Dutch SPs and what that means in terms of recovering the wastes to become usable products (bunker fuel or blend components) can be found in Chapter 3 and the relevant references.
85. Up to and including the moment where the mixing occurs the applicable rules that we need to refer to are Art. 10.54a Wm and the *Regeling scheiden en gescheiden houden van gevaarlijke afvalstoffen*, https://wetten.overheid.nl/BWBR0009515/2011-03-05.

unit can be used for Stage one of processing wastes coming within the scope of SP 58. The unit does not reduce contaminants, but only removes water and sediment from the input substances.[86]

**Figure 4.8 Comparison between processing according to law, Crafty's permit and in reality**

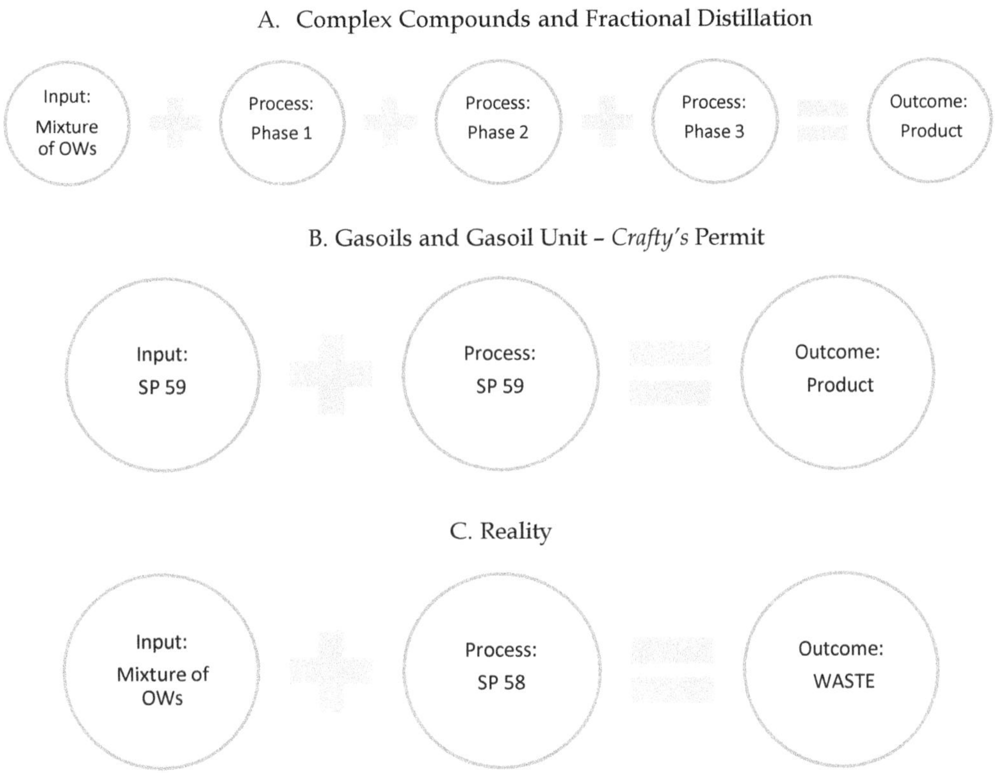


**Outcome:** From the above, we can see that there is a mismatch between the waste types Crafty handles and the process it applies to them. This is illustrated by Figure 4.8, which synthesises the information on waste streams, processes, and outcomes. The mismatch means that the outcome of *Crafty's* actions is a waste not a product. Using the crime-script tool we see all the logistical steps that lead to this outcome (Figure 4.9). In the *Pre-activity* scene, Crafty receives several different types of WOs, does not test for the harmful components in these wastes and then mixes them all together even where they belong to different categories of waste. Furthermore, the steps we looked at in *Act 2* concerning the manipulation of accompanying documents and company records conceal the mismatch between the

86. Criminal investigation file "Case 1" from the Andante project. Field Notes 20-21.10.2016; Field Notes 27.10.2016; Field Notes 28.10.2016.

nature of the waste oils and the technology being used to treat them, therefore, it is also included in this scene. That same manipulation also makes the labelling as a product of the top fraction possible in the *Post-activity* scene.

**Figure 4.9 Act 4 – Processing WOs, activities and actors organised in scenes from Pre-activity to Post-activity**

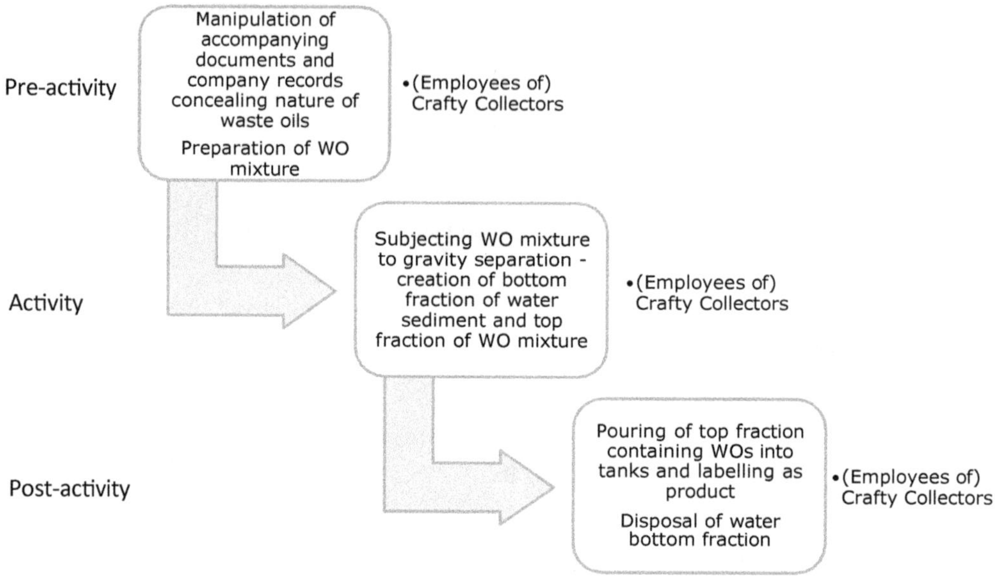


In the *Activity* scene, Crafty applies gravity separation to a mixture of several WOs, this is insufficient to treat them adequately and to generate a product. Therefore, the top fraction from the simple gravity separation process is still a waste. It is this portion of the outcome of the process that is labelled as a blend component in the *Post-activity* scene, ready to be sold on to Terminals and End Users in *Act 5*.

*Examining Offending and Enforcement Conditions*

Much like in the preceding *Act*, the means used in this portion of the criminal event are relatively simple. Crafty need only possess and use a gravity separation unit – one of the simpler forms of technology for treating waste oils. The inadequacy of this unit *vis à vis* the waste streams introduced into it are invisible to the untrained eye. In fact, we see how awareness of the implications of what is happening in this *Act* is not a prerequisite for Crafty to complete the sequence of actions, but it is necessary to sustain both the formal and potential systems of guardianship. The employees of Crafty Collectors need only mechanically operate the machinery used for processing the waste oils. They need not know which wastes may be treated according to which minimum standards in view of the applicable Sector-plans. Once more, the possible lack of awareness of the employees of this reality can be a facilitating factor as it hampers their intervention to stop the crime.

The formal guardians continue to pose a low risk in this *Act*: they could uncover the criminal actions in one of four ways. First, they could check whether the processing is in accordance with the law by looking at the accompanying documents of the incoming WOs and the company records to see whether there is a match between waste streams and technology. However, in this case they would discover no irregularities thanks to the actions that took place in *Act 2*. Second, they could take samples immediately prior to the processing to check what the nature of the wastes is. But this would lead to uncertain answers because of the mixing that happened in *Act 3*, and it would be a very costly procedure, often requiring the involvement of technical experts. As an alternative to carrying out the testing themselves, a third means of discovery would be to look at reports from testing done by Crafty of the WOs. Yet, we saw in *Act* 3 that Crafty only carried out limited testing of parameters that are interesting to look at for the mechanical functioning of ship engines. Finally, the guardians could venture further to look at the tank administration and retrace the original disposers or collectors from which the WOs arrived to find out the actual nature of the waste oils. Only at that point would they discover that there is a mismatch between the waste streams collected, Crafty's permit conditions and the gravity separation unit used to process them.

Once the top fraction has been poured into tanks, it is time for Crafty Collectors to make it sellable. The waste oils that emerge from the gravity separation process can be passed off as blend components given their physical properties. Therefore, by generating false documentation that certifies the wastes as blend components, Crafty gives itself the possibility to profit. If the wastes had been labelled according to their actual nature, Crafty would have to pay another waste treatment facility to process them with the appropriate technology.[87] Instead, by portraying the wastes as products, Crafty has the possibility to be paid. This means Crafty falsifies documents, thereby committing a violation of Article 225 WvS. Crafty has created a marketable product on paper and can proceed to sell it, so it gets in contact with potential buyers, which are of two kinds: a) Traders and Terminals, which use blend components to produce bunker fuel and then sell the bunkers on to ships; b) direct End Users (ships), by passing off the waste oils as ready-to-use bunker fuel. The labelling and sale of the wastes are part of the *Pre-activity* scene (see Figure 4.14).

87. The discrepancy between the characteristics of the WOs and the technology Crafty has means that Crafty would not be able to treat the wastes appropriately, but it may be able to partially transform them by removing silt and water. Yet, for the wastes to become products much more complex processing would have to occur, which would divide the components of the wastes into usable oil fractions and remove harmful substances. (Criminal investigation file "Case 1" from the Andante project. Field Notes 20-21.10.2016; Field Notes 27.10.2016; Field Notes 28.10.2016.)

Nevertheless, we must keep in mind that the formal guardian who would ordinarily have the responsibility to monitor Crafty's operations and uncover these irregularities is the same one who issued a permit which does not match the technology owned by Crafty. According to its permit obtained from Mr. Smith of Wasteland Province, Crafty Collectors owns and is legally allowed to use a unit for regenerating fuel oils and fuel oil residues. Had Mr. Smith or another employee of Wasteland Province carried out the necessary assessment of the characteristics of the technology possessed by Crafty and done so knowing what different types of technology look like and how they function, he would not have legally been able to issue Crafty the permit he did.

From the foregoing we can see that the physical tools and (mechanical) human capabilities necessary for the *Act* to be completed are simple; therefore, relatively little effort is required for this core portion of the crime event to take place. Yet, the overall technical nature of the regulations, as well as the complexity of waste management and bunker fuel production systems, make even such simple elements obscure to guardians and lower risks of detection substantially.

*Act 5 – Illegally Moving and Receiving Waste Oils Labelled as Products*

*Reconstructing the Crime Event*

In the *Activity* scene, Crafty delivers the WOs to Terminals and End Users under the guise of providing them blend components or bunker fuel, it does not attach the necessary documents – that would signal the true nature of the substances as wastes – to the movement itself. Therefore, we are presented here with a breach of Article 10.44 Wm, which requires all movements of hazardous waste to be accurately documented and notified. Moreover, the only entities that can handle waste oil must have a permit to do so, issued on the basis of having the requisite technology to safely treat the waste. Therefore, by delivering the WOs to Terminals and End Users, Crafty Collectors is also violating Article 10.37 Wm, which forbids delivery of wastes to unauthorised entities. It is also important to note that, on some occasions, these movements of waste occur across borders. Movement of hazardous wastes across borders within the EU is governed by Regulation (EC) 1013/2006, which defines movements of hazardous waste without appropriate notification as 'illegal shipments' in Article 2(35). This is criminalised under Dutch law.[88]

The documents that accompany the waste oils from Crafty to the various buyers portray the substances as blend components or bunker fuel. The labels do not correspond to reality. Instead, those documents should identify the substance being transported as WOs, with the related EURAL and international codes, and include all the details regarding their composition. Where such documentation

88. Art. 10.60 Wm.

would be present it would also mean that the Terminals and End Users could not receive the substances delivered by Crafty as they are not waste management facilities.

The main task of Traders using Terminals is to blend together different components at ratios that lead to sellable bunker fuel. They determine the ratios based on a limited set of parameters. The final blend that is sold on without much evidence of the presence of waste oils – all documents state that the bunker fuel has properties that make it suitable for an engine to run on. This blending as well as the burning of fuel oil both by End Users who directly received it from Crafty and those who purchase it from the terminals form the *Post-activity* scene. The scenes are brought together using the crime-script tool in Figure 4.10.[89]

**Figure 4.10** **Act 5 - Illegal Movement and receipt of WOs Labelled as Products, activities and actors organised in scenes from Pre-activity to Post-activity**

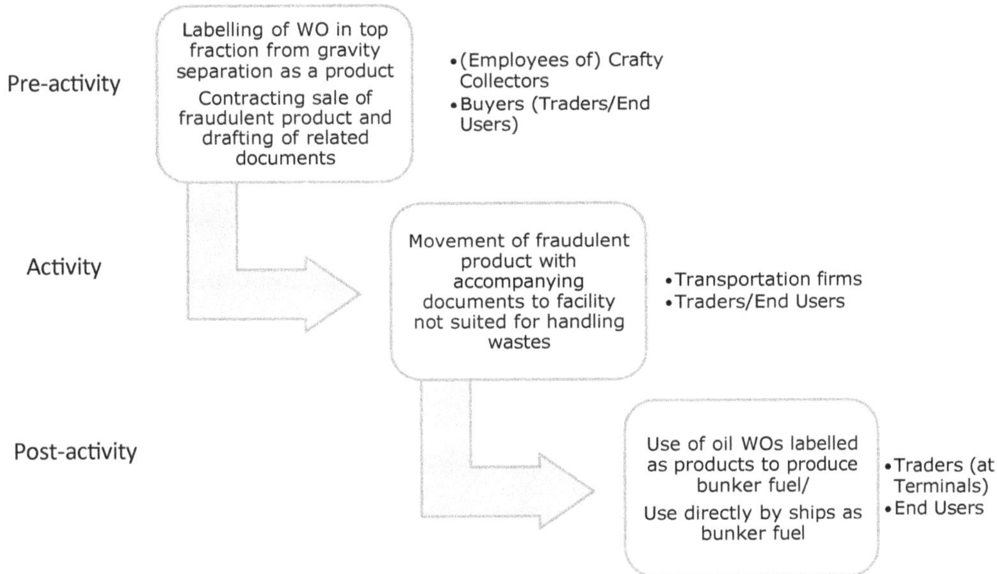


*Examining Offending and Enforcement Conditions*

In reviewing the prerequisites, we can first consider what tools are necessary in the *Pre-activity* scene where the wastes emerging from the gravity separation process are labelled internally – physical labelling of tanks containing the wastes – and externally – in the form of sales to interested parties – as products. Here we see that four elements are important: Firstly, Crafty Collectors operates as a waste collection and treatment facility, it is registered as such in the List of

89. Criminal investigation file "Case 1" from the Andante project. Field Notes 20-21.10.2016; Field Notes 27.10.2016; Field Notes 28.10.2016.

Waste Collectors.[90] Secondly, it has a permit, which allows it to treat *certain* wastes and transform them into usable blend components. Thirdly, Crafty manipulated documents and records in *Act 2*. Finally, Crafty generates false documents certifying the processed wastes as products. In terms of physical equipment, all Crafty needs is paperwork and a simple processing tank.

Then, knowledge returns in this scene as an important prerequisite in the completion of the criminal activity. The interaction with different buyers as well as the creation of the false documents requires that the employees of Crafty Collectors know what is desirable and permissible on the blend component market, as well as within the broader bunker fuel industry. Furthermore, they must also know how to make the labels certifying the 'product' according to the standards used in the industry- these are the safety data sheet and bunker delivery note. It may be the case that the employees making these labels and contracting the sale of the 'product' are not aware of the true nature of the substance they are marketing and selling. This is not a prerequisite for them to carry out this activity.[91] However, where such awareness would be present, they would individually be conscious of the fraudulent nature of their actions. Such awareness could give rise to the possibility for those employees to become guardians and frustrate the process by either refusing to compile fraudulent documentation or reporting the matter to formal guardians.

It is interesting to think about this with the concepts of compartmentalisation and instrumental rationality in mind.[92] The tasks of the employees do not require them to think further than their own discrete contribution to the process, therefore, they also cannot understand the consequences and implications of the broader process they are contributing to. It is from this vantage point of partial ignorance that they are disempowered as potential guardians.

The labelling that occurs in the *Pre-activity* scene is fundamental not only for Crafty to profit by selling its 'products', but because it has far-reaching implications in terms of guardianship during the *Activity* scene. The new label Crafty assigns to the WOs in the *Pre-activity* scene results in a substantial shift in applicable rules. In fact, when comparing the bunker fuel industry to the waste management services industry we can say that the former is virtually not regulated.[93]

---

90. See Section 2 of Chapter 3 for more information on the List of Waste Collectors. The collection of waste oil and ship waste is subject to a permit requirement under 10.48 Wm in conjunction with the *Bia* and a listing on the VIHB list under 10.45 Wm is not sufficient.
91. The notions of compartmentalization and instrumental rationality are discussed again in Section 3 of Chapter 5.
92. Bauman, Zygmunt. Modernity and the Holocaust. Cornell University Press, 2000.
93. See Chapter 3 for more details. Unlike waste management, bunker fuel production, movement and use are not strictly regulated activities. There is no central authority to which movements of blend components must be notified. There are also no formal guardianship structures that monitor the handling of bunker fuels generally. All that is required is the presence of documentation (albeit, it should be accurate) and the compliance with limitations on $SO_x$ and

Therefore, compliance in this *Act* is encouraged only by the threat of checks to the deliveries leaving Crafty's premises. As a waste collection and treatment facility, Crafty answers to and is checked by Wasteland Province, the ILT, Customs and Police.[94] The checks the formal guardians carry out would have to go beyond documentation and include the taking of samples to determine whether the transports are actually of suitable blend components or bunker fuel. Even where such samples are taken, it may not be the case that the results show a clear presence of waste oils, depending on which parameters are checked. Or the results may be incomprehensible to the authority conducting the check depending on their level of expertise.

The only way to ascertain the true nature of the substance being transported would be to trace back the journey undertaken by it through Crafty's tank administration, including an assessment of the technology used to process the wastes, through to the origins of the wastes. Again, the authorities conducting such an analysis would need to have sufficient expertise to see Crafty's misconduct. The manipulations undertaken in *Act 2* could mean that even looking into the tank administration may not lead to discovery of wrongdoing. The checks would need to go further back and trace the origins of the WOs (prior to entering Crafty's premises) and the related original documentation. The resources and expertise required for such checks to occur *and* be systematic are very high. Therefore, the risks of Crafty getting caught are correspondingly very low.

The above described challenges to developing a solid guardianship system are compounded by the actions that take place in the *Post-activity* scene, namely the use of the wastes labelled as fuel by Traders and End Users in their activities. Such use means that the physical evidence of the presence of waste in the deliveries from Crafty Collectors are blended or burned away. Nevertheless, much like Crafty Collectors, Terminals (where Traders have the physical blending take place) and ships have to record the movement of substances in and out of the tanks of their premises, i.e., they also have a tank administration. By reconstructing the tank administration, it is possible to identify where the components that make up the final product Traders sell to End Users or ships burn as fuel come from. Therefore, the substances could be traced back to Crafty Collectors through the tank administration and company registration systems that show when and by whom blend components or bunker fuel are delivered. The tank administration again emerges as a potential tool for exercising social control and guardianship.

---

$NO_x$. The latter obligation was not applicable at the time the case unfolded. The applicable limit for $SO_x$ after 2010 was 1%, before 2010 it was 1,5%. For $NO_x$, a tier system applies, based on engine year of construction.

94. Given the fact that the transports are originating from a waste management facility and sometimes have destinations across EU borders, other authorities empowered to monitor and sanction these activities are the ILT, Customs, and Police.

However, the tank administration tool can feasibly only be used by investigators *ex post facto.* In the course of the activities themselves, it would be highly unlikely that a Trader or End User would take the time to check the ultimate origins of the substance they are purchasing. Here we see how the elements discussed for the *Pre-activity* scene further the completion of the criminal act by inhibiting the exercise of social control by potential guardians. For Traders and End Users, it is more cost-efficient to trust the documentation that accompanies the blend components than conducting tests or tracing back the origins of the product they receive, because the latter courses of action would be costly and delay operations. In the case of Traders, a 'bad batch' of blend components can easily be tempered by mixing it with many other 'good batches', and it may even be advantageous to purchase a lower quality blend component (read: WO) at a competitive price to increase profit when selling the final product on to End Users. For End Users, the costs that would certainly be lost by delaying departure are of much graver concern than the costs of malfunctioning where the bunker is not of adequate quality, as the latter would often be covered by insurance.[95] That said, there have been instances where, upon recognising the hazardous nature of the fraudulent bunker fuel – whether through detection of certain odours or because of sickness of crew members–, ship captains have refused to sail with the bad bunkers and have contacted port authorities.[96] These are, however, rare and extreme cases. Traders and End Users could serve as potential guardians yet there are virtually no incentives for them to do so. What would be required of them – a thorough review of the true nature of the substances they benefit from using – would actually accentuate the pressures already placed upon them because of the economic dynamics of the bunker fuel and shipping industries.

Ultimately, what must be considered when looking at the *Post-activity* scene, which also coincides with the conclusion of the case, is that there are ship engines that are able to burn the wastes that are sold as blend components by Crafty. On some occasions, the quality is so bad that even these engines are not able to process what is fed into them. Yet, the crime can be repeated because there is a viable use for the fraudulently manufactured product. Viable use, however, should not be confused with environmentally sound consumption. The prohibition of processing the various wastes Crafty received in *Act 1* exists because only sophisticated technology can ensure that harmful substances are not released or are only released within legally acceptable standards when those wastes are burned. Neither the ship engines nor the gravity separation unit used by Crafty can accomplish this task.

95. The issue of time and efficiency and how it influences the constellation of incentives and pressures in the bunker fuel and shipping industries is discussed in Chapter 3.

96. This occurred outside of the investigations undertaken concerning Case 1. These examples were shared during a conversation with investigators that took place on 07.04.2016.

*Case 1 Conclusions and Reflections*

A number of features of the criminal event stand out when we take a birds-eye view of the case as a whole. We can consider these features as overall offending and enforcement conditions that are characteristic of this case. The first of these is the role of Crafty Collectors in the wider contexts of WO management and bunker fuel production. Crafty is materially and legally – through its permit, technology, and registration – identifiable as a firm that collects and treats WOs, making it a viable recipient for WOs in the eyes of other collectors, disposers, and guardians. This gives it the means and opportunity to engage in the criminal actions described above. Crafty is also a legitimate supplier of blend components and bunker fuel. The same permit conveys Crafty legitimacy because it combines with the policy and legislation-based idea that waste treatment can lead to manufacturing of products.

A second important feature relates to Crafty's internal functioning. The gravity separation tank, which Crafty uses for processing WOs, is important in two ways: a) it allows for some form of processing to occur, and b) it is a very simple and relatively inexpensive technology. The simplicity of the gravity separation tank lowers the efforts required from Crafty – the financial and human resources necessary to purchase and maintain such a unit are lower compared to the units Crafty would actually need to treat the wastes properly. At the same time, Crafty's rewards are increased because it can perform a service at a lower cost than would normally be required, so its profit margins go up. Yet, the simplicity of the tank is elusive for those looking into Crafty's operations without the necessary expertise. The tank's role within the much more complex and technical processes of WO management and fuel oil production creates obstacles to detection and comprehension of wrongdoing, thus lowering risks for Crafty.

Another feature is the existence and easy manipulation of documents and records that certify the movement of WOs into Crafty's premises. Although the documents are manipulated in *Act 2*, their function is paramount throughout the criminal event. Like in many other forms of organisational crime, a well-designed paper trail can provide an effective shield to the outside world for those who are behaving questionably. Where those who have the task of monitoring and checking an organisation do not have the time or resources to look beyond the paperwork, this tactic is an optimal means of concealment.

The above reflection now brings us to the question of guardianship and the role that the manipulation of documents that takes place in *Act 2* has in impairing formal systems of guardianship during the entirety of the criminal event, thus lowering risks for Crafty.

- In relation to *Act 1*, it is used as a means for exiting the crime scene, by making something that is forbidden – the receipt of WOs not covered by Crafty's permit – seem legitimate.
- In *Act 3*, it supports the mixing of WOs that should not be mixed together.

- In *Act 4,* the processing of complex WOs using gravity separation meant for simple oil-water compounds is legitimised by making the WOs appear to be simple oil-water compounds on paper.
- In *Act 5,* labelling, selling, and moving substances that continue to be WOs as products is possible because, on paper, they appeared to be different input compounds and were, therefore, treated correctly.

The above considerations bring us to the issue of knowledge and expertise, which is relevant both for offending and enforcement conditions. Knowledge and expertise have different dimensions: mechanical, chemical/technical, and legal. If we look at the offending conditions, specifically the manipulation of documents and records in *Act 2,* the actors involved need to know in which way to modify the documents to seem compliant. Therefore, chemical/technical and legal knowledge are necessary. Nevertheless, the resources (read: effort) required on the part of the perpetrator are quite low. It can be argued that, in the entire process, only one person needs to be conscious of the legal and chemical/technical significance of what is happening. That person can even direct the actions of others to implement the act of modifying documents and records in practice. Even supposing that the individual tasked with the latter also has some consciousness of the legal and chemical/technical significance of what he is doing, this is still a relatively small part of the larger process.

If we continue to explore this element of knowledge and expertise in relation to offending conditions, we see that much of the criminal event does not need to be carried out by specialised actors. Therefore, the costs and efforts for Crafty are correspondingly low. When we consider the means of perpetration, only *mechanical* knowledge and capacities are necessary to carry out the acts of moving, mixing and processing the waste oils. Awareness of the chemical/technical and legal significance of the actions that take place during the event only returns during *Act 5* where the final 'product' is sold on. Here, the focus is not so much on understanding what has happened to the WOs and whether it was compliant with the applicable rules. Rather, it is projected outwards towards the blend component market, which has very different criteria for what is acceptable and legal. Legal and chemical/technical expertise regarding adequate handling of WOs are unnecessary for carrying out the requisite tasks at this stage.

We can also look at the element of knowledge and expertise from the perspective of enforcement conditions. We have seen that the agencies tasked with issuing permits and monitoring compliance are local and provincial administrations, the latter when industrial and hazardous wastes are being handled. In this specific case, we have seen that understanding the legal and chemical meaning of certain actions and processes is an important factor in making guardianship successful. In fact, Crafty operated without an adequate permit and in violation of both the permit it *did* have and the generally applicable legislation for quite some time. This was possible also thanks to the lack of technical/chemical and legal expertise of the assigned formal guardian. Just like the employees and lorry drivers as potential guardians, the formal guardians require enough knowledge and expertise to be empowered to intervene against illegal conduct.

If we combine this lack of expertise with a paper-trail that gives apparent legitimacy to Crafty's operations, the system of guardianship is further jeopardised. Legal requirements of documenting and recording movements of waste are at the core of the existing system of guardianship. Being able to manipulate this paperwork so easily is already highly problematic as it lowers Crafty's risk of being detected. However, we have seen that there is also another paper trail, that of the tank administration, that can remove the veil created by the documents. It is the tank administration, combined with understanding the technical/chemical and legal significance of the process that has made it possible for criminal law enforcement agents to uncover the criminal acts we have analysed. We should also keep in mind that their technical/chemical understanding extends beyond the set of procedures observed in this case. What has supported the criminal investigations greatly, is a *contextualised understanding* about the wider processes of waste oil management and bunker fuel production. Knowing the intricacies of these and how they are technically and legally *supposed* to unfold makes it possible to identify signs that the licit path is not being followed. This is a good example of how having expertise can materialise into an important element of successful guardianship.[97]

Nevertheless, the use of tank administration documents to support enforcement is problematic in two respects: first, (potential) offenders may learn to also manipulate this documentation because of the actions of guardians.[98] Second,

97. An additional note here is that, although the accompanying documents and codes are modified, the origin or source of the wastes may not necessarily be altered in the LMA. So, Firm A may deliver waste oils to Crafty, and the records will still state that Firm A handed wastes over to Crafty, regardless of whether it is allowed to or not. The LMA itself does not automatically detect or signal when there is a mismatch between waste origin/type and collection/treatment processes. So, by looking into the data available through in the LMA, a guardian with sufficient knowledge about the reality of Crafty and the technical/chemical reality of waste oil management may be able to identify problematic deliveries remotely without even conducting checks. Indeed, in an interview with the investigating officers it was pointed out that this form of 'accurate record keeping' of illegalities was something that occurred quite frequently, but there was no systematic response (checking, investigating and punishing) of these irregularities. (Interview no. 7 on 20.02.2020)

98. This would be a form of displacement (See: Robert Barr and Ken Pease, "Crime Placement, Displacement, and Deflection," *Crime and Justice* 12 (1990); Ronald V. Clarke and David Weisburd, "Diffusion of Crime Control Benefits: Observations on the Reverse of Displacement" (2006); Derek B. Cornish and Ronald V. Clarke, "Understanding Crime Displacement: An Application of Rational Choice Theory," *Criminology* 25, no. 4 (1987); Shane D. Johnson, Rob T. Guerette, and Kate Bowers, "Crime Displacement: What We Know, What We Don't Know, and What It Means for Crime Reduction," *Journal of Experimental Criminology* 10, no. 4 (2014); Thomas Gabor, "Crime Displacement and Situational Prevention: Toward the Development of Some Principles," *Canadian Journal of Criminology* 32, no. 1 (1990).

reconstructing the illicit management of WOs using this tool is resource-intensive and can occur only *ex post facto*. Using this tool for investigation not only requires expertise, but a lot of time and concentration because each movement of waste needs to be traced back to its origin going through thousands of documents.[99] Even more importantly, the movement, and the possible environmental damage, will have already occurred. Therefore, it is important to think about which specific guardians, both formal and potential, should have the knowledge and expertise to intervene and which means they would require to intervene *preventively*.

Returning to a more general level, we see two elements that also recur in other forms of illegal waste activities in the process of bunker fuel production: the nature of waste oils and ship engines. Waste oils are present throughout the crime event, except for *Act 2*. The physical properties of WOs make them highly viable alternatives to adequate blend components for bunker fuel. If only looked at in terms of viscosity and flash point, they could easily be burned by a ship engine. This remains true throughout the process and can be seen as an important opportunity and source of rewards for Crafty. The other side of this is the existence of ship engines. Although we only see this element appear in the final *Act*, without it none of the other steps could materialise as there would be no purpose in manufacturing bunker fuel as a product. The ship engines are themselves a motor for the criminal process we have uncovered. These elements appear in several forms of illegal waste activities in the process of bunker fuel production.

## 4.3 Case 2: Producing Petrochemicals and Waste Oils

In the second criminal event we are exploring, the focus is on the production of petrochemicals by Pesky Producers (referred to in abbreviated form as Pesky), which operates in the UK. Pesky uses heavy aromatics coming from the Far East as the base component of its products.[100] When the heavy aromatics arrive at its premises, Pesky does not test them but simply begins processing them to make pesticides and fertilisers. Besides generating these products, one of the outcomes of the production process is sometimes a waste that has very similar physical characteristics to bunker fuel blend components.

Pesky discovers the chance to profit from this waste instead of having to pay for its treatment by a specialised firm: selling it as a REACH certified chemical that is used to make bunker fuel. Pesky is informed of this possibility by another petrochemical firm in its field, which also explains to Pesky how to forge the REACH certificate that it needs to pass its waste off as a product. In order to help it place this 'product' on the market, Pesky gets in touch with some blend component Traders. The Traders support the sale of Pesky's product by asking a

99. This was discussed in various conversations with investigating officers that took place on 02.10.2019, 16.10.2017 and 26.09.2017.
100. See note 103 below for an explanation of what heavy aromatics are.

firm specialised in testing blend components to evaluate a sample of it. However, those tests only show certain characteristics of the 'product' and cannot reveal its true nature as a waste.[101]

Once some willing buyers are found, Pesky delivers its wastes labelled as products to them overseas. During one of the deliveries in the Netherlands, the lorry driver becomes suspicious about the substance he is transporting: the smell is too strong, and he is concerned for his safety. The lorry driver contacts the authorities, who test the product and find it does not correspond to the certificate that it is travelling with.

In the following sections we analyse the various steps that form this criminal event. We do so by looking at four *Acts* (see Figure 4.11). *Act 1 – Producing (Fertilisers and Pesticides)* concerns the stage where Pesky uses heavy aromatics to make its products. During *Act 2 – Labelling Waste Oils as By-products* we see how Pesky transforms part of the outcome of its production process from a waste to a product on paper by using opportunities to do so that exist in the waste and chemicals legal frameworks. In *Act 3 – Limited Testing of Waste Oils*, Pesky collaborates with Traders and a testing firm to make its new product more attractive for the market by showing only what is good about it through limited testing. Finally, in *Act 4 – Illegal Movement and Receipt of Waste Oils labelled as REACH Products*, Pesky sells the waste oils and delivers them to Terminals under the guise of the REACH certificate.

101. Specification made by a member of the Andante team: "Testing is done on the specifications that are important to the buyers. Given the definition of waste (subjectively determined by the holder's intention), you can never demonstrate waste by testing. You can only show whether the substance meets the buyer's requirements for it. [author's translation from Dutch]." (Personal communication 05.10.2022).

**Figure 4.11 Overview of component Acts in Case 2**

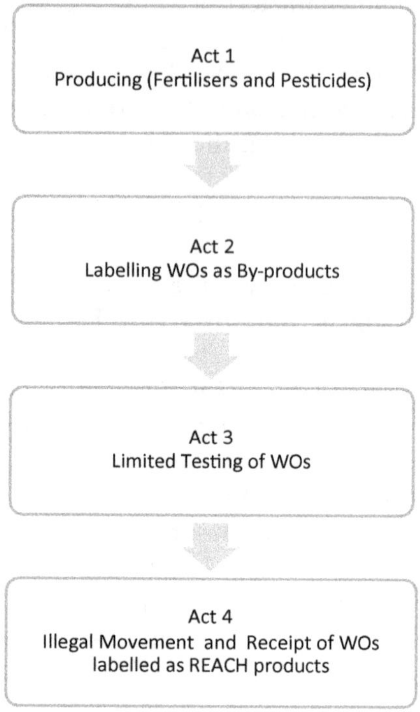


### *Act 1 – Producing (Fertilisers and Pesticides)*

*Reconstructing the Crime Event*

Pesky Producers is a firm in the petrochemical sector that produces fertilizers and pesticides.[102] It does so by refining heavy aromatics originating from the Far East.[103] When the heavy aromatics arrive, they are not thoroughly tested to ascertain what (hazardous) substances they contain and what their exact composition is.[104] The heavy aromatics are modified and cleaned through a series

102. To understand the relationship of this sector to waste oil management and bunker fuel production, see Section 1 of Chapter 3.
103. Heavy aromatics are the residues from the processes of purification and production of (para-xylene) and are used to make solvents in the petrochemical sector. Reza Sadeghbeigi, "Chapter 3 – Fcc Feed Characterization," in *Fluid Catalytic Cracking Handbook (Third Edition)*, ed. Reza Sadeghbeigi (Oxford: Butterworth-Heinemann, 2012); Shell Plc, "Aromatics," https://www.shell.com/business-customers/chemicals/our-products/aromatics.html; Haltermann-Carless, "Heavy Aromatic Solvents – 70 Years of Expertise," https://www.haltermann-carless.com/what-we-do/special-aromatics.
104. Different degrees and forms of testing yield different types of information. The information that is needed to set up the mechanical and chemical procedures to produce fertilisers and pesticides require one type of information whereas generating other petrochemical substances, requires a different technical set up that, in turn, depends on having other information about the input

of steps during which several chemical compounds are mixed in with the original substance.[105] Two types of materials emerge from this process: the first, found in the top fraction of the distillation column, is the desired final product – fertilizers or pesticides. The second, found in the bottom fraction is composed of what is left over, which is a waste. However, the bottom fraction is not *always* present when carrying out the chemical processing: its presence depends on the quality of the heavy aromatics that are being treated.

The lack of testing of the heavy aromatics and the fact that the bottom fraction is not always present are important factors to bear in mind for the classification of the bottom fraction as a waste instead of a by-product. We look at the issue of whether the bottom fraction is a waste or a by-product in *Act 2*. *Act 1* can be broken down into scenes using the crime script tool. Each scene includes an activity (in the box) and actors performing the activity (to the right of the box) (see Figure 4.12).

substance. In the situation described here, Pesky already has enough information about the heavy aromatics it receives to carry out its usual procedures for manufacturing fertilisers and pesticides. As we will see later, Pesky claims to also produce a blend component; however, in order to have done that, Pesky would have had to first test the heavy aromatics to gather *more* information, then it would have had to adjust the technical procedures accordingly to yield a substance with certain chemical and physical characteristics. Pesky cannot be sure to have produced that substance without the necessary prior testing, and it is highly unlikely or even impossible that the procedures that it did apply would actually generate that blend component.

105. Making pesticides and fertilisers requires altering an organic molecule, which may involve using one or several reagents and catalysts and should occur under controlled conditions, such as within a certain temperature range. The exact combination of reagents and catalysts depends on the characteristics of the organic molecules before the procedures are applied, as well as the desired outcome. Changyeol Song et al., "Enhanced Yield of Benzene, Toulene, and Xylene from the Co-Aromatization of Methane and Propane over Gallium Supported on Mesoporous Zsm-5 and Zsm-11," *Fuel* 251 (2019); Victor de O. Rodrigues and Arnaldo C. Faro Júnior, "On Catalyst Activation and Reaction Mechanisms in Propane Aromatization on Ga/Hzsm5 Catalysts," *Applied Catalysis A: General* 435-436 (2012); M. N. Akhtar et al., "Aromatization of Alkanes over Pt Promoted Conventional and Mesoporous Gallosilicates of Mel Zeolite," *Catalysis Today* 179, no. 1 (2012); Wikipedia contributors, "Petrochemical," Wikipedia, The Free Encyclopedia, https://en.wikipedia.org/w/index.php?title=Petrochemical&oldid=1068615653.

**Figure 4.12 Act 1 – Producing (Fertilisers and Pesticides), activities and actors organised in scenes from Pre-activity to Post-activity**

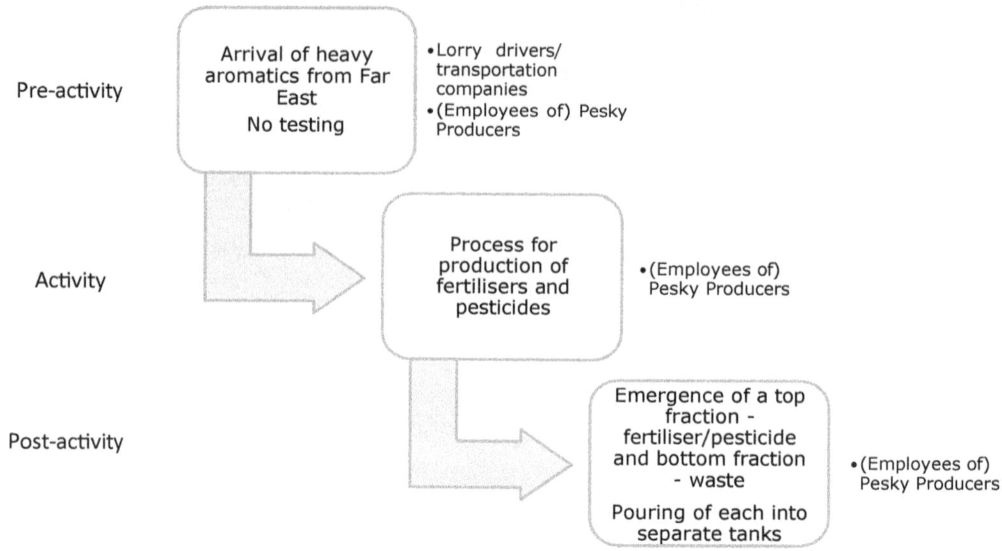


*Examining Offending and Enforcement Conditions*

In terms of physical prerequisites for offending, the actions that take place during this *Act* are the same as those that make up the legal process of manufacturing pesticides and fertilisers. Adequate machinery is required as well as the capacity to use the machinery. The illegal practices only concretely begin in *Act 2*, where Pesky labels the wastes in the bottom fraction as by-products. An interesting element to explore that creates a bridge between the ordinary, legal practice of producing pesticides and fertilisers to the illegal sale of wastes as by-products is knowledge about the nature and possible applications of the bottom fraction that emerges from the production process.

The information gathered from the criminal investigation authorities shows e-mail communication between Pesky Producers and another firm of its sector, Cunning Chemicals, discussing the bottom fraction as an interesting residue that looks a lot like a bunker fuel blend component. In fact, Pesky asks Cunning Chemicals how they deal with the costs of disposing of these residues, and if they have other ways of profitably getting rid of them. The steps that we uncover in *Act 2* follow on from this exchange between Pesky and Cunning Chemicals.

In terms of enforcement conditions, we know that Pesky Producers has obtained a permit for manufacturing fertilisers and pesticides from the competent administrative authority.[106] We must keep in mind that Pesky Producers is not a waste management firm and does not have a permit to treat (hazardous) wastes. Waste management firms must obtain permits from the UK Environment Agency directly and are monitored by this national entity.[107] Pesky's practices at this stage comply with the applicable rules, therefore, the system of guardianship, both formal and potential, would not be able to find grounds to intervene and stop Pesky's activities.

*Act 2 – Labelling Waste Oils as By-Products*

*Reconstructing the Crime Event*

Under EU and Dutch law, it is possible for certain substances to be labelled as by-products instead of wastes. This is the case for residues from certain production processes that are unintended outcomes of those processes. For such substances to be considered by-products, several criteria must be met.[108] We have discussed these in detail in Chapter 3, but it is helpful to have the list laid out here to understand why these rules are violated by Pesky in the course of the present crime event.

(a) further use of the substance or object is certain;
(b) the substance or object can be used directly without any further processing other than normal industrial practice;
(c) the substance or object is produced as an integral part of a production process;
(d) further use is lawful.

106. The following information relates to the application of REACH in the UK prior to Brexit. The current rules are substantially different as EU REACH no longer governs the management of chemicals in the UK. REACH in this paragraph refers to EU REACH prior to Brexit. The Department for Environment, Food and Rural Affairs (Defra) was the lead government department for REACH in the UK. The Chemicals Assessment Unit of the UK Environment Agency was also involved in implementing REACH. The national authority responsible for applying REACH was the Health and Safety Executive (Chemicals Regulation Directorate). This authority was also responsible for the implementation of the EU Regulation on labelling of hazardous and chemical substances (CLP). Companies that work with or manufacture petrochemicals, including companies that manufacture fertilisers classify as 'A1' installations, which must obtain their permit directly from the UK Environment Agency. The Environment Agency is then primarily responsible for enforcement. Part 2, Schedule 1, Regulation 2 (1), The Environmental Permitting Regulations (England and Wales) 2016, No. 1154. See also: UK Environment Agency, "Understanding the Meaning of Regulated Facility," Regulatory Guidance Series, No. RGN 2 (2015).

107. Chapter 5, Part 2, Schedule 1, Regulation 2 (1), The Environmental Permitting Regulations 2016 covers the issuing of permits for firms handling hazardous wastes and waste oils. Permits must be obtained from the UK Environment Agency.

108. Art. 5 Directive 2008/98/EC and Art. 1.1(7) Wm.

Before the application of the criteria, it is important to ascertain whether the substance in question is a production residue. We have already determined that the substance in the bottom fraction may be considered a production residue because it is not intentionally manufactured by Pesky – sometimes the residue is present and sometimes it is not; and Pesky cannot determine this beforehand. We also know that the intended use for the substance is, *in theory*, legal in accordance with (d): it should be used as a blend component for the production of bunker fuel. However, the testing of the substance by criminal investigators showed that its characteristics make it an unsuitable blend component. Therefore, the test under (a) – whether the residue's use is certain – must be answered in the negative. The substance does not have the qualities necessary for it to be used. In fact, the testing carried out by the police showed that for the substance to be used it would have had to go through several other processing steps to remove hazardous substances,[109] which means that (b) and (c) would also have to be answered in the negative. Pesky also does not test the heavy aromatics going into the production process, nor does it test the bottom fraction that is generated by the production process. Its assessment of whether the bottom fraction would be a good blend component is based on observing the physical characteristics of the substance. This lack of testing also makes it impossible for Pesky to be certain of the direct usability of the substance and of whether or not other steps would need to be taken to make it usable.

Despite the above considerations, Pesky Producers labels the waste oil that emerges from the pesticide and fertiliser production process a by-product. Specifically, they give it the name 'Washed Aromatic Residues' (WARs).[110] On its website, Pesky claims to be using an 'aromatic extraction unit' to produce these WARs. This unit is, supposedly, the next step after the pesticide and fertiliser production process, however, this unit is not actually in use. In fact, Pesky by-passes this unit and leaves the wastes in their original state.[111] Furthermore, Pesky attaches a REACH certificate to the fraudulently labelled WARs to add credence to the claim that it is generating a product. After consulting a fellow petrochemical firm, Pesky learns how to generate a false certificate for WARs. Pesky also includes

109. Criminal investigation file "Case 2" from the Andante project. Field Notes 03-04.11.2016; Field Notes 10.11.2016; Field Notes 11.11.2016.

110. According to the REACH registration reviewed by investigating officers, WARs should generally be produced through distillation of substances rich in aromatics, and they are used as diluents for pesticides. (Criminal investigation file "Case 2" from the Andante project. Field Notes 03-04.11.2016; Field Notes 10.11.2016; Field Notes 11.11.2016.)

111. Upon physical inspection, the investigating officers discovered that there was, in fact, such a unit at Pesky's premises. However, there were two paths available between the original pesticide and fertilizer manufacturing technology and the tanks where the wastes would end up. One path went through the aromatic extraction unit, and another was a series of tubes that skipped the unit and went straight into the tanks. The inspection revealed that the aromatic extraction unit was not in use and that the substances would simply flow through this series of tubes, leaving the wastes completely unaltered.

the relevant serial number in the REACH certificate and adds that the substance can be used as a blend component for bunker fuel production.[112]

Pesky did not possess the technology to carry out the procedure that is connected to the substance it claimed to have manufactured by issuing the certificate. The certificate itself was drawn up by using an existing template.

When police authorities took samples of the wastes labelled as WARs, they found that there were hazardous substances such as styrene that should not have been present according to the product description. They also collaborated with the ILT to trace back the serial number given in the REACH certificate and found that it corresponded to a joint-submission in the REACH database of approved chemicals. According to the joint submission, the technology needed to produce the substance to which the serial code was linked is a 'catalytic reformer fractionator'. Inspection of Pesky's premises showed that the firm did not possess any such technology and, therefore, could not have manufactured that product.[113] Therefore, even if Pesky had used the 'aromatic extraction unit' it *does* possess, it would not have been able to make WARs as described in the forged REACH certificate.

In Figure 4.13, *Act 2* is broken down into scenes. The *Activity scene*, where the actual forging of the certificate takes place, is the first criminal act we see in this case. It is in violation of Article 225 WvS, which punishes the generation and use of documents that are supposed to certify certain facts (i.e., the nature and composition of the substance) that do not correspond to those facts. In the *Post-activity* scene, Pesky makes further efforts to market its 'product' successfully by involving bunker fuel traders and a surveying company that publishes results of tested samples. This is the focus of *Act 3*.

112. A REACH certificate indicates the nature and characteristics of a substance. What is more important, however, is that a REACH certificate implies that the substance is one that is legally accepted and marketable and that the procedure used to make that substance has been approved as well. Substance and manufacturing procedure possess an indissoluble link under the REACH framework. See Chapter 3 for more details on REACH.

113. Criminal investigation file "Case 2" from the Andante project. Field Notes 03-04.11.2016; Field Notes 10.11.2016; Field Notes 11.11.2016.

**Figure 4.13** **Act 2 – Labelling WOs as By-products, activities and actors organised in scenes from Pre-activity to Post-activity**

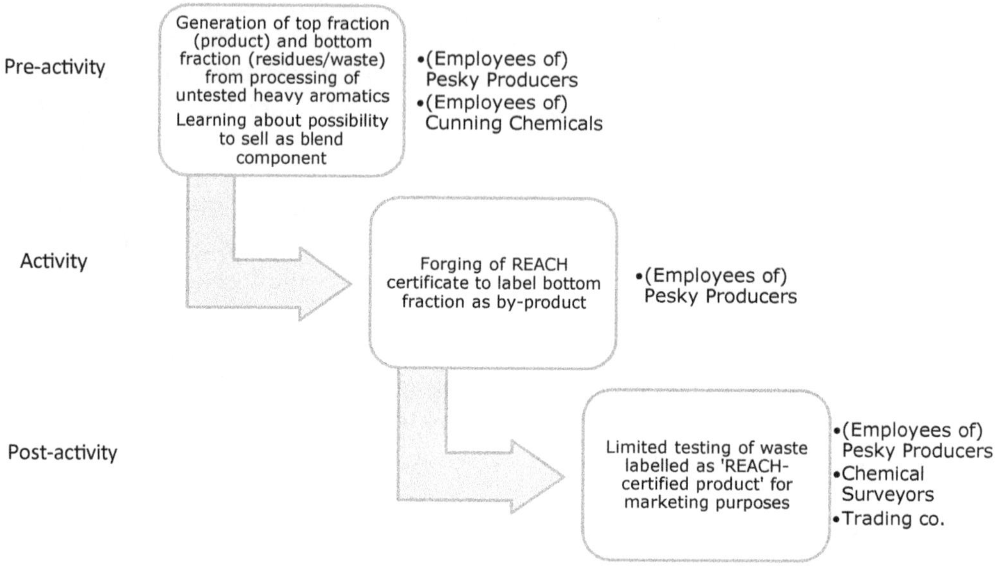


*Examining Offending and Enforcement Conditions*

Like in the case of collecting and processing wastes, a very important prerequisite for the criminal actions to be carried out successfully is the existence and easy manipulation of documents. Pesky is a petrochemical firm, therefore, no red flags are raised when, according to the documents it issues, it manufactures and sells petrochemical products like WARs. The physical instruments Pesky needs for making the certificates to substantiate this are simple and inexpensive.

However, we see that the most important prerequisites come in the form of knowledge. In fact, the first step that Pesky needs to take is recognising that the wastes that emerge from its normal production processes resemble bunker fuel blend components. The second step is knowing how to make these wastes appear to be legitimate blend components. At this stage, we see a particularly interesting aspect of the case: Pesky collaborates with and learns from Cunning Chemicals about how to forge a REACH certificate.[114] This collaboration is noteworthy also

114. This has also been observed in other cases. For example, police investigators stated that they noted several instances where different companies – whether blend component manufacturers (i.e., firms who handle petroleum or petrochemical substances that might be used as blend components) as well as traders communicated on specialised internet forums. They would share experiences about manufacturing legitimate blend components, specifically they would indicate how to make sure the blend component was suitable based on testing a limited set of parameters. (Criminal investigation file "Case 2" from the Andante project. Field Notes 03-04.11.2016; Field Notes 10.11.2016; Field Notes 11.11.2016.)

because it shows that opportunities and *modi operandi* can be learned in this form of crime.

In terms of potential guardians, the employees of Pesky Producers do not need to know the significance of their actions. They are merely required to pour substances into the processing units and then store the products and residues that emerge into tanks. There are, nevertheless, formal guardians who could intervene. They would first need to check the technology Pesky possesses and take samples of the substances leaving its premises to see whether the certificates Pesky issues reflect the reality of the 'products' they sell. The formal guardian at the front line is the administrative authority, which issued, and monitors Pesky's permit for producing petrochemicals. The national authority that oversees REACH registrations also has the possibility to check whether Pesky produces the WARs appropriately. National authorities in the countries to which Pesky delivers its wastes labelled as WARs also have access to the database of registered chemical substances and can verify whether substance and certificate match.[115]

We see that waste management legislation does not play a role at this stage of the criminal event. However, this is only partly true. In fact, the moment wastes are generated by Pesky, several legal obligations arise, which require Pesky to handle the wastes in certain ways; including applying adequate labelling, documentation, and the engagement of specialised waste management firms to collect and treat the wastes.[116] However, because the wastes do not exist on paper, this makes it difficult for any specialised authority to see and stop Pesky's actions.

*Act 3 – Limited Testing of Waste Oils Labelled as By-Products*

*Reconstructing the Crime Event*

During this *Act*, Pesky takes steps that help it to ensure it profits from its illegal actions. Pesky is in the business of selling fertilisers and pesticides, not bunker fuel blend components, therefore, it engages the services of a Trader – Trading co. Traders operate in the bunker fuel market; their task is to support the buying and selling of petroleum products, specifically blend components to make bunker fuel. They serve as intermediaries between the stage of bunker fuel production – which takes place at Terminals – ship owners or charterers, which ultimately consume bunker fuel.[117] Traders ensure that bunker fuel reaches those who need it, therefore, they are expected to work in the interest of End Users.

Nevertheless, the role of Trading co. is not so straightforward in this case. Pesky turns to Trading co. to help it place its new 'product' on the market. To

115. For more details about the EU-wide system of compliance and enforcement in relation to REACH, see Section 1 of this Chapter as well as Chapter 3.
116. Art. 3 Regulation 1013/2006.
117. To understand the role of Traders as well as their relationship to other actors in the bunker fuel and shipping sectors, see Sections 1 and 3 of Chapter 3.

support the sale of the 'product', Trading co. advises Pesky to make use of the services of Chemical Surveyors, a firm whose task is to test samples of petroleum products, including blend components.[118] These tests are trusted within the bunker industry and are used as a means to prove the quality of the products sold in this market. Testing is done by assessing the sample against certain parameters: Trading co. tells Chemical Surveyors which parameters should be applied when testing Pesky's sample. These parameters do not reveal the true nature of Pesky's product is a waste as they only look at aspects such as viscosity, flash-point, and density.[119] The tests do not include a search for hazardous substances such as styrene. The results of the tests are forwarded to Trading co. and to any Trader that is interested in purchasing Pesky's 'product'.[120] Figure 4.14 shows the component scenes of *Act 3*.

118. See Section 1 to understand the role of surveyors within the system of guardianship in the bunker fuel industry.
119. These parameters are interesting for blending substances into bunker fuel. The specifications under the ISO 8217 standards are focused on such parameters because they best reflect what is needed for optimal and efficient functioning of ship engines. For more details regarding the Standard applied to bunker fuel, see Chapter 3. It is important to underline that ISO 8217 is composed of several tables and that actors in the bunker fuel industry display an interest only in *part* of what the ISO Standard requires. Clause 5 Annex B of the Standard could be a useful tool for producers and consumers of bunker fuel to conduct thorough quality checking of the final product, based on diligent review of the production process. However, there is a general tendency to look only at a small selection of testing parameters as mentioned in the text, so that actors can remain willfully blind to what may be in the final blends.
120. Criminal investigation file "Case 2" from the Andante project. Field Notes 03-04.11.2016; Field Notes 10.11.2016; Field Notes 11.11.2016.

**Figure 4.14** **Act 3 – Limited testing of WOs labelled as by-products, activities and actors organised in scenes from Pre-activity to Post-activity**

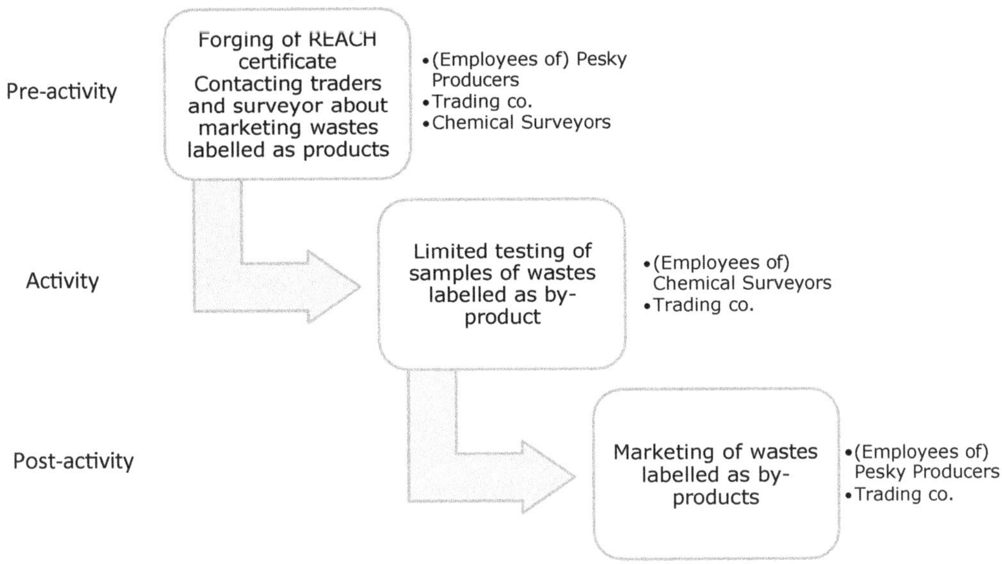


*Examining Offending and Enforcement Conditions*

There are some actors in the bunker fuel industry that exist to support adherence to the standards by independently testing products on the market. Chemical Surveyors is one such actor. Traders like Trading co. are also supposed to support the proper functioning of this market.[121]

As we saw from the reconstruction of *Act 3*, this system of guardianship does not necessarily guarantee that wrongful and questionable practices are discouraged and stopped. On the contrary, we can look at Chemical Surveyors' function in this *Act* as being an important prerequisite that furthers Pesky's offending. Although we cannot speak of complicity in legal terms, the fact that Chemical Surveyors is paid and given instructions by Trading co. – whose interest lies in gathering blend components on behalf of producers to then make bunker fuel to sell on – is a critical element in assessing the functioning of the system of guardianship. Trading co. could be a potential guardian because it could demand

121. The bunker fuel industry is virtually unregulated. What is used to assess whether a product is good (legitimate) or not are international standards, namely ISO 8217. (See Section 3 of Chapter 3 for details regarding the standard applied in the process of bunker fuel production and how this filters into the regulation of blend components. The testing that occurs is functional to compliance with the standard – the qualities of the substance that are relevant are those that make it a suitable blend component.) There are no governmental agencies that enforce these standards, they are agreed upon within the industry. (Enforcement in the realm of bunker fuel production is discussed in Section 1, above. For a more detailed discussion on the structure of the bunker fuel industry see Chapter 3.)

or encourage more thorough testing of substances that end up in its blends. However, the economic incentives in the bunker fuel production process steer Trading co. in the opposite direction: it can profit more by 'ignoring' the true nature of some of the components that enter its blends.[122]

In terms of offending conditions, the physical prerequisites are already part of the tools that the various actors have for their normal functioning. The simplest of these are the means of communication (telephone and e-mail) for the various actors to contact each other and make arrangements for testing and marketing the product. A sample of Pesky's wastes labelled as WARs is also needed, as are the instruments Chemical Surveyors uses for testing the sample.

However, if we move beyond physical prerequisites, we find a fundamental facilitator, which is the relationships between the different actors in the bunker fuel industry. Pesky's 'product' becomes reliable thanks to its connection to Chemical Surveyors through Trading Co. We can see two dimensions to this element: the first is the path of communication and collaboration between the various actors in this industry – which we already observed in *Act 2* between Pesky and Cunning Chemicals – and how it supports the industry's functioning. This network dimension is necessary for the smooth running of (legitimate) day-to-day business, but it also opens up gateways for learning about and conducting questionable and illegal practices.

The second dimension is that of trust. If there were no trust between Trading Co. and Chemical Surveyors and between both these actors and the customers on the bunker fuel market, the actions that we observed in this *Act* could not occur or would not have any facilitating function in the completion of the criminal event. The REACH certificate that is fraudulently generated and applied to the wastes adds another layer of trust and credibility.

Furthermore, knowledge returns in this *Act* as a prerequisite. Trading Co. knows which parameters to have tested so that potential customers will find the 'product' attractive, but it also knows which parameters not to test so that the true nature of the 'product' does not emerge. Pesky also needs to know who to contact to help it market its product: Trading Co. has the expertise to support the actual marketing of the 'product'. Having acquired legitimacy for its wastes to be seen and bought as bunker fuel blend components, Pesky sells and delivers the wastes to Terminals across the border as we see in *Act 4*.

122. For a more detailed discussion of the economic incentives and pressures in the bunker fuel production process, refer to Section 3 of Chapter 3.

### *Act 4 – Illegally Moving and Receiving Waste Oils Labelled as REACH Products*

*Reconstructing the Crime Event*

The final stage of the criminal event unfolds in *Act 4*. Pesky's efforts to generate a marketable product on paper leads to the sale of the wastes labelled as WARs to Terminals where the WARs will be blended with other components to make bunker fuel. The Terminals are located in other EU countries; therefore, the wastes move across borders, which is in violation of Regulation 1013/2006.[123] This provision classifies movements of hazardous wastes across borders without notification and the appropriate documentation as illegal. Furthermore, given that part of the shipment from Pesky travels through the Netherlands, we see a violation of Articles 10.37, 10.55 and 10.60 Wm, which prohibit the disposal of hazardous and industrial wastes by delivery to an unauthorised entity, without the necessary notifications, also across EU borders.[124]

The reconstruction of the criminal event by police investigators also uncovered the correspondence between Pesky and Cunning Chemicals, which we explored in *Acts 1* and 2. On the basis of this correspondence, the police determined that Pesky *knowingly* sold and delivered substances that are harmful to human health and the environment, thereby endangering both; and did so concealing the true hazardous nature of the substances. This is in violation of Article 174 WvS. As with the case on collecting and processing waste oils, once the WOs arrive at the Terminal they are blended with other components, making it difficult to trace back their original composition. Figure 4.15 breaks *Act 4* down into its component scenes.

123. Title 9 Wm.
124. Read with Arts. 10. 1 (3) and (4) and 10.45 Wm.

**Figure 4.15 Act 4 – Illegal Movement and Receipt of WOs labelled as by-products, activities and actors organised in scenes from Pre-activity to Post-activity**

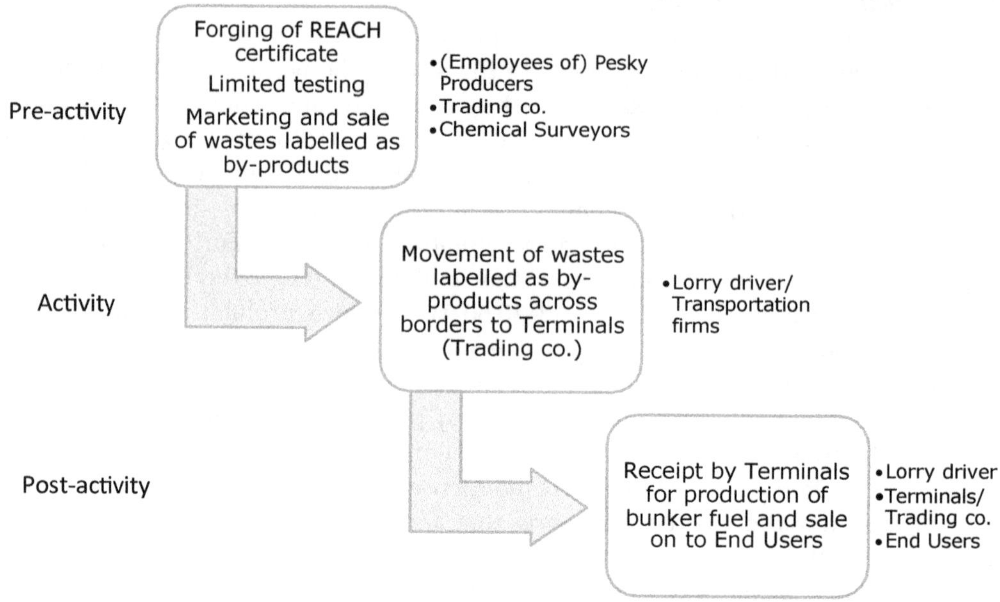


*Examining Offending and Enforcement Conditions*

This case is a prime example of how a potential guardian can frustrate the completion of the criminal act. One of the lorry drivers who was transporting the wastes labelled as by-products to a Terminal became alarmed by the strong smell of the substance in his cargo. He chose to alert the police, who tested the substance and ascertained its true nature. Yet, this is the exception rather than the rule in these types of cases. As discussed for Case 1, effective guardianship usually hinges on having sufficient expertise to see and understand that something has happened in contravention of the rules. In fact, it was the expertise matured by the criminal investigators that helped them see that the presence of styrene in the sample they tested was an indicator that the 'WARs' were actually wastes. What was also important in this case was the collaboration with the ILT and the use of the expertise of those agents in matters of applying REACH rules. The police force does not have access to the database of REACH registered substances and manufacturing processes, nor does it have experience with the enforcement of this body of rules.[125]

Concerning offending conditions, we can once more see the fundamental role that customers in the forms of Traders and ships (End Users) have in making the

125. See Section 1 above on enforcement in the bunker fuel production and waste oil management industries as well as Chapters 6 and 7 for the implications of how access to different databased influences guardianship.

entirety of the criminal event possible. Without the latter there would be no market for Pesky's fraudulent 'WARs'. Furthermore, the *way* Traders operate (through Terminals) to carry out blending conceals the true nature of those 'WARs'. The physical tools used in both the *Activity* and *Post-activity* scenes do not have to be manufactured for the specific purpose of offending, they are part of the normal functioning of each of the actors in their line of business. The knowledge required in these scenes relates only to what are the characteristics that are desirable for bunker fuel; and we saw in *Acts 2* and *3* (here part of the *Pre-activity* scene) that the REACH certificate and the test results provide Trading co. with all the information they need to be satisfied with their purchase of 'WARs' from Pesky.

*Case 2 Conclusions and Reflections*

Several insights can be gleaned by reflecting on our analysis of this second criminal event. Much like in Case 1, we are dealing with a specific type of actor, which has certain characteristics and possibilities. Pesky is a petrochemical production firm and this has two implications. First, (some of) its employees have know-how about petroleum products and their uses along with knowledge of and access to the networks through which these products are traded. Therefore, they are able to recognise the possibility to use waste oils as blend components and can also begin doing this practically. Second, Pesky directly deals with a petroleum product – the base ingredient for its manufacturing processes is petroleum, specifically heavy aromatics. Therefore, there is the potential that its residues *could* be a blend component for bunker fuel given that bunker fuel is composed of several types of residues from different petroleum treatment and refining processes.[126] Pesky has a permit and a history of legal commerce in petroleum-based products, which also facilitates credible access to the bunker fuel market.

Looking at the internal functioning of Pesky, we see that it does not use any additional technology to generate the wastes it labels and sells as WARs. In fact, no extra expenses are incurred – Pesky can simply proceed with its usual business of manufacturing fertilisers and pesticides. This 'usual' process sometimes generates wastes, which, instead of having a negative value as they would if handled in accordance with the law, have a positive value because they are redefined as products.[127] Materially, this requires very little efforts: the profit derives from creative labelling. We can connect this to a feature that is true of corporations in any sector: the constant pursuit of profit. Having this ultimate goal, a firm presented with a potential loss – costs for waste treatment – can be innovative to find a gain instead. It is not just companies that view their reality in this way. The

126. See Chapter 3 for more details on the composition of bunker fuel as well as the process of it manufacturing.

127. See Chapter 3 for a discussion on the economic characteristics of the waste management industry, where the negative value of waste is also discussed as a facilitating factor for criminogenesis within that industry.

following is a quote from Dutch policy guidance concerning the determination of whether a residue is a waste or a by-product:

> *The use of production residues becomes less attractive economically due to the burdens and costs that the waste status entails. Certainly, in the light of the policy objective to stimulate the use of production residues, it is undesirable that this use should be hindered by the waste legislation regime without there being any reason stemming from the goals pursued by waste legislation: the management of waste-related risks (such as illegal or uncontrolled landfill, discharge, or incineration and illegal or uncontrolled use of wastes) in order to protect the environment and human health. A qualification as waste material is then an unnecessary obstacle.*[128]

This quote gives us a taste of the culture within the waste management industry – the social space where both economic and state actors cross. Labelling something as a waste is seen as creating burdens, costs, and obstacles. And, although the goals that guide the formulation and application of waste legislation are recognised, this quote hints to a restrictive application of the legislation being supported in favour of profitable uses of residues. Combining this perspective with that of the bunker fuel production industry where bunker fuel is synonymous with 'mixture of useful residues' leads to a potentially dangerous symbiosis between these two industries.[129]

This interaction between two industries then brings us to reiterate the importance of the differences that exist in the systems of guardianship of the two industries as a facilitating factor. The 'burdensome' system of waste management, including agencies with strong mandates to monitor and enforce is absent already from *Act 2* of Case 2, when the by-product label and REACH certificate redefine the waste oils Pesky generates. The actors Pesky enters into contact with in

128. [Author's translation]. Regeling van de Staatssecretaris van Infrastructuur en Milieu, van 18 maart 2015, nr. IENM/BSK-2015/52417, houdende vaststelling van criteria ter nadere invulling van de voorwaarden als bedoeld in artikel 5 van de kaderrichtlijn afvalstoffen (Regeling criteria bijproducten kaderrichtlijn afvalstoffen), Staatscourant 2015, 7458. [Original: Met de lasten en kosten die de afvalstatus met zich meebrengt wordt het gebruik van productieresiduen economisch minder aantrekkelijk. Zeker in het licht van het beleidsdoel om het gebruik van productieresiduen te stimuleren, is het onwenselijk dat dit gebruik wordt belast met het regime van de afvalwetgeving zonder dat er een reden is vanuit het doel van de afvalwetgeving: de beheersing van afval-gerelateerde risico's voor milieu en menselijke gezondheid (zoals illegale of ongecontroleerde stort, lozing of verbranding en illegale of ongecontroleerde toepassing). Een kwalificatie als afvalstof is dan een onnodige belemmering.] The quote is connected to the implementation into Dutch waste policy of the CJEU ruling in the *Shell* case, which will be discussed in Section 3 of Chapter 5.

129. This observation is made 'externally', i.e., we cannot know that the policymakers formulating this guidance intended for it to be used as an excuse for questionable, harmful, or even criminal conduct within the waste management and bunker fuel production industries. Nor do we know if they were aware of such harmful potential. The aim is rather to show what perspectives and language are accessible to actors in the waste management industry, deriving from the guidance that policy makers provide. This point is addressed further in Chapter 5.

the world of bunker fuel support its economic success by helping it design the certificate it needs to make its product credible and desirable (Cunning Chemicals) and to contact other agents who will facilitate the sale of the 'WARs' (Trading Co. and Chemical Surveyors). There is no clear and strong system of guardianship, in fact; and what little monitoring does occur is on the basis of standards and goals that differ greatly from the imperatives that underlie waste management policies. The protection of the environment and human health are not parameters in the testing practices requested by Trading Co. and carried out by Chemical Surveyors. Their only interest lies in having products that are physically suitable for the fuelling of the engines of End Users.

Yet, the case of Pesky also shows us something important about the system of guardianship, something that can support strong and effective guardianship, in fact. Police investigators collaborated with administrative agents from the ILT to reconstruct the criminal event. While the fact that REACH databases are generally beyond the purview and expertise of police investigators could present an obstacle to effective guardianship, in this case this potential challenge was overcome with positive results. The existence of the REACH framework can be seen, on the one hand, as creating new possibilities for abuse or as an extra tool in the belt of companies that wish to fraudulently sell waste oils as blend component. On the other hand, this tool is neutralised in the face of well-informed and functioning collaborative guardianship structures.

*Overall Reflection and Conclusions*

In this Chapter, we learned about the situational conditions in which two cases of illegal waste activities in the process of producing bunker fuel occur. Using the conceptual and analytical tools of SCP and CSA, we were able to deconstruct the sequence of steps that make up the respective criminal events. We identified the tools used by the actors in each scene and which opportunities for crime the actors were faced with. In order to further reflect on our findings from the two cases, we can refer to the following theoretical statement:

***Crime will occur when: efforts & risks are low and rewards, provocations & excuses are high.***

This assertion can be expanded on by looking at each of the five elements separately to draw conclusions regarding what we may observe in the data.[130]

1. **Efforts** are lowered when: the target is easily accessible and manageable; the tools or means are accessible or affordable; the target is 'desirable' compared with other 'candidates'.

130. See Chapters 1 and 2 for more details about the theoretical concepts used here.

We saw in both cases that the characteristics of the targets – bunker fuel, waste oils, blend components – are fundamental conditions for the occurrence of the crimes. The physical properties of waste oils and blend components are very similar. The properties of bunker fuel – black and treacly – are such that it is very easy to mix in waste oils, which then become indistinguishable and undetectable within this mixture (this is also relevant for reducing risks). In fact, bunker fuel is, by definition, a complex and loosely determined mixture of several substances that can vary from one instance of production to another. The base components of bunker fuel are residual oils of various types: the residues that are left over from refining processes are more often than not processed into bunker fuel, which makes it easy to introduce other forms of residues, which are actually wastes.[131]

We can consider the (fraudulent) documentation that travels with the waste oils as a tool or means to complete the crimes. The documents and the instruments to modify or fraudulently generate them are easily accessible. The efforts that Crafty and Pesky need to make in respect of the documents are very low – simply using pens to change codes and/or using templates to manufacture product certifications. If we also consider the employees of the companies involved as *means* of perpetration, we can reaffirm that the skills and expertise required of them are merely mechanical. Neither firm must invest in specialised or highly qualified staff in order to carry out the criminal activities.

As regards the attractiveness of waste oils as opposed to other substances, we can see that the cost-cutting effects of using waste oils are very appealing. The alternatives are, on the one hand, treating them adequately and, therefore, incurring large costs. On the other hand, the alternative to using waste oils compared to other blend components also reduces costs for the production of bunker fuel. Therefore, from the perspective of both industries, use of inadequately treated waste oils instead of appropriately produced blend components is the more economically attractive option. Considering all the above, we can say that the **efforts necessary for perpetration are quite low.**

2. **Risks** are lowered when: guardians are not present; guardians cannot act or check; guardians do not act or check; crime is easily concealed or invisible; responsibility for crime is difficult to attribute; (internal) reporting is impossible or disadvantageous or non-advantageous; monitoring is difficult or not possible or undesirable.

The issue of guardianship was discussed extensively in both cases. We saw that the systems of guardianship are easily undermined. Two factors are important in this respect: the use of deception and the taking advantage of (a lack of) expertise. We see deception as the cornerstone of both of our cases: buyers and

131. See Chapter 3 for more details about bunker fuel and its production.

(formal) guardians are deceived into seeing waste oils as blend components through a variety of processes. The main means of deception is the manipulation of documents, which provides concealment and reduces the risk of detection.

We can also characterize the manipulation of documents as an abuse of trust. In fact, in the chemicals, bunker fuel, and waste management industries, documents are the agreed upon and trusted means of informing economic exchanges. That trust replaces the need to test each batch of substances that is the object of these exchanges: It promotes efficiency and stability and leaves space for deception. It has been argued that reliance on documents as a means of creating and maintaining trust within an industry supports the 'right to be ignorant' of the actors involved.[132] In such a system, it would seem burdensome and inefficient to take a deeper interest and ask more questions when purchasing a substance with a label that states it is a blend component from a company that has a license to treat wastes or produce petrochemicals. The custom and even the legal obligation to use documents relieves the actors in this setting of such obligations.

Trust also characterizes the relationship between the firms and their guardians. One of the main instruments for formal guardians to exercise oversight is by checking documents and records. Even where one would take interest in looking beyond the documentation, the second factor affecting, and inhibiting, guardianship is expertise. The concealment function of documents is compounded by the concealment effect that the complex and technical nature of the processes of waste oil management and bunker fuel production have. Both formal and potential guardians are inhibited in their ability to intervene due to their lack of expertise. We can speak of an asymmetry here: the tools necessary for the perpetration of the crime are relatively simple, while the legal and technological context in which they occur is very complex. This asymmetry contributes to lowering risks by making the crimes easy but invisible.

We should also consider the difficulties in tracing the origins of the component elements of bunker fuel as an important condition for lowering risks of detection. Once the waste oils are blended into bunker fuel, the efforts, and resources – both material and intellectual – required to identify at which stage wastes may have entered the production process are very high. The use of tank administration is currently the only way to do this, and it cannot be guaranteed in all cases that this will lead to a satisfactory and legally relevant determination of who is responsible for waste oils entering the process.

Regarding (internal) reporting and monitoring mechanisms, we have seen that potential guardianship is hindered by lack of expertise, much like formal guardianship. Yet, the waste oils management industry includes several state authorities to which reports could be made and that have strong legal mandates

132. Andrew Szasz, "Corporations, Organized Crime, and the Disposal of Hazardous Waste: An Examination of the Making of a Criminogenic Regulatory Structure," *Criminology* 24, no. 1 (1986). This notion is discussed in more detail in Chapter 5.

to intervene and monitor activities occurring in their sector. This is different for the bunker fuel production industry where there is little to no formal guardianship and the surveyors, who support oversight within this branch, have no authority to turn to when they witness wrongdoing. In theory, potential guardians could notify the formal guardians that operate in the waste sector, but this is problematic for two reasons. First, it is not automatically the case that knowing something is not correct in respect of a blend component means that it is a waste or that the person discovering this inaccuracy is aware of the fact that it could indicate that the blend component is a waste. Second, because these are two legally separate industries, potential guardians from the bunker fuel industry may be unfamiliar with the formal system of guardianship that is responsible for monitoring waste management. In general, the fact that these crimes are economically advantageous for almost all parties involved means that there are few incentives for reporting. All the above considerations mean that the **risks involved in this type of crime are quite low.**

3. **Rewards** are increased when: the target is accessible; manipulation is not costly and is worthwhile; target is not identifiable, traceable; there is a 'market' or use for the target; entering and being an actor in the system is not relatively disadvantageous or difficult; profitably functioning as an actor in the system is not difficult; one can easily benefit from actions – no loss of 'investment' (no fines or monitoring or guardianship).

In this respect, we can reiterate what was said in the discussion of 'efforts' above. The waste oils are easily accessible in that they form part of the ordinary operations of both Pesky and Crafty. Neither firm has to make extra efforts to obtain the waste oils; and their positions in the market as well as their relationship with other actors make it quite simple to trade their 'products'. The way they manipulate the waste oils are not excessively costly; on the contrary, in both cases we see that no or very simple technology is used to process the waste oils. The 'transformation' into products occurs thanks to paperwork, which is also inexpensive to generate.

Concerning the availability of a 'market' for the objects of the crime, we see that bunker fuel and the waste oils that end up in it have to be used in order for the crimes to take place. If there were no ship engines with the ability to burn these substances, there would be no opportunity to sell them profitably. We can extend this further to reflect on the fact that there is a *need* for fuel for these ships. Our global, consumer economy depends on the possibility to move large quantities of goods across seas and oceans and to do so at a reasonable price. The need for ships to run means our global economy also generates a need for appealingly priced bunker fuels.[133]

Entering the market is also not difficult in both Crafty and Pesky's cases. Each firm has some form of technology and permit to operate in industries adjacent to or overlapping with that of bunker fuel production. Entering their waste oils into the bunker fuel production process does not require them to make particular efforts. In Pesky's case, we even see how other actors in the system (Cunning Chemicals, Trading co., and Chemical Surveyors) actually facilitate its successful entry into the process. The network in the bunker fuel production industry is not impenetrable. In fact, it is characterised as a highly mobile market with new actors constantly entering and exiting it.[134] If we combine the foregoing with the low risks of detection and, therefore, punishment (loss of investment) discussed above, we can see that the **rewards for this type of crime are high.**

4. **Provocations** are increased when: there are pressures to earn (market); peer pressure; there are no clear signals that wrongdoing is punished/has consequences.

The information we analysed in this chapter concerning the two cases does not tell us much about the pressures that characterise the waste oils management services and bunker fuel production markets. We already discussed these in Chapter 3, where we saw that there is a lot of pressure within the waste management industry to cut costs given that the rules for treating hazardous waste oils are very stringent and require the application of very expensive technology. In the bunker fuel industry, pressure is particularly high at the stage where blend components are generated and sold. On a general level, we can say the Crafty and Pesky's practices give them competitive advantages. They do not incur the full costs of proper waste treatment and they can profit from their wastes by selling them as products.

Concerning the clear signals that wrongdoing is punished, what we discussed concerning risks and the operation of the system of guardianship shows that the reaction to questionable behaviour is rather weak. In fact, firms within the same sector even encourage each other to pursue these courses of action as Pesky's case clearly shows. The imperative of the bunker fuel production industry is to generate substances that will make ship engines run. There is little concern regarding how that happens. Even the waste management industry creates many possibilities for redefining waste. The discourse on reducing waste through recycling and recovery portrays the transformation of wastes as an admirable aim, which should

133. For a more detailed discussion on the dynamics and relationship between the bunker fuel and shipping sectors and how this molds the economic incentives and pressures in the bunker fuel production process, see Chapter 3.
134. See Section 3 of Chapter 3 for a more detailed exploration of the bunker fuel and blend component markets.

be encouraged and rewarded. In our discussion in Chapter 3 of the broader contextual conditions in which these crimes take place, this is discussed in more detail. Chapter 5 will build on this further as well. On the basis of these preliminary considerations, we can say that **provocations are relatively high**.

5. **Excuses** are increased when: there are no or only weak or ambiguous rules; there are ambiguous or no instructions; there is a lack of awareness of consequences; there is no support to comply.

The possibility of redefining waste as a product is an important factor when discussing excuses. This possibility is created and maintained by the legal framework. Although waste management legislation is quite stringent, there is plenty of room for ambiguity, especially due to the possibility of 'escaping' this legal framework through the transformation of wastes into products. We then see an important asymmetry playing a role here: that between the guardianship structures and legislation of the waste management industry and the bunker fuel production industry. Through the mere relabelling of a substance, rules and limitations melt away leaving space to the creative practices of those looking to make cheap fuel. In the world of bunker fuel production, there is very little in the way of instructions on how to handle which substance to ensure human and environmental protection. Rather, emphasis is placed on a limited set of physical characteristics that are related to the running of ship engines.

Awareness of consequences by the actors involved is challenging to assess given the data at our disposal. Yet, if we look at more generally applicable findings concerning environmental crime, we see that the remoteness of the harm in time and space means it is easy to do away with concerns about the impact of one's actions. Pollution is mostly not visible when it materialises; and the causal relationship between the actions we analysed in the two cases and the harms to human health and the environment are difficult to establish legally, but especially hard to grasp intellectually. The general societal consciousness of these problems is low and lacks thrust.[135] Although the actors involved may plausibly be aware, on some level, of the consequences of their actions, they operate in a general context of apathy and lack of resolve towards these issues, one where environmental damage is an undesired but supposedly inescapable externality of doing business; and doing business is the means of survival. This will be discussed in further detail in the coming chapters, but we can say that **excuses are relatively high**.

---

135. See, for example: Michael J. Lynch, "Green Criminology and Environmental Crime: Criminology That Matters in the Age of Global Ecological Collapse," *Journal of White Collar and Corporate Crime* 1, no. 1 (2020); Rob White, "Environmental Issues and the Criminological Imagination," *Theoretical Criminology* 7, no. 4 (2003); *Kriminologijo* 65, no. 4 (2014); Nigel South and Avi Brisman, *Routledge International Handbook of Green Criminology* (Routledge, 2013).

***

The foregoing reflections help us to develop a more detailed picture of how the waste oil management services and bunker fuel production industries function separately and together. We have seen how the mechanism comprised of motivation and opportunity concretely operates on a micro level to produce criminal actions and harmful activities. We have now also analysed the features – efforts, risks, rewards, provocations, and excuses – of the situation, which lead to the generation and interaction of the motivations and opportunities in these cases. However, these features are themselves the product of broader dynamics at play within and across the two industries, and in the wider societal context in which the industries exist. If we wish to explain these crimes better – also in order to develop appropriate interventions – then we must explore the broader industrial and societal contexts that give rise to the features we have identified and analysed here. We will do this in the next Chapter.

# 5 A Crime-Facilitative System at the Intersection of Two Symbiotic Industries

A series of questions remain unanswered after our analysis in Chapter 4. We unravelled two criminal events to expose some of the risks, rewards, efforts, excuses, and provocations that influenced the choices and behaviours of the perpetrators. Yet we are still left with several threads that lead beyond the individual circumstances of the cases towards wider, contextual forces. For example, we saw that, in many instances, the weakness or non-existence of systems of guardianship greatly diminished the risks faced by the perpetrators. This circumstance may be attributed, at least in part, to the specific incompetence or failings of a few individuals tasked with monitoring and enforcement. However, we also saw that there are aspects of the cases that would make it challenging for even the most honest and prepared guardians to exercise their powers effectively. These aspects can be traced back, to some degree, to the way the waste oil industry is structured and regulated. For instance, the highly complex and technical nature of the applicable legislation or the fragmentation of enforcement between different agencies operating at various levels are features of the industry, rather than individual circumstances.

Another element uncovered in Chapter 4 was that it appeared relatively simple to physically use waste oils as blend components: this would hold true generally given the characteristics of these substances. Furthermore, we saw that the legal possibilities of processing and transforming wastes complemented the physical possibility of doing so by providing a legal – albeit misapplied and abused – definition and justification for this process. Again, these possibilities exist beyond the criminal events we have examined – our understanding of how bunker fuel should be, or what we define as a waste oil are negotiated and influenced by government as well as market dynamics and players. The negotiation of these definitions – as well as the legal instruments that exist to crystallize them – occurs at a higher level than that of the individual waste collector or petrochemical firm. These latter actors operate in a broader system, and their actions only make sense *within* that system.[1] Therefore, we must now pull at those seemingly loose

1. To avoid confusion, it is important that we make a distinction between the various ways the term 'system' is used in this Chapter and the book generally. At the highest level of analysis,

threads that remain after our initial analysis of the criminal events. In doing so, we will discover that they lead us to much larger and more tangled, criminogenic balls of yarn. The attempt we make in this Chapter, then, is to begin untangling these threads too; and, by so doing, to continue unravelling the case of illegally introducing waste oils into the bunker fuel production process. Our analysis in this Chapter is structured by the notion of a crime-facilitative system, which has been defined in the following terms:

> *The corporate systems involved* [...] *present extremely tempting structural conditions – high incentives and opportunities coupled with low risks – that encourage and facilitate crime, both by system members and by outsiders who seek to enter or use the system for criminal purposes.*[2]

To explore how the object of our case study can be understood as a crime-facilitative system, we need to dissect this definition into different components. The structural conditions of the system generate:

1. Incentives
2. Opportunities
3. (Low) Risks

Furthermore, each of these elements can be qualified – they are such that they lead to extreme temptation to act criminally by:

a. Encouraging, and
b. Facilitating crime

The definition also includes a reference to actors – "members of the system and outsiders" – who commit crimes. It is important, then, to circumscribe what we indicate with the concept of 'system', what 'structural conditions' are, and who classifies as a 'system member' or 'outsider'.

In this Chapter, we begin by clarifying the various conceptual elements we have just listed. Section 1 delves into the literature from organisational criminology to

---

we can say that the processes of waste oil generation and management as well as bunker fuel production are part of a global system of industrial production and consumption, each of them being sub-systems with their own dynamics. Sometimes the two overlap. Within each industry there are rules and norms in place, some of which are generated by states. These rules are part of and give structure to a formal system of guardianship, which comprises different powers and tools. Those powers and tools are, in turn, used by agencies and individual actors, who are also part of the formal system of guardianship. Depending on the perspective or legislative basis, the system of guardianship pertains to one or the other industry or to both. In fact, the industries overlap economically, operationally, and legally. The system that is the focus of *this* Chapter, is all the factors – economic, operational, legal and so on – that are present at the *overlap between the two industries*.

2. Martin L Needleman and Carolyn Needleman, "Organizational Crime: Two Models of Criminogenesis," *The Sociological Quarterly* 20, no. 4 (1979). 521.

set up our theoretical outlook. Each later Section deals with different aspects of the crime-facilitative system: incentives, opportunities, and risks. The first aspect is discussed in Section 2 and is linked to the crime-encouraging character of crime-facilitative systems. In Section 3, opportunities are seen as both encouraging and facilitating crime. Risks are linked to the facilitating character of the system in Section 4. Each of the elements is also linked to other criminological concepts, with particular emphasis on those from situational crime prevention – risks, efforts, rewards, excuses, and provocations -, which we used in Chapter 4 to break down the two criminal events. The reason for this is to make the connection between the macro-level features of the system and the micro-level situational conditions explicit.

## 5.1 Crime-Facilitative Systems, Symbiotic Industries and Organisational Crime

The concept of 'crime-facilitative system' was developed as a critical reflection on the link between criminogenesis and the structural features of certain organisational systems, defined as "typically industries or professions".[3] This link had been initially postulated to explain crime by referring to organisational features of a system as opposed to personal motives of individuals; thereby breaking away from the seeming dependence on "high social status" – and the micro-focused explanations assumed to flow from this label – included in Sutherland's definition of white-collar crime.[4]

The link between structure and harmful behaviour highlighted how *economic, legal, organisational, and normative* features could be explored as influential in the decision to commit crime.[5] However, the creators of the crime-facilitative system

3. Ibid. 517.
4. The term was used by Sutherland in: Edwin H. Sutherland, "White-Collar Criminality," *American Sociological Review* 5, no. 1 (1940). Several authors have subsequently reflected on the concept and phenomenon of white-collar crime and their relationship to the status of offenders, taking different positions on the matter. See, for example, Gisela Bichler, Andrea Schoepfer, and Stacy Bush, "White Collars and Black Ties Interlocking Social Circles of Elite Corporate Offenders," *Journal of Contemporary Criminal Justice* 31, no. 3 (2015); Susan P. Shapiro, "Collaring the Crime, Not the Criminal: Reconsidering the Concept of White-Collar Crime," *American Sociological Review* 55, no. 3 (1990); Sally S Simpson and David Weisburd, *The Criminology of White-Collar Crime* (Springer, 2009); David Weisburd and Elin Waring, *White-Collar Crime and Criminal Careers* (Cambridge University Press, 2001); Hazel Croall, "Who Is the White-Collar Criminal?," *The British Journal of Criminology* 29, no. 2 (1989).
5. Needleman and Needleman, "Organizational Crime: Two Models of Criminogenesis." 517 – 520. The authors review the following studies and refer to the results as exceptional in that the focus of these studies is on industries that have singular features that are not generally common to many other industries or organisational systems, which are also characterised by crime. These systems are defined as 'crime coercive' by the authors. See: Harvey A Farberman, "A Criminogenic Market Structure: The Automobile Industry," ibid.16 (1975); Norman K Denzin, "Notes on the Criminogenic Hypothesis: A Case Study of the American Liquor Industry," *American Sociological Review* (1977); William N Leonard and Marvin Glenn Weber, "Automakers and Dealers: A

concept found that the research done until that point, which established that this link was too deterministic, making the relationship between organisational features and wrongdoing too unrealistically direct and insufficiently nuanced. In their proposal, they posed questions that encourage us to dig deeper and move away from a simplistic application of '*x*, *y*, *z* system features = crime'. They invite us to look at what mechanisms, deriving from the features of the system, transmit the influence towards criminal conduct and at how "routinized illegality" is "rationalized, protected and sustained" within such systems.[6]

We now have a few elements to work with to establish which 'system' we are talking about. It should be an industry or profession, which has some discernible economic, legal, organisational, and normative (structural) features. Such features have some influence on members of that system, and they are also intelligible to outsiders of the system who may take advantage of them for their own gain. In addition, the system enables the routinisation of practices or procedures as well as the gradual development of common definitions and rationalisations. We see that criminal activity can be *sustained*, further clarifying the fact that the system is not casual or momentary, rather it is durable and spans over a longer period of time. More importantly, the crimes or harms are not single incidents, instead they are common practices that routinely take place within the normal operation of the system.

The system we look at in our case study is born at the intersection of *two* industries – waste oil management services (WOMS) and bunker fuel production (BFP). While the structural features of each single industry contribute to facilitating and encouraging crime, it is *at* the overlap *between* the two that the 'separate' structural features come together symbiotically to produce crime. Therefore, when we refer to the concept of 'system' in the following pages, we are focused on the point at which the two industries meet, which necessarily requires us also to pay attention to certain aspects of each individual industry.

We already explored the structural features of the two separate industries in some detail in Chapter 3 and do not need to review those findings here. Some of the information and analysis presented there is useful now for our delineation of what the system we are looking at is. It is also useful for our analysis throughout the coming Sections of this Chapter. To avoid repetition, cross-references are made accordingly.

Each of the two industries includes a number of specialised actors that can be considered 'system members'. In that sense, we can refer back to Chapter 3 where we looked at the processes of bunker fuel production and waste oil management to see which types of firms operate at different stages. For example, waste collectors

---

Study of Criminogenic Market Forces," *Law and Society Review* (1970); Gilbert Geis, "The Heavy Electrical Equipment Anti-Trust Cases of 1961," in *Criminal Behavior Systems*, ed. M and Quinney Clinard, R (New York: Holt, Rinehart and Winston, 1967).

6. Needleman and Needleman, "Organizational Crime: Two Models of Criminogenesis." 518.

are members of the waste management system and traders are members of the bunker fuel production system. But, who classifies as an outsider? A simple answer would be – anyone who is not included in the lists made in Chapter 3. While this is not necessarily incorrect, we can draw a more precise and more useful distinction by focusing on the intersection between the two industries again. From the perspective of waste oil management, we can say that there are clear system members because these receive permits. However, if we look at the matter in terms of *function*, we can say that handling waste generally is an activity that is part of this industry, even improper or illegal handling of waste. Therefore, those firms that (either knowingly or not) use or handle wastes are, strictly speaking, outsiders because they do not have a permit, yet they participate in the system. These outsiders can use wastes that are cheaper than alternative products, thereby gaining an advantage in their own area of activity.

The picture is a little blurrier in the case of bunker fuel production. Because there is no *specialised* permit system in place, there are stages in the production process where anyone can be both an outsider and a system member. This is particularly the case for the stage where blend components are generated and sold.[7] In Chapter 3, we saw that the other stages of the process are highly demanding in terms of technology and investment, therefore there is a much more limited number of 'system members'.[8] Nevertheless, the distinction between members and outsiders proves to be highly useful because it captures the opportunities that exist at the intersection of the two industries, which is precisely where our crime-facilitative system operates. Waste handlers or generators can be seen simultaneously as outsiders *and* system members in the phase of blend component production. It is the flexibility in defining membership at this stage that gives them access to the bunker fuel industry. We explore this matter further in Section 5.4.

The issue of membership brings us to reflect on the concept of 'industry', which we have merely defined on the basis of two industrial processes until now. However, there is also a theoretical notion of industry, which is relevant for explaining criminogenesis. 'Industry' can be understood as a circumscribed setting where "organizational actors [pursue] similar goals in a common institutional

7. There is no legislation that specifically requires blend component producers to have permits for such activities. Many substances can be blend components, most often these are petrochemical substances of some kind – therefore, the firms that produce the blend components may – and mostly do – have permits for activities in relation to management of petrochemical substances. This is discussed in more detail in Section 3 of Chapter 3.
8. System membership for the bunker fuel industry is determined more by economic characteristics than legal boundaries. In Chapter 3, we saw that the various stages of bunker fuel production have different requirements: Stages I and III – where residues from petroleum refinement are generated and bunker fuel is blended – are virtual oligopolies. Therefore, membership is restricted based on economic power, and we witness a high degree of market concentration. Conversely, Stage II, where blend components are generated and traded, is highly competitive and the market is open. Stage II is where the overlap between the two industries materialises.

environment."[9] This concept has been used to uncover how goals and institutional arrangements at the intersection between government and business activities produce criminogenesis. While this relationship between state and economic actors is also relevant in our case,[10] we can re-work this notion of industry to understand the potency of the intersection between bunker fuel production and waste oil management in generating crime. At this intersection, we can say that organizational actors pursue *symbiotic* goals in an *overlapping* institutional environment. Therefore, we could argue that criminogenesis is the result of a crime-facilitative system born at the intersection of two symbiotic industries. Let us look at the two elements – symbiotic goals and overlapping institutional environment – in more detail.

The notion of symbiosis is not new in criminological explanation and is rooted in two perspectives, one focused on organisational crime and the other on organised crime. The first has already been mentioned in discussing 'industry' above and derives from the state-corporate crime concept. It focuses on the symbiosis between "institutions of political governance" and "institutions of economic production and distribution"[11] within a neoliberal society. The second has been developed to indicate one of the ways in which members of criminal organisations and legal actors relate to each other.

In the organised crime context, symbiosis is opposed to antithesis and is premised on the existence of demand for what is offered on an illegal market.[12] Illegal market refers, in that formulation, to drugs, prostitution and similar goods and services.[13] We could adapt that definition and see two 'illegal markets'

9. Elizabeth A Bradshaw, ""Obviously, We're All Oil Industry": The Criminogenic Structure of the Offshore Oil Industry," *Theoretical Criminology* 19, no. 3 (2015). 2.

10. The notion of state-corporate crime is used in the conclusions of Chapter 3 and then again in combination with the concept of the "Treadmill of Law" from green criminology in Chapter 7 to reflect on the influence of state-business dynamics in our case.

11. Ronald C Kramer, Raymond J Michalowski, and David Kauzlarich, "The Origins and Development of the Concept and Theory of State-Corporate Crime," *Crime & Delinquency* 48, no. 2 (2002). 270.

12. That is not to say that the notion of organized crime is used by criminologists and jurists only to look at activities connected to illegal markets, but for the purposes of the present analysis, which focuses on the notion of symbiosis, is usually connected to organized crime involvement in illegal markets and the relationship between organized criminals and other actors linked to that involvement.

13. Nikos Passas, "Cross-Border Crime and the Interface between Legal and Illegal Actors," in *Upperworld and Underworld in Cross-Border Crime*, ed. Petrus van Duyne, Klaus von Lampe, and Nikos Passas (Nijmegen: Wolf Legal Publishers, 2002). 22. For more perspectives on the relationship between organised crime and legal business, see: Vincenzo Ruggiero, *Organized and Corporate Crime in Europe: Offers That Can't Be Refused* (Dartmouth, 1996); Edward R. Kleemans and Henk G. Van de Bunt, "Organised Crime, Occupations and Opportunity," *Global Crime* 9, no. 3 (2008). Georgios A. Antonopoulos et al., "Counterfeit Goods Fraud: An Account of Its Financial Management," *European Journal on Criminal Policy and Research* 26, no. 3 (2020); Edward R Kleemans, "Organized Crime and the Visible Hand: A Theoretical Critique on the Economic Analysis of Organized Crime," *Criminology & Criminal Justice* 13, no. 5 (2013); M. Vere van Koppen, "Involvement Mechanisms for Organized Crime," *Crime, Law and Social Change* 59, no.

in our case: namely that for inadequate and inexpensive hazardous waste oil management services and that for inadequate and inexpensive blend components. While the illegal exchanges for drugs and prostitution require organised crime groups to manage and coordinate them, the 'products' in our case are actually more easily managed by legitimate actors because they appear to be legitimate and are part of those actors' normal activities.

Various forms of symbiosis are proposed to capture the relationship between legal actors and organised crime: outsourcing, collaboration, co-optation, reciprocity, systemic synergy, funding, legal interactions and legal actors committing organised crimes.[14] Of these typologies, reciprocity and systemic synergy are useful for us. The symbiosis in our case does not derive from the clear illegal nature of the product or service, thus excluding most other typologies. The symbiosis is hinged on mutual benefits for equal parties, which are features of reciprocity. Yet, we cannot say with any certainty that in all cases there is a clear knowledge of the illegalities on the part of all those involved, thus excluding the option of 'legal actors committing organised crimes'. Therefore, we can use the category of systemic synergy: "actors benefit each other while they go about their business independently promoting their interests and objectives [...] the synergy is a consequence of structural factors."[15] This is most relevant for our case because it indicates that the symbiosis can only be disrupted by changing those structural features that synergise. Those structural features can be identified by returning to the concept of industry: they are the goals and the institutional environment.

The overlapping institutional environment is composed of two types of 'institutions' (or structures). First, there is a normative-legal overlap by virtue of waste and chemicals legislation, where the juridical definition of substances can drift from waste to product.[16] Second, there is a corresponding economic-operational dimension to the overlap. The substances themselves have an economic value and a mechanical function that makes them handleable in both industries. Furthermore, they can be used by firms that are part of the structures of both industrial processes, as we saw when discussing system membership. As concerns the goals, they are symbiotic because managing waste oils at a low cost neatly corresponds with generating blend components at a low cost. Actors pursuing the former goal are able to do so thanks to the necessities (goals) of the

1 (2013); Derica Lambrechts and Michael Hector, "Environmental Organised Crime: The Dirty Business of Hazardous Waste Disposal and Limited State Capacity in Africa," *Politikon* (2016); Monica Massari and Paola Monzini, "Dirty Businesses in Italy: A Case-Study of Illegal Trafficking in Hazardous Waste," *Global crime* 6, no. 3-4 (2004); Tom Vander Beken and Stijn Van Daele, "Legitimate Businesses and Crime Vulnerabilities," *International journal of social economics* 35, no. 9/10 (2008).

14. Passas, "Cross-Border Crime and the Interface between Legal and Illegal Actors." 22-25.
15. Ibid. 24.
16. See Chapter 3 for a detailed discussion of the relevant legislation. This point is also elaborated on below in Section 5.3.

latter industry. It is a symbiotic relationship because there are mutual benefits to both industries and both types of actors. Actors from one industry are not more powerful than those from the other – making the relationship reciprocal.[17]

Before delving deeper into our analysis, we should note one last characteristic of a crime-facilitative system:

> *[It]does not necessarily benefit from the crimes it promotes through its structural conditions. The crimes may even be regarded as inimical to organisational goals; however, the measures necessary to control internal crime are felt by the system's policy makers to be potentially even more damaging to the system's goals (in most cases, the goal of profit making).*[18]

Therefore, crime is "an unwelcome but unavoidable *cost* of doing business."[19] This latter aspect is only partly addressed in this Chapter. What we see is that the range of goals pursued by system *members* does not include committing illegal acts *per se.* In fact, the criminal activities we are investigating occur to the detriment of some of the goals that they are required to pursue – such as environmental protection or good functioning of ship engines through provision of quality fuel. Yet, just as the creators of the concept point out, the goal of profit-making – and, possibly, other system goals – may be furthered by the criminal activities. The function of the system's goals in encouraging the pursuit of criminal paths to their achievement is discussed in the next Section and is connected to the high incentives that characterise a crime-facilitative system. The association between goals and incentives is discussed in relation to two other criminogenic factors, derived from the framework of situational crime prevention, namely provocations and rewards.

---

17. The question has been raised whether the distinction between the two industries is not artificial and whether the supposed overlap is not rather a sign of a larger, global conglomerate that comprises different specialized sectors. In Chapter 3, we saw that there may be some very large corporations, with subsidiaries across the globe, which are involved in many stages of the industrial processes. However, based on the research conducted for this study, no evidence was found that there is a general coordinating actor or set of actors that influences and controls the entirety of the bunker fuel production sector or the waste oil management sector, and there is no evidence whatsoever that both sectors are coordinated at a level that comprises them both. The notion of symbiosis should be reflected on in a nuanced manner. We may imagine a continuum of symbiosis, where being part of the same organization with procedures to coordinate several, interlinked sub-procedures may be one extreme and merely occasional, coincidental mutual benefits may be at the other. The system we discuss in this Chapter lies somewhere between these two extremes and its positioning is not necessarily fixed.
18. Needleman and Needleman, "Organizational Crime: Two Models of Criminogenesis." 521.
19. Ibid.

## 5.2 Encouraging Crime: Goals, Provocations, Incentives & Rewards

In order to determine what 'incentives' look like in practice, we need to have more information about the system itself. An incentive is a push or nudge towards a certain action: incentives motivate individuals. Motivation is understood here as the willingness to do something. However, the concepts of incentive and motivation are hollow – they tell us nothing about the nature or direction of the behaviour that they could lead to. The incentives in a crime-facilitative system encourage the pursuit of a *criminal path* towards a specific *goal*. Our task then becomes not simply the identification of incentives and motivating factors; rather we are interested in the direction or goal that they serve and how they encourage criminal behaviour in pursuit of that goal. The questions become: Which goals are (implicitly or explicitly) promoted within the system we are analysing? How is the *criminal* pursuit of these goals incentivised as opposed to the use of legal means? The second question may also be formulated differently: Under what circumstances does the motivation to act criminally prevail over the motivation to act within the boundaries of legal permissibility? To answer these questions, we must look at four aspects of the system: first, goals; second, (il-)legitimate opportunities; third, constraints and provocations; lastly, incentives and rewards.

*Goals*

The relationship between goals and (criminal) motivation has been repeatedly explored in the field of organisational criminology.[20] One perspective is that motivation emerges from the "symbolic constructions that define certain goals and activities as desirable."[21] Individuals learn what is desirable as well as what they should do to obtain that which they find desirable. Reaching goals means

20. E. Gross, "Organizational Crime-a Theoretical Perspective," in *Studies in Symbolic Interaction*, ed. Norman K Denzin (Greenwich, CT: JAI Press, 1978). Kathleen Daly, "Gender and Varieties of White-Collar Crime," *Criminology* 27, no. 4 (1989); David Weisburd, Elin Waring, and Ellen F Chayet, *White-Collar Crime and Criminal Careers* (Cambridge University Press, 2001); Marshall B Clinard, Peter C Yeager, and Ruth Blackburn Clinard, *Corporate Crime* (Routledge, 2017); James W Coleman and Linda L Ramos, "Subcultures and Deviant Behavior in the Organizational Context," *Research in the Sociology of Organizations* 15 (1998); Anne Jenkins and John Braithwaite, "Profits, Pressure and Corporate Lawbreaking," *Crime, Law and Social Change* 20, no. 3 (1993); Sally S. Simpson and Nicole Leeper Piquero, "Low Self-Control, Organizational Theory, and Corporate Crime," *Law & Society Review* 36, no. 3 (2002); Sally S. Simpson and Christopher S. Koper, "The Changing of the Guard: Top Management Characteristics, Organizational Strain, and Antitrust Offending," *Journal of Quantitative Criminology* 13, no. 4 (1997); Sally S Simpson, "Corporate Crime, Law, and Social Control," (2002); Robert Agnew, "Building on the Foundation of General Strain Theory: Specifying the Types of Strain Most Likely to Lead to Crime and Delinquency," *Journal of Research in Crime and Delinquency* 38, no. 4 (2001); Robert Agnew et al., "A New Test of Classic Strain Theory," *Justice Quarterly* 13, no. 4 (1996); ibid.
21. James William Coleman, "Toward an Integrated Theory of White-Collar Crime," *American Journal of Sociology* 93, no. 2 (1987). 410.

achieving success. By identifying the definition of success in a given group, community, or culture, we get an idea of the goals that are promoted in that social setting. We can also find out what behaviour is considered acceptable in the same way: Most actions and behaviours that are part of the pursuit of success are considered *normal* or even praiseworthy. The habitual patterns of social life – and the more or less explicit norms that crystallise these patterns – are equally natural. In this way, broader social structure defines goals, and the social structure of the group supports that definition and complements it with a definition of 'appropriate means'. A means of achieving the goals can also be seen as an opportunity. The *availability* of certain opportunities makes it possible to develop definitions about what suitable means of conduct look like.[22]

We can identify a number of goals that may be pursued by the actors in our case study based on a review of the context in which the crime events unfolded. These goals can be traced back to explicit statements or formulations in policy or legal texts; or they may be deduced from the way the relevant industries are organised and operate. The activities that we observed in Chapter 4 have been carried out in the industrial frameworks of bunker fuel production, petrochemical manufacturing, and waste oil management. All these areas of activity are part of a wider global(-ised) process of production and consumption based on neoliberal, free-market principles. Furthermore, they are shaped by operational, economic, and legal factors, which we explored in Chapter 3. The goals of the actors – the firms – involved in this system are summarised in Table 5.1.

**Table 5.1 The structurally established goals in the waste oil management and bunker fuel production industries.**

| Waste (Oil) Management | Bunker Fuel Production |
|---|---|
| Economic survival: maximisation of profit and minimisation of losses | Economic survival: maximisation of profit and minimisation of losses |
| Managing waste | Making bunker fuel |
| Environmentally-sound waste management, in accordance with applicable rules | Making bunker fuel according to applicable specifications and regulations |
| Efficient, profitable waste management | Cost-efficient making of bunker fuel |
| | Profitable sale of bunker fuel |

The *sources* of these goals are various and are 'located' at different levels: at the global, political economy level; societal or cultural level; and at the level of industry, itself partly global in nature, but also nationally contingent.

Let us consider the first goal on both lists: economic survival and maximisation of profit. We currently live in a society where it is assumed that the welfare of the

22. Ibid.

whole can be achieved by the aggregate realisation by each individual of his or her desires. These desires are selfishly pursued by competing with others. We need to compete because it is presumed that the resources necessary for the satisfaction of our desires are scarce, and their availability is unpredictable and uncertain. Scarcity and uncertainty make failure in achieving our desires – and, therefore, surviving – a possibility that we should try to avoid. The free market is the setting in which and structure whereby resources are optimally distributed for everyone's survival. It is assumed that exchanges in and through the free market ensure equality, freedom, and justice in our individual pursuit of survival and happiness, which make this way of living acceptable and accepted in our society.[23]

These cultural circumstances place us in a perpetual state of competition, where survival and winning are seen as one and the same. Winning is the ultimate goal, whatever the competition itself consists in.[24] Whether in sports, at school, work or in the global marketplace, we cycle, study, labour and exchange to dominate. In theory, this means we do the best cycling, get the best education, produce the best outputs, and develop the best products (at the lowest possible price). In practice, it means that whoever has an 'edge', wins. That 'edge' is not always the same as being the 'best', and can, in fact, come in very hazardous forms.

The case we are studying takes place in a specific industrial context, which is shaped by the cultural forces we have just described. While the pressure to win can be said to be all-pervasive in contemporary society, it is particularly evident in industry. In the two industries that form the setting of our case, the smallest 'unit' is always a firm. It is not the case that a single individual would generate waste oils

23. Ibid.
24. Ibid. 414-420: here Coleman traces the historical roots of the 'culture of competition' back to Hobbes and Locke, citing reflections from modern thinkers such as MacPherson, Wuthnow, Mills and Malcolm X (C. Wright Mills, *Situated Actions and Vocabularies of Motive* (Indianapolis: Bobbs-Merrill, 1970); C. B. MacPherson, *The Political Theory of Possessive Individualism* (Oxford, 1962); Robert Wuthnow, *The Consciousness Reformation* (1976); Malcolm Haley Alex Handler M. S. X, *The Autobiography of Malcolm X* (1965). He also refers to the work of Bonger, who is a prominent figure in the radical theory/criminology community where the link between capitalism and crime is repeatedly reaffirmed (W. A. Horton Henry P. Lindsey Edward Norcross Frank H. Bonger, *Criminality and Economic Conditions* (New York: Agathon Press, 1967). Other examples of criminological reflection following this current are: Raymond J. Michalowski, *Order, Law, and Crime: An Introduction to Criminology* (New York, N.Y.: Random House, 1985); William J. Chambliss, *Exploring Criminology* (New York: Macmillan, 1988). The culture of competition or contest in contemporary Western society is also explored by several other authors in different disicplines, such as: Michael Robert Karlberg, *Beyond the Culture of Contest: From Adversarialism to Mutualism in an Age of Interdependence* (Oxford: George Ronald, 2004); Gordon Fellman, "Rambo and the Dalai Lama: The Compulsion to Win and Its Threat to Human Survival," (1998); Alice Kehoe, "Conflict Is a Western Worldview," in *The Anthropology of Peace: Essays in Honor of E. Adamson Hoebel*, ed. E. Adamson; Rohrl Vivian J.; Nicholson M. E. R.; Zamora Mario D.; International Congress of Anthropological Ethnological Hoebel, Sciences (Williamsburg, Va.: Dept. of Anthropology, College of William and Mary, 1992); Walter J. Ong, *Fighting for Life: Contest, Sexuality, and Consciousness* (Ithaca: Cornell University Press, 2013); David Unesco General Conference Promoting Enduring Peace Adams, *The Seville Statement on Violence* (1994).

or handle them or produce, sell, or use bunker fuel.[25] Therefore, it is important for us to consider the characteristics of this basic unit – the firm or corporation – that are interesting when trying to identify goals and incentives. Corporations are legal fictions – they exist and can operate because the law allows it to be so. The law also requires corporations to be solvent to exist – profit, or at least an avoidance of losses, is necessary for survival.[26] Therefore, beyond the general societal push for winning and gaining, corporations are necessarily always concerned with making profit.[27]

However, making profit is dependent on the carrying out of some profitable activity. Consequently, we need to explore the activities that the firms in our case carry out to profit. Broadly, these activities are part of the processes of waste oil management and bunker fuel production (second row in Table 5.1). If we look at the rules applicable to these processes, we can further specify what other goals exist for these firms. For example, waste management is mostly regulated through environmental legislation. According to the applicable rules, waste management should be carried out *in order to* protect the environment and human health and *in a way that* does this to the greatest extent possible. Therefore, firms in this sector are supposed to profit by handling waste, and to do so in a way that does not harm

25. That is not to day that individuals are not involved in making decisions and acting, whether to the advantage of corporate interests or their own through their position within the corporation. However, the nature of the substances involved in our case means that a corporation will always be involved in some way, even if its function and relationship to the gains and harms may vary.
26. The notion of 'survival' needs to be contextualised when discussing corporate crime. Corporations have a potentially unlimited life span – there can be continuity even though corporate forms seem to 'perish'. The 'same' corporation may reincarnate under a different name. There are examples of this within the Dutch waste oil management sector: The Probo Koala case mentioned in Chapters 1 and 6 was connected to the operations of a firm, which at the time was called 'Amsterdam Port Services', and which no longer officially exists. However, investigations have shown that a company called 'Main' now occupies the facilities at the address that once belonged to Amsterdam Port Services, and, in fact, the owner remains the same as well, albeit this is well concealed through complicated veils and ownership structures. In that sense, the legal form takes a backstage role and profit or avoidance of losses can continue through always changing corporate vehicles. (For more information on Amsterdam Port Services and Main, see: Greenpeace & Amnesty International, "The Toxic Truth. About a Company Called Trafigura, a Ship Called Probo Koala and the Dumping of Toxic Waste in Cote d'Ivoire," (London: Amnesty International Secretariat, 2012).)
27. Refer also to note regarding the specific way 'strain' manifests for corporate actors 466below. It is also important to consider how the corporate form has peculiar characteristics that facilitate crime and harm, including reducing the impact of social control measures. See, for example: Gary Slapper and Steve Tombs, *Corporate Crime*, Longman Criminology Series (Harlow: Pearson Longman, 1999); Frank Pearce and Steve Tombs, "Ideology, Hegemony, and Empiricism: Compliance Theories of Regulation," *The British Journal of Criminology* 30, no. 4 (1990); G. Slapper, "Companies, Crime and Punishment," *Business Law Review -London-* 15, no. 5 (1994); Snider Laureen, "Cooperative Models and Corporate Crime: Panacea or Cop-Out?," *Crime & Delinquency* 36, no. 3 (1990); Henry Mintzberg, "Who Should Control the Corporation?," *International corporate governance: text, readings and cases / [a cura di] Robert I. Tricker* (1994); M. David Lundman Richard J. Ermann, *Corporate and Governmental Deviance* (New York: Oxford University Press, 1982); Kip Weisburd David Schlegel, "White-Collar Crime Reconsidered," (1992).

the environment and human health. (This can be seen in the third row of the left column in Table 5.1)

Bunker fuel production is unfettered by the same degree of environmental concern. There are some outer boundaries of permissibility, which are crystallised in legislation and are connected to mechanisms of state enforcement (see the third row of the right-hand column). Nevertheless, the norms and standards of this industry revolve around productivity and efficiency. A high degree of pressure also enters the bunker fuel industry through the monopsony condition that we analysed in Chapter 3: bunker fuel is destined first and foremost for cargo shipping, i.e., the backbone of our global consumer economy. The goal of 'efficiency' is revved up substantially because of this pressure, thereby influencing the economic dynamics, which, in turn, mould the *process* of bunker fuel production.

While we have been talking about goals, we have also been thinking of the means to achieve those goals, which may be termed goals in their own right. This goals-means relationship may be rather confusing for us, and maybe all the more so for those who operate within the industries themselves. One may imagine knowing that profit or avoiding losses is important to strive for, but also that environmental protection should be ensured. How may one weigh these goals or prioritise them? What routinized actions does one take in pursuit of those goals? The process whereby one decides to act in pursuit of one or multiple goals at the same time is intriguing – it is in that process that the choice to act using (il-)legitimate means is made. It is in that process that this decision is made routinely to the repeated detriment of at least part of those goals. The coming paragraphs take us through the choice between legitimate and illegitimate opportunities, which actors at the crossroads of waste oil management and bunker fuel production are faced with in pursuit of the goals we listed above.

*(Il-)Legitimate Opportunities*

Opportunities are potential courses of action made possible by a set of social conditions, and they can be attractive or unattractive. Courses of action have a physical dimension; but in our day to day lives we are also presented with opportunities that exist purely thanks to the existence of social relations. We can go to court to make a claim because a humanly created legal system exists, which allows for such claims to be made, for example. In fact, the law is considered the "most basic of all forces shaping the distribution of opportunities" in social reality.[28] Another source of opportunities, especially when considering potentially unethical or illegal conduct, is the "pattern of enforcement".[29] Knowing how a state or an organisation tends to enforce certain rules makes particular

28. Coleman, "Toward an Integrated Theory of White-Collar Crime", 425.
29. Ibid. 426.

opportunities more or less attractive because it influences the risks involved in choosing a potentially *illicit* course of action. The attractiveness of an opportunity is dependent on different factors: risks, potential gains, compatibility with rationalisations and individual beliefs, and the assessment emerging from the comparison of one opportunity against other courses of action.

Therefore, the attractiveness of an opportunity is not absolute or objective; it is based on two dimensions of *relative* attractiveness. First, each opportunity – legal or illegal – can be weighed against other opportunities to determine which is riskier and which could potentially yield greater rewards. The second dimension is the commensurability of each opportunity when tested against the definitions that one has of what is desirable and acceptable – in terms of both goals and the means to achieve such goals. Of course, the definition of what level of risk is acceptable or what amount of gain is worthwhile will also be contingent in a similar way.[30]

The attractiveness of opportunities is not just relative but variable depending on the context in which such opportunities present themselves. Indeed, the relative attractiveness of opportunities is tied to their variable distribution. This variation is itself contingent: for example, law and its enforcement are important determinants of how attractive opportunities are distributed. If a certain area of activity is tightly regulated and enforcement procedures are rigorously applied (i.e., making risks high), then there will be fewer opportunities for misconduct *and* those opportunities will often seem less appealing compared to compliance. Other possible factors that may influence the variation in the distribution of opportunities are the structure of a given industry; the characteristics of a specific organisation (intended as a single firm, even where it is very large and has a highly complex configuration involving several firms or organisational entities); or the features of an occupation.[31]

Much like the distribution of opportunities depends on the circumstances and structure of a specific industry, organisation, or profession, the fact that an opportunity is considered attractive and acceptable is also affected by the conditions and concepts that characterise these settings. If a legal or illegal opportunity does not exist practically or conceptually in a given industry, it will also *not* be consciously appealing.

Under the title 'goals' we discussed the bunker fuel production and waste oil management industries as sources of specific goals but also as vessels for the attainment of goals, i.e., as sources of opportunities. These industries incorporate the practices and customs that lead to profit, to environmental protection, and to the fuelling of ships that make globalised trade possible. We can see how the opportunities that the two industries provide overlap in Figure 5.1. In this

30. Ibid. 425.
31. Ibid. 427-432.

representation we can also see the difference in the overlap that *legal boundaries* create.

The waste management industry provides the legal opportunity to define substances as by-products or wastes, and then for wastes to be recovered and receive 'end-of-waste' status. Firms 1-5 in Figure 5.1 are all licenced waste oil management firms, but firm 3 is the only one that is legally equipped to transform waste oils into products by ending their waste status. Firm 2 may also do this, but the product it generates may not be legally acceptable on the bunker fuel market because the sulphur content is too high, for example. Firm 1 could be a licenced waste oil collector, which cannot transform wastes, and which operates within the boundaries of the legal framework on waste. Firms 4 and 5 may be licenced firms but they do not have the permit, or the technology specifically required to transform the wastes that enter their facilities into products. The difference between the two is determined by the rules on bunker fuel, which exclude the use of chemical wastes in the blending process. Because the definition of waste is nationally-determined just like the definition of the end-of-waste, it may be the case that something that is a waste in one country is taken to a country where it is not considered a waste and blended into bunker fuel – that would be firm 5.[32] An example of firm 4 would be Crafty Collectors from Chapter 4.

**Figure 5.1 Legitimate and illegitimate opportunities for goal attainment at the crossroads between waste oil management and bunker fuel production**

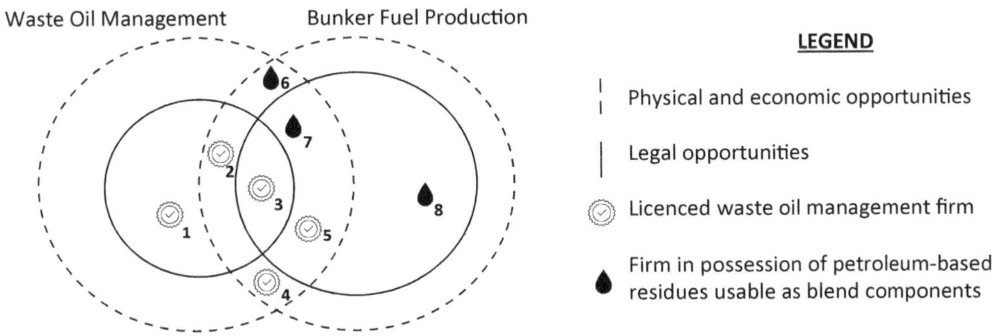


Firm 8 may be a firm in possession of a by-product in accordance with the law and firms 6 and 7 may be in possession of substances that *should* be labelled as wastes

32. In theory, EU and international rules are designed to avoid this very scenario, but this does not always work out in practice. There is, in fact, an EU-wide definition of waste as we saw in Chapter 3, however, because a substance may never become waste or may stop being a waste based on nationally appliable rules and policies. In Section 3, we see an example from the UK where governmental policy conveys the possibility of defining certain substances as products instead of wastes and where this is incompatible with the definition of that same substance in the Netherlands.

but are not. An example of firm 6 is Pesky Producers that claimed its residues were by-products instead of waste oils as we saw in Chapter 4.

The bunker fuel industry provides the legal opportunity to use several substances as blend components, with very few exclusionary criteria. That is why the inner circle on the side of bunker fuel is so wide. From a *legal* perspective, 'blend component', 'by-product', and 'recovered waste oil' are synonymous. From a *physical* perspective the substances indicated by these terms are also synonymous, however, even non-recovered waste oils and fraudulently labelled by-products would be acceptable – these substances would be those held by firms 4 and 6. Economically, there need be no distinction: all the cited substances may be economically exchanged. Nevertheless, there may be differential possibilities to profit or to reduce losses, if the definition of a substance is manipulated past the boundaries of legitimacy but within the scope of what is physically possible. The latter is the case for firms 4 and 6, which represent Crafty Collectors and Pesky Producers, respectively. Because they operate outside the demands of the rules applying to waste oil management, they can earn more or spend less than firms numbers 3 and 8. Firm 3 would be the only one in Figure 5.1 that could legitimately generate blend components from waste oils. And Firm 8 truly possesses a by-product. In that sense, firms 4 and 6 are *constrained* from achieving one of the goals outlined above through the legitimate opportunities that are structurally provided by the two industries. Yet they may still achieve that goal by making use of illegitimate means. Moreover, the mere existence of a legal overlap (where firm 3 is located) gives credibility to and conceals their illegal actions.

### *Constraints & Provocations*

The moment a firm is faced with a constraint on the path to achieving one of its goals, it may choose to pursue illegitimate means. To understand the mechanism behind this choice, it may be helpful for us to consider the concept of 'precipitators' as used in situational crime prevention. This concept captures several situational factors that induce and motivate individuals to commit crime.[33] Under the umbrella of precipitators, we find four categories of which one – provocations – is useful for our discussion on incentives.[34] Provocations are frustration-inducing conditions: In order to relieve the frustration, one may resort to criminal conduct.[35]

33. Derek Blaikie Cornish and Ronald V Clarke, "Opportunities, Precipitators and Criminal Decisions: A Reply to Wortley's Critique of Situational Crime Prevention," *Crime prevention studies* 16 (2003). 43.
34. The four categories are: prompts, pressure, permissibility and provocation. Prompts are signals that stimulate certain behaviour. Pressure in this framework means social pressure to act; for example, in alignment with a group of peers or by obeying a superior. Permissibility refers to the way certain actions may be perceived as legitimate and acceptable because of the way they are defined within a certain (social) setting. When criminal acts are seen as legitimate, they become more accessible to the perpetrator. Permissibility and pressure are discussed below when considering the issue of definitions and excuses. Prompts are not considered here. (ibid.)
35. Ibid. 43-45.

The notion of provocation is reminiscent of the concept of strain. From the theoretical perspective in which this latter concept is used,[36] crime is one of the possible behavioural responses to the frustration and strain that is felt by individuals when goals cannot be achieved because they lack the necessary means to do so. Different (sets of) individuals have different access to the structural means to achieve the goals set by society. When those means are inadequate for attaining the goals, these (sets of) individuals develop behaviours and practices to cope with the resulting frustration. Alternatively, the paths to achieve these goals may be blocked in some way for certain individuals, also leading to frustration. Innovation is one of the coping mechanisms used to counter frustration and it results in the search for alternative means. One form of alternative means (or innovation) is crime.[37]

Different groups or categories of individuals may also be subjected to *varying degrees of pressure for goal attainment*. Corporations are goal-seeking entities and are prone to pressures as their survival, by definition, depends on increasing profits, growth, and efficiency.[38] Corporations are constantly under pressure

---

36. This concept comes from a body of literature referred to as functional sociology, of which Émile Durkheim and Robert Merton are the foundational and most prominent exponents. The basic ideas underlying the work of functional sociologists is that industrialised societies tend to be organised in ways that generate social positions that are occupied by certain types of individuals or groups. These positions are organisational *roles*, which serve the organisational system and have identifiable properties that influence the individuals who occupy them. The concept of anomie was used by Durkheim to connect criminal conduct to the cultural flux occurring in industrialising societies whereby traditional roles were gradually being replaced and overtaken by modern ones. This flux generated instability in a previously predictable social structure, which, in turn, would weaken the power of moral authority (or institutions), which would then no longer be able to regulate conduct. Merton's instrumental anomie and his concept of strain are inspired by, but different to Durkheim's anomie. The starting point is still social structure, specifically its goal-setting and role-providing functions. However, his focus revolves around the idea of 'relative deprivation' as it manifests within a given social structure. Specifically, how social structure in 20th century America was inherently characterised by discrepancies in means-ends distributions that would produce strain and then crime. Some of the literature that is relevant to understand these important sociological concepts is: Emile Durkheim, "Suicide, a Study in Sociology," ([1897] 1951); Steven F. Rosenfeld Richard Messner, *Crime and the American Dream* (Australia: Wadsworth Cengage Learning, 2013); Albert Kircidel Cohen, *Delinquent Boys: The Culture of the Gang, by Albert K. Cohen* (New York: Free Press, 1967); R. A. Ohlin L. E. Cloward, *Delinquency and Opportunity* (USA: The Free Press of Glencoe, 1963); Merton Robert K., *Social Theory and Social Structure* (New York: Free Press, [1957] 1968); Steven Box, *Deviance, Reality and Society* (Cassell, 1986).
37. Nikos Passas, "Anomie and Corporate Deviance," *Contemporary Crises* 14, no. 2 (1990); Robert K. Merton, "Social Structure and Anomie," *Crime* (2003); Robert King Merton, *Opportunity Structure: The Emergence, Diffusion, and Differentiation of a Sociological Concept, 1930s-1950s* (New Brunswick, N.J: F. Adler & W.S. Laufer, 1995); Freda Laufer William S. Merton Robert King Adler, *The Legacy of Anomie Theory* (New Brunswick (N.J.); London: Transaction, 1995); Nikos Passas, "Global Anomie Theory and Crime," in *The Essential Criminology Reader*, ed. Stuart Henry and Mark Lanier (Boulder, CO: Westview Press, 2006).
38. "Anomie and Corporate Deviance." 161-162; Steven Box, "Power, Crime, and Mystification," (1983); Gary Slapper and Steve Tombs, *Corporate Crime* (Harlow: Longman, 1999). 129-136 and 141-149.

to succeed, but they also operate in uncertain environments where "legitimate opportunities for making profit are often limited and constrained."[39] Therefore, beyond the general and continuous pressure for profit maximisation corporations are subjected to, there may be particular circumstances in their institutional environments, which increase uncertainty or limit the means to achieve goals. In fact, it may even be the case that the *source of constraint* is the pursuit of *other goals*, which derive from the circumstances in the institutional environment in which the firms are located.

We can identify several sources of constraint in our case, which also generate further pressure and then frustration, on the road to making profit. These sources are located in the structure and functioning of the industries themselves – in that sense we can talk about 'structural means' from the definition of strain provided above. The waste oil management industry has been more and more stringently regulated over time. While it was initially very simple to obtain a permit and begin operating as a waste management firm, it gradually became more challenging and expensive to comply with the legally imposed requirements for this business. The profit one could make by performing relatively simple acts of collection and disposal was progressively made less attainable by requiring more sophisticated technology to be used. At the same time, other legitimate avenues for profit have emerged, namely those allowing for wastes to become products that can be sold on. Similarly, these avenues have become more and more stringently regulated in order to protect the environment and human health. Possessing the necessary technology and skilled labour to manage waste and (re-) create products imposes heavy financial burdens on firms in this sector.

A corollary to the maturation of the waste sector is that the widespread use of some substances in certain industrial processes is now inhibited because these same substances are currently considered wastes. Therefore, legal and technical measures are now a barrier to their use – these measures also generate costs across the board. Firms have suddenly become waste generators and handlers because definitions of waste have broadened. Other firms now must purchase 'wastes-turned-product' – i.e., they purchase not just the substance, but they pay for the process that stops it being a waste. This has been the case for blend components to make bunker fuel. Historically, the bunker fuel and blend component markets were scarcely regulated. It was, and still is, general practice to mix together substances that present the physical and chemical properties for engines to run smoothly. It was also common practice that these substances be oil residues of different kinds. The constraints in this industrial context have appeared in two forms. Firstly, many better quality 'residues' moved on to more profitable markets. Secondly, many residues entered the domain of waste legislation. It was no longer possible to use the remaining residues without expensive treatment because of the

39. Passas, "Anomie and Corporate Deviance." 162, Box, "Power, Crime, and Mystification." 35.

health and environmental impacts linked to such use. Therefore, profit for those who 'produced' residues and those who purchased them to make the final bunker fuel was also hindered.[40]

Another important source of constraint is connected to the development of a globalised consumer economy, which relies on supply-chains spread out across the planet. Manufacturing processes as well as the route between producer and consumer are physically connected by thousands of cargo ships. Maintaining this system requires low prices for bunker fuel. At the same time, waste oils are also produced at unprecedented rates because they emerge from the lubrication of machinery or they are the secondary product in many manufacturing processes where petroleum is one of the components.[41] On both sides of the equation there is mounting pressure to deal with waste and speedily fuel ships with minimum loss of profit.

From the foregoing we see how there may be friction due to the combined presence of several goals in two overlapping industries. This friction may then lead to frustration and strain, thus provoking criminal motivation and conduct. The general societal goal to win (and survive), which becomes the goal of maximisation of profits when applied to corporations, is strongly present due to the 'culture of competition'.[42] In the waste industry, the means to profit is the management of waste. In the bunker fuel industry, it is the production and sale of bunker fuel. Regulation has, over time, created obstacles to profit by imposing other goals: namely, the environmentally-sound management of waste and, to a lesser extent, bunker fuel production. Furthermore, increased pressure for cheap bunker fuel due to the need to minimise costs for cargo shipping as well as increased competition for cheap blend components,[43] have constrained profits in the bunker fuel industry.

*Incentives & Rewards*

By reflecting on the concepts of provocation, pressure, and strain, we can say that incentives may come in the form of opportunities to overcome pressure and frustration in pursuit of certain goals. These will be felt when the necessary (or legal) means to attain those goals are absent or constrained. In such a scenario, the

40. See Chapter 3 on the economic features of the industry for a more detailed analysis of these aspects. For a more detailed history of the development of the waste (oil) industry in the Netherlands, see: Wim Huisman, "Tussen Winst En Moraal: Achtergronden Van Regelnaleving En Regelovertreding Door Ondernemingen" (Boom Juridische uitgevers, 2001); ACM Spapens, "Vuile Olie: Een Onzichtbaar Probleem Met Grote Gevolgen," *Het tijdschrift voor de politie* 75, no. 8 (2013); Karin van Wingerde, *De Afschrikking Voorbij: Een Empirische Studie Naar Afschrikking, Generale Preventie En Regelnaleving in De Nederlandse Afvalbranche* (2012).
41. See Section 1 of Chapter 3 on petroleum as a common denominator across all the industries analysed in this case study.
42. Coleman, "Toward an Integrated Theory of White-Collar Crime." 414.
43. See Chapter 3 on the economic features of the industry for a more detailed analysis of these aspects.

pressure and frustration combine with availability of criminal means to achieve the desired goals. This availability of criminal means – under said conditions – is equal to an *incentive* for criminal behaviour.

We have identified some sources of frustration that actors in the system – at the intersection of waste oil management and bunker fuel production – may experience because the paths towards their goals are constrained in great part due to the financial burden that the legal framework on waste management has generated. Therefore, we have also established that they may be provoked into seeking opportunities for achieving the ultimate goal of profit maximisation – as well as the less nuanced goals of mechanical waste management and bunker fuel production – using alternative and, possibly, criminal means. However, criminal conduct will not be incentivised unless such opportunities materialise.[44]

An interesting notion in this respect is that of 'lure'. Lure refers to situations in which a person can take advantage of certain categories of economic transactions to enrich him or herself. Lure indicates courses of action that yield profit, which, consequently, attract or lure the attention of those who encounter them. This notion has been used to translate the concept of motivation and opportunity from rational choice theory – used to explain more traditional forms of crime – to white-collar crimes.[45] This notion of lure points out the importance of 'rewards' as a criminogenic condition. From a rational choice perspective, the choice to risk pursuing illegitimate means towards one's goals only makes sense if there is at least the impression that doing so will lead to goal attainment. At the overlap between waste oil management and bunker fuel production, the prospect of such rewards is so probable and predictable that it leads to a *routinised* pursuit of illegitimate means.

Applied to our case, we see that waste management firms (or firms in possession of waste oils) can be rewarded – they can profit or avoid losses and have a competitive advantage – by treating wastes improperly in four ways. First, they can receive payment calculated based on the application of appropriate procedures, which are quite costly, and then proceed to cut corners. Second, they generate *products* without following the necessary processes, according to the applicable rules. Third, they gain a competitive advantage on the blend component market when selling their 'products'. These blend components are often cheaper

44. Richard A. Cloward, "Illegitimate Means, Anomie, and Deviant Behavior," *American Sociological Review* 24, no. 2 (1959). See also the work of Braithwaite, which we will discuss in more detail below, regarding how the availability of illegal opportunities is essential for the generation of a criminal motivation: John Braithwaite, "Criminological Theory and Organizational Crime " *Justice Quarterly* 6, no. 3 (1989). 338.

45. M.L. Benson and S.S. Simpson, *Understanding White-Collar Crime: An Opportunity Perspective* (Routledge, 2015). 86-87. Neal Shover and Andrew Hochstetler, *Choosing White-Collar Crime* (Cambridge University Press, 2005). 27.

than those that are adequately produced. Lastly, firms buying these cheaper blend components profit by having to spend less money to make bunker fuel.[46]

The next questions are: What features of the system give rise to such criminal opportunities? What do these opportunities (for reward) look like concretely? How do these opportunities become psychologically accessible to the actors within the system?

## 5.3 Facilitating & Encouraging Crime: Opportunities, Efforts & Excuses

There are several aspects of the waste management and bunker fuel industries that facilitate and encourage criminal conduct. We can refer to these as opportunities to pursue the goals set within these industries using alternative means or as luring opportunities *within the legitimate system*. Drawing on the findings in Chapter 4, we consider two categories of opportunities at this stage by borrowing from the language of situational crime prevention: efforts and excuses. The opportunities captured by these two categories are, in large part, born at the intersection between the two industries. Therefore, we see that the pressures and provocations that are generated in each separate industry find solution at the point where the two meet and merge.

### *'Business as Usual': Efforts at the Crossroads between Waste Oils and Bunker Fuel*

Let us begin by considering the category of efforts, which we can succinctly define as the exertions that an offender has to make in order to complete a criminal act.[47] In Chapter 4, we saw that numerous actions undertaken by the perpetrators either corresponded to their usual day-to-day business activities or required very little action beyond those activities. They also did not entail peculiar expertise by those carrying them out. There are six elements we can consider under the heading of 'low efforts'. The first, and most fundamental, of these is the that very little needs to be done to make waste oils physically appear to be good quality blend components. This is because of the characteristics of both waste oils and of bunker fuel. They are similar in appearance, but they are also both characterised by a 'low product differentiation', which means it is difficult to distinguish their nature and quality without thorough investigation.[48]

46. These rewards are shown clearly in the crime-script analysis carried out in Chapter 4.
47. Ronald V. Clarke, "Situational Crime Prevention," *Crime and justice* 19, no. Building a Safer Society: Strategic Approaches to Crime Prevention (1995). 131. See Chapter 1 for a more general discussion of the various categories of situational crime prevention.
48. The economic characteristics of waste oils, blend components and bunker fuel are discussed in Chapter 3.

The second dimension of effort is economic. Waste treatment facilities like Crafty Collectors in Chapter 4 need not invest in expensive technology, machinery, or specialised personnel to carry out the fraudulent transformation of wastes. Crafty, in fact, only possessed a simple tank, which it used to carry out the 'treatment' processes. The tank – and the related permit – allowed it to keep up the appearance of being a legitimate treatment facility. What Crafty used to support this appearance was the simple means of manipulating the documentation of incoming wastes.

We now come to the third element, which shows how low efforts facilitate the commission of these crimes. The documents accompanying wastes are on paper and the electronic records of waste collection and treatment facilities are kept by the staff, based on the papers they accumulate from the deliveries of waste. Inspection authorities often check only the electronic records, which do not reveal the mismatch between wastes handled and the technology and permits of the firm. The documents themselves were merely 'corrected' – i.e., the codes of the incoming waste were fraudulently altered – using pens. We can also consider this a material dimension of effort, which, however, has its roots in the administrative set-up of the waste industry.

If we think of our case from an economic perspective, we identity a fourth element. The blend component market is highly competitive, which is one of the sources of pressure in our case study. However, it is also easily accessible. There are no peculiar legal or economic requirements for a firm to produce blend components. In fact, historically, blend components have almost always been residues of other processes. Furthermore, there is low product differentiation in this market as well, which is related to the low product differentiation characteristic of bunker fuel. The physical characteristics of bunker fuel and blend components make it very easy to pass wastes off as products.

The fifth element is linked to this economic aspect, and it is the social network in which the actors operate. The broader oil industry – from large oil companies to petrochemical and waste oil management firms – is a relatively small and specialised world. We saw in Chapter 3 how oil is the common denominator flowing from wells, through refinement procedures, into varied applications, including fuel, and then becoming waste. The actors that handle petroleum products have common knowledge and common contacts. This nearness in social and business terms facilitates the crimes we are analysing. The recognition that a waste may be used as a blend component comes with knowing the products in the oil industry well. The possibility of then bringing that waste into the blend component market without grave challenges is due to easily being able to identify and contact customers or traders. We saw this in Chapter 4 in the case of Pesky Producers, for example. The existence of this social and logistical network is further enhanced by the sharing of knowledge and experience, which, in turn, facilitates the commission of crime. Police authorities have identified several forums where instructions are exchanged among actors regarding how to 'transform' wastes into blend components and go about marketing them.[49]

Lastly, we should ponder on the fact that using 'residues' has been part of the bunker fuel blending process since it first began. Chronologically, the environmental concern and related legislation that led to these residues being considered harmful – thus unsuitable for use without adequate treatment – came later than the practice of actually using them.[50] This is a general characteristic of environmental harm in contemporary times. Many technologies and practices have been developed and used for long periods, and we have only relatively recently begun truly asking ourselves what their impact on our environment is. After all, we cannot say that we do not know that driving petrol fuelled cars contributes to environmental degradation, yet we go about our day-to-day lives 'ignoring' that fact. Our habits and common practices have a stronger hold on most of us than our environmental consciousness.[51]

We can reflect on this supposed ignorance using a few theoretical concepts: 'complaisance', 'de-coupling' and 'differential association'. Complaisance refers to the fact that mutual benefits, which fulfil the wishes or needs of those gaining them, create an opportunity for wrongdoing.[52] Potential guardianship is disrupted because it is more beneficial to participate or close an eye to the wrongdoing than to intervene and disrupt it. This has two dimensions: there can be complaisance on the part of the system's 'policy makers' (see the quote at the end of Section 1), or on the part of the firms carrying out the system's operations. Firms from both industries end up benefiting from this use of wastes, therefore, they are not inclined to disrupt this way of working. The perspective of policy makers is discussed in the concluding part of the Chapter. Complaisance is connected to the symbiosis and systemic synergy we discussed in Section 1.

---

49. See the conclusions of Chapter 4 for more details on the forums indicated here.
50. For details regarding the characteristics of the bunker fuel industry, see Chapter 3.
51. Ignorance and denial play interesting roles in the way society, policy-makers and academics perceive and problematise environmental damage or harm. This matter has been explored by several authors, some examples are: Malte Faber, Reiner Manstetten, and John LR Proops, "Humankind and the Environment: An Anatomy of Surprise and Ignorance," *Environmental values* 1, no. 3 (1992); Helen J Boon, "Climate Change Ignorance: An Unacceptable Legacy," *The Australian Educational Researcher* 42, no. 4 (2015); Sheldon Ungar, "Knowledge, Ignorance and the Popular Culture: Climate Change Versus the Ozone Hole," *Public Understanding of Science* 9, no. 3 (2000); Kevin Elliot, "Selective Ignorance in Environmental Research," *Routledge International handbook of ignorance studies* (2015); Orange Roughy and Australian Fisheries, "Ignorance, the Precautionary Principle, and Sustainability," *Ambio* 24, no. 2 (1995); Reece Walters, "Climate Change Denial: 'Making Ignorance Great Again'," in *Ignorance, Power and Harm: Agnotology and the Criminological Imagination*, ed. Alana Barton and Howard Davis (Cham: Springer International Publishing, 2018); Alana Barton, Howard Davis, and Holly White, "Agnotology and the Criminological Imagination," ibid.
52. Denzin, "Notes on the Criminogenic Hypothesis: A Case Study of the American Liquor Industry." 918.

Thanks to this complaisance, an informal structure emerges, which "contradicts or supersedes the formal structure"[53] and where definitions are re-worked. Under the cover of the formal structure, a different and illegal way of operating exists, which is accepted by all those involved. This informal structure can exist thanks to the customary involvement in the practices outlined above as well as the tacit approval that custom entails. Another way to reflect on this informal structure is through the concept of 'de-coupling', which derives from bringing together neo-institutional theory and the concepts of anomie and strain.

> *When operating in complex and competing institutional (or 'rule') environments, organizations are often formally organized so as to shear structure (the blueprint for organizational action) from action (what actually happens on the ground). That is, formal statements of how and why things should be done are decoupled from how they are actually done.*[54]
>
> *In decoupled organizations, 'institutionalized' organizational structures are adopted, where bureaucracy is deeply permeated by cognitive, normative and legal expectations from the environment. Highly institutionalized structures may, however, interfere with the organization's on-the-ground effectiveness. Under those conditions, [...] the organization and its leaders face a dilemma: adhere to environmental expectations at the expense of performance or reject the environmental demands at the expense of legitimacy. The strategy of decoupling allows organizations to have it both ways: the institutionalized structure is a symbolic display, while action within the organization proceeds largely independently from the structure.*[55]

From the foregoing, we could argue that the customary use of residues (wastes) in producing bunker fuel is a way for the involved firms to remain effective on the ground. Their manipulation of documents and perfunctory performance of treatment operations allow them to continue undisturbed in their practices because they not only conceal their activities from formal guardians, but they add to their legitimate and acceptable appearance. The choice to 'de-couple' may be more or less conscious depending on which level of internal organization and system structure we focus. It may be motivated by considerations of efficiency – which then includes a 'calculation' of efforts – or it may even result from 'alienation from the law'. The latter has been seen as contributing to motivating individuals and firms to act in concerted deviance.[56] Where the law is perceived as inadequate for the operational functioning of a system, it is collectively pushed aside in the day-to-day practices of system members. Of course, we cannot know which of

53. Ibid.
54. Susanne C. Monahan and Beth A. Quinn, "Beyond 'Bad Apples' and 'Weak Leaders': Toward a Neo-Institutional Explanation of Organizational Deviance," *Theoretical Criminology* 10, no. 3 (2006). 364.
55. Ibid. 374.
56. Denzin, "Notes on the Criminogenic Hypothesis: A Case Study of the American Liquor Industry." 919.

these sources of motivation supports the activities without interviewing the system members themselves.[57]

The informal structure exists within the formal one and does not match the contours of the formal one precisely. In fact, the informal structure exists among a specific group, which may ultimately include the majority of actors in a system. What is relevant here is that this group will always necessarily be a sub-group within the wider system. The sub-group then has its own (sub-) culture linked to its own informal structure. This means that the informal structure is not only functioning operationally and materially, but it also has a definitional dimension, which is diffused and maintained through the sub-culture. Within this sub-group and sub-culture, we also see the complaisance discussed above giving rise to a common understanding or definition of the activities that take place. Hence, the usefulness of the notion of differential association:[58] in this sub-group, the definitions applied to the use of wastes enables offending by equating wastes with residues, which are the *normal* components of bunker fuel blends.

*Excuses: 'Drifting' into Acceptable Definitions of Waste and Product*

The last element we have explored brings us to the question of definitions and excuses. It may be true that there are pressures, frustrations, and provocations within the waste oil and bunker fuel industries. It may also be true that these encourage or incentivise actors within these industries to seek alternative means for reaching their goals. We have seen that these means exist in practice because it takes little effort to cut corners at the intersection of these two industries. The low efforts required could make such opportunities attractive.[59] However, this attractiveness based on efforts does not necessarily make these options accessible to the actors involved in a psychological, cognitive, or definitional sense. For these actors to truly be incentivised to engage in criminal activities, they need to see these activities as desirable and appropriate.

The question of desirability or appropriateness leads us to consider the aspect of definitions and labels. The actors within the system not only have the possibility to choose from a range of behavioural possibilities but also from a variety of definitions they can apply to those behaviours. Some of these definitions are more favourable or conducive to law-breaking than others.[60] In the following

57. Although it may still be the case that the matter remains unclear even once we have data from such interviews.
58. Edwin H. Sutherland, *Principles of Criminology* (Chicago, Philadelphia: J.B. Lippincott Company, [1939] 1947). 6-8 (proposition 6).
59. Coleman, "Toward an Integrated Theory of White-Collar Crime." 424.
60. Sutherland, *Principles of Criminology*. 6-8 (proposition 6).See also Chapter 1 on situational crime prevention and consider the following quote: "[R]egard mundane offenders as remaining always only "receptive" to the idea of criminal involvement rather than unqualifiedly ready to offend. Because the readiness decision is a potentially revisable one, committing offenses in settings

paragraphs, we explore the issue of definitions from two perspectives. The first perspective considers the effect that the dominance of economic imperatives has on the way we draw the lines of acceptability in society generally. The second perspective centres on the definitional possibilities provided by the regulatory framework applicable to waste oil management and bunker fuel production specifically.

There are some general tendencies within our society that help us to define the margin of acceptability of certain behaviours or means of goal-achievement. We find ourselves in a specific cultural context where economic institutions have more power than non-economic ones. The imbalance in power between these institutions is such that there is a distortion in the culture and structure of society towards goals and practices in furtherance of material and economic imperatives.[61] Under such conditions, non-economic (or moral) institutions lose their strength and effectiveness.[62] The dominance of economic and profit goals opens the way for questionable (or even illegal) means to become acceptable and accepted. Ends justify the means. These means can then lead to, among other things, harm to humans or the environment, various forms of injustice and inequality, as well as (overt) violations of legal provisions.[63]

which exhibit few explicit moral markers helps to permit and excuse the actions taken. Hence the presence of "permissibility" or "excusability" cues in the crime setting may serve to confirm criminal readiness by helping to neutralize continuing moral qualms." (p. 64 Cornish and Clarke, "Opportunities, Precipitators and Criminal Decisions: A Reply to Wortley's Critique of Situational Crime Prevention.")

61. We return to this idea of power in the last Section of this Chapter.
62. This idea is central to the work that falls under the umbrella of 'institutional anomie theory' of which Messner and Rosenfled are the main proponents. See: S F Messner and R Rosenfeld, *Crime and the American Dream* (Cengage Learning, 2012). Mitchell B. Chamlin and John K. Cochran, "Assessing Messner and Rosenfeld's Institutional Anomie Theory: A Partial Test," *Criminology* 33, no. 3 (1995); Adam Marquart James Mullings Janet Trahan, "Fraud and the American Dream: Toward an Understanding of Fraud Victimization," *Deviant Behavior* 26, no. 6 (2005).
63. Green criminologists are particularly aware of this distortion. See, for example: Vincenzo Ruggiero and Nigel South, "Toxic State-Corporate Crimes, Neo-Liberalism and Green Criminology: The Hazards and Legacies of the Oil, Chemical and Mineral Industries," *International Journal for Crime, Justice and Social Democracy* 2, no. 2 (2013); Nigel South, "Green Criminology and Brown Crime: Despoliation, Disposal and De-Manufacturing in Global Resource Industries," in *Hazardous Waste and Pollution* (Springer, 2016); Vincenzo Ruggiero and Nigel South, "Green Criminology and Crimes of the Economy: Theory, Research and Praxis," *Critical Criminology* 21, no. 3 (2013); Vincenzo Ruggiero, *Power and Crime* (2015); *Crimes of the Economy – a Criminological Analysis of Economic Thought* (2015); Michael J. Lynch, Paul B. Stretesky, and Michael A. Long, "The Treadmill of Production and the Treadmill of Law: Propositions for Analyzing Law, Ecological Disorganization and Crime," *Capitalism Nature Socialism* 31, no. 1 (2020). On the more general distortion that economic imperatives lead to in neoliberal Western society see, for example: Karlberg, *Beyond the Culture of Contest: From Adversarialism to Mutualism in an Age of Interdependence*. Robert N. Bellah, *Habits of the Heart: Individualism and Commitment in American Life, with a New Preface* (Berkeley: University of California Press, 2008); Amitai Etzioni, *The New Golden Rule: Community and Morality in a Democratic Society* (New York: Basic Books, 1999).

This acceptability of questionable practices is further supported by the widely held and perpetuated assumption that the market itself can and will correct or redress situations and outcomes that are *truly* inimical to the aggregate welfare of all participants. Negative outcomes – or 'externalities' as they are known in economic terminology – can be ignored because they are merely unpleasant side-effects of walking the path to profit, survival, and freedom.[64] Right and wrong are not clear-cut categories based on moral considerations. Behaviour is legitimate not because of its inherent morality but because it supports one's advancement in material and economic terms.

The 'attractiveness' of a course of action as compared to another is highly influenced by these dominant economic imperatives. While profit equals survival generally for corporate entities, it is not just the threat of perishing that invites questionable actions in pursuit of profit. As we have seen, one need not be 'coerced' into crime, one may merely be highly tempted. Material gain is so mouth-watering, especially when it is so 'effortless', that moral hurdles are easily overcome and forgotten. In fact, they are replaced by the call to gain. The association 'material gain equals happiness' is firmly established in Western neoliberal culture. That same culture is the setting of the majority of contemporary business practices.[65] Furthermore, the fact that a competitive culture and market forms the backdrop of the crimes we are investigating makes illegal opportunities attractive because a 'callousness of attitude' can develop under these circumstances. Actors in the system have few scruples because their focus on survival and competitive advantage combines with the perception that "everyone is doing it" and, consequently, survival may actually be perceived as *depending* on wrongful behaviour.[66]

Let us now consider the blurring of lines within a specific area of activity. There may be features of an industry that legitimise some questionable or illegal courses

64. Outside of criminology specifically, this belief in the self-correcting feature of markets has been reflected on at length. See, for example: Karlberg, *Beyond the Culture of Contest: From Adversarialism to Mutualism in an Age of Interdependence*; D. R. Loy, "The Religion of the Market," *Journal- American Academy of Religion* 65, no. 2 (1997).This perspective has been reflected on by radical criminologists as well from the perspective of 'Structural Marxism', which focuses on the state's role in regulating harmful and wrongful behaviours (crimes). The main idea here is that states have a stake in the long-term protection of capitalist interests and not necessarily in the more temporary allegiance with any specific individual, group or corporation at a given time. This more insidious collusion relies on the assumed benefits of capitalism as well as the discounting of its routine harms. See, for example: R. M. Bohm, "Radical Criminology – an Explication," *Criminology* 19, no. 4 (1982); Jock Young, "Thinking Seriously About Crime," ed. Gregor McLennan and Jennie Pawson Mike Fitzagerald (London: Routledge, 1981); Michalowski, *Order, Law, and Crime: An Introduction to Criminology*; Chambliss, *Exploring Criminology*.

65. Globalisation means that the Western neoliberal model has been stretched in the matter of trade and business also to parts of the world that are culturally different in most other respects.

66. Denzin, "Notes on the Criminogenic Hypothesis: A Case Study of the American Liquor Industry." 919.

of action. Policy and legislation within the industry may even furnish the concrete tools for such legitimisation to occur. The concepts of 'drift' and 'neutralisation' are useful for us to understand this point further.[67] It is relevant for us to ponder on how laws and norms on a *societal level* may generate neutralisations.

> *The law contains the seeds of its own neutralization. [...] Criminal law is especially susceptible of neutralization because the conditions of applicability and thus inapplicability, are explicitly stated. "This means people can claim various kinds of exemptions in the belief that they are, under certain mitigating circumstances, not bound by the law. The classic example is" self-defense.*[68]

Law is, by nature, prescriptive and proscriptive – i.e., its function is to set out a clear set of guidelines of acceptable and unacceptable conduct. However, law is almost never absolute. Most pre- and proscriptions are accompanied by conditions for and exceptions to their applicability. The most basic limitations are geographic, temporal, and personal. Yet, many factors are relevant, and the presence or absence of these factors is almost always subject to interpretation not just in individual application, but officially through jurists and courts. It is these conditions and exceptions that blur the boundaries of what is acceptable within a certain area of activity to which a law applies.

Where this blurring materialises, so does the possibility for 'drift'. The latter notion has been defined as "an area of social structure in which control has been loosened."[69] Within this area "[t]he delinquent transiently exists in a limbo between convention and crime, responding to the demands of each."[70] This process of drifting between convention and crime, between legitimate and illegitimate choices and behaviours, is supported by the above-described process of neutralisation. Law creates the possibility for "unintended duplication, distortion, and extension of customary beliefs relating to when and under what circumstances exceptions are allowed."[71] Therefore, the control that laws and norms *should* guarantee are neutralised and this "depends partly on equivocation – the unwitting use of concepts in markedly different ways."[72]

---

67. Although (techniques of) neutralisation may emerge at different levels and within diverse, interactional – be it larger or smaller – group settings.
68. David Matza, *Delinquency and Drift* (New York: Routledge, 1964; repr., 1990). quoted in: M Lanier, *Essential Criminology* (New York: Routledge, 2015). 141.
69. Matza, Delinquency and Drift. quoted in: Lanier, Essential Criminology. 142.
70. Essential Criminology; ibid. 140-144.
71. Ibid.
72. Ibid. Other scholars have also focused on the role techniques of neutralisation play in both traditional and corporate crime, for example: Nicole Leeper Piquero, Stephen G. Tibbetts, and Michael B. Blankenship, "Examining the Role of Differential Association and Techniques of Neutralization in Explaining Corporate Crime," *Deviant Behavior* 26, no. 2 (2005); Shadd Maruna and Heith Copes, "What Have We Learned from Five Decades of Neutralization Research?," *Crime and justice* 32 (2005).

If we combine this understanding of drift and neutralisation with our considerations concerning crime-facilitative systems, we can posit the following: Incentives for criminal conduct may be generated through laws themselves. In fact, laws may open up opportunities to engage in certain behaviours; or to apply different meaning to certain courses of action. Law has a constitutive function. Without law there would be no waste, for example. Without law there would be no legally acceptable ways of handling waste nor to profit from that handling. Without law there would also be no exceptions to the applicability of the definition of waste. Without law there would be no parameters and processes for an object or substance to be differentially defined as a waste or a product. In the paragraphs below we delve into this further.

*Three Examples of the Blurred Boundaries between the Waste and Product Definitions*

The legal and policy framework of the EU and the Netherlands provide two avenues for considering wastes or residues as products. However, both are open to interpretation. We have already explored the legislative and policy framework in Chapter 3 and do not need to review it again here. Rather, our concern now is to immerse ourselves into this grey area that exists between the labels of waste and product – the grey area wherein we can drift from one side to the other. Just like the application of the definition of waste generally, attaching an end-of-waste or by-product label to an object or substance is a contentious process. It involves several – technical-scientific, economic, and legal – and sometimes competing considerations.

This labelling process is left to certain entities and is not an individual layman's exercise. There are some institutions that have the authority or the need to make use of the waste/product labels – it is their interpretation and their positioning within this grey area that is particularly relevant for our analysis. In the following paragraphs we look at examples of these different institutions applying the labels of waste and product in different ways. Besides the position they take and the explicit grounds on which they base their perspectives, we should also pay attention to the *assumptions* that underlie their drift towards the one or other direction. We reflect on this aspect further in the conclusions of the Section. We refer to the actors in these examples as 'institutions' because they populate the institutional environment of the industries, as indicated by the theoretical concepts we discussed in Section 1.

The first example centres around the waste/by-product distinction and the task of labelling is taken on by judicial authorities. The second example shows how this matter is dealt with by policy- and lawmakers and looks at the application of the end-of-waste label. In the third example, we analyse an exchange between firms working at the crossroads of the two industries. These companies try to define the substance they are handling – a waste – as a product.

**The *Shell* Case:[73] Waste or Product?**

In September 2006, Shell Netherlands delivered a batch of bunker fuel to a Belgian client. The delivery was completed by loading the fuel onto a ship, which had not been fully emptied from a previous load, and then transferring it to the client. The fuel and the substances from the previous load were mixed together, which meant that the fuel had become contaminated and made unsuitable for use.[74] Shell claimed that it had not been aware of the contamination before final delivery. The client returned the unsuitable fuel to Shell and demanded a refund. At this point, Shell chose to re-blend the returned substance before selling it once more. Shell was charged with illegally transporting hazardous waste across borders by the authorities in Rotterdam in relation to its moving the returned off-spec fuel from the client back to its blending facilities without the necessary (waste) documentation. The Court decided to request a preliminary ruling from the Court of Justice of the European Union (CJEU) to receive clarification on how to assign the label of waste or product in the case. The Court asked the CJEU whether the contaminated fuel that the client had returned to Shell after the first delivery had been a waste under EU law.

The Advocate General (AG) and the Court answered the question differently. Whereas AG Jääskinen took an approach that favours environmental protection through the application of the precautionary principle, the Court was more focused on the economic repercussions of having an exceedingly broad definition of waste. The contrast between these two opinions clearly mirrors the general struggle between the two goals that are pursued in this context. Environmental protection and profit maximisation appear to be at odds to the point that taking one perspective or the other results in a different definition of the same reality. Let us review the reasoning first of the AG and then the Court to understand this better.

AG Jääskinen begins by determining what factors need to be considered in applying the label of 'waste' to a substance. He refers to the lists[75] that accompany the Waste Framework Directive (WFD)[76] and states that a number of entries on

73. Joined Cases C- 241/12 and C-242/2012 Shell Nederland Verkoopmaatschappij BV and Shell Belgium [2013].

74. Ultimately, the fuel could not even be stored by the client because of its low flashpoint, which also indicated that it was off-specification – further proof of the fuel's unsuitability.

75. Commission Decision of 3 May 2000 replacing Decision 94/3/EC establishing a list of wastes pursuant to Art. 1(a) of Council Directive 75/442/EEC on waste and Council Decision 94/904/EC establishing a list of hazardous waste pursuant to Art. 1(4) of Council Directive 91/689/EEC on hazardous waste(notified under document number C(2000) 1147) (2000/532/EC). For more information about the Waste Directive and the List of Wastes, see Section 2 of Chapter 3.

76. The version of the Directive that was discussed in the case is no longer in force: Directive 2006/12/EC of the European Parliament and of the Council of 5 April 2006 on waste (OJ L 114, 27.4.2006, p. 9-21). This version was repealed and replaced by Directive 2008/98/EC, which is still in force (as amended by Directive (EU) 2018/851). (Directive 2008/98/EC of the European Parliament and of the Council of 19 November 2008 on waste and repealing certain Directives OJ

that list could be applicable to the off-spec fuel in the case. He then says that these are mere indications that the substance is a waste and are not conclusive evidence. The determination of whether something is a waste depends on the intention of the holder to 'discard' it.[77] The term discard can also include recovery of a waste because this is one of the operations allowed according to the WFD. The fact that Shell intended to blend the substance in order to sell it after it had been returned points towards it being a waste because the blending amounts to recovery.[78] The AG goes further and states that the fact that a substance may be put to re-use for economic purposes or the fact that it can be part of an industrial process does not preclude the substance from being classified as a waste.[79]

The composition of a substance does not *per se* determine the classification of that substance as a waste. However, the composition is relevant to determine whether a substance is *hazardous* waste, and it may serve as an indication of whether something should – is intended or required to – be discarded within the meaning of waste legislation.[80] He proceeds to consider the objective of environmental protection and applies the precautionary principle. He concludes that the concept of waste should *not* be interpreted restrictively.[81] So, the definition of 'by-product' should be restrictively interpreted. Accordingly, there should be *certainty* that the substance will be used and not mere possibility. Without such certainty, the substance should not be allowed to escape the waste definition and the obligations attached to it.[82] In support of his argument, the AG refers to the distinction between wastes and by-products and adds that by-products are, in any case, the result of other *intentional* production processes. The contamination in the case was accidental, therefore, the application of the logic behind the by-product exception is excluded.[83] He concludes stating:

> [*The*] [*w*]*aste* [*definition*] *does not to exclude substances and objects capable of recovery as fuel in an environmentally responsible manner. The possibility of re-use of a substance with modifications is not pertinent* [*to the determination of whether something is a waste or not*].[84]

---

L 312, 22.11.2008, p. 3-30; Directive (EU) 2018/851 of the European Parliament and of the Council of 30 May 2018 amending Directive 2008/98/EC on waste, OJ L 150, 14.6.2018, p. 109-140.) The 2008 version of the Directive incorporates this and other case-law in Art. 5 on by-products.

77. Joined Cases C- 241/12 and C-242/2012 *Shell Nederland Verkoopmaatschappij BV and Shell Belgium* [2013], Opinion of AG Jääskinen, Paras. 20-21.
78. Para. 25. This point may be objectionable in itself because recovery has to performed by licenced waste management firms using specific techniques and technology. This reasoning is emblematic of the exasperatingly tautological conundrum one enters when looking at whether waste oils and residues are, in fact, wastes or not when they are destined for the bunker fuel production process.
79. Para. 30.
80. Para. 31.
81. Para. 32.
82. Para. 35.
83. Para. 36.
84. Para. 36; C-418/97 *ARCO Chemie Nederland Ltd* [2000] ECR I – 4475.

However,

> *a non- intentionally manufactured mixture or compound is prima facie waste if the use to which it is intended to be put is not safe, in the absence of knowledge of its composition. This applies to products* [...] *whose qualities are important to human health and the environment.*[85]

The CJEU's reasoning takes the same point of departure by stating that the determination of whether something is a waste revolves around the intention of the holder to 'discard' it.[86] The Court also acknowledges that waste legislation is designed to protect human health and the environment, which means we also should consider the precautionary principle. Accordingly, the terms 'waste' and 'discard' cannot be interpreted restrictively.[87] At this point, the Court begins to take a different path to come to its conclusion, compared to the AG. It states that in order to determine whether something is a waste, the fact that the substance or object is considered 'burdensome' by the holder provides an indication to this effect. The burdensome nature of the object would make the holder inclined to dispose of it, which might then lead to harm to environment.[88]

The CJEU begins applying this reasoning to the facts of the case. It states that off-spec fuel is not *a priori* a banned or illegal substance that holders *must* dispose of or a substance that poses a specific risk.[89] In fact, it affirms that, although there is evidence that the off-spec fuel was a burden to Shell's client, that same client wanted to return it in exchange for a refund. The expectation or demand for a refund shows that it was not likely that the client would have disposed of it, especially given the economic value of the substance.[90] Furthermore, the Court takes into account Shell's claim that the substance, although unsuitable for that specific client, *could* have been sold on the market without modifications and that it has a very high commercial value.[91]

Additionally, the claim by Shell that it intended to blend the substance in the specific case so that it could sell it again and that it was sure of this sale is,

85. Para. 40.
86. Joined Cases C- 241/12 and C-242/2012 *Shell Nederland Verkoopmaatschappij BV and Belgian Shell NV* [2013], Paras. 37-38, Case C-188/07 Commune de Mesquer [2008] ECR I-4501, para. 53, Case C-263/05 Commission vs. Italy [2007] ECR I-11745, para. 32.
87. Commune de Mesquer, Paras. 38-39. For an overview of the CJEU's impact on the interpretation of the waste definition, see: Backes, Chris, "The Waste Framework Directive and the Circular Economy", in Peeters, Marjan, and Eliantonio, Mariolina, eds. *Research Handbook on EU Environmental Law. Cheltenham*: Edward Elgar Publishing Limited, 2020. Here the author also reflects on how the CJEU moves from more or less restrictive interpretations of 'waste' in its case-law and notes that the CJEU's position in the *Shell* case specifically is an example of the Court interpreting 'waste' restrictively to the advantage of economic considerations.
88. Para. 42.
89. Para. 43.
90. Para. 46.
91. Para. 49.

according to the CJEU, the determining factor in the case.[92] The purpose of EU law distinguishing between wastes and products is that of capturing and regulating those instances where marketable substances (which may bemade unintentionally, in the case of *by*-products) may still be traded legally by avoiding the waste definition. The CJEU claims that the broad definition of waste should not impede this possibility where it can be determined that the entity who wishes to trade the substance is certain of the use of such (by-)products.[93]

**End-of-Waste: Who Decides and How?**

In this example, the focus is on the application of the end-of-waste label. Under EU law, it is possible that a waste that has undergone recovery or recycling operations, which comply with certain criteria and conditions, may cease to be a waste.[94] Member States "may decide case by case where certain waste has ceased to be waste taking into account the applicable case law" if no "criteria have been set at the [Union] level" in accordance with the procedure set out in Article 6 WFD.[95] Let us briefly recall the conditions set in Article 6 for developing rules and procedures for 'ending wastes'.[96] Article 6(1) lists four elements:

a. There should be a common use of the recovered substance for specific purposes;
b. There should be demand or a market for it;
c. The substance meets the technical requirement for the purposes indicated in (a.) and any existing standards or applicable legislation;
d. The use of the substance should not lead to overall adverse effects on the environment or human health.

Similarly to the criteria for by-products, we see that the fact that there is a commercial value for the 'former waste' is an important factor for it to lose its waste status and re-enter the global production chain. This is, of course, a valuable aspect to consider because it would seem pointless and, ironically, wasteful to make something for which there is no use. Yet, the process of finding a use for something depends only in part on the qualities or properties of the substance or object itself. Much like the label of waste is dependent on the holder's intention to discard it, the '*end*' of waste depends on the (future) holder's intention to *use* it. So, the determination of where the boundary between a waste and non-waste

92. Para. 52.
93. Paras. 53 and 54.
94. Art. 6 Directive 2008/98/EC.
95. Art. 6(4) Directive 2008/98/EC. There are no Union-wide provisions concerning recovery of waste oils, therefore, some Member States have exercised their freedom under Art. 6 to formulate guidelines and rules according to which waste oils can be recovered and become bunker fuel blend components.
96. Art. 6 Directive 2008/98/EC is discussed in Section 2 of Chapter 3.

lies is highly arbitrary and subject to interpretation.[97] The interpretation itself is heavily dependent on the perspective and interests of the individual or entity making the decision of which label to apply. We return to this point later. Two issues need to be explored at this point: first, the *process* of formulating rules and procedures applicable to a certain waste stream for it to cease being waste. More specifically, who is involved in this process and in what way. Second, the actual outcome of this process, namely the end-of-waste criteria themselves as well as the consequences of their application in practice.

Regarding the former aspect, we can reflect on an example from the Netherlands. In accordance with EU law obligations, the Netherlands regularly formulates updated waste management plans and policies, which include specific rules and guidelines for the transformation and treatment of waste. These are included in the *Landelijk Afvalbeheerplan* (LAP), which we discussed in Chapters 3 and 4. In April 2016, the Ministry of Infrastructure and Water Management[98] invited a group of stakeholders to participate in the process of developing LAP 3, with a specific focus on the LAP entry concerning used waste oils (*afgewerkte olie*), which is now included in Sectorplan 56 of LAP 3.[99] The topic of the meeting: "*Einde afval voor vloeibare brandstoffen uit afvalstoffen*" – end of waste for liquid fuels from wastes. Among the invitees: two firms that had been repeatedly criminally convicted of illegally handling (hazardous) wastes. The stakeholders were asked to share their opinion on how to 'treat' the wastes. They also discussed the monitoring procedures that would be applicable to companies that would have the task of treating wastes. Specifically, the stakeholders were invited to give their opinion on how frequently checks should be conducted. Ultimately, the media attention on this matter disrupted the involvement of these two firms in the process.[100]

Let us now consider another example where we see actual guidelines developed for waste oils. In the UK, the Environment Agency has published a

97. The matter of how waste is defined has been discussed by different scholars, for example: Nicolas Michel de Sadeleer, "New Perspective on the Definition of Waste in Ec Law," *Journal of European Environmental & Planning Law* 1, no. 4 (2005); Mikael Drackner, "What Is Waste? To Whom?-an Anthropological Perspective on Garbage," *Waste management & research* 23, no. 3 (2005); Nicolas Michel de Sadeleer, "Ec Waste Law or How to Juggle with Legal Concepts: Drawing the Line between Waste, Residues, Secondary Materials, by-Products, Disposal and Recovery Operations," *Journal of European Environmental & Planning Law* 2, no. 6 (2005).

98. Ministerie van Infrastructuur en Milieu, now Ministry of Infrastructure and Water Management – Ministerie van Infrastructuur en Waterstaat – IenW.

99. Ministerie van Infrastructuur en Waterstaat, "Landelijk Afvalbeheerplan 2017 – 2029 (Tweede Wijziging) (Lap 3)," (2017). For more information on LAP, see Chapters 3 and 4.

100. Wilfried Koomen, *Beerput Nederland* (2017).This instance is discussed in the documentary "Beerput Nederland" [Literally: Cesspit Netherlands]. An anonymous tipster informed journalists that companies that had been previously criminally convicted for waste-related illegalities were part of this policy-making process. The journalists followed up the tip, also making use of the rights to access information under Dutch law (Wet van 31 oktober 1991, houdende regelen betreffende de openbaarheid van bestuur.)

*Quality Protocol* in which it lays out the "end of waste criteria for the production and use of Processed Fuel Oil (PFO), from waste lubricating oils."[101] In this protocol we find a table that matches categories of wastes (based on their EURAL codes and composition) to procedures that should, in theory, lead to the creation of what the Environment Agency has called Processed Fuel Oil. This PFO label was seen coming back in a number of investigations by the Dutch police authorities. Upon closer inspection, they noticed two things. First, they discovered a mismatch between waste stream characteristics and treatment processes. Similarly to what we saw in the case of Crafty Collectors, the procedures applied to the wastes are not suitable to actually remove the hazardous content adequately in order for the use of the PFO to be environmentally-sound. This was apparent from the policy documents and guidelines and did not even require examining the activities of the companies themselves. Second, they looked into the firms that were producing PFO and quickly discovered that their facilities were clearly inadequate for carrying out the processing of the wastes indicated by the EURAL codes mentioned in the policy document.[102] The data gathered does not allow us to make any declarations regarding who was involved in the making of the "Quality Protocol" and what expertise (or interests) they brought to the drawing board. Suffice to say, however, that by virtue of this protocol, hazardous waste oils are being legitimately – in the sense of in accordance with that particular policy – labelled as fuel (Firm 5 in Figure 5.1 is an example of this situation).

**Making a Product on Paper**

In the following example we should pay attention to two aspects: first, the *attitude* displayed by those involved towards the description and labelling of the substances they handle and sell. Second, the methods of manipulating the documents. Although the example is an exchange between individual agents of different organisations, they are still pertinent to see how macro-level system dynamics – especially the definitions and concepts available thanks to the structure of that system – filter into the day-to-day operations of the organisations.

An email exchange takes place between three parties. One is a recycler of waste oils, which is in possession of a substance that it wishes to sell as a blend component. That substance is, in fact, a waste oil, whose true nature was established through police investigations subsequent to its ultimate sale.[103] Next, we have an environmental bureau (or consultant). Environmental bureaus are either a department within large companies or independent consultative bodies to which firms can resort. They are private entities and have no formal guardianship

101. UK Environment Agency, "Guidance: Quality Protocol: Processed Fuel Oil (Pfo) – Sets out End of Waste Criteria for the Production and Use of Processed Fuel Oil from Waste Lubricating Oil.," ed. Northern Ireland Environment Agency (Oxon2011).
102. Field Notes (Visit and conversations with R. 1 and R. 5) 04.12.2018.
103. Criminal investigation file "Case 3" from the Andante project. Field Notes 04.12.2018.

responsibility stemming from the legislative framework. Their function is to assist companies with questions on compliance with rules and specifications applicable to their area of activity.[104] Part of their work is to make sure that the necessary documents are in order. The third party is a fuel oil trader.

The scenario plays out as follows: the recycling company (RC) has sold some 'blend components' (read: wastes) to the fuel trader (FT). The physical transfer of the 'product' requires appropriate accompanying documentation – a (material) safety data sheet (SDS). The nature of the product, certified by such documentation, is relevant for its handling by FT, including FTs blending or further sale of the product after the bunker fuel production process. FT communicates to RC that the documents, which have been sent in advance, are not appropriate for this purpose. An environmental bureau (EB) is solicited to help dealing with the matter.

E-mail Exchange I[105] – from Fuel Trader to Environmental Bureau

> If we want to store the product, we must have a correct SDS.
> Which parameters need to be analysed?
> What information do you need?
> What would it cost...?
> That SDS he gives us, however, does not correspond to the product.

E-mail Exchange II[106] – from EB back to FT

> If [RC] sends SDS in word format to [EB], [EB] will adapt the SDS to make it REACH compliant and send it to [FT] for approval.
> If [RC] sends SDS in word format to [EB], [EB] will adapt the SDS to make it REACH compliant and send it to [FT] for approval.

104. For more information on the role of environmental bureaus in the bunker fuel production process see Section 3 of Chapter 3 and Section 1 of Chapter 4.
105. [Author's translation] Original (in Dutch): "Indien wij het product willen opslagen moeten wij echter een correcte SDS hebben"
"Welke parameters moeten geanalyseerd worden?"
"Welke informatie hebben jullie nodig?"
"Wat zou het kosten...?"
"Die SDS die hij ons geeft, komt echter niet overeen met het product."
106. Original in English, reported verbatim with omission of certain details to protect anonymity.

E-mail Exchange III[107] – from EB to FT referring to the ultimate customer who will purchase the bunker fuel

> We are now told that the MSDS is inaccurate and we are asked to provide one that is relevant. This is proving to be difficult because we do not know their specifications or limits. We are left in the dark. Perhaps it would [be] better if we were to be given the specific technical limits as to what is or is not acceptable to your customer? By doing so *we can test the [product] to ensure that it meets the specification limits and create an MSDS that truly represents their needs.* [Emphasis added]

What we can see in the e-mail exchanges is that the attitude towards the compilation of documents is one that is functional to the efficient continuation of the business practices. The interest of the parties is not to bring the documents in conformity with the truth, rather they bring the 'truth' in line with their business needs *through* the documents. While the initial request (E-mail Exchange I) appears to lead to a rectification of documents in order to certify the actual qualities of the 'product' being sold, the later e-mails reveal that all parties involved are merely trying to apply a label that fits so the procedure can continue. The material safety data sheet is not being drawn up for the sake of deceiving the client. On the contrary, the client itself – FT – is complicit in creating an SDS that will complete the sale procedure without creating obstacles.

We can reflect on this example with the notion of 'compartmentalisation' in mind. The way the document is manipulated is not entirely dishonest. The documents are intended to reflect some (partial) test results. The label is not a pure work of fiction or fraud, in this sense. The actors themselves also do not seem to correspond to the image of scheming masterminds forging official documentation. Rather, there appears to be a pragmatic approach to the whole 'production process'. The right documents are merely another step in the assembly line before the product is sent out for use. The question before those involved at this stage of the 'production process' is not whether they are doing something wrong, immoral, illegal, or dishonest; they are merely doing what is needed to continue. We could say they display an 'instrumental rationality'.[108] Moreover, we can see this exchange as a good example of 'de-coupling' as discussed in the quote on page 189, specifically the fact that an "institutionalized structure

107. Original in English, reported verbatim with omission of certain details to protect anonymity. This e-mail was sent by EB to FT, summarizing the conversation with RC.
108. Of course, it is not possible to speak to the actual state of mind of those involved or their definition of their behaviour without interviewing them directly. The reflections here are mere inferences drawn from reviewing several exchanges of this kind in similar cases and considering the social context in which they are performed.

[can be] a symbolic display, while action within the organization proceeds largely independently from the structure."

*Reflections: Efforts and Excuses that Encourage and Facilitate Crime*

From the foregoing we have seen that the legal and policy framework legitimises the waste-to-product transformation process. This 'transformative process' is not only legitimised by the framework, it is promoted and encouraged. A big theme in the *current* approach to waste is the 'circular economy', which may be defined in the following terms: "A circular economy is based on the principles of designing out waste and pollution, keeping products and materials in use, and regenerating natural systems."[109] Let us consider a circular economy as an overarching theme in the policy and legal framework, which can also be seen as a structural mind-set.

Institutions, individuals, and firms to which the framework applies put the transformative process into action in different ways, depending also on their position and interests. We briefly reviewed the third example with the concepts of instrumental rationality and compartmentalisation in mind. We can extend our reflection further to all three examples. In each scenario, the actors navigated towards one of the shores of the grey area between the waste and product labels. Attaching a waste label was linked to heightened environmental concern and precaution, while the product label was assigned with economic or operational considerations at the fore. One might say that, in the process of protecting the environment, an instrumental decision in that direction would warrant a broader application of the 'waste' label. The more cautious we are in releasing recognisably harmful substances into the environment, the more we will contribute to its conservation. However, the application of the 'product' label is no less instrumentally rational in that sense. If we want to have a thriving economy, we cannot exclude perfectly tradable objects and substances from the market. The steps involved in bringing this about are merely functional to that aim.

Is there a problem here? If we develop a circular economy, maybe not. A circular economy is one that incorporates both imperatives – economic *and* environmental prosperity – and tries to make them coherent.[110] In such an economy we would be working towards these twin goals simultaneously, and

109. Ellen MacArthur Foundation, "Finding a Common Language — the Circular Economy Glossary," https://ellenmacarthurfoundation.org/topics/circular-economy-introduction/glossary.There is no single definition of 'circular economy', although the three elements included in the quote are re-iterated in several definitions. An attempt at devising a comprehensive and stable definition has been attempted, see: Gustavo Cattelan Nobre and Elaine Tavares, "The Quest for a Circular Economy Final Definition: A Scientific Perspective," *Journal of Cleaner Production* 314 (2021).

110. : "The Quest for a Circular Economy Final Definition: A Scientific Perspective." Communication from the Commission to the European Parliament, the Council, the European Economic and Social Committee and the Committee of the Regions A new Circular Economy Action Plan for a cleaner and more competitive Europe (COM/2020/98 final)

instrumental decisions would be characterised as functional to both aims. This case study could then be limited to looking at how the implementation of a circular economy will resolve the problems and crimes we have been investigating. Yet, we still have several things to consider and may not want to sing the praises of a circular economy just yet. In fact, if the criminal events analysed in Chapter 4 are considered *without* taking into account the values and goals of environmental protection, they are very good examples of *a* circular economy in action. Is it not true that waste is being 'eliminated'? Is it not true that new resources are not being used because they have been replaced by re-used ones? Wherein lies the problem, then?

The concept of 'compartmentalisation' could be useful for us here or we could also talk about 'sub-cultures' or 'differential association'. The proposal for a circular economy is implanted into a competitive neoliberal economy, where distribution of profit determines who wins and who loses, who survives and thrives, and who perishes. A corporation, by nature, will be lured towards the easiest avenue for profit. Again, this would be no problem if there were only one avenue to profit *and* protect the environment. However, at the crossroads between waste oil management and bunker fuel production there is a very – practically and psychologically – accessible, 'alternative' avenue for *greater* profits (and smaller losses). The bunker fuel industry is not characterised by the same concern and related stringent formal systems of guardianship of the waste oil management industry. The specifications firms adhere to in the bunker fuel realm promote productivity, efficiency, and maximum utility. It is also common practice to use 'residues' in the bunker fuel industry; and it is so *easy* to 'make' residues. It would be a pity to not jump at such an opportunity, after all.

The circumstances we have just described are reminiscent of a theoretical proposition, which we can adapt based on our discussion of incentives and constraints in Section 2: "[Constraint] of legitimate opportunities for the attainment of organizational or subunit goals fosters subculture formation within an industry."[111] Such subcultures are themselves illegitimate opportunities because they "transmit knowledge of how organizational actors can work together to break the law [...] and how to rationalize this behaviour as good, necessary, and inevitable."[112] This latter quote captures the criminogenic set up of efforts and excuses we discussed in this Section.

According to the theory of tipping points from which the above quotes derive, disrupting sub-cultures and their crime-facilitating effects requires adding more weight on one side of a social control scale. That weight comes in the form of

111. Braithwaite, "Criminological Theory and Organizational Crime", 339. In the original formulation constraints is "blockage" as Braithwaite remained closer to the original idea of strain, we have replaced it based on our considerations in the preceding section because profit was identified as one of several goals that may be partly constrained.

112. Ibid. 339.

shame: organisational actors may be shamed within a crime-prone subgroup into committing crime, plus they may be stigmatised by state enforcement agents as well as the public in a way that makes them reluctant to comply with the law. Alternatively, the shaming within the sub-group may be alleviated and disrupted by re-integrative shaming applied by state agents and society at large, which favours respect of the rules.[113]

We have seen that the incentive for sub-culture formation is generated by the pressures and provocations that exist because of the simultaneous pursuit of profit and environmental protection within a globalised neoliberal economy. We have also seen that these sub-cultures furnish the fertile ground for learning techniques and definitions favourable to offending. These circumstances are quite the opposite of what is considered an important feature of law-abiding industries according to the theory of tipping points: "Shaming of organisational crime by professional and industry peers is enhanced by vigorous commitments to industry and professional regulation, including the establishment of self-regulatory forums that forcefully denounce particular individuals and organisations adjudicated guilty of wrongdoing."[114] Now we can investigate the issue of social control and state interventions, and how they may tip the scale further in the direction of offending or whether they could somehow encourage compliance instead. We carry out this investigation with the following question in mind: How does the operation of 'controls' facilitate the crimes under study?

## 5.4 Facilitating Crime: Low Risks, Concealment and Capable Guardianship

The degree of risk faced by those who contemplate engaging in criminal behaviour is an important factor in the theoretical explanation of crime. We can equate low risks with unsuitable, incapable, or ineffective guardianship.[115] While this perspective remains applicable to organisational crime, the nature of organisational crime itself is important to grasping what 'low risks' look like in practice. To understand what is meant by 'nature of organisational crime', we refer to both the type of offender and the type of offence. There are, in fact, features of organisational offenders and offences that are particularly influential in lowering the risks of detection in organisational crime because they influence how controls operate. The narrower aspect of 'capable guardianship' is addressed in the second subsection, while the link between the nature of organisational crime and low risks is analysed in the subsection immediately below.

113. Ibid.
114. Ibid. 346.
115. The notion of 'incapable guardian' comes from the literature based routine activities theory and is used in the situational crime prevention framework. For a review of this literature see the discussion on situational crime prevention in Chapter 1.

### *'Blindness' in Organisational Crime: A Special Opportunity*

We can use the concept of technique for our analysis of the features of organisational crime to understand how they contribute to lowering risks. Techniques are "methods for accomplishing desired aims."[116] They are different for organisational crimes from the techniques employed in other types of crime-commission processes. This difference is a product of both the types of offence and the kinds of offenders that characterise organisational crimes. Therefore, by studying the techniques we can also find out how these particular offenders and offences uniquely lower the risks involved in the crime-commission equation.

Three features of organisational crime techniques differentiate them from those used in traditional forms of crime. First, offenders have legitimate access to the location where the crime is committed. Second, offenders are spatially separated from victims. Third, the actions of offenders have a superficial appearance of legitimacy.[117] The techniques themselves have been categorised into three forms: deception, abuse of trust, and concealment and conspiracy.[118] First we look at the combination of abuse of trust and concealment to reflect on how the nature of offenders reduces risks of detection in organisational crime. We see offenders – firms involved in handling waste oils – as 'authorised representatives' who hold 'powers', which facilitate the commission of crimes. Second, we consider the combination of deception and concealment techniques and how they materialise in the organisational offence of fraud. Thirdly, we reflect on how the peculiarities of organisational crimes and criminals influence the interventions we can adopt to prevent and respond. Guardians need to possess different skills, capacities, and attitudes to contrast organisational crimes as compared to traditional forms of crime.

#### *The 'Power to' Conceal in Organisational Crime: Legitimate Perpetrators as Authorised Representatives*

The technique of abuse of trust tells us about the special opportunity afforded to organisational offenders because it underlines the paradox that makes social control of them so challenging.[119] We can think of 'trust' in two ways: first, trust

116. Benson and Simpson, Understanding White-Collar Crime: An Opportunity Perspective.
117. Ibid. 101.
118. Ibid. 102.
119. It is important to note that Shapiro uses the notions of fiduciary and agency relationships to move away from the 'status' of offenders as a determining criminogenic factor in white-collar crimes. She criticizes the focus in the literature on the micro-level features of the offenders by offering a more organisational perspective, namely how the trust is socially organised and structurally creates opportunities for abuse. Although we speak of characteristics of offenders in this Section, the stance taken in this study is not altogether different from Shapiro's as the determining feature here is not status (or power connected to status), rather it is about the capacity, i.e., the organisationally conferred role. (Shapiro, "Collaring the Crime, Not the Criminal: Reconsidering the Concept of White-Collar Crime.")

can be seen as characterising fiduciary relationships. Therefore, understanding how trust operates in facilitating organisational crime becomes a matter of understanding fiduciary relationships. Secondly, we can take the notion of fiduciary relationships to a deeper level and see how the conferral of 'power' through these relationships plays a more structural and insidious role in facilitating organisation crime.

Abuse of trust implies that there is a fiduciary relationship, which is taken advantage of in some way.

> *A fiduciary relationship exists where a person has his interests served by another... the fiduciary is a functionary who, within the limits of his powers and duties, is independent of, and not controlled by, the person for whose benefit he acts. In this independence, this freedom from immediate control, lies the final and decisive characteristic of the fiduciary office.*[120]

Fiduciary relationships are a distinguishing feature of organisational crime because its perpetrators almost always have access to the crime-scene thanks to the role given to them through these relationships.[121] For example, waste oil management firms have been delegated the task of handling waste substances by the state. This delegation is formally sanctioned through the conferral of permits. The permit means that waste management firms are agents of the state. This delegation can also be described as the creation of an "agency relationship [where] individuals or organizations act on behalf of another (the 'principal')."[122]

Such an agency relationship is problematic because it is characterised by asymmetries. The waste management firm has more knowledge about waste management than the state (and the state's own principals, the citizens). Then, it has physical control over the waste substances and the means of treating and transforming them. Lastly, the waste management firm has ambivalent functions. On the one hand, its task is managing waste in accordance with the applicable legislation – the permit crystallises this task. On the other hand, the firm – like any corporation – aims to survive and grow through the accumulation of (ever-greater) profits and the avoidance of losses. We saw above that the former task may be seen as a hindrance to the latter; hence, the ambivalence.[123]

We can say that fiduciary or agency relationships put individuals and firms in positions of power, which can then be abused. The concept of power is frequently used by scholars who investigate how and why organisational crimes occur. Indeed, many use the label of 'crimes of the powerful' to refer to this category

120. Ibid. P. 347-348 citing Finn 1977 p. 12-13.
121. Ibid.; Benson and Simpson, Understanding White-Collar Crime: An Opportunity Perspective.
122. Shapiro, "Collaring the Crime, Not the Criminal: Reconsidering the Concept of White-Collar Crime." p. 348.
123. Ibid.; Benson and Simpson, Understanding White-Collar Crime: An Opportunity Perspective.

of phenomena.[124] For the present analysis, we can make a distinction between the notions of 'power to' and 'power over'. The latter denotes a relationship of dominance and subjugation, and it is the one that we commonly find in sociological and criminological explanations.[125] The former notion is broader in its conceptual scope, and it can be equated with the term 'capacity'. We see that 'power over' is a sub-category of the wider notion of 'power to'. In this sense, 'power over' is equal to the capacity to subjugate or dominate.

What powers (i.e., capacities) do the perpetrators in our case have, which facilitate the commission of crimes by lowering risks of detection? First and foremost, the perpetrators are *expected* to be present or take actions in the place and way we saw in Chapter 4. Their doing so does not raise any red flags or warrant suspicion by potential victims or guardians. It is partly the legitimacy of the perpetrators that makes organisational crimes possible, i.e., it creates an opportunity for them to occur, while at the same time rendering them invisible by lowering risks through concealment. Only those companies and agents who have the power – the legally and socially created *capacity* – to handle our money,

124. See, for example: Simon Mackenzie, "Systematic Crimes of the Powerful: Criminal Aspects of the Global Economy," *Social Justice* (2006); David Kauzlarich and Dawn L. Rothe, "Crimes of the Powerful," in *Encyclopedia of Criminology and Criminal Justice*, ed. Gerben Bruinsma and David Weisburd (New York, NY: Springer New York, 2014); Steve Tombs and Dave Whyte, "Unmasking the Crimes of the Powerful," *Critical criminology* 11, no. 3 (2003); Gregg Barak, *The Routledge International Handbook of the Crimes of the Powerful* (Routledge London, 2015); Frank Pearce, *Crimes of the Powerful: Marxism, Crime and Deviance* (Pluto Press London, 1976); David O Friedrichs, "Crimes of the Powerful and the Definition of Crime," *The Routledge international handbook of the crimes of the powerful* (2015). In fact, the status of the offenders is a relevant factor, or even a defining factor, according to Sutherland's conceptualisation of white-collar crime: 'High social status' is often equated with power in this case. Yet, an assumption underlies this association: the powerful are also those who are socially dominant within society. We cannot dispute that, in many cases, those who perpetrate or facilitate organisational crime occupy dominant positions due to their wealth, role or reputation within a certain social or situational setting. Nonetheless, this is definitely not the case for all acts and events, which fall under the umbrella of organisational crime. It may also not be the most relevant in the context of this case study. In the subsection below we return to this notion of power as domination when looking at the pattern of enforcement. (Sutherland, "White-Collar Criminality." Stanton Wheeler et al., "White Collar Crimes and Criminals," *Am. Crim. L. Rev.* 25 (1987).

125. A lot of the Radical or Marxist criminologists rely on the idea of 'power over' as part of their explanations of crime or criminal justice policy. However, much of this literature focuses on more traditional forms of crime or how traditional forms of crime are defined and prosecuted (see, for example: Richard Quinney, *The Social Reality of Crime* (Boston: Little, Brown, 1970); *Class, State, & Crime* (New York: Longman, 1980); William Jones Chambliss, "Toward a Political Economy of Crime," *Marx and law Marx and Law / ed. by Susan Easton, ISBN 0754627322* (2008). In the case of organisational crimes, this body of literature focuses more on the fact that offenders escape the 'criminal' label because many of the harms they produce are either not criminalised nor prosecuted (this was already a main argument furnished by Sutherland). Indeed, the 'power over' explanations for organisational crime have more to do with the 'power to' define, through policy and legislation, what organisational actors do as legal, acceptable, or merely a regulatory offence. This feature of organisational offending is not discussed in detail here but will be picked up on at the end of Chapter 6.

resources, goods, and wastes also have the possibility to do so fraudulently, negligently, or in any way that is dangerous or harmful. We can also reflect on this by using the concept of lure discussed in Section 2. Here, however, our focus is on how the *legitimacy* of the perpetrators also conceals the illegitimacy of their actions rather than how their position givens them material access to the means for profit. Organisational offenders that act as agents in fiduciary relationships are uniquely placed before the opportunity to *invisibly abuse* the powers entrusted to them, which can lure them to do so.

The second aspect of power that facilitates the commission of organisational crimes requires us to think about the relationship between power and language. Language – through legal arrangements – has a constitutive function in two ways in the crimes we explore. On the one hand, it defines certain behaviours as acceptable: for example, using certain substances to produce bunker fuel or making it possible to apply the label of waste or product to a substance. On the other hand, it provides the concrete means of perpetration. The concept of 'authorised speaker' helps us to discern this. Let us consider the following statements that analyse the relationship between language and power:

> *The power of words is nothing other than the delegated power of the spokesperson, and his speech* [...] *is no more than a testimony, and one among others, of the guarantee of delegation which is vested in him.*[126]

> [*T*]*he use of language, the manner as much as the substance of discourse, depends on the social position of the speaker, which governs the access he can have to the language of the institution, that is, to the official, orthodox and legitimate speech. It is the access to the legitimate instruments of expression, and therefore the participation in the authority of the institution, which makes all the difference – irreducible to discourse as such – between the straightforward imposture of masqueraders, who disguise a performative utterance as a descriptive or constative statement, and the authorized imposture of those who do the same thing with the authorization and the authority of an institution.*[127]

> *The authorized spokesperson is only able to use words to act on other agents and, through their action, on things themselves, because his speech concentrates within it the accumulated symbolic capital of the group which has delegated him and of which he is the authorized representative.*[128]

While the above statements are formulated reflecting on certain types of authorised speakers – teachers, ministers, and priests – they are applicable to social reality generally. Structures and institutions that populate and shape our social reality are powerful because we have delegated power to them through custom or explicit acts. This delegation of authority and power is comparable to the creation of fiduciary relationships. We structurally create fiduciary relationships in order to

126. Pierre Bourdieu, *Language and Symbolic Power* (Harvard University Press, 1991). 107.
127. Benson and Simpson, Understanding White-Collar Crime: An Opportunity Perspective. 109.
128. Ibid. 111.

support the functioning of our ever-more complex (social) reality and, thereby, structurally delegate authority and power. We must then trust that this power is exercised righteously, or at least in accordance with the guidelines we set. However, in delegating power we relinquish our own ability to evaluate its righteous exercise. We even shy away from making such evaluations. We replace our scrutiny with that of 'experts'. Experts themselves have been delegated power thanks to their knowledge, as certified by degrees and experience.

It is not surprising that, when confronted with the possibility to profit and avoid loss (i.e., to survive), those entities that have been awarded powers may choose to do so, even when this requires a questionable use of such power. A waste management firm is legally empowered to certify whether a substance is a waste or not. As concerns the waste management industry, we have created a system that excludes 'masqueraders' in the sense of the second quote above. You cannot handle waste unless you have a permit to do so. However, in drawing these exclusionary boundaries we have also endowed those who are within them with more power and more trust.

At the same time, no such clear boundary has been drawn in the process of bunker fuel production. There are no permit requirements. There are no clearly authorised speakers. Everyone has a say, as long as their 'point' seems relevant to the 'debate': i.e., as long as the blend components and bunker fuel seem to power engines, they are good enough and acceptable. In fact, the little authority that exists in *this* industry, in the form of fuel specifications and material safety data sheets, backed up by the opinions of surveyors and environmental bureaus, is almost all directed towards productivity, not environmental concern. Therefore, where the label of 'suitable blend component' or 'bunker fuel' is questioned, the parameters according to which the label is applied are quite different than those for waste.[129]

The asymmetry that exists in the two industries in this respect is a fundamental component of the symbiosis that emerges at their overlap. There is a narrow door through which wastes can escape and re-enter the global supply chain. The gatekeepers who can open this door are clearly marked, authorised speakers, in the form of waste management firms with permits. Their 'authority' is powerfully blinding. Once a waste has passed through that door and been consecrated into a product, little to no obstacles – protecting the environment and human health – exist on the other side when it enters the realm of bunker fuel production. That waste management firm is then as much an authorised speaker as any other firm, which brings blend components to the market.

129. It should be recalled that both ISO 8217 Clause 5 Annex B and Annex VI to MARPOL both require bunker fuel to be produced *without* using waste substances, yet the parameters that are focused on by operators in the industry make it possible to 'forget' this prohibition and still make a marketable product. Plus, the enforcement mechanisms of both ISO 8217 and MARPOL work very differently than those in the realm of waste management (see Chapter 3 and Section 1 of Chapter 4).

It is here that we can return to the concept of system members and outsiders within a crime-facilitative system, which we discussed in Section 1. System membership, granted to those entities who operationally allow the system to run, is a double-edged sword when seen from the perspective of the techniques of organisational crime. While membership is supposed to support the proper (legal) functioning of the system by excluding those who would act in contravention of the goals of environmental conservation and protection of human health, it becomes an opportunity for questionable behaviour as well as greater profit by concentrating power as well as knowledge and oversight. At the same time, the *lack* of a system of membership on the side of blend component production – which is supposed to promote competition that, in turn, would yield the best outcomes – generates a wild west-style market. Fool's gold can be traded at the price of real precious metals and plenty of fool's gold (read: waste) is simply waiting to be (re-)used.

The foregoing shows how organisational offenders that are granted specific powers and capacities are placed in alluring positions, which enable them to abuse the powers and trust that are structurally conferred upon them, and how that same conferral makes others blind to the abuse. The conferral, in fact, also entails relinquishing of authority and foregoing expertise, which, in turn manifest themselves in opportunities for fraud.

*The Duality of Documents: From Means of Guardianship to Means of Concealment through Acts of Fraud*

Linked to the power of waste management firms in labelling substances as wastes or products, is the means by which they concretely do this: by generating and using documents. Before looking into this means of both guardianship and perpetration, let us quickly return to the techniques of organisational crime, namely deception and concealment.

Deception is "the advantageous distortion of perceived reality" and refers to the manipulation of circumstances by the perpetrator that leads to a "discrepancy between appearance and reality".[130] This is a fundamental aspect of our case study – wastes appear to be suitable blend components although they are not. Deception is relational, in the sense that the manipulated reality must be perceived by someone. 'Someone' comprises both victims and guardians. In our case, many of the ultimate victims are often unaware even of the industrial processes in which this deception is carried out. However, other firms involved in waste oil management and bunker fuel production may be more or less aware of – and participants in – this act of deception. The way formal guardians are influenced by this deception is discussed later.

130. Ibid. 102.

Concealment and conspiracy are not unique to organisational crime, yet they take on a specific form in these cases. "For ordinary street offenders, concealment may be used to hide the offender's identity. In the case of white-collar crime, it is used to hide the crime."[131] The actions of perpetrators often (seemingly) overlap with legal and legitimate practices. *Maintaining* the appearance of legitimacy is the means through which unethical or illegal actions are concealed. One of the most common forms of organisational crime is fraud, which we also see in our case study. Fraud epitomises the techniques of concealment and deception in that it consists in an act of misrepresentation, which hinges on the falsely displayed reality being acceptable to the person who is being misled. The acceptability, in turn, rests on two things: the fact that the speaker displaying reality is authorised and the fact that the falsely displayed reality is easily mistaken for the truth.

Within the waste management industry, the means by which one can differentiate whether something is a waste or not, and what kind of waste it is, is through the use of documents. Labels and accompanying documents are elements of the waste management system by virtue of legal obligations.[132] Through these documents, firms make the nature of the substances they handle discernible to third parties, whether customers or guardians. Documents and labels are also linked to company records of its transactions. These records provide insight into the activities of the company to those who have the task of monitoring its activities. In this sense, appropriate documents are a means of guardianship as the lack thereof would signal questionable or wrongful practices.

Yet, documents are also a veil to guardianship. Documents, labels, and permits remove the onus to verify whether things are truly as they seem. As is indicated in the following quote regarding the hazardous waste industry in the United States:

> *the right to be ignorant has been structured into the regulatory scheme* [...] *the generator bears no obligation to know its contractual partner beyond assuring itself that the firm has been licensed, declared fit to handle hazardous waste by one of the states.*[133]

Such circumstances have been reflected on before in organisational criminology: for example, 'self-reporting' has been seen as a 'means' of perpetrating crime where industries depend on such a system for the effective implementation of regulations. Documenting is part of waste legislation and the act of documenting

131. Ibid. 107.
132. See Section 2 of Chapter 3 as well as Section 1 of Chapter 4 for more details regarding the legislative framework applicable to waste and how documents form part of the formal system of guardianship.
133. Andrew Szasz, "Corporations, Organized Crime, and the Disposal of Hazardous Waste: An Examination of the Making of a Criminogenic Regulatory Structure," *Criminology* 24, no. 1 (1986). 18.

is carried out by those same firms which turn out to be the main perpetrators of illegal waste activity.[134]

The above holds true also for the bunker fuel portion of our crime-facilitative system, albeit in a slightly different way. Although the formal system of guardianship for this realm of activities is not as demanding and controlling as for the waste management sector, documents are still an important and mandatory feature of it.[135] These documents – material safety data sheets, bunker delivery notes and REACH certificates – provide details about the qualities and hazards of blend components and bunker fuel. This information is given by the entities handling these substances based on results of sample-testing. Fraud in the sense of outright falsification of these documents is not something so common, yet still possible in the sense of certifying as products substances that are actually wastes. Misrepresentation and deception are, nevertheless, possible and do occur just like we saw in the last example in Section 5.3. The parameters considered most important by the industry do not reveal much in terms of environmental impact. Testing, then, can be partial – it can exclude what we do not 'want' to know and still indicate what we need to know according to these welfare-blind standards. Once more, documents – and the limited information they provide – give us an excuse not to know what lies behind them.

How is it possible that documents can play this dual role? And, what is it about organisational crimes that makes these techniques – deception and concealment by fraud – so pervasive and difficult to overcome? A partial answer may be that organisational crimes take place in a context where organisational actors (as well as guardians) must straddle complexity and efficiency at the same time. We need to trust documents – just like we need to trust the authorised speakers – because to not do so would cause our complex and speedy economic system to crumble. However, our push for efficiency and for profit is felt in the same way by the authorised representative who creates and uses those documents.

Let us briefly recall the story of the Ever Given, which was mentioned in Chapter 1, to get a sense of the impact that efficiency has in our case and how it creates blindness in organisational crimes. The global economy suffered losses in the several billions because of a few days' delay of hundreds of cargo ships. Indeed, losses were estimated at millions of dollars per minute.[136] That is the context that influences the specific flow of residues into bunker fuel; which we actually know to be the frequent flow of waste oils into bunker fuel. That is the general speed, the efficient rhythm, at which the actors in these industries

134. Denzin 918.

135. See Section 3 of Chapter 3 as well as Section 1 of Chapter 4 for more details regarding the legislative framework applicable to bunker fuel and blend components and how documents form part of the formal system of guardianship.

136. Estimates were at around 9.6 bn per day over a span of 6 days, also equated with 6.7m per minute. (Mary-Ann Russon, "The Cost of the Suez Canal Blockage," *BBC News* 2021.) More details on the case are also included in Chapter 1.

must operate daily, which includes consulting the documents that accompany the substances flowing through the engines of our global consumer economy. It is the same rhythm to which state authorities must adapt when exercising their guardianship functions. Guardians know on some level that there are potential tax dollars and euros flowing before them as they run spot checks on but an insignificant number of ships or terminals or 'blend component' transports. They need to be careful to not be exceedingly thorough because to check them all would set the national and global economy back by millions *per minute*.

And so, one must have faith in the documents before us, which certify the substances that ultimately bring the comforts and knick-knacks right up to our front door from across the globe; for the stunningly low prices we have become accustomed to. Our apparent 'good faith' – our ignorance as the quote above suggests – is justified by the same rationale as the bad faith – and knowingness – of those who conceal and deceive through the manipulation of documents. Think of the stressed out, heart attack-prone delivery man who double parks his subcontractor van outside your door. How he breathlessly brings you your package of unbelievably cheap plastic or bamboo [insert product name here]. That is the mode in which 'blend component' producers (i.e., waste handlers) and bunker fuel blenders function and it is the mode in which they relate to the tool we have given them to display compliance: the waste transport document and the safety data sheet.

*Knowledge and Expertise as Barriers to Guardianship*

How could we then remove the veils created by the manipulated or 'partial' documents? By verifying whether reality matches with what is being claimed. This is one of the fundamental tasks of the formal guardians in our cases. However, we saw in Chapter 4 how this is not a simple undertaking; on the contrary, the complexity of the processes of waste oil management and bunker fuel production – both inherent features of the two industries – create an obstacle to guardianship. If guardians do not have the necessary knowledge and expertise, they cannot tell the difference between an adequate means of treatment for certain wastes or of production of blend components from one that is not appropriate. They then rely on the authority of the speaker and the authorised speech – the documents – that describe the reality they are supposed to monitor.

Acquiring the necessary expertise and knowledge are themselves arduous and expensive tasks. This is one of the reasons why the notion of self-regulation is so appealing. Industries incorporate the process of knowledge and expertise development into their practices. It is an organic component of their business, and they are best placed to develop, enact, and evaluate the validity of their procedures and activities. Any individual or entity that is not part of that organic process will always be lagging behind and, therefore, will be hindered in making an assessment as to whether things are going the way they should. It is then easier to know what a 'form', label, or accompanying document should look like. Ignorance is bliss because it is much easier, cheaper, and faster.

Why then, do we not just allow all industries to self-regulate? Why must we have such stringent procedures when it comes to waste? Why must states assume the burden of raising up capable – i.e., knowledgeable and expert – *external* and formal guardians? The theory of tipping points discussed at the end of the previous Section proposes a system of guardianship built on these premises.[137] Consider the following propositions:

> *(a) In organisations with subcultures of resistance to law, crime is more likely to occur when organisational actors are morally isolated in sealed domains of responsibility and when concerted ignorance is built into organizational communication.*[138]
> *(b) Shaming and informal control [i.e., forms of self-regulation] of organisational crime by regulatory officials are facilitated by cooperative regulation backed by firm enforcement (as opposed to regulation that is cooperative and weak or confrontational and unforgiving).*[139]

If we consider proposition (a) when reflecting on the idea of self-regulation, we can see how there is a higher chance of domains being "sealed" when no external observers need to be catered to. Documents serve as a means of communicating something that is known internally to an entity that is ignorant because it is outside of the systems that the substances to which those documents are attached refer to. If the receiver of this communication (the guardian) has no understanding of the meaning behind the documents, i.e., if the guardian does not *fluently* speak the language that is being used to communicate, then the firm need not put effort into an accurate articulation. It can merely communicate superficially, in a de-coupled manner as we saw in Section 3. This superficial communication satisfies the requirement of having communicated, regardless of the content and depth of that communication. Domains can only be sealed, and ignorance can only become concerted where the entity standing on the other side of the organisational "walls of secrecy" has no real interest in acquainting itself with or an ability to understand what happens behind those walls. How is this interest awakened and sustained? To answer this question, we first must take a moment to also consider the second statement from the theory of tipping points.

Proposition (b) tells us that we need to capitalise on the expertise of industry as well as the intra-organisational reach of the shaming that can be performed in the industry (i.e., with*in* the walls of secrecy). However, reliance on self-regulation will only work to increase compliance when formal social controls incorporate a non-stigmatising attitude and are *strong*. What does regulatory strength look like in

137. See also the discussion on responsive regulation in Chapter 1 for more details on the theory of tipping points, also referred to as the integrated theory of organizational crime (ITOC).
138. Braithwaite, "Criminological Theory and Organizational Crime ". 352.
139. Ibid. 347.

the context of organisational crimes? (Keeping in mind that regulators often have an ingrained trust of both the authorised speaker and its authorised speech.) We can say that knowing what to look for or what it looks like when things go wrong make it possible for a guardian to capably perform its duties, i.e., be strong.

The cases analysed in Chapter 4 were investigated by very technically specialised police agents. These agents possess two characteristics that are instrumental to their operations. First, their expertise, which removes the veils created by deception and concealment achieved by manipulating documents and which counters the edge of perpetrators who are specialists in their field. Second, the nature of their role: they are adversaries of the perpetrators. The members of the Andante team assume that non-adversarial, regulatory officials do not have the requisite strength in the sense of proposition (b) mentioned above to make them effective.

However, this assumption may be misguided. An adversarial stance may be helpful; and it may also be a necessary component of a dynamic enforcement strategy. We will look at this point in Chapter 6. For now, we can say that the adversarial approach is useful only insofar as it provides leverage to act *against* the interest of the firms to profit by harming the environment. An adversarial attitude creates the necessary distance that avoids complacency and ignorance that risks being fostered in a cooperative relationship. However, the theory of tipping points starts from the premise that it may actually be possible for firms to be committed to regulatory aims and not just pure profit (as mentioned in the quote at the end of Section 3). That commitment is fostered because the regulatory relationship is not dyadic: the question of compliance is not fought or negotiated solely between the firm and the formal guardians. Cooperative regulatory approaches must be strengthened by the involvement of a third 'entity': "A cooperative and firm regulatory strategy is more likely to be achieved when the agency stands in the middle between a regulated industry and an organized countervailing constituency that wields some political power."[140] This 'organised', 'countervailing' constituency may be the source of encouragement or pressure that triggers the efforts of breaking past the walls of secrecy. This constituency can push for investment in and mobilisation of the resources necessary to exercise guardianship capably. What does the organized countervailing constituency look like in our case? And, how does it influence the pattern of enforcement that, in turn, affects the distribution and attractiveness of illegal opportunities?

### *Asymmetries and the Pattern of Enforcement*

We now address the question of enforcement more narrowly: we can meditate on the degree of risk of detection and punishment that enforcement creates in

140. Ibid. 347.

the context of our case study. We have already seen that one element in the system of guardianship is weakened by its own relative applicability. Different exceptions and interpretations are incorporated in the legal and regulatory means of guardianship – the label of waste can be applied and removed based on diverse (subjective) assessments and procedures. This ambiguity in using the waste or blend component label potentially disrupts the entire system of guardianship. Negotiations are enabled at different levels – policy, judicial and operational – making it all the more difficult for guardians to carry out their control activities. If, seemingly, there is no clear standard which they can refer to, what should they uphold? However, regardless of the line that guardians must ensure is not crossed, there are characteristics of the system of guardianship itself that are important in facilitating crime. We look at this from two angles: First, we explore the issue of formal guardianship in terms of the ability of and cooperation between different enforcement agencies – administrative and criminal – and the pattern that emerges from their operation. Second, we look at the discrepancy between the global nature of the crimes and harms in our case and the lack of a global response, also linked to the issue of displacement.

*Formal Guardians and the Pattern of Enforcement*

The pattern of enforcement has been referred to in the following terms: "A knowledge of the pattern of the state's enforcement efforts and the likelihood and severity of the punishment for different offences is [...] important to our understanding of the attractiveness of various opportunities."[141] Therefore, the pattern of enforcement is linked to *formal* guardianship in that the applicable rules and related enforcement efforts derive their authority from the state.

The regulatory frameworks on environmental protection, waste management and use of chemicals create a formal system of guardianship, which comprises different (delegated) powers and tools. The events studied in Chapter 4 also include activities that are generally pursuable under criminal law (e.g., fraud and illegal transport of hazardous waste across borders). Broadly speaking, we have two types of formal guardians: administrative authorities and criminal law enforcement agencies. In the Netherlands, these authorities also often work together as part of what is known as an 'integrated approach'.[142]

We saw in Chapter 4 that one of the facilitating elements in the crime commission process was the inability of administrative authorities to adequately monitor the activities of the firms involved. Their lack of expertise (or attention) meant the firms could continue undisturbed. In the case of Crafty Collectors, police authorities looked into the history of the permit-issuing process. Crafty was often caught acting in contravention of rules on waste management, yet

141. Coleman, "Toward an Integrated Theory of White-Collar Crime." 426.
142. The integrated approach is discussed in more detail in Chapter 6.

it was continually allowed to have new permits issued. Crafty was even given the possibility to formulate the conditions of the permit, with administrative authorities ultimately 'rubber-stamping' the self-imposed conditions. Collusion was suspected, but, ultimately, incapability was linked to lack of capacity (including lack of expertise) as opposed to malicious intentions.[143] The fact that Crafty was in contact with authorities several times, yet still able to continue committing crimes shows that familiarity with the state's pattern of enforcement did not deter wrongdoing. On the contrary, we could argue that it solidified the consciousness and resolve that wrongdoing would go unpunished. Numerous studies on (organisational) crime support the idea that awareness of scarcity of enforcement and penalties contributes to encouraging and facilitating crime.[144]

Another aspect of the pattern of enforcement that should be mentioned is that of prioritisation. States have limited resources, yet they have taken on immense responsibilities to regulate and control a wide array of behaviours and activities. It is not possible for states to deal with all issues with the same degree of effectiveness, and choices often must be made at different levels – by policymakers, but also by agents in the field who cannot respond or simply monitor every human endeavour it would be in their formal powers to deal with. The choices that are made reflect the priority that a state, agency, or individual may have. An issue that plagues the prevention and contrast of environmental harms generally is the lack of prioritisation *vis-à-vis* other crimes. Sometimes, this lack of prioritisation is so extreme that the harm is not even seen as such. Indeed, we often witness that there is little to no 'sense of urgency' in dealing with corporate and environmental crime alike.[145]

We can now return to the idea of an organised countervailing constituency mentioned before. The matter of lack of prioritisation has its roots in the absence of such a constituency or rather in the *relative* lack of it when compared to the organised constituency that favours an efficient and thriving system of globalised trade. Within the neoliberal framework, there is a strong and fairly cohesive contingent that promotes economic imperatives to the detriment of environmental

143. (Criminal investigation file "Case 1" from the Andante project. Field Notes 20-21.10.2016; Field Notes 27.10.2016; Field Notes 28.10.2016.)

144. Denzin, "Notes on the Criminogenic Hypothesis: A Case Study of the American Liquor Industry." 918. Criminologists have explored the idea of deterrence in cases of organisational crime. See, for example: Shover and Hochstetler, *Choosing White-Collar Crime*; Raymond Paternoster and Sally Simpson, "A Rational Choice Theory of Corporate Crime," in *Routine Activity and Rational Choice: Advances in Criminological Theory* (Routledge, 2017); Michael L. Benson and Sally S. Simpson, *White Collar Crime: An Opportunity Perspective*, vol. 2 (Hoboken: Routledge, 2009). Law and economics scholars have also discussed this question: Michael G Faure, "Effective, Proportional and Dissuasive Penalties in the Implementation of the Environmental Crime and Ship source Pollution Directives: Questions and Challenges," *European Energy and Environmental Law Review* (2010); Michael G Faure and Katarina Svatikova, "Criminal or Administrative Law to Protect the Environment? Evidence from Western Europe," *Journal of environmental law* 24, no. 2 (2012).

145. See note 480above citing sources from green criminology that pursue this line of thought.

conservation. This contingent in some ways prevents the formation of an equally strong *countervailing* group whose mission would include ensuring righteous exercise of authority by waste management firms as well as petrochemical producers and bunker fuel manufacturers. We saw how this manifested itself in the positioning of judicial authorities, policy makers, and economic actors in the three examples in Section 3. The same drift between profit and environmental conservation may be experienced by society at large and the currents produced at this macro level filter into the choice not just to define but also to prioritise the contrast of certain activities. These currents exist at a national level and produce national strategic agendas. But they also have a global manifestation, as we see in the paragraphs below.

*Asymmetries: Global Problems without Global Responses and the Risks of Displacement*
The majority of environmental harm has transnational dimensions, by definition. The 'environment' does not belong to a single nation, therefore, damage to the environment can rarely be said to have borders. This is especially true when we think of pollution generally and pollution of seas and air specifically.[146] However, the transnational nature of environmental harm in our case is determined not only by the effects of the crimes committed but also by the global character of the activities that underlie the crimes. We have looked at this as a structural feature of the industries in Chapter 3. Our focus here is on how this aspect of the activities impacts guardianship.

We can reflect on this issue using the notion of 'criminogenic asymmetries', which are "structural disjunctions, mismatches, and inequalities in the spheres of politics, culture, the economy and the law" that, *inter alia*, "reduce the ability of authorities to control illegal activities."[147] While our economy has become globalised, our legal systems (and often our interests) remain national. The crimes we are analysing are intimately linked to the current global system of production and consumption; they epitomise the negative side-effects of

146. For a discussion on these aspects of environmental crime, see: Rob White, "Researching Transnational Environmental Harm: Toward an Eco-Global Criminology," *International journal of comparative and applied criminal justice* 33, no. 2 (2009); Grant Pink, "Regulatory Responses to Transnational Environmental Crime: An Overview of Choices, Challenges and Culture," *Environmental Crime in Transnational Context* (2016); Raymond Michalowski and Kevin Bitten, "Transnational Environmental Crime," *Handbook of transnational crime and justice* (2005); Toine Spapens and Wim Huisman, "Tackling Cross-Border Environmental Crime: A 'Wicked Problem'," in *Environmental Crime in Transnational Context* (Routledge, 2016); Antal Berkes, "Cross-Border Pollution," in *The Routledge Handbook on Extraterritorial Human Rights Obligations* (Routledge, 2021).

147. Nikos Passas, "Global Anomie, Dysnomie, and Economic Crime: Hidden Consequences of Neoliberalism and Globalization in Russia and around the World," *Social Justice* (2000); "Globalization, Criminogenic Asymmetries and Economic Crime," *Eur. JL Reform* 1 (1999). "Cross-Border Crime and the Interface between Legal and Illegal Actors." 26.

globalisation. Attempts to resolve or reduce these effects suffer from the same weakness as those contrasting other harms deriving from globalisation.[148]

Let us try to scale our focus down slightly to help us grasp this more concretely. In Europe, there are five ports, which have large bunkering facilities: Rotterdam, Antwerp, Hamburg, Le Havre and Piraeus.[149] When one of these becomes 'unavailable', customers who wish to bunker can go to one of the other four with relative ease. Although waste legislation has a strong European coverage, applicable to all the countries where these ports are located, the way this legislation is interpreted, applied, and enforced varies among these places. To compound this aspect that derives from the nature of EU law (Directives) generally, we have the fact that the waste definition is itself open to interpretation, as we saw above. This increases the potential for differences. These asymmetries are often referred to as resulting in "pollution havens".[150]

By way of example, we could argue that the port of Rotterdam has gradually become more 'resistant' to the types of crime we are analysing, also thanks to continually strengthened and refined enforcement efforts. The same authorities which have contributed to this resistance have observed a shift, or 'displacement',[151] of the activities that had been taking place in Rotterdam (and the Netherlands, generally) to the other countries in Europe where bunkering ports and waste/petrochemical firms are located.[152]

---

148. Jude McCulloch and Sharon Pickering, *Borders and Crime: Pre-Crime, Mobility and Serious Harm in an Age of Globalization* (Springer, 2012); Nita Rudra, "Globalization and the Race to the Bottom in Developing Countries," *Cambridge Books* (2008); M Ramesh, "Globalisation and National Regulations: Race to the Bottom, Top, and Middle," *Deregulation and Its Discontents Rewriting the Rules in Asia* (2006); Shabina Arfat, "Globalisation and Human Rights: An Overview of Its Impact," *American journal of humanities and social sciences* 1, no. 1 (2013).
149. For more details on the bunker fuel industry see Chapter 3. For a recent exploration of the link between ports and crime, see: Sergi, Anna, Alexandria Reid, Luca Storti, and Marleen Easton. Ports, Crime and Security: Governing and Policing Seaports in a Changing World. 1st ed. Bristol University Press, 2021.
150. Lisa A Cave and Glenn C Blomquist, "Environmental Policy in the European Union: Fostering the Development of Pollution Havens?," *Ecological Economics* 65, no. 2 (2008).Literature on differential applicability of EU law and how this has a criminogenic effect/ negative side-effects. In Chapter 3 and in Section 3 of this chapter, we also saw that there are several definitions, not just that of waste, but also of 'end-of-waste' or 'by-product' that may be determined nationally, which means the potential for creating pollution havens is multiplied.
151. For more information on the notion of 'displacement', see: Robert Barr and Ken Pease, "Crime Placement, Displacement, and Deflection," *Crime and Justice* 12 (1990); Ronald V. Clarke and David Weisburd, "Diffusion of Crime Control Benefits: Observations on the Reverse of Displacement" (2006); Derek B. Cornish and Ronald V. Clarke, "Understanding Crime Displacement: An Application of Rational Choice Theory," *Criminology* 25, no. 4 (1987); Shane D. Johnson, Rob T. Guerette, and Kate Bowers, "Crime Displacement: What We Know, What We Don't Know, and What It Means for Crime Reduction," *Journal of Experimental Criminology* 10, no. 4 (2014); Thomas Gabor, "Crime Displacement and Situational Prevention: Toward the Development of Some Principles," *Canadian Journal of Criminology* 32, no. 1 (1990).
152. Conversation during meeting on 07.04.2016. It may also be interesting to consider that what may be witnessed is not necessarily displacement but 'diffusion of benefits' instead. See: Clarke,

In Chapter 6, we will reconstruct the process whereby these special efforts were triggered and then developed in the Netherlands. At the moment, it is important for us to consider the mechanisms behind increased and improved enforcement that the Dutch example represents. Increased and improved enforcement are the result of allowing, encouraging, and pressuring formal guardians to venture past the walls of secrecy that surround complex industries and to mature sufficient skills and expertise to intervene against crime and harm. The permission, encouragement, and pressure are the result of public outcry being systematically channelled into the state apparatus. An organised countervailing constituency arises and bolsters regulatory agents who become strong enough to react capably in the face of systematic organisational wrongdoing. In Belgium, Germany, France, and Greece no similar societal movement took place. The criminogenic asymmetry is not just the result of different laws or geographical limitations to administrative reach. It is rooted in the absence of a cross-border constituency that can and wants to organise itself against the environmental damage that affects all of us.

### *Conclusions*

In this Chapter, we have gradually reconstructed the elements that make up the crime-facilitative system, which is the context of the criminal events analysed in Chapter 4. We saw that low risks coupled with high incentives and opportunities facilitate and encourage criminal activities at the overlap between waste oil management and bunker fuel production. Now, we can add another layer of reflection focusing on the idea of symbiosis. An important aspect of symbiosis is the synergy between the goals that are pursued by the organisational actors in the two industries. We saw that these goals derive from the structures of the two sectors. In simplistic terms, these goals are: managing waste in an environmentally friendly manner and producing bunker fuel for the smooth running of ships.

However, there is a goal common to both these industries, namely that of profit maximisation, which we should not forget. Indeed, this latter, overarching goal, so intimately connected to the nature and purpose of the actors that populate the system – corporations – influences perceptions in pursuit of the two former goals. Employing means to achieve those *other* goals constrains efforts towards profit maximisation. Under such circumstances, actors become susceptible to illegal opportunities to maximise profits or reduce losses within their day-to-day business. The tension between the mixture of goals provokes such susceptibility. The possibility to release such tension by pursuing *some* of the goals of each industry in questionable ways is generated by the synergy of goals. Profitably treating waste oils finds its perfect synergetic counterpart in profitably generating

---

Ronald and David Weisburd (1994). "Diffusion of Crime Control Benefits: Observations on the Reverse of Displacement". Crime Prevention Studies, volume 2. Monsey, NY: Criminal Justice Press.

blend components, for profitable bunker fuel production. This is portrayed in Figure 5.2 below, which is a re-worked version of the overlapping circles discussed in Section 2. The continuous lines show the legally permissible activities in the two industries and the dotted lines show the economically and physically available opportunities. What is new in Figure 5.2 are the arrows labelled pressure, that show the drive towards profit maximisation and efficiency; as well as the arrows labelled constraint, which represent the policy goal of environmental preservation enshrined in legislation. The tension between pressure and constraint leads to the pressure being distributed towards the parts of the overlap where it can be resolved through the symbiosis that was just described.

**Figure 5.2 Symbioses and synergies that generate a crime-facilitative system at the overlap between WOM and BFP**

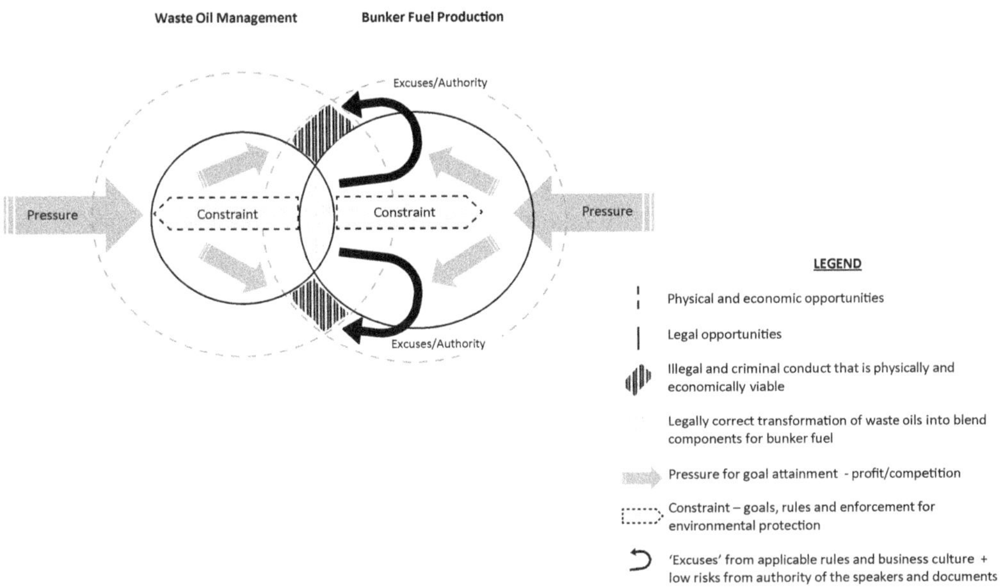


To complement the synergetic overlap of goals, we also saw that there is a synergy of opportunities at the crossroads between the two industries. Practically, legally, and psychologically taking advantage of these opportunities does not require great efforts. On the contrary, the ease with which actors can access these diverse opportunities cannot be overstated. In this respect, we explored the fundamental role of waste management and chemicals' legislation. We witnessed ambiguity in what classifies as waste. We also saw the instrumental nature of the assessment of whether waste has ceased to be such and can re-enter the global production chain. These two aspects belong to the normative-regulatory dimension of the symbiotic overlap between the two industries. They are fundamental in shaping the minds and practices of the actors working in the system. Similarly, there are normative, economic, and operational dimensions of the symbiotic overlap that add to the merely regulatory-normative one. Within the bunker fuel industry, for example, using residues is ultimately seen as 'business as usual'. The arrows going from the legitimate overlap towards the two *il*legitimate overlaps show how the normative-regulatory dimension of the symbiotic overlap provides the illegitimate practices that exist at the economic and operation overlap with the necessary 'excuses' to become acceptable or invisible.

The structural – "economic, legal, normative and organisational"- features of the system we have been exploring enter into a synergetic dance. The goals and institutional arrangements move at the same rhythm and intersect creating one pulsating system. System members – who are, at the same time, insiders *and* outsiders of the respective industries – can dance to the rhythm of the patterns that are generated by the system. It is quite natural and simple for waste management firms or waste oil holders to move smoothly from handling wastes to producing blend components. And, equally smoothly, bunker fuel producers absorb these components into their blending operations.

Measures to control or discourage such behaviour – and the structural conditions that facilitate them – are inappropriate. Guardians experience a degree of blindness merely due to the nature of offences and the offenders: the legitimacy of the actors and the capacity (the power) they have to define their activities in a way most favourable to themselves inhibits a true understanding of what they are doing. (Also shown with the arrows going from the legitimate overlap towards the two illegitimate overlaps in Figure 5.2.) This blindness is compounded by the complexity and technical nature on the activities and industries themselves. Guardians are further inhibited by the structures in which they themselves operate. Internally to one country, this may be the quality of the relationship between criminal and administrative authorities as well as the degree of prioritisation these harms receive in the enforcement agenda. Across borders, the disparity in legislation and enforcement arrangements hinders effective cooperation and uniform responses. Gaps are created by the structuration of the formal systems of guardianship as well as individual or organisational incapability. These gaps are visible to the actors in the system. Therefore, the attractiveness of the illegal opportunities to achieve profit maximisation within the context of waste management and bunker fuel production increases, as the risk of detection and punishment decreases; thus, fostering the synergies at the intersection of these two sectors.

Following from the last point, we can see that increasing the risks of detection and punishment is an important aspect to analyse as part of this case study. The organisation of formal systems of guardianship and whether formal guardians' capabilities are commensurate to the incentives and opportunities that facilitate criminogenesis are the central themes of the next Chapter.

# 6 Andante: Exploring an Example of Capable Guardianship

For a thorough study of our case, it is not enough to learn about criminogenesis. We also need to know about (capable) guardianship. Guardianship, first and foremost, as an important element *of* criminogenesis that, if altered and improved, can limit the occurrence of crime and harm. Guardianship also as the desire to contribute to progress and growth in societal well-being as opposed to bowing down to the dreadful status quo. The theoretical framework – situational crime prevention (SCP) – that structures this research is founded on the examination of guardianship as a factor in the crime-commission process. By looking at how guardianship may have been ineffective or inexistent in limiting crime, we can also reason our way towards some suggestions for its improvement.

In preceding Chapters, we saw different aspects of the system of guardianship that operates in our case: We looked at the broader policy and legal framework in Chapter 3. Then, we considered the enforcement conditions – both their merits and deficiencies – related to concrete criminal events in Chapter 4. Finally, we contemplated how the system of guardianship at different levels generates a degree of risk that contributes to facilitating crime in Chapter 5. The analysis carried out until now has mostly focused on answering the first main research question, which is: How and why do illegal waste oil management activities in the process of producing bunker fuel take place? We can now collect those different analyses together to generate some overall reflections on how guardianship needs to be strengthened with the aim of reducing illegal waste activity in the bunker fuel production process.

Nevertheless, in this Chapter we do more than just reflexively think about guardianship. We have direct information regarding the experience that a group of guardians has had. For several years, the Andante team has been learning about the crimes we have unpacked in Chapters 4 and 5 through their investigations. More importantly, they have learned about *contrasting* these crimes. They have done so, partly, based on the assumptions that underly SCP. Hence, Andante is a pertinent and insightful case for us to study through the lens of SCP. Combining the reflexive approach to guardianship with the analysis of the Andante experience will help us to answer the second main research question, which is: How can illegal waste oil management activities in the process of producing bunker fuel be limited?

Therefore, the aim of this Chapter is *not* to carry out an impact-evaluation of the work of the team.[1] "Evaluation research seeks to examine the consequences of the adoption of particular courses of action. It sets out to determine whether a particular policy or programme has been effective in achieving certain policy or programme goals."[2] The purpose of this Chapter is *different*. We look at Andante through the lenses of SCP as well as organisational criminology as a group of guardians. In SCP, *incapable* guardians contribute to increased incidences of crime. In similar vein, a crime-facilitative system in organisational criminology presupposes a low degree of risk of getting caught and punished for wrongdoing by guardians or controllers. Therefore, in this Chapter we are merely continuing to reflect on our case through these theoretical tools, but we are doing so by looking more closely at a real-life example of the 'guardian' portion of the problem-triangle as opposed to the 'targets' or 'offenders'.[3]

Before delving into the analysis of Andante as a group of guardians, we need to recall the concept of responsive regulation we looked at in Chapter 1. There we saw that criminal law enforcement – along with the punitive tools and the adversarial attitudes it presupposes – is *only oneof several* mechanisms used to foster corporate compliance. Nevertheless, this type of approach – whereby substantial fines are levied, criminal proceeds are removed, and corporate agents are held criminally accountable – is a *necessary* element of regulatory mixes. The tip of the responsive regulation pyramid gives strength and credibility to the

1. This decision is rooted in the methodological history of this study. I initially was in contact with Andante because I wanted to learn about the substantive results of their investigations. I was interested in the *modi operandi* that their dossiers documented. Naturally, I was exposed to their approach from the first day of my exploration, this is a normal consequence of interacting with data in a human context. However, over time, as I had more and more contact with the team members, and witnessed their work as a group of enforcement agents, as a group of individuals striving in their day-to-day efforts, this aspect became more and more interesting for me to observe and learn about. A lot of the information presented in this Section derives from the intensification of my conversations with the team members, which I had not anticipated at the start of the research. If had I avoided such conversations, as part of a narrow-minded resoluteness to *only* read the dossiers, I would have learned a lot less about the team and I would probably not have been invited to participate in so many of the team's activities. A large portion of the data that I collected thanks to the intensification of our conversations cannot be shared here in order to respect the focus that my research questions necessitate. That said, the data I collected – more or less advertently -was also not collected with the vision of carrying out a process evaluation of the team. No research design was developed with such a purpose in mind, nor were the data collected with the team being informed of any such aims. Therefore, although a lot of the data could be used for such a purpose, it would be methodologically and ethically dubious to do so. See Chapter 2 and the related annexes for further details about methodological choices and perspective.
2. Norman W. H. Blaikie, *Designing Social Research: The Logic of Anticipation*, 2nd ed. ed. (Cambridge, UK;: Polity Press, 2010), p. 74.
3. The crime-problem triangle is discussed in the concluding part of Chapter 3.

gradual, fair, and proportionate system that the entirety of the pyramid represents. We cannot be responsive towards corporate actors if we cannot deal with those organisations that act based on (amoral) cost-benefit assessments. We cannot be responsive if we do not have a range of tools at our disposal that credibly discourage wrongdoing, if firms persistently act in contravention to the law. Hence, it is important to take the time to reflect on the experience of a group of guardians who, formally, are designated at the top of the responsive regulation pyramid. Yet, indirectly, by looking at Andante we are also looking at the rest of the pyramid.

In the first Section of this Chapter, we review the narrative of Andante: how the team emerged, including the regulatory and enforcement conditions that prompted and contextualised its emergence. Through this narrative, we learn about what guardianship looked like in the context of our case before and during Andante's operation. The narrative then informs the analysis in the subsequent sections. Section 2 helps us deepen our understanding of Andante's work as guardians by using the notions of problem-oriented-policing and responsive regulation. Section 3 brings us back to the dynamic relationship between guardianship and criminogenesis. There we reflect on Andante through the lens of SCP. The aim is not to evaluate the results of the team's work; rather, we weave together the relevant criminological concepts, our insights on criminogenesis from preceding Chapters, and the information we have from the Andante experience to expand our understanding of the overall case and to build a more solid basis to make recommendations in Chapter 7.

## 6.1 Andante: An Overview

In this Section we consider the story of the Andante team. Several aspects are interesting for us: the way the team was formed; the questions it was set up to answer and the methods it has been using to answer these questions. We begin by exploring the team's biography, with special focus on the needs that gave rise to its creation. Then we zoom in on the team's approach and methods. Finally, we look at the team's legacy – what they have learned about both criminal events and enforcement. The data used in this Section come from the team itself: in-depth interviews with its members, observations of the day-to-day operations of the team, and documents that the team has developed for explaining its work to others.[4]

Before delving into the Andante story, it is helpful for us to situate Andante within the broader law enforcement context in the Netherlands in respect of waste legislation. Although the bunker fuel industry also includes some legally-regulated features, the powers the Andante team has used and the legal framework within

4. For a detailed overview of data collection, see Chapter 2 and the related annexes.

which it has operated with other agents is the one concerning waste management. We already looked at this in part in Section 1 of Chapter 4 in terms of the legal provisions and powers that structure the formal system of guardianship. Now we are more interested in the network of (formal) guardians and Andante's place within that network. Figure 6.1 portrays the system of guardianship in the Netherlands.

From left to right, we see different shades that help us distinguish the private from the public sector. An interesting agency in this respect are port authorities, which have powers that may be considered 'public', but the nature of these agencies is actually private, as they are organised into for-profit corporations. Within the clearly 'public' domain, there is a distinction between agencies that act through administrative law provisions and using administrative law measures and others that do so using criminal law powers and instruments. The ILT[5] disposes of both kinds of powers and is, in fact, at the forefront of the formal system of guardianship when it comes to waste management policy. In the public domain we can also make a distinction between the operational and the policy levels (shown at the bottom of Figure 6.1 with the dark grey partition).

**Figure 6.1 The agencies involved in the system of guardianship for waste management in the Netherlands**

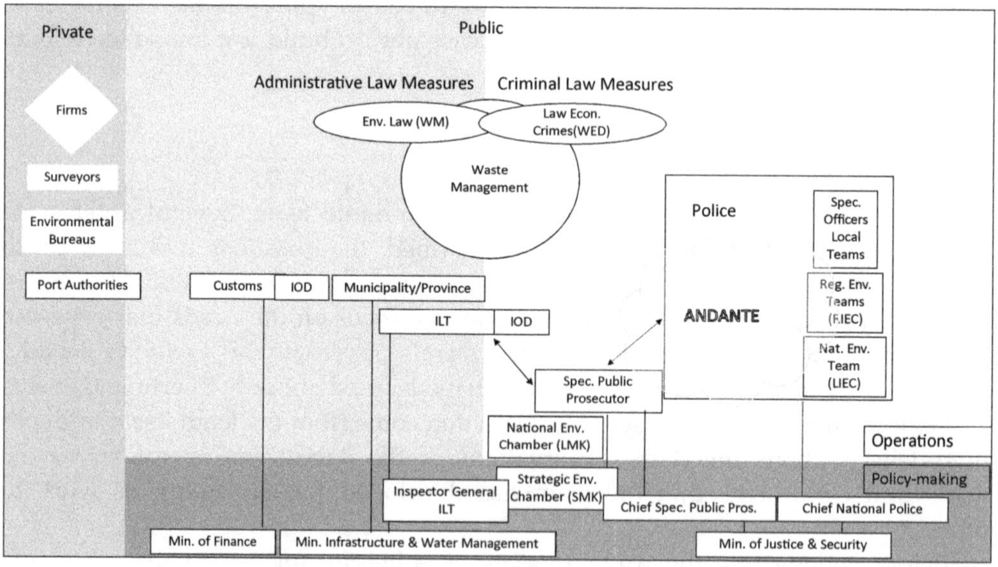


The hierarchical structure of command and control from the policy level down to the field agents has repercussions for the way enforcement is carried out in practice

5. *Inspectie, Leefomgeving en Transport* – Infrastructure, Environment and Transport. The ILT is discussed in more detail in Chapters 3 and 4.

because it creates separations and possibly contention when guardians have to work together. At the same time, it is an important factor to consider in reflecting on successful or necessary collaborative practices.

On the side of criminal law enforcement, we need to be aware that a lot has changed in the way the police corps is organised in the Netherlands in the last ten years. This process of change and reform is an important contextual factor in the formation of the Andante team. Currently, the Dutch police is divided into three levels: national, regional, and local. At each of these levels there are specialised figures in the field of environmental protection. There are ten specialised environmental teams at the regional level, which exercise their powers based on geographic scope. There is also a national unit (*Landelijke Eenheid*), under the aegis of the National Police (*Nationale Politie*), which is responsible for organised crime, 'subversive' crime and crimes having an international dimension connected to environmental harm. Furthermore, non-specialised local police units (*basisteams*) may also include individual team members who have specialised knowledge and tasks on environmental crimes. Any criminal case that emerges from the investigations of Police, Customs and ILT is overseen by a specialised public prosecutor from the National Public Prosecutor's Office for Financial, Economic and Environmental Crimes (*Functioneel Parket* – FP).

All the above cited authorities exercise their monitoring, investigation, and enforcement powers concurrently, which can lead to overlaps and fragmentation. To overcome this obstacle, two entities have been created: the Strategic Environmental Chamber (*Strategische Milieukamer* – SMK) and the National Environmental Chamber (*Landelijke Milieukamer* – LMK). The SMK is a national coordinating body that develops policy and sets priorities that guide the work of the agents working on the ground to respond to environmental crime, which extends beyond violations of waste management rules.[6] The LMK is also known as the Tactical Environmental Chamber because it supports the ordinary management of the casework, including the weighting of individual cases.

In Figure 6.1, we can see that Andante does not fit into any of the boxes that represent the agencies, which have just been enumerated. The members of the team are police officers who belonged to specific units before participating in Andante and who went back to those units. The units intended are those that fit into the clearly circumscribed boxes in the diagram. It was from its ambiguous positioning (i.e., outside the clear and standard structures of the police organisation) that Andante has investigated crimes; collaborated with the other

6. The Chair of the SMK is the Chief Public Prosecutor of the National Public Prosecutor's Office for Financial, Economic and Environmental Crimes (Functioneel Parket) and its other members lead the agencies the SMK coordinates. (Inspector General ILT, the Inspector General of the Netherlands Food and Consumer Product Safety Authority (NVWA), the Environmental Crime Portfolio Holder on behalf of the Force Command of the National Police of the Netherlands, and the Member of the South Holland Provincial Executive responsible for the Environment on behalf of the local authorities.

agencies portrayed above (as well as others abroad); and, ultimately, it is from this position that Andante has learned a great deal about the illegal waste activities that take place in the process of bunker fuel production.

*The History and Origins of the Andante Team*

> *And, in fact, this [Andante] is the outcome of it. And for years we have been busy with oil. Yeh well we, we were busy with oil, we were always busy with it, but Probo Koala triggered it. Then we started, because it was a big investigation, we also had the time because there was, the political urgency was there, the whole societal upheaval about the dumping in Abidjan. So, we had the time and we got the data and we started to really really get insight into 'why are they doing it, what is the earning model – the verdien model – what is driving these guys?'*[7]

The origins story of Andante is unsurprising for anyone who dabbles in corporate environmental crime. Under the calm surface of our economic system, callous attitudes and questionable practices run deep. Then, suddenly, we get a momentary glimpse into their devastating consequences. Death. Suffering. Destruction. And the cries of public outrage allow some of the barriers to action and justice to topple, even if briefly. Trailing the landmark case of the *Probo Koala,*[8] an integrated strategy to fight crime in the oil sector was initiated in the Netherlands. The experience and knowledge matured by some members of the police, the prosecution service, and the administrative branch of enforcement – ILT – were constructively channelled into concerted efforts.[9] While the case was being investigated and brought to criminal court, many resources were being mobilized to assure that such terrible events could be prevented in the future. One of the strategies pursued was that of setting up '*Waakzame Acties*': systematic checks of transports carried out by several enforcement agencies, both criminal and administrative. The transports were the connecting links between locations where oil and chemical wastes were produced, collected, stored, transformed, and then re-used in the production of bunker fuel. The authorities involved each had responsibilities, powers, and interests in the monitoring and enforcement of these transports from different perspectives.[10]

7. Interview 7 on 28.02.2020.
8. The facts of the *Probo Koala* case are summarised in Chapter 1. Please see the notes in that Chapter for the relevant secondary references. ECLI:NL:RBAMS:2010:BN2149; ECLI:NL:RBAMS: 2010:BN2068. Appeals: ECLI:NL:GHAMS:2011:BU9237; ECLI:NL:GHAMS:2011:BR0014.
9. Interview 1 on 05.09.2017 [Author's translation].
10. In Chapter 4, we saw which actors are involved in the formal system of guardianship in our case. There we also explored the legislative basis of their powers and what their tasks are. See also Figure 6.1 above and the related description.

*In principle, we went with all specialists together, from different agencies, so ILT, Customs, Police and, if necessary, we also had people from the municipality, the LMA;*[11] *so all those agencies put together at one location, and with the knowledge of all those agencies we would go look and see: 'ok, how do the transports – in the field of waste oil – look: who collects it; who brings it in; who processes it; what happens then, when it is processed; where does it go, to which terminal, from that terminal where does it go?'*

This approach bore many fruits, especially in the form of information about some of the activities and actors operating at the crossroads between waste management and bunker fuel production. Furthermore, parallel to the carrying out of systematic checks by state authorities, some scholars also began to take interest in the questions that injustices like the *Probo Koala* case raised. Studies – not just in criminology but also from specialists in more technical topics relevant to environmental protection – began to dissect the patterns of activity underlying the two industries. Their findings matched the evidence of systematic wrongdoing that *Waakzame Acties* had been demonstrating.[12]

While the results of the endeavours of both academics and enforcement agencies were a great advancement, they brought with them new questions and needs. Specifically, the collective checks led to the realization that laws were being systematically violated within the waste oil sector, thus triggering the demand to investigate and prosecute. However, in response to this demand, the existing structures appeared unsuitable and unprepared. And so it was that the process of learning and capacity building continued to progress into the formation of a team, specialized and specializ*ing* in contrasting these crimes. One of the agents involved from the start describes the sequence of events in the following terms.

*So, we did [Waakzame Acties] for three years, we got more and more knowledge of all the information, especially of all the flows, of the whole chain, [...] we saw from that information that a lot of wrong things happened – fraudulent actions – only the point was 'who is going to investigate and verbalize that now?' And that was never well thought through within the police – which team is going to do that, in the end.*

*So, there were teams for that, those are the regional environmental teams;*[13] *only they can't handle this kind of large investigations. And within our landelijke eenheid,*[14] *you don't have a team that deals with*

11. The LMA – *Landelijke Meldpunt Afvalstoffen* – is discussed in Chapters 3 and 4.
12. A de Buck et al., "Blends in beeld. Een analyse van de bunkerolieketen," (Delft: CE Delft, 2011); ACM Spapens, "Vuile Olie: Een Onzichtbaar Probleem Met Grote Gevolgen," *Het tijdschrift voor de politie* 75, no. 8 (2013). Inspectie Leefomgeving en Transport (ILT), "Heavy Fuel Oil for Sea-Going Vessels on-Road Fuels for West Africa Blended in the Netherlands," (2018).
13. The (re-)organisation of the police corps in the Netherlands is described in a document of the Minister for Security and Justice, see: Minister van Veiligheid en Justitie, "Inrichtingsplan Nationale Politie," ([2012] 2015). The relationship of the regional teams to the wider police organisation is visible in Figure 6.1 above.
14. See note 594above. The term *'landelijke eenheid'* is kept from the original quote because the Dutch police organization was re-structured in recent years and this aspect of Andante's historical

> *this kind of big environmental issues; and that was always the point: you have a lot of information about crimes, but nobody prosecuted it, nobody investigated it. [O]nly then the investigations always had to go to those regional environmental teams, and they couldn't carry them out, so they had to hire [a specialist] to help with the investigations there, so to speak.*
> *It would be best if there were specialist teams on multiple themes. Because now it's a [police] environmental team for each region, they need to know everything – a case with asbestos, then another case on soil. But you don't go into that with detailed specialisation, you go into it with a general specialisation. And these oil investigations require in-depth specialisation, more knowledge than general knowledge.*[15]

Specific capacities and resources were required to answer to the needs that the systematic checks revealed, and this was the starting point for the Andante team. That, and the insurmountable challenges of prosecuting complex environmental cases against large multinational corporations. The case against Trafigura – the culprits behind the events of the *Probo Koala* – was concluded with convictions and fines being levied against the corporate giant and its leadership.[16] However,

---

context is important in the story of the team and the *programma*. In 2013, the police corps was substantially reorganised based on the provisions of the Police Law of 2012 (*Wet van 12 juli 2012 tot vaststelling van een nieuwe Politiewet*). One of the aims of the reorganisation was reduce fragmentation by, amongst other things, bringing together a number of previously separate units and departments under a national corps (*landelijke eenheid*). The Andante team members themselves repeatedly said that the reorganisation was ongoing during their operation -"*weet je, we zitten in een reorganisatie*", is a sentence I heard at least ten times to contextualise both clever achievements and frustrating problems that the team faced (For example, this topic was extensively discussed with two officers from the team in a conversation on 12.04.2017). The reorganisation meant that many officers, across the country, were already being moved from one department to another. Andante could benefit from the temporary posting of officers before they were more permanently relocated to their unit of destination. On a website where the Andante *programma* is briefly described, the following is also stated: "Every disadvantage has its advantage. As a result of reorganisation, we have 20 unfilled vacancies, we do not exist in accounting terms, so we have no money. This fact makes us creative!" Andante had to exist outside the police organisation because the organisation was in flux. Politie NL – Politie Academie, "Andante: Foute Stookolie," https://www.politieacademie.nl/thema/opsporing/LaboratoriaOpsporing/Paginas/Andante-foute-stookolie-.aspx.

15. Other interviews (nos. 1-6) have looked more in depth into the kind of training and experience the Andante officers have gone through.
16. Both criminal and civil cases were brought to court in the Netherlands. The criminal cases were against Trafigura, its president director Claude Dauphin and one of its employees leading the blending operations. In 2010, Trafigura was convicted for the transportation of the waste in violation EU Regulation 1013/2006, and for concealing the hazardous nature of the waste. A fine of one million euros was imposed. The conviction was confirmed in 2011 upon appeal. Further appeals were lodged by Trafigura and the OM, but were withdrawn after a settlement was agreed, which made the appeal court's ruling final. Trafigura was obliged to pay the one-million-euro fine and agreed to contribute 300,000 euros to repairing the damage caused. The employee leading blending operations was initially subjected to a conditional sentence of six months' imprisonment and a fine of 25,000 euros. This was overruled in appeal proceedings. As part of the settlement with Trafigura, the employee withdrew a further appeal upon payment of 25,000 euros. The case against Claude Dauphin was withdrawn upon his payment of 67,000 euros. The civil case in the Netherlands was a collective action (ECLI:NL:GHAMS:2020:1157). The case

other similar cases rapidly ended in frustration and smoke. The complexity of the operations in the waste oil and bunker fuel sectors created evidentiary obstacles. The cases left too much room for persuasion to those who could afford the flashiest and most convincing teams of experts and lawyers. The enforcement agencies were not adequately prepared in the face of this: they did not know the inner workings of the industry well enough and did not have the conceptual tools to break it down in a way that was easily understandable for the court. It was too much too soon, they reflected. They needed to learn step by step.[17] Enter Andante.

> *[O]ur goal was to make, say, the entire industry visible, so to make the entire chain understandable [...] So, we started that: we made several steps, to make the chain visible, and in each step it had to be demonstrated, through investigations, that each part of the chain went wrong.*[18]

This approach to investigating is not the norm within the police organisation. It is reminiscent of a scientific analysis of social phenomena; possibly something that could be carried out by teams involved in problem-oriented policing, but, in this case, for organisational crime.[19] The exceptional nature of this approach required an equally exceptional set-up of the team itself. Therefore, in 2011, Andante was set up as a *programma:* a group of police officers, who explore a specific topic for a limited amount of time and who benefit from working with a prosecutor assigned to them.

Working in the context of a *programma* meant that the team had to design a strategy to answer their investigative research questions. They broke down their work into five stages, which reflected the process of fraudulently transforming wastes into products. We look at these different stages and what it means to work in a *programma* in more detail below when examining the methods of the team. At the moment, it is important for us to keep in mind that, for each of the five stages, the team would select a few representative cases following either systematic checks, formal complaints, or intelligence linked to preceding cases.[20] Each case was seen as more than an opportunity to investigate, prosecute, and convict. In fact, the main aim was that of learning about the pertinent stage in the fraudulent chain so that similar cases, which may emerge later, could be investigated better.

---

was appealed in 2020. Civil charges were also brought through a collective suit in the UK. In 2009, a settlement was reached and approved by the High Court whereby the 30,000 claimants would receive a share of the total agreed amount of 30,000 pounds. However, only 6,000 of the claimants received the money because of illegitimate practices by the organisation 'National Coordination of Toxic Waste Victims of Côte d'Ivoire', which falsely claimed to represent the claimants. *'Agouman v. Leigh'* (2009), High Court of Justice, [2016] EWHC 1324 (QB).

17. Memo 1; Memo 2; Field Notes 20-21.10.2016; Interview 1 on 05.09.2017 [Author's translation].
18. Interview 1 on 05.09.2017 [Author's translation].
19. Problem-oriented-policing is an approach to policing, which was developed in response to more traditional forms of offending. For a more detailed discussion of this, see Section 6.2 below.
20. Memo 2; Field Notes 20-21.10.2016.

Nevertheless, operating as a *programma* did not mean complete removal from the broader enforcement context. On the contrary, once *Waakzame Acties* had concluded, new initiatives were organised, namely *Zwarte Stromen* and *African Blends*. Both these initiatives had similar goals to their predecessor: collaboration between different state agencies to systematically monitor the waste oil branch, with *African Blends* being more focused on the shipment of waste oils to the African continent.[21] Below, we discuss *Zwarte Stromen* in more detail given that they were closely linked to Andante's functioning. The next subsection is dedicated to reviewing the team's aims, approach and methods in more detail.

*The Setup of Andante: Purpose and Context*

The Andante team has developed a series of documents through which its work is introduced and explained.[22] An important function of these documents is that of helping others to begin walking along the same investigative and capacity-building path they have been treading in the last decade.[23] In one such document, they share a set of explicit objectives, shown in an extract in Figure 6.2. Here we see a clear link between the actions undertaken prior to the creation of the team and the aims of the team itself. The first five goals are directly connected to the systematic wrongdoing uncovered through *Waakzame Acties*. They also show how Andante operates as a *criminal* law *enforcement* team. They focus on crimes; and they intend to enforce, prosecute, and deprive culprits of their illegally obtained gains.

Yet, the last two objectives reveal the uniqueness of Andante's approach. 'Structural change' indicates an attitude to intervention that goes beyond assigning

21. See: (ILT), "Heavy Fuel Oil for Sea-Going Vessels on-Road Fuels for West Africa Blended in the Netherlands."One of the officers describes the difference between the two types of systematic checks like this: "During our Waakzaam Acties and Zwarte Stromen Acties we have seen waste oils being processed (simple splitter fractionator – vacuum distillation) in a bottom and top fraction. We saw that the bottom fractions were used as a fuel oil components and the top fractions were blended in gasoline in Dutch terminals to be exported to West-Africa. Because these fractions can be considered waste and do not meet the European standards for gasoline they were exported to West Africa where there are limited regulations for gasoline. Andante concentrated to investigate the bottom fractions (fuel oil) and the ILT concentrated to investigate the top fractions (gasoline – African blends)." (Written comment from police agent on 15.04.2021).
22. See Table 1 in Annex II for a complete list of the documents that were shared with me by members of the Andante team, including a description. For a more detailed overview of the data that was selected and collected during the field work with the Andante team see Chapter 2 and the related annexes.
23. These documents are, for example, distributed to agents who join during the *Zwarte stromen* action days. During the briefing on the first morning, a presentation is given alongside the distribution of the documents. A lot of emphasis is placed on how awful the crimes are and on how unjust it is that the companies involved are enriching themselves at the expense of our health and the environment. The agents involved in the systematic checks are made aware that their work during the action days is linked to a wider process of learning about enforcement, and that the evidence they gather shows only part of a systematic problem in the fuel oil industry (Field Notes 25-26.09.2017.)

individual responsibility and even beyond the manipulation of costs and benefits in the immediate situations that contextualise criminal events. There is a recognition that the industrial structure of the fuel industry is a major component in facilitating those criminal events. The notion of a 'programmatic approach' is not further defined or clarified in the document.[24] Fortunately, other conversations and interviews give us a picture of what it entails, namely breaking down both the crimes and the industry into component processes; and using the chain-investigation method.[25] Overall, these objectives give us some insight into the ideology and assumptions underlying the work of the team. They want to deter and enforce in a more traditional sense, which we can look at through the SCP framework. However, they also want to do more, they want to change an industry. This reveals a more critical stance towards crime and enforcement, which is less common in mainstream policing, even of organisational crimes.

**Figure 6.2 Extract from "Blauwdruk Team Andante 2017 Engels", p. 3**

Andantes objectives:

- Getting an understanding of the criminal activities and networks in the fuel oil sector.
- Enforcement of (inter) national rules and legislation in relation to fuel oil trade.
- Prosecution of companies in the global trade in "filthy" fuel oil.
- Following the money flows within the international fuel oil trade.
- Deprivation of illegally obtained assets.
- Provoking structural changes within the fuel oil industry.
- Creating a programmatic approach of environmental investigations of the fuel oil sector.

As can be seen from the last portion of text Figure 6.2, the collaboration with other agencies is explicitly mentioned as a feature and strength of the way Andante operates. We saw in the preceding subsection, that Andante actually emerged

24. In the Netherlands, the concept of a '*programmatische aanpak*' (programmatic approach) is used in a very specific way within in the realm of environmental regulation and enforcement. In that context, a programma is a policy tool whereby ultimate objective can be achieved through various stage of implementation and local or or provincial authorities have more flexibility than usual in assessing compliance with permits because they use the parameters set out in the programma instead of rules formulated at national or European level, for example. An overview of the way '*programma*' and '*programmatische aanpak*' are used as well as the related legal instruments these notions are related to can be found at: https://iplo.nl/regelgeving/instrumenten/programma/kenmerken-programma/.
25. Memo 1; Memo 2; Field Notes 20-21.10.2016; Interview 1 on 05.09.2017 [Author's translation].

partly in response to evidence collected through *Waakzame Acties* and that it has continued to work in collaboration with others through *Zwarte Stromen*. These systematic checks are not unique to this particular story or field of enforcement. They are an example of a broader approach to and culture of enforcement in the Netherlands, known as the integrated approach.[26] The following paragraphs are dedicated to exploring the integrated approach as a contextualising feature of the work of the Andante team.

We can describe the integrated approach in the following terms: A multiplicity of actors having different perspectives, capacities and interests *collaborate* in order to reduce crime, unwanted behaviour and harm.[27] In practice, this collaboration has two dimensions. On the one hand, monitoring and enforcement activities are carried out in a collaborative, successive and graduated manner by both administrative and criminal law agencies. On the other hand, integrated approaches can be seen as a form of multi*disciplinary* practice in enforcement. The resources, expertise and access to different types of information that different agencies have are pooled together to generate more knowledge about certain crime areas or markets. Integrated approaches, particularly in the Dutch context, are often implemented based on the same assumptions that underlie SCP strategies, which means that they function on the basis of rational choice explanatory models. Therefore, the limitations inherent in the rational choice perspective are transported into the implementation of integrated approaches. Integrated

26. The Netherlands stands out as a country in which many efforts have been made to implement integrated approaches. This enforcement strategy was originally developed in response to organized crime activities such as drug and human trafficking. Dutch policymakers were inspired by the experience in combating organized crime matured in the United States and Italy. In those jurisdictions, the rootedness and pervasiveness of the *mafia* had impacted the integrity of the legal system. Departing from those experiences abroad, Dutch policymakers began learning about what it takes to prevent organized crime without resorting predominantly to repressive criminal law measures. Indeed, this approach was meant to resolve the issue that criminal law enforcement measures did not seem to function effectively. Hence, the original target of the integrated approach was organized crime, which in the Netherlands often took the form of transit crime. Over time, this strategy has come to characterize Dutch enforcement in a variety of sectors, especially where the crimes involved are considered as 'undermining' society, which is also a concept that was originally linked to organised crime. See note 28 below.
27. The approach has been defined in the following terms: "An approach based on joint responsibility for the police, the judiciary, the business community and government" [Author's translation]. The original (*"Een aanpak waarbij een gezamenlijke verantwoordelijkheid voor politie, justitie, bedrijfsleven en bestuur de basis vormt."*) quote is taken from p. 14 of Centrum voor Criminaliteitspreventie en Veiligheid, "Handboek Bestuurlijke Aanpak Georganiseerde Criminaliteit – Het Instrument in De Praktijk," (Utrecht: Colofon, 2010). See also: John Smits et al., "Bestuurlijke Aanpak Georganiseerde Criminaliteit," (Arena Consulting/Pro Facto, 2013). Toine Spapens, "Macro Networks, Collectives, and Business Processes: An Integrated Approach to Organized Crime," *Eur. J. Crime Crim. L. & Crim. Just.* 18 (2010); Maaike Peters and Antonius Spapens, "The Administrative Approach in the Netherlands," *Administrative approaches to prevent and tackle crime: Legal possibilities and practical application in EU Member States* (2015); Wim Huisman and Hans Nelen, "Gotham Unbound Dutch Style," *Crime, Law and Social Change* 48, no. 3 (2007).

approaches are often geared towards and lead to the implementation of policy and enforcement changes that target the balance of costs and benefits of situations and contexts.[28]

The Andante project emerged in this setting. Many features of the integrated approach can be seen in the work of the team, especially if we look at their involvement in *Waakzame Acties* and *Zwarte Stromen*. The team has actively sought out the collaboration of other state agencies. However, the team has also distinguished itself in its decisions to *exclude* some actors from the integration and *include others* that are normally not envisaged. In interviews and conversations, the team members have linked these decisions to the nature of the crimes and criminals themselves but also to the way state agencies function. Furthermore, the team has participated in collaborative spaces in a different way than may be considered the norm. Their work as a *programma* and their dedication to structural change have meant that they took advantage of the collaboration mainly as a means of building a widening pool of capable guardians. They looked past the successful investigation of cases as the sole purpose of the collaboration. Let us consider both the ways they have excluded some actors and included others.

Regarding the decision to exclude, two reasons emerged from conversations with team members and other criminal law enforcement agents: one linked to the organisational structure of state agencies and the other to organisational dynamics within an industry where state and business interact. Regarding the former, the integrated approach has limits because each agency has its own targets and structure to answer to. Cooperating with administrative authorities was described several times as a positive experience when it came to one-on-one interaction with agents in the field. However, as soon as work on 'shared' cases came to the attention of those further up the hierarchy of responsibility, the pressures and interests of middle management would create tension between the goals of administrative agencies and criminal law enforcement.[29] At this level of the organisations, the two branches of the state were no longer on the same team. Indirectly, they each had to compete to show how they were reaching their respective targets.[30]

---

28. Huisman and Nelen discuss the underlying (explanatory) assumptions behind the Dutch integrated and administrative approaches in: Hans Nelen and Wim Huisman, "Breaking the Power of Organized Crime? The Administrative Approach in Amsterdam," in *Organized Crime: Culture, Markets and Policies* (Springer, 2008).
29. Field Notes 25-26.09.2017; Field Notes 26-27.09.2017.
30. If the administrative authority could wrap up a case 'on its own', it would increase its own quota and the closed case would not enter the figures related to criminal law enforcement. Likewise, cases that had to shift or were caught by criminal law enforcement would not count as a success for the administrative agency. Both agencies would then have an interest in frustrating each other's efforts. Scholars from other disciplines have reflected on how Anthony Downs, *Inside Bureaucracy* (Boston: Little, Brown, 1967); Tenaw Gedefaw Abate, Rasmus Nielsen, and Max Nielsen, "Agency Rivalry in a Shared Regulatory Space and Its Impact on Social Welfare: The Case of Aquaculture Regulation," *Aquaculture Economics & Management* 22, no. 1 (2018); William

The second point of tension that impacts collaboration is the long-held belief that administrative authorities, especially at higher levels in the organisation, are subject to capture. Conversely, criminal law enforcement is thought to be blessed with independence and integrity.[31] The economic clout of the oil – and, generally, the transport sector – of industry has been referred to in linking corporate harm and illegalities to the Dutch system of politics and governance.[32] Let us consider a quote from one of the interviews with members of the Andante team in order to understand how this impacts (the attitude towards) collaboration.

> ***Interviewer:*** *And how is your relationship as criminal enforcement agents to the [waste oil and bunker fuel] branch?*
> ***R7b:*** *Communication on my part occurs only when we investigate, occurs when we investigate the companies. Not so much without investigation going on.*
> ***R7a:*** *And that's the same for me.. And if they want to have talks on policy or changes in permits, it's then the bevoegde gezag [competent authority] I'll point to, they should have the discussions there, or in politics, or in permit negotiations[...] And I always explain that we are the organization that looks*

---

A Niskanen, "The Peculiar Economics of Bureaucracy," *The American Economic Review* 58, no. 2 (1968); D. Martimort, "The Multiprincipal Nature of Government," *European Economic Review* 40, no. 3-5 (1996); W. E. Oates and R. M. Schwab, "Economic Competition among Jurisdictions – Efficiency Enhancing or Distortion Inducing," *Journal of Public Economics* 35, no. 3 (1988).

31. Interestingly, in some analyses of the implementation of integrated approaches in the Netherlands against organised crimes, the issue of capture has been reflected on critically. The argument has been that organised crime in the Netherlands does not have the same political aims or effects as it has in the United States and Italy. Using administrative measures in those countries has been a tool for limiting the spread of political influence of the *mafia* because organised crime has often functioned as a shadow state, undermining the legal state apparatus. The same cannot be said of the way Dutch organised crime has operated, which removes the socio-historical basis for administrative law measures to be taken for this type of crime, hence the critique. See: Nelen and Huisman, "Breaking the Power of Organized Crime? The Administrative Approach in Amsterdam." Symbioses between upper and underworld have not had the same *structural* impact in the Netherlands. Yet, one could argue that the relationship between corporations and the Dutch state might be more similar to that between the mafia and the Italian or American administration. However, that might mean that the impact of an 'administrative approach' would be wholly different, especially if we consider the reflections on authorised representatives mentioned in Section 5.4.

32. See Sections 5.3 and 5.4 and the related references for a discussion on the relationship between the oil sector and the Dutch government. See also Section 6.3 and Section 5.3 for a discussion on the negotiation of environmental and economic imperatives. An anecdote mentioned in conversation with the interviewees was that regarding the naming of the ministry that is responsible for environmental policy. The same ministry is also responsible for infrastructure and transport. In 2010, the question of how to name the ministry was discussed: should it be the 'ministry of environment and infrastructure' or the 'ministry of infrastructure and environment'? The latter was chosen and, since 2017, the *Ministerie van Infrastructuur en Milieu* is the *Ministerie van Infrastructuur en Waterstaat.* This anecdote was cited as an example of the tendency in Dutch politics to prioritise economic imperatives, including the image of the Netherlands as a country where transport and trade are the foundation of a flourishing economy and society. The environment has its place in policy and politics, and that is immediately *after 'Nederland verkeerstaat'*. (Field Notes 28.02.2020.)

*back [gestures], so we just come into play at the moment things have happened, and then we'll have an opinion about it. But we don't start beforehand and say this is approved by [the criminal law enforcement branch].*

*The policy makers also tend to be part of that game of and lobbying and influencing policy and permits. And so they organize sessions with the branch or with a certain firm and then put the problems on the table and see what solutions can be found. [criminal law enforcement agents] should not be at that table, that would influence our position, [...] it influences[their] objectivity. And it's also one-sided. It's only the companies, or the waste, but it's not other parts of society, say the environment.*

***R7b:** I was part of for a year, or one and a half year, in a working group between the branch, the authorities – ILT – and police. And we discussed what restrictions there should be for the waste oil industry. And the oil industry. And there you saw that the influence of the branch on the authorities was huge. On the one hand, I was glad to be there because I was the only critical voice in that group. The only one.*

***R7a:** But more on a principle level, police and prosecutor are not the persons who should be participating in policy making. We are law enforcers. So, give us the law and we will enforce. And we can discuss with the lawmakers about the quality of the law or it should be better, or broader, or whatever, or out of the way. But that's a conversation of the law maker and the law enforcer. But the subject of our enforcement shouldn't be at the table [in conversation with the companies] or that could be of conflict of our position we should take [later during prosecution].*

***R 7b**: I totally agree, but the opportunity to see that the influence was huge on the authorities, and that they dictated the authorities how the program should look like and the letters to the ministry how they should be*

***R 7a:** And be aware, at that table. there was not Greenpeace, there was no inhabitants of people living around the waste plant, or (...)*

***Interviewer:** Were they not invited, or did they not attend?*

***Both:** No No, not invited.*[33]

Reflecting on the views shared in these quotes, we can say that the members of the Andante team see integrated approaches as important tools to increase compliance. However, they believe that integrated approaches can only function under certain conditions. It is essential that there be a separation between state and business that guarantees the integrity of state organs. Therefore, the kind of integrated approaches whereby the collaboration directly includes the subjects of regulation – corporations – themselves is not acceptable from the team's perspective. In fact, this is the core of the argument of the Andante team members against *uncritical* reliance on integrated approaches. Integration can only be beneficial when it leads to business respecting the law, which in turn protects human and environmental welfare. Direct collaboration with business is unwise and contrary to that protection under certain circumstances. For example, in a context where business exerts power and pressure *vis-à-vis* the state and where other stakeholders

33. Interview 7 on 28.02.2020.

do not or cannot do the same, which is the set of circumstances that the notion of an 'organised countervailing constituency' that we discussed at the end of Chapter 5 tries to avoid or overcome. Hence, according to this view, criminal law enforcement should collaborate with other law enforcement agencies. And it should do so in a way that maintains the same integrity that the separation between state and business is generally supposed to uphold.[34]

Furthermore, the team members' perspective revolves around a specific conceptualisation of what the function of criminal law enforcement is. Especially in a context where business has the upper hand, it is imperative that criminal law agencies maintain the independence necessary to intervene when it is appropriate for them to do so: i.e., *after* criminal activities have taken place.[35] Avoiding dialogue with business as criminal law enforcement agents is, therefore, also rooted in a deep respect of the principle that criminal law should be used as an *ultimum remedium*. Ultimately, the belief motivating the team's decisions to exclude certain actors or avoid dialogue with business are based on the belief that repressive deterrence measures, and the agents that use them, should only come into play when the policymaker has failed due to incapability, collusion, or corruption.[36] It is based on these underlying ideas and assumptions that Andante has taken on its role as that of *supporting other state agencies* to learn from their experience. In that way, prevention can be achieved by the "*bevoegde gezag*", the competent authority.

At the same time, Andante has recognised how *other* stakeholders – direct victims, environmental conservation advocates, the broader public – do not as easily get an audience with the competent authority. Therefore, it is important to inform and empower these actors. They can counter the definitional, regulatory and enforcement tendencies, which over-reliance on dialogue with companies can have in shaping policy. That is the source of the decision of the Andante team to include other actors, especially the media and academia.[37] By building more public awareness and consensus about the harms, the team would no longer be alone in

34. We could use the notion of state-corporate crime to understand how the lack of separation can become problematic. We explore this idea further in Section 3.
35. In contrast with notions such as predictive policing, defined as "This approach means that police departments analyze statistical historic data to predict in what geographic areas there is an increased chance of criminal activity. This type of information can be used by law enforcers to efficiently deploy their resources to prevent criminal behavior." Meijer, and Wessels. "Predictive Policing: Review of Benefits and Drawbacks." *International Journal of Public Administration* 42, no. 12 (2019): 1031-1039.
36. Interview 7 on 28.02.2020 and Field Notes 28.02.2020.
37. Memo 1; Memo 2; Field Notes 20-21.10.2016; Interview 7 on 28.02.2020 and Field Notes 28.02.2020. The inclusion of media and scholars is not unique to Andante's version of the integrated approach, however, the way they have done it and the assumptions they have based this inclusion on are particularly interesting for our study, especially because of the relationship to the causes of environmental crime. See the last part of Section 6.3. for a deeper reflection on this point.

their interventions against it. Andante has potentially contributed to the formation of an 'organised countervailing constituency'.

Having reviewed how Andante came into existence and the foundations and context within which it developed, let us now review the methods and approach the team adopted for its functioning.

*The Methods of Andante: Programmatic Approach, Chain-Investigation and Capacity-Building*

> *They did it very cleverly with Andante, they made a* programma, *which has advantages and disadvantages. The advantage is that a programma is completely independent, and nobody has anything to say about it, except the prosecutor and the team leader. So, they can never really bother you. The disadvantage is, that you're not officially within the [police] organization, you're not an official detective team; so, you stay until the topic is finished, the programma is finished. And then you all have to go back to your own positions.*[38]

We can look at the way Andante was set up with reference to the notion of a *'programma'*, which has two dimensions: first, the relationship to the broader police organisation; and second, the approach and processes that are substantively undertaken. A *programma* is an organisational space where several agents can collaborate and learn about a specific topic. It removes the 'distractions' of day-to-day policing and makes resources available to focus and intensify efforts. It is interesting to see that this requires moving outside the usual organisational structures. From the interviews, the consequent 'outsider status' has two advantageous features: first, escaping the traditional chain of command that filters down pressures and specific orders. Second, having removed the usual performance-evaluation standards and related tasks, there is the freedom to ingeniously investigate and explore.[39] A *programma* is different from a project in its approach and purpose. Although temporary, a *programma* is set up to bring lasting change. A *programma* is designed to ensure that adequate time and

38. Interview 1 on 05.09.2017 [Author's translation].
39. However, being outsiders also means that, in the long-term, there are many risks. The officers that were interviewed could be categorised in two groups Some found the idea appealing at first, but they wanted and needed to continue growing professionally. If they desired a promotion or a raise, they needed to be within the traditional organisational structure. Their time with Andante was beneficial if kept brief. Ultimately, the skillset that is recognised as valuable by the broader police organisation did not seem to coincide with that developed while working in a *programma* for a long time. The second set of officers appeared more ideologically driven, almost to the point that the outsider status and the related disadvantages were worn as a badge of honour. They would be sacrificing themselves to fight injustice. Their belief in this cause, along with their appreciation for the technical nature of the work, seemed to be enough to keep them going. Examples of the former set can be seen in interviews 3, 4 and 6; examples of the latter show up in interviews 1, 2 and 5.

(human) resources are concentrated on an issue long enough to generate sufficient knowledge, which then leads to transforming the status quo. This is reflected in the aims of Andante portrayed in Figure 6.2 above.

A programmatic *approach* to environmental crime meant that the team had to develop a structure for their work, including goals, targets, and a plan of action. The initial mandate was of three years. At the end of that period – during which the focus had been mostly on the phenomenon of 'de-bunkering' – the team's mandate was extended. Based on their initial findings regarding de-bunkering, they developed and refined the concept of a chain-investigation, which is the core of team's approach.[40] While the nature of law and criminal justice requires the identification of clear targets for assigning responsibility, the companies and individuals that the team has been investigating are seen as part of a larger sequence of actions and operations. Each portion of the process has its unique criminogenic features and opportunities that need to be uncovered.

> *And if you have a good knowledge of that chain, if you have gathered more and more information – through checks and the like – and if you have knowledge of the topic, of the policy, of the legislation, then you also know exactly how the flows are going to go. You know who the players are; you know who the collectors are; who the transporters are; who the processors are; which terminals are involved; and then you recognize that this is how you check a ship with a certain cargo on board and you have that knowledge and experience and that information, then you know 'hey, this probably goes from a to b and I know about b – from my knowledge and experience – I know that b often doesn't work well, or that b often commits fraudulent acts.'*
> *So, at the moment you check a transport you already know, when you get the information from that transport, whether it is right or wrong, or what you need to check or follow to see if it is done properly.*[41]

This quote demonstrates a high degree of clarity and understanding about the way the bunker fuel and waste oil industries function. The interviewee connects this clarity and understating to the adoption of a programmatic approach and to the use of the chain-investigation technique. Both of these require a systematic dissection of the contexts and situations in which crimes occur, reminiscent of SCP, crime-script analysis, or problem-oriented policing. At the broadest level, the team separated the processes they observed into five stages, each of which would be looked at in turn:

1) **De-bunkering**: i.e. the *consequence* of using dirty oil. When ships had to get rid of bad fuel oil that had caused them trouble and damage, the Andante team and their collaborators would look at the history behind the suspicious batch and they would also go and look at the way the bad fuel was handled after

40. Memo 1; Memo 2; Field Notes 20-21.10.2016; See Report on De-bunkering cited in Table 1 in Annex II.
41. Interview 1 on 05.09.2017 [Author's translation].

it was discarded. Interestingly, both inquiries would often lead into the same procedures and actors.[42]

2) **Collection and treatment**: bad fuel or other waste oils have to be collected (and treated) by specialised entities. The inquiries into de-bunkering had often led the team to the same set of collectors, one of which is *Crafty*, who's activities we looked at in Chapter 4. The team saw that collection was a central node – all kinds of wastes were being brought to certain companies. These companies would also then be the ones providing blend components for the process of bunker fuel production. Several investigative observation operations, coupled with their accruing technical expertise, showed the investigators that the collected wastes did not match the permit and technology the companies had. And the combination of technology and wastes did not match the supposed products that the companies were producing and selling on.
3) **Distillation:** when following the flows from collection towards bunker fuel production, the team also saw that a lot of supposed blend components were coming from distillation processes that are undertaken in firms such as petrochemical manufacturers. This also was mirrored in the relevant scientific literature. However, they wanted to verify whether these flows were suffering from similar irregularities as those witnessed in the realm of waste oil collection. They found evidence of wrongdoing here too. *Pesky's* case in Chapter 4 is an example.
4) **Blending:** where did all the fraudulently manufactured blend components go? Terminals and traders are the nodes, in physical and economic terms, where several substances come together and are blended into bunker fuel. While following the blend components from the collection and distillation stages led *to* these nodes, examining the blending stage opened up the network in its entirety. By looking at blending, investigators had to find all the different sources of residues and blend components that make up bunker fuel. Oftentimes these sources were questionable. The full network of improper and illegal waste management started becoming visible at this point, and gradually extended further and further beyond the Netherlands.
5) **International:** it was no news to investigators that waste oil management and bunker fuel production – legal and illegal – are carried out in global networks. Yet, thanks to the preceding investigative efforts, the flow of wastes into bunker fuel that has been taking place across the world could now start to be effectively documented and proved. At the same time, the new question of building partnerships to counter these harmful activities in other parts of the world became more pressing. In fact, the team observed that, as

42. See Report on De-bunkering cited in Annex II. In the meantime, three convictions have returned from cases that focused on the de-bunkering stage of the process.

> their investigations and prosecutions intensified, many firms who had been moving their wastes through Rotterdam harbour began shifting routes towards Belgium or Denmark instead. They reflected that their activities had increased risks of detection and punishment for firms under Dutch jurisdiction, thereby leading to displacement to countries where risks were perceived as lower (e.g., Belgium).[43] Many efforts were made by Andante to engage authorities in these countries in dialogue, so that all together they could align standards and practices of enforcement in the different countries, inspired by the Dutch experience.[44]

These overarching stages provided a framework for the Andante team, which then began making efforts to pinpoint the connecting links between the various processes that these stages are composed of. They identified what the applicable rules were for the businesses involved. They reconstructed how the entirety of the process *should* look in accordance with those rules. Then they checked to see if this was happening at all times in practice.

We can summarise the results of their approach in three categories. First, they increased their own knowledge about the boundaries of permissibility in the sector, and the corresponding techniques used to cross those boundaries illegally. Second, they reconstructed the network – by looking at the *flows* of waste oils, blend components and bunker fuel – to arrive at the problematic nodes in the network where these substances are handled. Therefore, it is now much easier to perceive early warning signals of possible wrongdoing. Intervention points can be selected with more accuracy. The team even developed a computer program that automates the selection of potential intervention or investigation points.[45] Lastly, Andante helped increase the awareness of other agencies of possible wrongdoing in their area of competence and helped them build capacities to combat it.

Regarding the latter point, we should briefly note here that the way in which Andante collaborated with other state agencies is both interesting and important. This collaboration was most intensive during the continued systematic checks that the team members were a part of. These evolved from *Waakzame Acties*, which had been almost a form of exploratory research – an initial reading of reality and trying to devise categories and reconstruct processes. *Waakzame Acties* had helped to shape the subdivision into five stages for the *programma. Zwarte Stromen*, which

43. This is an assumption: in the sense that no research was conducted to verify whether the shift in location of streams and waste movements that was observed by the officers was truly 'caused' by their previous efforts in Rotterdam.
44. I personally observed the work with authorities from other countries during my field work (Field Notes 25-26.09.2017; Field Notes 26-27.09.2017).
45. This program concentrates the years of experience that the team has matured into a standardised mechanism that can see whether known 'offenders' are part of a particular flow of substances. The program is based on both patterns of activities the team has reconstructed as well as intelligence indications based on previously convicted or indicted firms.

was later managed under the leadership of the Andante team, has had a different function. These checks have generated new insights in terms of changing actors and routes of waste and bunker fuel flows. However, the pivotal focus of the Andante team during *Zwarte Stromen* has actually been that of building capacity in a broader spectrum of authorities and stakeholders. Through such capacity-building efforts, they have also refined their own investigative methods and tools. The Andante team members learned *alongside* and *from* the other agencies they worked with. For example, when they started looking at the 'distillation' stage, they saw an increasing number of cases where REACH-related documents were circulating. Their collaboration with ILT and RIVM was repeatedly mentioned as a positive learning opportunity for the team.[46]

Generally, the team members made it their aim to accompany individual agents to learn about the crimes and the contexts in which they occur, and to become more capable guardians. During *Zwarte Stromen,* for example, the members of the Andante team would actively observe which officers from other agencies or units showed particular enthusiasm for and interest in the work that they were carrying out collectively. They would invite these agents to take the time to learn along with them and encourage them in strengthening their investigative capabilities. While *Zwarte Stromen* was generally designed for both collective action and collective learning by all those involved, they also facilitated longer-term processes of building capacities in individual guardians. This capacity-building effort was consciously enacted by the team through and as part of the *programma.* It was designed in response to the fact that they saw there was a lack of capable guardians who could contrast crimes in the waste oil and bunker fuel sectors.

***

Just as originally planned, Andante is, at the time of writing, being rolled up and concluded.[47] A small fraction of the officers who were originally involved remain operational as part of the team. Their task is to conclude the dossiers of the cases that are already open. Most of the other officers have returned to their original departments. Some have entered retirement. What have they left behind? What are the outcomes of the team's work? Which changes have taken place during and after the team's operation, and how may such changes be connected to the Andante *programma?* What has not changed? The outcome that is easiest to identify comes in the form of the number of checks, of investigations, of convictions and the amount of illegal assets that have been confiscated.[48]

46. Field Notes 03-04.11.2016; Field Notes 25-26.09.2017; Field Notes 26-27.09.2017.
47. This was the situation at the beginning of 2020.
48. The total amount of confiscated assets from seven concluded cases was €9,340,500 (Total sum provided in written communication dated 15.04.2021). Four more cases were still being investigated or prosecuted and it was estimated that at least €13,992,805 could be confiscated from

However, there are four other areas in which the Andante team has accumulated experience and which we can reflect on. First, the organisational aspect of having a dedicated team of police officers that carries out specialised investigations in the field of environmental crime. Second, the substantive problem of knowing enough about the inner workings of a specific industry to make enforcement possible and effective. Third, the capacities and patterns of collaboration built with numerous agents and organisations, which we consider a procedural aspect of the team's operation. Each of these three is touched upon briefly in the paragraphs below. Lastly, there may be a more diffuse effect of contributing to added effectiveness in enforcement and regulation, which derives from the other three. However, this effect is challenging to establish and quantify, yet we try to capture it in Section 3 when we reflect on the work of Andante and its outcomes through the lens of SCP.

Organisationally, a formal, specialised detective team has been created at the national level.[49] For some time, it has been operating parallel to Andante. Its existence can be seen as tangentially linked to the Andante *programma*. The national team is supposed to complement the regional teams that already existed before. Its mandate is to take over the largest cases of environmental concern. Determining which cases are the largest relies on aspects like geographic scope – cases having international character, for example. Another criterion is that the crimes are seen as 'undermining' – a catch-all term that grows in scope (and ambiguity) in the Dutch law enforcement landscape. It has often been linked to organised and serious crime.[50] In the later stages of its operation, Andante has

---

the perpetrators upon conviction. See also the website of the Dutch public prosecution service at: Openbaar Ministerie, "Afvalstoffen in Stookolie (Dossier Andante)," https://www.om.nl/onderwerpen/strafrechtelijk-programma-andante.

49. A detective team is different from a *programma*, in terms of the resources and approach it has as well as its relationship to the broader police organization. In one interview, it was mentioned that a specialised detective team in the Netherlands usually consists of the following types of personnel: analysts, specialists, administrative support staff, leadership, detectives, intelligence officers Andante did not have all such roles within its team, it only had: specialists, detectives, intelligence officers and leadership (Interview 1 on 05.09.2017). Beyond the different roles, however, a specialised detective team is endowed with permanence – regardless of who may be part of the team, it is formalised within the police organisation, thereby also removing obstacles to moving up the career ladder that Andante members had, for example. Specialised detective teams are not unique to the Netherlands; indeed, they are part of a traditional form of policing.

50. The notion of *'ondermijnende criminaliteit'* [crime having and undermining character] is discussed in the following official documents: Openbaar Ministerie en Politie, "Rapportage Aanpak Georganiseerde Ondermijnende Criminaliteit 2018," (2019). "Kamerstukken Ii 2018-2019, 29 911, Nr. 212"; "Kamerstukken Ii 2017-2018, 29 911, Nr. 207." The concept of *ondermijnende criminaliteit* as well as its place in the Dutch law enforcement landscape has been reflected on critically. See, for example, Hans Boutellier et al., "Een Einde Aan Ondermijning," *Tijdschrift voor veiligheid* 19, no. 1 (2020); Emile Kolthoff and Sjaak Khonraad, "Ondermijnende Aspecten Van Georganiseerde Criminaliteit En De Rol Van De Bovenwereld," *Tijdschrift voor criminologie* 58, no. 2 (2016); E.W. Kolthoff, "De Geschiedenis Van Een Begrip," *Christen Democratische Verkenningen* 2019, no. 4 (2019).

collaborated with this national environmental team.[51] Indeed, some members of the new national team have spent some time working as part of Andante and/or participating in the systematic checks that continued after Andante was set up (*Zwarte Stromen*). This national team risks suffering from the same challenges as the pre-existing regional teams. The degree of specialisation of its officers is not related to the characteristics – technical, economic and regulatory – of the contexts and situations that facilitate the crimes they have to investigate. Rather, the supposed degree of harm or geographic scale of the crimes are the determining factors. The same set of officers would have to investigate cases of wildlife trafficking and chemical waste mismanagement when these occur in an international context, for example. Individual officers may have a degree of specialisation in one of these fields, but there is no thematic focus for the entire team.

Substantively, Andante has generated a wealth of knowledge about crime events in the waste oil and bunker fuel sectors; the *modi operandi* that are employed and the circumstances that facilitate them. This wealth has been distributed in several directions. The main and official recipient is the ILT. The ILT can now implement all the insights generated during Andante's lifespan in order to improve its own monitoring and enforcement activities. Indeed, the ILT is the competent authority that carries out these activities *preventively*. Outside the ILT and outside the Netherlands, other individual agents, who have been accompanied by Andante, can continue to make use of the capacities they built as they work in their area of competence. Numerous other authorities and agencies in the Netherlands, who have some interest in this field, have been involved during Andante's operation, especially through *Zwarte Stromen*. They can bring their baggage of knowledge and experience with them in their future endeavours. Abroad – in Germany, France, and Portugal, for example – police agents have made attempts to initiate and encourage more systematic involvement of their colleagues in these kinds of investigations, with mixed results.[52] Outside of the

For a discussion on the use of the administrative approach to *ondermijnende criminaliteit*, see: ACM Spapens, "Bestuurlijke Aanpak Van Ondermijning: Ervaringen in Nederland En Het Buitenland," *Tijdschrift voor Bijzonder Strafrecht en Handhaving* 2019, no. 2 (2019); Pieter Tops and Henny Schilders, "Naar Een Meervoudige Aanpak Van Ondermijning," *Tijdschrift voor de Politie* 78, no. 7 (2016).

51. Some cases identified during *Zwarte stromen* or through intelligence have been forwarded to the national team, for example. Or larger cases identified by Andante had to be sent to the national team. Sometimes Andante has been invited to consult with the team on the cases the latter is handling.

52. From a written communication with one of the leading investigating officers dated 15.04.2021, the following overview is shared: "In the Netherlands, during investigations and *Zwarte stromen acties*, we worked with roughly 100 other agents from the police and other authorities. The number of agents we have actually worked with abroad is more difficult to determine, alone during investigations I estimate 40-50. In addition, we have worked with various organizations abroad to propagate Andante's method and findings. I think we spoke to about 70-80 people from different authorities abroad."

traditional enforcement realm, journalists and academics have produced reports and studies (including this one) that give the insights the team has generated a new platform and a broader audience.[53]

Procedurally, the network of committed and interested individuals and organisations that the team tried to foster, also through *Zwarte Stromen*, risks losing the leadership and direction that Andante provided. While *Zwarte Stromen* is still part of the plans of both criminal and administrative enforcement agencies, no clear successor currently exists to maintain the focus and momentum developed thanks to Andante.[54] And, even though collaboration among different agencies has been a staple of Dutch enforcement practice for some time, there is no guarantee that the aims and approaches the team tried to infuse into these collaborative spaces will continue to be fostered. While systematic checks may continue to be carried out, the methodical learning focus and capacity building aims are no longer explicitly in place. Who will train and accompany the cadre of capable guardians – in the Netherlands and abroad – in the years to come? And who will learn about this process of widening the pool of capable guardians, and continue to document and share the related insights with others?

Another procedural dimension of the team's outcomes is their investigative method, the chain-investigation, so reminiscent of problem-oriented policing and CSA. It is unclear how their experience with such an approach is supposed to be shared and implemented into future (policing) practice, in the case of environmental crime and beyond. The team itself has made many efforts to document this aspect of their work. *This* book also shares their experiences with a broader public. However, what the team's experience has repeatedly revealed is that one can only truly learn *in the field* and by committing sufficient time to *continuous* learning. Policing manuals can convey information and knowledge that is pertinent right now, or rather was pertinent at the time of writing. However, capacity is built through practical experience gained alongside others who have already matured similar experience. The pace at which one learns can accelerate under such circumstances, thereby also making it possible to keep up with innovation on the part of the (criminal) reality one tries to learn about and intervene upon.[55]

---

53. For example, Wilfried Koomen, *Beerput Nederland* (2017).This instance is discussed in the documentary "Beerput Nederland" [Literally: Cesspit Netherlands]; Heel, Leon van 'Brandstofzwendel scheepvaart erger dan de eiercrisis' AD 28 September 2017.
54. Field Notes 28.02.2020.
55. Literature on collective learning. It may be interesting to look into the issue of 'collective learning' that I use to indicate the process of knowledge generation and sharing in which several individuals and even groups of individuals can partake from and contribute to. There are different disciplines that touch upon this issue. For example, the areas of human resource development, (adult) education and organisation/management studies have been reviewed in: Tara Fenwick, "Understanding Relations of Individual—Collective Learning in Work: A Review of Research," *Management learning* 39, no. 3 (2008); Thomas N Garavan and Alma McCarthy, "Collective Learning Processes and Human Resource Development," *Advances in developing*

The chain-investigation is a tool that can be applied to different types of complex (organisational) crimes, but it is itself embedded in a *'way of policing'* that needs to be fostered. The structure of the police or enforcement organisation needs to enable such forms of investigation. Enabling means giving the space to reconstruct the chains of events and processes at different levels, instead of demanding only immediate (re-)action and increasing numbers of convictions.[56] And the mind-set towards enforcement also needs to be conducive to this way of analysing crimes or societal problems. An attitude of learning, which patiently goes past the immediate gratification of quickly pinpointing culpability down to individual firms or persons, is key to structural change. Potential offenders may change their *modi operandi*, structural arrangements and forces may generate shifts in criminal practices. Will enforcement agencies be able to dedicate sufficient resources to learning systematically about these new characteristics of criminal events? Will they be able to build capacities and patterns of action that respond to crimes in a sustained and sustainable manner? Will the state apparatus allow and encourage this way of working? Some Andante team members fear that that will not be the case, as can be seen in the quote below.

***Interviewer:*** *So, what are the main challenges that you imagine in making things change?*

***Interviewee 7a:*** *The main challenge is now keeping the capacity going.*

***R 7b:*** *Our own organizations, (smiling) are they motivated enough to give us room and capacity to do our thing?*

***R 7a:*** *And to learn from what we have learned and to make it last. Otherwise, it's just 3,4 6 years of a lot of fun (haha) but it's away in 2-3 years and then it's gone. And it's not only about fuel oil, but it's just the way you take the things and the way you try to sort out in the environmental criminal enforcement system. And we think we have come up a viable way of having something to say and having some effect within that world. And if you talk about fuel oil or about other kinds of environmentally bad*

---

*human resources* 10, no. 4 (2008); John Hayes and Christopher W Allinson, "Cognitive Style and the Theory and Practice of Individual and Collective Learning in Organizations," *Human relations* 51, no. 7 (1998). Another perspective is that of 'group learning', explored in: Deborah W Kilgore, "Understanding Learning in Social Movements: A Theory of Collective Learning," *International journal of lifelong education* 18, no. 3 (1999).

56. The proponents of system's theory highlight that the goals of a system or subsystem, as well as the way these goals are translated into concrete targets and indicators for system members to evaluate their success are important factors for understanding how a system operates in practice. The way goals and targets are articulated and interpreted may lead to adverse outcomes compared to the wishes of those who set up or develop the policy for a specific system. See, for example, Donella H. Wright Diana Meadows, *Thinking in Systems: A Primer* (2015).More about targets and goals as distorting a system organization, refer to systems literature. System's theory has also been applied specifically to the criminal justice system (in the USA) in: Freda Adler, Gerhard OW Mueller, and William S Laufer, *Criminology and the Criminal Justice System* (McGraw-Hill New York, NY, 2007). There is also interesting literature in the field of public administration in this respect, such as: Amanda Rutherford and Kenneth J Meier, "Managerial Goals in a Performance-Driven System: Theory and Empirical Tests in Higher Education," *Public Administration* 93, no. 1 (2015).

*effects that are taking place, we should learn from that. The problem is how to get others enthusiastic about this way and we thought, 'well [if you show them everything] we have done and the success we had and the amount of cases we dealt with.' But, no one is interested really in the enforcement of criminal environmental law, it's a very select, small world. A lot of people and even policy makers who are responsible for making environmental policy are also responsible for economic policy. And they are not interested in too much criticism on the environment and the actions of firms and people that have also connections with the success of Rotterdam harbor or Schiphol or Nederland* distributie land *[Netherlands, distribution country]. So, and that's the same with politics. Everyone thinks that fiscal fraud should be attacked because people are walking away with our money. But no one is really interested in high quality fuel oil if that means that transportation is getting more expensive and so all our goods are getting more expensive, because 70% of all goods we see moving around have been shipped across the oceans nowadays. So, everything is dependent on that. And you see that also makes even within our own organizations that, that they're not really interested. [...] you know, environment, it's always politic, it's always economics.*

***R7b:*** *But we learned also positive things, I think it's important if you concentrate on a branch in the waste [sector] that you have to have information, knowledge, (eh) specialism, endurance, and that is what we did with Andante and that's an example.*[57]

Information, knowledge, specialism and endurance. That is what is needed, according to a veteran Andante team member, to keep going, to keep learning and to keep contrasting crimes in the waste oil and bunker fuel sector and beyond. Which conceptual tools can help us make sense of how Andante achieved this? Can these tools also help us see what a potential way forward could be to make sure learning and contrasting of crime continue? Of course, Andante did not do it alone, nor can the efforts to contrast these crimes have an effect if carried out alone. How did Andante work with others? How has that contributed to strengthening enforcement and facilitating compliance? All these points are addressed in Section 2. The second respondent in the quote also mentioned something else – an obstacle to enforcement, and obstacle to learning. That obstacle is the political resistance to putting environmental conservation above economic imperatives, when it turns out that economic patterns are detrimental to the environment. This point is addressed in Section 3.

## 6.2 Andante through the Lenses of Problem-Oriented Policing and Responsive Regulation

In this Section we continue meditating on the work of the Andante team by unpacking their characteristics as guardians. By using the concepts of problem-oriented policing and responsive regulation, we can systematise our understanding of how Andante as a team and as a *programma* have operated.

57. Interview 7 on 28.02.2020.

Guardians can be defined as capable from two perspectives, one internal and one external. From an internal perspective, we can look at how guardians and guardianship are formed, how they are organised and how they may grow and evolve in the face of their goals and tasks. Given that the goals and tasks of guardians are linked to the reduction of crime,[58] the external perspective requires us to see how guardians may have been (*in*)capable in the face of such crimes.

In preceding Chapters, we saw that there were two important factors that inhibited adequate guardianship (by state authorities) in the criminal events under study. First, there was the issue of knowledge. The crimes occur in an industrial context where mechanical, technical/chemical, and legal knowledge are all important for truly grasping the significance of the activities that are taking place. In Andante's story, we saw that lacking this knowledge created obstacles for state authorities, whether those enforcing criminal law or administrative law. Second, we have the problem of 'authorised representatives'. Firms operating in these economic sectors have the permits, technology, and registrations to do so. They are also embedded in an industrial network where they are accepted as legitimate traders. Moreover, the beliefs about what 'business as usual' looks like in this network are rather distant from the environmental conservation aims that (waste) legislation tries to pursue. State-mandated guardians do not have direct access to 'crime scenes': they rely on the trustworthiness and expertise of the authorised representatives. They can only monitor externally. They are practically inhibited from detecting wrongdoing, but also cognitively impaired by the authority and expertise of the firms themselves. These two factors are essential to bear in mind for our discussion of guardianship in the coming paragraphs.[59]

The issue of 'knowledge' is central to the ideas of problem-oriented policing – striving for in-depth knowledge, experience and analysis are features of problem-oriented policing that distinguish it from other forms of policing. The concept of responsive regulation is not as focused on this aspect, although our reading of Andante through responsive regulation shows us how knowledge as part of the capacities of *all* guardians is important in a holistic approach to regulation. The problem of authorised representatives is difficult to insert into the discussion of problem-oriented policing, mainly because the latter has been developed for more traditional forms of crime. However, overcoming the challenge of authorised representatives is fundamental to proposals such as responsive regulation, one of the aims of which is to strike a balance between encouraging corporate innovation while ensuring the protection of welfare interests. We go into more depth in the respective subsections.

58. For a definition of 'guardian' and 'guardianship', see Chapter 1.
59. For detailed findings on this see the analysis of 'offending and enforcement conditions' in Chapter 4 and the discussion on 'low risks' in Chapter 5.

### *Andante as Problem-Oriented-Policing*[60]

A field of practice that has been closely linked to SCP is that of problem-oriented-policing (POP). At the core of the original proposal for POP lay the question of the effectiveness of policing activities in reducing crime and making a population feel safe. At the time, police were concerned with apprehending and punishing criminals. Reactionary policing was the norm: its preventive force depended on *ex post facto* interventions that would incapacitate as well as deter potential repeat or future offenders. In contrast to this type of policing, POP imagined *true prevention* through police agencies, which would, in turn, collaborate with other, both state and non-state, actors. This form of policing would rely on a deeper understanding of the root causes of crime and ground its preventive strategies in such an understanding.[61]

POP is far from the mainstream approach to policing in most of the world. In fact, what is labelled as 'incident-driven policing' in the POP literature continues to be the norm. Members of the Andante team have spoken about incident-driven policing as inimical to investigating and prosecuting cases of organisational and environmental crime. They explained how both the way the police organisation is structured as well as the tactics and tools that specialised officers are given are not suitable for these kinds of crime.[62] Therefore, there are parallels in the sources of dissatisfaction that generated the impulse for both a new problem-oriented policing model and in the creation and development of the Andante *programma.* These parallels serve as the common starting point to look at Andante through the lenses of POP: many of the characteristics of the team resemble aspects of POP units as described in the literature, probably because both phenomena react to common deficiencies in traditional law enforcement.

For the purposes of our analysis in this Chapter, we can say that the defining feature of problem-oriented policing is that it is truly preventative as opposed to reactive. Prevention through problem-oriented policing aims to resolve root causes

60. A few months into the start of the field work for this research, the concept of problem-oriented policing continually returned to my mind when I tried to describe the operation of the Andante team. I even mentioned it to the team members several times: they nodded in recognition of something familiar, but the team members had not been set up as a problem-oriented-policing unit and, therefore, could not explicitly label themselves in this way.

61. Herman Goldstein, "Improving Policing: A Problem-Oriented Approach," *Crime & Delinquency Crime & Delinquency* 25, no. 2 (1979).

62. John E. Eck Michael S. Scott, Johannes Knutsson, Herman Goldstein, "Problem-Oriented Policing," in *Environmental Criminology and Crime Analysis*, ed. Richard Wortley and Michael Townsley (Oxon: Routledge, 2017); Anthony Allan Braga, *Problem-Oriented Policing and Crime Prevention* (Criminal Justice Press Monsey, NY, 2008); Michael S Scott, *Problem-Oriented Policing: Reflections on the First 20 Years* (US Department of Justice, Office of Community Oriented Policing Services, 2000); Rachel Boba Santos Roberto G. Cops Program United States Department of Justice Office of Community Oriented Policing Services Santos, *A Police Organizational Model for Crime Reduction: Institutionalizing Problem Solving, Analysis, and Accountability* (Washington, D.C.: U.S. Dept. of Justice, Office of Community Oriented Policing Services, 2011).

as opposed to contributing to prevention merely through general and specific deterrence or incapacitation. In that sense, problem-oriented policing is coherent with the aims and logic of strategies like responsive regulation but, differently to them, it places police agents at the centre of a profound and nuanced process of change.

The story we reviewed in Section 1 has already shown us how the Andante *programma* has many affinities with problem-oriented policing, based on this broader definition of problem-oriented policing. Now we can take the Andante-problem-oriented policing juxtaposition one step further. Problem-oriented policing has been discussed in the literature in reference to ten elements, which are specific to POP in contrast to other types of policing.[63] Here we list these ten elements and apply each of them to the Andante experience. This application shows us the links to the broader learning on problem-oriented-policing, with which we can further build on the strengths of Andante and try to suggest remedies for some of its limitations.

1. **Clustering of similar incidents defined as a problem:** The subdivision into the five stages – from de-bunkering to international – that we saw in Section 1 corresponds well to this aspect of problem-oriented policing. The focus on crimes in the bunker fuel sector that was the basis for the Andante *programma* was a form of clustering. Yet the five stages allowed for an even deeper analysis of the characteristics of criminal events. Each stage had its own peculiar 'problems' for the team to study.
2. **Microscopic examination (using crime analysis skills and techniques):** Clustering facilitates a detailed zooming in and analysis. The recognition by Andante that *structural* factors need to be changed shows their approach to crime-reduction. Andante's work is an effort at social science, not just policing.
3. **The drive to develop new and more effective responses to the crime problem**: Among their goals (see Figure 6.2) Andante cites the improvement of enforcement of environmental law. At every step of the way, Andante was dissatisfied with the tools, practices and strategies that traditional policing offered them. Indeed, the favoured tactic of so many police units of the last decades – phone-tapping – was scorned as a waste of time in several conversations. Andante always returned to the organisational and economic processes underlying the crimes and sought new ways of 'infiltrating' them intellectually to understand and respond better.
4. **Commitment to generating preventive responses:** Again, the recognition of *structural* causes of crime, including the structural deficiencies of enforcement practices that facilitate crime, meant that Andante did not just prevent trough

63. John E. Eck Michael S. Scott, Johannes Knutsson, Herman Goldstein, "Problem-Oriented Policing," in Environmental Criminology and Crime Analysis, ed. Richard Wortley and Michael Townsley (Oxon: Routledge, 2017).

deterrence and remedial measures *ex post facto*. They even chose to look at smaller cases in order to facilitate learning gradually instead of 'going after the big fish' to attempt spectacular convictions.[64]

5. **Commitment to generating responses that are not dependent on the criminal justice system:** "We 'move' the Code of Criminal Procedure 'to one side' and make grateful use of the powers offered to us by the Economic Crimes Act." Even in their policing, Andante has explicitly preferred to leave traditional criminal law measures aside in order to deal with the crime problems at hand more effectively.[65] Their continuous pursuit of collaboration with other state agencies and their wish to empower them are signs of wanting to reduce the use of the criminal justice system. Here it is important to add that the set-up of the Dutch enforcement system facilitates this enormously: corporations may be held criminally accountable; the behaviour of businesses that puts health and environment at risk is connected by law to both administrative and criminal law; the lines between administrative and criminal law agencies and measures are not overly rigid and enable many forms of collaboration.[66]
6. **Commitment to generating responses that engage other public agencies, the community, and the private sector:** This element is clearly formulated based on the original range of phenomena to which problem-oriented-policing was applied, namely more traditional forms of offending. The private sector there can be, for example, workplaces where offenders are employed or business premises that are the setting of criminal activities. However, organisational crimes – specifically, corporate crimes – involve the private sector in a completely different way. The private sector may, in fact, coincide with the offender. Alternatively, the private sector may involve consultancies or auditing firms, which have specific mandates and guardianship roles.[67] Furthermore, as we see in the coming subsection, public agencies – specifically administrative authorities – are almost always already involved or have an official relationship with perpetrators. The question, therefore, is rather how these authorities could benefit from the learning being matured by a problem-oriented policing team. Lastly, the community is somewhat different too. While there may be a nearby 'local' community

64. Before Andante was formed and while the *Probo Koala* court case was nearing its end, some agents who later became members of the team attempted to go after larger firms, but these cases proved to be too difficult, prompting the need for a *programma*. This is also discussed in Section 1.
65. *"We het wetboek van strafvordering 'links' laten liggen en wij dankbaar gebruik maken van de bevoegdheden die de Wet op Economische Delicten ons biedt."* – quoted from Academie, "Andante: Foute Stookolie". The *Wet op de Economische Delicten* (Law on Economic Crimes) is discussed in Chapters 3 and 4.
66. See Section 1 of Chapter 4 for an overview of the formal system of guardianship in the Netherlands.
67. See also the adapted problem-triangle for organizational crimes in Chapter 1.

that is somehow consciously, directly affected by the criminal practices of corporations, it is more often the case that communities are oblivious to crimes. That is, unless the crimes lead to scandal-like harm.

7 In this last respect, Andante has made efforts to make invisible practices visible and intelligible for both the wider population and policymakers. Their problem-oriented approach has made them experts in their own right regarding the technical, chemical and legal details of the processes involved. Their own voice has been strengthened through such building of expertise. But they have gone further to involve media and academics to increase visibility and understandability of the currents that underlie the functioning of our global economic system. By trying to multiply the eyes and the voices involved, they have made steps that can be described under this sixth problem-oriented-policing element.

7. **Commitment to *implementing* new strategies and responses** (i.e., not just theorising but going back into the field to enact the strategies): We can certainly see that, as Andante moved through each of the five stages of the *programma*, it brought the insights from the previous stages into its work on the subsequent ones. Insights regarding known offenders, logistical nodes, *modi operandi*, but also in their investigative techniques and collaboration with other state agencies. For example, once they saw the importance of REACH certificates, they intensified their collaboration with the ILT and RIVM, as well as with the relevant authorities in other EU countries in this respect. However, their powers were still limited – they could only mobilise some individuals outside of the team itself. The new strategies they could imagine and articulate required much more widespread and systematic implementation. Their relative isolation, which helped them so much in focusing down into the details of the crime-problems, became an obstacle when they had to distribute their knowledge and practices.

8. **Commitment to rigorously evaluating the effectiveness of the strategies and their implementation:** Here is where we begin to see differences between Andante and the problem-oriented policing model. Andante was never set up as a formal problem-oriented policing unit. Intuitively – and possibly from part of their training- the team implemented the above aspects of problem-oriented policing into their work – this is a sign of their ingeniousness and drive to both develop themselves and really deal with the crime-problem. Nevertheless, they did not consciously consider the evaluation aspect, nor did they necessarily have the resources for this. However much more time they could dedicate to learning compared to officers working according to the normal policing patterns, they could not *self*-reflect. At a later stage of their operation, they tried to have regular internal briefings, where they attempted to foster collective exchange and reflections. But the briefings focused mostly on the logistical distribution

of investigative tasks and updates on the progress of a given dossier. The broader police organisation also did not require or encourage any such practices. Taken a step further, the relevant ministries, linked to both police and administrative authorities, did not create the spaces for reflecting and learning systematically about these enforcement practices. They coordinated well when it came to action and following up of that action into investigation and sometimes even policymaking. But this did not extend to the growth and specialisation of the agencies themselves. Moreover, parameters for any kind of evaluation were never established nor consistently used for such purposes.

9. **Commitment to reporting the results of such evaluation for collective learning:**[68] Due to the lack of systematic (self-)evaluation, reporting is not something we could expect to see much of in this case. Yet, the Andante team did their best to communicate what they were doing to others. First and foremost, with the aim of accompanying them to pursue the same goal of contrasting crimes in the waste oil and bunker fuel sectors. In action-research terminology, they lacked a dedicated resource person, who could take on the responsibility of accumulating, systematising, and distributing knowledge about the work they were doing.
10. **Commitment to building a body of knowledge that supports further professionalisation of the police:**[69] Just like the preceding two points, this aspect of problem-oriented policing is largely absent from the Andante story. That is not for lack of trying and vision. At all times, professionalisation of the police and of state agencies has been an important aim of the *programma*, but the team was just not institutionally supported in this endeavour. Usually, making formal and explicit arrangements for problem-oriented policing units means that steps are taken at higher levels in the police organisation, which then also provide for appropriate subsequent training to be organised based on the unit's work. This was not set up in the case of Andante.

While the overlap between problem-oriented policing and Andante is not perfect, we have now managed to articulate their exceptional work more clearly thanks to the POP elements. Nevertheless, the POP concept can only take us so far in understanding how the work of Andante relates to the criminogenic features that were identified in previous chapters. Because we have been discussion *corporate* environmental crimes, we need to now consider insights from the literature on responsive regulation. This body of work can help us to understand Andante's

68. Herman Goldstein and Susmilch C. E., "Experimenting with the Probelm-Oriented Approach to Improve Police Service: A Report and Some Reflections on Two Case Studies," (Madison, WI: University of Wisconsin, Law School, 1982).
69. The Center for Problem-Oriented Policing has been established in furtherance of this goal: www.popcenter.org.

relationship with other guardians and with 'authorised representatives' – the firms in the waste oil and bunker fuel industries – better.

*Andante and Responsive Regulation*

Responsive regulation aims to make compliance and deterrence part of a coherent system. Compliance and deterrence meant as strategies, approaches, attitudes, and techniques but also as forms of guardianship carried out by different types of actors.[70] In that sense, responsive regulation is, by definition, about more than just police work. Both Section 1 of this Chapter and the first part of the current Section have shown us that Andante, although formally a police team, is about more than just police work too. The *programma* has involved more than traditional police work, and it has been more than the work that can be done through the police as an institution and enforcement agency. The notion of responsive regulation can help us to highlight the efforts of the Andante team and the outcomes of the *programma* through a wider lens in three ways. First, it can help us understand how Andante may have contributed to a broader strengthening of a variety of measures that lie further down than the tip of the enforcement pyramid, i.e., those measures (and actors) whose objective is to encourage firms to comply. Second, responsive regulation can also show us where gaps may have been left by Andante in increasing compliance in the waste oil and bunker fuel sectors. Lastly, the Andante story may, conversely, show us limitations of the responsive regulation model.

The breadth of Andante's contribution is rooted in two interconnected aspects: the first is their assessment of the conditions that facilitated the crimes before the *programma* was set up, namely the incapability of *all* formal guardians in the face of systematic criminal practices. The second is the vision of the team: concerted and collective efforts to contrast crime are needed in the face of concerted collective criminal practices. The lack thereof leaves gaps that are appetising to motivated offenders. Not just poor quality of but also asymmetries in enforcement facilitate crime. These two aspects are also partly present in the underlying assumptions of responsive regulation, albeit with a different character.

Responsive regulation shares a degree of pragmatism with the Andante team's approach. Prevention cannot wait for *ex post facto* intervention by police – it must take place *before* harm occurs and not depend on the hypothetical strength of deterrence. Therefore, prevention measures must first trigger the industry or firm to act appropriately; second, they can depend on external powers of constituencies, consultancies, and then administrative authorities. (The distinction between external and internal is shown with the grey labels on the right in Figure 6.3.) The latter will then begin by advising, signalling mistakes, supporting firms

70. For a more detailed overview of responsive regulation, see Chapter 1.

to take steps towards compliance and then start discouraging violations using sanctions. Only after such initial attempts at deterrence fail, does the iron fist of policing begin to enter the picture, in a third stage. This strategy of moving from the bottom to the top of the pyramid, which can be seen in Figure 6.3 covering rows 2 to 5 starting from the bottom of the pyramid, places a substantial burden on administrative authorities. However, we saw in Chapters 4, 5 and in the first Section in this Chapter that administrative authorities have been far from prepared to carry out all such tasks. Indeed, all rows of the pyramid were, to some extent, weak. The pyramid model, like the Andante approach, assumes that a range of authorities must *all* be *equally strong* in preventing and contrasting crime.[71]

**Figure 6.3 Adapted responsive regulation pyramid**

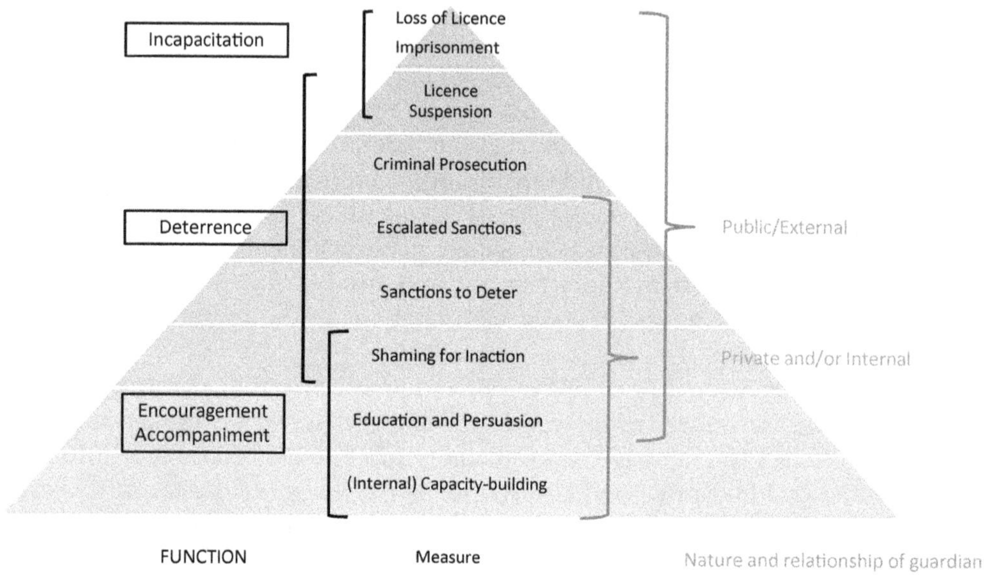


Andante could have remained at the top of the pyramid and hoped that, by aggressively chasing and punishing perpetrators, the latter's perception of risks would increase so much that crime would stop. They could have focused on only improving policing practices. But they took a broader approach. (One that is also more respectful of the principle of criminal law as *ultimum remedium*.) They wanted to empower others. They tried to re-construct the base of the pyramid so that criminal law enforcement measures could stably take their place at the top,

71. This is also reflected in the way the discourse on responsive regulation has evolved from focusing on the 'vertical' movement from one type of measure to another towards more 'horizontal' maneuvers that look at enforcement as something that happens in networks that are composed of both private and public actors. See also notes 78 and 79 below.

where they belong. Therefore, Andante's action outside of the standard policing model is comprehensible through the logic of responsive regulation.

At this point, we also see three limitations to using the responsive regulation lens to look at Andante. The first two relate to the responsive regulation concept. Responsive regulation describes a framework for generating compliance, but it does not capture the process of *generating capable guardians*. Furthermore, responsive regulation does not question the rules that are enforced or the way those rules are created, including the definitions of harmfulness and wrongfulness that those rules crystallise.[72] This point regarding definitions of crime and harm is addressed in the second part of Section 3. The third limitation relates to Andante: the team incorporated the logic of responsive regulation into its goals and practices, but it consciously avoided a fundamental premise of responsive regulation, which concerns the attitude regulators have towards firms.

Let us begin with the last point. Re-integrative shaming – the process whereby regulators relate to the regulated entities to encourage them into compliance instead of stigmatising them into submission – underlies the functioning of responsive regulation. The members of the Andante team could not have been more distant from such an attitude towards offenders. They viewed firms and their managers as *imm*oral rational calculators, always seeking the next opportunity to profit at the expense of society. They imagined themselves as the adversaries of perpetrators of injustice.[73] They also prized their independence and integrity, which was linked to their distance from the perpetrators. Moreover, they viewed the non-adversarial relationship between the administrative branch and corporations with a high degree of scepticism, as we saw in the discussion on integrated approaches in Section 1.

From the perspective of responsive regulation, this attitude towards corporations and this approach to enforcement, if widespread, can lead to more regulatory resistance and more harmful practices instead of less.[74] Of course, responsive regulation *does* connect measures and actors at the top of the pyramid to the determination that the firm in question is behaving like an amoral rational calculator, which perceives low risks of getting caught when offending. But responsive regulation also insists on a gradual approach, whereby fairness and

72. Although when one looks through other publications by Braithwaite on regulatory capitalism and his republican theory of criminal justice or the notion of enforced self-regulation, there are a number of arguments made that also concern this aspect. (John Pettit Philip Braithwaite, *Not Just Deserts: A Republican Theory of Criminal Justice* (Oxford: Clarendon Press, 2010); John Braithwaite, "Enforced Self-Regulation: A New Strategy for Corporate Crime Control," *Michigan Law Review* 80, no. 7 (1982).Unfortunately, the practices that have built upon responsive regulation – and, especially, the pyramid – are often lacking any consideration of these more fundamental premises of the approach. This has been the trigger for scholars who advocate for 'really responsive regulation' (see note 660 below).
73. Interview 7 on 28.02.2020.
74. Braithwaite articulates this idea in his theory of tipping points, which then underlies his later work on responsive regulation. This theory is briefly discussed in Chapter 5.

proportionality demand a more cooperative attitude to begin with. We cannot gage this aspect of responsive regulation functioning in practice from the Andante experience because we are methodologically precluded from doing so.[75] But from the dossiers of their criminal investigations, we can see that at least *some* administrative authorities did not deter, yet they also did not encourage firms to comply.[76] We may conclude that the scepticism of the Andante team members is quite understandable, even if their experience is not representative of the entirety of administrative enforcement of the two industries. Nevertheless, such scepticism should not permeate all measures and actors that Andante have been supporting and strengthening. For the principles of responsive regulation to work in practice, a non-stigmatising attitude also needs to be cultivated by regulators (at the bottom of the pyramid).

The solution Andante found to the deficiencies of guardianship – from its institutional location and based on its assumptions about both offending and enforcement – was that of capacity- and tool-building. As noted above, this process is not adequately described within the responsive regulation paradigm. Collaboration between state agencies is important, especially in view of the functioning of the mechanisms of fairness and proportionality. But that stops short of the underlying processes of guardian *formation*. Our review of Andante through the concept of problem-oriented policing already took us a long way in this regard: the action-research dynamic underlying problem-oriented policing also characterises the way Andante worked as a team and with others. They often looked to improve their collective monitoring and investigative practices based on new learnings about crimes and criminogenesis. A very concrete result of these efforts comes in the form of a checklist that the team refined over the years, and which was shared with different authorities, in the Netherlands and abroad. This checklist can be used by field agents who conduct checks of vehicles that transport chemicals or wastes. It facilitates the identification of suspicious activities.[77] The later-developed computer program mentioned in Section 1 elevates this further facilitates and automates the checking of much larger batches of transports. These

75. By definition, the cases we looked at showed indications of criminal conduct. The sample was skewed to show those instances where previous attempts at encouraging compliance, whether they had been carried out in the spirit of responsive regulation or not, had failed. Even when observing the collaboration between Andante and administrative authorities during *Zwarte Stromen*, the leadership of Andante as a police team gave a specific character to the activities carried out by all the agents and agencies involved. For example, the morning briefings made it very clear that the aim of the checks was to "catch the bad guys". Hence, even if there are authorities who have been successfully adopting a responsive regulation approach in the Netherlands in respect of firms in the waste oil and bunker fuel sectors, the data regarding that is not available for this study.

76. The example, in Chapter 4, of *Crafty Collectors'* relationship with the administrative authorities is clear in this respect. There was an authority whose task it was to monitor and enforce, but they did not do so.

77. See Checklist cited in Table 1 in Annex II.

examples show a very practical way of collaborating to strengthen a variety of regulators.

Yet even problem-oriented policing and these examples do not adequately capture what Andante has tried to achieve. Developing tools such as the checklist or the computer program are superficial manifestations of a deeper engagement that builds *human* resources. Resources that possess knowledge, skills, qualities and who have matured a degree of experience, which makes them capable guardians. The strong focus of responsive regulation on the relationship between regulators and corporations leaves little room to analyse this building of human resources. Indeed, the resources that are built in responsive regulation are the ones in the business sectors themselves. The processes of education, accompaniment, checking, and sanctioning serve to shape corporations and their employees to steer them away from rule violation and into compliance. Andante has worked on training the regulators, not the regulated. They have tried to take the necessary step *before* direct engagement with business, which then makes a responsive regulation approach possible and effective.[78]

There is another aspect of the Andante *programma* that deserves attention, which can be addressed through the concepts from the literature on responsive regulation and enforced self-regulation. This aspect centres around overcoming the problem of 'authorised representatives' in the context of organisational crimes. In enforced self-regulation, rulemaking by firms and governments is linked up to broader constituencies in order to avoid the dangers of collusion and capture. This linking up is transposed into the concept of responsive regulation by referring to tripartite regulation, i.e., involving state, business and third parties.[79] The

78. It would be important to look into the ways that regulators and enforcement agents are trained to carry out their activities. This issue is not specifically focused on in the criminological literature and is also not central to the body of work around corporate regulation. It would seem that there is an assumption that the state and its agents are naturally 'capable' to carry out their tasks. At the same time, the incapability of the state seems to be central to proposals for self-regulation by the industry. The fields of public management and public administration may be interesting to look into in this respect. See, for example: Claire A. Dunlop, Jonathan C. Kamkhaji, and Claudio M. Radaelli, "Regulators and Reform: A Quasi-Experimental Assessment of the Effects of Training Inspectors," *International Public Management Journal* 18, no. 2 (2015). There is some literature looking at new forms of police training that may also be interesting Michael T Rossler and Michael J Suttmoeller, "Is All Police Academy Training Created Equally? Comparing Natural Resource Officer and General Police Academy Training," *The Police Journal* 91, no. 2 (2018).in this regard, for example: Craig Paterson, "Adding Value? A Review of the International Literature on the Role of Higher Education in Police Training and Education," *Police Practice and Research* 12, no. 4 (2011).

79. The various constellations of business-state-public have been reflected on by different scholars. Beyond the work of Braithwaite, we find the notion of meta-regulation, which is closer to the idea of enforced self-regulation and places more emphasis on the how the responsibility of rule-*making* can be adequately allocated. See, for example: Peter Grabosky, "Meta-Regulation," *Regulatory theory: Foundations and applications* (2017); Christine Parker, "Meta-Regulation: Legal Accountability for Corporate Social Responsibility," (2007); Colin Scott, "Speaking Softly without Big Sticks: Meta-Regulation and Public Sector Audit," *Law & Policy* 25, no. 3 (2003); Christine

broader constituency or third parties provide the necessary pressures through their 'weight' against *both* government *and* business. The broader constituency and third parties but also democratise regulation by defining what a population wants and needs. According to the mechanics of enforced self-regulation and responsive regulation, this weight must be adequately distributed for the pressure and definitions to actually materialise. Sometimes the practices in need of regulation should be scrutinised at global or national level because of the nature and magnitude of harm that they cause or because of how widespread those practices are. Sometimes, local residents are in a better position to monitor and demand regulation and enforcement of certain rules against specific firms. Oftentimes a combined activation of constituencies at different levels may prove most fruitful.[80]

Andante has triggered these types of pressure-inducing and definitional mechanisms by actively engaging media and academics in their pursuits. How can a constituency act to regulate (as a third party) if it is unaware of the problem? Because the crimes are so far removed from public consciousness and the harm

---

Parker, "Twenty Years of Responsive Regulation: An Appreciation and Appraisal," *Regulation & Governance* 7, no. 1 (2013).

Other fields of inquiry that build on the ideas of responsive regulation are 'really responsive regulation' and 'smart regulation'. Really responsive regulation tries to incorporate a more critical perspective whereby reflexiveness and learning need to become part of the process of devising both rules and enforcement procedures. Examples of this are:

Robert Baldwin and Julia Black, "Really Responsive Regulation," *The modern law review* 71, no. 1 (2008); Peter Mascini and Eelco Van Wijk, "Responsive Regulation at the Dutch Food and Consumer Product Safety Authority: An Empirical Assessment of Assumptions Underlying the Theory," *Regulation & Governance* 3, no. 1 (2009); Julia Black and Robert Baldwin, "Really Responsive Risk-Based Regulation," *Law & policy* 32, no. 2 (2010).

Smart regulation is about the exchanges and dynamics between several types of guardians – these are administrative and criminal law authorities, but also consultancies or other private entities as well as internal agents of firms or industries, and the public at large. Examples from this branch of literature are: Neil Gunningham, "Strategizing Compliance and Enforcement: Responsive Regulation and Beyond," *Explaining compliance: business responses to regulation* (2011); Neil Gunningham and Darren Sinclair, "Smart Regulation," *Regulatory theory: Foundations and applications* (2017); Peter Van Gossum, Bas Arts, and Kris Verheyen, "From "Smart Regulation" to "Regulatory Arrangements"," *Policy Sciences* 43, no. 3 (2010); Judith Van Erp and Wim Huisman, "Smart Regulation and Enforcement of Illegal Disposal of Electronic Waste," *Criminology & Pub. Pol'y* 9 (2010).

80. Braithwaite, "Enforced Self-Regulation: A New Strategy for Corporate Crime Control." In the literature on smart regulation, the tripartite arrangement is taken a step further through the notion of a 'social licence', which is combined with a legal and an economic licence. The argument is as follows: for a firm to operate it needs to have at its disposal not just a permit in a strict sense (the legal licence), but it must also be economically viable and socially accepted. The social licence functions through the other two licences as the public can demand legal licences to be withdrawn or, at least, altered (for example, we can campaign for lower carbon emissions that are regulated through legal instruments). The public can also use the market – the economic licence – to express preferences by boycotting certain products or producers, for example. This social licence is comparable to the organised countervailing constituency that Braithwaite talks about in his theory of tipping points. (Neil Gunningham, Robert A Kagan, and Dorothy Thornton, "Social License and Environmental Protection: Why Businesses Go Beyond Compliance," *Law & Social Inquiry* 29, no. 2 (2004).

is so diffuse and 'invisible', the so-called third party is effectively precluded from exercising its regulatory potential. Collective conscience – which can also then awaken individual consciences in the remaining two parties – [81] has been absent. In that sense, Andante has mobilised not just the state actors at the base of the regulatory pyramid but also the third parties that can really contribute to complete functioning of the pyramid model and enforced self-regulation.

We also previously saw that the issue of 'authorised representatives' has different facets. Corporations or industry representatives have been part of policy and legislation-making conversations with government. In Section 1 here and in Chapter 5 we saw that no such opportunity was offered to wider constituencies or NGOs, for example. So, authorised speakers generate veils not just through their individual activities carried out behind a permit, but they participate in the definition-making in a way that further shields them from the pressures and definitions of the public. This more insidious – and even less visible – functioning of authority is linked to a more deeply rooted structural arrangement, which we try to unpack using the state-corporate crime concept in Chapter 7. Before that, we try to understand how Andante's functioning as guardians, which we explored in this Section, may influence the future criminogenic conditions within the sectors they have been active in.

## 6.3 Andante through the Lens of Situational Crime Prevention

In this Section the focus shifts back to the relationship between guardianship and the incidence of crime. The aim is to see, through the lens of SCP,[82] how we can better understand the outcomes of the Andante *programma* in view of the criminogenic conditions, which we explored in Chapters 3 to 5, that characterise the crimes.

Let us now look at the categories of techniques that can be devised in response to specific crime events: increasing risks; increasing efforts, reducing rewards, reducing provocations; and removing excuses.[83] It is important to restate that this analysis is *not* an *impact*-evaluation of the work of Andante, nor a process-evaluation of the functioning of the team members.[84] Indeed, the reflections in this

81. In Chapter 3, we looked at how the intervention triangle may be adapted for organisational crimes. Accordingly, the logic of routine activities theory and responsive regulation may be combined to see how this tripartite system of guardianship may function in practice.
82. The use of SCP to understand the effects of environmental law enforcement is not new, see: Huisman, Wim, and Judith van Erp. "Opportunities for Environmental Crime: A Test of Situational Crime Prevention Theory." *British Journal of Criminology* 53, no. 6 (2013): 1178.
83. For a detailed discussion of SCP, see Chapter 1. The full table of the 25 Techniques of SCP can be found in Annex I.
84. To some extent, one could speak of a process evaluation in the sense trying to determine whether the team reached its own goals as they are articulated in their own materials, such as the list presented in Figure 6.2 above. For an overview of the different forms of evaluation, see: Nelen, H. & Leeuw, F.L., Evaluating Counterterrorism: The Case of the Netherlands. in *Evaluation and*

Section generally should *not* be taken as an analysis of cause and effect. The setup of this study does not allow us to draw conclusions that causally link the actions of the Andante team or any of its individual members to specific results,[85] beyond the legal measures taken against specific companies or persons.[86] Even when referring to *those* measures, we cannot make any definitive claims as to how they have impacted the prospective and subjective assessments of would-be offenders in the bunker fuel and waste oil sectors. Therefore, the categories used in this section should be taken as heuristic tools – they are merely helpful for systematising the insights that derive from our inquiry into the work of the Andante team.

*Increasing Risks*

We can characterise the work of Andante mainly using this category of SCP techniques. Police activities are, by their nature, geared towards the detection and punishment of offenders. Yet the particular approach that the members of the team have had towards this goal is remarkable. Prevention of harm and *reducing the involvement of policeand public prosecution* have been the ultimate aims of the team members. They recognised that their intervention as criminal law enforcers, especially when it comes to environmental crime, is often too little too late.[87] Indeed, the way in which the team has sought to 'increase risks' is through the empowerment of several agencies and agents, with particular regard for administrative authorities as well as partners beyond national borders. Learning more about the conditions and techniques that facilitate crime has definitely increased their *own* effectiveness as a police investigative team. Nevertheless, the aim has always been that of bringing this learning *beyond* the team – and beyond the police organisation – to spread and strengthen the guardianship function that several types of actors can have.

More concretely, we can say that the participation of the team in carrying out and improving systematic checks of transports and other activities has increased risks. Enforcement agents have been more present and more visible than before the checks were carried out. They are now also better able to detect wrongdoing thanks to the knowledge and capacities acquired over time. Therefore, actors in the waste oil and bunker fuel sectors may perceive a higher chance of being detected when breaking the law, at least in the Netherlands.

Beyond improved and increased detection, the efforts made by Andante have furthered prosecution and conviction. Starting with the cases investigated by the team itself, we can say that offenders, who may have avoided punishment in

---

*turbulent times. Comparative Policy Evaluation.* Transaction Publishers, New Brunswick London, 2013, p. 179-197.

85. Arguably, causation is an inadequate notion in the field of social science generally. My approach to explanations and causation can be found in Chapter 2.
86. At the end of Section 6.1., we saw the details regarding the outcomes of the team's work.
87. Memo 1; Memo 2; Field Notes 20-21.10.2016.

absence of the team, have now lost permits, paid fines or been convicted.[88] This is something that other actors in the respective industrial branches may perceive. The experience and expertise the team has built through the application of the chain-investigation method has also generally improved their effectiveness as they have progressed, thereby also increasing the possibility to punish offenders in the long term. Their means of sharing their experience and expertise has further improved the chances that offenders receive some form of punishment or response from agencies that monitor and enforce rules in the waste oil and bunker fuel sectors. Moreover, the efforts made to engage international partners is a step towards decreasing the disparity in enforcement that national borders create; thereby impacting one of the most important criminogenic opportunities for this type of crime. Indeed, Andante has been conscious of the criminogenic asymmetries that so often facilitate cross-border and environmental crime and the potential for displacement that these asymmetries create.[89]

Ultimately, the dedication to capacity building of Andante has led to an increase – both qualitative and quantitative – in capable guardians. In turn, it has become more challenging for would-be offenders to deceive guardians. Capable guardians could possibly now operate more consistently across agencies, across the territory of the Netherlands, but also across the globe.[90] However, there is a limit to this increase in risks. The capability of guardians is always relative to the ingeniousness of the offenders. Innovation in offending requires corresponding innovation in interventions. One of the defining features and biggest strengths of Andante has been their dedication to continuous learning. Their focused scrutiny of the two industries over several years has meant that they could observe their evolution. Andante made efforts to catch up with the branch, to help others catch up with it, and then together to *keep up* with changing trends and actors. If similar efforts are not continued, the "period of crime-lag" may be just that: a phase followed by a renewed increase thanks to innovation in *modi operandi*.[91]

---

88. See Section 6.1.
89. See, for example, the objective to effect structural change in Figure 6.2.
90. Of the officers from other countries who have learned with Andante, three sets – in Germany, France and Portugal – have begun implementing the insights they gained. Co-operation with Belgium took a bit longer, but towards the end of Andante's operation, it seemed that similar measures to the Dutch ones were being implemented there too. In the case of Belgium, part of the cooperation occurred through a Joint Investigation Team.
91. In their discussion of crime-facilitative systems, Needleman and Needleman also talk about crime-resistant systems. Regarding crime-resistance, they hypothesise that there may be situations where structural change only leads to a temporary reduction in crime (crime-lag). Conversely, there may be cases where the structural changes have a more permanent effect. They suggest that research should be done to see which kind of changes lead to which kind of outcome. (Martin L Needleman and Carolyn Needleman, "Organizational Crime: Two Models of Criminogenesis," *The Sociological Quarterly* 20, no. 4 (1979). Innovation in *modi operandi* may not be sufficiently anticipated by the structural change, depending on the nature of the innovation – how fundamental it is in relation to its contextualising forces. At the same time, innovation in *modi operandi* is just one way that motivated offenders may continue committing crime even

*Increasing Efforts*

One of the salient features of the criminal events we have been exploring is that they are carried out in an economic context where the use of residues and wastes is part of a 'normal' business model. The *routineness* of these practices is an important facilitating condition. We could argue that these entrenched "traditions of commerce"[92] have, at least to some extent, been disturbed or disrupted by the actions of the Andante team. The team's investigations have problematised these practices at different levels. A debate about the appropriateness of using certain (waste) substances as blend components has been fostered, and we see evidence of this even in parliamentary proceedings and media coverage, for example.[93] The veil of unknowingness that has covered these activities, which are at the background of our economic system, has been lifted. Therefore, the actors in these sectors have to make attempts to change their ways. It is no longer acceptable to continue as they have. Of course, they may choose to change the way they offend and conceal their offending. But this still remains an effort they need to make.

Furthermore, the link between activities performed by waste management firms, the technology they use to carry these activities out, and the permits that sanction them has been strengthened. We could argue, therefore, that Andante's work has contributed to altering market dynamics in the industry. A source of 'low efforts' in the cases we analysed was the simplicity of the technology in respect of the substances being handled. A firm could make a relatively low investment in waste treatment technology and claim to be doing more with that technology than they were actually able to. Incapable guardians would not have been able to see this. By strengthening guardianship, Andante has, indirectly, impacted the efforts firms need to make to continue participating in this business, whether legitimately or illegitimately. The nature of their intentions is something we cannot assess, but firms will need to make larger investments in technology to treat hazardous waste oils if they want to at least appear to be following the rules of the industry. There is even a concrete example of impacting market dynamics through the functioning of the permit as a mechanism of enforcement and compliance. A firm, which had one of the larger market shares in waste oil collection and treatment in the Netherlands, has been the object of Andante's investigations. It has lost its permit as a consequence of the team's efforts.[94] It is no longer allowed to operate in the

after interventions have been implemented (at different levels). The literature on displacement (mentioned in Chapters 4 and 5) for example, explores various forms of displacement that may take place when *situational* conditions are altered. It may be worth exploring the idea of displacement when structural change happens.

92. Ibid. p. 524-525.

93. For example, Wilfried Koomen, *Beerput Nederland* (2017); "Kamerstukken II 2012-2013, 33450, 4." "Kamerstukken II 2013-2014, 33450, 5"; "Kamerstukken II 2013-2014, 31409, 58." "Kamerstukken II 2016-2017, 31409, 124"; "Kamerstukken II 2016-2017, D29117." "Kamerstukken II 2017-2018, 620"; "Kamerstukken II 2017-2018, Z12969."

94. Ontwerpbeschikking ambtshalve gedeeltelijk intrekken vergunning van Wubben Handelsmaatschappij BV, Gedeputeerde Staten van Noord-Brabant, 8 December 2016.

Dutch market. This is a visible illustration of the economic effect of the team's work.

Let us take this idea further and beyond the functioning of the permit as a regulatory mechanism. We could argue that Andante's efforts may have contributed to more broadly affecting the markets in which waste oils and bunker fuel are traded. Environmental consciousness has increased generally in the last years and decades. We live in the time of 'Fridays for Future'. More and more, we as a society take ownership of the negative consequences that our (economic) lives have on the planet and on our health.[95] By making the questionable practices and harms of the waste and bunker fuel industries more visible and intelligible, Andante has contributed to increasing the amount and accuracy of information available in the market. We *all* can act based on that information. We can choose not to support firms that ship their products across the oceans burning bunker fuel. We can scrutinise waste management firms more closely. We can campaign for more stringent regulations and more effective enforcement. Andante's contribution has gone beyond strengthening the enforcement of state-generated rules by state agents, it has also *potentially* empowered market participants.

*Reducing Rewards*

The most direct link between reduction of rewards and the work of Andante are the profits that have been removed from firms following successful conviction. The Dutch criminal law framework is set up to reduce and remove the rewards that derive from criminal activities through both the application of fines and the confiscation of criminal assets. Following a criminal conviction, article 9 of the Dutch Criminal Code states that a forfeiture can be imposed as a sanction, regardless of the imposition of other sanctions.[96] Article 33a indicates which types of objects and property may be subject to forfeiture. The first point in the list of Article 33a is the most relevant for us because it indicates that "items belonging to the offender or which he can use for his own benefit, in whole or in part, and

95. There is some interesting literature regarding the mounting environmental consciousness we have been witnessing in recent years, including the media attention dedicated to environmental protection movements: Ruth E. McKie, "Climate Change Counter Movement Neutralization Techniques: A Typology to Examine the Climate Change Counter Movement," *Sociological Inquiry* 89, no. 2 (2019); Anna Di Ronco, James Allen-Robertson, and Nigel South, "Representing Environmental Harm and Resistance on Twitter: The Case of the Tap Pipeline in Italy," *Crime, Media, Culture* 15, no. 1 (2019); Jenalee Kluttz and Pierre Walter, "Conceptualizing Learning in the Climate Justice Movement," *Adult Education Quarterly* 68, no. 2 (2018); Olivia Hasler, Reece Walters, and Rob White, "In and against the State: The Dynamics of Environmental Activism," *Critical Criminology* 28, no. 3 (2020). The effects of environmental activism on policy and structural economic practices are, nevertheless, challenging to ascertain as is demonstrated in: John Muñoz, Susan Olzak, and Sarah A. Soule, "Going Green: Environmental Protest, Policy, and Co2 Emissions in U.S. States, 1990–2007," *Sociological Forum* 33, no. 2 (2018).

96. *Wet van 3 maart 1881 Wetboek van Strafrecht*. The relevant criminal law provisions applicable to the cases studied in this book are discussed in Section 1 of Chapter 4.

which have been obtained wholly or mainly through or from the proceeds of the offence" may be confiscated.[97]

Beyond confiscation, fines can be imposed that are commensurate to the harm caused by the crime in accordance with Article 6 Law on Economic Crimes (WED).[98] Depending on the nature of the offence – its classification in the WED, its seriousness and whether it has been carried out several times by the offender – a monetary fine of either the fourth or fifth category is applicable, which in 2020 could amount to a maximum of € 21,750 and € 87,000, respectively.

That said, as with all other SCP categories, a more *indirect* link to the reduction of rewards is that of Andante's contribution to raising more and more capable guardians. These guardians, in turn, can intervene against culpable firms and remove their profits.[99] Likewise, more capable guardians mean more possibilities to discourage and disrupt criminal activities and events, therefore, an overall reduction in the rewards from crime.

Nevertheless, we should remember that in our case study rewards are mainly the result of *structural* conditions that influence the specific costs and benefits of situations. To explore the potential contribution of Andante's work regarding the reduction of rewards means we need to consider such structural factors. To start with, waste crime is facilitated by the negative value of wastes. Collection and treatment firms are commonly paid before they carry out treatment services. That payment is based on the claims these firms make about what they are able to do and the technology they appear to have. As discussed for increasing efforts, strengthening the 'permit-technology-substance link' by making monitoring of compliance with permits more stringent and effective, means that some firms need to invest more in order to comply. The profit margins such firms have been maintaining by receiving payment for services they did not and could not offer correspondingly decrease. Violating the law is still a possible choice; but firms need to invest in order to appear legitimate, and their overall profits are negatively impacted as a consequence. This effect could gradually extend beyond the Netherlands.

97. Furthermore, Art. 36e(1) WvS states that "At the request of the public prosecutor, a separate court decision may impose on a person convicted of a criminal offence the obligation to pay a sum of money to the state for the deprivation of illegally obtained benefit." [Author's translation] and Art. 23(7) adds: "Upon conviction of a legal person, if the fine category determined for the offence does not allow for appropriate punishment, a fine may be imposed up to the amount of the next higher category. If a fine of the sixth category may be imposed for the offence and that fine category does not allow for appropriate punishment, a fine may be imposed up to a maximum of 10 per cent of the legal entity's annual turnover in the financial year preceding the judgment or criminal order." [Author's translation]

98. Wet van 22 juni 1950, houdende vaststelling van regelen voor de opsporing, de vervolging en de berechting van economische delicten. The WED is discussed in more detail in Chapters 3 and 4.

99. Fines and other measures to remove profit may not only be used by criminal law enforcement agencies. For more details about the range of measures available to regulators in the Netherlands, see Section 1 of Chapter 4.

In a globalised world, disparities in regulation and enforcement are important facilitating factors for corporations to increase profits and escape the criminal label. These disparities are a feature of the waste management industry, and attempts have already been made to address them through instruments like the Basel Convention on the transboundary movement of hazardous wastes. However, the Convention is not a guarantee of harmonised implementation, application and enforcement. But it is a common basis from which to harmonise. Within the European context, the network of guardians Andante has been trying to build and foster can readily refer to Regulation 1013/2006,[100] which implements the Basel Convention into EU law. Over time, the Basel Convention can be used more and more as a levelling instrument that, when coherently enforced following the example of teams like Andante, can further remove disparities, i.e., criminogenic asymmetries, that have made it cheaper to manage wastes in one location compared to another.

A corresponding and related effect can be imagined in the bunker fuel industry. Blend components that were coming from the waste oil sector may increase in price because corners are not cut as easily. Consequently, the costs of compliance may spill-over into the bunker fuel sector. The old business models would no longer be viable. The rewards of making dirty fuel would decrease as the price of blend components increases. In fact, we could anticipate a general increase in the costs of doing business in both industries, first in the Netherlands, but then gradually over larger and larger portions of the world, if interventions similar to Andante's are progressively expanded. Of course, the asymmetry between the waste industry, which is tightly regulated, and the bunker fuel sector where there is almost only self-regulation, is not removed through this spill-over effect. Therefore, depriving the bunker fuel production process of cheap blend components without removing the opportunity that the lack of proper regulation creates could be problematic. Pressure functions as a motivator as we saw in Chapter 5, therefore, reducing rewards in the context of overlapping symbiotic industries needs to be accomplished cautiously because firms may be motivated to seek new paths to profit, which are even more problematic.

*Reducing Provocations*

In Chapter 5, we conceptualised 'provocations' in the context of our case study by referring to the pressures for profit maximisation and growth that corporations face as economic actors. We saw that waste legislation coupled with a shift in market conditions in the blend component trade have led to an increase in such

100. For a more detailed review of the Basel Convention and the Regulation, see Chapter 3. Basel Convention on the Control of Transboundary Movements of Hazardous Wastes and their Disposal (adopted 22 March 1989, entered into force 5 May 1992) (1989), 28 ILM 657; Regulation (EC) 1013/2006 of the European Parliament and of the Council of 14 June 2006 on shipments of waste, OJ L 190, p. 1, 12.07.2006.

pressures, thereby making illegitimate opportunities to profit more and more attractive. Andante's efforts to investigate criminal activities and to increase the supply of capable guardians have contributed to decreasing the supply and attractiveness of these illegitimate opportunities, at least in theory. The competitive advantage firms may have had by engaging in illegal practices like the ones we have been analysing has been correspondingly reduced.

We should *not overstate* the consequences of Andante's work in respect of this SCP category. Firstly, we cannot estimate such consequences with any degree of accuracy. Secondly, and maybe more importantly, impacting this facilitating condition requires structural changes that lie beyond the reach of any single investigative team. The economic circumstances that make criminal activities attractive are tied to wider processes of global production and consumption. We saw in Chapter 3 that a strong source of pressure to make cheap bunker fuel derives from our globalised consumer economy. Indeed, there is nothing illegal or seemingly illegitimate in the demand for cheaper and 'faster' products. On the contrary, we often take this trend as a sign of a healthy and thriving economic reality. It is challenging to effect change where no problem is perceived in the first place. Similarly, we should not forget that the flow of oil wastes is equally pervasive and invisible. Oil wastes are linked to so many production processes because oil is the basic component of innumerable products as well as the means whereby machinery and means of transport are fuelled and lubricated as we saw in Chapter 3. A systematic increase in the price of treatment of oil wastes will have an impact on the economy, but we may not be aware of the impact on our health and environment in the same way.

Therefore, reducing provocations is a category that is fraught with challenges; provocations may, paradoxically, *increase* with improved enforcement. Steps actually need to be taken to match such an increase with a bolstering of democratic debate that would help to channel frustrations in the market towards environmentally friendly innovation as opposed to criminal and harmful practices. And here again we see the important contribution of Andante, which we cannot overestimate or estimate at all, but we can recognise. Andante has at the very least tried to foster this debate by increasing awareness and making more information available.

*Removing Excuses*

A lot of effort has been made by the team with regard to this category of interventions. One of the main facilitators of crime in this sector originates in the ambiguity and flexibility of definitions of what is a waste, a product, a blend component or bunker fuel. A flexibility, which is compounded by the ambiguity and murkiness of the physical substances themselves. The lack of clear definitions leads to a lack of 'clear instructions', which allows 'consciences' to remain dormant.[101] The breadth of the spectrum of acceptability is too wide because there is plenty of room for interpretation.

Much of the work of the team has been that of entering into conversation with authorities at different levels and in different places to explain and see together how the processes and labels being applied to wastes and harmful substances are often not correct. Part of that endeavour has included broadening the responsibility for guardianship to include society at large. Journalists, documentary film makers and academics have been called upon to take the time to investigate these crimes and industries and then share what they learned with the general public. The definition of waste, of harm, has been reviewed not just with the help of technical experts and scientists, but through democratic mechanisms that alert us all to harmful practices that go unnoticed and that fuel our consumer economy.

However, the other source of 'excuses' is the realm of bunker fuel where definitions of the product revolve around efficiency as opposed to conservation. Andante has had little chance to intervene in this respect. Legislation is scarce; therefore, it is difficult to even have a platform in which to debate what should be in that legislation. Waste legislation, however ambiguous, has to be interpreted and applied in favour of environmental protection. Bunker fuel specifications are very detailed but are simply not meant to protect human health and the environment. Indeed, bunker fuel producers and consumers have no need for excuses or absolutions when they perpetrate harm.[102]

*Situational Crime Prevention and Fostering Compliance: Providing Opportunities*

This new category of SCP includes five techniques: facilitating compliance, forgiving past offences, subsidising desired outcomes and legalising behaviours or shifting their regulation away from criminal law.[103] It is interesting because it shows us a very different approach to limiting crime and harm than the one that underlies SCP traditionally but also, and especially, the work of the Andante team. Indeed, it is challenging to characterise the work of the team using any of the techniques that are part of this new category. This is partly attributable to the institutional 'location' of the team, they are not in a position to legalise, forgive or subsidise, for example. However, we could argue that their attitude and ideology as a team and as a criminal law enforcement entity precludes the consideration of such techniques. Saying this does not equal to tacit approval of the proposed techniques. In fact, it is worthwhile to take the time to see how these techniques would look if applied to cases of organisational or environmental crime, and to generally meditate on the implications of implementing them. However, in the

101. These are techniques numbers 22 and 23 in the 25 techniques table, which can be found in Annex I.
102. The rules applicable in the bunker fuel sector are discussed in Section 3 of Chapter 3.
103. For a more detailed discussion of this new set of techniques, see Chapter 1.

same spirit as the paragraphs above, these techniques offer us a heuristic tool to mediate on the work of Andante. This meditation reveals the limitations of the team, which derive partly from their ideological and institutional characteristics.

The team has set "provoking structural change in the fuel oil industry" as one of its objectives (see Figure 6.2 above). We saw in this Section that their efforts, even if multiplied by the extension of their techniques of investigation and enforcement across the globe, are all mostly geared towards increasing risks of detection and punishment. In the rational choice model this is covered by the 'costs', especially the formal costs, of certain behaviours.[104] This link to costs is the same for measures that increase efforts and reduce rewards. Thus, these are ways of *discouraging* criminal activities that depend on external (state) action, which is very expensive financially and in terms of the energy that is required to 'keep up' with the motivated offenders. However, when we reviewed the work of the team under the categories of reducing provocations and removing excuses two things became clear. First, the extraordinariness of the approach Andante has had. They have attempted to dive deep into the definitional realm by questioning the link between labels, profit and harm. They have attempted to make space for (democratic) debate. Second, the limitedness of their reach, if not supported by others. Provoking structural change requires the mobilisation of those who are formed by and, in turn, reproduce the structures of the industry. A large component of these structures is the business world, the companies themselves. They can be pushed into corners with the threat of punishment, but will that suffice?

In the quotes we looked at in Section 6.1, we saw that Andante does not understand its role as that of changing companies through direct, cooperative dialogue. They are a criminal law enforcement team that should be available to intervene *after* crime has occurred. Their preventative efforts are rooted in doing their best to capably intervene, within their function. At most, the team helped other guardians become capable enough to ensure compliance with the law and protection of the citizens and the environment. It is these *other* guardians that have to be prepared and not naïve when dealing with the economic portion of an industry. Policymakers, regulatory agencies and administrative authorities can act in ways conceptualised in the sixth category of SCP. They can facilitate, subsidise, provide alternatives, legalise and forgive, but they must do so knowing enough about the industry so that the result is *less* harm. That is where Andante's experience and our exploration of criminogenesis in this study reveal the limitations of this new SCP category.

Unfortunately, we need to be sceptical about almost all the techniques that belong to this new category when trying to implement it through regulatory

104. The rational choice perspective is discussed in Chapter 1 in more detail, both in respect of traditional and organisational offending.

techniques. Let us explore each in turn. 'Legalising behaviours' is one of the *problems* in our case. Waste management is already primarily dealt with through regulatory law. The waste definition legalises a lot of harm because it makes certain waste management practices perfectly acceptable; and it is vague enough that less acceptable practices become invisible. The bunker fuel sector is scarcely regulated, so there is not much to legalise; in fact, this is part of the challenge. 'Forgiving' and 'subsidising' although not (legally) explicit, seem to already be part of the patterns of these industries. Companies are given a lot of room for manoeuvre, even when their track record should preclude them from continuing to act and profit in the waste industry.[105] The almost complete privatisation of the waste sector leads to reaping the benefits of the market conditions that make waste management extremely lucrative. This may not be a formal subsidy, but it is a mouth-watering opportunity. Not to speak of the freedom from constraint and controls that bunker fuel production is given. 'Alternatives' are exactly what firms in these sectors look for: alternative ways of treating wastes, alternative ways of making bunker fuel. Indeed, they are innovators in this respect. Maybe the alternative to protect the environment should be 'subsidised' instead?

'Facilitating compliance' is, however, difficult to argue with. We should not be blind to the fact that the complexity of waste legislation as well as the generally challenging nature of ensuring environmental protection in our modern industrial reality make compliance far from simple. So yes, many, many efforts need to be made to support compliance by assisting and consistently learning together and improving these compliance efforts. And authorities and individuals outside the firms themselves have tremendous responsibility in this respect. We cannot facilitate compliance by delegating to the expertise of the economic chunk of an industry. 'External' actors need to be as much part of the innovation as the economic sector itself, and continually contribute with social, environmental and ethical considerations.[106] Andante and any others that follow in their footsteps can help us in that regard, but only to an extent. So, the question remains, how do we provide opportunities to comply or do less harm, beyond hiking up the costs of crime? How do we do so cognisant of the wider forces that define harm and acceptability and, in turn, shape regulatory and enforcement structures and patterns? Answers to these questions require a much deeper exploration of the structural forces that sustain criminogenesis and which, if altered, could maintain justice by truly preventing harm. This is now discussed briefly in the conclusions

105. For example, previously indicted or convicted firms who have done considerable harm are still allowed to be part of policymaking negotiations and contribute with their expert knowledge to the making of the rules that are supposed to protect us. A concrete example of this was presented in Section 3 of Chapter 5.

106. This task can, of course, partly be accomplished through NGOs and other civil society organisations.

of this Chapter and will be an important aspect of the final reflections that are articulated in Chapter 7.

*Conclusions*

What the story of Andante shows us is important not just in relation to the cases where they themselves intervened and were successful. Or even for the cases that came to the team's attention but did not lead to a conviction or an investigation in the first place. Indeed, the insights we can draw from reflecting on the experience of the Andante team can extend past designing interventions to prevent crime in the waste oil and bunker fuel sectors. These insights are pertinent to responding to corporate environmental crime more generally. Many of the challenges the team faced are not so different from those faced by others who try to contrast these forms of crime.[107] And the way they have overcome those challenges can inspire other potential guardians of human health and the environment.

When they started their work, the first challenge the team encountered was that they could not effectively respond as criminal law enforcement agents, as members of the wider police organisation. They were not prepared. The actors who should have been working at the top of the regulatory pyramid could not exercise the necessary deterrent function. And, at this initial stage, they also witnessed that there was a general lack of competence within state organs to respond to this type of crime. The state's ability to recognise and confront these problems, through both criminal and administrative law powers was very poor in comparison to the systematicity of the crimes themselves. In SCP terms, motivated offenders did not need to make disproportionate efforts to carry out and conceal criminal activities, nor did they face high risks of being caught and punished.

Indeed, at the start of Andante's operation, we can say that it was not just the top of the regulatory pyramid that was not credibly deterring. Those state agents working at the bottom of the regulatory pyramid, who are supposed to educate and support compliance or even reward good practice, *they* were unprepared for such tasks. Hence, Andante's efforts tried to address these deficiencies. They wanted to increase the deterrent potential of the criminal law enforcement organisation. *And* they wanted to make sure that those agents that were supposed to be in direct contact with business could be prepared to carry out their tasks appropriately and in favour of environmental protection. Andante endeavoured to strengthen the integrity of the relationship between state and business by trying to build up capable guardians that would cater to the entirety of the regulatory pyramid.

107. For a more detailed review of interventions in the context of corporate environmental crime, see Chapter 1.

Of course, Andante's reach has been partial. Such partial reach is connected to the fact that the administrative branch of the state is first in line to encourage and facilitate compliance. Therefore, in addition to their own explicit refusal to be in direct negotiation with firms, they have been structurally impeded in getting involved with directly making the industries change. Furthermore, the actual (illegitimate) practices that produce harm are carried out *by* firms. The economic portion of the industry – the corporations themselves and not just the state – must take ownership of the task of protecting human health and the environment when performing their activities. To expect anything different would be the same as expecting a parent to continue making decisions for a child even once that child is an adult. Corporations and their agents need to take responsibility for the consequences of their activities. The state and its agencies must then provide what corporations – as they are currently legally designed – cannot: ethical principles and independent scientific enquiry to counter the instrumentalization of technology moved by the push for profit maximisation.

It is at this point that we can pause to meditate on how the relationship between states and companies – within environmentally sensitive industrial sectors but also beyond – leads to outcomes that may be judged differently under different perspectives. If we think about this relationship and then the more concrete activity of enforcement by state agents, we can talk about effective regulatory strategies and practices: From this perspective, 'regulating' is about making sure that whatever the relevant policy position is, it gets implemented. Another perspective is that focusing on harms and injustices, regardless of policy positions and legal definitions. If we look at the Andante experience solely from the former perspective, we may be inclined to minimise their achievement by focusing merely on how many firms were held (criminally) liable and try to estimate the temporary increased risk their expertise-building generated.

However, Andante's efforts can only truly be understood through the second, zemiological perspective. Andante's efforts have been targeted at questioning the *content* of the law. The team has tried to highlight that, often, those same firms that are committing crimes are called upon by policymakers to help in drafting legislation. Legislation becomes a means to shield oneself from the criminal label and the related sanctions, in the course of making profit. But beyond this blatant collusion there is a more subtle problem. Without addressing this more subtle problem, we may never really be able to address environmental crimes and harms adequately. Andante's focus on *structural* causes acknowledges this problem. And Andante's selective inclusion of state and non-state partners into their process may reflect the understanding that structural problems are also connected to the way state enforcement is organised and carried out. Let's take this argument further.

Policies, legislation, and enforcement practices are developed in a wider global context where business interests are prioritised over and above welfare considerations. In the era of neoliberal democracies, states may no longer be custodians of the *victims* of business activities – the environment and human health.[108] It could be argued that states have become complicit in the drive to bolster the economy; they reproduce and regurgitate the same scientific and technical evidence constructed by the research and development departments of large corporations. Within this political-economic setup, the act of administering society turns out to be a purely bureaucratic or technocratic endeavour; instead of one charged with political and ideological significance.

The setup also means that implicit decisions that favour immediate economic prosperity over and above environmental conservation are the basis of policymaking. These decisions as policies are then simply implemented through the executive, i.e., through the agencies that carry out enforcement. In their implementation of the rules, these agencies are, in truth, still caught in the tension between profit and preservation, yet they are not designed to resolve this tension politically. In fact, the question of regulation that is delegated to them is one formulated as needing *technical* solutions. These technical solutions are supposedly devoid of ideological and political value. The disowning of political responsibility makes room for collaborative spaces between state agencies and business, which become the venues where *technical, neutral* solutions to problems can mature.

Therefore, through this apolitical delegation of their regulatory functions, states risk generating 'hegemonic apparatuses' instead of guardians of human and environmental welfare. While seemingly addressing the 'bad behaviour' of firms, law enforcement merely lends credibility to the state by making it appear as if they are resolving the issue of ensuring compliance with environmental protection rules. However, this same endowment of credibility means that it becomes impossible to question the decisions that have *already* been made about which interests should be protected and which should be prioritised above others. That is why regulatory agencies can be seen as *hegemonic* apparatuses.[109] They do not favour the powerful elite segments of society by forcefully suppressing opposition and defending existing dominant positions. Rather, they diffuse opposition and generate consent in favour of the powerful by giving the impression that a fair struggle against the powerful is already underway.

---

108. See the crime-problem triangle discussed in the conclusions of Chapter 3 to see the distinction between different types of guardians in organisational crime. What is being referred to here specifically is the distinction between the custodians of the *targets* in criminal activities – which in our case are waste oils, blend components and accompanying documents – and the victims, which are human health and the environment. States and their agencies are only indirectly custodians of the targets because the targets are usually legitimately controlled by waste generators or management firms, or other entities involved in bunker fuel production. The guardianship function of states derives from the mandate to protect human health and the environment from mismanagement of those targets.

109. Rialine Mahon, "Regulatory Agencies: Captive Agents or Hegemonic Apparatuses," *Studies in Political Economy* 1, no. 1 (1979); Frank Pearce and Steve Tombs, "Ideology, Hegemony, and Empiricism: Compliance Theories of Regulation," *The British Journal of Criminology* 30, no. 4 (1990).

In the same Gramscian vein that sprouted the concept of regulatory agencies as hegemonic apparatuses, we can think of Andante as a team of 'counter-hegemonic organic intellectuals'.[110] One of the ways consent and hegemony are generated in favour of dominant classes is through the work of intellectuals (which are not the same as academics), who are able to influence morality, culture, politics and policy. The Andante team broke free of the ideological chains that make states enablers of economic growth instead of custodians of welfare. Although agents *of* the state, they resisted assimilation and neutralisation – to use critical terminology – and questioned the dominant frames of reference. They actively engaged in the production of (scientific) knowledge to contrast the mainstream ideology whereby the interests of business prevail over the environment. Andante is the embryonic form of a more conscious guardianship, not just technically capable and materially resourced, but with a new mindset and attitude. They have been committed to justice and to human and environmental welfare, beyond the limitations of conviction rates and beyond the confines of subservient laws. From them we can and must learn.

110. Quintin Hoare and Geoffrey Nowell-Smith, *Selections from Prison Notebooks* (Lawrence & Wishart, 2005). One could draw parallels between this notion and that of 'moral entrepreneurs' from the labelling literature (see: Becker, *Outsiders: Studies in the Sociology of Deviance*, 1963).

# 7 Conclusions

April 2015, Faculty of Law, Maastricht University: I am standing in front of the assessment committee that will decide whether I get a chance to carry out my PhD research on organised waste trafficking. As part of my lightning speed presentation to convince them, I have brought an old mobile phone, which I have been keeping in one of the drawers in my childhood bedroom for the preceding ten years. This phone – old before its time with 'just' a colour screen and no 'smarts' – is my way of bringing the message home to the respectable academics who I am speaking to. I kept it in a drawer and did not discard it because, although useless, my treating it as a waste would have triggered a series of events in which I did not want to be involved.

As part of this five-minute presentation, I manage to tell the alternative story of the phone. In the case that I had discarded it, it would have found its way into a large container in the company of old computers, televisions, laptops, and other electric and electronic waste. That container would have been loaded onto a ship at a port and then would have ended up on the coast of a developing country, maybe Ghana. There, 'the disadvantaged' would have torn the phone and its companions apart using methods that are far from safe, inhaling toxic fumes, to retrieve the components that could so preciously be re-used, recovered, or recycled. I rattled on, explaining how crime-networks were facilitating activities of this kind. My research was going to focus on reconstructing these chains of events and mapping those networks, trying to describe and explain the phenomenon further; hoping to change things for the better.

I did not realise, at that time, that my focus would gradually shift from the phone to the container and the ship that it would have travelled on – if I had, indeed, discarded it. In fact, before the phone had even reached me more than a decade earlier, it had already been on such a ship along with thousands of tonnes of other goods. All these ships carrying the trash and treasure of the modern world were virtually invisible to me, and even more invisible was the fuel that they were running on.

Fast forward to July 2022, a news article reads "Mass use of chemical wastes in marine fuel":[1] the experience of reading the lines that follow is bittersweet. The topic – what I have become accustomed to calling 'my' topic – is clearly still relevant, important, urgent even. But how awful that no real improvement seems to have materialised in all these years. And now I ask myself: why have the waste oil and bunker fuel sectors not changed? What is taking them so long? What is taking us as a society so long to do something about this?

It is at that point that I remind myself that we are talking about repeated and systematic wrongdoing that serves not just the interests of the single firms involved in any one crime event. Indeed, our entire economic system creates incentives, pressures, and definitions that encourage and facilitate these illegal waste management activities. Without intervening at that global, macro level, we cannot expect any major shift. But before a sigh filled with powerlessness escapes my mouth, I remember that there are other, smaller-scale factors that facilitate crime and that shape the immediate situational context in which firms in the (Dutch) waste oil and bunker fuel sectors operate in. Those factors may be easier to alter so that crimes are more difficult to carry out. Then, hopefulness invades me as I recall the various people who I have spoken to since beginning my research and who are eager to bring about change. It's not just the police officers and public prosecutor from Andante, who gave me access to their work and the worlds of waste oil and bunker fuel in the first place. There are several other agents, who I have met through Andante, who work in the Netherlands and abroad. Then there are the students who I spoke to about my work, whose indignation is palpable when they hear about these crimes and harms. Lastly, there is every single person who is first puzzled when I mention the words 'bunker fuel' and who then immediately look at their clothes, the phone in their hand and the objects that surround them wherever we may be sitting while we have our conversation. They briefly visualise a gigantic ship sailing across the ocean carrying those very objects, emitting some tremendously toxic black smoke into the air. (Although I then explain it is never that obvious or visible.)

## 7.1 Summary and Overview of the Book

This book traced the process backwards before those toxins are emitted and explained how the flow of fuel is entwined with the flow of waste oils. In Chapter 3, these physical flows were outlined and then set in their regulatory and economic context. There we saw how waste (oil) management is a technically-demanding economic activity, which depends upon skills and machinery as much as the willingness to act in accordance with the letter and spirit of the law.

1. Tom Claessens and Mira Sys, "Chemisch Afval Wordt Massaal Gebruikt Als Scheepsbrandstof," *Follow the Money* 2022.

Without the latter, the environment and human health become the victims of greed and inadequacy. Bunker fuel production was also described as a highly specialised activity, which, however, is subject to less state intervention. It provides the economic release for the frustrations of both the waste oil management and (cargo) shipping sectors. The uncontainable search for profit, which cannot be hemmed by the tight margins of those two industries can be smoothly blended away into the fuels of the third. Chapter 4 delved into the details of how this happens by reducing two crime events into tiny dissectible acts: the tools as well as the situational conditions of commission were brought to the fore. Chapter 5 combined the insights from the preceding chapters: it articulated the link between the situational circumstances that characterise crimes and the contextual structures and industrial dynamics, in which they are set. Chapter 6 focused on measures that can limit illicit waste oil management activities in the bunker fuel production process. The example of the Andante team was used to reflect on what may or may not contribute to limiting this form of corporate environmental crime. The analysis was carried out to answer two main research questions:

1. How and why do illegal waste oil management activities in the process of producing bunker fuel take place?
2. How can illegal waste oil management activities in the process of producing bunker fuel be limited?

These two questions were broken down into 10 sub-questions. Table 7.1 summarises the answers to those sub-questions and indicates in which Chapter the answers were developed. In the next Sections, we build on the answers and draw broader implications, which are also relevant for developing (new) interventions.

**Table 7.1** Summary of the answers to the research questions and overview of related book Chapters

| Research Questions | Relevant Chapters & Summary |
| --- | --- |
| a. What do illegal waste oil management (WOM) activities in the process of bunker fuel production (BFP) look like? | – **Chapter 4:** Two crime events were broken down into Acts and then into Pre-Activity, Activity and Post-Activity scenes using crime-script analysis. This two-tier deconstruction helped to identify which actions were essential to completing different portions of the crimes and how the different steps link up and become complex criminal events. Unpacking the complexity in this way allowed us to see how each scene included specific opportunities and facilitators for crime as well as points of intervention. |
| b. During which steps of the broader BFP and WOM processes do these illegal activities occur? | – **Chapter 3:** We situated the criminal activities within their broader industrial contexts. The crucial steps in the waste oil management process are those where the waste label is applied and removed: where the intention to discard meets the intention to use substances in new ways. In the process of bunker fuel production, the fundamental step is that where blend components are generated and selected as elements of bunker fuel blends. |
| c. Which logistical steps and which actions are undertaken by the actors involved? | – **Chapter 4:** The scripting process described in relation to question (a) above made it possible to scrutinise discrete acts, such as the forging of documents; he communication between different entities to decide on what label to give to a substance; or simply mixing substances together. |
| d. What types of actors are involved? | – **Chapter 3** also helped to see which actors operate within the waste oil and bunker fuel industries and, especially, at the *crucial* moments in the industrial processes where crime is more likely to occur. We saw the legal definitions as well as the economic roles the actors have in their structural settings.<br>– **Chapter 4** showed us how the actors carry out their activities in practice and, especially, how they deviate from the applicable rules in their activities. The focus was narrowed down to a waste management firm, which both collected and treated wastes (Case 1) and a petrochemical manufacturer that sold wastes as blend components (Case 2). In Chapter 4, we also saw how these two firms interacted with other companies and entities, including formal guardians, and how those interactions were connected to their opportunities to offend. |
| e. What types of activities do they engage in? | – **Chapter 3** explained what the *legal,* routine activities are in the waste oil management and bunker fuel production industries.<br>– **Chapter 4** demonstrated how legitimate actors engaged in those same routine activities but did so *illegally.* |

| Research Questions | Relevant Chapters & Summary |
| --- | --- |
| f. What tools do they use to complete these activities? | – **Chapter 4** gave an overview of objects, practices and technical processes that were used in the two cases as means to complete the criminal events. These ranged from pens to alter the waste code on documents, to tanks where wastes are treated improperly, and transports of wastes across borders.<br>– **Chapter 5** took us to a more conceptual understanding of 'tools'. There we saw how the definitional universe in which actors from the waste oil management and bunker fuel production industries are immersed makes it possible, acceptable, and appealing to produce environmental harms. |
| g. What factors, at different levels of analysis, influence – facilitate or constrain – the actors involved in undertaking the abovementioned logistical steps towards crime-commission? | – **Chapter 3** mapped the routine flows and activities that organise the daily business lives of the actors involved in illegal waste oil management. There we also saw the pressures, incentives, and definitions, which contextualise criminal activities. ***[Macro-level]***<br>– **Chapter 4** zoomed-in on how those routine activities crystallise into micro-level situational opportunities that lower risks of detection as well as reducing efforts for committing crime, while increasing rewards and provocations and providing excuses for illegal conduct. ***[Micro-level]***<br>– **Chapter 5** returned to the structural level to make the connection between the situational circumstances and the institutional dynamics at the overlap between the two industries. Those institutional dynamics were shown to be symbiotic, thereby generating a crime-facilitative system. ***[Macro-level]*** |
| h. What internal as well as external regulations and mechanisms for supervision and control exist that apply to the WOM and BFP sectors? | – **Chapter 3** outlined the foundational rules that apply to two economic areas of activity. There we saw what is both permissible and desirable as well as what is prohibited in the fields of waste oil management and bunker fuel production.<br>– **Chapter 4** went into the details of which agencies have powers to monitor waste oil management and bunker fuel production activities in the Netherlands. There we saw which kinds of powers they dispose of, including their tools for enforcement. |
| i. How are these regulations and mechanisms interpreted, applied, and enforced? | – **Chapter 3** concluded with a reflection on how enforcement of two nationally regulated but globally operational industries is ultimately asymmetric as well as fragmented and, therefore, encourages criminal symbioses.<br>– **Chapter 4** connected specific enforcement powers and efforts to the two criminal cases that were broken down using crime-script analysis. |

| Research Questions | Relevant Chapters & Summary |
| --- | --- |
| | – **Chapter 6** delved deep into the way a group of criminal law enforcement agents came into existence and operated to contrast illegal waste oil management activities in the process of bunker fuel production. The way *this team* interpreted, applied, and enforced regulation and mechanisms was the focus in that Chapter. |
| j. How can these regulations and mechanisms influence – facilitate or constrain – the occurrence of the criminal activities that take place in the WOM and BFP sectors? | – **Chapter 4** included the analysis of data through which we could see the contribution enforcement agents made to either facilitating or constraining illegal activities. Furthermore, we saw how legally mandated tools such as documents and record-keeping could be manipulated to conceal criminal actions.<br>– **Chapter 5** explored the way regulations and mechanisms of enforcement contribute to facilitating crime in combination with other criminogenic conditions. Where incentives, pressures and frustrations for goal attainment are high, regulations can furnish the means to define illegalities away and regulatory mechanisms can backfire to create veils of ignorance, which lower risks of detection. Symbioses between state and business favour interpretations, application and enforcement practices that are more conducive to environmental harm than protection.<br>– **Chapter 6** used the notions of problem-oriented policing, responsive regulation, and SCP as lenses through which to reflect on Andante's contributions to the fight against one type of corporate environmental crime. These bodies of literature provide theoretical and empirical insights into the relationship between regulations, enforcement mechanisms and crime: this was the key through which the story of Andante was reflected on. |

## 7.2 Developing Crime-Resistance: Intervening at Multi-Level Pinch-Points to Inhibit Crime-Commission

In Chapter 5, we used the notion of a crime-facilitative system to understand the structural dynamics that shape the situations in which illegal waste oil management activities unfold. A system that is crime-facilitative may be transformed into one that resists crime by "develop[ing] protective mechanisms to neutralize criminogenesis, because in-system crime is an undesired side effect of normal activity rather than being essential to the organization's goals."[2] The generation of such protective mechanisms would lead to the emergence of a crime-resistant system, which is described as follows: "[the] structural conditions deter illegal acts by members of the corporate system and/or those they come in contact with [such] as customers or clients. Crime control is adopted as an organizational goal."[3]

The analyses in preceding Chapters revealed the structural and situational features, which would have to be manipulated and altered to generate the deterrent effects that would then produce a crime-resistant system. The goal of this Section is to zero-in on the pinch-points of intervention that were identified at both the situational and structural levels and to articulate some suggestions for interventions. Implementing such interventions could lead to an increase in crime-resistance in the system that exists at the overlap between the waste oil management and bunker fuel production industries.

In Figure 7.1, we see the combined processes of waste oil management and bunker fuel production in simplified form. The image brings together the pinch-points for intervention that were uncovered in Chapter 4 by using crime-script analysis and contextualises them using the findings from Chapters 3 and 5, so that they can assume their full significance. Five contextualised pinch-points for intervention emerge from this integrated (multi-level) script. A list of the interventions is provided below and then each is explored in more detail in its own subsection.

The first point of intervention that became clear (labelled with the number one in Figure 7.1) was the vulnerability of documents to manipulation. One way to inhibit offending would be to focus on the physical vulnerability of the documents. Another way of altering this aspect of both situation and structure would be to change the conversation behind the waste-labelling process: involving different actors that can provide both insight and oversight.

The second point of intervention is the boundary between the waste oil management industry and those industries where former wastes or mis-labelled wastes are used as products. The porousness of that boundary weakens the

2. Martin L Needleman and Carolyn Needleman, "Organizational Crime: Two Models of Criminogenesis," *The Sociological Quarterly* 20, no. 4 (1979), p. 526.
3. Ibid.

rules and controls that apply to waste management. The moments in the crime-commission process where this becomes clear, and which can be practically intervened upon, are when wastes are treated and recovered or where they are labelled as by-products. This point is indicated with the number two in Figure 7.1.

The third point of intervention is the bunker fuel industry itself (number three in Figure 7.1). The lack of hard law instruments prescribing which substances are allowed in bunker fuel and governing the production process of this substance leave too much space for harmful and wrongful behaviour. The lack of prescriptions also facilitates the concealment of wrongdoing.

Number four in Figure 7.1 points to the consumption of bunker fuel. If there were no ships that could consume bunker fuel as it is currently produced (i.e., often containing wastes) then these crimes would simply not be possible. The existence of ships of this kind, as well as the structural conditions that constrain both the change in the quality of fuel that is habitually used and the updating of the engine technology of the ships themselves fall under this point of intervention.

The broadest point of intervention in Figure 7.1 is number five – it is the current set up of our globalised economy. Although plenty of literature in both organisational and green criminology already points to neoliberalism as a force at the level of political economy, which fosters and facilitates harm, in this case this force appears even more evidently as both waste generation and bunker fuel consumption are intimately linked to the current globalised trade system. It could even be argued that this force could compromise any and all other efforts to intervene.

**Figure 7.1 Intervention script for illegal waste oil management activities in the process of bunker fuel production: five pinch-points for intervention**

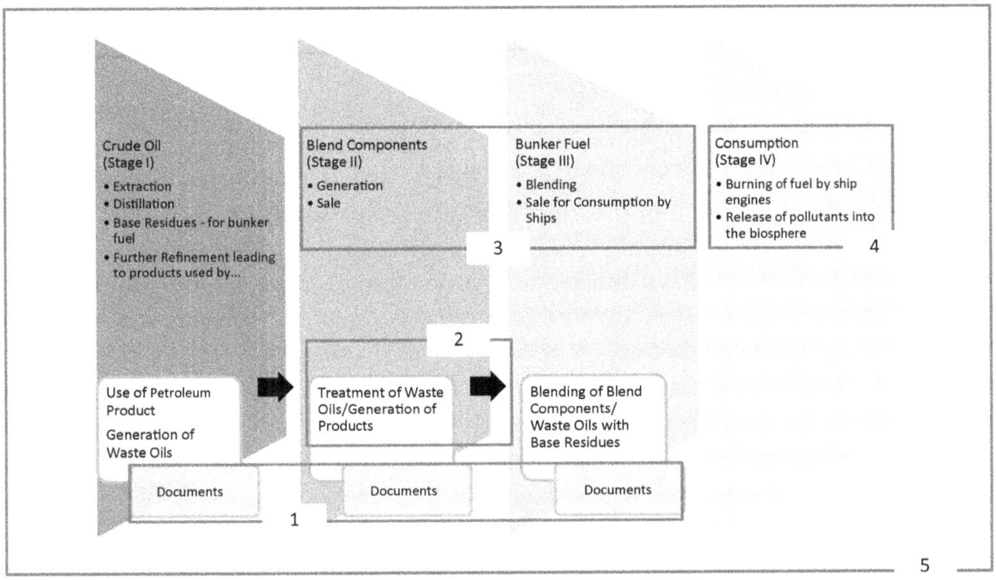


*Pinch-point 1: Documents as Targets, Tools & Means of Guardianship*

Documents are an important element of the crime-commission process, and they can be viewed from different angles. They are a *target* for offenders as they are fraudulently manipulated, which transforms them into a *tool of crime-commission* and concealment. They are also a *means of guardianship* that can be strengthened to increase the chances of detection. When referring to documents we have three types: documents that accompany the movement of wastes; documents that certify and accompany products; and documents that record the tank administration of both waste oil management firms and firms handling blend components and bunker fuel. The focus here is on the first two types – those accompanying wastes, products, and by-products. (The logic of the system, which is proposed below, could, however, accommodate the inclusion of tank administration documents too.)

We focus on documents because they are key in the practical unfoldment of the crimes, but they are also an *interpretative* key to the underlying concepts and definitions that give significance to what these crimes are in their specific social, legal, technical, and economic context. Documents are a vehicle of meaning – they crystallise the definitions and interests of the parties to the exchanges, and they do so in a way that is coherent with the broader (formal) system of meaning that includes economic activities involving waste oil management and bunker fuel production.

This dual nature of documents underlies the first proposal for intervention: the creation of an electronic document network (EDN). The 'electronic' portion is connected to one dimension of documents, namely their practical function in the crime commission process. Documents are a target that can be 'hardened' in order to increase efforts within SCP terminology. They can then preserve their intended function, which is to operate as a means of guardianship, if they are digitalised earlier in the waste management process and with more advanced technologies. The 'network' portion of the EDN hints to the involvement of a broader set of actors, who may take on more responsibility for exercising guardianship, whether they be public or private actors. Access to information could increase the potential for exercising oversight. Plus, the active involvement of more actors would include dialogue and debate on how certain substances should be labelled, whether they are wastes or not and what types of waste. The proposal for the EDN is broken down into ten recommendations:

1. All documents connected to waste oils should be drawn up electronically and recorded in a database that is accessible to several connected parties – the electronic document network (EDN). All movements can be 'checked in' and be tracked in real time.
2. Entries cannot be changed *ex post*. The integrity of the entry should be safeguarded through blockchain-like mechanisms.[4]
3. The first label and document are created by and entered into the system by *waste generators* instead of waste collectors or other specialised waste management firms. If a firm thinks it is handling a by-product, this should also be recorded.
4. The entry by waste or by-product generators also includes information on the (industrial) processes that led to the production of the waste/by-product and potentially connects users of the primary products of those processes to the information about the waste that is tied to the products they use.
5. When wastes/by-products go through treatment and they end up being re-used as part of other products or processes, this is also recorded and visible to those who use the ultimate products as well.
6. Formal guardians – administrative and criminal law authorities – all have access to the information regarding the movement of wastes/by-products and some details regarding the entities that have handled them.
7. Other stakeholders may also access the information about the movements; as well as very limited information about the entities that have handled the wastes.

4. See proposals such as: Matthias Daub, Steve Cheng, Axel Domeyer, and Martin Lundqvist, "Using Blockchain to Improve Data Management in the Public Sector," (McKinsey & Company, 2017); Vipul H Navadkar, Ajinkya Nighot, and Rahul Wantmure, "Overview of Blockchain Technology in Government/Public Sectors," *International Research Journal of Engineering and Technology* 5, no. 6 (2018); F Rizal Batubara, Jolien Ubacht, and Marijn Janssen, "Challenges of Blockchain Technology Adoption for E-Government: A Systematic Literature Review" (paper presented at the Proceedings of the 19th annual international conference on digital government research: governance in the data age, 2018).

8. Input of records in the EDN is regulated according to clear criteria. Visualisation rights for information in the EDN is also regulated based on the role of the person or entity that wishes to see the information (e.g., consumer, stakeholder, authority, other firms involved in process).
9. The system can learn – also through input of intelligence-based algorithms[5] – and generate automatic signals when questionable activities take place. These signals can lead to advice, investigations, warnings, and sanctions, depending on the circumstances.
10. The reach of the system would have to reflect the movement of the relevant substances, which means the system should operate across the definitions of waste and (by-) product; and across national borders ultimately, applying outside and beyond the EU.

*Pinch-point 2: Falling Apart at the Seams – The Weaknesses of Waste Definitions*

One of the fundamental issues that has become apparent in this book is that the waste management industry has been assigned and carries out tasks of monumental importance in the quest to protect human health and the environment. At the same time, the weight of the waste industry is matched by the ambiguity of its definitional basis. The functioning of the entire waste management system is predicated on the distinction between waste and non-waste: the line between these two concepts has been drawn through technical means that rely on aspects like composition and hazardous effects of substances. However, at its core, the notion of waste is subjectively determined because it revolves around the existence or lack of use for a substance or object. The desirability of such use is itself contingent on both material or physical characteristics of the substances and the way they can be employed as well as the acceptability of such use. And so, it seems that there can be an endless debate about the true nature of a substance and whether it should be a waste or not. In absence of clear definitional lines, a more important issue appears to be that of who is involved in formulating the definitions and what these actors consider important aspects in determining both usefulness and acceptability of use.

While it may be argued that the waste/non-waste definition is ultimately determined – or at least checked – through systems that protect collective well-being, i.e., by democratically accountable states; in practice, it is waste generators and managers that are tasked with this privilege. Waste generators and managers, which are corporate entities at the cross-roads between the industries of origin of the wastes and the potential industries of destination, with opportunities to profit on both sides. The current means of connecting the industry of origin and the industry of destination through waste management firms in the Netherlands is the

5. Inspiration could be drawn from approaches such as 'risk terrain modeling'. See, for example, Leslie W. Kennedy, Joel M. Caplan, and Eric Piza, "Risk Clusters, Hotspots, and Spatial Intelligence: Risk Terrain Modeling as an Algorithm for Police Resource Allocation Strategies," *Journal of Quantitative Criminology* 27, no. 3 (2011).

*Landelijke Afvalbeheerplan* (LAP). All EU countries have their own version of the LAP.[6] The LAP is highly technical in nature and focuses on waste streams, which reflects the sectoral nature of waste legislation more generally.

Waste legislation has historically developed in reactionary fashion. A substance is generated – or has habitually been generated – and only *after* its generation a debate begins about how it can safely be handled. The private sector produces, and the public sector responds. As part of this response, the first step is the recognition of the environmental burden of the waste; the second step is the transformation of this burden into an economic one, which can be absolved through the carrying out of technical procedures. The economic burden falls on waste generators and managers. In the logic of waste management, recovery, re-use, and recycling are all solutions to the problem of waste having *already* been generated.

By-products follow a different logic: the usefulness of the substance is the first to be assessed, but its potentially negative impact on health and the environment may remove it from the industrial realm. This removal is coupled with it being assigned a negative economic value so it can be dealt with through waste management procedures. In this setup, the threat of an economic burden lingers over the waste generator at the same time as the potential for profit, if the substance can indeed be characterised as a by-product.

In both scenarios, escaping or avoiding the waste label is connected to the resolution of an economically charged problem. While economic considerations are not the only ones that directors and employees of both waste-generating and -managing firms include in their decision making, they most certainly can have an impact. If waste were a definitive and unquestionable label, if there were no escape from the burdens and responsibilities that this label implies, then those in possession of wastes could be inclined to handle wastes differently. The fact that this escape is possible and profitable is a form of lure. And the lure extends to the other side of the waste border – those who can use 'non-wastes' may also profit. This potential common benefit means there is fertile ground for collusion or concerted ignorance.

If the industries of destination are prone to 'ignoring' the waste problem or are structured in a way that makes this ignorance possible and even appealing, then the waste/non-waste distinction loses its protective function. An instrument like the LAP, which gives detailed instructions about how waste streams may truly and safely become products for specific industries, cannot capture the complexity of the structure of the industries of destination. It focuses solely on the physical flow aspects. However, the analysis in this book shows that the actors who handle wastes and bunker fuels are not just handling physical substances. Rather, they operate in situations and contexts that are characterised by a myriad of incentives, pressures, and definitions. *The LAP does not resolve these structurally generated*

6. See Chapter 3.

*conditions and it does not help companies that find themselves being subjected to these forces to evaluate the consequences of their activities.* If on the other side of the waste border there were clear rules geared towards protection of the environment and human health, with related compliance and enforcement mechanisms, the LAP may have sufficed. Sadly, this is often not the case.

In view of the foregoing, it seems that three avenues could be pursued: the first is extending the reach of waste management rules and safeguards. When substances go from the waste industry into other sectors as products, there should be greater caution and more stringent rules and checks that apply to former wastes. A second – and more appropriate – option is that of systematically studying the movement of wastes to see where they end up as 'products' and to then encourage increased controls and oversight in the industries of destination more generally, which in our case would be the bunker fuel and shipping sectors. A third option would be to focus on the other border to the waste industry, the one before which wastes are generated in the first place. If less waste is created, it also will be less likely to cause harm because it is improperly managed. The challenge here is that waste-generating industries need to be encouraged to review their processes and products to truly contribute to environmental preservation by minimising waste, and not simply stop labelling substances as wastes to avoid costs. Regulatory agencies would also have to mature the commensurate technical skills and strategies to understand the dynamics of waste *generation* and not just waste management.

*Pinch-point 3: Banishing Bad Bunkers: Regulating the Bunker Fuel Production Process (Worldwide)*

There is an all-too obvious absence in the industrial worlds we have immersed ourselves in throughout this book: detailed, stringent, and enforceable regulation of the bunker fuel sector. There are no clear prescriptions of what can and should be in bunker fuel nor what its manufacturing process should look like. There are also no obvious technical reasons for this to be the situation: the lack of regulation is explainable only in reference to the economic and political dynamics that are linked to bunker fuel production and consumption worldwide. Bunker fuel can be purchased and taken on board at a port. The fact that bunker fuel consumption is tied to these locations also circumscribes the regulation and enforcement measures that can be undertaken in respect of the product itself.

Ports are important nodes in the globalised system of trade. That system has been relying on the process of containerisation more and more. In the last 30 years, the success of ports around the world in attracting revenue has been determined, to a great extent, by their capacity to quickly and efficiently handle huge numbers of container shipments, and act as hubs for incoming and outgoing movements of goods and materials. The success of a port is often also the success of the region it serves; and having appropriate and appealing bunkering facilities partly contributes to that success. Appealing is an important descriptor here because the containerisation trend has also meant that a ship can swiftly decide to switch to a different port in order to access a given region at a specific time. Competition among ports is fierce and potentially deadly for the communities that invest heavily in port infrastructure in the hope of generating future revenue but are then left stranded.[7]

Without concerted and homogenous action at the level of a (sub-) continent or worldwide, regulation of bunker fuel is unimaginable. A more troubling aspect of this is that the international body that should be at the forefront of such global regulatory efforts – the IMO – is, in fact, highly dominated by industry figures.[8] As things stand, the benefits from the current system are accrued by the same individuals and entities who are in a position to influence its structure. And the discontent that the current system generates is not urgently or uniformly felt by a contingent strong or cohesive enough to counter the current balance of powers.

In connection to the presence of wastes in bunker fuel specifically, it would already be helpful if procedures were developed to test for the presence of such wastes. EU and international rules prohibit the use of wastes but do not give indications as to how such presence can be determined.[9] A first step then would be the collaboration with authorities and experts who know enough about the management of waste oils to create ways to identify and test for wastes in bunker fuel. This would also be coherent with the suggestions made in respect of the waste industry: collaboration across the definitional lines of waste and non-waste to study the flows that cross them, with a focus on environmental protection and reduction of toxins instead of merely celebrating the re-use of material resources.

*Pinch-point 4: Technical Innovations in the Shipping Sector*

Among the most popular and often-cited interventions in both the shipping sector – as well as any other industry concerned with emissions from fossil fuel-powered vehicles – is innovation in engine technology. Such innovation can target three different aspects of the combustion/propulsion mechanism.

1. **Engines can be designed to run on 'cleaner' fuels**. Cleaner is a relative term because it depends on what types of emissions from combustion one

7. A common practice in this sector is to invest heavily even though there is no demand for the port facilities so that the newly built or improved port will attract large numbers of ships. Hercules Haralambides, "Globalization, Public Sector Reform, and the Role of Ports in International Supply Chains," *Maritime Economics & Logistics* 19, no. 1 (2017).
8. Ibid.; Nicholas Gaskell and Craig Forrest, "Marine Pollution Damage in Australia: Implementing the Bunker Oil Convention 2001 and the Supplementary Fund Protocol 2003," *University of Queensland Law Journal, The* 27, no. 2 (2008); Rebecca Prentiss Pskowski, "Bad Bunker: Fuel Contamination Claims, Imo 2020, and the Houston Problem," *Tul. Mar. LJ* 44 (2019).
9. See Chapter 3.

is targeting. Already since the 1950s, the shipping sector has included several ships that can burn Liquefied Natural Gas (LNG) instead of bunker fuel. LNG is not carbon based, therefore, $CO_2$ as well as $SO_x$ and $NO_x$ emissions are greatly reduced when this fuel is used. However, engines powered by LNG pose their own alarming risks. LNG engines suffer from what is known as 'methane slip', a commonly recorded problem whereby unburned gas leaks from the engine. Methane has a global warming potential[10] 86 times higher than $CO_2$. The use of LNG also poses other challenges: most ports, ships and seafarers are not equipped and experienced in its use, which can lead to further risks. Transforming the global fleet into one that would run exclusively on LNG would mean changes in infrastructure and habits, themselves requiring the expenditure of many resources. Such a structural overhaul is not guaranteed to lead to an overall benefit to the environment. Furthermore, one source of LNG has been shale gas, which brings with it a series of environmental problems and has been linked to severe injustices, especially in the US.[11]

More recently, new, alternative fuels are being designed and tested. These fuels are essentially man-made evolutions of LNG and they have become particularly appealing as the already relatively high prices of LNG soared in the aftermath of the Russian invasion of Ukraine in early 2022. Naturally generated LNG is a non-renewable fossil fuel composed of methane. However, there are now a series of products on the market that are also made of methane and are comparable to LNG, these are knows as Synthetic Natural Gases (SNG), which can be used for ships fitted with engines that burn LNG. SNG can be created from the gasification of biomass (hence it also being called Bio-SNG). Similar products are Biomethane or biogas, which are yielded from a fermentation process instead. The result is the same liquefied methane that LNG or Bio-SNG is composed of, but Biogas actually has a high $CO_2$ content, which leads to questions about the environmental impact of its production. Plus, let us not forget that 'biomass' is another word for 'waste'. The wastes in question are those from the handling of animals (e.g., cow manure) and from household wastes. Many of the reflections about the waste industry discussed in this book are also applicable to these two specific wastes, albeit tailored to the relevant substances and actors. There is also another methane fuel known

10. "[T]he cumulative radiative forcing, both direct and indirect effects, over a specified time horizon resulting from the emission of a unit mass of gas related to some reference gas [CO2: (IPCC 1996)]"Science Direct, "Global Warming Potential," https://www.sciencedirect.com/topics/earth-and-planetary-sciences/global-warming-potential.
11. Jack A Lampkin and Tanya Wyatt, "Utilising Principles of Earth Jurisprudence to Prevent Environmental Harm: Applying a Case Study of Unconventional Hydraulic Fracturing for Shale Gas in the United Kingdom," *Critical Criminology* 28, no. 3 (2020); Paul Stretesky and Philipp Grimmer, "Shale Gas Development and Crime: A Review of the Literature," *The Extractive Industries and Society* 7, no. 3 (2020).

as Power-to-Gas (PtG-LNG), which is created through electrolysis. All of these LNG alternatives pose the same risks once injected into engines, specifically the engines are prone to 'methane slip'.[12]

2. **Engines can be (retro-) fitted with additional parts that 'purify' the emissions from fuel combustion.** These parts are known as scrubbers. Scrubbers became an increasingly sought-after solution when the limits to $SO_x$ emissions at international and EU levels crystallised. In anticipation of the 2020 Sulphur cap, scrubbers were marketed as the alternative to new fuels. The IMO specifically indicates that, from 2020, a ship may only bunker fuel that has the applicable $SO_x$ content, but that there is an exception where a ship has been fitted with the recognised scrubber technology.[13] Some industry experts have debated about the costs and benefits of fitting old ships with scrubbers versus simply purchasing low-sulphur fuels: it seems that the higher costs of these fuels may still be lower than the roughly $4 million investment that is required for such retro-fitting (per ship), especially as low-sulphur fuels take up larger market shares and become more widely available. New ships may be built with scrubbers from the start, which may lead to relatively lowers costs, but this would still be a debatable cost-efficient solution.[14]

   Many argue that an industry-wide acceptance of the new low-sulphur fuels would actually lower costs for all. The debate also highlights the pernicious structure of the shipping industry: costs for scrubbers or updates to engines fall on ship owners whereas individual bunker fuel purchases are usually carried out by charterers. Some argue that charterers may be more willing to use ships with scrubbers in order to then pay less for fuel costs, thereby giving scrubber-fitted ships (and their owners) a competitive advantage. Yet, the more pressing point is that $SO_x$ emissions are only part of the problem. While the industry wastes time debating the scrubber versus fuel point, other contaminants are still being released into the air and waters, without this being considered a problem from a legal perspective.

3. Another alternative to address this pinch-point is to **entirely change the way ships are powered**. This option would possibly require a complete overhaul of the entire global shipping fleet, which is not unproblematic. Ship-breaking (and ship-making) are incredibly resource intensive processes, which

---

12. Deutsches Zentrum für Luft- und Raumfahrt Shell Deutschland, Technische Universität Hamburg, "Shell Lng Study: Liquefied Natural Gas – New Energy for Ships and Trucks?," (2019).
13. Yewen Gu and Stein W Wallace, "Scrubber: A Potentially Overestimated Compliance Method for the Emission Control Areas: The Importance of Involving a Ship's Sailing Pattern in the Evaluation," *Transportation Research Part D: Transport and Environment* 55 (2017).
14. IMO, "Imo 2020 – Cutting Sulphur Oxide Emissions," https://www.imo.org/en/MediaCentre/HotTopics/Pages/Sulphur-2020.aspx.

potentially produce all sorts of harms and injustice.[15] However, this possibility should at least be considered. As we begin seeing more electric cars and energy efficient homes being built, we need to also consider how a similar logic may be applied to shipping, but still be mindful of the potentially negative side effects that each alternative brings with it.

*Pinch-point 5: Symbioses that Sustain Harm – The State-Corporate Nexus at the Cross-Roads between Waste Oil Management and Bunker Fuel Production*

As long as the interventions at the micro or even industry level (e.g., new technologies and legislation or market incentives) are implemented within a globalised, neoliberal, consumption driven capitalist system, they are at risk of being distorted. Those interventions may even end up serving interests other than – or possibly inimical to – environmental protection. This idea is not new, but this case study confirms it, especially when looking at how waste management legislation fails once it begins overlapping with other industries that are so fundamental to the 'system'. We cannot develop policies and practices conducive to environmental preservation until and unless we modify our economic system more fundamentally.

An example of this was cited in Chapter 1, namely the connection between very low sulphur oil (VLSO) and the 'wasted' kerosene from a decreased number in flights after the breakout of COVID-19. Physical, economic, and regulatory structures have been in place for decades to welcome 'residues' into bunker fuel and power the global economy. These structures have only deepened as the flows have intensified in the last 30 years. Hazards cannot continue to circulate so easily if we *really* want to conserve natural resources.

The link between neoliberalism and organisational crime has been discussed in the literature on state-corporate crime. We already drew on this body of work on in Chapter 5 to understand the symbioses that underly the crime-facilitative system that exists at the overlap between waste oil management and bunker fuel production. We now take that analysis a level higher in relation to our fifth pinch-point for intervention by using the specific notion of state-*facilitated* state-corporate crime.

State-facilitated state-corporate crimes are those instances where state institutions have failed to intervene in cases of harmful or deviant conduct by private actors. The reasons behind this failure can range from actual collusion between the state (agencies) and the private actors involved to (in-) action in pursuit of goals "whose attainment would be hampered by aggressive

15. Karin van Wingerde and Lieselot Bisschop, "Waste Away. Examining Systemic Drivers of Global Waste Trafficking Based on a Comparative Analysis of Two Dutch Cases," *Erasmus L. Rev.* 12 (2019); Jasmien Claeys and Lieselot Bisschop, "Een Schip Op Het Strand Is Een Baken in Zee," *Tijdschrift voor Criminologie* 60, no. 1 (2018).

regulation".[16] This latter specification of the relationship between state intervention and the goals common to both political and economic institutions is reminiscent of one of the elements of a crime-facilitative system. In a crime-facilitative system, "the measures necessary to control internal crime are felt by the system's policy makers to be potentially even more damaging to the system's goals (in most cases, the goal of profit making)."[17]

We could argue that the political institutions that develop environmental protection and waste management policies do not necessarily intend for waste to be managed improperly. However, they operate in a context where corporate profits may increase from such improper management. Similarly, it is likely *not* the conscious aim of bunker fuel producers to make low quality fuel; yet, doing so increases their profit margins and releases pressure they feel from the shipping sector to fuel global trade as inexpensively as possible.[18]

Understanding the state-corporate nexus in relation to our case study and as an element of criminogenesis that can be "pinched" for intervention means that we need to meditate on a few aspects: first, we should think about the goals that are common to both political and economic institutions in the system that contextualises our case study. Then we need to contemplate the possibility that there may be conditions under which interventions (in the structural conditions of) the system could be perceived as inimical to those goals. The actors in our case study act in pursuit of goals in three main domains: fuelling the shipping sector; producing bunker fuel; and managing waste oils. Both economic and state institutions have some stake in these three domains. Let us explore each in turn.

Shipping is an important activity for the global economy. The most commonly practiced form of it is cargo shipping, which is the bedrock of modern trade and commerce. Facilitating the smooth functioning of trade and commerce is seen as an important prerogative of the state. We tremble at the idea of economic depression, and states have taken on the task of ensuring we remain economically prosperous, even when markets fail.[19] Therefore, any measures that facilitate cargo shipping

16. Kramer, Michalowski, and Kauzlarich, "The Origins and Development of the Concept and Theory of State-Corporate Crime." 272.
17. Needleman and Needleman, "Organizational Crime: Two Models of Criminogenesis." 521.
18. This is discussed in more detail in Chapter 3.
19. For recent criminological reflections about the state-business relationships connected to economic and financial crises, see: Ifeanyi Ezeonu, "Market Criminology: A Critical Engagement with Primitive Accumulation in the Petroleum Extraction Industry in Africa," *The Handbook of White-Collar Crime* (2019); Vincenzo Ruggiero and Nigel South, "Critical Criminology and Crimes against the Environment," *Critical Criminology* 18, no. 4 (2010). David O Friedrichs and Dawn L Rothe, "State-Corporate Crime and Major Financial Institutions: Interrogating an Absence," *State Crime Journal* 3, no. 2 (2014); Steve Tombs, "State-Corporate Symbiosis in the Production of Crime and Harm," ibid. (2012); Wim Huisman, "Corporate Crime and Crisis: Causation Scenarios," in *Economic Crisis and Crime*, ed. Mathieu Deflem, Sociology of Crime, Law and Deviance (Emerald Group Publishing Limited, 2011); Henry N Pontell, William K Black, and Gilbert Geis, "Too Big to Fail, Too Powerful to Jail? On the Absence of Criminal Prosecutions after the 2008 Financial Meltdown," *Crime, Law and Social Change* 61, no. 1 (2014); Ayreen NRN Alibux, "Criminogenic

are beneficial to state institutions. Cargo shipping thrives on low prices of bunker fuel. A natural consequence of this is that practices that keep those prices low are favourable to the aims of institutions of government. Hence, intervening to disrupt those practices could be perceived as inimical to those aims and, as such, unattractive.

Producing bunker fuel is the next domain we can explore. Here we find two dimensions. The first is linked to the argument from the preceding paragraph: Low costs for bunker fuel production equal economic prosperity for all in the form of cheap products for consumers and a thriving global trade. The second dimension concerns the link between the state and powerful economic actors in the broader oil industry. A number of scholars and journalists have reflected on the relationship between state and oil: they claim the economic power wielded by the oil sector has often shielded it from aggressive control by the state.[20] In the Netherlands in particular, the dependency of the state on the economic might of the oil sector has also been documented.[21] But before we allow ourselves to be mystified by the concept and workings of 'power', let us recall two of the fundamental features of oil flows we explored in Chapter 3, namely that petroleum reserves are finite, and that petroleum has generated pervasive regimes of living given the diversity of its applications. We are hooked on oil. Bunker fuel

Conditions, Bribery and the Economic Crisis in the Eu: A Macro Level Analysis," *European journal of criminology* 13, no. 1 (2016).

20. Among green criminologists, this link between oil and crime is often discussed. See, for example: Ruggiero and South, "Critical Criminology and Crimes against the Environment"; Ezeonu, "Market Criminology: A Critical Engagement with Primitive Accumulation in the Petroleum Extraction Industry in Africa"; Michael J Lynch, Averi Fegadel, and Michael A Long, "Green Criminology and State-Corporate Crime: The Ecocide-Genocide Nexus with Examples from Nigeria," *Journal of Genocide Research* 23, no. 2 (2021); Bradshaw, ""Obviously, We're All Oil Industry": The Criminogenic Structure of the Offshore Oil Industry"; Matthew B Greife and Paul B Stretesky, "Treadmill of Production and State Variations in Civil and Criminal Liability for Oil Discharges in Navigable Waters," *Routledge International Handbook of Green Criminology. London: Routledge* (2013).

21. The history of repeated harmful practices against the environment and human health, attributable to firms in the oil, waste oil and chemical waste sectors spans more than half a century. Examples include the facilities set up by Shell in Moerdijk in 1969. Moerdijk and the surrounding are have also been the setting of several incidents involving companies like Remondis, Chemie-Pack and Uniser. Harmful substances were released into the environment, whether intentionally or due to failures in following appropriate safety procedures. The government's inaction in the face of these blatant failures to protect welfare interests has also been documented and explained. In great part, the relationship between business and government has been characterised at the very least as collusive. (Some examples of criminological analyses of this relaitonship are: Chrisje Brants and Theo de Roos, "Pollution, Press, and the Penal Process: The Case of Uniser in the Netherlands," *Crime and Social Justice*, no. 21/22 (1984); Judith Gabriël van Erp, "Toezicht in De Open Samenleving: Maatschappelijke Controle Op Multinationale Ondernemingen," (2016); C Brants, "The System's Rigged—or Is It?," *Crime, Law and Social Change* 21, no. 2 (1994); Wim Huisman and Elies van Sliedregt, "Rogue Traders: Dutch Businessmen, International Crimes and Corporate Complicity," *Journal of International Criminal Justice* 8, no. 3 (2010); Henk van de Bunt and Wim Huisman, "Organizational Crime in the Netherlands," *Crime and Justice* 35 (2007).

production is merely one of the many manifestations of this addiction. We have not yet evolved into a society that gives us the benefits of modernity without the troubling side-effects that the fossil fuel foundations of modernity bring along.

Waste management is the third domain to which we can apply the notion of state-facilitated state-corporate crime. Waste management is, in fact, a state prerogative.[22] This services sector was created by the state through policy and legislation. Indeed, we can say that waste management epitomises the relationships described by the concept of state-facilitated state-corporate crime because the state has set goals and established procedures, which must ultimately be attained through and implemented by private economic actors. Progressive and growing delegation of this task to economic actors has also led to an asymmetry between the expertise of the state and that of firms operating in the waste management sector. As legislation has become more stringent to protect the environment, waste management processes have become more complex and technical.

We could argue that waste management is an example of another form of dependency: regulatory as opposed to physical and economic. The more we, as a society, want to protect human health and the environment, the more pressure we exert on (political) institutions to enact this collective desire. The more states try to implement this in practice, the more they become reliant on private actors to turn the desired vision into reality, as well as to generate innovative solutions. States may develop more rules, standards, and targets, but they will always depend on business to ultimately achieve their goals; and they may not always have the material and human resources to see and understand when this is happening correctly and justly. Regulation may be rather 'aggressive' to use the state-corporate crime terminology; but monitoring and enforcement may simply not be adequate to keep up and to ensure compliance or avoid harm.

From the foregoing we can conclude that there are several conditions in the waste oil and bunker fuel industries that make them individually vulnerable to state-facilitated state-corporate crime. Imagine then how much more vulnerable they are at the points at which they overlap. This susceptibility to state-corporate crime now brings us back to the idea of developing a crime-resistant system, which requires developing "protective mechanisms to neutralize criminogenesis" premised on the fact that "in-system crime is an undesired side effect of normal activity rather than being essential to the organization's goals."

We addressed five pinch-points in this Section that, if intervened upon, could contribute to neutralising criminogenesis. But we can take this discussion further in two ways. First, we can think about other insights that emerged in this book, specifically those from Chapter 6 on Andante, to identify additional criminogenesis-neutralising mechanisms. Second, we can consider the following

22. See Chapter 3 for a more thorough discussion of the waste industry.

questions connected to the notion of both crime-resistance and state-corporate crime: How can we characterise the relationship between the structural features of the system that facilitate criminal activities and the organisational goals in the bunker fuel production and waste oil management industries, given what we have just said about the symbioses between goals and institutional environments at their overlap? And how can this relationship between structural facilitators and the functioning of the 'system' impact both existing and suggested measures for supervision and control?

## 7.3 Halting the Treadmill of Law: Learning Experiences from Criminal Law Enforcement and Beyond

The 'Treadmill of Law' notion was developed by a group of criminologists to reflect on how forces at the level of political economy can affect and vitiate regulatory efforts, which are supposed to contribute to environmental conservation. In true green criminological spirit,[23] those scholars have drawn from other fields of knowledge in generating the Treadmill of Law (ToL) concept. The ToL operationalises what we discussed at the end of the preceding Section: it shows how the weakness of responses to environmental crimes is rooted in the role that the state plays in a neoliberal economy. The state facilitates capital accumulation and must, therefore, avoid standing in the way of that accumulation by not becoming overly disruptive when harmful (and even criminal) practices occur; nor overly supportive of the efforts of those who fight against environmental degradation. The state's function in such a setup is better understood by looking at the background to the ToL concept.

The notion of 'Treadmill of Production' (ToP) was coined in the 1980s and was itself the outcome of the multidisciplinary exploration of a paradox. How was it possible that with growing innovation in science and technology, we were not witnessing the corresponding expected increases in human welfare and prosperity? A lot of economic theories matured prior to the mid-twentieth century had anticipated that human beings would be healthier and happier, across the globe, thanks to the (economic) advancement of humanity as a civilisation. Yet what was frequently observed (already several decades ago and still today) was that growth in economic and technological terms resulted in a lot of harm to the environment and human health. Also, it did not lead to an adequate distribution of benefits, whether material or otherwise. When trying to generate or re-work (economic) models to understand this, researchers always came up short of an answer.

However, by combining insights from numerous disciplines, one thing became very clear. The capitalist mode of production and consumption – the supposed

23. See Chapter 1 for a more general discussion on green criminology as a field of inquiry.

motor of growth and prosperity – was itself the generator of degradation and harm. The ToP theory posits that a fundamental conflict exists between capitalism and nature. The goal of capitalism is unending growth through accelerated production, which is ultimately unattainable (and probably also undesirable). By taking natural organisms as a means of comparison, we can see that growth is common to all, but it is always limited and circumscribed by the other aims of the organisms themselves as well as by the environments, which they inhabit. Because capitalism neither provides nor accepts limits to what is enough or what is too much, and only pushes for increases in production and consumption, it leads to the destruction of nature. To fuel and accelerate production we need energy; and to reduce costs of production we need to eliminate expenses, namely labour. These two needs lead to ever more extraction of resources and introduction of pollutants, especially chemicals and fossil fuels.[24] Part of the theory is connected to the role of states and regulation and sees them as functional to the expansion of the ToP.

The Treadmill of *Law*, in turn, indicates the "ways in which environmental laws and regulations reflect and reinforce economic relations that legitimize and replicate ToP practices, relationships, and interests, and contribute to expansion of the ToP".[25] This is achieved through the dynamic relationship between three sets of actors: producers who contribute to ecological disorganisation and their lobbyists; state agents who generate regulations and laws; and citizens as well as civil society groups that demand environmental protection. Partly drawing on the materialist theory of law, ToL proponents say that these three sets of actors are in conflict about the content and implementation of environmental rules. In addition, they say that the notion of state-corporate crime should awaken us to the power dynamics between these sets of actors because they are relevant in understanding and predicting the *outcome* of their 'conflict' over regulation. The outcome is that "producers oppose environmental regulations, including criminal regulations, which place constraints on production and accumulation" and "treadmill actors [can] attempt to employ the ToL to oppose both more stringent environmental regulations and efforts to define ecological disorganization as a crime to protect their economic interests."[26]

Building on the premise of the state-corporate nexus that was articulated in the preceding Section, we can see how the nexus influences *responses* specifically. The

24. Allan Schnaiberg, "The Environment: From Surplus to Scarcity," (1980); Allan Schnaiberg, David N. Pellow, and Adam Weinberg, "The Treadmill of Production and the Environmental State," in *The Environmental State under Pressure*, ed. Arthur P. J. Mol and Frederick H. Buttel, *Research in Social Problems and Public Policy* (Emerald Group Publishing Limited, 2002).

25. Michael J. Lynch, Paul B. Stretesky, and Michael A. Long, "The Treadmill of Production and the Treadmill of Law: Propositions for Analyzing Law, Ecological Disorganization and Crime," *Capitalism Nature Socialism* 31, no. 1 (2020). 109.

26. Ibid.110. It is important to note that the authors have just begun elaborating this concept and it cannot be considered a fully-fledged theory. They also specify that conflicts can arise within each of the three sets outlined, which increases makes it even more complex to truly predict what the outcome will be in terms of the regulatory landscape.

creators of the ToL idea have formulated three propositions to delineate how the treadmill operates in practice.[27]

- **Proposition 1:** "The ToL will oppose (through state-corporate crime, if necessary) enhancements of environmental regulations that criminalize ecologically destructive behaviors of the ToP and its agents."[28]
- **Proposition 2:** "The state's enforcement of criminal environmental laws will not change production trends or limit ToP expansion."[29]
- **Proposition 3:** "Actors who threaten the ToP are likely to be defined as "green" deviants and criminals."[30]

What is common to all three is that there is an underlying paradox whereby the treadmill's movement is, in truth, the source of inertia. Rules are devised and applied – there is visible regulatory activity; but the ultimate result is that the balance of powers stays the same. Resources are extracted from the Earth and toxins are released into the biosphere, regardless of how many new laws or mechanisms for supervision or control are established. In fact, the establishment of these regulatory devices facilitates the continued destruction of the environment by making it appear as if something is being done to conserve it instead.

In the following paragraphs, we use the three propositions to take a further look at the findings from this research and discover how to foster crime-resistance by disrupting the operation of the ToL. We address the propositions starting from the third one and moving back through to the first one. In the following paragraphs, we pay attention to how each proposition has played out in the case study. We also consider how the findings from the case study can provide insights into the ways that the ToL can be disrupted. Furthermore, as we come to the end of the book, it is helpful to consider the way the ToL is operating *today* and what that means for the implementation and potential effectiveness of any interventions or suggestions that are articulated in this Chapter.

*Disruption through Civil Society Mobilisation*

Proposition 3 suggests that where the inertia fostered by the treadmill is overtly fought against, steps may be taken to quell the counter-treadmill flames. While this research has not looked at civil society specifically, the theoretical ideas that have informed the analysis in preceding Chapters all assign a role to civil society in the process of criminogenesis and its neutralisation.[31] Therefore, while we have

27. Ibid. See also: Michael J. Lynch and Michael A. Long, "Green Criminology: Capitalism, Green Crime and Justice, and Environmental Destruction," *Annual Review of Criminology* 5, no. 1 (2022).
28. Lynch, Stretesky, and Long, "The Treadmill of Production and the Treadmill of Law: Propositions for Analyzing Law, Ecological Disorganization and Crime", p. 110.
29. Ibid. p. 112.
30. Ibid. p. 114.
31. Civil society featured in the crime-problem triangle (connected to SCP, RAT and POP) discussed in the conclusions of Chapter 3. The 'organised countervailing constituency' mentioned in the

not reviewed any detailed data on this aspect of the ToL's operation in preceding Chapters, we can consider how this feature of the ToL operates today and what that means for the development of responses to illegal waste oil management activities in the process of bunker fuel production.

As these conclusions are being written,[32] environmental activists are receiving harsh criticism for voicing the distress of an entire generation. A group of activists in Germany has been protesting and demonstrating against climate change with hunger strikes and, most recently, by forcing the shutdown of one of Berlin's airports. They call themselves 'The Last Generation' (*"Die Letzte Generation"*) and have come under fire by politicians, journalists and even climate change scientists for being too disruptive to honest people's daily lives. A number have been arrested.[33] These protesters are 'merely' requesting the following: a reduction of the speed limit on German motorways to 100 km/h; and the assurance of affordable public transport. Their actions at BER airport have tried to call attention to the fact that air travel is one of the largest contributors to $CO_2$ emissions.[34] Two *hours* of an airport being shut down were responded to with the following words: "Anyone who deliberately puts others in danger for their worldview is not an activist but a criminal."[35]

The ToL theory as well as the other frameworks listed above that assign a role to civil society in contributing to the control of crime see efforts like those of the Last Generation among those necessary to begin shifting perspectives and provoke meaningful change. However, these recent events also leave one in painful contemplation. What would happen if instead of a reduction of speed limits, the request being made were that the fuel powering the thousands of cargo ships circling our oceans be of higher (less polluting) quality and that state

theory of tipping points in Chapter 5 could be seen as coinciding or overlapping with the civil society groups indicated in Proposition. Responsive regulation, discussed in Chapters 1 and 6, acknowledges the need for tripartite regulatory efforts that involve not just business and government but civil society too.

32. November 2022.

33. The Last Generation began mobilising against the (in-)action of the German government in 2021, prior to the elections for the new Chancellor. After having received audience with the new Chancellor – Olaf Scholz – and having, in their words, ascertained that "[he] showed no awareness of the existential threat to society posed by the climate emergency", they began organising blockades of some of Germany's most used motorways. [Author's translation] (original: *"kein Bewusstsein für die existenzielle Bedrohung der Gesellschaft durch den Klimanotfall erkennen ließ"*). (See their website at: https://letztegeneration.de/). They are connected to a wider, global network of organisations that are mobilising to create awareness of and try to halt the climate crisis. This network is called the a22 network (See their website at: https://a22network.org/de/).

34. Tagesschau, "Harte Strafen für Aktivisten gefordert" 24 November 2022. "Scharfe Kritik an Flughafen-Blockade" 25 November 2022. Deutsche Welle, "Berlin airport briefly shut down by climate protesters" 24 November 2022.

35. These were the words of the Minister for Internal Affairs of the state of Brandenburg, Michael Stübgen, a member of the CDU (Christian Democratic) party. (Reported in: Tagesschau, "Harte Strafen für Aktivisten gefordert" 24 November 2022.)

enforcement agendas should prioritise fighting the types of crimes explored in this book?

There seems to be a huge chasm between the state and civil society organisations as well as between civil society organisations and businesses. But more importantly, it seems civil society organisations are not backed up by society at large. The isolation of 'green' activists crucially influences the potential for change in sectors that are so fundamental to the functioning of the global economy such as those we have been exploring in this book. As long as environmental conservation is perceived as a 'fringe' interest, as a cause that only some of us have a stake in fighting for, then the energies necessary to sustain the process of change will not be released. We need to accept that our lives *must* be disrupted by the process of transformation from the status quo to sustainability because it is the way we currently live our lives that requires the health of our planet and its inhabitants to deteriorate.

*Disruption through Improved Enforcement*

Proposition 2 defines the ineffectiveness of enforcement in relation to the state's ability to change production trends. An important issue to discuss in this respect is that of 'detection'. States that endeavour to regulate industrial activities such as waste oil management and bunker fuel production- as well as controlling their negative outcomes – require a wealth of knowledge. This knowledge is of two types: The first is *information* about what is happening – which substances are being handled by which entities and how. The second is about the *meaning* and implications of what is happening. What are the consequences of certain substances being handled in certain ways? Why is it useful under certain perspectives for a substance to be used in a particular manner?

Regarding the first type of knowledge, i.e., information about what is happening in the waste oil and bunker fuel industries, we can draw on the literature on regulation to reflect on the findings from preceding chapters. Six proposals that should enhance the abilities of the state to observe the activities in the two industries we have been discussing throughout the book and, especially, to detect non-compliance are enumerated below. The rationale behind these proposals is below each of them: These rationales are by reflecting on the findings from preceding chapters in light of a proposal for 'really' responsive regulation, which adds to the ideas of responsive regulation we explored in Chapters 1 and 6. In that proposal, the authors develop a list of several questions, the answers to which can help to pinpoint what needs to be improved to strengthen detection and the accumulation of information about regulated industries. The relevant questions are also included in the discussion on rationale.[36]

36. For full list of questions, see the table on really responsive regulation reproduced in Annex I. Robert Baldwin and Julia Black, "Really Responsive Regulation," *The Modern Law Review* 71, no. 1 (2008).

1. **Strengthening the 'physical tools' used for entering information on waste generation and movement in a centralised database (see pinch-point 1 on documents, Section 1 above).**
2. **Developing means to de-couple data collection from punishment (e.g., cultivate and reward accurate data collection specifically).**

<u>Rationale</u>: Guiding Question: *Do regulatees supply accurate data on their activities?* Both cases in Chapter 4 demonstrated that the main mechanism used to collect data on waste flows in the Netherlands – the updating of records through the *Landelijke Meldpunt Afavalstoffen*[37] – relies on waste collectors' willingness and ability to label wastes appropriately. Not applying an appropriate waste label facilitates the concealment of profitable, but illegal activities. An enforcement agency or policy maker that wishes to develop a targeted and effective strategy based on the accurate documentation of waste flows cannot do so.

3. **Using intelligence-based and computerized means of narrowing down the pool of candidates for inspection to reduce challenges posed by an extensive community (see pinch-point 1 on documents, Section 1 above).**

<u>Rationale</u>: Guiding Question: *Do detection processes reveal the extent of undesirable as well as non-compliant activity?* Monitoring and inspection activities do not always reveal the true extent of non-compliance. The regulated community is extensive, which means that there is an asymmetry between the breadth of what could or should be inspected and the resources available to carry out such inspections. Wastes and products can move in smaller quantities on thousands of vehicles – on road, rail, and ships. The ratio of (capable) inspectors to transports is low. Randomised spot-checking can only deliver a partial account of non-compliance.[38]

4. **Prioritising the formulation of EU-wide standards for recovery of waste oils and for defining by-products. The movement of these substances is clearly a cross-border phenomenon.**

<u>Rationale</u>: Guiding Question: *How do institutional relationships/divisions of powers or roles impact on detection?* The regulated activities occur across borders. While waste management rules across Member States have been approximated through EU rules, the main legislative tool used is a Directive, which then delegates powers to states to formulate guidelines on how the waste definition should be (dis-)applied to certain substances. Therefore, the basis for enforcement is already uneven. The natural differences in enforcement that exist because of individual and agency level disparities is then exacerbated in an EU context.

---

37. See Chapters 3 and 4 for more details about the LMA.
38. Robert Baldwin, Martin Cave, and Martin Lodge, Understanding Regulation: Theory, Strategy, and Practice, (Oxford: Oxford University Press, 2012).

5. **Reviewing rules on information exchange between authorities of different kinds (administrative, criminal) and how they can be harmonised across the EU where the activities that are targeted are primarily of an economic/ industrial nature.**

**Rationale**: Guiding Question: *How do institutional relationships/divisions of powers or roles impact on detection?* Building on the rationale outlined for point 4 above, we should also consider that exchanging information is particularly problematic because of diverse regimes applying to sensitive information and how authorities can handle it in the EU and beyond.[39]

To underline why this is important, we should recall that, in the Netherlands, the relationship between different state agencies an important positive factor in the Andante story because of it shaped detection and enforcement activities. Inspections were carried out *together* and information could be shared relatively freely during the inspections as well as later on – during the investigative stage. Different agencies have access to different information databases, e.g., waste movements versus REACH registrations. By working together, the agents could follow flows as they are recorded through such disparate systems. They could also benefit from the wisdom and expertise of each agency in relation to the specific substances and processes.

6. **Taking a clear and uncompromising position in favour of environmental protection, which spills over into industries of origin and destination of wastes to overcome the resource/hazard ambivalence in waste management policy and practice**

**Rationale**: Guiding Question: *Are there ideas/cultures/traditions – within the regulated population or the regulatory body – that impact on effective detection?* There are discrepancies in the attitudes and definitions of what desirable or undesirable behaviour may be between states and business. The waste/product distinction is subjective, albeit accompanied by certain common standards and rules. In the bunker fuel production industry, 'residues' from any oil refining or use have been employed as blend components for decades. The attitudinal setting in this

39. There is a new proposal for a Regulation to replace Regulation 1013/2006 on the transboundary shipment of waste (see Chapter 3 for a discussion on that piece of legislation), which includes improved mechanisms for exchanging information in Art. 26, specifically paragraph 2 states: "The Commission shall operate a central system that allows for the electronic submission and exchange of information and documents referred to in paragraph 1. That central system shall provide a hub that shall be used for the exchange in real time of the information and documents referred to in paragraph 1 between existing national systems for electronic data interchange." This could be similar the EDN proposed in Section 1 above. (Proposal for a Regulation of the European Parliament and of the COUNCIL on shipments of waste and amending Regulations (EU) No 1257/2013 and (EU) No 2020/1056 (COM/2021/709 final).

industry is one where productivity takes the fore. In the waste management sector, environmental protection has a much more important role to play. However, here the useful/useless distinction is also paramount and may obfuscate the need to exercise caution against hazards. Regulatory agents may also be sensitive to matters of productivity and usefulness, but their mandate derives from the public policy objectives of the state, which is connected to the environmental conservation aims of waste management legislation.

Detection is only one part of the enforcement process, albeit a crucial one if harms and crimes are to be prevented and if states need to strengthen their ability to interact with and react to business practices on equal footing. Another important aspect is tied to the second type of knowledge that states need, namely understanding of industry dynamics and implications. The Andante *programma* delivers two important insights in this respect that have to do with the analytical and learning practices that the team employed.

Andante was set up as a *programma* mainly for the purpose of analysing the factors underlying repeated offending the in the waste oil and bunker fuel sectors. In Chapter 6, we saw how they divided the *programma* into different stages to sharpen their analyses. Here we should instead pay attention to a more structural element that made it possible for them to gather enough information for the analyses to be carried out in the first place. The Dutch regulatory framework for environmentally sensitive activities and to deal with corporate and environmental crimes has served the analytical aims of Andante as well. The Law on Economic Crimes (WED) is a gateway to streams of information about a company's transactions (this is then also connected to the first type of knowledge discussed above). The threshold the WED imposes for accessing that information is lower than that of general criminal procedure. Because environmental and corporate crime are premised on misrepresenting business transactions, the WED is a vital tool for both reading the reality of an industry and for holding firms accountable.

Now to the second aspect. Learning was a really important aim and characteristic of the Andante team, but we also saw that the lack of *continued, institutional* learning is likely going to lead to a fizzling out of the progress made thanks to the team's work.[40] Andante explicitly focused on learning instead of convictions. Each case they investigated was, first and foremost, functional to understanding both the legitimate industry practices and the criminal *modi operandi*. The lack of a successful conviction at the end of an investigation was not a signal of failure, rather an opportunity to formulate more refined learning questions.

40. This type of 'loss of learing' has also been confirmed in recent findings from a study of the responses to 'undermining' (*ondermijnend*) crime in the Netherlands. See: Hans Nelen, Karin van Wingerde, Roland Moerland, Lieselot Bisschop, *Koers bepalen. Over de lessen van de versterking aanpak georganiseerde drugscriminaliteit*. Den Haag: Boom Criminologie, 2023.

What is really remarkable is that, in order to achieve these learning objectives, Andante operated through a peculiar relationship with the usual state structures. They were not a regular unit within the standard hierarchy of the police organisation (see how they are depicted in Figure 6.1 in Chapter 6). Rather, the individual members of the team were formally members of their units of origin and were on loan to the *programma* for (part of) its duration. Consequently, agents were not exposed to the pressures and routines that often hamper the effectiveness of guardians – they had time to learn and did not have to fulfil conviction quotas. More recent trends in regulatory practice and in the study of corporate regulation confirm that there needs to be continuous space for analysis and learning by state agents, if regulation is to be really responsive. Ideally, this space is not just among operational level agents but characterises all bureaucratic echelons all the way to the circle of policy makers.[41]

Therefore, this 'removal' from the patterns of day-to-day enforcement practices was both a blessing and a curse. The members of the Andante team often shared their feeling of isolation: the fact that they felt 'different' and differently treated than colleagues who focused on more mainstream criminal activities. Indeed, Andante being set up as a temporary *programma* as opposed to a fully-fledged problem-oriented policing unit is quite telling in this regard.[42] The generalist approach to environmental crime and the *ad hoc* nature of thorough approaches to understanding criminogenesis in cases of ecological disorganisation is a symptom that 'green' resistance remains the exception rather than the rule. Andante's own attitude towards this isolation can be characterised as ambivalent. On the one hand, team members displayed pride in knowing they were going against the grain; they also expressed cynicism about the independence of other state agents or agencies. On the other hand, they actively grappled with the need to expand their reach to encourage others to take up the precious tasks of analysis and learning they had been responsible for.

These last insights from the Andante experience lead us back to the paradox highlighted through the ToL concept: for the effectiveness of enforcement agents to increase, they needed to be *removed* from the routine structures. This removal, however, also means that their reach and possibility to effect structural change will always be limited. The existence of this paradox may be linked to more fundamental arrangements that hinder the formulation, implementation, and enforcement of policies, which prevent and address environmental degradation. These more fundamental arrangements can be seen as the way state-corporate

41. Robert Baldwin and Julia Black, "Really Responsive Regulation," *The Modern Law Review* 71, no. 1 (2008).
42. That is not to suggest a conscious avoidance of this set up. Problem-oriented policing is generally not the standard model for policing, and there may be several factors to justify *not* making this choice. Yet, a choice was made to do something, i.e., to set up a *programma* with all the advantages and disadvantages that that entailed.

nexus is organised, i.e., the way these actors interact and what kind of dynamics exist between them. These dynamics can be symbiotic and lead to harmful or criminal activities and we explored this type of symbiosis in the conclusions of Chapter 5 as well as in the discussion on state-corporate crime at the end of the previous Section in this Chapter. However, the symbiosis also manifests itself through the definitional framework that is shared by actors at the state-corporate nexus. In the context of the ToL, this definitional framework is the focus of Proposition 1.

*Disruption through Shifts in Frameworks and Definitional Processes*

Proposition 1 of the ToL focuses on the way environmental harms are legally defined. The issue of definition has cut across the entirety of this book. Specifically, we have repeatedly returned to the question of whether a substance is a blend component for bunker fuel or a waste oil, to the contrast between useful and useless, between productive and unproductive. These dualities have traversed the case study and have already been identified as facilitators of crime.

A number of years have passed since the facts of the two cases analysed in Chapter 4 unfolded, and the dualities persist, albeit they are embedded in a context of renewed resolve to combat climate change. Policymakers have been devising innovative structural solutions to the waste problem and these solutions turn out to be an important example of the potential perils and pitfalls of the ToL's operation. What has been happening is not a remarkable increase in the detection of illegalities in the waste sectors or criminalisation of wrongful conduct in the waste oil and bunker fuel sectors. The shift seems to be moving more in the direction of accommodating productivity over wastefulness in ways that could increase risks, if naively applied.

The notion of a circular economy is currently the most popular answer to the problem of waste management. It has become more prevalent in the time after the events that are analysed in the book, and it features as the headliner for policy programmes at EU and national level.[43] Unfortunately, the circular economy may not live up to the hype, as one group of scholars warns:[44]

43. It has been interesting to see how the website on the topic of 'waste' of the Directorate-General for the environment of the European Commission has evolved during the time span in which I conducted this research. In 2015 the image at the top of this page was a downward-facing pyramid representing the waste hierarchy, which places waste prevention at the top and disposal at the bottom. Today, in 2022, the first item on the website is a circle where waste is the last element before the cycle that the circle symbolizes begins again. 'Waste prevention and management' are seen as one step in a resource efficient process of 'extraction-production-consumption-waste generation'. that shows how resources can be re-used to 'avoid waste'. DG Environment European Commission, "Waste Prevention and Management," https://ec.europa.eu/environment/green-growth/waste-prevention-and-management/index_en.htm.

44. See also: Hervé Corvellec, Alison F. Stowell, and Nils Johansson, "Critiques of the Circular Economy," *Journal of Industrial Ecology* 26, no. 2 (2022); Weston Baxter, Marco Aurisicchio, and Peter Childs, "Contaminated Interaction: Another Barrier to Circular Material Flows," ibid.21,

> *The concept [of a circular economy] appears to decouple economic growth from resource use as well as promoting waste reduction or minimization. Hence, its use in both practitioner and academic literatures tends to be approbatory, uncritical, descriptive and deeply normative.*
>
> *[T]o effect a circular economy driven by producers through either industrial symbiosis or cradle-to-cradle manufacturing*[45] *would require radical transformations to the economic order, including fundamental recasting of manufacture, retail, consumption and property rights. Beyond the ideal, in the messy world of how circularity is being enacted in actual economies, post-consumer wastes have become the basis for circular economies.*[46]

In the scramble to resolve the grave challenges that our current industrial set up has generated quickly enough to quell the complaint of rising environmental consciousness and fear, policymakers may have bought into the circular economy slogan too quickly. What is striking is that the emergencies of climate change and resource scarcity are being responded to frenetically instead of through thoughtful, science-based reflection. If the system that we are building *relies on* waste as an alternative resource, there is reason to suspect that it will actually generate *demand for* waste. Such demand seems to be the opposite of one of the proclaimed aims of this new approach, namely waste *prevention*, although it does fulfil the aim of waste *reduction or minimization*.

The superficial application of 'circularity' feels appealing because it is a classic case of wanting our cake and eating it too. How amazing that we can continue to live like there is no tomorrow by munching on yesterday! As the first quote makes clear, academics and practitioners alike are intoxicated by the exciting prospects; and uncritical of the supposed solutions. True, healthy circularity is premised on fundamental shifts as is made clear by the second quote; and one should expect more resistance from all quarters. Truly transformative policies would be expected to trigger responses like the ones thrown at civil society groups like the Last

no. 3 (2017); Martin Calisto Friant, Walter J. V. Vermeulen, and Roberta Salomone, "Analysing European Union Circular Economy Policies: Words Versus Actions," *Sustainable Production and Consumption* 27 (2021); Edurne A. Inigo and Vincent Blok, "Strengthening the Socio-Ethical Foundations of the Circular Economy: Lessons from Responsible Research and Innovation," *Journal of Cleaner Production* 233 (2019).

45. Industrial symbiosis is "an innovative approach that brings together companies from different sectors in an effort to promote the valorisation of waste, improvement of resource efficiency and reduction of environmental impact. ("Science Direct, "Industrial Symbiosis," https://www.sciencedirect.com/topics/engineering/industrial-symbiosis.) "design and production of products of all types in such a way that at the end of their life, they can be truly recycled (upcycled), imitating nature's cycle with everything either recycled or returned to the earth, directly or indirectly through food, as a completely safe, nontoxic, and biodegradable nutrient. With cradle to cradle, all the components of a product feed another product, the earth or animal, or become fuel." Andrew Sherratt, "Cradle to Cradle," in *Encyclopedia of Corporate Social Responsibility*, ed. Samuel O. Idowu, et al. (Berlin, Heidelberg: Springer Berlin Heidelberg, 2013).
46. Nicky Gregson et al., "Interrogating the Circular Economy: The Moral Economy of Resource Recovery in the EU," *Economy and Society* 44, no. 2 (2015).

Generation mentioned above. These fundamental shifts need us to re-think the notions of waste and of resource, of prosperity and healthy economies, of legal and illegal. These fundamental shifts should actually lead to the dismantling of the ToL and the ToP in their current form. How do we go about making these more fundamental shifts? How do we go about developing a crime-resistant system that does not merely define crime (and waste) away by applying new labels but that is based on regulatory structures and mechanisms that are truly conducive to environmental preservation?

*Disruption through Collaboration*

The reflections on the three propositions articulated above show how the ToL invalidates at least part of the responses that are necessary to limit illegal waste oil management activities in the process of bunker fuel production. What this discussion has also tried to show is that the operation of the ToL is not the work of an all-powerful evil master or cabal; the assertions in this Section are not borne of bleak cynicism about the power of 'the system'. The problem is much more subtle and complex than that. The ToL impacts some elements of what would make enforcement effective, thereby reducing their potential to neutralise criminogenesis and build crime resistance. But the ToL is itself the product of *deeper* dynamics. It operates because of a fundamentally unhealthy relationship between the state, the economy and civil society – a relationship where growth and innovation are not properly combined with prosperity and learning. A relationship where what is law is not necessarily what is just. The modern industrialised society we live in is not the product of planned, perfected, and purposeful designs. Rather the state-corporate nexus has changed and evolved through the forces of history to the point where the distinction between the 'state' and the 'corporate' portions are hard to untangle from each other, where each of them is both the chicken and the egg from which modernity has evolved. But untangling states from business is no longer the most pressing issue. The problem at hand is effectively dealing with the perilous consequences of this relationship. A relationship that will continue to produce harm because:

> *[R]egulatory institutions, institutions of state provision of infrastructure and redistribution, have succeeded in generating more dynamic markets of increasingly global reach, [and] not only is this creating greater swags of wealth, it is also creating bigger swells of crisis. No sooner does the world feel that it has done rather well in coping with the crisis of the closing of the ozone hole, than it is overwhelmed by the much larger crisis of global warming sending waves crashing into the birthplace of capitalism in the low country of the Netherlands.*[47]

47. Braithwaite, John. *Regulatory capitalism: How it works, ideas for making it work better*. Edward Elgar Publishing, 2008, p. 197.

The above quote is taken from the concluding pages of a treatise on regulatory capitalism. The author argues that to speak of neoliberalism (as we have partly done in this book too), is inaccurate as it too easily convinces us of the overwhelming power of the corporate portion of the state-corporate nexus. Instead, he shows another way to understand the current political-economic setup: this nexus is populated by a myriad of both public and private actors that are connected to each other through networks. Those networks alternately deliver us what he terms "markets of vice and virtue"; and the way to flip from vice to virtue is through the resources located in those networks:

> *When the weak cannot defeat the strong, they can still mobilize private governance that builds out from the islands of civility that persist in the most corrupt and war-torn societies in the world. [...] [T]he most promising ways of regulating islands of incivility are from islands of civility rather than through central state coercion.*[48]

Halting the ToL, which also means halting the ToP and the resulting environmental harms and injustices, requires the fostering of these islands of civility. I would argue that an example of such an island of civility has been the Andante *programma* and the Andante team. But islands, like Andante, are isolated. So, as we come to the end of this journey, we need to contemplate how the enthusiasm, the knowledge, skills, and capacities that have been developed through islands of civility like the Andante *programma* can be transferred onto the mainland.

The ToL and ToP concepts are premised on the idea that social factions are in conflict with one another in their pursuit of power. Therefore, disrupting the treadmills means strengthening the actors who vie for environmental protection enough so that they can counter the power of those producing harm.[49] The notion of regulatory capitalism – which is conceptually and philosophically connected to responsive regulation and the theory of tipping points – makes similar proposals. However, the proponent of the idea of regulatory capitalism as the concept through which to understand our political economy setup then goes a step further and challenges an even more fundamental assumption and arrangement.

> *All nodes of separated private, public or hybrid governance need enough autonomy so that they cannot be dominated by other nodes of governance. Equally, each needs enough capacity to check abuse of power by other nodes so that a multiplicity of separated powers can network to check any node of power from dominating all the others. But of course [...] it is more important that they influence one another with strength-building pyramids than with regulatory pyramids [of sanctions]. The participatory nature of deliberative denizenship is a better vehicle for capacity building and adult learning than*

48. Ibid. p. 206-207.
49. Lynch, Stretesky, and Long, "The Treadmill of Production and the Treadmill of Law: Propositions for Analyzing Law, Ecological Disorganization and Crime".

> *non-conversational voting. Responsiveness and integrity [...] is enabled by a society with a strong state, strong markets and strong civil society, where the strengths of each institution enable the governance capabilities of the other institutions.*[50]

So, we need to disrupt the three aspects that allow the ToL to continue operating. We can reduce the power imbalances between state and business through improved enforcement, an embryonic example of which is Andante. We need to support the efforts of civil society organisations that actively contest the status quo. We need to question prevailing definitions of economic health and environmental justice. Yet all of this will not be enough if we do not foster cooperation among states, business, and society at large; cooperation premised on a common vision of what we are striving for.

In this book, we have come to realise that the problem of illegal waste oil management activities in the process of bunker fuel production might be limited. This realisation has been possible thanks to the use of the literature on (organisational) criminology. By drawing on that body of work, we devised several targeted interventions in Section 2 as well as structural arrangements at the state-corporate nexus that enable the ToL. Implementing those interventions and actively disrupting the ToL's foundational arrangement may take us a long way towards a crime-resistant system. But the challenges of today, the urgent matter of stalling the climate crisis that is connected to polluting activities like the ones that have been discussed in this book find few answers in this body of scholarship. The most fundamental normative issues that need to be addressed lie beyond the scope of this doctoral dissertation. In the humble acceptance and embrace of that limitation, a few words can be offered to complement the findings presented in this book, which may provide some guidance as to what we still need to research in criminology and beyond in order to limit environmental injustice.

> *All of the earth's inhabitants deserve the opportunity to enjoy the fruits of a global society advancing in harmony with the natural world. To create such a society, people everywhere must be empowered to participate in the constructive processes that will give rise to it. Building capacity in individuals, communities, and institutions to contribute effectively to transformational change is therefore an indispensable element of effective environmental action.*
>
> *The gulf between intention and action is one of the central challenges facing humanity today. This gap can be bridged; individuals, communities, and nations are contributing their share toward this goal*

50. Braithwaite. *Regulatory capitalism: How it works, ideas for making it work better*, p. 205. Please note that the notion of 'deliberative denizenship' is used by Braithwaite to capture a specific process, namely that where individuals that have access to different networks may participate in each of them to advance a specific goal. Deliberative denizenship functions alongside both deliberative democracy and contestatory citizenship. Denizens have plural identities that given them access to multiple deliberative spaces, which allows them to widen the circles in which matters are discussed, i.e., by extending the potential for participatory governance. See p. 202-205.

*every day. Yet for action to rise to the scales required, far stronger consensus and collective will among the nations is needed around the values demanded by the current stage of humanity's development. It also calls for much greater resolve in putting those values into practice, recommitting to that which is beneficial to the common good and discarding whatever stands in the way of answering the moral and practical call of the present hour. This is a high endeavor indeed, and its benefits a priceless legacy that must be left to the generations to come.*[51]

51. Bahá'í International Community, "One Planet, One Habitation: A Bahá'í Perspective on Recasting Humanity's Relationship with the Natural World" (New York, 2022), p. 5 and 20.

# Annex I – Additional Materials

## Twenty-five Techniques of Situational Crime Prevention

TWENTY FIVE TECHNIQUES OF SITUATIONAL PREVENTION

| Increase the Effort | Increase the Risks | Reduce the Rewards | Reduce Provocations | Remove Excuses |
|---|---|---|---|---|
| **1. Target harden**<br>▪ Steering column locks and immobilisers<br>▪ Anti-robbery screens<br>▪ Tamper-proof packaging | 6. Extend guardianship<br>▪ Take routine precautions: go out in group at night, leave signs of occupancy, carry phone<br>▪ "Cocoon" neighborhood watch | 11. Conceal targets<br>▪ Off-street parking<br>▪ Gender-neutral phone directories<br>▪ Unmarked bullion trucks | 16. Reduce frustrations and stress<br>▪ Efficient queues and polite service<br>▪ Expanded seating<br>▪ Soothing music/muted lights | 21. Set rules<br>▪ Rental agreements<br>▪ Harassment codes<br>▪ Hotel registration |
| 2. Control access to facilities<br>▪ Entry phones<br>▪ Electronic card access<br>▪ Baggage screening | 7. Assist natural surveillance<br>▪ Improved street lighting<br>▪ Defensible space design<br>▪ Support whistleblowers | 12. Remove targets<br>▪ Removable car radio<br>▪ Women's refuges<br>▪ Pre-paid cards for pay phones | 17. Avoid disputes<br>▪ Separate enclosures for rival soccer fans<br>▪ Reduce crowding in pubs<br>▪ Fixed cab fares | 22. Post instructions<br>▪ "No Parking"<br>▪ "Private Property"<br>▪ "Extinguish camp fires" |
| 3. Screen exits<br>▪ Ticket needed for exit<br>▪ Export documents<br>▪ Electronic merchandise tags | 8. Reduce anonymity<br>▪ Taxi driver IDs<br>▪ "How's my driving?" decals<br>▪ School uniforms | 13. Identify property<br>▪ Property marking<br>▪ Vehicle licensing and parts marking<br>▪ Cattle branding | 18. Reduce emotional arousal<br>▪ Controls on violent pornography<br>▪ Enforce good behavior on soccer field<br>▪ Prohibit racial slurs | 23. Alert conscience<br>▪ Roadside speed display boards<br>▪ Signatures for customs declarations<br>▪ "Shoplifting is stealing" |
| 4. Deflect offenders<br>▪ Street closures<br>▪ Separate bathrooms for women<br>▪ Disperse pubs | 9. Utilize place managers<br>▪ CCTV for double-deck buses<br>▪ Two clerks for convenience stores<br>▪ Reward vigilance | 14. Disrupt markets<br>▪ Monitor pawn shops<br>▪ Controls on classified ads.<br>▪ License street vendors | 19. Neutralize peer pressure<br>▪ "Idiots drink and drive"<br>▪ "It's OK to say No"<br>▪ Disperse troublemakers at school | 24. Assist compliance<br>▪ Easy library checkout<br>▪ Public lavatories<br>▪ Litter bins |
| 5. Control tools/ weapons<br>▪ "Smart" guns<br>▪ Disabling stolen cell phones<br>▪ Restrict spray paint sales to juveniles | 10. Strengthen formal surveillance<br>▪ Red light cameras<br>▪ Burglar alarms<br>▪ Security guards | 15. Deny benefits<br>▪ Ink merchandise tags<br>▪ Graffiti cleaning<br>▪ Speed humps | 20. Discourage imitation<br>▪ Rapid repair of vandalism<br>▪ V-chips in TVs<br>▪ Censor details of modus operandi | 25. Control drugs and alcohol<br>▪ Breathalyzers in pubs<br>▪ Server intervention<br>▪ Alcohol-free events |

Source: Arizona State University – Center for Problem-Oriented Policing: https://popcenter.asu.edu/content/25-techniques-0 (Last accessed: 8 August 2022)

## Really Responsive Regulation – DREAM Framework

| | Detection | Response | Enforcement | Assessment | Modification |
|---|---|---|---|---|---|
| **Compliance Response** | 1. Are objectives clear?<br>2. Do regulatees supply accurate data on their activities?<br>3. Do detection processes reveal the extent of undesirable as well as noncompliant activity? | 1.Does the regulator have the tools to deal with the full variety of compliance responses? | 1. Are objectives clear? 2. Do enforcement strategies deal with 'off screen' activities? 3. Are strategies optimally targeted? | 1. Are objectives clear?<br>2. Can compliance records be measured and related to outcome objectives? | 1. Can changes be made when achieving objectives will require new tools/strategies? |
| **Attitudinal Setting** | 1. Are there ideas/cultures/ traditions - within the regulated population or the regulatory body - that impact on effective detection? | 1. Do ideas/culture s traditions affect the potential use of certain tools? | 1. Do ideas/ cultures/ traditions affect the potential use of certain strategies? | 1.Is assessment undermined by ideas/ cultures/ traditions (eg that may corrupt data supply/ quality)? | 1. Are cultures consistent with a capacity and inclination to modify when necessary? 2. Is there awareness of the need to change tools/strategies in the policymaking culture? |
| **Logics of Tools and Strategies** | 1. Do different tools/strategies operate harmoniously to facilitate detection? | 1. Are tools consistent or at tension? | 1. Are strategies consistent or at tension? 2. Are positive combinations of strategy exploited? 3. Are known weaknesses of strategies dealt with? | 1. Do the various assessment procedures operate consistently? | 1. When modifications are carried out are interactions of logics taken into account? |
| **Regime Performance** | 1. Are objectives clear? 2. Is the regulator confident about the accuracy of the detection system? | 1. Does the system allow the performance of particular tools to be measured? | 1. Are objectives clear? 2. Does the system allow the performance of particular strategies to be measured? 3.Can needs to adjust strategy be assessed? | 1.Are objectives clear? 2. Do assessment methods link closely to objectives? | 1. Are modifications based on evidence from assessments? |
| **Change** | 1. Are objectives clear?<br>2. Can the detection regime cope with changes in objectives/operational | 1. Can new tools be resourced/ legislated for? | 1. Can strategies be adjusted to cope with new risks and risk creators? | 1. Can assessment methods be adjusted to cope with new risks risk creators/ objectives etc.? | 1. Can modifications be introduced quickly enough to cope with changes in risk/ objectives etc.? |

Source: Robert Baldwin and Julia Black, "Really Responsive Regulation," *The Modern Law Review* 71, no. 1 (2008).

# Annex II – Field Work

## Field Work Overview

| # | Date | Location | Event/Description | Relevant Documentation [Name of Document for Citation] |
|---|---|---|---|---|
| 1 | 14.12.2015 | Rotterdam | Conversation to establish contact regarding research (R1, R12, Hans Nelen and Roland Moerland) | |
| 2 | 02.03.2016 | Maastricht | Dinner and conversation with R1, Hans Nelen and Roland Moerland the evening before guest lecture – getting to know more of his work and perspective | |
| 3 | 07.04.2016 | Rotterdam | Meeting R1, R2, Hans Nelen and Roland Moerland | [Memo_1] (See Table above) |
| 4 | 21.07.2016 | Amsterdam | Field Visit/Dossier Review | [Memo_2] (See Table above) |
| 5 | 22.07.2016 | | | |
| 6 | 20.10.2016 | Amsterdam | Field Visit/Dossier Review | [Field Notes 20-21.10.2016] |
| 7 | 21.10.2016 | Amsterdam | Field Visit/Dossier Review | |
| 8 | 27.10.2016 | Amsterdam | Field Visit/Dossier Review | [Field Notes 27.10.2016] |
| 9 | 28.10.2016 | Amsterdam | Field Visit/Dossier Review | [Field Notes 28.10.2016] |
| 10 | 03.11.2016 | Amsterdam | Field Visit/Dossier Review | [Field Notes 03-04.11.2016] |
| 11 | 04.11.2016 | Amsterdam | Field Visit/Dossier Review Expert Interview R.1 on 4.11.2016. | |
| 12 | 10.11.2016 | Amsterdam | Field Visit/Dossier Review | [Field Notes 10.11.2016] |
| 13 | 11.11.2016 | Amsterdam | Field Visit/Dossier Review | [Field Notes 11.11.2016] |
| 14 | 17.11.2016 | Amsterdam | Field Visit/Dossier Review | [Field Notes 17.11.2016] |
| 15 | 18.11.2016 | Amsterdam | Field Visit/Dossier Review | [Field Notes 18.11.2016] |

| # | Date | Location | Event/Description | Relevant Documentation [Name of Document for Citation] |
|---|---|---|---|---|
| 16 | 24.11.2016 | Amsterdam | Field Visit/Dossier Review | [Field Notes 24.11.2016] |
| 17 | 25.11.2016 | Amsterdam | Field Visit/Dossier Review | No new notes taken, see other documents. |
| 18 | 01.12.2016 | Amsterdam | Field Visit/Dossier Review | [Field Notes 01.12.2016] |
| 19 | 02.12.2016 | Amsterdam | Field Visit/Dossier Review | No new notes taken, see other documents. |
| 20 | 08.12.2016 | Rotterdam | Meeting R2, R7 and R1 | |
| 21 | 09.12.2016 | Rotterdam | Field Visit – Zwartestromen | |
| 22 | 15.12.2016 | Amsterdam | Field Visit/Dossier Review | No new notes taken, see other documents. |
| 23 | 16.12.2016 | Amsterdam | Field Visit/Dossier Review | No new notes taken, see other documents. |
| 24 | 12.04.2017 | Maastricht | R2 and R7 visiting in Maastricht with Roland Moerland and Kim Geurtjens | |
| 25 | 29.08.2017 | Amsterdam | Field Visit/Dossier Review | [Field Notes 29.08.2017a-c] |
| 26 | 05.09.2017 | Amsterdam | Field Visit/Dossier Review<br>Interview #1 (R2) | [Field Notes 05.09.2017a-d]<br>Recording Interview 1<br>[Transcript Interview 1]<br>[Interview 1 Notes] |
| 27 | 13.09.2017 | Amsterdam | Field Visit/Dossier Review<br>Viewing first full cut documentary "Beerput Nederland" | [Field Notes 13.09.2017a-d] |
| 28 | 19.09.2017 | Amsterdam | Field Visit/Dossier Review<br>Interview #2 (R4) | [Field Notes 19.09.2017]<br>Recording Interview 2<br>[Transcript Interview 2]<br>[Interview 2 Notes] |
| 29 | 25.09.2017 | Willemstad | Field Visit – Zwartestromen<br>[Systematic checks/action days with different enforcement agencies] | [Field Notes 25.09.2017a -d]<br>[Field Notes 25-26.09.2017]<br>[Field Notes 26.09.2017 b-d]<br>[Field Notes 26-27.09.2017] |
| 30 | 26.09.2017 | Willemstad | Field Visit – Zwartestromen | [Field Notes 27.09.2017b-d] |
| 31 | 27.09.2017 | Willemstad | Field Visit – Zwartestromen | |
| 32 | 28.09.2017 | Willemstad | Field Visit – Zwartestromen | |
| 33 | 02.10.2017 | Amsterdam | Field Visit/Dossier Review<br>Interview #3 (R6) | [Field Notes 02.10.2017]<br>Recording Interview 3<br>[Transcript Interview 3] |

| # | Date | Location | Event/Description | Relevant Documentation [Name of Document for Citation] |
|---|---|---|---|---|
| | | | | [Interview 3 Notes] |
| 34 | 09.10.2017 | Amsterdam | Field Visit/Dossier Review<br>Interview #4 (R8) | [Field Notes 09.10.2017a-c]<br>Recording Interview 4<br>[Transcript Interview 4]<br>[Interview 4 Notes] |
| 35 | 16.10.2017 | Amsterdam | Field Visit/Dossier Review<br>Interview #5 (R3) | [Field Notes 16.10.2017a-b]<br>Recording Interview 5<br>[Transcript Interview 5]<br>[Interview 5 Notes] |
| 36 | 24.10.2017 | Amsterdam | Field Visit/Dossier Review<br>Interview #6 (R9) | [Field Notes 24.10.2017a-d]<br>Recording Interview 6<br>[Transcript Interview 6]<br>[Interview 6 Notes] |
| 37 | 31.10.2017 | Amsterdam | | [Field Notes 31.10.2017a-h] |
| 38 | 29.11.2017 | Amsterdam | Sinterklaas visit | N/A |
| 39 | 14.12.2017 | Driebergen | Milieuchefs (R10 and R11) | |
| 40 | 21.12.2017 | Amsterdam | Christmas Party | N/A |
| 41 | 04.12.2018 | Amsterdam | | [Field Notes 04.12.2018] |
| 42 | 02.10.2019 | Duesseldorf | R2 and R3 | [Field Notes 02.10.2019] |
| 43 | 28.02.2020 | Amsterdam | Conversation about work done so far with R2 and R1.<br>Interview #7 (R1 and R2)<br>There are two recordings because we took a break half way through as I needed to feed Lara. The break is noted down in the transcript, which includes both parts in a single document. | [Field Notes 28.02.2020]<br>Recording Interview 7a<br>Recording Interview 7b<br>[Transcript Interview 7]<br>[Interview 7 Notes] |

## Documents from/on Field Work

| Date | Location | Event/Description | Personal Notes/Documents Received |
|---|---|---|---|
| 07.04.2016 | Rotterdam, Funktioneel Parket | Meeting R1, R2, Hans Nelen, Roland Moerland, Giulia – overview of work and history of Andante – looking at what possible points of interest are for the research | [Memo_1] |
| 21.-22.07.2016 | Amsterdam (Office Andante Police Team) | First encounter with the team and visiting the offices of the team – Memo on cases and overview of work of the team so far | [Memo_2]<br>De-bunkering Report *Tactische Analyse* – Confidential Report of Phase I Andante |
| 09.2016 | - | - | [Memo_2b] |
| 12.2016 | Amsterdam | General points taken from notes in notebooks during field visits in 2016 | [Memo_3] |
| 10.2016 | Amsterdam | Summarized electronic memo taken from notes in notebooks during field visits in 2016 on *Case 1* | [Memo_4] |
| 10.2016 | Amsterdam | Summarized electronic memo taken from notes in notebooks during field visits in 2016 on *Case 2* | [Memo_5] |
| 11.2016 | Amsterdam | Summarized electronic memo taken from notes in notebooks during field visits in 2016 on *Case 3* | [Memo_6] |
| Received 25.04.2016 | N/A | Email Communication | Kamerstukken II 2015-2016 31409 nr. 111 |
| Received 15.12.2015 | N/A | Email Communication | Journal article – Proposal for a Dutch Environmental Authority (G.A. Biezeveld & M.C. Stoové. "Naar een Nederlandse Omgevingsautoriteit Een pleidooi voor onafhankelijk milieutoezicht" *Tijdschrift voor Toezicht* 2011 (2) 3. |

| Date | Location | Event/Description | Personal Notes/Documents Received |
|---|---|---|---|
| Received 26.10.2016 | N/A | Email Communication | Six judgments from cases similar to those investigated by Andante. |
| Received 10.11.2016 | N/A | Email Communication | One judgment from a case similar to those investigated by Andante. |
| Received 01.12.2016 | N/A | Email Communication | Femke de Vries "Leidt transparantie tot meer vertrouwen in de toezichthouder?" REDE in verkorte vorm uitgesproken op 29 maart 2016 Bij de aanvaarding van het ambt van hoogleraar Toezicht aan de Faculteit Rechtsgeleerdheid vande Rijksuniversiteit Groningen |
| Received December 2 016 | | | Money laundering pamphlet |
| Received 05.09.2017 | N/A | Email Communication | Surveyor statement |
| Received 05.09.2017 | N/A | Email Communication | ISO Standard 8216 |
| Received 27.09.2017 | Willemstad | Printouts from R3 | |
| Received 09.10.2017 | N/A | Email Communication | Prof dr. G. van Calster, Onderzoeksrapport "Handelingen aan boord van de Probo Koala in het kader van Nederlandse, Europese en internationale regelgeving" Internationale en Europeesrechtelijke verplichtingen ten aanzien van handhaving in de zeescheepvaart Prof. Ch.W. Backes, Dr. A.B. Blomberg, Mr. H.M. Dotinga m.m.v. Prof. A.H.A. Soons |
| Received 10.10.2017 | N/A | Email Communication | Andante – the Basics ENGLISH read only (PPT) – presentation prepared by the Andante team to give an overview of their work to international 'partners'. Presentation is in English and has been shared also to provide |

| Date | Location | Event/Description | Personal Notes/Documents Received |
|---|---|---|---|
| | | | an overview of the relevant legal provisions. |
| Received 11.10.2017 | N/A | Email Communication – Sending of documents developed by the Andante Team to share internally and externally. Describe and instruct on the history, approach, needs and goals of the team. Are supposed to encourage others to support and learn along. | Betrekken van partners in 4 stappen<br>Bijlage Checklist Transportmiddel<br>Bijlage IGP vragenlijst_n-e<br>Bijlage IGP vragenlijst<br>Bijlage Ketenonderzoek<br>Blauwdruk Team Andante 2016 02 15<br>Blauwdruk Team Andante 2016 02 15 Engels<br>Blauwdruk Team Andante 2016 07 15 Engels<br>Checklist docx Transportmiddel_n-e<br>Ketenonderzoek_n-e |
| Received 11.10.2017 | N/A | Email communication | Ontwikkelingen Zwarte Stromen 2017-2018 – document concerning the actions "Zwartestromen" |
| 16.10.2017 | N/A | Email Communication | Bakker, M.H. Broekman & J. "Milieurisico's Van Specifieke Stoffen in Bunkerolie in Zeeschepen: Onderzoek Van De Literatuur En De Reach-Dossiers." Bilthoven: Rijksinstituut voor Volksgesondheid en Milieu (RIVM), 2016 |
| Received 04.12.2018 | Amsterdam | Printouts from R3 | |
| Received 04.12.2018 | Amsterdam | | |
| Received 02.10.2019 | Duesseldorf | PowerPoints shared by R3 and R2 via USB stick | |

# Annex III – Details on Waste Oils and Bunker Fuel

### Overview of sector-plans from the *Landelijke Afvalbeheerplan* concerning waste oils

| Sectorplan | | Typering | Minimumstandaard bewerking |
|---|---|---|---|
| 53 | Scheepsafvalstoffen | Olie- en vethoudend scheepsafval; ladingrestanten en afval van lading; ladinggerelateerde afvalstoffen, overig afval uit vaartuigen | Geen minimum standaarden (verwerking van deze afvalstoffen wordt in andere sectorplannen beschreven) |
| 56 | Afgewerkte olie | Afgewerkte olie categorie I en II, ≤ 5 volume-% sediment èn ≤ 10 volume-% water | Regenereren tot basisolie<br><br>Wanneer regeneratie vanwege technische redenen of ontwikkelingen in de markt economisch niet haalbaar is, *mag categorie I en II olie worden opgewerkt tot gasolie of een gelijkwaardige brandstof*[30, 31, X] |
| 57 | Halogeenhoudende afgewerkte olie | Afgedankte smeer- of systeemolie met een gehalte aan organische halogeenverbindingen van meer dan 1.000 mg/kg, ≤5 volume-% sediment én ≤10 volume-% water (= afgewerkte oliecategorie III) | *Nuttige toepassing met hoofdgebruik als brandstof.*[X]<br><br>Daarnaast is verbranden met terugwinning van chloor door gespecialiseerde bedrijven eveneens toegestaan |
| 58 | Olie/water/slib mengsels en oliehoudende slibben | Olie-, water- en slibmengsels, ballastwater, bilgewater, oliehoudend waswater en oliehoudend afvalwater | Scheiden in een oliefractie, een slib/zandfractie en een waterfractie<br><br>*Voor de oliefractie die resteert na scheiding van ows-mengsels: hoofdgebruik als brandstof*[X] |
| 59 | Vloeibare brandstof- en olierestanten | | *Nuttige toepassing met hoofdgebruik als brandstof* |
| 60 | Oliehoudende boorspoeling en boorgruis | Boorspoeling op oliebasis | Destillatie tot een voor het oorspronkelijke doel herbruikbare olie en tot een minerale stof |

Source: de Buck, A, ME Smit, Jasper Faber, and Anouk van Grinsven. "Blends in beeld. Een analyse van de bunkerolieketen." Delft: CE Delft, 2011, p. 62

### (Waste) oil substances found in bunker fuel

| Typering | Herkomst | Rest-stroom | Inzet als | Mogelijke bestanddelen | Aandachts-punten/ eigenschappen |
|---|---|---|---|---|---|
| Resin residues | Productie van kunststoffen, synthetische harsen, rubber (verf, inkt, etc.) | Ja | Cutter-stock | Aromaten, terpenen, Naftaleen, Fenolverbindingen | Laag vlampunt |
| Ethyleenkraker-residu | Residuen van ethyleenkrakers | Ja | Residuale brandstof | Hogere naftalenen | Slechte mengbaarheid met stookolie |
| Ethyleenkraker-zijstroom | Zijstroom van ethyleen-kraker | Ja | Cutter-stock | Styreen Naftaleen (> 10%) Alkyl-naftalenen Cresolen Dicyclo-pentadieen | Polymerisatie van styreen-monomeer tot polystyreen Stank |
| Bruinkoolteer, steenkoolteer[11] | Reststroom van productie cokes/ kolenvergassing | Ja | Residuale brandstof | PAK's, hogere fenolen, cresolen | Slechte mengbaarheid met stookolie |
| Afgewerkte (smeer-)olie | Reststroom na gebruik smeerolie | Ja | Cutter-stock | Fosfor, zink, calcium, magnesium | |
| Residuen biodiesel | Reststroom productie biodiesel | Ja | Cutter-stock | Organische zuren | |
| Heavy Crude Oil | Zware ruwe olie, die voor bitumen-productie wordt gebruikt | | Brandstof | | |
| Shale oil | Olie uit leisteen of teerzanden | | Residuale brandstof | Hogere fenolen, arseen | Slechte mengbaarheid met stookolie |

Source: de Buck, A, ME Smit, Jasper Faber, and Anouk van Grinsven. "Blends in beeld. Een analyse van de bunkerolieketen." Delft: CE Delft, 2011, p. 8.

# Bibliography

## Primary Sources


Communication from the Commission to the European Parliament, the Council, the European Economic and Social Committee and the Committee of the Regions A new Circular Economy Action Plan for a cleaner and more competitive Europe (COM/2020/98 final)

Proposal for a Regulation of the European Parliament and of the COUNCIL on shipments of waste and amending Regulations (EU) No 1257/2013 and (EU) No 2020/1056 (COM/2021/709 final)

"Kamerstukken II 2017-2018, 29 911, Nr. 207."

"Kamerstukken II 2017-2018, 620 ".

"Kamerstukken II 2017-2018, Z12969."

"Kamerstukken II 2018-2019, 29 911, Nr. 212."

"Kamerstukken II 2012-2013, 33450, 4."

"Kamerstukken II 2013-2014, 31409, 58."

"Kamerstukken II 2013-2014, 33450, 5."

"Kamerstukken II 2016-2017, 31409, 124."

"Kamerstukken II 2016-2017, D29117."


## Books and Articles


Abate, Tenaw Gedefaw, Rasmus Nielsen, and Max Nielsen. "Agency Rivalry in a Shared Regulatory Space and Its Impact on Social Welfare: The Case of Aquaculture Regulation." *Aquaculture Economics & Management* 22, no. 1 (2018/01/02 2018): 27-48.

Adams, David Unesco General Conference Promoting Enduring Peace. *The Seville Statement on Violence.* 1994.

Adler, Freda Laufer William S. Merton Robert King. *The Legacy of Anomie Theory.* New Brunswick (N.J.); London: Transaction, 1995.

Adler, Freda, Gerhard OW Mueller, and William S Laufer. *Criminology and the Criminal Justice System.* McGraw-Hill New York, NY, 2007.

Agnew, Robert. "Building on the Foundation of General Strain Theory: Specifying the Types of Strain Most Likely to Lead to Crime and Delinquency." *Journal of Research in Crime and Delinquency* 38, no. 4 (2001): 319-61.

Agnew, Robert, Francis T. Cullen, Velmer S. Burton, T. David Evans, and R. Gregory Dunaway. "A New Test of Classic Strain Theory." *Justice Quarterly* 13, no. 4 (1996/12/01 1996): 681-704.

Akhtar, M. N., N. Al-Yassir, S. Al-Khattaf, and Jiří Čejka. "Aromatization of Alkanes over Pt Promoted Conventional and Mesoporous Gallosilicates of Mel Zeolite." *Catalysis Today* 179, no. 1 (2012/01/05/ 2012): 61-72.

Alaranta, Joonas, and Topi Turunen. "Drawing a Line between European Waste and Chemicals Regulation." *Review of European, Comparative & International Environmental Law* 26, no. 2 (2017): 163-73.

———. "How to Reach a Safe Circular Economy?—Perspectives on Reconciling the Waste, Product and Chemicals Regulation." *Journal of Environmental Law* 33, no. 1 (2021): 113-36.

Albanese, J. "Corporate Criminology: Explaining Deviance of Business and Political Organizations." *Journal of criminal justice* 12, no. 1 (1984): 11-20.

Alibux, Ayreen NRN. "Criminogenic Conditions, Bribery and the Economic Crisis in the Eu: A Macro Level Analysis." *European journal of criminology* 13, no. 1 (2016): 29-49.

Almer, Christian, and Timo Goeschl. "The Sopranos Redux: The Empirical Economics of Waste Crime." *Regional Studies* 49, no. 11 (2015): 1908-21.

Antonopoulos, Georgios A., Alexandra Hall, Joanna Large, and Anqi Shen. "Counterfeit Goods Fraud: An Account of Its Financial Management." *European Journal on Criminal Policy and Research* 26, no. 3 (2020/09/01 2020): 357-78.

Appel, Hannah, Arthur Mason, and Michael Watts. *Subterranean Estates: Life Worlds of Oil and Gas.* Cornell University Press, 2015.

Arfaoui, Nabila, Eric Brouillat, and Maïder Saint Jean. "Policy Design and Technological Substitution: Investigating the Reach Regulation in an Agent-Based Model." *Ecological Economics* 107 (2014): 347-65.

Arfat, Shabina. "Globalisation and Human Rights: An Overview of Its Impact." *American journal of humanities and social sciences* 1, no. 1 (2013): 18-24.

Ayres, Ian, and John Braithwaite. *Responsive Regulation: Transcending the Deregulation Debate.* Oxford University Press, 1992.

Babcock, Hope M. "A Risky Business: Generation of Nuclear Power and Deepwater Drilling for Offshore Oil and Gas." *Colum. J. Envtl. L.* 37 (2012): 63.

Backes, Chris. "The Waste Framework Directive and the Circular Economy." In *Research Handbook on EU Environmental Law*: Edward Elgar Publishing, 2020.

Baird, Jim, Robin Curry, and Paulo Cruz. "An Overview of Waste Crime, Its Characteristics, and the Vulnerability of the EU Waste Sector." *Waste Management & Research* 32, no. 2 (2014): 97-105.

Baldwin, Robert, and Julia Black. "Really Responsive Regulation." *The Modern Law Review* 71, no. 1 (2008): 59-94.

Baldwin, Robert, Martin Cave, and Martin Lodge. *Understanding Regulation: Theory, Strategy, and Practice.* Oxford: Oxford University Press, 2012.

Barak, Gregg. *The Routledge International Handbook of the Crimes of the Powerful.* Routledge London, 2015.

Barr, Robert, and Ken Pease. "Crime Placement, Displacement, and Deflection." *Crime and Justice* 12 (1990): 277-318.

Barton, Alana, Howard Davis, and Holly White. "Agnotology and the Criminological Imagination." In *Ignorance, Power and Harm: Agnotology and the Criminological Imagination*, edited by Alana Barton and Howard Davis, 13-35. Cham: Springer International Publishing, 2018.

Bascom, Willard. "The Disposal of Waste in the Ocean." *Scientific American* 231, no. 2 (1974): 16-25.

Bassey, Michael. "Pedagogic Research: On the Relative Merits of Search for Generalisation and Study of Single Events." *Oxford review of education* 7, no. 1 (1981): 73-94.

Batubara, F Rizal, Jolien Ubacht, and Marijn Janssen. "Challenges of Blockchain Technology Adoption for E-Government: A Systematic Literature Review." Paper presented at the Proceedings of the 19th annual international conference on digital government research: governance in the data age, 2018.

Baxter, Weston, Marco Aurisicchio, and Peter Childs. "Contaminated Interaction: Another Barrier to Circular Material Flows." *Journal of Industrial Ecology* 21, no. 3 (2017): 507-16.

Beaver, Kevin M., James C. Barnes, and Brian B. Boutwell. *The Nurture Versus Biosocial Debate in Criminology: On the Origins of Criminal Behavior and Criminality.* Los Angeles: SAGE, 2014.

Beck, Brian J. "Liability of Marine Surveyors for Loss of Surveyed Vessels: When Someone Other Than the Captain Goes Down with the Ship." *Notre Dame L. Rev.* 64 (1989): 246.
Becker, Howard Saul. *Outsiders.* N.Y.: Fress Press, 1966.
———. *Tricks of the Trade: How to Think About Your Research While You're Doing It.* Chicago: Univ. of Chicago Press, 2011.
Beirne, Piers, and Nigel South. *Issues in Green Criminology.* Routledge, 2013.
Bellah, Robert N. *Habits of the Heart: Individualism and Commitment in American Life.* Berkeley: University of California Press, 2008.
Benson, M.L., and Sally S. Simpson. *Understanding White-Collar Crime: An Opportunity Perspective.* Routledge, 2015. Berkes, Antal. "Cross-Border Pollution." In *The Routledge Handbook on Extraterritorial Human Rights Obligations*, 434-46: Routledge, 2021.
Bichler, Gisela, Andrea Schoepfer, and Stacy Bush. "White Collars and Black Ties Interlocking Social Circles of Elite Corporate Offenders." *Journal of Contemporary Criminal Justice* 31, no. 3 (2015): 279-96.
Bisschop, Lieselot. "Corporate Environmental Responsibility and Criminology." *Crime Law and Social Change* 53, no. 4 (May 2010): 349-64.
———. "Is It All Going to Waste? Illegal Transports of E-Waste in a European Trade Hub." *Crime Law and Social Change* 58, no. 3 (Oct 2012): 221-49.
Black, Julia, and Robert Baldwin. "Really Responsive Risk-Based Regulation." *Law & policy* 32, no. 2 (2010): 181-213.
Blaikie, Norman W. H. *Designing Social Research: The Logic of Anticipation.* 2nd ed. ed. Cambridge, UK;: Polity Press, 2010.
Blair, Roger D, and Jeffrey L Harrison. *Monopsony in Law and Economics.* Cambridge University Press, 2010.
Block, Alan A., and Thomas J. Bernard. "Crime in the Waste Oil Industry." *Deviant Behavior* 9, no. 2 (1988/04/01 1988): 113-29.
Block, Walter E, and Roy Whitehead. "Environmental Justice Risks in the Petroleum Industry." In *Philosophy of Law*, 257-80: Springer, 2019.
Boba, Rachel. "Crime Analysis and Crime Mapping." Sage Publications Inc., 2005.
Bohm, R. M. "Radical Criminology – an Explication." . *Criminology* 19, no. 4 (1982): 565-89.
Bonger, W. A. Horton Henry P. Lindsey Edward Norcross Frank H. *Criminality and Economic Conditions.* New York: Agathon Press, 1967.
Boon, Helen J. "Climate Change Ignorance: An Unacceptable Legacy." *The Australian Educational Researcher* 42, no. 4 (2015): 405-27.
Borrion, Hervé. "Quality Assurance in Crime Scripting." *Crime Science* 2, no. 1 (2013): 6.
Bourdieu, Pierre. *Language and Symbolic Power.* Harvard University Press, 1991.
Boutellier, Hans, Ronald van Steden, Yarin Eski, and Mauro Boelens. "Een Einde Aan Ondermijning." *Tijdschrift voor veiligheid* 19, no. 1 (2020): 3.
Box, Steven. *Deviance, Reality and Society.* : Cassell, 1986.
———. "Power, Crime, and Mystification." . (1983).
Bradshaw, Elizabeth A. ""Obviously, We're All Oil Industry": The Criminogenic Structure of the Offshore Oil Industry." *Theoretical Criminology* 19, no. 3 (2015): 376-95.
Braga, Anthony Allan. *Problem-Oriented Policing and Crime Prevention.* Criminal Justice Press Monsey, NY, 2008.
Braithwaite, John. "Criminological Theory and Organizational Crime ". *Justice Quarterly* 6, no. 3 (1989): 333-58.
———. "Enforced Self-Regulation: A New Strategy for Corporate Crime Control." *Michigan Law Review* 80, no. 7 (1982): 1466-507.
———. *Regulatory Capitalism: How It Works, Ideas for Making It Work Better.* Edward Elgar Publishing, 2008.
Braithwaite, John, and Peter Drahos. *Global Business Regulation.* Cambridge University Press, 2000.
Braithwaite, John Pettit Philip. *Not Just Deserts: A Republican Theory of Criminal Justice.* Oxford: Clarendon Press, 2010.

Brantingham, P. J., Brantingham, P. L., and Andresen, M. A. "The Geometry of Crime and Crime Pattern Theory." In *Environmental Criminology and Crime Analysis*, edited by Richard and Townsley Wortley, Michael. Oxon: Routledge, 2017.
Brants, C. "The System's Rigged—or Is It?". *Crime, Law and Social Change* 21, no. 2 (1994): 103-25.
Brants, Chrisje, and Theo de Roos. "Pollution, Press, and the Penal Process: The Case of Uniser in the Netherlands." *Crime and Social Justice*, no. 21/22 (1984): 128-45.
Brayley, Helen Cockbain Eleanor Laycock Gloria K. "The Value of Crime Scripting: Deconstructing Internal Child Sex Trafficking." . *Policing*, no. 5 (2011): 132-43.
Breyer, Stephen G. *Regulation and Its Reform*. Cambridge, Mass.: Harvard University Press, 1982. doi:10.4159/9780674028760.
Brisman, Avi, and Nigel South. "A Green-Cultural Criminology: An Exploratory Outline." *Crime Media Culture* 9, no. 2 (Aug 2013): 115-35.
Britannica, The Editors of Encyclopaedia. "Charter Party (Contract)." In *Encyclopedia Britannica*, 2018.
Bullock, Karen Clarke R. V. G. Tilley Nick. "Situational Prevention of Organised Crimes." . (2013).
Bullock, Karen, Ronald V. Clarke, and Nick Tilley. *Situational Prevention of Organised Crimes*. Taylor & Francis, 2010.
Burgess, Robert L., and Ronald L. Akers. "A Differential Association-Reinforcement Theory of Criminal Behavior." *Social Problems* 14, no. 2 (1966): 128-47.
Burton, S., McGregor, M. Enhancing SARA: a new approach in an increasingly complex world. *Crime Sci* 7, 4 (2018).
Calisto Friant, Martin, Walter J. V. Vermeulen, and Roberta Salomone. "Analysing European Union Circular Economy Policies: Words Versus Actions." *Sustainable Production and Consumption* 27 (2021/07/01/ 2021): 337-53.
Cave, Lisa A, and Glenn C Blomquist. "Environmental Policy in the European Union: Fostering the Development of Pollution Havens?". *Ecological Economics* 65, no. 2 (2008): 253-61.
Chainey, Spencer P., and Arantza Alonso Berbotto. "A Structured Methodical Process for Populating a Crime Script of Organized Crime Activity Using Osint." *Trends in Organized Crime* (2021/08/23 2021).
Chalmers, A. F. *What Is This Thing Called Science?* Indianapolis: Hackett Publishing Company, Inc., 2015.
Chambliss, William. "State Organized Crime." *Making law: The State. Law, and Structural Contradictions* (1993): 290-314.
Chambliss, William J. *Exploring Criminology*. New York: Macmillan, 1988.
Chambliss, William Jones. "Toward a Political Economy of Crime." . *Marx and law Marx and Law / ed. by Susan Easton*, (2008): 339-60.
Chamlin, Mitchell B., and John K. Cochran. "Assessing Messner and Rosenfeld's Institutional Anomie Theory: A Partial Test." *Criminology* 33, no. 3 (1995): 411-29.
Cheyne, Ilona. "The Definition of Waste in EC Law." *Journal of Environmental Law* 14, no. 1 (January 1, 2002 2002): 61-73.
Claeys, Jasmien, and Lieselot Bisschop. "Een Schip Op Het Strand Is Een Baken in Zee." *Tijdschrift voor Criminologie* 60, no. 1 (2018): 3-33.
Clarke, Derek B. Cornish and Ronald V. "The Rational Choice Perspective." In *Environmental Criminology and Crime Analysis*, edited by Richard Wortley and Michael Townsley. Oxon: Routledge, 2017.
Clarke, Martha J. Smith and Ronald V. "Situational Crime Prevention: Classifying Techniques Using "Good Enough" Theory." In *The Oxford Handbook of Crime Prevention*, edited by Brandon C. Welsh Martha J. Smith Ronald V. Clarke David P. Farrington: Oxford University Press, 2012.
Clarke, Ronald V., & Felson, M., ed. *Routine Activity and Rational Choice: Advances in Criminological Theory*: Routledge., 1993.

Clarke, Ronald V. "Situational Crime Prevention: Theoretical Background and Current Practice." In *Handbook on Crime and Deviance*, 259-76: Springer, 2009.

Clarke, Ronald V. "Situational Crime Prevention." In *Environmental Criminology and Crime Analysis*, edited by Richard and Townsley Wortley, Michael. Oxon: Routledge, 2017.

———. "Situational Crime Prevention." *Crime and justice* 19, no. Building a Safer Society: Strategic Approaches to Crime Prevention (1995): 91-150.

Clarke, Ronald V., and David Weisburd. "Diffusion of Crime Control Benefits: Observations on the Reverse of Displacement." 2006.

Clarke, Ronald V. G., and Marcus Felson. *Routine Activity and Rational Choice.* Vol. 5: Transaction Publishers, 1993.

Clinard, Marshall B, Peter C Yeager, and Ruth Blackburn Clinard. *Corporate Crime.* Routledge, 2017.

Clinard, Marshall Barron Yeager Peter C. *Corporate Crime.* New Brunswick, NJ: Transaction Publ, 2006.

Cloward, R. A. Ohlin L. E. *Delinquency and Opportunity.* USA: The Free Press of Glencoe, 1963.

Cloward, Richard A. "Illegitimate Means, Anomie, and Deviant Behavior." *American Sociological Review* 24, no. 2 (1959): 164-76.

Cockett, Neil. *Neil Cockett on Bunkers.* London; Hong Kong: LLP, 1997.

Cohen, Albert Kircidel. *Delinquent Boys: The Culture of the Gang, by Albert K. Cohen.* New York: Free Press, 1967.

Coleman, Clive, and Jenny Moynihan. Understanding Crime Data: Haunted by the Dark Figure. Crime and Justice. Buckingham: Open University Press, 1996.

Coleman, James W, and Linda L Ramos. "Subcultures and Deviant Behavior in the Organizational Context." *Research in the Sociology of Organizations* 15 (1998): 3-34.

Coleman, James William. "Toward an Integrated Theory of White-Collar Crime." *American Journal of Sociology* 93, no. 2 (1987): 406-39.

Coll, Steve. *Private Empire: Exxonmobil and American Power.* Penguin, 2012.

Cornish, Derek B. "Crimes as Scripts." Paper presented at the Proceedings of the international seminar on environmental criminology and crime analysis, 1994.

———. "The Procedural Analysis of Offending and Its Relevance for Situational Prevention." *Crime prevention studies* 3 (1994): 151-96.

Cornish, Derek B., and Ronald V. Clarke. "Understanding Crime Displacement: An Application of Rational Choice Theory." *Criminology* 25, no. 4 (1987): 933-48.

Cornish, Derek Blaikie, and Ronald V Clarke. "Opportunities, Precipitators and Criminal Decisions: A Reply to Wortley's Critique of Situational Crime Prevention." *Crime prevention studies* 16 (2003): 41-96.

Corvellec, Hervé, Alison F. Stowell, and Nils Johansson. "Critiques of the Circular Economy." *Journal of Industrial Ecology* 26, no. 2 (2022): 421-32.

Cresswell, J. *Research Design.* Sage Publications, 2014.

Croall, Hazel. "Who Is the White-Collar Criminal?". *The British Journal of Criminology* 29, no. 2 (1989): 157-74.

Crowe, Timothy D., and Institute National Crime Prevention. *Crime Prevention through Environmental Design: Applications of Architectural Design and Space Management Concepts.* 2nd ed. ed. Boston, Mass: Butterworth-Heinemann, 2000.

D'Amato, A. "Illegal Waste Disposal in the Time of the Mafia: A Tale of Enforcement and Social Well Being." *Journal of Environmental Planning and Management* 55, no. 5 (2012): 637-55.

Daly, Kathleen. "Gender and Varieties of White-Collar Crime." *Criminology* 27, no. 4 (1989): 769-94.

de Buck, A, ME Smit, Jasper Faber, and Anouk van Grinsven. "Blends in beeld. Een analyse van de bunkerolieketen." Delft: CE Delft, 2011.

De Haan, Willem, and Jaco Vos. "A Crying Shame: The over-Rationalized Conception of Man in the Rational Choice Perspective." *Theoretical Criminology* 7, no. 1 (2003): 29-54.

de Sadeleer, Nicolas Michel. "EC Waste Law or How to Juggle with Legal Concepts: Drawing the Line between Waste, Residues, Secondary Materials, by-Products, Disposal and Recovery Operations." *Journal of European Environmental & Planning Law* 2, no. 6 (2005): 458-77.

———. "New Perspective on the Definition of Waste in EC Law." *Journal of European Environmental & Planning Law* 1, no. 4 (2005): 46-58.

Dehghanniri, Hashem, and Hervé Borrion. "Crime Scripting: A Systematic Review." *European Journal of Criminology* 18, no. 4 (2021): 504-25.

Denzin, Norman K. "Notes on the Criminogenic Hypothesis: A Case Study of the American Liquor Industry." *American Sociological Review* (1977): 905-20.

Dherani, M., D. Pope, M. Mascarenhas, K. R. Smith, M. Weber, and N. Bruce. "Indoor Air Pollution from Unprocessed Solid Fuel Use and Pneumonia Risk in Children Aged under Five Years: A Systematic Review and Meta-Analysis." . *Bull World Health Organ* 86, no. 5 (May 2008): 390-98c.

Di Ronco, Anna, James Allen-Robertson, and Nigel South. "Representing Environmental Harm and Resistance on Twitter: The Case of the Tap Pipeline in Italy." *Crime, Media, Culture* 15, no. 1 (2019): 143-68.

Dorn, Nicholas, Stijn Van Daele, and Tom Vander Beken. "Reducing Vulnerabilities to Crime of the European Waste Management Industry: The Research Base and the Prospects for Policy." *Eur. J. Crime Crim. L. & Crim. Just.* 15 (2007): 23.

Downs, Anthony. *Inside Bureaucracy.* Boston: Little, Brown, 1967.

Drackner, Mikael. "What Is Waste? To Whom?-an Anthropological Perspective on Garbage." *Waste management & research* 23, no. 3 (2005): 175-81.

Dukes, Graham, John Braithwaite, and James P Moloney. *Pharmaceuticals, Corporate Crime and Public Health.* Edward Elgar Publishing, 2014.

Dunlop, Claire A., Jonathan C. Kamkhaji, and Claudio M. Radaelli. "Regulators and Reform: A Quasi-Experimental Assessment of the Effects of Training Inspectors." *International Public Management Journal* 18, no. 2 (2015/04/03 2015): 304-22.

Durkheim, Emile. "Suicide, a Study in Sociology." . ([1897] 1951).

Durkheim, Émile, Sarah A. Solovay, John Henry Mueller, and George Edward Gordon Sir Catlin. *The Rules of Sociological Method.* A Free Press Paperback. 8th ed. ed. New York: Free Press, 1966.

Ekblom, Paul. "The Conjunction of Criminal Opportunity: A Framework for Crime Reduction Toolkits." *Policing and Reducing Crime Unit Research, Development and Statistics Directorate Home Office: London, UK* (2001).

———. "Deconstructing Cpted... and Reconstructing It for Practice, Knowledge Management and Research." *European Journal on Criminal Policy and Research* 17, no. 1 (2011): 7-28.

———. *Design against Crime: Crime Proofing Everyday Products*. Boulder, Colo.: Lynne Rienner Publishers, 2012.

Elliot, Kevin. "Selective Ignorance in Environmental Research." *Routledge International handbook of ignorance studies* (2015): 165-73.

Ermann, M. David Lundman Richard J. *Corporate and Governmental Deviance.* New York: Oxford University Press, 1982.

Etzioni, Amitai. *The New Golden Rule: Community and Morality in a Democratic Society.* New York: Basic Books, 1999.

Ewart, W. D. *Bunkers: A Guide for the Ship Operator.* London: Fairplay Publications, 1982.

Eze, I. C., E. Schaffner, E. Fischer, T. Schikowski, M. Adam, M. Imboden, M. Tsai, *et al.* "Long-Term Air Pollution Exposure and Diabetes in a Population-Based Swiss Cohort." . *Environ Int* 70 (Sep 2014): 95-105.

Ezeonu, Ifeanyi. "Market Criminology: A Critical Engagement with Primitive Accumulation in the Petroleum Extraction Industry in Africa." *The Handbook of White-Collar Crime* (2019): 398-417.

Faber, Malte, Reiner Manstetten, and John LR Proops. "Humankind and the Environment: An Anatomy of Surprise and Ignorance." *Environmental values* 1, no. 3 (1992): 217-41.

Farberman, Harvey A. "A Criminogenic Market Structure: The Automobile Industry." *The Sociological Quarterly* 16, no. 4 (1975): 438-57.
Farrell, Graham. "Situational Crime Prevention and Its Discontents: Rational Choice and Harm Reduction Versus 'Cultural Criminology'." In *Crime Opportunity Theories*, 343-69: Routledge, 2017.
Faure, Michael. "The Development of Environmental Criminal Law in the EU and Its Member States." *Review of European, Comparative & International Environmental Law* 26, no. 2 (2017): 139-46.
Faure, Michael G. "Effective, Proportional and Dissuasive Penalties in the Implementation of the Environmental Crime and Shipsource Pollution Directives: Questions and Challenges." *European Energy and Environmental Law Review* (2010): 256-78.
Faure, Michael G, and Katarina Svatikova. "Criminal or Administrative Law to Protect the Environment? Evidence from Western Europe." *Journal of environmental law* 24, no. 2 (2012): 253-86.
Faure, Michael, Morag Goodwin, and Franziska Weber. "The Regulator's Dilemma: Caught between the Need for Flexibility & the Demands for Forseeability-Reassessing the Lex Certa Principle." *Alb. LJ Sci. & Tech.* 24 (2013): 283.
Fellman, Gordon. "Rambo and the Dalai Lama: The Compulsion to Win and Its Threat to Human Survival." . (1998).
Felson, Marcus. "Linking Criminal Choices, Routine Activities, Informal Control, and Criminal Outcomes." In *The Reasoning Criminal*, 119-28: Springer, 1986.
———. "Routine Activities and Crime Prevention:: Armchair Concepts and Practical Action." In *Crime Opportunity Theories*, 483-87: Routledge, 2017.
———. "The Routine Activity Approach." In *Enviornmental Criminology and Crime Analysis*, edited by Richard & Townsley Wortley, Michael. Oxon: Routledge, 2017.
Felson, Marcus Cohen Lawrence E. "Human Ecology and Crime: A Routine Activity Approach." *Human Ecology* 8, no. 4 (1980): 389-406.
Fenwick, Tara. "Understanding Relations of Individual—Collective Learning in Work: A Review of Research." *Management learning* 39, no. 3 (2008): 227-43.
Ferrell, Jeff Hayward Keith J. Morrison Wayne Presdee Mike. *Cultural Criminology Unleashed.* 2016.
Feyerabend, Paul. *Against Method.* London: Verso, 2010.
Firestone, Jeremy, and James Corbett. "Maritime Transportation: A Third Way for Port and Environmental Security." Paper presented at the Widener L. Symp. J., 2002.
Fisher, Christopher Lux Jonathan. *Bunkers: An Analysis of the Practical, Technical and Legal Issues.* Banbury: Petrospot Ltd, 2004.
Focquaert, Farah. "Neurobiology and Crime: A Neuro-Ethical Perspective." *Journal of Criminal Justice* 65 (2019/11/01/ 2019): 101533.
Freilich, Joshua D., and Graeme R. Newman. "Providing Opportunities: A Sixth Column for the Techniques of Situational Crime Prevention." In *Organized Crime, Corruption and Crime Prevention: Essays in Honor of Ernesto U. Savona*, edited by Stefano Caneppele and Francesco Calderoni, 33-42. Cham: Springer International Publishing, 2014.
Friedrichs, David O. "Crimes of the Powerful and the Definition of Crime." *The Routledge international handbook of the crimes of the powerful* (2015): 39-49.
Friedrichs, David O, and Dawn L Rothe. "State-Corporate Crime and Major Financial Institutions: Interrogating an Absence." *State Crime Journal* 3, no. 2 (2014): 146-62.
Gabor, Thomas. "Crime Displacement and Situational Prevention: Toward the Development of Some Principles." *Canadian Journal of Criminology* 32, no. 1 (1990): 41-73.
Galley, Michael. "Ship Registration, Owner Anonymity and Sub-Standard Shipping." In *Shipbreaking: Hazards and Liabilities*, 99-115: Springer, 2014.
Garavan, Thomas N, and Alma McCarthy. "Collective Learning Processes and Human Resource Development." *Advances in developing human resources* 10, no. 4 (2008): 451-71.
Garland, David. "Governmentality and the Problem of Crime: Foucault, Criminology, Sociology." *Criminological Perspectives. Essential Readings* (2003): 456-66.

Garland, David, and Richard Sparks. "Criminology, Social Theory and the Challenge of Our Times." *Brit. J. Criminology* 40 (2000): 189.

Gaskell, Nicholas, and Craig Forrest. "Marine Pollution Damage in Australia: Implementing the Bunker Oil Convention 2001 and the Supplementary Fund Protocol 2003." *University of Queensland Law Journal, The* 27, no. 2 (2008): 103-65.

Gehring, Thomas, and Benjamin Faude. "A Theory of Emerging Order within Institutional Complexes: How Competition among Regulatory International Institutions Leads to Institutional Adaptation and Division of Labor." *The Review of International Organizations* 9, no. 4 (2014/12/01 2014): 471-98.

Geis, Gilbert. "The Heavy Electrical Equipment Anti-Trust Cases of 1961." In *Criminal Behavior Systems*, edited by M and Quinney Clinard, R. New York: Holt, Rinehart and Winston, 1967.

Geldermann, Jutta, Christina Jahn, Thomas Spengler, and Otto Rentz. "Proposal for an Integrated Approach for the Assessment of Cross-Media Aspects Relevant for the Determination of "Best Available Techniques" Bat in the European Union." *The International Journal of Life Cycle Assessment* 4, no. 2 (1999/03/01 1999): 94-106.

Gibbs, Carole, Meredith L Gore, Edmund F McGarrell, and Louie Rivers. "Introducing Conservation Criminology Towards Interdisciplinary Scholarship on Environmental Crimes and Risks." *British Journal of Criminology* 50, no. 1 (2010): 124-44.

Gilmour, Nicholas. "Understanding Money Laundering–a Crime Script Approach." *Eur. Rev. Organ. Crime* 1, no. 2 (2014): 35-56.

Goffman, Erving. *Stigma: Notes on the Management of Spoiled Identity.* London: Penguin, 9999.

Goldstein, Herman. "Improving Policing: A Problem-Oriented Approach." . *Crime & Delinquency Crime & Delinquency* 25, no. 2 (1979): 236-58.

Goode, William J. Hatt P. K. *Methods in Social Research.* New York1 952.

Gottfredson, Michael R. Hirschi Travis. *A General Theory of Crime.* Stanford, Calif.: Stanford Univ. Press, 1998.

Grabosky, Peter. "Meta-Regulation." *Regulatory theory: Foundations and applications* (2017): 149-62.

Grabosky, Peter N. "Green Markets: Environmental Regulation by the Private Sector." *Law & Policy* 16, no. 4 (1994): 419-48.

Gregory, Kimberly K. "Basel Convention and the International Trade of Hazardous Waste: The Road to the Destruction of Public Health and the Environment Is Paved with Good Intentions, The." *Currents: Int'l Trade LJ* 10 (2001): 80.

Gregson, Nicky, Mike Crang, Sara Fuller, and Helen Holmes. "Interrogating the Circular Economy: The Moral Economy of Resource Recovery in the Eu." *Economy and Society* 44, no. 2 (2015/04/03 2015): 218-43.

Greife, Matthew B, and Paul B Stretesky. "Treadmill of Production and State Variations in Civil and Criminal Liability for Oil Discharges in Navigable Waters." *Routledge International Handbook of Green Criminology. London: Routledge* (2013): 150-66.

Gross, E. "Organizational Crime-a Theoretical Perspective." In *Studies in Symbolic Interaction*, edited by Norman K Denzin, 55–85. Greenwich, CT: JAI Press, 1978.

Gu, Yewen, and Stein W Wallace. "Scrubber: A Potentially Overestimated Compliance Method for the Emission Control Areas: The Importance of Involving a Ship's Sailing Pattern in the Evaluation." *Transportation Research Part D: Transport and Environment* 55 (2017): 51-66.

Gunningham, Neil. "Strategizing Compliance and Enforcement: Responsive Regulation and Beyond." *Explaining compliance: business responses to regulation* (2011): 199-221.

Gunningham, Neil, Peter N Grabosky, and Darren Sinclair. *Smart Regulation: Designing Environmental Policy.* Vol. 514: Clarendon Press Oxford, 1998.

Gunningham, Neil, Robert A Kagan, and Dorothy Thornton. "Social License and Environmental Protection: Why Businesses Go Beyond Compliance." *Law & Social Inquiry* 29, no. 2 (2004): 307-41.

Gunningham, Neil, and Darren Sinclair. "Smart Regulation." In *Regulatory Theory*, edited by Peter Drahos. Foundations and Applications, 133-48: ANU Press, 2017.

Häder, Donat-P. "Dumping of Toxic Waste into the Oceans." In *Anthropogenic Pollution of Aquatic Ecosystems*, 353-71: Springer, 2021.

Hancock, Graham, and Gloria Laycock. "Organised Crime and Crime Scripts: Prospects for Disruption." In *Situational Prevention of Organised Crimes*, edited by Karen Bullock, Ronald V. G. Clarke and Nick Tilley, 172-93. Collumpton: Willan Publishing, 2010.

Haralambides, Hercules. "Globalization, Public Sector Reform, and the Role of Ports in International Supply Chains." *Maritime Economics & Logistics* 19, no. 1 (2017/03/01 2017): 1-51.

Hasler, Olivia, Reece Walters, and Rob White. "In and against the State: The Dynamics of Environmental Activism." *Critical Criminology* 28, no. 3 (2020/09/01 2020): 517-31.

Hayes, John, and Christopher W Allinson. "Cognitive Style and the Theory and Practice of Individual and Collective Learning in Organizations." *Human relations* 51, no. 7 (1998): 847-71.

Heine, Dirk, and Susanne Gäde. "Unilaterally Removing Implicit Subsidies for Maritime Fuels." *International Economics and Economic Policy* 15, no. 2 (2018/04/01 2018): 523-45.

Hoare, Quintin, and Geoffrey Nowell-Smith. *Selections from Prison Notebooks*. Lawrence & Wishart, 2005.

Hoecke, Mark van. *Methodologies of Legal Research: What Kind of Method for What Kind of Discipline?* Oxford: Hart, 2013.

Howitt, Dennis. *Forensic and Criminal Psychology*. London;: Prentice Hall, 2002.

Huisman, Wim. "Corporate Crime and Crisis: Causation Scenarios." In *Economic Crisis and Crime*, edited by Mathieu Deflem. Sociology of Crime, Law and Deviance, 107-25: Emerald Group Publishing Limited, 2011.

———. "Tussen Winst En Moraal: Achtergronden Van Regelnaleving En Regelovertreding Door Ondernemingen." Boom Juridische uitgevers, 2001.

Huisman, Wim, and Hans Nelen. "Gotham Unbound Dutch Style." *Crime, Law and Social Change* 48, no. 3 (2007): 87-103.

Huisman, Wim, and Judith van Erp. "Opportunities for Environmental Crime: A Test of Situational Crime Prevention Theory." *British Journal of Criminology* 53, no. 6 (2013): 1178.

Huisman, Wim, and Elies van Sliedregt. "Rogue Traders: Dutch Businessmen, International Crimes and Corporate Complicity." *Journal of International Criminal Justice* 8, no. 3 (2010): 803-28.

Hutchings, Alice, and Thomas J Holt. "A Crime Script Analysis of the Online Stolen Data Market." *British Journal of Criminology* 55, no. 3 (2015): 596-614.

Inigo, Edurne A., and Vincent Blok. "Strengthening the Socio-Ethical Foundations of the Circular Economy: Lessons from Responsible Research and Innovation." *Journal of Cleaner Production* 233 (2019/10/01/ 2019): 280-91.

Janssen, MPM, and FA van Broekhuizen. "Waste Handling and Reach: Recycling of Materials Containing Svhcs: Daily Practice Challenges." (2017).

Jarrell, Melissa Luisa. *Environmental Crime and the Media: News Coverage of Petroleum Refining Industry Violations*. LFB Scholarly Pub., 2007.

Jeffery, C. Ray. *Crime Prevention through Environmental Design*. Beverly Hills [Calif.]: Sage Publications, 1971.

Jenkins, Anne, and John Braithwaite. "Profits, Pressure and Corporate Lawbreaking." *Crime, Law and Social Change* 20, no. 3 (1993/10/01 1993): 221-32.

Johnson, Shane D., Rob T. Guerette, and Kate Bowers. "Crime Displacement: What We Know, What We Don't Know, and What It Means for Crime Reduction." *Journal of Experimental Criminology* 10, no. 4 (2014/12/01 2014): 549-71.

K., Merton Robert. *Social Theory and Social Structure*. New York: Free Press, [1957] 1968.

Kagan, Robert A., and John T. Scholz. "The "Criminology of the Corporation" and Regulatory Enforcement Strategies." In *Enforcing Regulation*, 67-95: Springer Netherlands: Dordrecht, 1984.

Karlberg, Michael Robert. *Beyond the Culture of Contest: From Adversarialism to Mutualism in an Age of Interdependence*. Oxford: George Ronald, 2004.

Kauzlarich, David, and Dawn L. Rothe. "Crimes of the Powerful." In *Encyclopedia of Criminology and Criminal Justice*, edited by Gerben Bruinsma and David Weisburd, 778-86. New York, NY: Springer New York, 2014.

Kehoe, Alice. "Conflict Is a Western Worldview." In *The Anthropology of Peace: Essays in Honor of E. Adamson Hoebel*, edited by E. Adamson; Rohrl Vivian J.; Nicholson M. E. R.; Zamora Mario D.; International Congress of Anthropological Ethnological Hoebel, Sciences, 55-66. Williamsburg, Va.: Dept. of Anthropology, College of William and Mary, 1992.

Kelishadi, R., and P. Poursafa. "Air Pollution and Non-Respiratory Health Hazards for Children." . *Arch Med Sci* 6, no. 4 (Aug 30 2010): 483-95.

Kennedy, Leslie W., Joel M. Caplan, and Eric Piza. "Risk Clusters, Hotspots, and Spatial Intelligence: Risk Terrain Modeling as an Algorithm for Police Resource Allocation Strategies." *Journal of Quantitative Criminology* 27, no. 3 (2011/09/01 2011): 339-62.

Khan, Sabaa Ahmad. "E-Products, E-Waste and the Basel Convention: Regulatory Challenges and Impossibilities of International Environmental Law." *Review of European, Comparative & International Environmental Law* (2016): n/a-n/a.

Kilgore, Deborah W. "Understanding Learning in Social Movements: A Theory of Collective Learning." *International journal of lifelong education* 18, no. 3 (1999): 191-202.

Kleemans, Edward R. "Organized Crime and the Visible Hand: A Theoretical Critique on the Economic Analysis of Organized Crime." *Criminology & Criminal Justice* 13, no. 5 (2013): 615-29.

Kleemans, Edward R., and Henk G. Van de Bunt. "Organised Crime, Occupations and Opportunity." *Global Crime* 9, no. 3 (2008/08/01 2008): 185-97.

Kluttz, Jenalee, and Pierre Walter. "Conceptualizing Learning in the Climate Justice Movement." *Adult Education Quarterly* 68, no. 2 (2018): 91-107.

Kolthoff, E.W. "De Geschiedenis Van Een Begrip." *Christen Democratische Verkenningen* 2019, no. 4 (2019-12-18 2019): 63 – 69.

Kolthoff, Emile, and Sjaak Khonraad. "Ondermijnende Aspecten Van Georganiseerde Criminaliteit En De Rol Van De Bovenwereld." *Tijdschrift voor criminologie* 58, no. 2 (2016).

Koons, Judith E. "Earth Jurisprudence and the Story of Oil: Intergenerational Justice for the Post-Petroleum Period." *USFL Rev.* 46 (2011): 93.

Kramer, Ronald C. "Corporate Crime: An Organizational Perspective." *White-collar and economic crime* (1982): 75-94.

Kramer, Ronald C, Raymond J Michalowski, and David Kauzlarich. "The Origins and Development of the Concept and Theory of State-Corporate Crime." *Crime & Delinquency* 48, no. 2 (2002): 263-82.

Krueger, Jonathan. "The Basel Convention and the International Trade in Hazardous Wastes." *Yearbook of international co-operation on environment and development* 2002 (2001): 43-51.

Kuhn, Thomas S. *The Structure of Scientific Revolutions.* : University of Chicago Press, 1970.

Kummer, Katharina. "The International Regulation of Transboundary Traffic in Hazardous Wastes: The 1989 Basel Convention." *International and Comparative Law Quarterly* 41, no. 03 (1992): 530-62.

Lacoste, Julie, and Pierre Tremblay. "Crime and Innovation: A Script Analysis of Patterns in Check Forgery." *Crime Prevention Studies* 16 (2003): 169-96.

Lambrechts, Derica, and Michael Hector. "Environmental Organised Crime: The Dirty Business of Hazardous Waste Disposal and Limited State Capacity in Africa." *Politikon* (2016): 1-18.

Lampkin, Jack A, and Tanya Wyatt. "Utilising Principles of Earth Jurisprudence to Prevent Environmental Harm: Applying a Case Study of Unconventional Hydraulic Fracturing for Shale Gas in the United Kingdom." *Critical Criminology* 28, no. 3 (2020): 501-16.

Lanier, M. *Essential Criminology.* New York: Routledge, 2015.

Lantsman, Leonid. *Seaport Vulnerability to Criminal Networks: A Mixed Method Approach to Measuring Criminological Vulnerability in the Top 30 Us Container Ports.* City University of New York, 2017.

Laureen, Snider. "Cooperative Models and Corporate Crime: Panacea or Cop-Out?" . *Crime & Delinquency* 36, no. 3 (1990): 373-90.

Lea, John. "Emerging Issues in Green Criminology: Exploring Power, Justice and Harm." *British Journal of Criminology* 54, no. 4 (Jul 2014): 691-96.

Leclerc, Benoit. "Crime Scripts." In *Environmental Criminology and Crime Analysis*, edited by Richard Wortley and Michael Townsley, 119-41. Abingdon: Routledge, 2017.

———. "Script Analysis for Crime Controllers: Extending the Reach of Situational Crime Prevention." In *Organized Crime, Corruption and Crime Prevention*, 13-20: Springer, 2014.

Leclerc, Benoit and Danielle Reynald. "When scripts and guardians unite: A script model to facilitate intevention of capable guardians in public settings." *Security Journal* 30, no. 3 (2016): 793-806

Leclerc, Benoit and Richard Wortley. *Cognition and Crime: Offender Decision Making and Script Analyses / Edited by Benoit Leclerc and Richard Wortley.* Crime Science Series (Routledge (Firm)). Edited by Benoit LeClerc and Richard Wortley. Abingdon, Oxon; New York: Routledge, 2014.

LeCompte, Margaret Diane Preissle Judith Tesch Renata Goetz Judith Preissle. *Ethnography and Qualitative Design in Educational Research.* Bingley, U.K.: Emerald Group Pub., 2008.

Leffler, William L. *Petroleum Refining for the Non-Technical Person.* Tulsa, Okla., USA: PennWell Books, 1985.

Leonard, William N, and Marvin Glenn Weber. "Automakers and Dealers: A Study of Criminogenic Market Forces." *Law and Society Review* (1970): 407-24.

Lewin, Kurt. "Action Research and Minority Problems." *Journal of Social Issues* 2, no. 4 (1946): 34-46.

Lewis, Paul. "Realism, Causality and the Problem of Social Structure." *Journal for the theory of Social Behaviour* 30, no. 3 (2000): 249-68.

Liddick, Don. "The Traffic in Garbage and Hazardous Wastes: An Overview." *Trends in Organized Crime* 13, no. 2-3 (2010): 134-46.

Ling, Shichun, Rebecca Umbach, and Adrian Raine. "Biological Explanations of Criminal Behavior." *Psychology, Crime & Law* 25, no. 6 (2019/07/03 2019): 626-40.

Lord, Nicholas, Jon Spencer, Elisa Bellotti, and Katie Benson. "A Script Analysis of the Distribution of Counterfeit Alcohol across Two European Jurisdictions." *Trends in Organized Crime* 20, no. 3 (2017): 252-72.

Loy, D. R. "The Religion of the Market." . *Journal- American Academy of Religion* 65, no. 2 (1997): 275-90.

Lynch, Michael J, Averi Fegadel, and Michael A Long. "Green Criminology and State-Corporate Crime: The Ecocide-Genocide Nexus with Examples from Nigeria." *Journal of Genocide Research* 23, no. 2 (2021): 236-56.

Lynch, Michael J, Paul B Stretesky, and Ronald G Burns. "Slippery Business: Race, Class, and Legal Determinants of Penalties against Petroleum Refineries." *Journal of Black Studies* 34, no. 3 (2004): 421-40.

Lynch, Michael J. "Green Criminology and Environmental Crime: Criminology That Matters in the Age of Global Ecological Collapse." *Journal of White Collar and Corporate Crime* 1, no. 1 (2020): 50-61.

———. "The Meaning of Green: Contrasting Criminological Perspectives." *Theoretical criminology* 7, no. 2 (2003): 217-38.

Lynch, Michael J., and Michael A. Long. "Green Criminology: Capitalism, Green Crime and Justice, and Environmental Destruction." *Annual Review of Criminology* 5, no. 1 (2022): 255-76.

Lynch, Michael J., and Paul B. Stretesky. "Similarities between Green Criminology and Green Science: Toward a Typology of Green Criminology." *International Journal of Comparative and Applied Criminal Justice* 35, no. 4 (2011/11/01 2011): 293-306.

Lynch, Michael J., Paul B. Stretesky, and Michael A. Long. "The Treadmill of Production and the Treadmill of Law: Propositions for Analyzing Law, Ecological Disorganization and Crime." *Capitalism Nature Socialism* 31, no. 1 (2020/01/02 2020): 107-22.

Mackenzie, Simon. "Systematic Crimes of the Powerful: Criminal Aspects of the Global Economy." *Social Justice* (2006): 162-82.

MacPherson, C. B. *The Political Theory of Possessive Individualism.* : Oxford, 1962.

Maguire, Mike, and Susan McVie. "The Oxford Handbook of Criminology." Essay. In Crime Data and Criminal Statistics: A Critical Reflection. Oxford University Press, 2017.

Maguire, Mike. "The Oxford Handbook of Criminology." Essay. In Criminal Statistics and the Construction of Crime. Oxford University Press, 2012,

Mahon, Rialine. "Regulatory Agencies: Captive Agents or Hegemonic Apparatuses." *Studies in Political Economy* 1, no. 1 (1979/01/01 1979): 162-200.

Makkai, Toni, and John Braithwaite. "The Limits of the Economic Analysis of Regulation: An Empirical Case and a Case for Empiricism*." *Law & Policy* 15, no. 4 (1993): 271-91.

Mandiberg, Susan F., and Michael G. Faure. "A Graduated Punishment Approach to Environmental Crimes: Beyond Vindication of Administrative Authority in the United States and Europe." *Columbia journal of environmental law.* 34, no. 2 (2009): 447.

Mansell, John NK. *Flag State Responsibility: Historical Development and Contemporary Issues.* Springer Science & Business Media, 2009.

Martimort, D. "The Multiprincipal Nature of Government." . *European Economic Review* 40, no. 3-5 (Apr 1996): 673-85.

Maruna, Shadd, and Heith Copes. "What Have We Learned from Five Decades of Neutralization Research?". *Crime and justice* 32 (2005): 221-320.

Mascini, Peter. "Why Was the Enforcement Pyramid So Influential? And What Price Was Paid?". *Regulation & Governance* 7, no. 1 (2013): 48-60.

Mascini, Peter, and Eelco Van Wijk. "Responsive Regulation at the Dutch Food and Consumer Product Safety Authority: An Empirical Assessment of Assumptions Underlying the Theory." *Regulation & Governance* 3, no. 1 (2009): 27-47.

Massari, Monica. "Ecomafias and Waste Entrepreneurs in the Italian Market." Paper presented at the 6th cross-border crime colloquium held in berlin, germany, 2004.

Massari, Monica, and Paola Monzini. "Dirty Businesses in Italy: A Case-Study of Illegal Trafficking in Hazardous Waste." *Global crime* 6, no. 3-4 (2004): 285-304.

Matza, David. *Delinquency and Drift.* New York: Routledge, 1964. 1990.

McConville, Mike Chui Wing Hong. *Research Methods for Law.* Edinburgh: Edinburgh University Press, 2017.

McCulloch, Jude, and Sharon Pickering. *Borders and Crime: Pre-Crime, Mobility and Serious Harm in an Age of Globalization.* Springer, 2012.

McKie, Ruth E. "Climate Change Counter Movement Neutralization Techniques: A Typology to Examine the Climate Change Counter Movement." *Sociological Inquiry* 89, no. 2 (2019): 288-316.

Meadows, Donella H. Wright Diana. *Thinking in Systems: A Primer.* 2015.

Meadows, Donella Hager Randers Joerrgen Meadows Dennis L. *Limits to Growth the 30-Year Update.* London: Earthscan, 2012.

Merton, Robert K. "Social Structure and Anomie." *Crime* (2003): 201-12.

Merton, Robert King. *Opportunity Structure: The Emergence, Diffusion, and Differentiation of a Sociological Concept, 1930s-1950s.* New Brunswick, N.J: F. Adler & W.S. Laufer, 1995.

Mesko, Gorazd, Nigel South, and Rob White. "Special Issue: Green Criminology Editors' Introduction." *Crime Law and Social Change* 59, no. 3 (Apr 2013): 249-50.

Messner, S F, and R Rosenfeld. *Crime and the American Dream.* Cengage Learning, 2012.

Messner, Steven F. Rosenfeld Richard. *Crime and the American Dream.* Australia: Wadsworth Cengage Learning, 2013.

Michael S. Scott, John E. Eck, Johannes Knutsson, Herman Goldstein. "Problem-Oriented Policing." In *Environmental Criminology and Crime Analysis*, edited by Richard Wortley and Michael Townsley, 227-58. Oxon: Routledge, 2017.

Michalowski, Raymond, and Kevin Bitten. "Transnational Environmental Crime." *Handbook of transnational crime and justice* (2005): 139-59.
Michalowski, Raymond J, and Ronald C Kramer. "The Space between Laws: The Problem of Corporate Crime in a Transnational Context." *Social Problems* 34, no. 1 (1987): 34-53.
———. *State-Corporate Crime: Wrongdoing at the Intersection of Business and Government.* Rutgers University Press, 2006.
Michalowski, Raymond J. *Order, Law, and Crime: An Introduction to Criminology.* New York, N.Y.: Random House, 1985.
Mills, C. Wright. *Situated Actions and Vocabularies of Motive.* Indianapolis: Bobbs-Merrill, 1970.
Mintzberg, Henry. "Who Should Control the Corporation?" . *International corporate governance: text, readings and cases / [a cura di] Robert I. Tricker* (1994).
Mitchell, J. Clyde. "Case and Situation Analysis." . *sociol rev The Sociological Review* 31, no. 2 (1983): 187-211.
Monahan, Susanne C., and Beth A. Quinn. "Beyond 'Bad Apples' and 'Weak Leaders': Toward a Neo-Institutional Explanation of Organizational Deviance." *Theoretical Criminology* 10, no. 3 (2006): 361-85.
Moreto, William D, and Ronald V Clarke. "Script Analysis of the Transnational Illegal Market in Endangered Species." *Cognition and Crime: Offender Decision Making and Script Analyses* (2013): 209.
Morrison, W. "What Is Crime? Contrasting Definitions and Perspectives." In *Criminology*, edited by Chris Hale, K. Hayward, A. Wahidin, and E. Wincup. Oxford: Oxford University Press, 2013.
Muehlemann, Samuel, Paul Ryan, and Stefan C. Wolter. "Monopsony Power, Pay Structure, and Training." *ILR Review* 66, no. 5 (2013): 1097-114.
Muñoz, John, Susan Olzak, and Sarah A. Soule. "Going Green: Environmental Protest, Policy, and Co2 Emissions in U.S. States, 1990–2007." *Sociological Forum* 33, no. 2 (2018): 403-21.
Nash, Hazel Ann. "The Revised Directive on Waste: Resolving Legislative Tensions in Waste Management?". *Journal of Environmental Law* 21, no. 1 (January 1, 2009 2009): 139-49.
Navadkar, Vipul H, Ajinkya Nighot, and Rahul Wantmure. "Overview of Blockchain Technology in Government/Public Sectors." *International Research Journal of Engineering and Technology* 5, no. 6 (2018): 2287-92.
Needleman, Martin L, and Carolyn Needleman. "Organizational Crime: Two Models of Criminogenesis." *The Sociological Quarterly* 20, no. 4 (1979): 517-28.
Negret, Carlos Felipe Llinás. "Pretending to Be Liberian and Panamanian; Flags of Convenience and the Weakening of the Nation State on the High Seas." *J. Mar. L. & Com.* 47 (2016): 1.
Nelen, H., Karin van Wingerde, Roland Moerland, Lieselot Bisschop, Lessen van de versterking van de aanpak georganiseerde drugcriminaliteit. Den Haag: Boom Criminologie, 2023
Nelen, Hans, and Wim Huisman. "Breaking the Power of Organized Crime? The Administrative Approach in Amsterdam." In *Organized Crime: Culture, Markets and Policies*, 207-18: Springer, 2008.
Newell, Pete. *Globalization and the Environment: Capitalism, Ecology and Power.* John Wiley & Sons, 2013.
Newman, Oscar. *Defensible Space: Crime Prevention through Urban Design.* New York: Collier Books, 1973.
Niskanen, William A. "The Peculiar Economics of Bureaucracy." *The American Economic Review* 58, no. 2 (1968): 293-305.
Nobre, Gustavo Cattelan, and Elaine Tavares. "The Quest for a Circular Economy Final Definition: A Scientific Perspective." *Journal of Cleaner Production* 314 (2021/09/10/ 2021): 127973.
Nurse, Angus. "Exploring Green Criminology: Towards a Green Criminological Revolution." *Journal of Environmental Law* 27, no. 2 (Jul 2015): 368-72.

O'Rourke, Dara, and Sarah Connolly. "Just Oil? The Distribution of Environmental and Social Impacts of Oil Production and Consumption." *Annual Review of Environment and Resources* 28, no. 1 (2003): 587-617.

Oates, W. E., and R. M. Schwab. "Economic Competition among Jurisdictions – Efficiency Enhancing or Distortion Inducing." . *Journal of Public Economics* 35, no. 3 (Apr 1988): 333-54.

Oberthür, Sebastian. "Institutional Interaction to Address Greenhouse Gas Emissions from International Transport: Icao, Imo and the Kyoto Protocol." *Climate Policy* 3, no. 3 (2003/01/01 2003): 191-205.

Ogus, Anthony Ian. *Regulation: Legal Form and Economic Theory.* Clarendon Law Series. Oxford: Clarendon Press, 1994.

Ong, Walter J. *Fighting for Life: Contest, Sexuality, and Consciousness.* Ithaca: Cornell University Press, 2013.

Parker, Christine. "Meta-Regulation: Legal Accountability for Corporate Social Responsibility." (2007).

———. "Twenty Years of Responsive Regulation: An Appreciation and Appraisal." *Regulation & Governance* 7, no. 1 (2013): 2-13.

Parker, Christine, and Vibeke Lehmann Nielsen. *Explaining Compliance: Business Responses to Regulation.* Edward Elgar Publishing, 2011.

Passas, Nikos. "Anomie and Corporate Deviance." *Contemporary Crises* 14, no. 2 (1990): 157-78.

———. "Cross-Border Crime and the Interface between Legal and Illegal Actors." In *Upperworld and Underworld in Cross-Border Crime*, edited by Petrus van Duyne, Klaus von Lampe and Nikos Passas, 11-41. Nijmegen: Wolf Legal Publishers, 2002.

———. "Global Anomie Theory and Crime." In *The Essential Criminology Reader*, edited by Stuart Henry and Mark Lanier, 174-82. Boulder, CO: Westview Press, 2006.

———. "Global Anomie, Dysnomie, and Economic Crime: Hidden Consequences of Neoliberalism and Globalization in Russia and around the World." *Social Justice* (2000): 16-44.

———. "Globalization, Criminogenic Asymmetries and Economic Crime." *Eur. JL Reform* 1 (1999): 399.

Paternoster, Raymond, and Sally S. Simpson. "A Rational Choice Theory of Corporate Crime." In *Routine Activity and Rational Choice: Advances in Criminological Theory*, 37-58: Routledge, 2017.

Paterson, Craig. "Adding Value? A Review of the International Literature on the Role of Higher Education in Police Training and Education." *Police Practice and Research* 12, no. 4 (2011/08/01 2011): 286-97.

Pawson, R. A. Y. "Middle-Range Realism." *European Journal of Sociology* 41, no. 2 (2000): 283-325.

Pawson, Ray. "The Abc of Evaluation." *American Journal of Evaluation* 26, no. 4 (2005): 582-83.

Pawson, Ray Tilley Nick. *Realistic Evaluation.* London: Sage, 2007.

Pearce, Frank. *Crimes of the Powerful: Marxism, Crime and Deviance.* Pluto Press London, 1976.

———. "Issues in Green Criminology: Confronting Harms against Environments, Humanity and Other Animals." *Theoretical Criminology* 13, no. 2 (May 2009): 277-80.

Pearce, Frank, and Steve Tombs. "Ideology, Hegemony, and Empiricism: Compliance Theories of Regulation." *The British Journal of Criminology* 30, no. 4 (1990): 423-43.

Peters, Maaike, and Antonius Spapens. "The Administrative Approach in the Netherlands." *Administrative approaches to prevent and tackle crime: Legal possibilities and practical application in EU Member States* (2015): 265-306.

Pink, Grant. "Regulatory Responses to Transnational Environmental Crime: An Overview of Choices, Challenges and Culture." *Environmental Crime in Transnational Context* (2016): 117-39.

Piquero, Alexis Russell Tibbetts Stephen G. *Rational Choice and Criminal Behavior: Recent Research and Future Challenges.* New York: Routledge, 2012.

Piquero, Nicole Leeper, Stephen G. Tibbetts, and Michael B. Blankenship. "Examining the Role of Differential Association and Techniques of Neutralization in Explaining Corporate Crime." *Deviant Behavior* 26, no. 2 (2005): 159-88.

Poggi, Laura, Tomaso Gaggero, Marco Gaiotti, Enrico Ravina, and Cesare Mario Rizzo. "Recent Developments in Remote Inspections of Ship Structures." *International Journal of Naval Architecture and Ocean Engineering* 12 (2020/01/01/ 2020): 881-91.

Pontell, Henry N, William K Black, and Gilbert Geis. "Too Big to Fail, Too Powerful to Jail? On the Absence of Criminal Prosecutions after the 2008 Financial Meltdown." *Crime, Law and Social Change* 61, no. 1 (2014): 1-13.

Psaraftis, Harilaos N., and Christos A. Kontovas. "Decarbonization of Maritime Transport: Is There Light at the End of the Tunnel?". *Sustainability* 13, no. 1 (2021): 237.

Pskowski, Rebecca Prentiss. "Bad Bunker: Fuel Contamination Claims, Imo 2020, and the Houston Problem." *Tul. Mar. LJ* 44 (2019): 217.

Quinney, Richard. *Class, State, & Crime.* New York: Longman, 1980.

———. *The Social Reality of Crime.* [in French] Boston: Little, Brown, 1970.

Rahim, Mia Mahmudur, Md Tarikul Islam, and Sanjaya Kuruppu. "Regulating Global Shipping Corporations' Accountability for Reducing Greenhouse Gas Emissions in the Seas." *Marine Policy* 69 (2016): 159-70.

Ramesh, M. "Globalisation and National Regulations: Race to the Bottom, Top, and Middle." *Deregulation and Its Discontents Rewriting the Rules in Asia* (2006).

Rice, P. "Harmonization of Criminal Environmental Liability Throughout the Eu." *Environmental Claims Journal* 15, no. 2 (2003): 281-86.

Richardson, Genevra, A. I. Ogus, and Paul Burrows. *Policing Pollution: A Study of Regulation and Enforcement.* Oxford Socio-Legal Studies. Oxford [Oxfordshire] New York: Clarendon Press; Oxford University Press, 1982.

Rodrigues, Victor de O., and Arnaldo C. Faro Júnior. "On Catalyst Activation and Reaction Mechanisms in Propane Aromatization on Ga/Hzsm5 Catalysts." *Applied Catalysis A: General* 435-436 (2012/09/05/ 2012): 68-77.

Rogers, James A. "Ocean Dumping." *Envtl. L.* 7 (1976): 1.

Rossler, Michael T, and Michael J Suttmoeller. "Is All Police Academy Training Created Equally? Comparing Natural Resource Officer and General Police Academy Training." *The Police Journal* 91, no. 2 (2018): 107-22.

Roughy, Orange, and Australian Fisheries. "Ignorance, the Precautionary Principle, and Sustainability." *Ambio* 24, no. 2 (1995): 92-97.

Rudra, Nita. "Globalization and the Race to the Bottom in Developing Countries." *Cambridge Books* (2008).

Ruggiero, Vincenzo. *Crimes of the Economy – a Criminological Analysis of Economic Thought.* 2015.

———. *Power and Crime.* 2015.

———. *Organized and Corporate Crime in Europe: Offers That Can't Be Refused.* Dartmouth, 1996.

Ruggiero, Vincenzo, and Nigel South. "Critical Criminology and Crimes against the Environment." *Critical Criminology* 18, no. 4 (2010): 245-50.

———. "Green Criminology and Crimes of the Economy: Theory, Research and Praxis." *Critical Criminology* 21, no. 3 (2013): 359-73.

———. "Green Criminology and Dirty Collar Crime." *Critical Criminology* 18, no. 4 (Dec 2010): 251-62.

———. "Toxic State-Corporate Crimes, Neo-Liberalism and Green Criminology: The Hazards and Legacies of the Oil, Chemical and Mineral Industries." *International Journal for Crime, Justice and Social Democracy* 2, no. 2 (2013): 12-26.

Rutherford, Amanda, and Kenneth J Meier. "Managerial Goals in a Performance-Driven System: Theory and Empirical Tests in Higher Education." *Public Administration* 93, no. 1 (2015): 17-33.

Sadeghbeigi, Reza. "Chapter 3 – Fcc Feed Characterization." In *Fluid Catalytic Cracking Handbook (Third Edition)*, edited by Reza Sadeghbeigi, 51-86. Oxford: Butterworth-Heinemann, 2012.

Salter, Michael Mason Julie. *Writing Law Dissertations: An Introduction and Guide to the Conduct of Legal Research.* Harlow: Longman, 2011.

Sampson, Helen, Michael Bloor, Susan Baker, and Katrin Dahlgren. "Greener Shipping? A Consideration of the Issues Associated with the Introduction of Emission Control Areas." *Maritime Policy & Management* 43, no. 3 (2016/04/02 2016): 295-308.

Santos, Rachel Boba Santos Roberto G. Cops Program United States Department of Justice Office of Community Oriented Policing Services. *A Police Organizational Model for Crime Reduction: Institutionalizing Problem Solving, Analysis, and Accountability.* Washington, D.C.: U.S. Dept. of Justice, Office of Community Oriented Policing Services, 2011.

Schlegel, Kip Weisburd David. "White-Collar Crime Reconsidered." . (1992).

Schmidt, Holger. "A Green Branch of Criminology? Thoughts on Green Criminology." *Kriminologisches Journal* 45, no. 4 (2013 2013): 260-78.

Schnaiberg, Allan. "The Environment: From Surplus to Scarcity." (1980).

Schnaiberg, Allan, David N. Pellow, and Adam Weinberg. "The Treadmill of Production and the Environmental State." In *The Environmental State under Pressure*, edited by Arthur P. J. Mol and Frederick H. Buttel. Research in Social Problems and Public Policy, 15-32: Emerald Group Publishing Limited, 2002.

Schoenberger, Harald. "Integrated Pollution Prevention and Control in Large Industrial Installations on the Basis of Best Available Techniques – the Sevilla Process." *Journal of Cleaner Production* 17, no. 16 (2009/11/01/ 2009): 1526-29.

Schofield, J. W. "Increasing the Generalizability of Qualitative Research ". In *Social Research: Philosophy, Politics and Practice*, edited by M. Hammersley, 200-25. London: Sage 1993.

Scholz, John T. "Cooperation, Deterrence, and the Ecology of Regulatory Enforcement." *Law & Society Review* 18, no. 2 (1984): 179-224.

Schrager, Laura Shill, and James F. Short. "Toward a Sociology of Organizational Crime." *Social Problems* 25, no. 4 (1978): 407-19.

Schwirn, Kathrin, Doris Voelker, Wiebke Galert, Joris Quik, and Lars Tietjen. "Environmental Risk Assessment of Nanomaterials in the Light of New Obligations under the Reach Regulation: Which Challenges Remain and How to Approach Them?". *Integrated Environmental Assessment and Management* 16, no. 5 (2020): 706-17.

Scotford, Eloise. "Trash or Treasure: Policy Tensions in EC Waste Regulation." *Journal of Environmental Law* 19, no. 3 (January 1, 2007 2007): 367-88.

Scott, Colin. "Speaking Softly without Big Sticks: Meta-Regulation and Public Sector Audit." *Law & Policy* 25, no. 3 (2003): 203-19.

Scott, Michael S. *Problem-Oriented Policing: Reflections on the First 20 Years.* US Department of Justice, Office of Community Oriented Policing Services, 2000.

Selin, Henrik, Yiqi Zhang, Rebecca Dunn, Noelle E. Selin, and Alexis K. H. Lau. "Mitigation of Co2 Emissions from International Shipping through National Allocation." *Environmental Research Letters* 16, no. 4 (2021/03/24 2021): 045009.

Sergi, Anna, and Alexandria Reid. *Ports, Crime and Security: Governing and Policing Seaports in a Changing World.* Policy Press, 2021.

Shapiro, Susan P. "Collaring the Crime, Not the Criminal: Reconsidering the Concept of White-Collar Crime." *American Sociological Review* 55, no. 3 (1990): 346-65.

Sherratt, Andrew. "Cradle to Cradle." In *Encyclopedia of Corporate Social Responsibility*, edited by Samuel O. Idowu, Nicholas Capaldi, Liangrong Zu and Ananda Das Gupta, 630-38. Berlin, Heidelberg: Springer Berlin Heidelberg, 2013.

Shi, Yubing. "Are Greenhouse Gas Emissions from International Shipping a Type of Marine Pollution?". *Marine Pollution Bulletin* 113, no. 1 (2016/12/15/ 2016): 187-92.

———. "Reducing Greenhouse Gas Emissions from International Shipping: Is It Time to Consider Market-Based Measures?". *Marine Policy* 64 (2016/02/01/ 2016): 123-34.

Shmelev, SE, and John R Powell. "Ecological–Economic Modelling for Strategic Regional Waste Management Systems." *Ecological Economics* 59, no. 1 (2006): 115-30.

Shover, Neal, and Andrew Hochstetler. *Choosing White-Collar Crime.* Cambridge University Press, 2005.

Simpson, Sally S. "Corporate Crime, Law, and Social Control." (2002).

Simpson, Sally S, and David Weisburd. *The Criminology of White-Collar Crime.* Springer, 2009.

Simpson, Sally S., and Christopher S. Koper. "The Changing of the Guard: Top Management Characteristics, Organizational Strain, and Antitrust Offending." *Journal of Quantitative Criminology* 13, no. 4 (1997/12/01 1997): 373-404.

Simpson, Sally S., and Nicole Leeper Piquero. "Low Self-Control, Organizational Theory, and Corporate Crime." *Law & Society Review* 36, no. 3 (2002): 509-48.

Slapper, G. "Companies, Crime and Punishment." . *Business Law Review -London-* 15, no. 5 (1994): 126.

Slapper, Gary, and Steve Tombs. *Corporate Crime.* Harlow: Longman, 1999.

Smil, Vaclav. *Energy and Civilization: A History.* Cambridge, Mass; London: The MIT [Massachusetts Institute of Technology] Press, 2018.

———. *Oil: A Beginner's Guide.* : Oneworld Publications, 2018.

Song, Changyeol, Min Yeong Gim, Yong Hyun Lim, and Do Heui Kim. "Enhanced Yield of Benzene, Toulene, and Xylene from the Co-Aromatization of Methane and Propane over Gallium Supported on Mesoporous Zsm-5 and Zsm-11." *Fuel* 251 (2019/09/01/ 2019): 404-12.

South, Nigel. "Green Criminology and Brown Crime: Despoliation, Disposal and De-Manufacturing in Global Resource Industries." In *Hazardous Waste and Pollution*, 11-25: Springer, 2016.

———. "Green Criminology Environmental Crime Prevention and the Gaps between Law, Legitimacy and Justice." *Revija Za Kriminalistiko in Kriminologijo* 65, no. 4 (Oct-Dec 2014): 373-81.

———. "A Green Field for Criminology? A Proposal for a Perspective." *Theoretical Criminology* 2, no. 2 (1998): 211-33.

South, Nigel, and Avi Brisman. *Routledge International Handbook of Green Criminology.* Routledge, 2013.

South, Nigel, Avi Brisman, and Piers Beirne. "A Guide to a Green Criminology." *The Routledge international handbook of green criminology* (2013): 27-42.

Spapens, Toine (ACM). "Bestuurlijke Aanpak Van Ondermijning: Ervaringen in Nederland En Het Buitenland." *Tijdschrift voor Bijzonder Strafrecht en Handhaving* 2019, no. 2 (2019): 85-92.

———. "Vuile Olie: Een Onzichtbaar Probleem Met Grote Gevolgen." *Het tijdschrift voor de politie* 75, no. 8 (2013): 20-21.

———. "Macro Networks, Collectives, and Business Processes: An Integrated Approach to Organized Crime." *Eur. J. Crime Crim. L. & Crim. Just.* 18 (2010): 185.

Spapens, Toine, and Wim Huisman. "Tackling Cross-Border Environmental Crime: A 'Wicked Problem'." In *Environmental Crime in Transnational Context*, 43-58: Routledge, 2016.

Speight, James G. "3 – Unconventional Gas." In *Natural Gas (Second Edition)*, edited by James G. Speight, 59-98. Boston: Gulf Professional Publishing, 2019.

Spencer, Dale C, and Amy Fitzgerald. "Three Ecologies, Transversality and Victimization: The Case of the British Petroleum Oil Spill." *Crime, Law and Social Change* 59, no. 2 (2013): 209-23.

Stake, Robert E. "Qualitative Case Studies." In *The Sage Handbook of Qualitative Research*, edited by Norman K. Lincoln Yvonna S. Denzin, 443-66. Thousand Oaks: Sage Publications, 2005.

Steenmans, Katrien. "Extended Producer Responsibility: An Assessment of Recent Amendments to the European Union Waste Frameworks Directive." *Law Env't & Dev. J.* 15 (2019): 108.

Stewart, R. "EU Legislation Relating to Electronic Waste: The Weee and Rohs Directives and the Reach Regulations." In *Waste Electrical and Electronic Equipment (Weee) Handbook*, 17-52: Elsevier, 2012.

Stretesky, Paul B, Michael A Long, and Michael J Lynch. *The Treadmill of Crime: Political Economy and Green Criminology*. Routledge, 2013.

———. "Does Environmental Enforcement Slow the Treadmill of Production? The Relationship between Large Monetary Penalties, Ecological Disorganization and Toxic Releases within Offending Corporations." *Journal of Crime and Justice* 36, no. 2 (2013/07/01 2013): 233-47.

Stretesky, Paul, and Philipp Grimmer. "Shale Gas Development and Crime: A Review of the Literature." *The Extractive Industries and Society* 7, no. 3 (2020): 1147-57.

Sutherland, Edwin H. *Principles of Criminology*. Chicago, Philadelphia: J.B. Lippincott Company, [1939] 1947.

———. "White-Collar Criminality." *American Sociological Review* 5, no. 1 (1940): 1-12.

Sutherland, Edwin Hardin, Gilbert Geis, and Colin Goff. *White Collar Crime: The Uncut Version*. Vol. 58, New Haven, CT: Yale University Press 1983.

Szasz, Andrew. "Corporations, Organized Crime, and the Disposal of Hazardous Waste: An Examination of the Making of a Criminogenic Regulatory Structure." *Criminology* 24, no. 1 (1986): 1-27.

Tikhonova, Irina, Tatiana Guseva, Eugene Averochkin, and Kirill Shchelchkov. "Best Available Techniques and Best Environmental Management Practices: Collaboration between Industries and Regions." *Procedia Environmental Science, Engineering and Management* 8, no. 2 (2021): 495-505.

Tombs, Steve. "State-Corporate Symbiosis in the Production of Crime and Harm." *State Crime Journal* (2012): 170-95.

Tombs, Steve, and Dave Whyte. "Unmasking the Crimes of the Powerful." *Critical criminology* 11, no. 3 (2003): 217-36.

Tompson, Lisa, and Spencer Chainey. "Profiling Illegal Waste Activity: Using Crime Scripts as a Data Collection and Analytical Strategy." *European Journal on Criminal Policy and Research* 17, no. 3 (Sep 2011): 179-201.

Tønnensen, Ivar. "Controlling Bunker Costs." Arendal, Norway: Gard Services AS, 2002.

Tops, Pieter, and Henny Schilders. "Naar Een Meervoudige Aanpak Van Ondermijning." *Tijdschrift voor de Politie* 78, no. 7 (2016): 12-15.

Townsley, Richard Wortley and Michael, ed. *Environmental Criminology and Crime Analysis*. Edited by Richard Wortley. Second ed, Crime Science Series. Oxon: Routledge, 2017.

Trahan, Adam Marquart James Mullings Janet. "Fraud and the American Dream: Toward an Understanding of Fraud Victimization." . *deviant behav Deviant Behavior* 26, no. 6 (2005): 601-20.

Trowbridge, Charles L. "History, Development, and Characteristics of the Charter Concept." *Tul. L. Rev.* 49 (1974): 743.

Ungar, Sheldon. "Knowledge, Ignorance and the Popular Culture: Climate Change Versus the Ozone Hole." *Public Understanding of Science* 9, no. 3 (2000): 297.

van de Bunt, Henk, and Wim Huisman. "Organizational Crime in the Netherlands." *Crime and Justice* 35 (2007/01/01 2007): 217-60.

van Erp, Judith. "Toezicht in De Open Samenleving: Maatschappelijke Controle Op Multinationale Ondernemingen." (2016).

van Erp, Judith, and Wim Huisman. "Smart Regulation and Enforcement of Illegal Disposal of Electronic Waste." *Criminology & Public Policy* 9, no. 3 (2010): 579-90.

van Gossum, Peter, Bas Arts, and Kris Verheyen. "From "Smart Regulation" to "Regulatory Arrangements"." *Policy Sciences* 43, no. 3 (2010): 245-61.

van Koppen, M. Vere. "Involvement Mechanisms for Organized Crime." *Crime, Law and Social Change* 59, no. 1 (2013/02/01 2013): 1-20.

van Leeuwen, Judith, and Kristine Kern. "The External Dimension of European Union Marine Governance: Institutional Interplay between the EU and the International Maritime Organization." *Global Environmental Politics* 13, no. 1 (2013): 69-87.

van Wingerde, Karin, and Lieselot Bisschop. "Waste Away. Examining Systemic Drivers of Global Waste Trafficking Based on a Comparative Analysis of Two Dutch Cases." *Erasmus L. Rev.* 12 (2019): 80.

van Wingerde, Karin. *De Afschrikking Voorbij: Een Empirische Studie Naar Afschrikking, Generale Preventie En Regelnaleving in De Nederlandse Afvalbranche.* 2012.

Vander Beken, Tom. *The European Waste Industry and Crime Vulnerabilities.* Maklu, 2007.

Vander Beken, Tom, and Stijn Van Daele. "Legitimate Businesses and Crime Vulnerabilities." *International journal of social economics* 35, no. 9/10 (2008): 739-50.

Walters, Reece. "Climate Change Denial: 'Making Ignorance Great Again'." In *Ignorance, Power and Harm: Agnotology and the Criminological Imagination*, edited by Alana Barton and Howard Davis, 163-87. Cham: Springer International Publishing, 2018.

Weisburd, David, and Elin Waring. *White-Collar Crime and Criminal Careers.* Cambridge University Press, 2001.

Wheeler, Stanton, David Weisburd, Elin Waring, and Nancy Bode. "White Collar Crimes and Criminals." *Am. Crim. L. Rev.* 25 (1987): 331.

White, Rob.. *Transnational Environmental Crime: Toward and Eco-Global Criminology.* 2011.

———.. *Crimes against Nature: Environmental Criminology and Ecological Justice.* Routledge, 2013.

———. "Environmental Issues and the Criminological Imagination." *Theoretical Criminology* 7, no. 4 (2003): 483-506.

———. *Global Environmental Harm: Criminological Perspectives.* Routledge, 2013.

———. "Researching Transnational Environmental Harm: Toward an Eco-Global Criminology." *International journal of comparative and applied criminal justice* 33, no. 2 (2009): 229-48.

———, ed. *Transnational Environmental Crime: Toward an Eco-Global Criminology*: Routledge, 2011.

———. "What Is to Be Done About Environmental Crime?". Chap. 20 In *The Routledge Handbook of International Crime and Justice Studies*, edited by Bruce Arrigo and Heather Bersot, 445-86. Abingdon: Routledge, 2014.

White, Rob, and Diane Heckenberg. *Green Criminology: An Introduction to the Study of Environmental Harm.* New York; London: Routledge, Taylor & Francis Group, 2014.

———. "Key Vulnerabilities and Limitations in the Management of Hazardous Waste and Its Disposal: A Checklist Assessment Tool." *Journal of Environmental Protection* 2, no. 09 (2011): 1257.

White, Rob, and Social Work. "Dealing with Environmental Harm: Green Criminology and Environmental Law Enforcement." Tasmanian Institute of Law Enforcement Studies (TILES), Accessed 15th February, 2009.

Whitehead Roy Jr., and Walter Block. "Environmental Justice Risks in the Petroleum Industry." *Wm. & Mary Envtl. L. & Pol'y Rev.* 24 (2000): 67.

Whyte, William Foote Whyte King Kathleen. *Learning from the Field: A Guide from Experience.* Beverly Hills, Calif.: Sage, 1984.

Williams, E Spencer, Julie Panko, and Dennis J Paustenbach. "The European Union's Reach Regulation: A Review of Its History and Requirements." *Critical reviews in toxicology* 39, no. 7 (2009): 553-75.

Wincup, Emma, Kathy Salter Hampson, Ella Holdsworth, and Joanna Large. Criminological Research: Understanding Qualitative Methods (version 2nd edition.). London: SAGE Publications, 2017.

Wong, M. H. "Export of Toxic Chemicals – a Review of the Case of Uncontrolled Electronic-Waste Recycling." *Environmental pollution* 149, no. 2 (2007): 131-40.

Wortley, Richard. "Situational Precipitators of Crime." In *Environmental Criminology and Crime Analysis*, edited by Richard Wortley and Michael Townsley. Oxon: Routledge, 2017.

Wortley, Richard, and Lorraine Mazerolle. *Environmental Criminology and Crime Analysis.* Willan, 2013.

Wuthnow, Robert. *The Consciousness Reformation.* 1976.

Wyatt, Tanya. "Issues in Green Criminology: Confronting Harms against Environments, Humanity and Other Animals." *British Journal of Criminology* 48, no. 5 (Sep 2008): 697-99.

X, Malcolm Haley Alex Handler M. S. *The Autobiography of Malcolm X.* 1965.

Yin, Robert K. *Applications of Case Study Research.* Sage, 2011.
———. *Case Study Research: Design and Methods.* Sage publications, 2013.
Young, Jock. "Searching for a New Criminology of Everyday Life: A Review Of'the Culture of Control'." Review of Searching for a New Criminology of Everyday Life: A Review of 'The Culture of Control', David Garland. *The British Journal of Criminology* 43, no. 1 (2003): 228-43.
Young, Jock "Thinking Seriously About Crime." edited by Gregor McLennan and Jennie Pawson Mike Fitzagerald. London: Routledge, 1981.
Zanella, Marco. "Script Analysis of Corruption in Public Procurement." In *Cognition and Crime: Offender Decision Making and Script Analyses*, edited by Benoit Wortley Richard Leclerc, 164-85. Abingdon Routledge, 2014.
Zhu, Ling. "Compensation Issues under the Bunkers Convention." *WMU Journal of Maritime Affairs* 7, no. 1 (2008): 303-16.

## Reports

BIMCO [Baltic and International Maritime Council] & IBIA [International Bunker Industry Association] "Bimco & Ibia Bunekring Guide." 2018.
Agency, UK Environment. "Guidance: Quality Protocol: Processed Fuel Oil (Pfo) – Sets out End of Waste Criteria for the Production and Use of Processed Fuel Oil from Waste Lubricating Oil.", edited by Northern Ireland Environment Agency. Oxon, 2011.
———. "Understanding the Meaning of Regulated Facility." 2015.
Antoine Pinasseau, Benoit Zerger, Joze Roth, Michele Canova, Serge Roudier. "Best Available Techniques (Bat) Reference Document for Waste Treatment ", edited by European IPPC Bureau. Seville, Spain: European Union, 2018.
Bakker, M.H. Broekman & J. "Milieurisico's Van Specifieke Stoffen in Bunkerolie in Zeeschepen: Onderzoek Van De Literatuur En De Reach-Dossiers." Bilthoven: Rijksinstituut voor Volksgesondheid en Milieu (RIVM), 2016.
Clarke, Ronald V. & Eck, John. "Become a Problem Solving Crime Analyst – in 55 Small Steps." London: Jill Dando Institute of Crime Science, University College London, 2003.
Centrum voor Criminaliteitspreventie en Veiligheid,. "Handboek Bestuurlijke Aanpak Georganiseerde Criminaliteit – Het Instrument in De Praktijk." Utrecht: Colofon, 2010.
Commissie, Hulshof. "Rapport Van Bevindingen Naar Aanleiding Van Het Onderzoek Van De Gang Van Zaken Rond Aankomst, Verblijf En Vertrek Van De Probo Koala in Juli 2006 Te Amsterdam ", edited by Requested by Gemeente Amsterdam, 2006.
ECHA, [European Chemicals Agency]. "Guidance on the Compilation of Safety Data Sheets (Version 4.0)." 2020.
E., Herman Goldstein and Susmilch C. "Experimenting with the Probelm-Oriented Approach to Improve Police Service: A Report and Some Reflections on Two Case Studies." Madison, WI: University of Wisconsin, Law School, 1982.
European Commission. "Commission Notice on Technical Guidance on the Classification of Waste ", 2018.
———. "Commission Notice on Technical Guidance on the Classification of Waste (2018/C 124/01)." 2018.
———. "Guidance on the Interpretation of Key Provisions of Directive 2008/98/EC on Waste." 2012.
Greenpeace & Amnesty International. "The Toxic Truth. About a Company Called Trafigura, a Ship Called Probo Koala and the Dumping of Toxic Waste in Cote D'ivoire." London: Amnesty International International Secretariat, 2012.
Inspectie Leefomegeving en Transport. "Heavy Fuel Oil for Sea-Going Vessels on-Road Fuels for West Africa Blended in the Netherlands." 2018.
Minister van Veiligheid en Justitie. "Inrichtingsplan Nationale Politie." [2012] 2015.

Ministerie van Infrastructuur en Waterstaat. "Bijlage 1 – Convenant Inzake De Samenwerking Tussen Het Ministerie Van Infrastructuur En Waterstaat Het Ministerie Van Financien Buj De Uitvoering Van Wettelijke Taken Op Het Beliedsterrein Van Het Ministerie Van Infrastructuur En Waterstaat Door De Douane." 2018.

———. "Convenant Inzake De Samenwerking Tussen Het Ministerie Van Infrastructuur En Waterstaat Het Ministerie Van Financien Buj De Uitvoering Van Wettelijke Taken Op Het Beliedsterrein Van Het Ministerie Van Infrastructuur En Waterstaat Door De Douane." 2018.

———. "Landelijk Afvalbeheerplan 2017 – 2029 (Tweede Wijziging) (Lap 3)." 2017.

United Nations. "Report of the Special Rapporteur on the Adverse Effects of the Movement and Dumping of Toxic and Dangerous Products and Wastes on the Enjoyment of Human Rights, Okechukwu Ibeanu." 2009.

———. "Review of Maritime Transport 2020 " In *Review of Maritime Transport*, edited by United Nations Conference on Trade and Development. New York, 2020.

OECD. "Review of Maritime Transport." 2021.

OECD and International Transport Forum. "Navigating Towards Cleaner Maritime Shipping: Lessons from the Nordic Region." 2020.

Politie, Openbaar Ministerie en. "Rapportage Aanpak Georganiseerde Ondermijnende Criminaliteit 2018." 2019.

"Scuffing & Red Deposits after Fuel Transition: Causes and Solutions." In *Marine lubricants information bulletin* Chevron Marine Products LLC, 2021.

Shell Deutschland, Deutsches Zentrum für Luft- und Raumfahrt, Technische Universität Hamburg. "Shell Lng Study: Liquefied Natural Gas – New Energy for Ships and Trucks?", 2019.

Smits, John, Anna Sibma, Josien Roodnat, and Bert Schudde. "Bestuurlijke Aanpak Georganiseerde Criminaliteit." Arena Consulting/Pro Facto, 2013.

Staring, Richard; Bisschop, Lieselot; Roks, Robby; Brein, Elisabeth; van de Bunt, Henk. "Drug Crime in the Port of Rotterdam." Rotterdam: City of Rotterdam Department of Public Safety; Public Prosecutor's Office; Police; Customs; Erasmus University Rotterdam, 2019.

Steve Cheng, Matthias Daub, Axel Domeyer, and Martin Lundqvist. "Using Blockchain to Improve Data Management in the Public Sector." McKinsey & Company, 2017.

Trafigura. "Trafigura & the Probo Koala." 2016.

Tweede Kamer, VROM "Probo Koala in Amsterdam, Feitenrelaas En Relevante Wetgeving." 2006.

UNEP. "Environmental Audit of the Sites Affected by the Dumping of Toxic Wastes from the "Probo Koala"." 2018.

## Web Pages

Academie, Politie NL – Politie. "Andante: Foute Stookolie." https://www.politieacademie.nl/thema/opsporing/LaboratoriaOpsporing/Paginas/Andante-foute-stookolie-.aspx

Agency, Environmental Protection. "Learn About Ocean Dumping." https://www.epa.gov/ocean-dumping/learn-about-ocean-dumping#:~:text=The%20Ocean%20Dumping%20Ban%20Act,at%20sea%20using%20shipboard%20incinerators.

Bahá'í International Community, "One Planet, One Habitation: A Bahá'í Perspective on Recasting Humanity's Relationship with the Natural World" (New York, 2022), available at: https://www.datocms-assets.com/6348/1655300643-bic_new_york_one_planet_one_habitation_statement_2022.pdf.

BBC. "Fractional Distillation." https://www.bbc.co.uk/bitesize/guides/zyvc6fr/revision/1.

contributors, Wikipedia. "Petrochemical." Wikipedia, The Free Encyclopedia, https://en.wikipedia.org/w/index.php?title=Petrochemical&oldid=1068615653

Science Direct. "Global Warming Potential." https://www.sciencedirect.com/topics/earth-and-planetary-sciences/global-warming-potential.

———. "Industrial Symbiosis." https://www.sciencedirect.com/topics/engineering/industrial-symbiosis.

Shell Plc. "Aromatics." https://www.shell.com/business-customers/chemicals/our-products/aromatics.html.

Douane (Ministerie van Financiën). "40.04.00 Overbrenging Afvalstoffen (Evoa)." https://www.belastingdienst.nl/bibliotheek/handboeken/html/boeken/HVGEM/overbrenging_afvalstoffen_evoa_-de_handhaving_van_de_afvalstoffenwetgeving.html.

Ellen MacArthur Foundation. "Finding a Common Language — the Circular Economy Glossary." https://ellenmacarthurfoundation.org/topics/circular-economy-introduction/glossary.

European Commission – DG Environment,. "Air Pollution and Climate Change." https://ec.europa.eu/environment/integration/research/newsalert/pdf/24si_en.pdf.

European Commission – DG Environment. "Waste Prevention and Management." https://ec.europa.eu/environment/green-growth/waste-prevention-and-management/index_en.htm.

Haltermann-Carless. "Heavy Aromatic Solvents – 70 Years of Expertise." https://www.haltermann-carless.com/what-we-do/special-aromatics.

IMO. "Imo 2020 – Cutting Sulphur Oxide Emissions." https://www.imo.org/en/MediaCentre/HotTopics/Pages/Sulphur-2020.aspx.

IMO. "Fourth Greenhouse Gas Study 2020." https://www.imo.org/en/OurWork/Environment/Pages/Fourth-IMO-Greenhouse-Gas-Study-2020.aspx.

Inspectie Leefomgenving en Transport (Ministerie van Infrastructuur en Waterstaat). "Marine Fuels Quality." https://english.ilent.nl/themes/l/legislation-merchant-shipping/marine-fuels-quality.

———. "Toezicht En Interventies." https://www.ilent.nl/onderwerpen/afvaltransport-evoa/toezicht-en-handhaving/toezicht-en-interventies.

International Air Transport Association, 'Airline Industry Statistics Confirm 2020 Was Worst Year on Record' Press Release, 3 August 2021, https://www.iata.org/en/pressroom/pr/2021-08-03-01/#:~:text=North%20America%3A%20401.7%20million%20passengers,passengers%2C%20down%2060.6%25%20over%202019.

National Geographic,. "Biosphere."

OECD. "Ocean Shipping and Shipbuilding." https://www.oecd.org/ocean/topics/ocean-shipping/.

Openbaar Ministerie. "Afvalstoffen in Stookolie (Dossier Andante)." https://www.om.nl/onderwerpen/strafrechtelijk-programma-andante.

Patterson, Warren. "Marine Fuels & Imo 2020: So Much for All the Hype." In *THINK Economic and Financial Analysis*, edited by ING, https://think.ing.com/articles/marine-fuels-imo-2020-so-much-for-all-the-hype, 21 July 2020.

Rijksoverheid. "Handhaving Reach En Clp." https://chemischestoffengoedgeregeld.nl/content/handhaving.

Rijkswaterstaat (Ministerie van Infrastructuur en Waterstaat). "Lap 2." https://lap3.nl/overig/lap-archief/lap-2-0/.

———. "Oliehoudend Afval." https://lap3.nl/sectorplannen/oliehoudend/.

UNEP. "Un Environment Releases Independent Audit of Sites Affected by Toxic Waste Dump in Côte D'ivoire." news release, 30 January 2018, 2018, https://www.unenvironment.org/news-and-stories/press-release/un-environment-releases-independent-audit-sites-affected-toxic-waste.

WHO. "Ambient (Outdoor) Air Pollution." https://www.who.int/news-room/fact-sheets/detail/ambient-(outdoor)-air-quality-and-health.

Wikipedia. "Impact of the Covid-19 Pandemic on Aviation."

## Newspapers and Documentaries

"Air Travel Down 60 Per Cent, as Airline Industry Losses Top $370 Billion: Icao." *UN News*, 15 January 2021.

Degnarain, Nisha. "Bp Confirms It Supplied Fuel to Mauritius Oil Spill Ship but Denies Fuel Was Cause." *Forbes*, 23 January 2021.

———. "New Images Released of Engine Damage Caused by Experimental Low Sulfur Ship Fuel Vlsfo." *Forbes*, 24 January 2021.

———. "Satellites Make New Discovery About Mauritius Oil Spill Ship Wakashio." *Forbes*, 22 January 2021.

Deutsche Welle, "Berlin airport briefly shut down by climate protesters" 24 November 2022.

Harper, Justin. "Suez Blockage Is Holding up $9.6bn of Goods a Day." *BBC News*, 26 March 2021.

Koomen, Wilfried. *Beerput Nederland*. 2017.

Marasi News,. "Clean Arctic Alliance: How Did Super Pollutant 'Frankenstein' Fuels Come to Market?", 29 January 2020.

Marijnissen, Hans. "Zaak-Shell: Testcase Voor Aanpak Vervuilde Stookolie." *Trouw*, 2013.

Mira Sys, Tom Claessens. "Chemisch Afval Wordt Massaal Gebruikt Als Scheepsbrandstof." *Follow the Money*, 2022.

Pearce, Fred. "How 16 Ships Create as Much Pollution as All the Cars in the World." *The Daily Mail*, 2013.

Plester, Jeremy. "Dirty Diesel: Why Ships Are the Worst Offenders." *The Guardian*, 2017.

Rasmijn, Ariën. "Zware Stookolie Gelekt in Binnenwater Aruba." *Caribisch Netwerk*, 2015.

Russon, Mary-Ann. "The Cost of the Suez Canal Blockage." *BBC News*, 29 March 2021.

———. "The Cost of the Suez Canal Blockage." *BBC News*, 2021.

Tagesschau, "Harte Strafen für Aktivisten gefordert" 24 November 2022.

———. "Scharfe Kritik an Flughafen-Blockade" 25 November 2022.

Vidal, John. "The World's Largest Cruise Ship and Its Supersized Pollution Problem." *The Guardian*, 2016.

www.ingramcontent.com/pod-product-compliance
Lightning Source LLC
Chambersburg PA
CBHW080933240926
51849CB00003BA/443
* 9 7 8 9 4 6 2 3 6 7 3 8 8 *